THE ANNALS OF
THE KING'S ROYAL
RIFLE CORPS

THE ANNALS OF THE KING'S ROYAL RIFLE CORPS

THE ANNALS OF THE KING'S ROYAL RIFLE CORPS

VOLUME VII
1943–1965

BY
MAJOR GENERAL G. H. MILLS,
CB, OBE

CELER ET AUDAX CLUB
WINCHESTER

First published in Great Britain 1979
by Celer et Audax Club, Peninsula Barracks
Winchester Hampshire

© *Celer et Audax Club* 1979

ISBN 0 9506676 0 9

Photoset by Woolaston Parker, Leicester.
Printed and bound in Great Britain by
Biddles of Guildford

CONTENTS

MAPS

ILLUSTRATIONS

PREFACE

This is the final volume of The Annals of The King's Royal Rifle Corps. For those who do not hold the first five volumes, this and its predecessor, published in 1971 as Volume VI, are a Regimental History in themselves. In them the period from 1919 to 1965 is covered in detail, and in the last chapter of this volume a summary is given of what The King's Royal Rifle Corps contributed over two centuries to the Army, and what it brought to The Royal Green Jackets.

It is 14 years since that new Regiment was voluntarily created from the battalions of the three old Regiments, and the standing of Riflemen has never been higher in the eyes of the Army or the nation. It is with pride that old 60th Riflemen see that their heirs have retained all that is best in their 200-year-old inheritance.

The material in this volume has come from official and other histories, war diaries, the KRRC Chronicles and private letters. The author would like to express his thanks to Lt Col R. F. Nixon for assistance with material and in many other fields, to Lt Col P. B. Earle for reading the manuscript and offering valuable comments, to Michael Hills and John Holmes for their help over production. He is grateful for Ministry of Defence assistance, where the help of Lt Col D. A. Johnson of the Press Office and officials of the Map Library in particular has been invaluable.

Winchester   G.H.M.
1979

REGIMENTAL SUCCESSION OF COLONELS IN CHIEF COLONELS COMMANDANT AND LIEUTENANT COLONELS

1943—1965

COLONELS IN CHIEF

His Majesty King George VI 1936–52
Her Majesty Queen Elizabeth II 1953

COLONELS COMMANDANT

1ST BATTALION

1938
Major General Sir Hereward Wake, Bt, CB, CMG, DSO
1946
Major General H. O. Curtis, CB, DSO, MC
1954
Lieutenant General Sir Euan A. B. Miller, KCB, KBE, DSO, MC

2ND BATTALION

1937
Major General Sir John Davidson, KCMG, CB, DSO
1946
General Sir Evelyn H. Barker, KCB, KBE, DSO, MC
1955
General Sir George W. E. J. Erskine, GCB, KBE, DSO

2ND GREEN JACKETS, THE KING'S ROYAL RIFLE CORPS

1958
Lieutenant General Sir Euan A. B. Miller, KCB, KBE, DSO, MC
1961
General Sir George W. E. J. Erskine, GCB, KBE, DSO
1965
Major General E. A. W. Williams, CB, CBE, MC

LIEUTENANT COLONELS IN COMMAND
(Regular Battalions)
1ST BATTALION

J. L. Corbett-Winder, MC	Jan 1943
W. D. Keown-Boyd	Jul 1943
E. A. W. Williams, MC	Jan 1944
J. C. Hope, DSO, MC (Died of wounds)	Mar 1945
H. R. G. Howard (local Lt Col)	Apr 1945
S. C. F. De Salis, DSO	Aug 1945
T. L. Timpson	Mar 1946
C. T. Mitford-Slade	Mar 1948
K. H. Collen	Jan 1951
R. F. L. Chance, MC	Oct 1953
H. A. Hope, OBE, MC	Oct 1956

2ND BATTALION

W. Heathcoat-Amory, DSO	Aug 1942
R. B. Littledale, DSO (Killed in action)	Jul 1944
R. H. W. S. Hastings, DSO, MC (Rifle Brigade)	Sep 1944
C. d'A. P. Consett, DSO, MC	Jan 1945
E. G. V. Northey	Jul 1945
C. H. Gurney, OBE	Jan 1947
C. T. Mitford-Slade	Oct 1947
J. L. Corbett-Winder, OBE, MC	Aug 1947
	and Dec 1947

The Hon M. F. Douglas-Pennant, DSO, MBE	Mar 1951
E. A. W. Williams, OBE, MC	Oct 1953
J. F. C. Mellor, DSO	Oct 1955

2ND GREEN JACKETS, THE KING'S ROYAL RIFLE CORPS

T. H. Acton, OBE (Rifle Brigade)	Jan 1959
J. H. P. Curtis, MC	Mar 1961
G. H. Mills, OBE	Mar 1963
E. N. D. Bramall, OBE, MC	Jan 1965

CHAPTER I
ACROSS THE MEDITERRANEAN INTO ITALY

(Maps: pages 8 and 12)

In his Mansion House speech of November 1942, celebrating the Allied landings in North Africa and the victory at Alamein, Winston Churchill had said, 'It certainly is the end of the beginning'.

Now, in the early summer of 1943, there was a brief pause for the British armies, and those American forces alongside them, right across the world. In the Arakan the Japanese thrust had ground to a halt under the monsoon's downpour. The conditions in any event made the Far East unsuitable for Green Jacket battalions while they remained in their motor battalion role with armour. A few Riflemen were, however, serving at regimental duty in South East Asia; of these Lt Col K. H. Collen, with the King's African Rifles, and future Warrant Officers Pope and Robbins, with the West African Divisions, will appear later in our story.

The recent victory in Tunisia would have seemed a mirage only a year earlier in the swirling dust of the Gazala battles. The Mediterranean in its summer blue—long a whirlpool of convoy actions, with Malta at its vortex—had overnight become a less certain Axis moat with the ensuing rise in Allied sea and air power. In an ironic reversal of history, Carthage was poised to destroy Rome, but with more humanity. However, the Germans, after their bitter Stalingrad winter, would not let their faltering ally, stripped of her empire, slide easily out of the mistaken partnership. Equally exacting to the Allies were the demands of Stalin for a second front in Europe to take the German pressure off him: Churchill replied that such a front had long been draining Axis resources away from Europe—most recently with their Tunisian loss of a quarter of a million soldiers—yet the Prime Minister was to be beset by echoes of this 'Second Front Now!' cry in the Commons and the country, regardless of its practicability, until the Normandy landings. The expedient Soviet 1939 pact with Hitler was conveniently forgotten by the political Left, and there was a genuine wish by both Western Allies to help their Eastern partner.

Since for the first time the strategic initiative had been secured by the Allies, their aims must briefly be considered, without too deep involvement in all the arguments of the respective American and British political and military strategists. In so doing it must be borne in mind that, because of the lead time necessary in assigning, training and assembling forces for combined operations, strategic decisions over the Sicily ('Husky') and Salerno ('Avalanche') landings had each to be taken before the previous operations had made certain the factors on which they were based. At the Casablanca Conference in January 1943 decisions had to be made on what campaigns to initiate in the European theatre.

1

American strategy was direct and simplistic: Germany was the most powerful opponent; therefore attack her by landing in North West Europe and driving on Berlin without wasting resources on diversions in the Mediterranean.

However, in January the Germans still held pockets of resistance at Stalingrad and our 1 Army was bogged down in the mud of Tunisia; it was unlikely that we should clear North Africa before summer, since Tripoli had only fallen on 23 January, the day before the famous Allied stipulation of 'unconditional surrender' by the Axis partners was made. General Alan Brooke, CIGS, made the British Mediterranean strategy for 1943 clear: we had neither the time nor the resources to make a successful landing in North West Europe until 1944—the Dieppe raid had yielded many costly lessons. We could draw off German forces from France and deny them to the East front. Opening the Mediterranean would save shipping, it would ensure that the Allied resources of all three Services assembled there could be fully used, however delayed our African victory, and it should enable us to knock the weakest opponent, Italy, out of the war. This concept was eventually accepted by the Americans and loyally pursued, but always with noses twitching for any scent indicating that Churchill might—in Gallipoli vein—be straying off into the Balkans or Central Europe. These upright soldiers served their United States better than that nation had supported them between the wars, but they naturally, after generations of isolationism, had no knowledge of European power politics, while their Commander in Chief, Roosevelt, saw Stalin as a mere avuncular party protagonist, whom he could handle better than any British imperial apologist; he little realized the centuries-old and far from benign Russian imperial dream now intensified by Marxism.

Sicily was then selected as the first objective, as being the greatest threat to the sea route, just in range from Malta and Tunisia for our fighters and the greatest blow to Italian morale if lost. Sardinia and Corsica were eventually assigned to the French to take. The 'Husky' landing in the South East of Sicily was to take place in July's best moon phase.

Turning to the Axis defenders, there were two schools of thought among the Germans, conveniently labelled by the names of the generals concerned. Kesselring, originally a Luftwaffe commander and responsible for supplying all the Mediterranean and African fronts since the end of 1941, had now increased his status, from liaison with the Italian High Command and with Mussolini, to that of C in C of German forces of all three Services in the Mediterranean. He believed that it was better for Germany to keep the large though ill-equipped Italian forces in being by stiffening the Italian defences with German divisions and resources, since 800,000 Italians were being used for internal security from the South of France to the Balkans, an equal number on home defence, and over 200,000 on the East front. If they collapsed, German troops would have to be diverted, for Hitler was not prepared to let the world see the precedent of a dictator and his fascist regime falling. The Italian peninsula should be held as far South as possible, since this gave airfields, such as the important Foggia complex, or at least denied their use against Balkan oilfields or Southern German industry to the Allies. Rommel's views, based on field rather than staff work with (and notionally under) Italian commanders, and with a certain weariness of Mediterranean problems, were cynically tough. Southern Italy with its ineffective leaders should be written off as too weak and vulnerable to assault landings from sea and air. A defensive Pisa-Rimini line should be established across the top of the peninsula, using the head of the Apennines. Behind this Germany would milk the rich Po valley and the industry of Turin and Milan. This view was partially accepted, in that six divisions were to be brought initially from the East, followed by as many from France; this in turn led on to the construction of the Gothic Line, through which 1st Battalion The King's Royal Rifle Corps was to battle in September 1944, and also to the more immediate presence of German troops ready to pounce on many Riflemen, prisoners of war since desert reverses, who were in Northern Italian camps. Kesselring, however, was to be responsible for the command of the remaining German troops when they were forced to withdraw from Sicily and the South; from this task, brilliantly carried out by use of terrain, and later weather, derives the River Sangro action of the 2nd Battalion and the River Garigliano and East Coast patrolling of the 11th Battalion from September 1943 to May 1944. Superimposed on these two tasks Hitler ordered the preparation of a contingency plan, to be carried out by Rommel from a Munich HQ. As finally approved at the end of August 1943, the Italian fleet and planes were to be seized and their soldiers disarmed, if they were not prepared, as Kesselring hoped, to fight on alongside the Germans. Rommel sharply interpreted disarmament as to be followed by shipping Italian soldiers as prisoners to work in Germany.

On the Allied side the Trident Conference in Washington DC was held in May 1943. It sought to establish strategic objectives after the projected fall of Sicily, although those landings were not due until July. The North African campaign at least was ending, and based on this certain factor, the invasion of North West France ('Overlord') was fixed for 1 May 1944 and to be given top priority. The Americans, anxious to force the British from any further indirect approaches, had warned that strategic priority might be given to defeating Japan— unforgiven by the US Navy and the public in general for her Pearl Harbour attack—if 'Overlord' was not firmly endorsed by the British. Operations could continue to eliminate Italy and tie down as many Germans as possible, but four US and three British experienced divisions and most of the landing craft must leave for the UK by 1 November 1943. Thus was laid down at this early stage the conditions under which Allied soldiers were to fight throughout the Italian campaign—low priority for equipment, a successive drain away of experienced divisions and insufficient landing craft to permit use of the sea to outflank the strong defensive positions, open to the Germans almost anywhere up the peninsula. However, complete air superiority was to be built up, and in all respects the Burma front fared worse.

The 'Husky' landings in South East Sicily started on the night of 9 July 1943 under the command of General Alexander, 15 Army Group. Messina at the narrows was finally found evacuated on the night 16/17 August. On the right the experienced but cautious 8 Army had become embroiled with short German defensive lines, based on Mount Etna's slopes, while General Patton's US 7 Army, using the only armoured division on the island, just beat Montgomery to the town. The élan and hustle of the Americans, even against a largely Italian opposition, were a surprise after the Gafsa reverse in Tunisia, and the seeds of the constant rivalry between Patton, Bradley and Montgomery were sown in this campaign. On a higher plane, the Mediterranean sea route was secure, the success of the assault landing techniques gave valuable experience and confidence for 'Overlord', the Canadians had laid the ghost of Dieppe and a striking political change had taken place. Mussolini had been outvoted in the Fascist Grand Council and arrested by Marshal Badoglio on the King's orders two days afterwards; even though he was rescued later, he was a broken man and the Italian collapse was inevitable. One of the consequences of 'Husky' was that Hitler stopped his limited Russian offensive, and from now on first-class German divisions were drawn away from that front and from France. Redoubtable divisions like 1 Para, Hermann Göring, 16 and 26 Panzer, and 15 and 29 Panzer Grenadier successively came into play; the supreme tactical lessons of Sicily had been the brilliant German evacuation across the Straits to the toe of Italy, largely by day despite air inferiority, and their ability to improvise one defensive line after another.

Concurrently with the Sicily fighting, Allied planning was proceeding for the next step. With Mussolini's fall, risks could be taken to try for the political prize of Rome before Christmas. Churchill was all for this, and British naval support including carriers was assigned to Eisenhower at AFHQ, while General Marshall was busy steering US resources back to the UK.

8 Army, after an embarrassing barrage on to an empty coast, crossed into Calabria on 3 September and moved up the toe, with small amphibious hooks, against demolitions lightly covered. The main assault was to be made on 9 September on the Salerno beaches South of Naples ('Avalanche'), executed by General Clark's 5 Army, with General McCreery's X (Br) Corps on the left; these beaches were just in fighter range from Sicily. 1 (Br) Airborne Division was to land by sea in the port of Taranto, if conditions—including the surrender of the Italian fleet—seemed right, with HQ V (Br) Corps and 78 Division to follow.

Meanwhile feverish political activity had been taking place. Italian emissaries had secretly signed an instrument of unconditional surrender in Sicily on 3 September 1943. Naturally, the Allies were not prepared to reveal the date of 'Avalanche' in case of duplicity or leakage, and in the event the Italian High Command had made virtually no contingency plans to meet the inevitable and long-prepared German reaction. Badoglio had expected a slightly later landing, and there was an hour's delay before he confirmed on Radio Roma Eisenhower's announcement of the Armistice on the evening of 8 September over Algiers Radio. By the evening of 9 September, the date of 'Avalanche', the Italian Army had laid down its arms, after only local resistance, and its equipment made the Germans much more mobile. The King and Badoglio, leaving no instructions, were en route for the Allied camp, and the fleet sailed to Malta to surrender. No less than 16 German divisions had by now been drawn into Italy, equally divided between Rommel's Army Group 'B' in the North, concentrating on the future Gothic Line, and Kesselring's Army Group South, to oppose any landings and make a fighting withdrawal under pressure up the peninsula.

10 German Army had sensed that the Salerno beaches were a likely Allied objective and had moved the battle-tried 16 Panzer Division from the East coast, just in time to disarm the Italian coastal division and to be on alert before the first Allied landings took place on 9 September. The beach-heads thus achieved were shallow, and British and Americans (because of 'Trident' decisions, much weaker than for 'Husky') found themselves overlooked by a great arc of hills, too far

inland to be easily won. There was a real danger that General von Vietinghoff might concentrate his troops in time to destroy the beach-heads before our 8 Army could link up past the unending demolitions in Calabria. Rommel's two Panzer divisions were held in the North to deal with Slovene partisans, who were threatening Trieste communications with acquired Italian arms, but six Panzer or Panzer Grenadier (PG) divisions were moving in for the kill. In the event naval gunfire, airborne and seaborne reinforcements and five hundred Strategic Air Force bombers enabled the gallant ground forces to hold on, and on 16 September patrols of our 5 and 8 Armies met. German troops were withdrawing slowly Northwards to the Volturno river, giving time for demolition and delayed charges to create havoc in Naples and for the preparation of the Gustav Line behind the Garigliano and Sangro rivers, which the battalions of the 60th were shortly to meet.

With the clarification of the strategic priorities between the Mediterranean and North West Europe campaigns, and with the establishment of our 5 and 8 Armies in too great strength in Italy for the Germans to eject them, it is indeed time to return to the Motor Battalions of the King's Royal Rifle Corps on the Southern shores of that ancient sea. After the fall of Tunis in May 1943, the victory parade, and the end of the desert war in which they had played such a full part, the 1st and 2nd Battalions drove back to the area of Tripoli. They were sufficiently close to hold a regimental parade alongside each other in great heat on 10 June; Maj Gen G. W. E. J. Erskine, late 60th and GOC 7 Armoured Division, inspected both battalions and addressed them on behalf of the Colonels Commandant. On 21 June both battalions lined a route out of Tripoli to salute and cheer HM King George VI, in his open car; speaking to each Commanding Officer in turn, our Colonel in Chief remarked that, while he had visited the 2nd in England, he was pleased to get his first glimpse of the 1st. Both battalions had moved to camps in refreshing areas, where the warm sea gently cooled the sun-baked rocks and opportunities for leave and courses were seized. The 1st, on the disbandment of 7 Motor Brigade, joined 2 Armoured Brigade of 1 Armoured Division, our 2nd Battalion's old formation, and in so doing was destined to remain in the Mediterranean for the next four years. Lt Col W. D. Keown-Boyd relieved Lt Col J. L. Corbett-Winder after the latter's excellent leadership of the 1st in their first encounters with the problems of hill warfare in Tunisia. With the 1st's departure to guard prisoners-of-war at Medjez-el-Bab on 1 August, we shall leave them to concentrate successively on the 2nd, and later the 11th, far to the East near Aleppo in Syria. Since the 2nd fought only on the East coast of Italy, which was isolated by mountains from the Naples–Rome axis, we shall first cover their actions until they re-embarked for Britain; the general narrative will be resumed with the story of the 11th, who fought under both 5 and 8 Armies.

At the end of the North African Campaign in May 1943, 4 Light Armoured Brigade became a standard independent armoured brigade consisting of 44th Royal Tank Regiment, 3rd and 4th County of London Yeomanry (CLY), and 2nd Battalion, The King's Royal Rifle Corps. Throughout the Sicilian Campaign, the armoured regiments were placed under command of Infantry divisions and the Battalion was left behind in a pleasant spot on the coast a few miles West of Tripoli, where it spent the remaining months of the summer training, playing games and swimming. On 16 September the Brigade was ordered to concentrate at Taranto in Southern Italy, and rumour had it that the Brigadier was demanding the immediate despatch of his motor battalion from its life of leisure beside the Mediterranean.

During this period, there were numerous changes in the Battalion. Maj H. R. Woods left to command 9 DLI, which he did with notable success until he was killed leading an attack during the first days of the Normandy campaign. One of the outstanding officers of the Regiment, he had won a DSO and an MC and Bar in the Desert and his death was a sad loss. His place as second in command was taken by Maj M. F. Douglas-Pennant. Maj D. J. Graham-Campbell, Capts F. O. Green-Wilkinson and R. H. Willis Fleming and Lts P. Gjertson, J. J. Walters and L. Asquith left for other appointments. Capt J. G. Harries became Adjutant, being replaced as Signals Officer by Lt M. J. L. Stow. Capt R. F. Nixon took over HQ Company and Capt H. B. S. Gunn D Company.

Meanwhile over in Italy our 5 and 8 Armies had linked, and command of the sea was assured with the surrender of the Italian fleet. Since the Apennine spine demanded that each coast should have its own ports and lines of communication, the harbours of Taranto, Brindisi and Bari were needed on the Adriatic side. The enemy in that area had been reduced to a single battalion, so part of 1 Airborne Division were landed on 9 September by cruiser directly into Taranto, and moved Northwards with eyes on the Foggia airfields.

Not unpredictably, after four months of inactivity, the 2nd Battalion's orders to move arrived without warning on 19 September. Nine days later the Battalion began disembarking from American LSTs at Taranto, having driven to Bizerta (the port of Tunis), some 600 miles from Tripoli, where vehicles and equipment to bring it up to scale had been issued. A considerable rear party, consisting of most of HQ Company and much of the support company (D Company), had to be left behind in Tunisia owing to shortage of shipping; they did not rejoin the Battalion until 25 October.

On 2 October, Maj H. C. J. Hunt—subsequently to gain world renown by leading the successful expedition to Everest—joined the Battalion and took over command of D Company. He arrived during the evening, but unfortunately many of his Riflemen were in no fit state to receive their new commander, having managed to get hold of large quantities of local and very strong wine which they had drunk as if it were weak beer. In spite of its having been rushed to Italy in precipitous haste, there appeared to be no particular need for the Battalion, and on 8 October it moved North to Foggia, where it took up a defensive position against a possible counter-attack on to the vital airfields located there. On the 28th a further move North was ordered to defend the Forward Maintenance Area at Termoli against somewhat improbable seaborne raids. By now the rains had arrived. The soil was heavy clay, and any movement in vehicles off the roads was almost impossible, as these were little more than tracks and generally ran along the tops of ridges; finding anywhere to harbour the Battalion was therefore extremely difficult, and while it was quite easy to get off the road into a dripping orchard, the reverse journey could take several hours.

Meanwhile, over on the West coast, Naples, its docks shattered by demolition, had been occupied on 1 October; a brilliant Allied joint effort, however, enabled 5 Army to start maintenance through the port a fortnight later. On 12 October that Army assaulted across the River Volturno, and had taken all the German positions covering it after a week of heavy fighting. The weather had broken simultaneously across the peninsula, the mud, swollen rivers and bad flying conditions helping the defender. Since Hitler, with his armies in Russia in full retreat for the Dnieper, had decided to hold a line, the Gustav, at its economical narrowest point, linking the rivers Garigliano and Sangro, the Germans were fighting dogged rearguard actions to allow time for the line's preparation. As they had as many fresh divisions again in Northern Italy, they could relieve or reinforce tired formations quicker than could the Allies, with their shipping limitations.

On the East coast Termoli had been taken by an assault landing, and 78 Division was advancing, after a repulsed Panzer attack on 6 October. In 8 Army V Corps commanded the coastal Route 16 thrust, while XIII Corps handled the slow Route 17 advance in the hilly centre. Alexander was straining his human and logistic resources to the utmost to seize his next objective, Rome, and the neighbouring airfield, road and rail network before the divisions and landing craft were withdrawn in November for 'Overlord'. However, the weather, enemy resistance and the dictates of road and port capacity slowed all movement and it was not until 4 November that V Corps were firmly over the River Trigno and advancing on the Eastern end of the Gustav Line, the River Sangro, where the 2nd Battalion, to which we return, was about to be committed.

Early in November, Lt G. M. Wood and eight Sergeants joined the Battalion from England, and at the same time Major M. F. Douglas-Pennant left to take over command of 5 Infantry Division Reconnaissance Regiment, where skilled leadership won him the DSO; Major Hunt took his place as second in command. On 4 November the Brigade was ordered to advance North towards the River Sangro. The weather by this time was appalling, and almost any movement off the roads was impossible for ordinary vehicles and very difficult even for tanks and carriers. The coastal plain up which ran Route 16, the main axis of advance, was interspersed by a series of knife-back ridges and deep streams, of which the Germans took full advantage by blowing the bridges and culverts and mining their approaches. Progress was slow, with a troop of tanks supporting with fire a motor company on foot; there was only one road, and it was not possible to advance on a wider front. By 6 November, B Company under command of 44 RTR had established a bridgehead across the Sinello, but by early afternoon the advance was held up by enemy tanks and infantry and the Battalion was ordered to lay on a full-scale attack. This was put in at 1530 hrs with A Company on the left of the road and B Company on the right. The attack was supported by one squadron of 44 RTR and three Regiments of Artillery; Colonel Heathcoat-Amory co-ordinated the attack by walking straight up the middle of the road in line with the leading platoons. By 1730 hrs the first objective, a crossroads just South of Scerni, was taken; five prisoners were captured as well as two machine-guns—our own casualties were two wounded. It was by now dark, but C Company passed through to clear the main village of Scerni, which ran due East from the crossroads and was to be our main base for the rest of the campaign in Italy. Fortunately, it had been little damaged by shelling, and so most of the battalion was able to get under some form of cover against the bitter weather. The advance was now continued by the infantry of 78 Division and the Battalion was concentrated in Scerni for a very well-deserved rest and clean-up. In this action

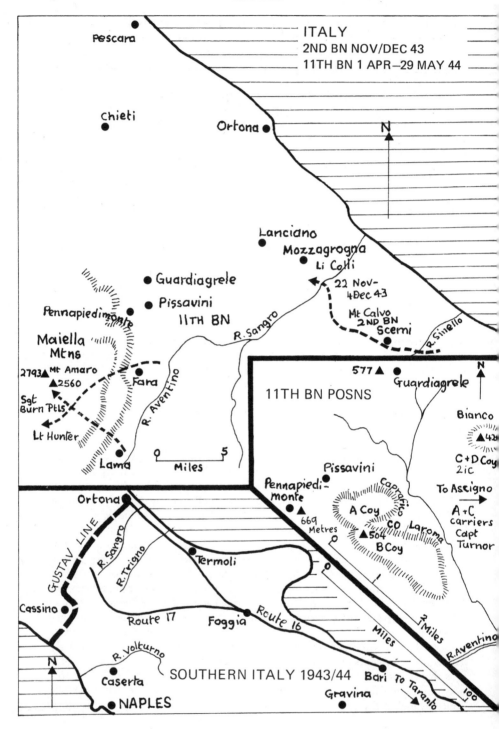

ITALY
2ND BN NOV/DEC 43
11TH BN 1 APR—29 MAY 44

Corporal Curtis of 7 Platoon and Corporal Watts of 8 Platoon, both in B
Company, did exceptionally well, and the latter was awarded a Military Medal for
his leadership.

On 15 November the 2nd Battalion relieved 2 Lancashire Fusiliers on Monte
Calvo, coming under command of 36 Brigade, 78 Division. The position covered
the last ridge overlooking the River Sangro which was held in great strength by
the Germans. Preparations for the battle were greatly delayed by the weather, but
Maj Hunt and Capt D. F. Fletcher took a patrol down to the river bank and found
that it was impossible to ford vehicles across it.

The River Sangro itself was a typical *torrente*, whose wide shingle bed, cut
with summer water channels, could fill with great rapidity at each mountain
rainstorm: during the battle the spate was to reach seven knots. The alluvial
plain was composed of bottomless mud and was sown with mines, covered by
fire from the main German position on the Li Colli ridge, which in turn had been
mined, wired and dotted with concrete emplacements by Italian forced labour.
The ridge was held by the German 65 Infantry Division, and, because 8 Army
operations were delayed by rain more than once, 26 Panzer and 90 PG were
moving up in depth. Our 78 Division had reached the river on 8 November and
had been patrolling vigorously up to the ridge in preparation for the bridgehead,
which 36 Brigade of the Division established on the night of 19 November. The
plan had been to pass in 8 Indian Division to take Mozzagrogna, and then for 4
Armoured Brigade and 78 Division to surprise the Germans by climbing the Li
Colli ridge in an area where the defenders had sited no anti-tank guns, thinking it
too steep for our armour. 4 Armoured would then sweep right down the ridge to
the sea, and open Route 16, while on the left the New Zealanders would make for
Chieti to threaten the lateral to distant Rome.

However, on 20 November rain fell endlessly, no bridge could be built nor the
Indians passed in, and the New Zealanders were only finally to make a crossing
on the 27th. In this desperate situation it was a case of trickling in battalions to
strengthen and if possible expand the 36 Brigade bridgehead. Thus 2nd 60th,
which should have played a classic motor-battalion role with their armoured
regiments in clearing the Li Colli ridge, were at little notice drawn in to try to
extend the 36 Brigade position from the river valley up the nearest escarpment.
Lt J. F. Gammell, who was commanding a platoon in B Company, has described
the part played by the 2nd Battalion.

> At 1500 hrs on 21 November we had orders that we were to cross early next
> morning to attack Casa Casone, about 1,000 yards beyond the river. Casa
> Casone was a strongly built house standing on the edge of the main
> escarpment which ran parallel to the Sangro River; the escarpment was
> climbable on foot almost anywhere.
>
> Owing to the operation being planned so late, there was no opportunity for
> a reconnaissance of the objective, except through field glasses. For the same
> reason little information could be gleaned about the area from other sources.
> However, we were quite accustomed to these 'operations of opportunity',
> which are a motor battalion's job. The Battalion moved off by companies,
> starting at 2200 hrs, and marched a very slippery and wet six miles to the
> river, where most people were able to get a little sleep while a suitable fording
> place was being reconnoitred.

C Company crossed first and took up a covering position on the far side, and A and B Companies passed through them on to their start line.

We had a half-hour concentration from four regiments, Royal Artillery, but as these same guns had other work to do that night we could not get them until 0500 hrs, a little late to ensure the attack being finished before first light. The 'fireworks' started punctually and it was an impressive sight as we waited on the start line for the gunners to finish. The Casa stood out faintly in the moonlight and the escarpment looked as high and unclimbable as the cliffs of Dover. When the time came for us to close up behind the concentration, we moved forward. Very soon after the guns stopped a good many German machine guns and mortars opened up on us while we were still a distance from the escarpment. Corporal Curtis, one of the few remaining Rangers' men, was killed here.

A Company on our right had apparently just failed to reach the top of the escarpment, which was by now well covered by enemy close-range fire and enfiladed from both flanks. Both forward companies were, therefore, ordered to consolidate on the line they had reached.

The forward platoon of B Company which had reached the foot of the escarpment was eventually withdrawn under cover of a smoke screen, but it was evening before some of the wounded could be collected and brought back. Alan Holmes (later reported killed) and his runner were found to be missing.

The 23rd passed with a good deal of shelling from both sides; meanwhile a plan was made for renewal of the attack that night. C Company attacked the position at first moonlight, about 0230 hrs, with A Company in Battalion reserve.

The advance was unsupported by artillery as it was hoped to catch the Hun by surprise. However, the enemy did not wait for us this time, and slipped away into the thick country behind, and our patrols the next morning reported him digging in about two miles back on the main ridge. The rest of the day was spent in consolidation on the escarpment and the evacuation of casualties by Bailey bridge.

Lt Gammell was himself wounded in the action, and was awarded the MC for his leadership during it, and Sgt Brown of D Company received the MM. In addition to Maj Holmes, the Battalion lost three Riflemen killed and 12 wounded. Maj Holmes, of whom nothing more was ever heard, was the last of those outstanding Eton masters in the 2nd Battalion, and had commanded B Company with distinction since Alamein.

The river was very swollen by the 23 November spate and it was difficult to get supplies across, as the Bailey bridge, which had been built with great courage by the Royal Engineers, was partly underwater and continually shelled. However, thanks to Maj Hunt's heroic efforts a mule train was got across with blankets and rations, but at a cost of two Riflemen being killed and two wounded by shellfire at the bridge. The Battalion, now under command of 21 Brigade, 8 Indian Division, remained on this very exposed and uncomfortable position until the 29th, when it was relieved by the 13/15 Punjabis. Although there was no active contact during this period, the area was heavily mined, and was subject both to shellfire and aerial bombardment. Lt P. E. Curtis, a son of Maj Gen H. O.

Curtis, later Colonel Commandant, and a brother of Maj J. H. P. Curtis, and a Rifleman were killed by an anti-personnel mine. On 27 November a small farmhouse, which was occupied by Lt D. T. T. Jackson's Platoon, received a direct hit from a bomb, as a result of which he and 12 Riflemen were badly wounded and Sgt Meredith, his Platoon Sergeant, was killed. On the same day Lt P. B. D. Cochrane and his driver were blown up in their carrier by an anti-tank mine, the driver being killed. Unfortunately, both Lts Jackson and Cochrane subsequently died of their wounds. These casualties, especially the deaths of these excellent young officers and the loss of Maj A. T. G. Holmes, were a sad blow, coming as they did in the last action the Battalion was to fight in Italy.

The part played by the 2nd had been most useful, for, in their successful attack up the escarpment early on 24 November, they had secured elbow-room for their 4 Armoured Brigade. On 29 November those tanks and the Irish Brigade of 78 Division climbed the ridge, and the next day had cut Route 16 to the Adriatic in a series of spirited actions.

On 4 December the 2nd pulled back to Scerni, which had housed the echelon throughout the Sangro battle, with no tasks other than to provide working parties to carry ammunition and salvage any worth-while equipment from the battlefield. Christmas was celebrated in traditional style, the Italian population, who now were very friendly, being as hospitable as their limited resources allowed. On 1 January 1944 the welcome news was received that the Battalion, together with the rest of 4 Armoured Brigade, was to return to England. Unfortunately, this meant leaving behind in Italy all ranks who had joined from England during the last nine months, and involved 5 officers and 65 other ranks. Maj Hunt also left to take over command of 11 KRRC.

The Battalion moved first to Taranto, where all vehicles and stores were handed in. The Quartermaster, Capt R. F. Bird, was faced with the difficult problem of how to dispose of considerable quantities of rum which he had never officially received; the HQ Company officers mess gallantly came to his aid, but at least one officer has never since been able to bear the smell of it. From Taranto the Battalion moved in a very dilapidated train through seemingly endless tunnels to Naples, a journey made even less enjoyable by the news that a civilian train had broken down on the same line a few days previously and all the passengers had been suffocated. After a few days in a transit camp, the 2nd Battalion consisting of 31 officers and 639 other ranks embarked on HMT *Almanzora* and after an uneventful voyage docked at Glasgow on 9 February 1944, two years since they had first encountered Rommel near Agedabia.

It is now more than time to take up the account of our 11th Battalion; we last heard of them in the previous Volume, as they were withdrawn after successful action on the Miteiriya Ridge during the battle of El Alamein in October 1942. During January 1943 the 11th moved from Egypt to Aafrine, near Aleppo in Syria. Having handed over its equipment to help the 2nd Battalion during Alamein, it still had only half its authorized vehicles, but a steady and progressive programme of training and courses prepared the Battalion for 9 Armoured Brigade exercises in May. The emphasis on fitness is shown by its gaining first place in 10 Armoured Division athletics and the introduction of hill warfare training from June onwards. In July Lt Col C. M. Gurney was appointed 2IC of 7 Armoured Brigade and was relieved as Commanding Officer by Lt Col C. d'A. P.

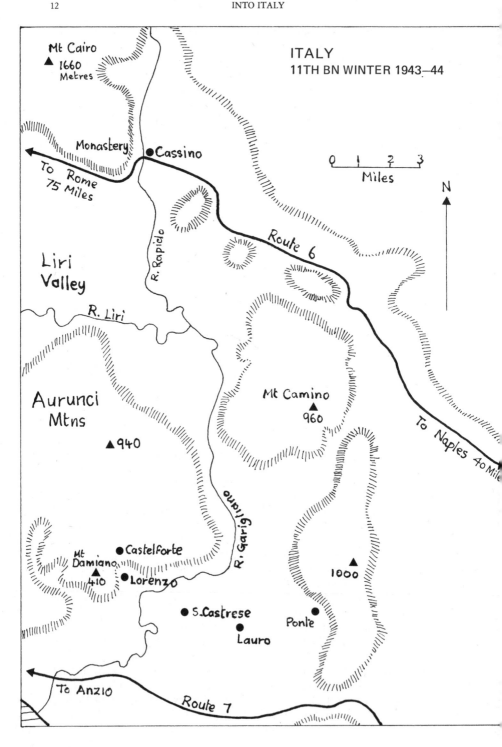

Mt Cairo
▲ 1660
Metres

ITALY
11TH BN WINTER 1943—44

Monastery
● Cassino

To Rome
75 Miles

0   1   2   3
Miles

N

Route 6

R. Rapido

Liri
Valley

R. Liri

Aurunci
Mtns

▲940

Mt Camino
▲
960

To Naples 40 Miles

R. Garigliano

Mt
Damiano
▲
410

● Castelforte

●Lorenzo

▲
1000

● S.Castrese

Ponte
●

● Lauro

To Anzio

Route 7

Consett, DSO, MC, who had joined as 2IC in April. All sensible preparations for a probable Mediterranean role continued to be made; hill and night training were given much emphasis, scales of kit for dismounted action were studied and mine and sniper courses were run.

At last on 16 September 1943 the 11th Battalion left Syria for Egypt, where the 1098 equipment was made up to scale. On 18 October the Battalion embarked in SS *Karoa* and marched to billets on arrival in Taranto, Italy, on the 22nd. The transport ship limped into Brindisi on the same day after striking a mine; 12 vehicles were damaged by sea-water. On 4 November the 11th started to move across the peninsula to Caserta, and were visited there by General Erskine on the 7th, as D Company was being reorganized on to a three-platoon basis, with the remaining Riflemen going to make up the other companies to strength. General Erskine's 7 Armoured Division had just reached the River Garigliano in the coastal sector, with 46 Division next inland; further still 56 Division was up against Monte Camino on the East bank of the river, where its tributary, the Rapido, came due South from Monte Cassino and its ancient monastery. All the bridges had been destroyed, approaches were mined, and vehicles, limited by mud to roads and tracks, were shelled from across the river. Route 7 on the coast was in any event not hard to block, and the apparently easier Route 6 had to wind round the foot of Cassino after crossing the Rapido and before entering the Liri Valley; this in its turn was dominated by the Aurunci Mountains to the South, while pill boxes were being constructed across the valley in depth, to prevent a rapid passage through the Gustav Line to Rome. However, 5 Army had first, by combined American and British effort, in their initial experience of Italian mountain warfare, to clear Route 6 up to the Rapido against the first-class German divisions overlooking them from successive heights.

To allow 7 Armoured Division to be withdrawn and to return to England, and to let 56 Division concentrate against Monte Camino, the 11th Battalion, under 23 Armoured Brigade, took over positions opposite the lower Garigliano within a week of arriving at Caserta. The chronicler of the Battalion's actions in Italy was Lt J. D. W. Hunter, and edited quotations interspersed in our narrative will be from his excellent account:

> Mention 'Italy' to a Rifleman of the 11th Battalion and what will the name conjure up? A picture of bare hillsides, with no vestige of cover against the weather; of low cloud and driving rain; of mules loaded with 'compo' rations, and the Indian muleteers who seemed to be even more obstinate than the mules; of 'stand-to' in a slit trench with a foot of water in the bottom; of bad 'vino' and worse cognac; and above all of patrols—night after night slithering into unexpected ditches, waiting in ambush for the Boche, who seldom turned up, coming back with the occasional prisoner or the occasional casualty. It was a static, sticky, slimy war with more casualties than kudos and more mud than was good for morale. There were no spectacular advances, no daring jock-columns; just sitting and waiting, and getting wet.

On 12 November 1943 Battalion HQ, with A, B and D Companies, formed a firm base at Ponte, while C Company patrolled forward to the river two miles away. Only essential vehicles were allowed forward and the point of this was reinforced the next day, when three of our water trucks, allowed through another unit's road block, found themselves halted by demolitions. They were unable to turn round because the rear truck was rapidly shelled and set on fire, and the first casualties were sustained. However, within two days C Company had ambushed and shot up Germans in small boats, plying between wooden jetties on the Garigliano. A Company loaded donkeys with a mortar and ammunition, using panniers better suited to peasant provender, and, in imitation of the long-drawn cries of the Italian drover, 'wandered out into no-man's-land sounding like rather rusty opera singers practising their scales, intermingled with which were other words more vehement than operatic'; the shoot, despite its logistic difficulties, was eventually successful.

On 23 November the 11th Battalion moved nearer the river, with Headquarters, A and C Companies at Lauro, West of Ponte.

B Company was at San Castrese, about a mile and a half from the river and even nearer an obstinate little body of Boche, commanded by one, Lieutenant Arnst, who lived in two villages in a loop on our side of the Garigliano. They would not have been difficult to evict, probably, but were left there to give us something to do. Arnst's boys did a good bit of patrolling and accordingly we produced a nightly quota of standing patrols and ambushes. One night Capt A. R. Turnor, returning from an A Company patrol, met a body of men quite close to our lines. Both parties thought that the others were friendly, but fortunately Tony tumbled on the truth before the Boche did, and his patrol quietly disarmed them. The four prisoners were from the German 94 Infantry Division and included a Pole, whose earlier Dachau experiences encouraged him to give much local information. C Company were meanwhile locating and engaging an enemy-held house.

These early skirmishes were the prelude to increasingly sharp patrol actions. The first gallant attempt by 5 Army to take Monte Camino had failed by mid-November. There was now to be a properly co-ordinated British and American attack, and it was important for the 11th Battalion to give the impression of all the preliminaries to an assault crossing over the lower Garigliano as a diversion. The river valley was observed by the enemy and German artillery and mortars had the range of every point, so Lt Col Consett's plan was designed to make as much use of firepower and carrier movement as possible, while ensuring that the small dismounted element would be glimpsed only briefly before last light, so that its size could not be properly assessed. After two days of elaborate planning and observation of routes and last-light timings, the diversionary patrol action went in on the late afternoon of 1 December.

C Company carriers, despite difficulty in the muddy lanes, got into action and had a spirited fire fight with Spandaus at 300 yards range. B Company carriers had similar mud problems, but also engaged a hamlet; heavy shelling and mortaring seriously wounded one crew member. All the while two regiments of guns and our mortars were carrying out an elaborate fireplan, which included flanking smoke. An A Company platoon fighting patrol, representing the just visible spearhead of an imaginary infantry attack at dusk, moved off on time over a series of ditches and, after swinging from North West to West, just failed to cut off the forward German section as it sped from the flaming hamlet. Another enemy section was driven back with casualties by grenades and sub-machine-gun fire; the hamlet was found to be no longer occupied and the patrol withdrew, its mission accomplished, under heavy shell-fire. The six bogged carriers were expertly recovered the next night and, thanks to skilful use of a motor battalion's full resources—not least intelligence applied to the conservation of our men's lives—a most successful part of a much wider deception plan was executed with only one Rifleman wounded.

Nearly every night from now on there were sharp patrol actions with casualties to one side or the other. One C Company patrol crept forward with an OP and harassed a German farm with three-inch mortar fire, while a Rifleman in another patrol was wounded by an 'S' mine. On 3 December B Company patrolled into the previously mentioned hamlet, which had been reoccupied by the enemy, and interrupted the sentries' conversation with a grenade at short range. Three actions, however, were at particularly close quarters, as now detailed.

Another notable patrol was carried out in broad daylight by 11 Platoon. Their task was to find out whether another house was occupied, and if so to harass it. It was, and they did. Lt P. H. Lawrence and Cpl Angus got right up to the house unobserved and were finally fired on from a hole in the wall. Peter inserted a grenade in the hole while Cpl Angus sprayed the windows with a tommy gun. Simultaneously the remainder of the patrol opened up on the other side of the house with two Brens, and put down 2″ mortar smoke to cover the withdrawal of the 'assault' party, which took place without incident. It was one of those rare occasions when everything goes according to plan.

During this period RSM James was lost, dying on an enemy position. He had gallantly insisted on taking part in a night patrol, led by Lt D. J. Longstaffe, B Company, to find out whether a ruined house was still occupied. Operating from a firm base, these two crawled up to the road running along the crest of the ridge. Two rifle shots were directed at them, which went well over their heads. RSM James replied with a burst of tommy-gun fire and Lt Longstaffe threw a grenade, whereupon Spandaus opened from left and right, and other fire and grenades came from the front. Lt Longstaffe was badly wounded in the right hand, and RSM James doubled up and rolled down the slope towards the enemy positions, calling out, 'I've been hit'. Verey lights went up and the fire intensified, but Lt Longstaffe, in spite of his wound and precarious position, remained for some time trying to find RSM James, before crawling back. A second patrol that night failed to find the RSM. Lt Longstaffe received the MC for his gallantry.

On 13 December a B Company standing patrol was attacked soon after midnight. Enemy machine-gun and mortar fire was brought down on them, and, despite the patrol replying with Bren and grenades, the commander, Sgt Hardwick, and three Riflemen were killed. A first-light carrier patrol by C Company encountered mines laid during the night, and Sgt Stone and two Riflemen were killed, with several other casualties. Unfortunately, as the 11th was relieved that night and went back to rest, there was no chance to retaliate.

The 11th Battalion rested, and in its training sensibly concentrated on house and street fighting, until the end of December 1943. We must meanwhile examine just enough of General Alexander's strategy to understand the Battalion's modest but essential role in the winter offensive that followed. If German formations were to be drawn away from Russia and from the 'Overlord' landings, pressure in Italy must be maintained despite weather and terrain; and yet the agreed priorities of the 'Overlord' timetable were already biting. Divisions were returning to England, and landing craft, already delayed, must follow them.

Briefly, after the last hills down to the River Rapido had been cleared, the French would threaten the enemy's Northern flank in the Apennines, while X British Corps, reinforced by 5 Division from 8 Army, would cross the lower Garigliano and seize the hills South of the Liri Valley. As the German reserves were drawn forward to cover these two widely separated threats, the Americans would try to force the Rapido below Cassino and advance up the Liri Valley. With all German reserves hopefully drawn forward an Allied landing would be made at Anzio in their rear. In all of this the 11th Battalion was used by X Corps on diversionary tasks and in the classic motor-battalion role of holding a wide front by aggressive patrolling, thus releasing the heavy infantry for the assault crossings.

On the night of 4 January 1944 the 11th relieved an Infantry battalion on the Garigliano, further up near Monte Camino. It should be noted that the approaches to the river lay under enemy observation throughout this period, and, even by night, restriction to roads and tracks meant that all movement was likely to be accurately shelled. On 11 January an enemy patrol of 12 crossed the river and was seen off by A Company with the capture of a Polish prisoner, who reported on the thwarted desire of his fellow-countrymen to escape forced service in the Wehrmacht. Indeed, the admirable Polish Corps was steadily reinforced by its countrymen who evaded their German masters.

On the night of 17 January the X Corps river crossings went in over ground well known to our patrols in December, while that Battalion further up-river carried out diversionary tasks, building up from a fire programme to simulated assault crossing preparations the next night. After much heavy fighting, and with great bridge and raft difficulties, X Corps established a bridgehead in the hills over the lower Garigliano; by 21 January Kesselring's reserve mobile divisions were successively drawn away from the Anzio area. The 11th was withdrawn on the night of 19 January for short-lived and over-optimistic planning under 23 Armoured Brigade for a drive up the Liri Valley. The failure of the gallant, but inadequately prepared, American assault over the Rapido soon put a stop to this, and on 22 January the 11th found itself relieving a 5 Division battalion in depth on the coastal flank of the bridgehead, where it stayed for a week of minor patrolling.

Meanwhile the Anzio landing had taken place successfully on 22 January, but the enemy rapidly ringed the beach-head with an anti-tank screen and soon concentrated his mobile forces in a series of vicious counter-attacks against us. In Hitler's anxiety to demonstrate the vulnerability of assault landings, German divisions from East and West were drawn to Italy. The strength of Cassino, however, defied the successive gallantry of American and later 4 Indian Division and New Zealand assaults in their desperate attempts to link up with the beach-head during the remaining winter months.

46 Division had defeated a series of very heavy attacks on their sector of the X Corps bridgehead. During one of these D Company 1/4 Hampshires was loaned to 2 Coldstream, who were under intense pressure in the hills North of

Castelforte. The Company's determined stand triumphed when, outnumbered four to one, Capt H. S. Killick, attached from the 60th, led the Reserve Platoon in a bayonet charge which rounded up 110 Germans. Capt Killick, awarded the MC, was wounded; he will eventually return as the Commander of C Company, 1st 60th.

During this period the 11th Battalion took its turn in the line within the X Corps bridgehead, first of all on Monte Damiano, a wretchedly bleak feature, covering a German infiltration route. On 15 February, the day of the first bombing of the Monastery at Cassino, Maj Hunt, who, after leaving the 2nd Battalion, had been 2IC for a short time, relieved Lt Col Consett in command; the latter was to command yet a third battalion of The King's Royal Rifle Corps before the end of the war. By this time 56 Division had had to be withdrawn from the bridgehead to reinforce Anzio, and it was a question of holding wide fronts in the hills West of the Garigliano by intensive patrolling. The 11th relieved a Commando with the role of covering a gap between the river and their Lorenzo position. The first task was to patrol Northwards and to find out how far forward of Castelforte the enemy had worked. On the night of 22 February an A Company patrol led by Lt R. Farnsworth, attached from The Rifle Brigade,

> penetrated almost to Castelforte up the main road, crossing two barricades before coming under heavy fire. Bob was badly wounded in both legs and fell in the middle of the road. The remainder of the patrol returned the fire as best it could but became temporarily disorganised. Bob Farnsworth was rescued by Rfn Cozens, who picked up him up under the noses of the Boche and carried him back across the barricades, loaded him on to an abandoned farm cart and trundled him back to our lines, making a noise like a troop of 'Tiger' tanks, which drew fire from both sides.

For this gallant rescue under heavy fire Rfn Cozens received a well-deserved MM.

On the night of 2 March 1944 Lt H. W. Fowler, one of our American platoon commanders, led a platoon fighting patrol against two successive houses. The first was found clear, and, from a firm base, the second was approached. After spotting an anti-tank gun Lt Fowler saw three figures at an open door. A heavy exchange of fire between our tommy-guns and grenades and enemy machine-guns followed, with enemy seen running back. Not being able to cross the road because of a machine-gun firing down it at 100 yards range, the patrol withdrew safely and brought down mortar-fire on the house. Two nights later the 11th Battalion was relieved by American infantry and spent till 28 March resting and training, the only interruption being a momentary stand-to, when Cassino town was bombed on 15 March, in the vain hope that the Armoured Brigade might be needed in the Liri Valley. On 29 March the 11th moved Eastwards over the Apennines to join V Corps on the Adriatic front. Behind them the beach-head defenders at Anzio had inflicted heavy casualties on the recently arrived German 14 Army's attacking divisions, and the Germans in Cassino appeared to be equally impregnable until a new plan and better weather were forthcoming.

It had now been decided to rationalize the Allied front, with 5 Army concentrating the American and French divisions on the coastal flank; 8 Army was moving across the Apennines to the Cassino sector and would command the

British, Commonwealth and Polish divisions in the great May 1944 offensive. Operations on the Adriatic coast, on a line South West from Ortona, were left to V Corps alone; the Germans had equally thinned out, their Jäger troops up in the mountains linking with the two grenadier divisions by the sea. The task of the 11th Battalion was to hold a four-mile front covering the exits from Guardiagrele and in particular the large village of Pennapiedimonte, from which a steep gorge ran Westward into the snowy Maiella Mountains. The companies, moving forward on the night of 1 April 1944, held a series of steep plateaux, at over 1200 feet; on the right were C and D Companies under the 2IC, Maj The Hon T. D. Freeman-Mitford; next were the carrier platoons under Captain Turnor, with A and B Companies on the left under the CO. On their left flank was the Reconaissance Regiment of Lt Col M. F. Douglas-Pennant. Very few vehicles were taken forward, and since German patrols had been active—and indeed had dominated the area—sleep was snatched fitfully by day and every night was dedicated to exhausting patrol work. Our story, which can only hint at the skill and courage at platoon and section level, will show how the 11th, over nearly two months without relief, gradually pushed the enemy back on to the defensive. Individually, these characteristics were evinced at all levels, since the CO, his Company Commanders and Warrant Officers, all joined in the task of patrolling; as might be expected, Lt Col Hunt applied his special skills to the rock and snow on the mountain flank. Working with the 11th were Italian partisans, whose local knowledge and ability to move about in daylight without normally drawing fire were invaluable.

At 0615 hours on 6 April the enemy put in a carefully planned raid on the forward platoon of A Company. This platoon had inherited a position whereby the HQ and rear section held a house, which could not support the forward sections in their nicknamed houses owing to thick trees. Previous enemy raids, using small arms, had always been beaten off, but this time the Germans used an anti-tank gun, first on 'Blue Shutters' and then on 'OP House'. Despite a desperate defence the enemy closed in, using smoke, and within twenty minutes it was all over. When the platoon commander crawled forward, he found Rifleman Herring killed in the nearer house and the rest wounded by fallen masonry; in 'Blue Shutters', of a section of seven, there remained only the body of Rifleman Moore. This raid showed clearly the wealth of information the enemy had been allowed to build up. Our platoon positions was rapidly concentrated within mines and wire, and fire trenches dug outside buildings to avoid the casualties caused by flying bricks. The battalion became determined to wrest control of no-man's-land from the enemy.

On the night of 9 April, Lt Neale and a patrol of B Company ambushed and killed a German, shot by Rfn Walsh, at the mined 'Blue Shutters'. A Company got their revenge two nights later, when Sgt Dayton earned the MM with a classic section ambush covering a bridge. He allowed a German patrol, 30 strong, to move cautiously forward by bounds, until his two Brens and tommy-guns could catch the leaders on the bridge. Although he had three Riflemen wounded during the action, a good many casualties had been inflicted in the confusion among the enemy on the bridge. Next day two bodies found there were identified as a new Company Commander of the Grenadier Regiment opposite and one of his corporals.

On the night of 18 April a C Company patrol under Lt Lawrence, with Sgt Parker, used a PIAT to cause heavy damage to a house, known to be occupied. Despite the patrol commander's efforts to enter from the first floor, Spandau fire from supporting positions and barricading prevented a break-in. Two nights later Lt Lawrence with CSM Waldron repeated the PIAT attack on another house, whence the Spandau fire had earlier come; the PIAT's hollow-charge bombs, fired at very short range, were the only house-breaking weapon in a platoon's armoury, but were more likely to cause brickbat casualties inside than effect a breach. The occupants of the house were silenced with no casualties to our side, but two A Company Riflemen were captured, when their section patrol was overrun by an enemy platoon in poor visibility. After first light our snipers, who were persistently on watch, killed a German in a village opposite. The next evening Lt J. C. Armitage with a section from B Company caught a half-platoon of Germans on a bridge; three were seen to fall, and our partisans found much equipment in the area next day.

For some nights reconnaissance of the small village of Pissavini, used as a patrol base and believed occupied by a German platoon, had been intensified. A carefully planned company raid was put in on the night of 1 May by A Company, under Maj J. A. H. Powell; the company had been rested in the echelon area prior to this. They moved forward slowly through thick olive groves and broken, hilly country, their movement covered by the noise of a 9th Manchester MMG diversion. The two assault platoons were halted, while the Company Commander got the third into its position to provide covering fire, and concentrations by three-inch mortars were giving useful guidance to the objective. The order to move on apparently never reached Lt I. G. E. Pollock, and this first-class officer was killed by Spandau fire when moving forward later towards the noise of fighting. Meanwhile, working to the prearranged time-table, Maj Powell and the remaining assault platoon engaged their half of the objective. Ten PIAT rounds were put into the main house at 40 yards range, and then 3 Platoon went in, two sections up; a Spandau which opened up was knocked out by Sgt Turnor. Maj Powell and Cpl Gallimore took two prisoners outside the house, and the enemy on this side moved off to a shower of grenades from Lt C. E. W. House and the reserve section. On the left L/Cpl Gorman's men shot another of the enemy and had cleared the position, when the red withdrawal Verey light went up, as prearranged with the CSM, at 0200 hours. A prisoner said that all the six Germans in the house with him had been killed or wounded by PIAT fire; if 4 Platoon had been able to join in the assault the whole position would have probably been cleared. As it was the sad loss of its commander, Lt Pollock, who had won his MC at Alamein, cast a shadow over an otherwise successful raid, carried out in difficult conditions of terrain and visibility. Maj Powell was awarded the MC for his leadership in the action.

All through May our patrols were out, building up information, or clashing with the enemy, with casualties to both sides. When Lt S. F. Williams followed up an unusually bold enemy patrol in the late afternoon, his men inflicted two casualties for the regretted loss of L/Cpl Purcell, but when the Germans repeated their 'Blue Shutters' pattern of raid in the same area they wasted much ammunition on empty buildings. One B Company patrol of CSM Stokes, Sgt Freshwater and two Riflemen went forward to find out whether Pissavini had been reoccupied. After observing the main house for some time, the two senior ranks were caught by a Spandau at point-blank range when they moved forward. CSM Stokes managed to crawl back wounded to his men, but Sgt Freshwater, after using his tommy-gun and grenades, never reappeared. Revenge was, however, exacted by our snipers next day when two Germans were successively shot down in the doorway of that house.

From now on our patrols started to penetrate more deeply into the enemy positions, always inhibited by steep ravines or thick country. The supreme challenge was, however, in the moutains to the West, and it was here that Lt Col Hunt showed his ability to pick a select few and train them, with the leadership qualities he was later to display on Everest. Starting as early as 12 April, he had taken Lt Hunter and two Riflemen, vainly looking down for a route into the rear of Pennapiedimonte but thwarted by the sheer gorge. Attention was next paid to an approach up the gorge from Fara, and Lt Hunter led a deep patrol in search of the aerial ropeway used to supply German OPs on the highest peaks; it was seen by moonlight, but it was not to be cut without the use of wings. It was therefore decided to establish a patrol base with the Household Cavalry Regiment at Lama, and look for tasks nearer home. Although the great Allied attack around Cassino had started on 11 May, the Jäger were continuing to move around and prepare positions in the Maiella with the studied nonchalance of those who believe themselves invulnerable specialists. Apart from Lt Col Hunt, only Sgt Burn had been trained as a mountaineer, and it was to him that it fell to jolt the complaisance of the enemy's ski troops.

On the 18th May Sgt Burn took out a patrol to establish an O.P. and return the following night. It consisted of Cpl Angus M.M. of C Company (who had taken part in Lt Lawrence's Garigliano house patrol), L/Cpl Prebble, D Company, Rfn Clarke, B Company and an Italian patriot. Clarke carried a sniper's rifle. By morning the patrol was established in a rocky outcrop known as the Grotta Canosa. As it grew light they realised that they were very much in the thick of it. There was continuous enemy movement all the morning and most of the afternoon on three sides of them up to within 300 yards away. The patrol kept a careful log of events, which was despatched by pigeon just before they left.

They were unable to brew up or drink, as the rock was bare and the nearest patch of snow about 20 yards away in the open. Enemy movement ceased at 1830 hrs. At 1930 hrs two men were seen for a few moments before disappearing about 1000 yards away. An hour later our patrol prepared to leave, when one of them spotted two men 300 yards away from them. The patrol could easily have withdrawn unobserved. The two Boche were on the ridge where most of the activity had taken place during the day. It might easily conceal their night positions. Certainly there were Boche positions on the flanks.

The patrol commander decided to put them in the bag. Cautiously, fully loaded, in order not to leave anything behind if they had to withdraw in a hurry, the patrol moved forward. Both parties saw each other at the same time. They were 20 yards apart on a ridge, one side of which dropped steeply into a ravine several hundred feet deep. The enemy fired and disappeared behind cover.

1 His Majesty King George VI, Colonel in Chief of the Regiment, greeting Lt Col J. L. Corbett-Winder, MC, Commanding the 1st Battalion, at Tripoli on 21 June 1943

2 1st Battalion near Tripoli, 10 June 1943

Left to Right—Lt Col J. L. Corbett-Winder, MC; Maj A. G. L. Goschen, MC; Maj Gen G. W. E. J. Erskine, DSO; and Rfn Brown.

3 2nd Battalion near Tripoli, 10 June 1943

Left to Right—Capt J. G. Harries; Maj H. R. Woods, DSO, MC; Maj Gen G. W. E. J. Erskine, DSO; Lt Col W. Heathcoat-Amory, DSO; Capt R. F. Nixon; Lt J. M. L. Stow.

Sgt Burn saw that in the half-light they might give him the slip. The alarm would be given and he would probably be cut off. He looked round and saw a rock some 30 yards away from which he thought he could shoot. The intervening ground was devoid of cover. He left the remainder of the patrol and dashed across the open space under heavy fire from two machine pistols at close range. He reached cover and emptied two tommy gun magazines. One of the men fell. The other dived for what he thought, in the bad light, was a depression in the ground. It was in fact the edge of the ravine. He is a doubtful survivor. The first man, although wounded, made an effort to get his machine pistol into action again, and was promptly despatched by Clarke, the sniper. The patrol removed his papers and withdrew unhurt.

The dead man was Lt Lukas Zwiauer, a battery commander in a Mountain Artillery regiment, wearing the Edelweiss, the coveted mountain insignia, in his hat.

Sgt Burn received the M.M. for this patrol.

At 7500 feet, close to the peak of Monte Amaro, this was one of the highest actions ever fought by Riflemen.

After this the German mountain troops reacted very strongly, using larger patrols, pushing positions forward and employing patrol dogs. They did not abandon the Maiella until events on the West coast made their position untenable. On 11 May the great Allied series of attacks had started; in a splendid succession of infiltrating attacks, the French Corps moved forward from the Garigliano bridgehead, where the 11th Battalion had earlier been, through the Aurunci Mountains to seize the southern end of the Gustav Line. On 18 May Polish troops, from the hard-won crest of Monte Cairo to the North, entered the Cassino monastery. On 23 May the Canadian Corps broke through the defences in depth up the Liri Valley, the Hitler Line, and on the same day the Allied forces in Anzio started their break-out, turning almost immediately to make their main thrust towards Rome.

Naturally, in V Corps on the Adriatic a very close watch on any German attempt to withdraw troops to reinforce the West was maintained. On the morning of 23 May a sniper from the Manchesters walked through Pennapiedimonte without meeting any enemy. To follow this up a patrol under Lt J. G. Harrison, with 2 Sergeants and 18 Riflemen was sent out and stayed out till dawn the next day. Pissavini was found unoccupied, but the ridge forward of that was occupied by a strong and aggressive force of the enemy at dusk, and only careful leadership brought our patrol back unscathed. The next day the 11th was ordered to conduct two more probes, which were carried out by B Company. Lt J. C. Armitage and 15 Riflemen worked round the heavily mined Pissavini towards the ridge beyond. Casualties, including the Platoon Commander, were suffered from mines, shelling and from Spandaus, one of which sadly killed Cpl Halls, MM. Stretcher-bearer parties were sent forward from advanced Company HQ, and 8 Platoon under Lt M. H. H. Partridge was ordered to try to continue the advance right-handed round the minefield. They were pinned down by Spandaus, and an artillery DF was brought down on them. Eventually a badly wounded Rifleman was recovered, and both platoons withdrew, having suffered a total of two killed and nine wounded. On the other flank the remaining platoon under Lt

P. B. Tillard moved forward by bounds under heavy shell-fire, until the fire section under Sgt Park was pinned by accurate small-arms fire; both sections had finally to withdraw with great difficulty under fire, but only one man was wounded. That night a platoon under Lt M. L. Lejeune, one of our American officers, endeavoured to shoot up some of the new positions located during the day, but the well-dug-in Germans won the fire-fight and inflicted six casualties on us.

On 24 May Lt The Earl of Sondes skilfully took a patrol of 15 deep into enemy territory and lay up till the next morning observing without being seen. It became clear that the enemy were holding new positions strongly, with new minefields well covered, and that no withdrawal had taken place. Our patrols had wrested this information for V Corps with considerable courage and at no small cost. For the next few days a careful watch was kept by listening patrols, and in the mountains Lt Hunter and Sgt Burn were up observing the considerable enemy movement.

On 28 May 1944 the 11th Battalion was relieved, and, after handing in all equipment, embarked on 10 June for Egypt with its Armoured Brigade. It was ironic that just as Rome had fallen and the battered German armies were streaming Northwards, one of the formations which could have best harried them was leaving the country. However, towards the Allied victory the 11th had done their bit. By constant and aggressive patrolling they had dominated a brigade's width of front and allowed the concentration of the heavy infantry for the offensive in the West. The Colonels Commandant, Generals Davidson and Wake, summed it up well in their signal to Lt Col Hunt:

> We wish to congratulate you and all Riflemen under your command on the gallant and memorable record of the Battalion during the last eight months almost continuous campaigning in Italy. Let there be no disappointment that you are not still taking part in the victorious advance. You helped pave the way and have earned a rest, which we hope you are enjoying. The Regiment sends you hearty greetings.

CHAPTER II

THE REGIMENTAL HOME FRONT
AND
THE PRISONERS OF WAR

If we were concerned only with battalions rather than with the history of the Regiment, it would now be tempting to switch the narrative straight from the Mediterranean to the Normandy landings, and to drive North Eastward, following the actions of our 2nd and 12th Battalions. But the 800 Riflemen of a battalion in the field did not get there by accident, and it is just as important to study how all the members of the Regimental team combined to raise, maintain and train the battalions of The King's Royal Rifle Corps; in so doing it will convey in outline something of the life of a beleaguered island at war.

In the chapter 'The Regimental Family' of the previous volume a description was given of the training machine, through which each recruit passed. This mentioned that the 60th element of the Rifle Depot moved from Bushfield Camp, Winchester, to Fulford, on the outskirts of York, and became 27 Primary Training Centre (PTC); conveniently alongside it was the Green Jacket OCTU for 60th and Rifle Brigade officer cadet training, and a few miles North was 1 MTB, KRRC at Strensall, for specialist and continuation training.

These moves took place in Autumn 1942, as the South of England started to receive American forces. Officers and Riflemen who had completed training at 1 MTB then normally moved on to one of our battalions of Territorial origin, billeted in winter in a motley collection of requisitioned buildings, and often in tented camps in the summer with their armoured regiments. In the chapter referred to we saw how with little national help or backing our Territorials kept their battalions going during the period between the wars, and how in the year after the Munich crisis that cadre allowed a second battalion to be formed from each original regiment, all as part of The King's Royal Rifle Corps. Thus Queen Victoria's Rifles provided our 7th and 8th Battalions, The Rangers our 9th and 10th Battalions and The Queen's Westminsters our 11th and 12th Battalions; the Regiment owes them a deep debt of gratitude for the quality of Riflemen of all ranks whom they had raised before the outbreak of war. Thereafter the Depot or PTC was fed by Ministry of Labour call-up, usually from our traditional recruiting areas, and by a smaller number of volunteers, enlisting early, before call-up, on a Regular engagement to make certain of coming to the Regiment; some of these came through our Young Soldiers Battalion in the early war years. Of the original or 1st Territorial battalions, all three went into action—the 7th at Calais in 1940, the 9th in Greece, Crete and the Western Desert, until casualties forced disbandment, and the 11th, as we have just seen, in Egypt and Italy, and later in Greece. Of the 2nd Territorial battalions, the 8th missed Normandy by a hair's breadth, the 10th took over the 1 MTB role and the 12th alone was in action in

North West Europe. All of the home team, however, made an invaluable contribution to the field training of individual reinforcements for the Regiment, and indeed from 1942 onwards pre-war Territorials were providing a cadre of officers, Warrant Officers and NCOs at all levels across the Regiment.

Using what battalion material still exists, and dependent on the historical conscience of a series of harassed wartime Adjutants, we shall try to reconstruct the pattern of events which brought our element of the Army at home, under GHQ Home Forces, from mobilization in 1939 to the Normandy landings in 1944.

For the Territorial Army the first phase was towards embodiment; let us start with one battalion and weave in the rest. On 23 and 24 August 1939 HQ of the 12th Battalion at 18 Caxton Street, SW1, received certain codewords and within eight hours the prearranged 30 key men had reported. Under the CO, Lt Col S. R. Savill, these included the future Minister and *Daily Telegraph* Editor, 2/Lt W. F. Deedes as MTO, no doubt relying more on initiative than that sonorous chapter of King's Regulations on Impressment of Carriages. On 27 August orders were received to call up a further 6 Officers and 300 Riflemen, and within 24 hours more than this number had been embodied. Vulnerable Points (VPs) were at once manned, interestingly before the raising of the RAF Regiment, at Northolt airfield and the RAF Depot, Uxbridge, as well as at important Southern Railway bridges. On 1 September the remaining Riflemen were embodied and living in such requisitioned property as the Westminster Garage, Petty France, and Watney's Gymnasium, with a canteen opening a few days later in the former. Riflemen received 3 shillings a day subsistence allowance and fed at the Army and Navy Stores, where regimental cooks were also being trained. Officers received 3 shillings and 9 pence a day and messed at Chandos Court in Caxton Street. Hardly lured by this monetary distinction, 16 potential officers immediately applied for commissions, an indication of the recruiting value of our London Territorial link; they included several well-known actors, mentioned in the earlier volume, and such Regimental characters as Henry Crookenden, later prominent in Association affairs after his wartime wounding; they reappeared as 2/Lts in February 1940 after enduring the 'redcoat' OCTU process before our own was formed.

The second phase for those at home, while the BEF was moving over to France, was that of guarding VPs in the grim black-out and cold winter of the 'Phoney War'. The 8th, 10th and 12th played box and cox, usually in the East of London, taking on an exhausting series of guards for a month at a time. The 10th started in the Docks under Lt Col R. L. Bennett, but then was moved into reserve in support of the police, and to do some training; billets were often schools, since many children had been evacuated from industrial areas to the country. The 12th had a similar break from VPs at Pinner, but the movements of the 8th, under Lt Col H. W. Butler, can at this stage only be picked up when relieved by the 12th in Hampstead in December. After Christmas the very cold weather was made worse by a severe flu epidemic; at its height on 1 February 1940 173 men were in hospital and 137 on sick leave from the 12th alone. An unrelenting round of guards in the Docks and at Woolwich Arsenal was enlivened only when a sentry shot at and missed a cyclist who failed to respond to repeated challenges; he turned out to be, in that very different era, an electrician concerned about his lateness for work. Boredom had taken the place of the first flush of the previous autumn's enthusiasm, but, after the rumblings from Norway, this was rapidly to be dispelled in May as the Germans raced from Sedan towards the Channel.

In April 1940 the 10th had moved to provide the outer screen against parachutists around the Royal Ordnance Factories at Waltham Abbey and Enfield, while the 8th were responsible for defence inside them; one company complete concentrated on wiring tasks. Old P14 rifles were being issued to the 12th, when suddenly on 10 May all leave, the regularity of which—coupled with employment in the Regiment's main recruiting area—had been the winter's only consolation, was cancelled. Slit trenches were dug by all battalions, and, while the 12th manned road blocks and learnt about Molotov cocktails as one of the few weapons available against German armour, the 10th practised occupying the line of the River Lea, against the possibility of the enemy landing in Essex to march on London. In June Lt Col A. G. Bennett, whose crisp efficiency as WTO and Adjutant we noted 10 years earlier, relieved his namesake as CO; the remainder of the summer was spent, with heavy restrictions on leave and platoons at very short notice, on increasingly higher level training within 3 London Infantry Brigade and in co-operation with the Home Guard. The 12th had moved via Cambridgeshire to Staffordshire in the same month and the first bombs fell near by.

France had fallen, and our island was now under increasing attack. With a move to St Donat's Castle in South Wales, the 12th suffered its first casualties on 7 August 1940, one Rifleman dying and others being wounded by 40-pound anti-personnel bombs on the MT lines. On 7 September our battalions stood to on receipt of the invasion codeword 'Cromwell' in company with the rest of the poorly equipped but resolute Army at home; thanks largely to the Royal Navy and the Royal Air Force no invasion came. The 10th spent September fighting fires caused by incendiary bombs in the Silvertown area, but gradually our battalions found their rightful home as motor battalions in the armoured divisions, which were beginning to be formed, in the first instance for mobile defence in depth against an invasion.

The 7th had been reformed, with great help from 1 MTB, after its action at Calais and, under Lt Col The Hon D. O. Trench, joined the Support Group of 9 Armoured Division at Whittlebury, Northamptonshire, from Tidworth; it was easy for Maj Douglas-Pennant to do the recces as it was his home area. The 8th moved into 28 Armoured Brigade of the same Division at Northampton, and the 10th joined 20 Armoured Brigade of 6 Armoured Division at Trowbridge, Wilts, in a mobile reserve role, with particular emphasis on such airfields as Lyneham. Lt Col H. C. E. Mauduit, MC, had assumed command of the 12th, now at Keele, Staffordshire, in 30 Armoured Brigade. From the static duties of a sentry in the early VPs Riflemen would eagerly speed up their reactions to the 25 m.p.h. battle. First, motor-battalion roles, doctrine and drills had to be worked out. Then they had to be taught to commanders, down to corporals commanding each section, in its unarmoured 15 cwt truck, or carrier crew. For every battalion at home 1941 was a year of intensive training, and it was through their efforts that the large drafts which reached the desert in 1942 could replace battle casualties without much further training. Training with tanks for the first time was much on everybody's mind, since the first great Home Forces exercise 'Bumper' was due at the end of September 1941. In this great wartime manoeuvre the 7th Battalion fought a hard defensive battle in the Buckinghamshire area, being employed as a battalion concentrated, while the 8th, two years ahead of battalions overseas, was loaned 81 white scout cars and took part in the armoured encounters. None had trained harder with armour than the 10th, who had spent all spring and summer in the Thetford area after useful winter work on Salisbury Plain. The 12th had started its long Yorkshire sojourn at Ampleforth in June and, lest it be thought that the Regiment had lost its old capacity for enjoyment and self-help, one of the number of concerts held in aid of the KRRC Prisoner of War Fund is noted at this time; the star, as often before, was the actress Evelyn Laye, whose actor husband, Frank Lawton, had been commissioned after serving in the battalion as a Rifleman. The 12th's CO was now Lt Col C. Dalby, and in the 8th Lt Col W. D. Davies had relieved Lt Col Butler, who assumed the appointment of Equerry to the King of the Hellenes.

If 1941 had been the first year in which all our battalions got down to the motor role, 1942 might be recalled as the year of the Battle School, Battle Drill and other detailed infantry work, although our work with armour went from strength to strength. An excellent reason for joining one of the many overseas drafts of the next year or so was that England seemed to be becoming an even higher risk to remain in. The motor-cycle was shortly to be formally declared by the Army Council to be a lethal weapon, having inflicted higher casualties on our Army than any but the most severe enemy actions. Other transport, particularly the carrier with its characteristic of rolling over if not kept straight on a slope, caused a steady drain. The reaction of raw troops coming under fire in the early years had taught the need for battle indoctrination, and the necessity to handle weapons realistically called for field firing with live ammunition; a further trickle of casualties on this training, and in the street fighting areas, made out of bomb-ruined enclaves in Battersea and in such cities as Southampton, was the regretted but inevitable concomitant of realistic preparation for battle to save the lives of the majority.

Battle Drill at section and platoon level was excellent in intent, and in essence is still used throughout our Infantry. Instead of thumbing through the pages of *Infantry Section Leading*, the junior NCO on first contact with the enemy had a logical series of actions by which to try to regain the initiative, which would be known and understood not only by his platoon commander but by his own Riflemen. Its admirable purpose tended later to get obscured when the more wooden, square-bound element of the Army tried to focus on the drill aspects. Competitions were held, when the fact that the Bren Gunner had not come to attention, indicating that he was firing, or that the No 2 Bomber had taken a pace too many, might rule out of court the best section in practical field terms.

Battle Schools, to train unit instructors how to harden their men, to build up and maintain team morale and to encourage aggressive initiative under field conditions, were also admirable in intent, and soon every Division formed one, and every unit, as now, made an assault course. This was in a sense a return to the schools found behind the front in World War I, and at times drew in self-styled experts of the more bullying blood and bayonet type. However, the general effect on the battle readiness of the Army was sound, and, in the contest of wits with the long-calloused German panzer grenadier or parachutist, a certain hardness was essential—the Queensberry rules, in the absence of a referee, had to be discarded. It is worth noting that the young platoon commanders of the 11th Battalion, whose work on patrol round Italian farmhouses in 1943 and 1944 we have just examined, were all trained under this system. One of the developing experts at this game in 1942 was Maj F. de R. Dawson, modest and gentle as is so often the case with a first-class boxer and rifle shot. He left the 10th Battalion to instruct at the 6 Armoured Divisional Battle School and then went on to advanced commando work in Scotland. Impatient to put theory into practice, he transferred to the Yorkshire Dragoons, was with them at Anzio and was killed commanding a company in the breaking of the Gothic Line in 1944.

All was not work, however, in 1942, and the 12th sent 200 Riflemen away to a 'stand-down' camp in Scarborough during August. There were memorable lectures on Alam Halfa by Lt Col Renton, RB, whose views as GOC 7 Armoured Division on desert tactics had not coincided with those of the newly arrived General Montgomery; for 1 MTB this included a light-hearted DEWS ('Desert Exercise Without Sand') in the Yorkshire Wolds.

Equally ribald were the songs of Lt (QM) C. Timson, who was posted from the 10th to 1 MTB in advance of the battalion relief described later. This fine Rifleman, who was to die sadly early as Secretary of The Riflemen's Aid Society after the war, used to end his repertoire with an irrepressible twinkle to the chorus, redolent of Southend: 'I carnt get me winkle aht, anybody 'ere gotter skewer?'

1943 was, more seriously, a year of change for the Regiment. There had been fortunately rather fewer casualties in the final desert advance than expected and the days of expansion to motor brigades were clearly over. Other regiments, who had temporarily lent a battalion to the motor role, reverted to lorried infantry, and the lessons of Tunisia put renewed emphasis on the Vickers machine-gun and the 4·2-inch mortar, wielded by the Manchesters, Middlesex, Cheshires and Royal Northumberland Fusiliers. To these and to other Infantry regiments in Central Mediterranean Forces, or indeed at home, would go any of our officers and men, if they stayed too long unclaimed in reinforcement units. It could well have been that the regimental system might have been abandoned altogether at this period—which the Americans in fact did do, on grounds of posting expediency—if it had not been for the saner counsel of the Director of Organization (now Manning) from 1943–5, Maj Gen J. F. Hare, CB, DSO. A descendant of generations of distinguished 60th Riflemen, he insisted that his staff should try to keep together those who were recruited and trained together, or at least in company with which they had something in common. He could not control theatre staffs, but the 1943 mutiny at Naples—caused by the injudicious posting of Highlanders to an English division when their own 51st was going home—did at least bear out his policy, to which our Infantry and Armour owe much.

The first battalion to feel the changes was the 10th. Lt Col A. G. Bennett had commanded it through another intensive training year, with mountain work in Wales, armoured training on the Berkshire Downs and street fighting in Southampton. In January 1943 he handed over this tough and well-trained team to Lt Col G. E. R. C. Osborne, lately Chief Instructor to 1 MTB, with which after a move to Bridlington it merged. For the remainder of the war it carried out continuation and specialist training and prepared all overseas drafts, in co-operation with 2 MTB (RB), at Retford under Lt Col V. Turner, VC. Although the 10th did not see action as a unit, its well-trained individuals were thereafter to be found across the whole Regiment.

The 7th Battalion had moved with its Armoured Brigade to Yorkshire in autumn 1942, but in April 1943 the unwelcome process of disbandment began two days after Lt Col Trench and his Adjutant had been called to the War Office with nominal rolls. Only 60 Riflemen went to our 8th and 12th Battalions; of the remainder, 100 went to the Kensingtons and all the rest to 2/7 Middlesex. The 7th had taken great pains to reform after Calais, and it was a curt and ungracious end to the life of a good battalion. Lt Col Trench was later to be most helpful to all Riflemen in transit up and down Italy.

The 8th had ended their long stay in Northampton and had moved with their Armoured Brigade to Morpeth, Northumberland, where in January 1943 Lt Col C. T. Mitford-Slade became CO. Simultaneously Lt Col R. G. R. Oxley took over the 12th, still in Yorkshire. Very much in the mind of both COs was the forthcoming GHQ Exercise 'Spartan' and an intensive work-up was put in hand for the 8th. The accent was on the battalion forming a pivot of manoeuvre with its new six-pounder anti-tank guns, and the professional programme included a series of cloth model exercises and TEWTS to get the deployment drills right before each exercise. In the event the 8th held a long front, once up to 18,000 yards, on the Aynho canal and did indeed form a pivot for their withdrawing armour. One of the dangers of massive movement by night without lights was brought out when Lt M. G. Dacres Dixon lost his arm after hitting a stationary tank on his motor-cycle. 'Spartan' was on a vast scale, and entailed the Canadians trying to advance over the upper Thames towards Huntingdon. The defensively minded saw in it a rehearsal of how a German invasion might be resisted; in the minds of most it was the first thoughts on how our armoured forces might take on panzer divisions in North West Europe, and to some it was a duel for who should command our invasion forces. Neither commander won that post, although it was nine months before Montgomery came home from Italy, but for those at home 'Bumper' and 'Spartan' had something of the distinction of battle honours.

While the pattern of individual and collective training continued, 1943 might be thought of as the year of courses. The turning of the Germans to defence in Europe put mine warfare, particularly lifting, top of the list, with street fighting and sniping not far behind. It was also the year in which veterans returned with lessons of past fighting, whether as formations due for 'Overlord' or as individuals under the 'Python' (home posting after a long period overseas) scheme; in the 1st Battalion there were still surviving Riflemen who had joined in Burma six or more years earlier. Some like Capt J. Holdsworth had been wounded severely enough to require home posting, rather than the normal Mediterranean technique of patching up and sending forward again; others, like Maj J. C. Hope, had a short spell of passing on hard-won battle techniques as instructors, or, like his brother, Maj H. A. Hope, an escaped prisoner of war from Italy, went on to the Staff College. All of these three and many other Riflemen insisted on going back into action and, as we shall see, many paid a high price for their unselfishness.

After 'Spartan' our battalions moved, the 12th to Warminster for the summer, and thence on to Northumberland in January 1944, where it was to remain until its 'Overlord' move. The 8th moved off 'Spartan' to Ampleforth, with again great emphasis on the pivot and its anti-tank guns in all armoured work; this was of course derived from the Rifle Brigade's famous 'Snipe' action at the end of Alamein and our 2nd's similar tactics at the time, both somewhat marred by the vulnerability of our armour. Sartorial changes were also being made; early in the year the modified 1942 pattern of Battle Dress was introduced, with every inch of surplus cloth removed, as in the officer's Service Dress of the period, and the blouse now revealed a multitude of buttons, which in the 60th's case were to be Rifle pattern. The khaki side hat had been replaced by a khaki beret, and unofficially the rifle green beret—later to be worn by all Riflemen and Light Infantrymen—was pioneered by our officers.

It was ordained by the Q Staff that the camouflaged oilskin gas cape, the rolling of which in such a way as to allow quick release over equipment was a recruit's early nightmare, was not to be used as a 'rainproof'. In fact, it was the one really waterproof item issued during the war, and in the field preserved many a Rifleman from pneumonia, while his inadequate groundsheet served as the outer cover of his bedding roll. Attention to dress was not inappropriate in the 8th, as in September 1943 they moved with their division to King's Lynn in Norfolk. There they mounted a Royal Guard of 5 officers and 120 men on York Cottage, Sandringham, with a troop of armoured cars and one of Light Anti-Aircraft (LAA). While the rest of the 8th were pulling the vital sugar beet, the guard was to protect HM King George VI against a parachute or submarine-landed assassination attempt. Since these guards continued until the end of January 1944 and were the first close and prolonged contact of the Colonel in Chief with his Regiment, the letter from the Equerry is given in full:

> The King desires me to write and say how pleased he was with the manner in which the troops under your command carried out their duties during His Majesty's visit to Appleton.
>
> It was apparent to The King that considerable trouble had been taken to instruct the Riflemen in duties with which hitherto they were not familiar! The results were most satisfactory, and contributed largely to the enjoyment of The King's visit.
>
> His Majesty, therefore, was very pleased to have an opportunity of inspecting the Guard on parade this morning, and the bearing and turnout was a source of great satisfaction to Him.

The 'unfamiliar duties' were as volunteer beaters out shooting.

A final guard was mounted in April, but the tempo towards 'Overlord' was building up and the 8th had spent two winter months back at Morpeth with a considerable exercise on the Wolds. Lt Col Mitford-Slade's care as a trainer is shown in a very thoughtful analysis of the lessons; the higher aspects, of the advantages of a reverse slope position (provided mines and wire can prevent it being rushed) are covered, as well as the details of platoon and section field routine. The 8th was now very well trained, and at the end of May 1944 was told that it would be mobilized by the end of June. Orders came to move on 6 July to East Anglia, but the destination of Pembroke Dock in Wales was given three days later. However, on arrival and about to embark for Normandy, the 8th was sadly held back. Maj P. J. Bradford took over a complete company to 8 RB, and his DSO and MC, and the MC of Lt M. Raymond and the MMs of Sgts Barton and Stonell, speak much for the quality of our 8th Battalion.

Over in Normandy the 'dog-fight' phase of Montgomery's battle had been unduly prolonged around Caen and in the bocage country to the West, and casualties in both Green Jacket regiments were beginning to mount; our 2nd Battalion alone had already lost a third of its officers and 80 Riflemen. The casualties to 8 RB in the 'Goodwood' battle were another drain, and on 3 August the War Office ordered three drafts to be despatched, each of the strength and composition of a Company with its reinforcements. The excellence of all ranks received was gratefully acknowledged by all the Green Jacket battalions. In mid September 1944 our 8th moved to Newmarket, and Lt Col Mitford-Slade, who had done so much to prepare it for war, was posted as a GSOI to India. The new CO, Lt Col W. Heathcoat-Amory, DSO, after a long tour in command of the 2nd, arrived on 2 October, and drew up a directive on the 8th's new role of training wounded Riflemen for both Green Jacket regiments. With the percipience of one with much field experience, he stressed that they would be dealing with trained soldiers, who must not be bored by elementary instruction. The pattern was to be that of rehabilitation for a minimum of three weeks; thereafter fitness and marksmanship were to be coupled with refresher training according to specialist or other experience. They would receive new drafts from our 10th Battalion or 9 RB and wounded from both regiments, and despatch those fit to our battalions in 21 Army Group. In such a way Lt D. M. Stileman, RB, who had been shot with 8 RB on the Bourgebus Ridge during 'Goodwood', and who was a Company Commander and 2IC of distinction with the 60th 20 years later, is seen as coming from hospital to spend from March to May 45 with our 8th Battalion. At that period the task of running a special course of Czech reinforcements for their motor battalion was also discharged.

From VE day in May 45, through the summer of the post-war election and VJ day, the 8th slowly ran down, until the CO was posted to command 27 PTC; with the gradual reversion to the pre-war training system and deployment we shall leave them, grateful for uncomplaining good work from all Riflemen.

There is another part of the Regiment, who continued to resist the enemy at the closest quarters throughout the war—our prisoners of war; and what a long feat of endurance it was for those taken at Calais in 1940! Official doctrine on what to do when captured in the lectures of 1939 was erroneously based on the 1914–18 experience. It had then been impossible to break back through the trench lines, and the best chance was to wait till inside a camp in Germany, before making a properly organized bid for neutral Holland. The factors were now different; before long only Spain, Portugal, Switzerland and Sweden were unoccupied in the West, and in the first one risked imprisonment. From 1941 until the last months of the war the Germans could hold many of their prisoners deep in Poland, involving hundreds of miles of travel through territory where every male of fighting age was the immediate focus of police attention on the railways. The very nature of the countryside, with its bitter winters, the huge open fields and the bare pinewoods, made foot movement and the finding of hides extremely difficult.

Prisoners captured in the desert were handed over to the Italians, and with their 1943 collapse there was a matter of hours when camps were unguarded before the Germans took over and moved the inmates North. Unfortunately, some senior British officers mistakenly ordered a stand-fast in the thought that Allied landings in North Italy would rapidly make contact. Two survivors of the Sidi Rezegh battle managed to get away: Lt Col S. C. F. De Salis, DSO, after assistance from the Italians near Piacenza, made his way by bicycle, bus and on foot to Switzerland, in time to be Liaison Officer to the Belgians in North West Europe; Maj H. A. Hope, MC, took the long trail down the Apennines until getting through the lines in the Maiella Mountains, near where the 11th was to hold a sector later. After the Staff College he returned to Italy as DAA & QMG of 2 Armoured Brigade, which included the 1st Battalion. Lt Col de Bruyne OBE, taken near Gazala, operated with the partisans for over a year before escaping over the Gothic Line in October 44.

It was, however, into the hands of the Germans that all our prisoners of war sooner or later fell. The record of some German individuals and groups was grim indeed, but there was a certain respect for regulations and conventions which made the Wehrmacht Camp Commandants and their staff on the whole not altogether inhuman. Oppression came more often through the increasingly demented orders of Hitler, and the ultimate danger of escape bids was to fall into the hands of the Gestapo. The early months of captivity became a question of survival on starvation rations until the Red Cross and Regimental parcels eventually arrived; with the breakdown of the German economy under air attack the last few months also brought the question of bare survival to the fore. Under the Geneva Convention soldiers were required to work, and for those who were billeted on farms there was some possibility of augmenting rations with fresh vegetables, although under the regime of a hard taskmaster one might regret being so far from regimental help. Labour in factories or mines was grimmer.

Officers were not allowed to work, and were kept concentrated in Offizierslager (Oflags). While the health or inclinations of some might move them to interest themselves in hobbies and correspondence courses, there was a hard core who took seriously the injunction that the duty of an officer is to escape. In our Army at that time it would have been generally admitted that no group did more to tie down German manpower and resources by escape and the threat of escape than Green Jacket officers.

The largest single contingent of our prisoners was from the survivors of the 2nd Battalion and the Queen Victoria's Rifles (7 KRRC) after their Calais fight. Exhausted and in many cases wounded, they resolutely endured the long march to Germany under Feld Gendarmerie brutality in that burning summer of 1940. Two slipped away early in the march and finally over the Channel, both earning the MC. Capt E. A. W. Williams later commanded the 1st Battalion in Italy, and Lt T. S. Lucas found his métier as Air Liaison Officer to the Americans in the same theatre. For the rest it was a question of surviving that first hungry and cold winter. High morale was necessary, and fortunately there were leaders of the right calibre to pull camps and groups within them into teams. Prominent in this was Lt Col E. A. B. Miller, MC, the 2nd's Commanding Officer, who played a most valuable role right until the end, when, as Senior Officer Oflag IX A/H he shepherded his officers safely into the hands of the Americans in April 1945. With him at that time was Lt Col R. Boileau, who had played the same role with his Rangers of the 9th Battalion, captured in Greece and Crete. With Col Holland and Lt Col Gamble—whose son was later commissioned into the Regiment—they delayed the march after leaving camp until their Allies could overtake them.

Rather like launching a man on Everest or into space, the officer whose escape plan was approved by the camp committee was supported by a host of specialists, who in many cases were sacrificing their own chances in the interests of the camp. There were self-taught specialists in disguise and tailoring, in currency and document production, in security, diversion and staff planning, and in all the techniques which eventually had to be co-ordinated into the efficient launching of an individual or small group out of the camp. It is, therefore, impossible to name the members of each supporting team, and it must be sufficient to say that Green Jacket prisoners formed a cohesive, cheerful and effective group in any camp where two or more were gathered together, helping to sustain the morale of their fellows and a potential threat to their captors.

In view of the great difficulties, few escape attempts from the Germans succeeded, and it would be right to name first, as the most honoured of all our Riflemen escapers, Lt A. M. Sinclair. Commissioned in the summer of 1939, he had done magnificent work with the 2nd Battalion at Calais. The citation for his posthumous DSO is the only one to be quoted in this Volume, and that in full, in recognition of the exceptional nature of his service.

From the moment he was taken prisoner at Calais in 1940 until he was shot in attempting to escape in daylight on the 25th September, 1944, Lieutenant Sinclair devoted the whole of his energies to the task of escaping and so returning to continue the fight. He never deviated from this set purpose and, in spite of setbacks and the hardest of luck, his courage and determination never wavered.

In all, he made no fewer than seven great attempts to escape, each one having been planned to the smallest detail, entailing months of preparation and careful calculation. Even after being wounded in September, 1943, during one of these magnificent efforts, he never gave up, but began to prepare for his next attempt almost before he had recovered from his wound.

On four separate occasions he was successful in getting out of the camp—a most difficult and hazardous undertaking from Oflag IVc, which was a 'Straflager' for persistent escapers—and he spent more months of freedom in Germany and other occupied European countries than any other prisoner-of-war. On each of these four occasions, when complete freedom seemed to be within his grasp, he was dogged by just that bit of bad luck that turned the scales against him.

The benefit of his experience was always available to any fellow prisoner-of-war wishing to escape and many successful escapers have testified to the great help he gave them in their planning.

No less than fourteen Senior Officers (including General Fortune) have recorded in their official reports that Lieutenant Sinclair was the most outstanding escaper they had known. His sustained gallantry and courage, his never-failing enthusiasm and his steadfastness of purpose were an inspiration to all.

A brief mention must be made of other 60th Riflemen, who never gave the Germans an easy moment, starting with the march from Calais.

Lt M. J. Gilliat made the first of several gallant escape attempts after Calais. Maj J. S. Poole, a distinguished veteran of World War I (when he had successfully escaped), nearly got through again from the line of march; after recapture his advice and help to other escapers and the effect of his leadership on morale were invaluable.

There were two mass escapes involving officers of the Regiment, that at Warburg, when 28 got over the wire and 3 reached England, and the escape by 60 officers through a tunnel from Eichstatt. At Warburg Lt Gilliat played a leading part; he was accompanied both in this and at Eichstatt by Lt P. Pardoe, who also escaped during the train journey there from Posen. Lt P. H. Parker also took part in the tunnel escape, and these three ended up in the security prison at Colditz. Happily they survived, Gilliat to be Private Secretary to HM The Queen Mother, Pardoe to command the Rifle Depot and Parker to be High Sheriff of Oxfordshire. Mass escapes of this kind naturally diverted German attention and resources on a wide scale, regardless of ultimate success.

Posen was another camp where 60th Riflemen made a great deal of difficulty for their captors. Lt Sinclair, besides recapture near the Dutch and Swiss borders, penetrated South over the mountains as far as Bulgaria with Maj R. B. Littledale before they were arrested. The latter escaped yet again on the way back at Prague, but was recaptured there when driven back from the Lichtenstein border with Switzerland by terrible snow conditions.

These two were routed on to Colditz with the other 60th officers already mentioned, and Rfn Cohen, who was an orderly there. From that grim castle Maj Littledale incredibly broke out in October 1942 and reached Switzerland. Not content to loiter there, he pressed on through the risks of France and Spain to England, for which and for his gallantry in the field he was awarded the DSO. It would have been easy for him to spend the rest of the war at home on the staff, but he was a field soldier and pressed to return to the reformed 2nd Battalion. Of his distinguished services in Normandy and his tragic loss in the pursuit North the next chapter will tell.

Lt E. G. B. Davies-Scourfield, who was awarded the MC for his work with the 2nd Battalion at Calais, also broke out of Posen; he was not easy for the Germans to pick up again, being for nine months in the care of the gallant Polish underground movement where he involved himself in dangerous propaganda distribution. At a disadvantage in starting from a camp in Eastern Europe, he was eventually recaptured trying to make his way through Austria to Switzerland, and was sent to Colditz. On a happier note, he survived to command a Green Jacket battalion some twenty years later and to be their Regimental Colonel. His ever-present sense of fun, modesty and leadership have since made him a most successful Secretary of the Boys' Clubs of Great Britain.

Although separation from their officers, and the lack of time to organize escaping between exhausting working parties, created favourable escape conditions for few soldiers, the names of three Riflemen must be particularly mentioned. Rfn F. Chapman escaped from a camp in Northern Italy on the 1943 capitulation. Evading the Germans, he decided not to move off with his fellows to Switzerland but stayed behind to organize a band of partisans. Despite the open nature of the Po Valley, his band successfully carried out sabotage and was a decided thorn in the Fascist and German sides. In January 1945 he was, however, betrayed and shot by the Fascists. In recognition of his 18 months of gallant services the War Office officially recorded Rfn Chapman as 'Killed in Action, while at large in enemy-occupied Italy'.

A very distinguished and successful escape was by Rfn Hossington (incorrectly noted as 'Rfn Harington' on Page 93 of these Annals, Volume VI).

Captured with the 2nd Battalion at Calais on 26 May 1940, he endured brutality and starvation by the Feld Gendarmerie on the forced march through France. Shipped in equally bad conditions by cattle truck to Poland, he moved from Stalag XXIB to a camp where intense labour on a canal was enforced despite low rations.

Escaping in October 1940 with a Sapper comrade, the two of them dealt with three Germans on their railway-line route, killing an armed policeman. From their first contact with the Polish population, they were never refused help nor ever let down. Delayed in the Warsaw area, while identity documents were prepared, they taught themselves Polish and how to ski.

Eventually on 1 February 1941 they marched with their Polish guide for 18 hours, covering 40 miles over the Carpathian Mountains into Slovakia. Mist, icy conditions and the threat of German border patrols were overcome, in addition to the physical challenge to weakened men. Crossing occupied Slovakia in a car driven by yet another Pole, they made their way into Hungary on foot.

Handed over in Budapest to the British Legation, by their splendid guide, they were escorted by the Foreign Service via Belgrade to Salonika and Athens. Crossing by escorted convoy to Alexandria, they reported to GHQ Middle East Forces in Cairo on 14 March 1941, having crossed the Balkans only weeks before Hitler's invasion.

Rifleman Hossington brought back much valuable information, including a map of German deployment marked by the Poles, sewn into his cap. For this outstanding act of courage, pertinacity and devotion to duty he was awarded the Distinguished Conduct Medal.

L/Cpl Illingworth, a commission candidate with Queen Victoria's Rifles, used his fluent French when escaping soon after capture at Calais. After he had made his way across France and Spain to Portugal, the ship taking him back to England was involved in the sinking of the *Bismarck*. After commissioning, he gallantly went against all private medical advice to the Middle East but died after being invalided home.

Behind our prisoners of war, and indeed Riflemen everywhere, was a highly efficient and devotedly caring part of the Regimental family.

After the loss of two battalions at Calais in 1940, Lt Col R. A. T. Eve, commanding the Rifle Depot, formed a Green Jacket Prisoner of War Parcel Depot Committee, with Mrs Eve as Honorary Organizer. She later handed over to Mrs H. O. Curtis, who sadly lost two of her four sons in the war. Brig Gen F. G. Willan as Treasurer raised £35,000 to finance the scheme, which received parcels from relatives and supplemented them, before preparing them for despatch via the Red Cross to our prisoners of war, ultimately 2000. The Hon Mrs Johnstone skilfully purchased, with all the attendant ration coupon and accounting difficulties, the large amount of goods required. Within this organization a devoted team of Green Jacket wives and Winchester friends busied themselves on the expert business of packing.

The Ladies' Guild formed a War Committee, of which HH Princess Helena Victoria was Chairman, with Ladies Davidson and Wake as Vice Presidents. From their Winchester office, presided over by Miss Buchanan Riddell, 85,000 comforts such as gloves, socks and scarves went out to our battalions, as well as blankets to returning prisoners. Nearly 6000 families of Riflemen were on their register, for whom 18,000 garments were provided. Toys from Canada and the USA were directed to the children of casualties or prisoners of war.

The Hospital Visiting Scheme of the Ladies' Guild, started by Lady Eastwood, was later run by Mrs Sinclair, who had another son in the Rifle Brigade as well as our Lt A. M. Sinclair. 118 visitors covered all Britain, including nearly 400 hospitals; the needs of our Riflemen in hospital were thus rapidly met. The work in the London area, organized by Mrs Harker, was naturally particularly heavy.

Behind all this the Riflemen's Aid Society provided funds for the Guild and dealt with 4500 applications for help from past and present Riflemen and their families. For 13 years, including the war, Miss Pooley, as Assistant Secretary at 32 Ecclestone Square, despite losing her house and the cousin with whom she lived in the Blitz, maintained invaluable continuity by interview and correspondence.

The many grateful letters from Riflemen, some of which were quoted in the 1945 Chronicle, speak for themselves. This side of the Regiment's work may best be summed up in a quotation from one of them:

> Riflemen are convinced that their 'Home Front' in the war was certainly the best and most efficient organization of its kind.

Turning now to our two Battalions who were to fight to the victorious end in North West Europe, it will be remembered from the previous chapter that the 2nd had sailed from Italy for England in February 1944.

On disembarkation at Glasgow, the Battalion moved by train to Worthing, where the rest of 4 Armoured Brigade was concentrated. After a month's leave, the task of reorganizing and re-equipping in preparation for the invasion of North West Europe began. There were many changes, both in personnel and in equipment. Maj R. B. Littledale, who had been awarded the DSO for his most gallant escape from a German POW Camp, joined as second in command. Capt J. G. Harries left for a staff appointment, and his place as Adjutant was taken over by Capt R. F. Nixon. Maj J. H. P. Curtis and Lts I. C. Scott and D. Hartog were posted to 10 KRRC, who in return sent a draft of 13 officers and 250 other ranks, bringing the Battalion strength up to 39 officers and 896 other ranks. The Company Commanders were Majs C. W. Morris, A Company; D. Fletcher, B Company; R. C. Gibbs, MC, C Company; and F. G. Bernays, D (Support) Company. The principal Warrant Officers were RSM F. Voysey, RQMS S. Cooper, DCM, and CSMs Hunt (A), Knights (B), Atkins, MM (C), Saunders (D) and Ford (HQ). In the place of their old 15-cwt trucks, American Half Track personnel carriers were issued, a great improvement not only because of their much-increased cross-country performance but also because their armour plating gave at least some protection against shell splinters and small arms.

The as yet untried 12th Battalion was equally making preparations. On the more intellectual plane, German Army organization was studied at Cambridge by the 2IC, Maj F. J. R. Coleridge, who was later to be Vice Provost of Eton, and the Signals officer, Lt S. J. McWatters, who, from house tutor at the same school, was to fill two headmasterships. In March a Battalion waterproofing cadre was organized, with waterproof material and grease, for wading vehicles ashore across the as yet undesignated beaches somewhere on the North West coast of the Continent. After moving to the Newmarket area there were several exercises at full strength with 7 Armoured Division, newly returned from Italy. After more street fighting practice the 12th at long last received White scout cars, the wheeled version of the 2nd's armoured International half-tracks, in place of their unarmoured 15 cwt section trucks.

The Company Commanders for the invasion were Majs P. H. Jackson (A), W. F. Deedes (B), H. R. Cleaver (C), P. W. Redway (D), with Capt S. J. Constance as Adjutant. Under them was a first-class team of platoon commanders, Warrant Officers and NCOs, who had received all that England could give them in training; it was now time to put it into practice.

Across the Channel von Runstedt had superiority in land forces, despite the drain on the East Front and the 26 divisions which had now been drawn down into Italy, as the Allies advanced to take Rome. However, in addition to massive air and sea superiority, we had the initiative and therefore the possibility of a concentration of force, provided we could maintain the element of surprise. A vast deception plan, indicating that our major thrust would be in the Pas de Calais, was successfully mounted. Travel to Ireland had been stopped in February 1944, and in April a strip 10 miles deep along our South and East coasts was closed to visitors. Marshalling areas were prepared inland from all our ports and harbours, and no one was more in the thick of this than that older Rifleman, Maj Gen H. O. Curtis, responsible for Hampshire and Dorset.

The Germans had still not fully understood that our need for fighter cover would limit the areas we could use for major landings, and von Runstedt had his infantry divisions strung along all the coast to beyond Bordeaux with his armoured reserve, fortunately for us, dispersed and well back. Rommel's arrival to command Army Group B, stretching from Holland to Brittany, had seen a great improvement in the beach defences; but he had not been allowed fully to implement his theory—which somewhat ignored the effect of naval bombard-ment—of packing his coastal areas with troops, and having counter-attack forces close behind them. Thus, when our invasion started on 6 June 1944, there were two German infantry divisions manning the defences across the whole of our Allied front instead of the earlier one. 21 Panzer Division had moved into closer reserve in the Caen-Falaise area, but the other armour was East of the River Orne or well to the South, and would have a gruelling advance against our air attacks and the French Resistance.

The three beaches allotted to 2 (British) Army were each to be stormed by an infantry division, supported by an independent armoured brigade. On the right, or West, 8 Armoured, without our 12th Battalion for the landing, was to discharge this role opposite Bayeux. 4 Armoured Brigade, complete with our 2nd Battalion, were to be follow-up troops on the Eastern beaches opposite Caen.

Although motor battalions were not suitable for an assault landing, there were Green Jackets, present or future, at all levels in the first phase. Six platoons of the 52nd Light Infantry in gliders, who seized the Orne bridges, were the first formed body of Allied Troops to land on D day, and were joined by 60th and other Riflemen in the Light Infantry Parachute Battalion. For the sea-borne landing Commanding Officers with combat experience were at a premium, and the 60th provided two, Lt Col G. W. White and Lt Col H. R. Woods, DSO, MC; the former had a most desperate struggle to get his battered battalion over the sea-wall before the rising tide drowned his wounded. Lt Col Woods was killed just as his DLI battalion had captured their final objective at Tilly a week later; he had commanded them with distinction, always from the front, through the battles in Sicily, and his Geordies had taken all their objectives on D day.

General Montgomery had given a D day objective to include Bayeux and Caen; the latter was then to be held as flank protection against German armoured formations moving from the East, while the bridgehead was enlarged South and West. In practice Caen was not taken for a month and the early expansion South from the original bridgehead had to be made with the city as a flank threat rather than a screen. With this in mind we shall move in the next chapter with our battalions across the Channel and, after the bitter fighting of Normandy, advance rapidly with them into the Low Countries.

CHAPTER III
FROM NORMANDY TO THE LOW COUNTRIES

(Maps: pages 40, 42, 46, 52, 60, 68 and 70)

Since this is a history of the Regiment rather than of the Army, just sufficient explanation will be given of the setting in which our two Battalions fought in the complicated Normandy battles for their role to be understood. We start with the 2nd, who were the first to cross the Channel.

Great secrecy was maintained about the actual details of the invasion, but by the end of May all vehicles had been water-proofed and it was clear that action was imminent. This was confirmed when on the 25th General Montgomery visited the Battalion and gave an inspiring address to all ranks in which he forecast a great victory. On 4 June the Battalion moved into a marshalling area just outside Southampton, where all contact with the outside world was sealed off and maps were issued followed by a full briefing. HQ, A and C Companies embarked on American LSTs (Landing Ships Tank) on the 8th, and arrived off the French coast by mid-afternoon on the 9th. Ships of all types and sizes were everywhere, and LSTs had to wait their turn to beach. After a considerable delay, disembarkation began at 2100 hrs, by which time it was pitch dark, and was not completed until 0100 hrs. The beach organization appeared to be in considerable confusion, which was not helped by almost continuous air attacks; however, ultimately the way was found to the harbour area some two miles inland, where the first two companies were joined by C Company on the next day.

On 11 June the Motor Companies were put under command of their respective Armoured Regiments, with whom they remained for most of the Normandy Campaign and subsequent pursuit into Belgium. The affiliations were A Company to 3 City of London Yeomanry (shortly to be merged with the 4th to form 3/4 CLY), B Company to 44 RTR and C Company to The Royal Scots Greys. The remainder of the Battalion under Major Bernays, consisting of D Company and most of the Echelon, arrived on 16 June. During this period of the Campaign the Brigade was deployed in various counter-attack roles, frequently with armoured regiments under command of an Infantry division, so that the motor companies had little work to do. The Battalion, without its three motor companies, was given various defensive positions to hold with the remaining anti-tank and machine-gun platoons of D Company.

Perhaps fortunately, none of the expected German counter-attacks material-ized, and apart from occasional shelling and night bombing there was little activity. The most exciting moment was unquestionably when Battalion HQ and D Company, whilst sealing off a German underground strong-point which was still holding out, were shelled by HMS *Nelson*, which had been asked to knock out the strong-point with her heavy guns but unfortunately, owing to a slight error in map reading, took on our farmhouse instead. Luckily, no one was hurt and as communications were for once working well, the necessary adjustments were soon made with the desired result.

By mid-June 1944 the first phase, that of the build-up of the bridgehead forces to a size at which they could not be pushed back into the sea, had been won by the Allies. Against Montgomery's 20 divisions, Rommel had 18 weak ones and the armour immediately at his disposal had been tied down; under naval gunfire, air attack and continuous shelling the Wehrmacht was suffering terrible losses, even if this was not apparent to the Allies trying to push forward in the thick hedgerow country. It was important for Montgomery to draw German reserve formations on to the British, to allow the Americans, first to secure the peninsula and port of Cherbourg, and then to advance South and East round the British pivot.

To this end, after the first XXX Corps thrust at Villers Bocage had been driven back, he directed VIII Corps to attack across the River Odon, South East of Tilly; he hoped that the Corps would then turn East and establish itself on the ridge South of Caen. Simultaneously in the German camp Hitler had decided to send to Normandy a Corps of two SS Panzer divisions, which had made a high reputation on the East Front, to split the bridgehead by a drive starting West of Caumont. Fortunately included in the British plan was an advance by 49 Division to protect the West flank of the Odon thrust; it was in turn the West flank of this division that our 12th Battalion was to protect in its first action.

The 12th had marshalled at West Ham and embarked in two ships in the Royal Albert and West India Docks on 13 June 1944; on 16 June they started landing in Normandy. They then joined 8 Armoured Brigade, whose armoured regiments were 4th/7th Dragoon Guards, 13th/18th Hussars and Sherwood Rangers Yeomanry (SRY), with the Essex Yeomanry as gunner support; the tanks were still supporting the infantry brigades at this stage, so the 12th dug in against possible counter-attack. This and subsequent extracts are taken from the valuable account by the 2IC, Maj Coleridge:

> On June 25th 49 Division launched an attack through Fontenay-le-Pesnil and Tessel Wood directed on Vendes and Rauray. By nightfall this attack had captured half of Tessel Wood and had not completely cleared Fontenay. Next day one Battalion of the Division and one Armoured Regiment were ordered to attack Rauray from Tessel Wood. This involved an exposed right flank in very thick country. 12th K.R.R.C. were given the job of protecting this flank and pushing on as far as possible towards Rauray. After a night move the Battalion arrived at Tessel Wood by first light. It had not been an easy march. It was a pitch dark night and the vehicles, except for some Scout cars and one Anti-Tank Platoon, had to be left to the north of Fontenay, as the village was not clear of the enemy. (Tessel Wood lies to the south of Fontenay). However the village was successfully by-passed and the few vehicles followed by a difficult ford.
>
> With the light came the snipers, and for the rest of the day in this dense country they were an intermittent nuisance. The main enemy resistance in the area between Tessel Wood and Rauray were some six to ten Tiger tanks, each with an attendant party of infantry well dug in. Progress from the corner of Tessel Wood was slow, as the armour could be of little help to us in that

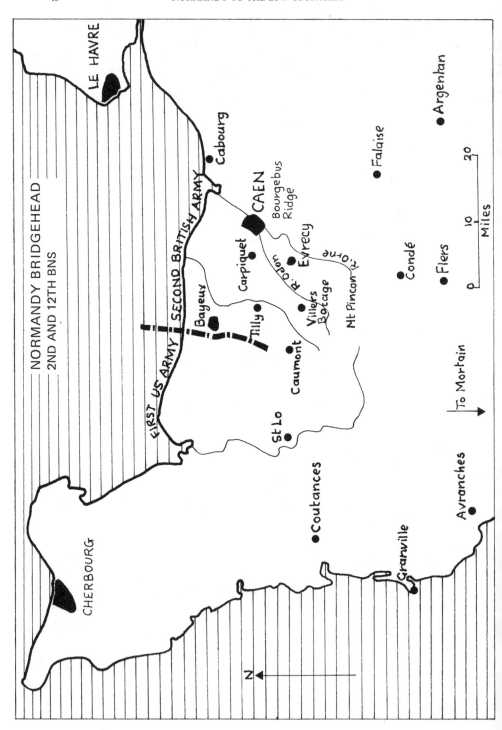

particular area. But we kept going fast enough to protect the infantry attack aimed at Rauray. The chief trouble was communication. The enemy picked off the 18 Sets of all the leading platoons, and it was impossible to know how far they got in these small fields with such limited visibility. Consequently the Gunners could not support them properly and their own mortars found it difficult.

Wireless operators could be spotted if their aerials were up, and the Germans were using the classic Rifleman's tactic of selective shooting.

In fact two platoons of B Company, who had been passed through, penetrated along the river to Le Manoir church, where Lt B. S. Newton had the spire fall at his feet and Lt R. D. Green had his helmet removed by a ricochet from a Tiger tank. A Company had previously been held up by another Tiger and infantry; in this engagement the Company Commander, Maj Jackson, and a platoon commander had been wounded. C Company had also been finally brought to a halt; Lt J. Becke had been killed while gallantly running across to warn our tanks, which were driving into a trap, and the other two platoon commanders wounded. It was to be an additional sadness that his only brother, Lt M. Becke, was later killed with 8 RB. At the end of the day 6 Officers and 32 Riflemen had become casualties.

When the church was reached the 49 Division advance on our left started to peter out and the 12th was ordered to withdraw; this was well carried out under cover of an excellent smoke-screen, laid by the Essex Yeomanry and our mortars. The 12th Battalion's action had not been in vain, since, with a cleared flank, Rauray was taken next day; this allowed 15 Scottish Division to form a firm defensive position facing West on the ridge against the SS Panzer attacks which came in on 29 June. The German armour had been rapidly drawn away from their own intended offensive, when on 28 June 11 Armoured started moving South over a captured Odon bridge, directed on Pt 112. Our 2nd Battalion became involved in this probe, and on 28 June B Company under command of 44 RTR crossed the Odon and advanced to North East of Evrecy against heavy opposition from tanks and self-propelled guns, supported by infantry. Little progress was made, and at 1730 hours the next day a strong counter-attack was launched, as a result of which 12 tanks were lost and B Company suffered several casualties, including Lt D. D. Strachan, and had two half-tracks destroyed. The bocage country of Normandy was very unsuitable for armour, being densely wooded, with small fields surrounded by thick hedges; these provided perfect cover for the German infantry, who were well provided with Panzerfausts, the German tank-destroying rocket or bazooka. The banks were vehicle obstacles; indeed the CO of the 12th had had to have a gap blown to allow his scout car forward in their recent advance.

On 30 June B Company was withdrawn when our 2 Army decided to pull all the armour back North of the Odon in view of the concentration of enemy armour. In effect the Odon probe had diverted the German armour from its offensive and had inflicted heavy casualties on it; our armour was still intact and could be used again in the Caen area.

While our 12th had nearly a fortnight out of the battle, on 3 July the 2nd Battalion was again concentrated and took up a defensive position on the forward

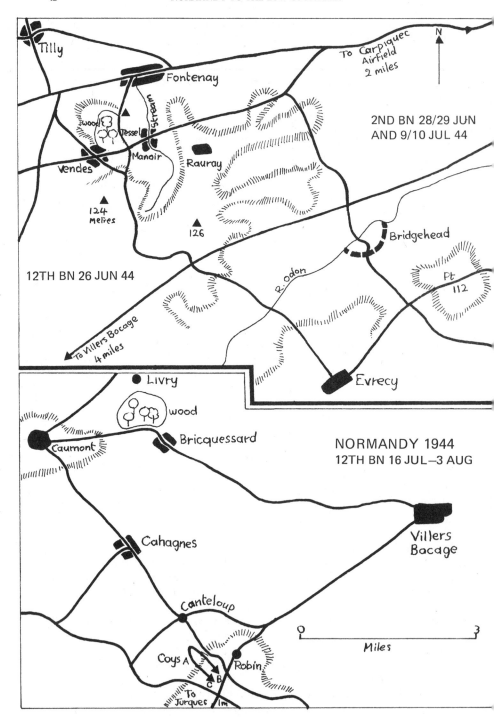

edges of Carpiquet airfield overlooking the city of Caen. As it was in full view of the enemy, the area was subjected to considerable shelling, although luckily without casualties. From here on the evening of the 7th they had a grandstand view of an attack on the unfortunate town by 450 four-engined bombers, which dropped more than 2000 tons of bombs. A great cloud of dust and smoke rose high into the air, and as they were down-wind a dense fog of dust soon completely blanketed their positions. The next day the ruins of the city were occupied, but the further suburbs were still in enemy hands.

On 9 July orders were given for an attack in support of the Greys across the River Odon. The plan was for 43 Division to take the high ground immediately to the South of the river, after which the Greys supported by the Battalion would pass through and exploit. In the event, the attack never got off the ground, the infantry meeting very heavy opposition and making no headway. The Battalion sat all day South of the river being shelled and mortared, and at 1830 hours A and C Companies were ordered to join their Armoured Regiments and the remainder of the Battalion was withdrawn back across the river. At 2000 hours very heavy shelling and mortaring was brought down on the forward companies, and the infantry of 43 Division, having suffered very heavy casualties, started to stream back. The situation was, to put it mildly, confusing, and Tiger tanks could be seen advancing and starting to fire at our vehicles. Fortunately, however, the German attack lost momentum, and strong action by senior officers soon restored the situation. During this action Maj C. W. Morris and Lt B. M. W. Jackson were both killed, and C Company order group received a direct hit by a shell, wounding Maj R. C. Gibbs, Lts E. N. W. Bramall and D. S. B. Hopkins, and killing Capt D. G. Wright and Company Sergeant Major Atkins; altogether it was a disastrous day with no counterbalancing achievement. On the next morning A and C Companies were withdrawn across the river and rejoined the Battalion. One of the problems at this time was to find space in which to deploy the Battalion when it was not in action. There were so many troops in the area that every field behind the front line had its occupants, most of whom appeared to be gunners—who were not good neighbours, not only because they prevented any form of rest by firing continuous fireplans but also because they attracted counter-battery fire from the enemy. Another unattractive feature was the ubiquitous stink of rotting flesh. Normandy is rich in dairy farms, which meant that many thousands of cows had been killed by shelling and left to rot in the fields. For the rest of the month—although always at short notice for various counter-attack plans—the 2nd Battalion was not involved in any actual fighting, and was able to carry out a certain amount of training and reorganization. Since landing in France, the 2nd Battalion's casualties had been 10 officers and 78 other ranks.

Every loss was regretted, but none more so than Lt Bertie Jackson, who was known widely throughout the Regiment and was held in affectionate respect in the 2nd Battalion. At 4 foot 10 inches in height he was certainly the smallest officer in the Infantry, if not the Army, and only intense efforts had won him that place. He had already been twice wounded with the 2nd in North Africa, but insisted on returning to his platoon; Sgt Usher, his Platoon Sergeant, should have the last word: 'We had been together nearly 18 months and to me he was not only my Officer but my friend . . . he will always be an example of courage and loyalty to us.'

With the fall of Caen Montgomery moved the three British armoured divisions into the airborne bridgehead East of the River Orne. His aim was to seize the commanding high ground, the Bourgebus Ridge, to the South of the city and exploit to Falaise. The attack, Operation 'Goodwood', went in on 18 July, preceded by 'carpet' bombing of unprecedented weight, but delay at a railway embankment, the survival of a few Tigers and 88s on the flanks and the arrival of Panthers on the Ridge just thwarted our more vulnerable armour, who were held up with very heavy losses. Our thrust had, however, met the requirement of drawing the enemy armour away from the Americans, who after clearing the Cherbourg peninsula, were poised to break out. Only two Panzer divisions with no heavy tanks were opposite them, while seven Panzer divisions and all the Tigers and Panthers were now opposite the British, five being East of the Orne. The armoured brigades, which contained our two battalions, played their part in assisting the American break-through west of St Lô, first by taking over a sector to enable them to concentrate and then by pressure on the inside of the vast left wheel which the break-out became.

Maj Coleridge takes up the account:

The 12th had been resting but on the 16th July we returned to work again with a vengeance. 8 Armoured Brigade was ordered to take over part of the line just east of Caumont from our American Allies to release them for more mobile operations further West. From them we inherited a fully dug position in dense country in the area of Livry. The forward positions were in such close contact with the enemy that in some cases we even shared the same hedge. We had the reassuring presence of the tanks behind, but this was hardly the country for them. So we settled down to learn a new game and, when we had learnt it, to make some experiments of our own. The chief feature was, of course, patrolling, and we sent out 33 patrols during our fortnight at Livry. The Germans were at some strength opposite us in and around Briquessard and they did not like our inquisitiveness. One good result was that the enemy reduced his patrols to nothing as time went on. We learnt enough about his habits in delivering rations, etc., to make their distribution a very hazardous proceeding on the last few nights, and the Essex Yeomanry lent us noble aid throughout the time. They fired a lot of rounds and our neighbours on the right, who could see the results when we could not, were much impressed. The enemy threw shells and mortar bombs at us daily in varying quantities. Our casualties were mercifully light.

After the news of the American break-through we were anxious to get moving ourselves and leave our old friends—Oxford Circus, Piccadilly Circus, etc.—for some less familiar grounds. At last, on 31 July, the move came. We were to follow behind a Battalion down the road Caumont–Cahagnes–Canteloup. At Canteloup we were to pass through and make for the two big cross roads near Robin which commanded the main road to Jurques. B Company (Maj Deedes) was in the lead and passed through 4th Worcesters soon after midnight. He had not gone far when his leading troops—and indeed the whole Company—could see the enemy guns firing from a few hundred yards away. Patrols revealed that the enemy was there in some strength and no further progress was made until a Battalion attack was laid on in daylight. The problem was to get up a steepish hill, through the enemy, then down the reverse slope to the two cross roads. The country was still very thick. All three companies were deployed for this operation. B Company were to stay containing the enemy while A and C Companies worked round the right flank, with C Company in the lead. Soon after the start the enemy counter-attacked with one or two tanks and about 100 infantry between us and the nearest battalion of 214 Brigade. This attack was driven off, but it imposed a long delay. However the forward move got under way again and with the assistance of two troops of the 4th/7th, B Company were soon on the high ground by the Robin cross roads and C Company got forward to dominate the southerly cross roads, leaving A Company to deal with enemy pockets known to be still behind us.

The next day, against fairly heavy shelling and mortaring and in close contact with the enemy, the 12th continued the operation to secure the two cross roads. On the right an enemy counter-attack at one moment threatened to cut off C Company, and a feature on the left was still held, with the odd Tiger and S.P. gun firing. CSM MacDonald was wounded while leading a patrol to locate a sniper behind Battalion HQ. By evening B Company was far enough forward to deny one of the cross roads, and on 2 August 7 Armoured Division started moving through; the next day the 12th was withdrawn.

The Battalion was suffering from much-weakened motor platoons, and also from the inevitable difficulty of an armoured brigade working with an infantry division. The Brigade Commander wanted the motor companies out with armoured regiments, while Division wanted to misuse them concentrated on heavy infantry tasks.

Mt. Pincon fell after much bitter fighting, but the way forward was barred by strong pockets of enemy, who could still cover the road running over the southern slopes of Mt. Pincon to Le Plessis Grimoult. And it was here that our next battle was fought, on August 7th. The Battalion's task was to clear a large chateau and its thickly-wooded grounds between the main road and a village called Danvou which lay about a mile to the South. Beyond this village was a squadron of 43rd Reconnaissance Regiment. Our area was about a mile long, half a mile wide and terribly thick. The knowledge about the numbers of enemy in it was very limited. And at the time we ourselves were very much below strength. The plan was to secure the main road along the north edge, then the village of Danvou at the south end, and finally clear up the jungle in between.

A Company got control of the road without much difficulty, but C Company, who went after Danvou and the chateau area, was immediately counter-attacked before it had time to dig in properly and two sections were overrun. To restore this situation B Company and two troops of 4th/7th, who had come under command, were committed. They seized and consolidated a big cross tracks near the chateau, and here Roger Green's platoon and the remaining C Company section spent a trying day under mortar and shell fire, but there was no further nonsense by the enemy infantry. The rest of B Company were put on the ground in depth to prevent enemy infiltration. So the position was roughly this: A Company secure at the North end of our area,

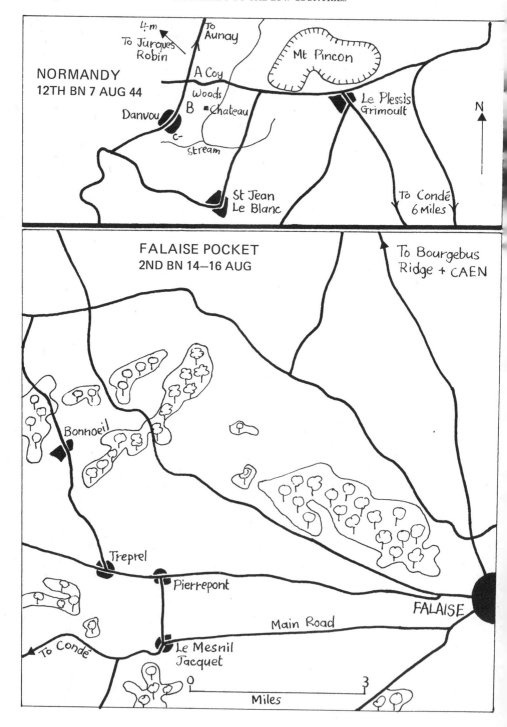

B Company scattered in platoon areas in the centre and C Company less one platoon in the village of Danvou. Then and for the rest of the day we set about likely enemy positions with guns, machine guns and mortars. Observation was almost nil, and at the time we didn't know what damage had been done; but a few days later we had the satisfaction of discovering that a lot of Germans had been killed. As many of them were out of their positions, it seems likely that they had been staging more than one counter-attack and had each time been dissuaded. During the night 4th Worcester took over from us and by 0430 we were all back in reserve.

Two days later, when the situation South of Mt. Pincon and in Le Plessis Grimoult had been clarified, we moved forward. In front of us the leading troops, supported by our own Armoured Regiments, were hammering their way down the approaches to Condé sur Noireau, while further East the stage was being set for the last act in the destruction of the German Seventh Army. It was here that Lt Col The Hon M. G. Edwardes, R.B., took over the Battalion in succession to Lt Col R. G. R. Oxley, who had left to take a Staff appointment.

Our next move was to St. Jean le Blanc, a few miles to the South-west, where we took over a position from the Worcesters. This faced South, and opposite us was the northern edge of the enemy, who had not been involved in the Mt. Pincon fighting nor in the fighting further West. In fact they formed a small 'pocket' of their own. Just as we were leaving for this move, two stray shells landed in D Company. Maj Paul Redway, the Company Commander, was badly wounded and his signaller, Cpl Read, killed.

The take-over was smooth and we remained here for two days, until a long daylight patrol by Lt John Peyton established what had already been suspected—that the enemy had had enough and was pulling back before he lost his escape route through Condé.

The 24 hours astride 7 August 1944 was a disastrous period for the Germans in Normandy. Their armoured reserves were defeated in an attempt to cut through the American drive by a thrust from Mortain to the sea. The Americans had fitted teeth on their tanks which allowed them to take each hedge by the roots, and were working in columns across country, each with aircraft overhead waiting to pounce. The Germans were caught on the roads and shattered. The fall of Mt Pincon removed the defensive pivot which the Germans might have used, and South of Caen the Canadians and British had barely been held after a night advance towards Falaise. The German pocket now forming, as the American armour started to race East and then North towards Argentan, called for a rapid German withdrawal. However, in the aftermath of the 20 July assassination attempt, von Kluge, who had replaced the wounded Rommel, did not dare put this course early enough to the infuriated Führer.

The 2nd Battalion eventually came into the scene on the North side of the Falaise pocket after resting during the latter half of July.

On 29 July, Lt Col W. Heathcoat-Amory, DSO, who had commanded the battalion with such success from before Alamein, handed over to Lt Col R. B. Littledale, DSO, and returned to England to assume command of the 8th Battalion. His departure was a great sadness to all ranks, for his leadership had been outstanding and his imperturbable calmness had restored many a tricky situation; however, no one could deny that he had more than earned a less arduous appointment. Maj H. R. W. Vernon, MBE, arrived from 21 Army Group HQ to take over as second in command, and Maj H. Wake, MC, took over A Company.

On the same day the Brigade came under command of VIII Corps, which was exerting pressure on the extreme right flank of the British front in support of the major American attack, which resulted in the break-out and outflanking movement culminating in the destruction of the German armies in France. Although the battalion moved with the Brigade, it was not involved in any major attack, each of the Armoured Regiments operating under command of one of the Brigades of 3 Division, and the motor companies were therefore not required. On 12 August the Brigade was again switched from the extreme right to the left, coming under command of 53 Division. The American breakthrough in the West was by now well under way, and the Germans had at last realized that their positions in Normandy were no longer tenable. The withdrawal had begun, but since they had very little motorized transport, and relied much on horse-drawn vehicles, the few roads leading out of the pocket soon became almost impassable. An American column from the South and the British from the North were both converging as fast as possible on Falaise; a juncture there would cut off all remaining troops left in the pocket, so the Germans were putting up a desperate fight to keep open their one remaining escape route. On 14 August the Battalion, with a squadron of 44 RTR under command, was ordered to attack to the South directed on to the village of Bonnoeil, which was taken with little resistance, and on the next day 3/4 CLY with A Company under command continued the advance. Maj Wake described the fighting:

The country was damnably thick and close and anything but suitable for tanks. The German infantry are well armed with bazookas and enjoy knocking out our tanks from ten yards range from thick hedgerows, orchards, lanes, etc., and our tanks can do nothing about it. Real infantry country, and so A Company led the advance all day (15 August), giving the tanks close protection and combing the thick bits and detecting and picking up mines in the lanes. A slow business indeed.

No. 4 Platoon, commanded by Nigel Laing, began in the early morning by riding on a troop of four tanks, but the Boche soon stopped that. Working up the hedges and through the farms all day in really hot sun on his flat feet, supported by his troops, Nigel did well to round up twenty-six Germans, killing four. The Germans did not give in easily, continuing to fire until you got right up to them, and he only had two casualties.

Riding up in a tank to see him (the ground was quite impossible for any of our vehicles—huge hedges with deep ditches, banks and wire—never saw such a fox-hunting nightmare in your life), four Germans wearing steel helmets suddenly emerged out of the undergrowth of a wood in front of us. The gunner of the tank opened up, quite rightly, with his .5 Browning instantaneously, and shot two of them. However, instead of being a bazooka party, a rather worried Rifleman Hyde of mine appeared behind them and complained that one bullet had gone through his hair, another into his arm, and would we mind leaving his . . . prisoners alone! Lesson: Always remove a Jerry's helmet. . . .

No. 2 Platoon, under Robin Lewin, did wonderfully. I put him under command of B Squadron of the Yeomanry to help them, as Nigel was helping A Squadron. B Squadron came to the village of Treprel on the right, which was full of determined Huns. Robin, with his 30 men, was ordered to clear it, because it lay on the road down which Brigade Headquarters behind us intended moving.

Robin was thoroughly enjoying himself. He had already taken one German officer prisoner who said there were 50 more in the village, and well could I believe it. They kept on potting at us from every house and orchard and you could not see them. In spite of civilians, we got Hugh Barrow, R. H. A., to fairly shell the place. Civilians were running about between trying to salvage stuff out of their burning houses.

There were mines about, but one splendid tank came up the road to help us. He was missed by bazookas which landed quite near me, and I thought it was a mine going off at first.

One Boche, sniping from behind an apple tree, gave himself up, and Col Ronnie seized his rifle and fairly pumped him for information in what I thought was an unhealthy place. However, they were such rotten shots or they would have hit us. I think they were rather shaken. Cpl Mutlow lay down and had a look down the road. I saw the spandau bullets whip past him and hit the wall of the house behind him. I shouted to him, but he was slow and didn't realise he was being shot at. The next burst got him in the arm and the leg, so we patched him up in the very same house where there were about ten French people. It didn't seem real in a fight to be drinking wine out of a wine glass with people who, in spite of the fact that our shelling had thoroughly knocked about their house, didn't seem to realise there was a war on.

I left Robin tackling an immense German tank and got Peter Gosse, my second-in-command, to help him, with a section of Sandy Fletcher's carriers (No. 1 Platoon). The advance could not wait, so the village was by-passed and my third platoon, No. 3, commanded by Graham Brice, took the lead. Robin Lewin ended by taking 38 prisoners, killing one, the remainder escaping to the South. The Germans then shelled the village very heavily.

Pierrepont was the next village, and that was soon mopped up, and at last light we reached our objective—the main road running East to Falaise, down which the Boches were escaping. We had advanced about five miles, and were we tired!

During the afternoon 44 RTR with B Company under command moved up on the right of the CLY and by last light had cut the main road from Condé to Falaise, South West of Treprel.

Next morning the advance continued against increasing opposition. Maj D. F. Fletcher, who had been with the Battalion since Alamein, and Lt D. F. Wyndham, both of B Company, were killed by a heavy mortar fire whilst doing a reconnaissance, and later in the day Lt H. S. Elgar was wounded whilst fighting off a counter-attack during which the company suffered 20 other casualties. During the same day, a C Company half-track received a direct hit, killing Lt G.

M. Shawyer and seriously wounding Capt D. E. Ellis and Lt J. Allen: the Company also had 12 other casualties from shell and mortar fire.

A Company were again in action:

I put Graham Brice's platoon under command of C Squadron, County of London Yeomanry, and they moved off out of leaguer before first light. Then bad news arrived from Graham Brice. His tanks were held up by determined Boches in houses astride the road. He went well ahead of the tank and, forcing his way into the houses, killed and captured quite a few. However, an 88 mm 100 yards further up the road fired an air burst down the road and knocked out one complete section. Cpl Gibbs was badly wounded and five others, and Rfn Clark killed outright.

Rfn Hett of Graham Brice's platoon, did frightfully well, and without orders and under exceptionally heavy shell fire went to the help of Rfn Sullivan, who was wounded, and not only brought him back but two other wounded men as well, and then went back to report to Graham.

Graham, with only 12 men in his platoon, continued the fight well into the enemy's camp. Entirely through his efforts the tanks got up on to their objective.

Lt J. G. Brice was later awarded the MC for the day's action.

For the next two days the Brigade continued to push South against heavy opposition, but by the afternoon of 21 August the end was in sight. Maj Vernon wrote of the scene which confronted the Battalion:

The sight that met us was beyond all possible description. The whole country was packed with destroyed and abandoned transport, wagons and equipment. Hundreds and hundreds of them were piled high on the tracks, in the fields, everywhere; dead Germans in their thousands lay about; and worse than anything were the dead horses. There were thousands of them, and bits of them, all over the area, stinking to high heaven. Many of us had seen most of the bloodiest battlefields of this war, in Europe, and North Africa, but no one had seen anything to compare with this chaos, this filth, this bloody destruction, and above all this stench.

There was very little fighting, as the Germans were too demoralised to put up any serious resistance. Prisoners came in their thousands and were guarded and marched back to their cages—men who were hardly men; they had lived through ten days of indescribable terror; they had had loosed on them every horror of modern war, and were the comparatively few survivors of the proud German Seventh Army. We joined up with the Americans to our South at midday the next day.

The account of the advance into Belgium owes much to Maj H. R. W. Vernon, who was 2IC and acting Commanding Officer during the period.

On 25 August the Brigade set off in pursuit of the fleeing Germans. Initially the advance was slow because of the mass of derelict equipment and dead animals which blocked all roads leading out of the destruction area, but by the 28th the Seine was reached and the Brigade concentrated on the Eastern bank. The next morning the advance continued with the motor companies under command of the armoured regiments. A Company and 3/4 CLY were in the lead directed on to

Gournay. Just short of the town Lt A. K. H. Fletcher and his carriers, leading the tanks through a thick wood, met a German SP gun pulling out. Firing their ·5 Brownings, they captured the gun and killed or captured most of the crew; A Company and the CLY then captured the town to the delight of the inhabitants.

C Company with the Greys had a brush at Grumesnil en route. When the leading platoon under Lt A. D. Stow suffered casualties on the South West approach, Lt P. W. M. Dean's platoon infiltrated from the South East, killing some Germans and capturing 20 others without loss. The same platoon, covered by their tanks, collected about 80 prisoners later in the evening from a burning village. By last light the Brigade was beyond Gournay on three sides, with the CLY to the North West, 44 RTR to the North East and The Greys to the West, each with their motor company under command.

After a brush in the night, when some Germans were killed, B Company lost the leading carrier to an anti-tank gun at first light the next day. The Company, however, in conjunction with a troop of CLY, soon rounded up 50 prisoners. The Brigade's advance continued that day towards Grandvilliers. Stragglers were being rounded up on all sides by the Free French, but the more determined of the Germans were seizing horses or bicycles at weapon point in a desperate effort to make their escape; it was difficult to tell who were Germans willing to surrender and who were formed bodies under their officers merely resting. After the capture of Grandvilliers B Company was ordered to clear a deep gulley where there were reported to be 'a few dead-beat Germans wanting to give themselves up'. Maj J. F. C. Mellor took Lt E. C. Phillips and his carrier platoon on their feet, without support, and the dozen Riflemen found that the 'dead-beat' Germans were about 200 under their officers. When one of the German officers was about to turn the tables, realizing how few British there were, Maj Mellor had to shoot him from the hip with a rifle while the platoon sergeant shot another with his Sten; the rest then laid down their arms. Since prisoners could not be sent back over the jammed roads, they were normally handed over to the local Free French, who, with a few captured weapons, could keep them rounded up till the follow-up troops arrived.

The advance which followed was one of continual confusion because the German troops, who had been deployed all along the Channel coast, were now being outflanked by the British and American forces to the South and were endeavouring to make their escape with all possible speed. As a result, the German withdrawal roads and the British axes of advance were frequently in conflict so that a series of minor battles developed at many road intersections. Further, as more Germans became cut off from the Fatherland, pressure on the Allied lines of communications built up and many attacks were launched in an effort to break through.

One such battle was that for the village of Airaines on the South bank of the Somme between Amiens and Abbeville. Orders were received in the early morning of 1 September for the Battalion less three motor companies but with an anti-tank Battery, RA, under command to occupy and hold the village against any enemy approaching from the North West. The village was some eight miles from our night leaguer, and the only information about the enemy was that a considerable force had been seen North West of the village by the RAF at dusk on the previous evening. Lt Col Littledale, with Maj Bernays and the anti-tank

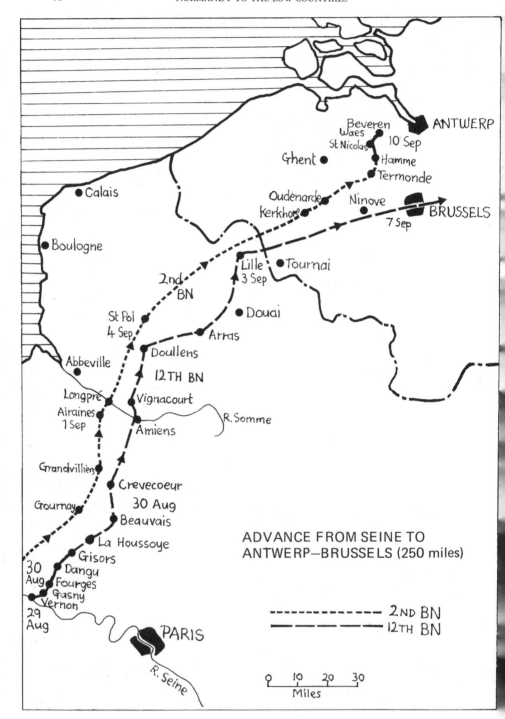

ANTWERP

Beveren
Waes
St Nicolas
10 Sep
Hamme
Termonde

Ghent

Oudenarde
Kerkhove
Ninove
BRUSSELS
7 Sep

Calais

Boulogne

Lille
3 Sep
Tournai

2nd
BN

Douai

St Pol
4 Sep

Arras

Abbeville

Doullens

12TH BN

Longpré
Vignacourt

Airaines
1 Sep

Amiens

R. Somme

Grandvilliers

Crevecoeur
30 Aug

Gournay

Beauvais

La Houssoye

Gisors
30
Aug
Dangu
Fourges
Gasny
Vernon
29
Aug

PARIS

R. Seine

ADVANCE FROM SEINE TO
ANTWERP—BRUSSELS (250 miles)

- - - - - - - - - 2ND BN
———————— 12TH BN

0   10   20   30
Miles

4 American Officers in the 60th near Tripoli, July 1943

Left to Right—Lts G. G. Thomson, S. J. O. Alsop, T. R. Ellsworth, H. W. Fowler, T. W. Braden. Ellsworth's dog 'Watling Street' in foreground.

5 A Company, 2nd Battalion, Advance Guard with RTR tanks in Normandy, August 1944
(drawn by Rfn Leach, A Company)

6 *(below)* Rfn Fink MM, 11th Battalion, with his Projector Infantry Anti-Tank, Athens, January 1945

7 *(right)* 1st Battalion Mortars in action, Mezzano, Italy, January 1945.

Left to Right—L/Cpl Crathern, Rfn Howarth and Ikin.

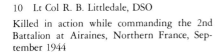

9   Inspection of 12th Battalion by Lt Gen Sir Evelyn Barker, KBE, CB, DSO, MC

Humber scout car and International half-track drive-past at Hannover, Germany, August 1945

8   1st Battalion Signallers checking lines, Mezzano, Italy, January 1945

Left to Right—Rfn Greenwood and Gess.

10   Lt Col R. B. Littledale, DSO

Killed in action while commanding the 2nd Battalion at Airaines, Northern France, September 1944

11   Lt Col J. C. Hope, DSO, MC

Died of wounds received while commanding the 1st Battalion at Finale, Northern Italy, April 1945

Battery Commander, and an escort of machine-gun carriers, moved off as soon as possible to reconnoitre the village, but as the carriers were slow in getting started, Col Littledale in his scout car went on ahead. Just as they were about to reach the village a German anti-tank gun opened up at point-blank range, killing immediately the Colonel, his driver and the Battery commander. Maj Bernays managed to get away and organized the remainder of his company as a screen round the Southern approaches to the village. The CLY with A Company under command were then ordered to attack the village from the North East.

Maj Wake led his three motor platoons up the valley to the edge of the village, covered by his carrier platoon (Lt Fletcher) and supported by a squadron of the Yeomanry. Lt Bramall was wounded and Lt Lewin narrowly missed being killed. The Germans fought extremely well, and against their accurate fire from the houses and the high ground on both sides, A Company were unable to force an entry into the town before dark. Lt Lord St Just's platoon had, however, inflicted many casualties on the enemy, and under cover of darkness the Company pulled out, having killed or captured 52 Germans, but suffering few casualties themselves.

Lt Col Littledale's death was a great blow to the Battalion, who knew of his magnificent escaping record since his capture at Calais. Although he had only commanded for just over a month, he had been with it since its return from Italy and his determination to destroy the Nazis and all they stood for, together with his quiet charm of manner, had endeared him to all ranks. It seemed so unnecessary, in that Airaines had no particular tactical significance and it was just chance that the German force had arrived in the village during the night and, unable to escape, had turned it into a strong-point. It was this very unexpectedness which had caused the Colonel to go on ahead of his escort and thus run headlong into the German defences. Patrols took the last 20 Germans prisoner next day, and the Mayor led a moving funeral procession of the whole village behind the coffins of their liberators.

In the meantime C Company, with The Greys, were trying to find a way across the Somme. Lt The Hon T. Trenchard found a footbridge intact opposite Longpré, which was seized after knocking out four 20-mm guns which fired at point-blank range until their crews had been killed or wounded. To extricate an OP tank, the bridge had to be crossed in full view of the enemy holding the far bank. In this operation 5 Germans were killed and 30 taken prisoner for the loss of only 2 wounded: Lt Trenchard was awarded the MC for his leadership in this battle.

On 3 and 4 September the advance continued, with the Brigade having the task of protecting the left flank of the British Army; the Germans to the West were reported to be abandoning their V2 rocket sites. There was little if any opposition, and many of the Germans were very willing to give themselves up in order to escape from the not so tender mercy of the French Maquis; however, as it was still impossible to guard prisoners on the advance, many were handed over to the local authorities. On 5 September the Brigade advanced 85 miles from St Pol into Belgium; but while the French has been most welcoming in their reception of the Allies, the Belgians were positively ecstatic. Cheering crowds, flowers, kisses and even champagne greeted our columns at every village. On the other hand, it was considered tactful not to enquire too closely into the fate of 'collaborators' who in some places were to be seen being frogmarched round the main square, the women with their heads shaven, and, judging by their expression, with little doubt as to the fate which awaited them after the briefest of summary trials. This enthusiastic reception, exciting and exhilarating though it was, undoubtedly held up the advance, and was more responsible for preventing us reaching Ghent than any action of the enemy. By the evening the CLY with A Company were at Oudenarde, 44 RTR with B Company, now under command of Maj J. F. C. Mellor, who had joined the Battalion on 21 August, at Kerkhove and The Greys with C Company at Avelghem. By now the Brigade had a completely open left flank in an area in which there were known to be large numbers of Germans, and it was therefore ordered to face West and protect the Corps axis from that direction. At first light battle positions were taken up on a front of 15 miles on the high ground between the River Escaut and the Lys Canal. It was not long before a stream of Germans began moving East along the whole brigade front, on which the only infantry were the motor companies of the Battalion, and so it was quite impossible to prevent some infiltration between the villages and along hedgerows. In spite of heavy losses the Germans continued to try to break through, and the tanks swept their areas over and over again. During the afternoon A Company captured 100 prisoners and a German convoy at Oudenarde, but it was clear that it would not be possible to hold such an extended line during the night, and the Armoured Regiments were ordered to fall back on to the line of the River Escaut to prevent any major crossing of it. The Germans tried several times to reach the bridges and attacked our tanks with bazookas. B Company in particular had heavy fighting protecting 44 RTR, and C Company collected 500 prisoners and 12 German vehicles, destroying many more. At first light the Armoured Regiments counter-attacked, driving the enemy back on to the high ground: they were relieved in the afternoon by a Brigade of 15 Scottish Division and pulled back to prepare for a further advance on the next day.

The Battalion got orders to move to Termonde at first light on 8 September and take over the town. The importance of Termonde was that the most northerly bridge left intact over the Scheldt was here, and our primary task was to guard this bridge. The Battalion arrived that afternoon, and got into houses for the first time since D day. B Company, with an anti-tank platoon and machine-gun platoon under command, was responsible for the North of the town where the bridge was. Carrier patrols went well North and failed to make contact with the enemy, except for a small party of Germans, shot up by A Company while attempting to swim the river. A Company was responsible for the South and East of the town, while one platoon of D Coy was responsible for the main road from the West. C Company were protecting 4th RHA to the South of the town.

That morning there had been a large funeral of about 30 Belgian children who had been murdered in cold blood by the SS. This was a reprisal for the activities of the Belgian 'Brigade Blanc', who had by force of arms prevented the Germans from blowing the bridge, and held it against all attacks—a great contribution to the Allied advance.

The advance was continued at first light by A Company and 44 RTR, with the remainder of the Battalion following immediately behind. Hamme was captured early, and by 11 am A Company reported St Nicholas was clear, and the Battalion were ordered to take it over, with 44 RTR in support.

The sight which greeted the Battalion at St Nicholas was indescribable. The whole population of some 60,000 was cheering in a seething mass in the square; so dense was the crowd that it was impossible to move. Every tank and every truck had about 20 Belgians on it with bunches of flowers, baskets of fruit and wine and every good thing for 'Les Tommies'. The perimeter was some four to five miles, and the problem was how best to defend it with three weak motor companies and one support company. In fact, the main approaches only were covered, and a screen of carriers was sent out to give warning of any enemy. The tanks backed up the motor platoons, and provided a squadron in reserve.

At about 2 pm the carriers reported German vehicles approaching the town from the North East. The Burgomaster was asked to clear all the people from the streets, and this was done in under half an hour, a most remarkable feat. A German half-track and another vehicle came up to the edge of the town; as it came round a bend in the road it was fired at by an anti-tank platoon and machine-gun platoon of D Company at about 800 yards range. Both vehicles were left blazing and all the occupants were killed. Other vehicles were reported coming in from the East, and Maj Gibbs, who was doing a reconnaissance, narrowly escaped being captured.

The next morning the Battalion and The Greys advanced up two routes to Beveren Waes, some four miles to the East. The town was occupied, and the welcome there was just as enthusiastic as at St Nicholas. We took over the town, with a squadron of Greys in support, while the rest of the Greys, with C Company under command, took over the North and East. After 36 hours the Battalion was relieved by a battalion of The Queens and was withdrawn to a pleasant wood near Booischot for a much-needed rest and reorganization.

Since the beginning of the break-out in Normandy, the Battalion had been almost continually on the move, and apart from covering a great many miles, there had been numerous changes in personnel. The five days pause which followed was therefore very welcome and enabled much necessary work to be carried out on the vehicles and weapons. On 14 September Lt Col R. H. W. S. Hastings, DSO, MC, a Rifle Brigade officer whose youthful appearance belied a forceful personality, backed by much battle experience both in the desert and in command of an Infantry battalion in Italy, arrived to take over command of the Battalion from Maj Vernon, who had been acting Commanding Officer since the death of Lt Col Littledale.

Now that we have seen the 2nd Battalion race from Normandy into Belgium—the ultimate compensation for the frustration of Calais in 1940—we must take up the 12th's story. The 2nd, in 4 Armoured Brigade, had been on the left of the British Armoured advance, running roughly parallel to the 12th, with 11 Armoured Division initially in between. To the right of the 12th was Guards Armoured Division, and gradually these two divisions with their superior punch drew ahead of the two armoured brigades, but all enjoyed the fruits of victory despite the saddening losses en route.

The 12th Battalion had passed slowly through the Falaise pocket, with all its litter of bodies and equipment, on 21 August and felt very far behind the leaders, who were approaching Paris. During the move to the Seine crossing at Vernon their LO at Brigade, Lt M. E. Healey-Pendarves, was unfortunately killed while directing traffic at night. On 28 August the 12th crossed the Seine and joined 8

Armoured Brigade, which was to advance next day; Maj Coleridge continues his account:

The 29th opened in floods of rain which continued on and off throughout the day. The Brigade's centre line was Gasny–Fourges–Dangu–Gisors. Orders were to clear as far as possible and 20 miles was the target for the day. Order of march—13/18 H. with B Company, S.R.Y. with C Company, Tac Brigade H.Q., 147 R.T.R., 12th K.R.R.C. less two companies, 4/7 D.G. The centre line lay along a river valley with high ground on both sides. The Germans put up resistance at all the villages along the route. B Company had a lot of work to do in these villages. So, too, did C Company, who were employed in a left hook movement to threaten the enemy on the centre line with the fear of being outflanked. By the end of the day the Brigade had got as far as Quesney, and 13/18 H. with B Company were sent racing on to Dangu to secure the crossings of the river to ensure an easy start to the next day's pursuit. In the gathering gloom B Company, who shared the town with a lot of Germans, took over and consolidated the bridge from the tanks, who had found it intact. The enemy gave no trouble during the night, and on taking stock in the morning, O.C. B Company found that he had acquired several very welcome bottles, a paymaster's safe with anything up to 5,000,000 francs, and as many horses as he wanted. For the first time we learnt the problem caused by prisoners taken by an Armoured Brigade. The 20 miles had been achieved at little cost to the tanks or ourselves, though we mourned the death of Cameron (Lt C. A. S.) Bailey, killed by a stray mortar bomb. The day had demanded determination and opportunism, and the Brigade had shown both in plenty. On our left 11 Armoured Division had forged ahead over good country, and our own activities had made it easier for the Guards Armoured Division to come into the battle on our right.

Next day the hunt was on again. Centre line Gisors–Lalandelle–Beauvais–Crevecoeur and 'get as far as you can'. All three Motor Companies were under command of their Armoured Regiments. The plan was:—one route as far as Gisors with 4/7 D.G. and A Company in the lead; 13/18 H. with B Company were to switch off via La Houssoye and rejoin at Beauvais, S.R.Y. with C Company to protect the left flank. It seemed an ambitious programme, but we sorted out the maps and sallied forth at first light. To everyone's surprise the enemy made no stand at Gisors and had not had time to blow the bridges. The surprise came from the population, who turned out in force. This was the first sizeable town through which we had been the pioneers of Liberation.

We rocketed along the centre line from village to village at astonishing speed. The locals all told of the enemy having recently left in a great hurry. And then quite suddenly we all realised with a jerk that Beauvais was getting very close. 13/18 Hussars on the southern route reported strong enemy positions just beyond La Houssoye. The other Armour were sent off round the North across country to get astride the roads North from Beauvais while the rest of us went on down the centre line. Just outside Beauvais the enemy had an S.P. gun or two and there was talk of a few tanks, and it seemed they meant to make a stand. The A Company command vehicle was hit by an S.P. gun and Jimmie (Maj R. R. H.) James, his driver and his Intelligence Corporal were all killed. This was a terrible blow for the Battalion, who otherwise had a very lucky day. This gun was knocked out by 4/7 D.G., who also got the enemy transport here. The way to the town seemed open.

With mixed feelings the leading Squadron and A Company started off down the main street. The citizens of Beauvais had been waiting for this occasion for a very long time and were not going to miss their fun. It was a harassing time for Nigel (Capt N. C. C.) Trench, who had just taken over the Company. At the North end of the town the leading tanks were actually fighting German tanks, and A Company were supposed to clear the town and picquet the route. This meant one Motor Company strung over about three miles of road lined with cheering and enthusiastic Frenchmen. Some brought gifts, others brought news of Germans (all grossly exaggerated), others wanted help for the Maquis, others cried, all were excited. However the Squadron and A Company managed it, and by the time Battalion H.Q. arrived the civilians were organised. Flags were out, the wine had been dug up from its hiding places and the whole fruit crop had been picked. There were also a surprising number of eggs. An unsuspected use of the armour on a White Scout Car soon became apparent. Mercifully the column kept gently moving except for one agonizing halt. It needed a strong-minded man to refuse the fifteenth and sixteenth drink—and they were all different sorts. But we moved on again just in time, leaving A Company 'in control' of the route.

During 31 August the Brigade was pinched out by 11 Armoured Division, which had moved ahead and expanded on to their centre line. The role now given for the advance over the Somme was for 8 Armoured to cover the left flank of that division.

There was no opposition until we were over the Somme, when Tanks met some enemy at Flesselles. While this was being tidied up, 4/7 D.G. branched off to the left, directed on Doullens via Vignacourt and Canaples. There were some enemy on both routes, but they were either dealt with or by-passed (we had one hideous cross-country jaunt behind the tanks) until Doullens was reached on the main route and Canaples on the other. Doullens appeared to be a stiffish proposition, and it was getting late. But 13/8 H. went right round the town and attacked it from the North, while B and C Companies sailed in from the South, supported by the S.R.Y. This clinched the matter, and the armour pushed on about five miles, leaving us in possession of the town until relieved some time next day. Meanwhile 4/7 D.G. had defeated the enemy at Canaples and joined the rest of the Brigade forward. A lot of retreating enemy had been shot up during the day, and the prisoner problem by nightfall was acute. One Gilbert and Sullivan turn must not be forgotten. The Colonel had just finished orders when an air O.P. flew very low overhead and dropped him a message which said 'There are three Boche in a shell-hole 30 yards away from you.' And sure enough there were. During the night the prisoners rolled in. By the time we found some kind person to take them off our hands they had risen to 240, and we handed 40 more to the local Frenchmen.

After a static day on 2 September, the advance was resumed through Arras, over Vimy Ridge and past the 1914–18 cemeteries. The Brigade halted while two squadrons 4/7 DG with A and B Companies reconnoitred Lille. Its population of 200,000 turned out in force to welcome their first liberators, and it was as well that there was no opposition, since vehicles were covered with the cheering French; it was with difficulty in the evening that Troopers and Riflemen were able to withdraw from the copiously bestowed wine and embraces and leave town for a well-earned rest.

11 Armoured Division had entered the invaluable port of Antwerp on 4 September and there was a short pause while the 12th Battalion, like the 2nd, faced West in case the German 15 Army tried to break out from the coastal strip; the remnants of the battered 7 Army had been swept aside by the British, and many had fallen into American hands in the Mons area. However, only Maj D. A. Colls and C Company were lucky, and after some awkward bargaining assisted in the surrender of a German regiment under its Colonel, a total of 2500 prisoners taken in three days.

On 6 September the advance continued through Tournai, and the next day through the already liberated Brussels and Louvain to Aarscht.

On the 8th we were back at work again. The Guards had forced the Albert Canal at Beringen and 8 Armoured Brigade was ordered to pass over as quickly as possible and strike North West for Gheel. The Brigade started at dawn, but was held up short of the bridge for some time as the Guards were still fighting hard in and about the coal mine to the North of the town. Eventually we crossed about midday and pushed through the Guards, with 4/7 D.G. and A Company in the lead. There were still enemy about in the woods near the bridge and more enemy in the woods near Oostham, which lay on our centre line. Towards evening some of 4/7 D.G. and A Company got into Oostham. There were obviously enemy all round the village, and so B Company were brought up to take over part of the town. There they were joined by B Squadron 4/7 D.G. and our own Tac H.Q. This village lay on the line of retreat for the Germans left on the Albert Canal North of Beringen, so they were naturally very interested in it. Next morning C Company were also brought up to take care of yet more of Oostham with the hope of clearing a route for the Armour to go through and strike North.

But before they did this, there had been an unpleasant alarum behind. The A1 Echelons of the Brigade, which had harboured near some woods just off the centre line, were sharply attacked soon after daylight by a determined party of Germans who were thought to be making for the bridge itself. Many ammunition and petrol lorries were fired and a dense cloud of smoke filled the sky. C Company carriers were the first to the rescue, followed shortly by some tanks of 13/18H. and the rest of C Company. What had been a rather unpleasant situation was quickly righted and the enemy driven off before C Company were actually employed. A post-mortem showed that our own L.A.D., under Reg Broad, had done nobly. They had done a bit of wood clearing, killed some Germans, and taken some prisoners without any casualties to themselves. It was great testimony of their initiative and alertness. We had, unfortunately, two casualties among the A1 personnel but no vehicles were lost.

After this C Company went forward to join A and B Companies. Oostham was not pleasant during the day. There were plenty of Huns in the woods and they had several S.P. guns with them. We lost three Officers during the day. Richard (Lt R. C.) Luxmoore, who had done so much to train our snipers, was himself killed while sniping—a very sad loss indeed. Arthur (Lt R. A. J.) Alcock and David (Lt D. C. W.) Bampfylde were both wounded when an S.P. gun shelled the houses and set fire to two half-tracks. We also lost one 6-pdr. by shell-fire. By the afternoon it was clear that no progress in that direction would be made by the armour, and the Battalion was accordingly ordered to pull out of the village. This operation, which started about 1900 hrs, was not easy, but was well carried out. B and C Companies got out fairly easily and rejoined the 13/18 H., and 4/7 D.G. respectively. A Company were last out, and the enemy, who were thought to be planning an attack that night, gave them little peace. But it was managed in the end for the loss of one 6-pdr. which was on the North side of the village and could not be got out. Battalion H.Q., A and D Companies joined the Brigade to the Northeast of Beringen. The 13/18 H. Group was left to hold the main Bourg Leopold Road. A captured German medical orderly revealed the satisfying news that his men round Oostham had gone far from unscathed at our hands.

The interest now centred in Bourg Leopold, and the Oostham area was left to the Germans. As the Guards were threatening the Escaut Canal on the right and 50 Division had secured a bridgehead over the Albert Canal near Gheel, the future for these particular Germans was not very bright. But Bourg Leopold had to be taken. An excursion round the East side on the 10th September by 4/7 D.G. proved it to be occupied. C Company had a long patrol into the edge of the town, whose object was to remove an anti-tank gun which had knocked out two tanks. They found no enemy on the East side and the gun had gone when they reached its lair. Next day civilians reported that the enemy had gone. So B Company and a Squadron of 13/18 H. were ordered to go up the line of the Beringen–Leopold main road and see what really was the form. The following sentence appeared in the Daily Telegraph: 'The great barracks of Bourg Leopold, converted into a strong point by the Germans, were stormed by the Belgian Army.' Without wishing to belittle our Allies, Bourg Leopold was actually liberated by one Squadron of 13/18 H. and B. Company, supported by O.C. D Company, who had come in the back way in his jeep. The Belgians subsequently took over from this party. And that was the battle of the Belgian Aldershot. Six prisoners were taken, of whom two were marines in plain clothes, thought to be members of the school staff.

It is a pleasant twist of fortune that Maj Deedes of B Company later became responsible for *Telegraph* accuracy as its Editor.

With the move of the 12th into the near-by pine-woods for rest and much-needed vehicle maintenance, the one giddy phase of the campaign was at an end. Although another great advance, from the Rhine, was to come in 1945; the civil populace would then see us glumly as conquerors rather than as liberators.

The question now posed to the Allies was whether they could keep up the momentum of the advance, so as to cross the Rhine and cripple Germany by seizing her centre of industry, the Ruhr, before the Germans could reorganize their defences. The Allied situation in early September was dominated by the

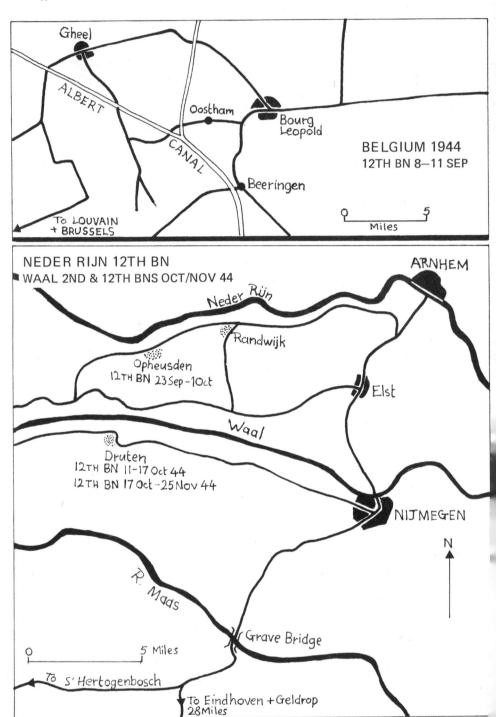

Gheel

ALBERT

Oostham

Bourg
Leopold

CANAL

BELGIUM 1944
12TH BN 8—11 SEP

Beeringen

To LOUVAIN
+ BRUSSELS

0   5
Miles

NEDER RIJN 12TH BN
WAAL 2ND & 12TH BNS OCT/NOV 44

ARNHEM

Neder Rijn

Randwijk

Opheusden
12TH BN 23 Sep - 10 ct

Elst

Waal

Druten
12TH BN 11-17 Oct 44
12TH BN 17 Oct - 25 Nov 44

NIJMEGEN

N

R. Maas

Grave Bridge

0   5 Miles

To S' Hertogenbosch

To Eindhoven + Geldrop
28 Miles

long logistic haul from Normandy. Working from the left, 1 Canadian Army was starting to clear the Channel ports, Dempsey's 2 Army had one corps grounded for logistic reasons on the Seine and another committed in Flanders to driving German 15 Army back to the Scheldt; there lack of naval intervention would allow it to cross at the mouth and deny the Scheldt approaches to Antwerp, the only port whose resources could quickly solve Allied logistic problems; of the British, only XXX Corps, in Northern Belgium, was available to go for the Rhine at Arnhem, and thence to the Ruhr from the North. To the immediate right 1 US Army had not received the petrol to keep pace with the British initially, but on 10 September were approaching the 1939 Siegfried Line defences in the Aachen area. Despite being accorded a lower logistic priority, Patton's 3 US Army was probing forward across the Moselle. Far to the South 7 US Army, including all the excellent French divisions, had been withdrawn at a critical time from Italy and its leading troops linked with Patton, on 10 September, after driving up the Rhine valley from their Mediterranean beach-heads.

A German pocket held out for several months from the Rhine to the Vosges. It was into these wooded hills that 2 SAS had parachuted to disrupt communications in September, with Maj D. R. Reynolds as 2IC and Lt D. G. Dill, who had served with him in our 10th Battalion, in the August advance party. When the SAS withdrew Lt Dill stayed behind to contact Maj Reynolds, who had been wounded. They were captured with Lt Whatley-Smith and after a winter in Gestapo hands—where their high morale was admired by their fellows—were shot in cold blood by their captors before American forces could free them. Maj Ian Fenwick, whose 'Trubshaw' cartoons had convulsed wartime England, was also killed, after leading his Squadron of 1 SAS brilliantly for three months behind the lines in France.

The one uncommitted force, which would not initially add to Eisenhower's logistic problems, comprised the two US Airborne Divisions and 1 British Airborne Division. These were now allotted to Montgomery, who assigned to the Americans as objectives the bridges in the areas of Eindhoven and Nijmegen and to the British the great Rhine bridge at Arnhem. Landings were to start on 17 September 1944, and XXX Corps was to link with them up the single embanked main road through country which permitted little or no vehicle movement off roads or tracks.

For the Germans there was the desperate necessity of buying time while the outdated pill-boxes of the Siegfried Line could be covered again by new mines and wire and troops raised to man them. The German genius for ruthless improvisation in defeat came to the fore. The Channel port garrisons won time by forcing the Allies to continue maintenance from Normandy. Back at home Volksgrenadier divisions capable of static defence of the Reich with a minimum of equipment were being raised. 15 Army slipped across the mouth of the Scheldt, so that not only was Antwerp's port unapproachable, but a potential threat to the Arnhem axis could develop from the West. Of most immediate interest to XXX Corps, Student, the airborne expert, was put in command of a new 1 Parachute Army, created on 4 September from a medley of parachutists and Luftwaffe ground crews; he was, as his new troops arrived, to fill the gap between Antwerp and the reviving 7 Army in the Aachen area, on the initial line of the Albert Canal and those water obstacles to the North. By chance General

Model's HQ was in the Arnhem suburbs, and the very reserve he needed, the re-equipping 9 and 10 SS Panzer Divisions, was near by. In the race to maintain the thrust across the Rhine or to thwart it, the Germans had the shorter communications and the incentive of defending the Fatherland; in their temporary success at Arnhem they were to let the Russians sprawl even further across Europe.

The operations of our two battalions in the XXX Corps were linked throughout Autumn 1944 with what became a British salient stretching North beyond Nijmegen; indeed, the 2nd did not leave the Maas until 17 February 1945. The principal role in each case was to hold a wide front, usually backed by armour, to protect the West or East flanks of the salient. This relieved infantry brigades to take part in the deliberate tidying operations, which successively cleared South Holland and the Antwerp approaches and later the area between the Maas and the Rhine, an essential preliminary to the March 1944 assault crossing over the latter. Both battalions would be involved in the heavy fighting to break the Schlieffen Line in the final phase of that clearance.

The Allied airborne operation 'Market Garden' started on 17 September 1944, and the advance of XXX Corps, led by Guards Armoured Division on a one-tank front, began that afternoon. The initial airdrops were in general successful, and by the 19th the leading Guards tanks had reached the Southern edge of Nijmegen to find the Americans under pressure from the Reichswald to their East; it was not until the evening of the 20th that Americans and British seized both approaches to the Nijmegen bridge and the first tanks crossed. Almost simultaneously German armour broke through the last gallant surviving parachutists at the Arnhem bridge and moved South to block the main road at Elst. Thereafter the only faint hope of retaining a bridge-head across the Rhine lay in the battered but magnificently courageous 3000 airborne troops West of Arnhem.

In XXX Corps our 12th Battalion, with under command A Squadron, 13/18H, was under 43 Division Reconnaissance Regiment, as the leading group of that Division behind the Guards. The intention had been to cross at Arnhem and wheel right to seize and hold three key bridges. With no information other than that the airdrop had been successful, the 12th moved up the main road towards Eindhoven on the morning of 20 September. A German counter-attack on Eindhoven from the East seemed possible, so the group took up a flank guard line astride Geldrop and carriers patrolled forward, to find nothing but American parachutists. On the evening of 21 September, after 11 Armoured Division had come up on the right, the group moved slowly through Eindhoven and over the intact Grave bridge, where the nature of the obstacle brought home what the airborne troops had achieved; the enemy were close to the road in places and tracer was flying about. For a brief period on 22 September the 12th was warned to be ready to race with 13/18H for the Arnhem bridge, so little was known of the position there.

However, late on the 23rd attention focused on trying to support the remaining 1 Airborne bridgehead on the North bank of the Lower Rhine below Arnhem. Accordingly the group was to form a flank guard at the narrowest point between the Waal and the Neder Rijn. The plan was to hold three villages as firm bases with A, C and B Companies, from which 43 Recce could patrol forward, and these were occupied without opposition on the night of the 23rd. The next day a short advance West was ordered, to cover an axis for 43 Division towards the ferry site to the beleagured and reducing bridgehead. Sadly, Maj W. A. Young-Smith, a recent arrival from the 8th Battalion, was killed when reconnoitring as A Company skirmished into Opheusden; this village on the South bank of the Neder Rijn was to become the most North Westerly position of 21 Army Group, as B Company joined A to look after the thick garden approaches on the West side. From the Neder Rijn an open meadow stretched up to the usual Dutch embanked road, which held back winter and spring floods; behind this was a paradise of apple and pear orchards, but around each village the gardens gave many hidden approaches. Before B Company's arrival, A Company had seen off a strong German platoon without loss, wounding the officer, inflicting casualties and taking a prisoner as they withdrew.

On the night of 25 September the last gallant survivors of 1 Airborne were ferried back across the river, and on the next a German battalion crossed to seize Randwijk to the East, held by 43 Recce. They were only expelled by a brigade counter-attack; on the 12th's river front, patrolling and harassing fire by machine-guns and mortars, the latter moved from position to position in a wheelbarrow by Sgt Hicks, kept the enemy firmly on the North bank. On 1 October the 12th was relieved by 501 US Airborne Regiment and moved South of Nijmegen for a fortnight's rest, including the despatch of parties to the Brigade Rest Camp at Louvain.

Meanwhile the role of our 2nd Battalion had been to guard the flank of XXX Corps, first on the East and then on the West. On 18 September the Brigade, less the CLY and 44 RTR, took over the line of the Junction Canal in the Bree area, a front of 15 miles, from an American reconnaissance unit; their task was to link with 1 US Army. This was a role with which the battalion was to become only too familiar during the next two months, that of covering large sectors of the front, thereby releasing other formations for decisive battles elsewhere. A motor battalion was very suited to this task, because with its good communications and fire power, it could cover larger fronts than a normal infantry battalion, whilst its shortage of riflemen on the ground was a distinct disadvantage in set-piece attacks. The Armoured Regiments could do little to assist, other than by being in reserve to launch counter-attacks should this be necessary, and the brunt of the defence fell on the Riflemen. It was possible to watch the Northern sector of the front from some high ground, but the rest of the area was heavily wooded and mined. There was a considerable amount of close-range firing on both sides, and B Company had a sharp encounter with some enemy in a large factory in which they had to establish a Gunner OP. Two-inch mortar HE was much used, but when the Germans withdrew on 21 September an inspection of their dug-outs showed how bomb-proof they were. They left a legacy of mines, which caught an A Company carrier on the towpath.

On the 26th, having handed over our front to the Royals, the Brigade relieved 8 Brigade of 3 Division along the Bois Le Duc and Wessem Canals, South East of Eindhoven. C Company occupied the town of Weert itself, and B Company was responsible for the village of Schoor. The Battalion front was some 7000 yards long, most of which was overlooked by the enemy, who had the advantage of the higher bank. This led to the Battalion being split up into platoon groups, supported in daylight by the tanks of the CLY and the guns of 4 RHA but at night more or less isolated. The Germans were very active and, realizing that we held the advantage by day, constantly patrolled our positions at night, imposing considerable strain on our scattered forces. The task was to harass the enemy as effectively as possible and to prevent any large-scale crossing of the Canal. The maximum use was made of our three-inch mortars and Vickers machine-guns, the latter using the new Mark 8Z ammunition, which gave them a range of 4500 yards. Lts J. H. Powe and F. H. Scobie, the Platoon Commanders, fired many belts of ammunition each night at likely supply routes and headquarters, hopefully estimating that one in every 10,000 rounds might have killed a German quartermaster or at least a colour sergeant coming up with the rations.

To begin with, the Germans definitely had the upper hand at night, but, despite increasing tiredness through lack of sleep, our very good young platoon commanders, supplemented with patrols found from every part of the Battalion, fairly quickly turned the tables. Switching positions and using trip flares and anti-personnel mines, Lt R. O. Lewin's platoon killed a German CSM and Cpl Diggines of B Company got his opposite number in ambush, while Capt P. M. Gosse took the war to the enemy, killing a probable five. By day Lt Bramall worked his platoon right on to the canal bank in a large wood and began to dominate the far side, shooting up several enemy, including a bazooka party. Lt Trenchard had to withdraw when an aggressive bull gave away his whereabouts in a ditch, drawing down a creeping accompaniment of mortar-fire; as they finally sortied his Bren Gunner had to shoot the bull as it charged. However, they soon afterwards caught an enemy patrol in another ditch, killing the officer, taking a prisoner and inflicting casualties. The enemy had good OPs and their night patrols were always pressing civilians for our whereabouts. Maj Mellor, armed with a pistol, nightly expected a follow-up to the many enquiries for his HQ—they were rebuffed when they did call—and Battalion HQ received a sudden shelling, which inflicted casualties on the RAP. Capt Nixon, as Adjutant, was caught washing without a stitch on, and had to organize a rapid move. On 8 October 7 US Armoured Division took over our sector of the front.

After three days rest and maintenance, the Battalion was given the task of covering 6000 yards of the South Bank of the Waal at Druten, on the left flank of the Arnhem salient, and facing North to harass enemy movement on the North Bank. There was, in fact, little activity, because the enemy opposite us were more interested in the American Airborne Division, which faced West on the North bank, and with whom they were in close contact, than our somewhat long-range and probably very inaccurate sniping across the 200-yard-wide river. On 16 October Maj J. Holdsworth, MC, took over command of B Company from Maj Mellor, who was required for a staff appointment. On the 17th the Battalion was relieved by 12 KRRC, and was ordered to take over a sector of the front just North of Poppel on the Belgian/Dutch frontier. This lay West of Eindhoven, and the move was in preparation for the big offensive, which was about to be launched with the object of clearing Holland South of the Waal and of course the Antwerp approaches. They were now linking 2 Army with 1 Canadian Army.

The 2nd Battalion took over their new position from four battalions of General (E. H.) 'Bubbles' Barker's 49 Division, whose advance had come to a stop in the middle of a forest, where they had dug deep trenches and were surrounded by a large number of enemy only 200 yards away. It was impossible to get vehicles anywhere near the position, and for once the battalion had to operate in a conventional infantry defensive role, with colour sergeants bringing up the main hot meal of the day after dark and departing before first light, having also served breakfast. Our task was to prevent the enemy from realizing that a relief had taken place and in particular the weakness of the relieving force, which caused concern to Polish troops on our flank; the maximum patrol activity was therefore ordered, and as usual the machine-guns and three-inch mortars made up in fire-power what we lacked in manpower. A patrol by Lt Bramall captured a prisoner and brought back some useful information without casualties, but a fighting patrol by Lt P. W. M. Dean was less fortunate. Its task was to clear a section of the wood on A Company's right with the support of three troops of 4 RHA and our own mortars and MMGs. It started off well, taking two prisoners, and clearing the wood without difficulty until it had almost reached its objective, when a Spandau opened up at ten yards range, wounding the patrol commander and five Riflemen, one of whom subsequently died of his wounds. The platoon, now led by Cpl Green, who was later awarded the MM, went on, taking four more prisoners, killing several Germans and finally cleared the wood. On the same night a German patrol blundered into B Company's position and seven prisoners were taken without loss. Maj Bernays, who spoke fluent German, did some useful interrogation of the prisoners, as a result of which most of their positions were accurately located and continually harassed by all available weapons. The enemy's retaliation was confined to intermittent shelling and mortaring, which was of little more than nuisance value and caused very few casualties: it was clear that these were not very good or enthusiastic Germans!

On 25 October, threatened by the advance of XII Corps towards 's Hertogenbosch, the enemy drew back, felling a number of trees across the road, which they booby-trapped, and scattered Schu mines, a small wooden mine which was hard to detect but had sufficient force to blow off a foot. The Battalion, supported by 44 RTR, was ordered to follow up and maintain the maximum pressure on the retreating enemy. Contact was regained on the 25th by a patrol led by Lt G. B. Benson, and early on the next morning the advance was continued with C Company leading. Lt H. S. H. Stanley's platoon was held up by an enemy position along the line of a small stream, the bridge over which had been blown. C Company launched a successful attack supported by a squadron of tanks, which drove the enemy back; six prisoners were taken, who confirmed that the enemy had taken up positions on the Southern outskirts of Goirle immediately to the North. At first light on the next day, B Company passed through C Company with two platoons leading on either side of the road. The right-hand platoon reached the outskirts of the village, when it was fired on by some Spandaus and the Platoon Commander, Lt J. Q. P. Curzon, was wounded, but not seriously. The left-hand platoon, led by Lt J. L. Lowther, was advancing up a lane towards a factory when the enemy opened up with machine-guns at close range, wounding the Platoon Commander, who, taking cover in a ditch, was again wounded by a Schu mine. The Platoon Sergeant, Sgt Birch, rushed forward to help him and was killed by Spandau fire, and two other NCOs also going to help were wounded. We had lost a good platoon commander, who despite his wounds insisted on seeing his men bandaged, and one of the bravest sergeants in the battalion. Eventually the platoon was withdrawn under cover of smoke and the casualties evacuated by carriers. This unfortunate incident showed clearly that Goirle was held in strength and, with the limited forces at our disposal, it could not be taken by frontal assault; it was therefore decided to try to outflank it with B Company supported by a squadron of tanks. The going was appalling, and soon all the half-tracks, most of the carriers and even some of the tanks were hopelessly bogged under the very noses of the enemy, who fortunately took very little notice of them. This was not before Lt E. C. Phillips with his carrier platoon and supported by a troop of tanks had taken several prisoners and killed a German company sergeant major, who charged the carriers with his rifle at the high port! However, by now it was getting dark and orders were received to stay in our present positions for the night.

On the following morning, 27 October, early patrols confirmed that the enemy were still present, but at 1230 hours two deserters came into the A Company position with information that the enemy had pulled back. Lt Bramall immediately set off with a section patrol to confirm whether Goirle had been evacuated. Unfortunately, in avoiding a suspicious road block, Cpl Martin stepped on a Schu mine in the plough and lost a foot; in helping him back, Lt Bramall was lucky that another mine, on which he stepped, did not go off. Despite this casualty, the patrol passed on into the village, and found it clear of enemy except for some deserters, who gave themselves up. Both they and a Dutchman, who arrived on a motor-cycle, said that Tilburg had also been abandoned. Lt Bramall, therefore, went forward on the latter's pillion and confirmed this. As he returned another patrol, led by Lt C. A. Humphreys, also became involved in a minefield and suffered seven casualties, including two stretcher-bearers, who had gone to the assistance of the wounded. On the next day the Brigade moved through the outskirts of Tilburg and continued down the road towards Breda. The road passed through thick wooded country, mostly of pines, and although the opposition was not strong there was continual skirmishing and sniping to clear the centre line. The Battalion, supported this time by the Greys, cleared the village of Reijen, and some prisoners were taken. A Company continued to the North, coming up against some strong opposition at a bridge which crossed a canal at Dongen; Lt Humphreys' platoon did very well, killing several Germans and taking 12 prisoners, with only one casualty themselves. On the 29th the rest of the Brigade withdrew, leaving us under the Greys; a patrol led by Lt A. K. H. Fletcher was shot up, suffering three casualties, including its leader. During the day information was received that we should rejoin the Brigade back in the Weert area, where we were to relieve an American formation.

Hardly had the Battalion deployed along the Canals around Weert when we were ordered to hand over our positions there to 158 Brigade and were to concentrate around the village of Tungelroij just to the South. The relief took place on 1 November and the Brigade moved into Corps reserve. A welcome draft of reinforcements arrived, including Lts C. T. C. Tatham and R. A. Soames (A Company), P. R. Smalley, R. H. Burton and M. S. M. Robinson (B Company) and M. J. F. Morrison (C Company). Training started interspersed with a certain amount of social activities in the evening. Games were played, and D Company Football XI beat Weert by the conclusive score of 13–Nil. On the 14th an attack was launched with the object of clearing the enemy who were still holding out West of the Maas. The armoured regiments were deployed in support of 49 Division and on the 21st the Battalion was ordered to pass through 49 Division Reconnaissance Regiment directed on to Tongerloo, West of Venlo, with the Greys in support. Starting at 1400 hours, the advance was slow owing to the completely saturated state of the ground and numerous mines. A patrol led by Lt J. G. R. Allen in the early hours of the next day reported the village to be clear of enemy, and it was occupied without opposition by 0930 hours. On 24 November the Battalion moved back to Leende on the main road from Weert to Eindhoven to continue its interrupted training programme. On the 29th the award of the MC to Lts The Hon T. Trenchard and M. A. C. Beaman was announced, and the MM to CSM R. Goss. Battalion HQ led a somewhat cramped existence in a building called Bond's Hotel, and the Companies all managed to find suitable covered accommodation, which, in view of the wet and cold weather, was most necessary. The locals were somewhat colourless, and were remarkable for being very bad at football; the village priest forbade the local girls to dance with the dissolute soldiery—perhaps a wise precaution—but otherwise they were friendly and helpful. Training proceeded apace, and the 2IC, Maj Vernon, ran an officers' cadre for all below the rank of Captain; this was a salutary but unpopular measure, which forced all subalterns away from their evening poker to listen to the Adjutant lecturing on courts-martial, Capt G. S. Palmer on the duties of a company second in command and the orderly room sergeant (Sgt Buffey) on pay.

Priority within 21 Army Group during October and November 1944 had gone to clearance of the Scheldt approaches to Antwerp, but the first convoy did not reach that city until 28 November. Meanwhile it will be remembered that the 12th Battalion had relieved the 2nd South of the Waal on 17 October, after a day spent on protecting the Grave bridge. Owing to pitch darkness and a difficult road, only the recce parties saw much of the 2nd, but all were grateful that relief in the line could on this occasion be on a one-for-one basis, since establishments and tactics of course matched. North of the Waal the line facing West from the Neder Rijn was held by the Americans, who no longer had such a firm hold on Opheusden, which the 12th had handed over to them a fortnight earlier. South of the Waal the 12th held a line facing North astride Druten, where the embanked road runs close to the river, and two brick factories down on the water's edge, at points where the road runs 1000 yards back from the river. By day no movement could be made outside the invulnerable factories since shelling was prompt and accurate, but at night patrols had to watch the river for attempted crossings along the 8000-yard front, to its junction with a reconnaissance regiment further West. When the Americans attacked to improve their front, the 12th extended their line West, and were able to overlook German-held territory from enfilade, using 16 OPs by day; Lt Hill as LO with the Americans had ensured mutual exchange of information and of targets. At night machine-guns, mortars and the supporting field regiment were harassing German supply movement, while the Dutch Underground gave their daily bulletin by phone from behind the enemy lines or through Capt Vickery, a British officer, who had been working with the Dutch for some time.

During this period there were three brushes with enemy who had landed, all in a desolate farm and orchard named Vincentshoef. The first time we won

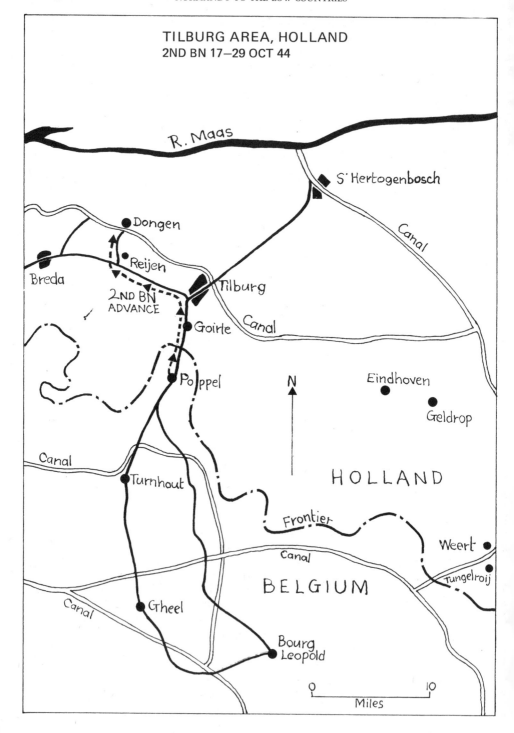

TILBURG AREA, HOLLAND
2ND BN 17–29 OCT 44

handsomely, killing two, including the leader, and wounding some more without casualties to ourselves. The second round was unsatisfactory. The enemy sent out two parties who, when contact was made, were on opposite sides of our patrol. After a lot of shooting the enemy cleared off and threw grenades from a very safe range; even though in the moonlight he could see a wounded man being attended to, he made no attempt to gain an identification. The wounded man was the patrol commander, Lt A. H. C. Hill, who had done excellent work during his short time in the battalion; our fatal casualty was Cpl Nutt, killed instantly. The Germans were thought to have had some wounded, but, if so, they got them all away without trouble. The third affray was a scuffle on a dark night, which unfortunately ended in the death of Cpl Ewing.

In the middle of November the land between the two embanked roads became flooded; previous to this a boat-sinking operation had been mounted, with the ·5 Browning as the most practical weapon, but now there was less likelihood of small boats crossing. During the period the odd flying bomb, Antwerp-bound, passed overhead, and a few V2s were seen, launched, from a distance. The main bombardment of London had of course finished with the clearance of the Pas de Calais sites.

As things became quieter, training started with a series of three-day courses back at the echelon. Sadly, RSM Kenrick, to whom the 12th owed a great deal, was accidentally shot in the head during an exercise with live ammunition. 8 Armoured Brigade had moved South to take part in the capture of Geilenkirchen, so for the last fortnight the Battalion came under the Canadians.

On 25 November the 12th moved off to rejoin their brigade North West of Geilenkirchen, entering Germany for the first time, having a splendid 100-mile run over the open roads—so unlike the September congestion, and showing how much of a backwater the salient had become. On 29 November 1944 the Dorsets were relieved on the extreme left of the 43 Division front, and the 12th occupied the two villages of Birgden and Kreuzrath; they were about a mile and a half of bare ground apart, overlooked by the enemy, who at Birgden was only 100 yards from the village. Movement by day was confined to within the villages, with unpredictable shelling, and by night German special patrol groups came forward boldly, which meant that echelon vehicles had to move up and back under escort. A vehicle of another unit which ignored this discipline was knocked out well behind Birgden.

The only consolations of an unremitting round of patrols—which on the wide and featureless front never happened to lay successful ambush—were the secure cellars and the excellent supply of poultry and pigs. L/Cpl Lane, the Battalion butcher, was unaccustomedly up from B Echelon dealing with the pork. The villages had been much knocked about, and on a windy night were eerie places, with rattling doors and banging shutters. To the regret of all who remembered his lively sense of rhythm on the drums while in England, or his cheerful leadership in war, Lt G. A. S. Callingham was killed one night while commanding his platoon in Birgden. The next night, 3 December, the 12th was relieved and paid a brief visit back over the Dutch border to Heerleheide for hot pithead baths, before joining a brigade of 52 Lowland Division as their reserve battalion on the edge of Geilenkirchen. Continuous reconnaissance was made of a projected attack to the River Roer, but a sea of mud killed the operation. All

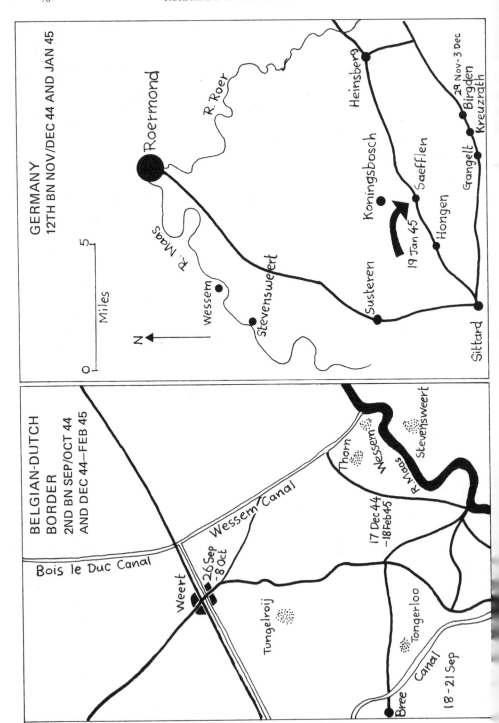

livestock had long been eaten and only the coal stocks in cellars of the ruined houses made life tolerable. The 12th were not sorry to leave for their old billets on the evening of 17 December, and noticed increased enemy air activity as they drove back.

Surprisingly it was not till 18 December 1944 that the 12th heard the news of von Runstedt's offensive in the Ardennes and linked it with the air activity they had seen. This offensive had started at dawn on 16 December, when, under a barrage of 2000 guns, 14 German infantry divisions attacked 5 US divisions holding a 100-mile front. The German forces had been building up secretly since the plan was first outlined at the end of October; Eisenhower's policy of attacking all along the front had dispersed his effort, so that the Allies had posed no threat, which would have prevented the creation of such an enemy reserve. Despite the surprise the Americans fought well, and they made quick moves of armour to St Vith and of airborne and armoured troops to Bastogne. This response, in a country of hilly woods, denied the key communication centres to the panzer columns, in the case of Bastogne permanently. Cross-country movement ate up precious fuel, and, although the offensive came very close to Allied petrol dumps, the strike towards Antwerp just failed to reach the Meuse, foundering initially more on fuel shortage than on Allied offensive action. It did, however, split the front, of which the Northern flank was put temporarily under Montgomery and forced XXX British Corps to be diverted from the planned Reichswald offensive to take up a stop line on the Meuse. As the weather improved the Allied air effort was able to cripple the German armoured columns confined to the forest roads and tracks, and on 27 December the German spearheads closest to the Meuse were struggling back Eastward and the gallant American defenders of Bastogne had been relieved from the South. In the event Hitler's gamble, despite the flurry it had caused in the Allied camp, had enabled his last great armoured reserve to be defeated West of the Rhine; the final assault on Germany could therefore be made with greater risks taken than ever before.

Although our 12th Battalion had at first felt itself too far North to be involved, 8 Armoured Brigade pointed out that a German thrust along the British/American boundary at Geilenkirchen was a possible diversion; indeed, just such a project was in the German mind. Accordingly the period astride Christmas was spent digging eight separate battalion stop-line positions in ground increasingly frozen. This accomplished, a very cheerful delayed Christmas was spent in Brunsum, a friendly Dutch mining town; the draw for the first 28-day home-leave vacancies was a momentous occasion, while the necessary cadres were run and snow camouflage considered. Before turning to the 12th's part in the clearing of the Rhineland we shall, however, look at the final phase of the Regiment's Winter defensive role in Holland, that of the 2nd Battalion on the River Maas.

It had been hoped that the 2nd Battalion might have been left in peace for Christmas but this was not to be, and on 17 December the Brigade was placed under command of 11 Armoured Division to take the place of its own Armoured Brigade (29th) which had returned to Belgium to re-equip. The Battalion was ordered to relieve a battalion of the Lorried Infantry Brigade facing East across the River Maas. C Company occupied Wessem, a small hamlet right on the West bank. Battalion HQ and A Company occupied Thorn, a slightly larger village on some high ground three-quarters of a mile back from the river bank—a somewhat unusual arrangement, in that both HQs occupied a very comfortable nunnery whose only disadvantage was that it was in front of the forward platoon position, while D Company was in a series of large farm buildings on the same high ground but a mile to the South, with B Company in reserve in a village a mile to the rear. During the day the area could be covered by fire, but at night the position became a series of isolated company strong-points with large unprotected gaps between them.

It was now very cold, and there were heavy falls of snow, so that white denim overalls were issued as camouflage suits; a further complication was that in both morning and evening a thick mist reduced visibility to zero. The 2nd Battalion's predecessors had been content to shut themselves up in their village fortresses at night, with the result that German patrols had been at liberty to cross the river at will and shoot up our positions with comparative ease; a heavy programme of counter-patrols was immediately put into effect, with the result that enemy activities noticeably decreased. At the same time plans were made to cross the river with our own patrols and inflict on the Germans opposite us the same treatment which they had successfully been giving us. The first of them, a reconnaissance to find out the practicability of landing on the far bank, and to what extent it was watched by the enemy, was a complete success, Capt P. M. Gosse and a Rifleman having paddled themselves across in an inflatable rubber dinghy and landed on the far bank without any interference. Similar patrols were also carried out by Lts C. T. C. Tatham and D. P. Dixon. The climax to this was a raid led by Maj John Holdsworth and Capt Teddy Phillips which not only shot up enemy positions but even brought back the first prisoner from the East bank; awed by their sinister white garb, he hastily declared himself a Saxon rather than a German.

On 24 December Lt Col Hastings was struck down with diphtheria and had to be evacuated. During the comparatively short time during which he had commanded the Battalion he had shown himself to be an outstanding leader; not only was he full of energy and aggressive ideas, but his meticulous eye for detail undoubtedly raised the standard of turnout, and saluting reached almost a pre-war standard of excellence. Maj Vernon again took over command until 13 January when Lt Col C. D'A. P. Consett, DSO, MC—a celebrated 1st Battalion figure of desert days, who had also commanded the 11th in Italy—arrived to relieve him. On 16 January 7 Armoured Division launched an offensive from the Sittard area, driving North between the Maas and Roer rivers with the object of eliminating the enemy in that area. As the advance was straight across their front, it was obvious that the 2nd Battalion would soon be squeezed out; this did indeed happen, but not before 3 Commando made a massive raid across the river on our front on the 19th to seize Stevensweert on the opposite bank; however, they were too late, the enemy having already departed.

Before our two Battalions' resumption of the offensive role, which will take them over the Rhine with 21 Army Group to the two great North German cities of Hamburg and Hannover in ultimate victory, it is appropriate to take stock of their contribution since the Normandy landings. The keynote is surely flexibility, which stemmed only partially from the wireless communications and the section vehicles of the establishment. More significant was the quality of the leadership at all levels; through constant Green Jacket effort by Capts the Hon J. K. Ritchie and R. P. Cave in the Colonel Commandants' office, good young officers had been recruited, and they and their NCOs had been well trained by experienced Regular, Supplementary Reserve and Territorial officers, and the initiative of their Riflemen encouraged.

Serving, as the two Battalions had throughout, in independent armoured brigades, it was only in the race from Normandy that they were let loose in the full motor role with their affiliated armoured regiments, attacking as a company or supporting squadrons with platoons. Each time their Brigade came under command of an infantry division they had to do most of the work as a battalion, since so often, as in the bocage or the soggy ground of the Low Countries, the tanks had to act as a reserve in depth. Our battalions then took over very wide fronts, often releasing an infantry brigade or at least a battalion for a concentrated task elsewhere.

Here above all the quality of leadership showed, for the 270 or usually fewer Riflemen of the nine motor platoons would have to do the work of at least 100 more men of the heavy infantry. True, the greater number of LMGs in the carrier platoons gave increased defensive fire-power, but the secret lay in the offensive patrolling, aimed at keeping the enemy so much at arm's length that he could not find out our low strength. Careful Company use of built-up intelligence in the planning phase was the basis, but the ultimate strength lay in the first-class young subalterns and their NCOs and Riflemen, who courageously and skilfully took the war to the enemy, night after night, through the hedgerows of the Summer and over the mud and frost of the Autumn and Winter.

The 2nd and 12th Battalions had not gone unscathed, but not all our North West Europe casualties were to be with the Regiment.

The distinguished work of officers killed with the Special Air Service has already been mentioned, to which must be added the name of Sgt Thorpe, killed with 2 SAS in Germany. When this new Regiment was raised again after the war, there were normally thereafter to be first-class Green Jacket officers and NCOs serving a Tour with it.

Lt L. N. Mosseri, another of our officers from America, was killed with the French Commandos in the Vosges, in the region where the SAS had been operating; French citizenship had encouraged his transfer to that Army.

Capt H. Stringer and Lts R. J. N. Ellis and M. Becke were attached to 8 RB and fell during the fighting in the Low Countries. Lt E. H. Taylor was killed, while attached to the Middlesex, in the same area.

Officers at an armoured brigade HQ were often in the thick of the fighting. Lt G. R. Ferguson had been killed at Alamein, and Capt J. W. Fawcus fell in the Rhineland battles.

Far across the world, against the Japanese, there were other sad losses. Maj the Hon T. Freeman-Mitford, as a pre-war Queen's Westminster, had worked his way up to be 2IC of our 11th Battalion. Going from the Staff College to Burma, he had declined a staff post and was killed while 2IC to a battalion, gaining jungle experience before command. Capt (QM) J. P. Archer died of fever contracted in the jungle with the Gambia Regiment.

Some there were who became impatient to get to grips with the enemy during the long period of waiting before D day in Normandy. Lt T. G. P. Peyton fell in the brilliant St Nazaire raid as a Commando, and Lt R. J. M. Peters was killed crossing the Irrawaddy in Burma with his Special Boat Section.

Many of our Riflemen must have been killed in action with other Regiments; since, unlike our officers, they were posted, not attached, we must honour them in thought, their names being on the roll of the units with which they died.

CHAPTER IV
VICTORY AND ITS
AFTERMATH IN GERMANY

(Maps: pages 70, 78, 84, 90 and 94)

The position of Germany was now desperate, for the Yalta Conference in early February 1945 showed that there would be no weakening of the Allies' resolve to enforce unconditional surrender by offensives on both fronts. In the face of this, Hitler gave priority to holding the Russians on the River Oder, East of Berlin. Thinking that it would take the Americans up to two months to recover from his Ardennes offensive, he moved half of his panzer divisions to the East and allocated virtually all of his tank-production to that front. The collapse of the German railways under air attack forced him to fight on West of the Rhine, since only by using that river could war materials enter or leave the Ruhr industrial complex. He relied on the difficulty of the Eifel country and on his ability to flood the River Roer from its dammed headwaters, backed by the refurbished Siegfried Line; on the Northern flank were the recently organized defences on the rides through the gloomy Reichswald, close to the Dutch border. Although the German people feared being overrun by the Russians above all, Hitler required the maximum resistance on behalf of his Reich on all fronts; in particular, any commander who allowed a Rhine bridge to fall intact into Allied hands was to be shot. The best that von Runstedt could do in the face of this rigid policy was to try to create a reserve in the flat Rhineland plain North East of Aachen.

Hitler had, however, underestimated the power of the Americans, who were now receiving a fresh division each week and no longer had an ammunition shortage. Their confidence had been enhanced by the way in which they had ejected the SS divisions from the Ardennes. There was no question of waiting for the Spring in Eisenhower's mind; he intended to make a two-pronged envelopment of the Ruhr with Bradley's Army Group in the South, moving on Kassel, and with Montgomery's 21 Army Group, including 9 US Army in the North. First, the Rhineland approaches to the river would have to be cleared in successive phases, starting in the North.

A limited preliminary action to the Rhineland battle was the clearance of the flat country lying between the Maas and the Roer, North of Sittard; its effect on the enemy, holding the Maas opposite the 2nd Battalion, was noted at the end of the previous chapter. 7 Armoured Division were to break through near Susteren, after which 8 Armoured Brigade less the SRY were to pass through and turn Eastwards behind the enemy lines. Once there the Brigade was to await the attack of 52 Lowland Division with the SRY from the South. The Operation was named 'Blackcock'.

On 12 January 1945 the Motor Companies of the 12th Battalion joined their Armoured Regiments: A to 4/7 DG, B to 13/18H and C to SRY. In the early stages of the operation the ground had thawed, which meant that movement was largely confined to roads, where any knocked-out vehicle made a block. 7 Armoured Division had a hard two-day fight before they were able to break through on 19 January; the leading troops of 8 Armoured Brigade (A Squadron 4/7 DG and A Company) then turned off to the right to make for Koningsbosch during the night.

Maj Coleridge wrote:

The road was very bad and narrow and there were disorganised parties of enemy all over the place. For instance, at one point, the leading tanks having passed, some Germans put mines on the road and caught one of the later tanks who had every right to assume the road was clear. But the 4/7 and A Company did extremely well and got through to the Koningsbosch area.

At dawn A Company had, thanks to the Armoured Vehicles R.E. and the Essex Yeomanry, a noisy and victorious entry to a small village near Koningsbosch. On arrival the place appeared empty, but the Company ferrets soon produced a nice number of nervous Germans from cellars. Later in the day the houses were heavily shelled and five Riflemen were wounded.

Meanwhile further back on the same route the 13/18 Group was not so lucky. A roving S.P., of which several were very bravely handled by the Germans throughout the operation, had knocked out a tank and blocked the only road. Passage across country was impossible. In front of the block was B Company and most of the Regiment, behind was the reserve Squadron and R.H.Q. Lt Dick (R.P.) Hornby's platoon was also behind; he had got his guns into action very quickly and chased off the S.P. The C.O. of 13/18 Hussars eventually rejoined his leading elements in a Weasel, and was provided by B Company with a half-track and a bed. Together they formed a strong-point at a track junction in the woods near Koningsbosch and had not much attention from the Hun.

52 Lowland Division and the S.R.Y. Group now made the frontal assault through Hongen and got through to Saeffelen, the next village to Koningsbosch. After a mine-lifting patrol from either end, provided by A and C Companies respectively, had met between the two villages, the way was now open to Koningsbosch on a shorter and much more satisfactory road, and the Brigade no longer had to use the 7 Armoured Division centre-line.

The story of the rest of the operation is soon told. 43 Division came up on the right of 52 Division and relentless pressure cleared right up to Heinsberg and the Roer. For our part the Motor Companies were used almost exclusively for protecting the tanks at night. C Company had more of this than the others. Snow on the ground and consistently low temperatures were trying, and some mockery was thrown at D Company and Battalion H.Q. firmly and warmly ensconced in Sittard in Holland.

After the battle we collected again at Wehr, which is just inside Germany near Sittard. A Company had gone off with 4/7 Dragoon Guards to assist 102 U.S. Division in tackling the Siegfried Line near Geilenkirchen. On paper it looked a formidable job, but 'Blackcock' influenced the enemy not to hold it strongly, and eventually 102 U.S. Division captured all its objectives without a fight. Neither 4/7 Dragoon Guards nor A Company were employed. Meanwhile at Wehr we had carried out a bit of maintenance and had run a cadre on the use of Wasp equipment (flame-throwers). It was here that we got our first warning about operation 'Veritable', the great battle through the Reichswald Forest and across the more open country beyond to the Rhine.

Montgomery's Rhineland plan was for XXX British Corps, under command 1 Canadian Army, to attack through the Reichswald in the North (Operation 'Veritable'); shortly afterwards 9 US Army was to launch a converging attack across the Roer. In the event, however, the blowing of the last Roer dam on 9 February caused flooding which delayed the American attack until the 23rd. During this fortnight the British and Canadians, having drawn off von Runstedt's reserve, found their opposition on the narrow Cleve–Goch front growing from the original one to nine German divisions. Accordingly when the Americans struck they had no difficulty in reaching the Rhine near Düsseldorf in two days and, as we shall see, of making contact with our 12th Battalion on 3 March near Geldern.

The XXX Corps attack started on 8 February, when five divisions, supported by 1000 guns, attacked through the Reichswald defences, held by one division. 15 Scottish Division succeeded in reaching the defended town of Cleve on the 9th, only to find that the town has been mistakenly bombed with HE instead of incendiaries; this turned it into an impassable mixture of craters and rubble, which the Germans, with all their Cassino and Stalingrad expertise, hastened to reinforce. Only two metalled roads, partially covered with flood-water, led to the front, and movement in the thawing countryside was impossible for vehicles. Not fully appreciating the movement situation, Corps brought forward two mobile columns of 43 Division; these included the 12th Battalion's 8 Armoured Brigade, which merely served to jam the Scottish centre line. Meanwhile, with their Southern Roer flank secure, the Germans were racing their reserve of two armoured and two parachute divisions North to the Goch–Cleve area. The XXX Corps operation became a series of deliberate operations to clear the Cleve area and the Reichswald itself, making log 'Corduroy' tracks, before seizing the escarpment North of Goch.

On 1 February the 12th Battalion moved from the Sittard area South of the Roer, first West into Belgium and then finally North into the Nijmegen area of Holland. Until arrival South of Goch the 2IC, Maj F. J. R. Coleridge, was in command, since the Commanding Officer was one of those home on leave. Throughout this phase A, B and C Companies were with their normal armoured regiments, who were each supporting a brigade of 43 Division. In such close country and at night it was very necessary for the tanks to have close protection against short-range anti-tank weapons, and a motor platoon was often allocated to a squadron.

The operation started on the 8th, but it was not till the evening of the 9th that the S.R.Y. Group set off from Nijmegen for Cleve with 129 Brigade. The Germans had flooded everything north of the road to Cleve, and to the south of it lay the Reichswald, where the numerous tracks soon became little better than quagmires. The main road round the south of the forest was not yet clear. So all movement was virtually confined to the one road, over which 48 hours later there was 3ft of water near Kranenberg. To give some idea of conditions on this road, Battalion H.Q.'s journey on the 10th is a good example. We

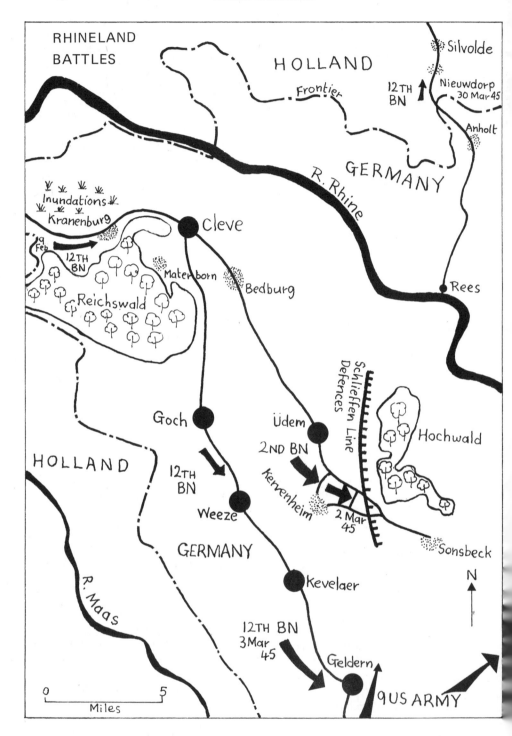

accomplished 9 miles in 16 hours. (And once more we rejoiced that the Luftwaffe was no longer a power in the land.) However, C Company and the rest of their party had got through to Cleve the night before. Far from being clear, the town contained a number of enemy. As it grew light, a party of Germans on a small hill overlooking the main road into Cleve opened up on C Company's vehicles which were jammed on the road unable to move. Capt John Garne, commanding in Maj Derek Colls' absence on leave, led C Company in some very spirited retaliation, for which he was subsequently awarded the M.C. and Sgt Lawrence the M.M. The vehicles were all saved and casualties inflicted on the enemy. Subsequently the hill was completed cleared by some flame-throwers. Mike (Lt M. H.) Hewlett was killed by a sniper as he moved from post to post encouraging his platoon, a very sad loss for the Battalion.

Meanwhile 214 Brigade and the 4/7 Dragoon Guards Group had followed up the centre line as far as Kranenberg. Thence they turned south after an interval and arrived in Materborn, a southern suburb of Cleve, after a difficult drive through the mud of the Reichswald. Materborn also was not clear, and but for the prompt action of Donald (Lt D. F.) Campbell and his platoon, who were moving with the leading Troop of tanks, more than one tank might have been lost in the dark.

The Cleve area was eventually cleared completely by 11 February, and 43 Division pushed on with the original plan. But there was to be no quick break-out or mad rush for the Rhine. Owing to the weather conditions and our very precarious lines of supply (at one time the only communication with Nijmegen was by boat), the enemy had time to collect reserves of parachutists and artillery and organize his defence. The slogging got harder from day to day and the German artillery put up performances which none of us had heard before. Somewhere or another by day and by night some part of 43 Division was attacking, and with all those attacks went part of 8 Armoured Brigade. For us at this time the main job was protection of tanks, and the Companies were generally split, with a motor platoon with each squadron. C Company spent two days together near Bedburg Asylum guarding the left flank of the Division, and on another occasion they made a fourth infantry company for a battalion which had had a lot of casualties. B Company were once prepared for a Company attack, but it was cancelled. A Company remained split throughout and their platoons did many difficult jobs with great success. In fact once something more like a section than a platoon cleared a group of houses for the tanks. D Company commander had to motor almost as far to visit his platoons as anyone from Battalion H.Q. to visit the Companies. Lt Joe (J. A.) Floyd and his M.G. platoon had one particularly arduous period under 8 Middlesex, for which they were highly praised by the M.G. battalion commander.

By the 18th the escarpment overlooking Goch had been finally won, and there ensued a short pause while the attack on the town was planned. In this the Brigade had no great part, and it was not till the exploitation south of Goch started that the Battalion had any major commitments. Then on the 25th we were once more reunited and sent off next day to take over part of the line south of Goch from two Battalions of 53 Division, our first contact with this Division. All vehicles, except for a few for Battalion H.Q. and a wireless carrier per Company, were left in Goch and the Battalion moved up on foot. The woods were not attractive places, and the enemy hindered the relief with some unpleasant shelling which cost us nine Riflemen wounded. Next day A and C Companies were pulled out for an operation with the S.R.Y., and in exchange the Colonel got a Squadron of the Reconnaissance Regiment and a Company from 1st Oxs and Bucks—a curious mixed command. Towards evening enemy activity slackened off a little, and Lt Andrew (A. G.) Burnaby-Atkins went out on a reconnaissance patrol. He found that the enemy had gone, leaving a number of dead behind.

Thus we stayed until March 2nd, when it was found that the enemy had left Weeze during the previous night—a place he had defended with great determination. So a force was hurriedly collected to pursue them. 1st Oxs and Bucks (the 43rd Light Infantry) in Kangaroos and the 4/7 Dragoon Guards were both available. A Company had not returned from the S.R.Y. and could not be got in time, so B Company went off instead.

The enemy had made extensive demolitions, and it was these rather than enemy fire which dictated the rate of advance. The Oxs and Bucks dismounted, got through to Kevelaer during the night, and were joined in the morning by the leading elements of 4/7 Dragoon Guards. But again demolitions played their part, and the advance did not really get going for several hours. When it did, it was not long before contact was made with the Americans (south west of Geldern) who had come racing up from the south after their break across the Roer.

First contact between Allied armies, who have learnt by bitter experience to keep a finger on the trigger, is always a ticklish moment. One method of effecting it on 3 March 1945 comes from an account by Maj Deedes, OC B Company:

The leading Squadron of the 4/7 Dragoon Guards and B Company spent a wet night on the home side of a large crater, mined and covered by two anti tank guns and a spandau. Benjy (Lt B.) Yeats-Brown had been wounded for the second time. A lot of vehicles were bogged.

Across the orchard, where we were eating breakfast, snatches of a familiar voice could be heard addressing the Regimental C.O. in homely terms. '. . . must crack on, old boy'. . . all gone away . . . bound to pack in . . .' O Group of the squadron leader selected to crack on was commendably short. 'Whips out . . .,' he said without enthusiasm. Soon we were bowling down the main road through Kevelaer towards Geldern, Andrew Burnaby-Atkins' carrier leading, some Honey tanks, a Troop, squadron leader, myself and the rest. Senior and Staff Officers stood on the corners swinging their arms vigorously eastwards, signifying late again over the start line.

Light opposition. That is, some Germans, mostly without weapons, some shells and, more formidable, a German N.A.A.F.I. cart towed by an old horse. Not all the whips in XXX Corps could get Riflemen past a cart laden with chocolate and Wehrmacht goodies. Very sensibly they dismissed the coachman, handed the reins over to a driver op., and sandwiched it between the leading carriers.

Nothing of note occurred until 3 miles short of Geldern. I had raised the sliding seat of my Humber scout car to one notch from the bottom. A muffled voice rang up and said, 'Lots of Yerman ranks 500 yards to our right.' 'German or Sherman, did he say?' I asked the operator with my finger still on the presser switch, 'Sherman', bawled Henry (Capt H. R.) James over the air from the rear. Such a relief.

Andrew Burnaby-Atkins was very quick indeed. American 9 Army had not featured very big in my O Group, on account of time, but he made a rapid simple plan, based on a child-like faith in the tanks containing Americans and not Germans. Aided by Rfn Crossman, he constructed a banner of the fluorescent aircraft recognition panel; then, as if leading a procession of invisible hunger marchers, these two advanced through the mist towards the faint outline of tanks.

Andrew left no news of his intention. The rest of the platoon moved off to the N.A.A.F.I. cart. When the Squadron Leader and I arrived at the head of the column everyone was eating chocolate. There was no Andrew, no Crossman and fog blotted out the tanks. We decided to walk over and see for ourselves. We plodded through ploughed fields towards the sound of furious, incessant firing.

Andrew's meeting had been eventful. Coloured American troops, manning about 50 Sherman tanks drawn up along the road to our right, had followed his advance suspiciously. 'Boy, we'sa certainly had you covered,' they chortled when he arrived. A German O.P. in Geldern Church tower, surprised to see an aircraft cerise panel moving vertically across a field, had loosed a salvo of Nebelwerfer which flung Andrew to the ground and made his nose bleed.

Rfn Crossman, who is not dressy by nature and was soiled by three days and nights in action, said a few words to mark the occasion. 'So you ain't washed neither,' he observed in sour Virginian to the negro commander of the leading tank.

By the time we arrived, Andrew had got past the tanks which, nose to tail, were firing hard at the rooftops of Geldern. Little piles of 75 mm. cases and Browning empties beside each tank showed how well they were getting on. Encouraged, we passed through, and found Andrew in mixed company near the R.H.Q. of the American tanks.

He had contacted a Staff Officer of the U.S. Division, who was interested in us and anxious to discuss Army boundaries. Our orders had been to take Geldern, but the 9th U.S. Army seemed so keen that one hesitated to press the claim of a squadron and company group.

The Staff Officer generously allotted me a minor road for the Brigade, well off to the left. By this time U.S. infantry in very great strength were swarming through the town's outskirts, under this remarkable carpet of over-head direct fire from the tanks. The noise and fury were terrible. There were quite a lot of casualties caused by determined German sniping from the top storeys of houses further back, and shells were falling. It seemed folly to stop it all.

With fitting reluctance I accepted a modified Army boundary, which left us well outside this frenzy.

After that the pursuit turned eastwards towards the Rhine and 8 Armoured Brigade was fairly soon squeezed out, and by 9 March was completely clear of the battle. It had been a hectic month and nobody was sorry to see it over. But it had been a real tonic to see the élite parachutists coming in as prisoners in their hundreds.

Considering the amount of shelling, the Battalion had been extraordinarily lucky in casualties to men and machines, but we did not escape our losses. One direct hit on an A Company half-track which had a complete section on board at the time was a particularly sad incident.

Turning back to the 2nd Battalion, it will be remembered from the previous chapter that the enemy had left the Maas bank opposite Wessem under the pressure of the drive from Sittard, in which the 12th had been involved. After staying in the Thorn–Wessem area for nearly a month, which saw the tempo progress from duck-shooting with Lt Gen Barker, late 60th and Commander VIII Corps, to intensive field firing, the 2nd moved to the 4 Armoured Brigade concentration area in Tilburg on 18 February 1945. It might be helpful at this stage to bring the command organization up to date. Lt Col Consett was Commanding Officer, with Maj H. Wake as his 2IC. At Battalion HQ Capt Nixon was Adjutant, with Capt Bramall as IO and Lt M. J. L. Stow as Signal Officer. Company Commanders were Capt Gosse (A), Maj Holdsworth (B), Maj Gibbs (C), while the anti-tank guns and MMGs of Maj Bernays' D Company were usually allotted to the motor companies; Capt H. B. S. Gunn commanded all the three-inch mortars when centralized.

On 24 February the Battalion moved up to a concentration area on the Southern edge of the Reichswald forest. Map-reading was almost impossible, as new log tracks had been cut through the forest and what few roads had existed were almost impassable. Inevitably their guides lost their way, and there was a somewhat tense scene when the commander of 3 British Infantry Division met the Battalion convoy struggling up his Division's only Down Route. On the 26th Üdem, a fair-sized German town, was captured by 3 Canadian Division. The 2nd Battalion had once more come under command of 11 Armoured Division in place of 29 Armoured Brigade, and the plan was for The Greys and KSLI to do a night attack, advancing some 3000 yards across an anti-tank ditch and piercing the defences to the South West of the town. The Battalion with 44 RTR would pass through the KSLI at first light and seize a feature of high ground to the South and East of the town, an advance of some 2500 yards.

The Battalion moved off at 0600 hrs on 27 February, with B Company riding on the tanks of B Squadron, followed by Battalion HQ, whose half-tracks could only keep up by being towed by the command tanks of the 44th—a somewhat uncomfortable method of cross-country movement.

Maj Wake, 2IC, now takes up the account:

> As it grew light the centre line became impassable with mud, and A Company and C Company de-trucked and walked up to join their squadrons on foot. The CO himself had had to leave his vehicle at Buchholt and walked the whole way to the railway, where he met the leading platoon commander of the KSLI, made his plan and gave Maj Holdsworth his final orders. These were to work along the road, clearing up the farms and woods on the right of the road with his squadron of tanks shooting him in from the open ground on the left of the road. His objective was the triangle of roads at 'Bergen', 2000 yards further on.

B Company reached the long wood 200 yards short of Welleshof Farm (about halfway to the objective) having bagged 80 German parachute troops. The Motor Platoons, under Lts D. M. Goddard, M. S. M. Robinson and R. H. Burton, did extraordinarily well, but had themselves had a few men killed and wounded. B Squadron had one tank knocked out by an 88 mm. from the high ground in front, and having little room to manoeuvre south of the railway, were unable to get on or support B Company. B Company carriers under Teddy Phillips and Peter (2/Lt P. R.)) Smalley, had now managed to get up, and Rfn Hands was killed here by heavy enemy mortar and shell-fire. Capt Teddy Phillips was to be heard giving an excellent running commentary on the doings of his carriers until it was abruptly ended by the shattering announcement, 'By God, I've been hit!' However the damage was trivial, much to everyone's relief.

It was, therefore, decided to pass A Company through B Company on to the next wood, nicknamed 'Hippo Wood', South of Tokatshof Farm. They were mortared and Nebelwerfered very hard indeed, but they captured Welleshof Farm and Hippo Wood, killing 3 Germans and collecting 37 prisoners. Harry Stanley, as 2IC, did great work, and the three Motor Platoon commanders, Lts I. M. P. Evans, C. T. Tatham and C. A. Humphreys all did well.

Time had flown and the men had been on their feet since first light, fighting hard, crawling down ditches full of water, eating nothing and being shelled as hard as most Rats can remember. As it grew dark, A Company carried on with A Squadron, and finally dug in at the furthest corner of the 'Bergen' triangle of roads. In this they were greatly assisted by the CLY and the Herefords, who had come through the Canadians in Udem and South over the railway and were working their way East along the high ground to our North, eventually to capture Gochfort Berg at the cost of 12 tanks.

In the dark, C Company moved up through B and A Companies and went on to the next bend in the road 600 yards further South-East Dennis. (Lt D. P.) Dixon had gone on a patrol and contacted the Herefords along the railway to the North and put them in the picture. Hugh Elgar, with 12 Platoon, patrolled right on to Tofurtzhof Farm. The Company finally dug in in the dark on its objective in spite of two SP guns and two 20 mm. guns firing tracer down the road. Eight more prisoners were taken, and Sgt Cox and Rfn Joseph were wounded.

The whole length of road was lit up by explosive 20 mm. tracer and mortared and shelled all night very unpleasantly. At about midnight the Regina Rifles, an affiliated Canadian Regiment, wearing the same cap badges as ourselves, arrived to take over, but the Companies remained where they were dug in, and by the grace of God had no casualties from the shelling. The Regina Rifles just put their Companies alongside and in front of ours and suffered quite a few casualties.

Thus ended a very exhausting day, during which the Battalion and 44 Tanks had advanced about 4000 yards against parachute troops and SP guns which fought well and shot straight. We steadily drove them back, and for remarkably few casualties took 128 prisoners. In spite of slight ups and downs in the country, water seemed to be lying everywhere and the going across country was practically impossible. The Battalion's carriers and half-tracks could only just get up along the lanes through the thick pine woods and farms.

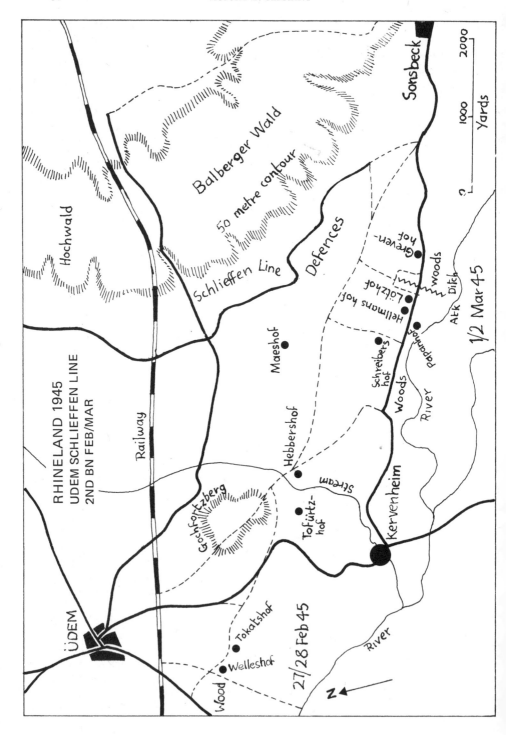

RHINELAND 1945
UDEM SCHLIEFFEN LINE
2ND BN FEB/MAR

The Doctor, Malcolm Mitchell, in particular deserves a mention, for, having had to leave his ambulances behind, he walked the whole way to Battalion HQ and there set up his RAP and tended all the wounded, with the Padre, Leslie Morrison, helping him.

The next morning, 28 February, no one was quite sure what first light would bring. There were anxious moments on the Gochfort Berg hill on our left, where another six CLY tanks were brewed up and the Herefords began attracting all the guns that we had drawn all night. However, with much smoke, they held firm, and to our delight the 44th knocked out an SP gun just in front of C Company as it tried to make off.

Being relieved by the Regina Rifles, the Battalion then moved back North a little to a drier bit of ground, but alas! not before Dennis Dixon, of C Company, had been badly wounded by a mortar bomb.

The 2nd, spending the last day of February reorganizing and catching up with lost sleep, had before it the Schlieffen defence line, the last before the Rhine in the Wesel area, where Montgomery hoped to make his assault crossings. The line was marked clearly on the defence overprint, based on aerial photography, as a network of fire trenches, anti tank ditches, minefields and machine gun emplacements, normally the subject for a series of deliberate infantry assaults. However, despite the flat, heavy going between large defended farms and woods, all overlooked from the Baalberg ridge, a fascine crossing had been made over the first stream; 15/19 H and the Herefords had exploited beyond it during the night 28 February/1 March while the sappers built a Bailey bridge.

The plan was for the Canadians to attack the Schlieffen Line on our left, North of the railway. On our right, 3 British Division were to capture Kervenheim. 4 Armoured Brigade were to pass through 15/19 H and advance two up with the Greys and KSLI on the left, South of the railway, and the 44th Tanks and 2nd 60th along the Sonsbeck Road. The KSLI and ourselves were to be carried in Kangaroos and all four regiments were to concentrate and form up just over the bridge. Matters were complicated by the Battalion being on the extreme right on the Corps boundary, while 3 Division were in a different Corps. This made liaison very difficult.

While the Battalion slept the sleep of the dead, the Kangaroos arrived in the very small hours of the morning of 1 March. After breakfast we looked at them and sent nine to each A and C Companies and six to B Company and one for Battalion HQ. They were ordinary Sherman tanks without their turrets, and with track extensions designed to carry 10 men and their equipment. The idea of being carried in tanks as opposed to on tanks appealed to all. It was not only novel to us, but we knew that we were the first Motor Battalion ever to be so carried—the modern motorised infantry. It was exciting to think that we could advance, oblivious of bursting shells or spandaus and by-passing or overrunning German positions, but we also wondered what would happen if we ran into an anti tank gun. Well, 44 Tanks would be advancing alongside us.

At 1330 hours the two regiments moved off, companies with squadrons of the same letter, in the order A, C and B.

Moving up to the bridge in broad daylight and forming up the other side in full view of the enemy's high ground not surprisingly brought a large number of shells crashing around us, but the armour kept the splinters out and there was great comfort in numbers. What was left of the Monmouths we saw in the woods, and we passed a good few Germans looking very green.

The plan was for A Squadron to get into position at Schreiberhof to cover the assault by C Squadron and C Company to the first objective.

A Squadron got badly bogged and could not get to their fire positions in time. Turning South, an anti tank gun soon stopped them, one shot going through one of A Squadron's tanks on which Sgt Barker and a number of our men were actually riding. They were blown off but unhurt, though some of the crew were unable to get out before the tank caught fire. The remainder of the tanks and Kangaroos, in trying to take cover, got stuck all over the place, and finally A Company had to march up on its feet, having lost a great deal of its equipment in the Kangaroos.

C Company and C Squadron didn't wait for A Squadron to give support, and went on bald-headed to Papenhof. All the Kangaroos got there, but only five tanks out of C Squadron's 15. Barnaby (Lt G. B.) Benson put his 11 Platoon at the cross-roads just short of Papenhof, which Bobby (Lt M. J. F.) Morrison held with 10 Platoon, while Hugh Elgar carried on with 12 Platoon to Hellmanshof, a farmhouse, which proved more troublesome. On approaching it, he came under heavy fire and took his platoon back for a moment. He then charged the place in his Kangaroos, successfully capturing it. For this gallant action he was awarded the Military Cross. Sgt Pickford also distinguished himself. The platoon killed two Germans, wounded two others and took eight prisoners of war who informed us that the cross-roads beyond Lötzhof were held.

The Germans were not slow to see what was happening, and accurately shelled these obvious targets. They also enjoyed sniping the Colonel's HQ from the direction of Maeshof.

Meanwhile Maj Wake had the remainder of Battalion HQ, including the RAP, just East of the bridge. One shell narrowly missed Malcolm Mitchell, the Doctor, killing one of his ambulance orderlies, and they were surprised to see 30 Germans surrender out of their woods. B Company remained in this area in reserve until it grew dark, when they moved up to relieve C Company at Papenhof, taking over at 2 am.

A Company in the meantime had passed through C Company, and in the dark Ian Evans and Charles Humphreys had captured Lötzhof and the next cross-roads, where the enemy's Schlieffen Line trenches began. There they were shelled hard and they made the best use of the available cover. They turned the German civilians out of their houses, and some of these were killed and wounded by German shells. Two A Squadron tanks thought that they had been bazooked, but next morning we saw that it was mines on the side of the road that had blown off their tracks.

It soon grew light; there were lots of Germans about who shot accurately, and having us under complete observation made ample use of their artillery. The Colonel went to Brigade HQ and nobody moved.

On his return, it was apparent that the 'powers that be' at the back had their whips out and, though it seemed impossible to us, were still hopeful of a break-through. So it was planned for B Company to pass through C and A and to make a frontal attack against, and through, the Schlieffen Line up to Brevenhof, 1000 yards further East. An artillery plan was made, and H hour fixed at 1400 hours.

At that hour Mike Robinson led 7 Platoon down the road while Dick Burton and David Goddard took 6 and 8 Platoons through the woods on the right. This necessitated crossing the anti tank ditch full of water and getting wet through. The men had not seen their vehicles for twenty-four hours and had had little, if anything, to eat and no blankets or sleep. It was surprising to find the Germans had not blown the road across the ditch, though they had blown it further down, and some of B Squadron's tanks gave close support from the road. 7 Platoon took the next farmhouse beyond the ditch, but not without casualties. It was at this moment that John Holdsworth led his men against the next house where there was a very troublesome German with a spandau machine gun. He was mortally wounded, and though Sgt Flanagan brought him in and made him comfortable, he died shortly afterwards. The other two platoons had meanwhile done very well and had captured Brauerhof, the next farmhouse beyond the troublesome one from where they could see 5 enemy tanks and 100 infantry. They found a goose all ready cooked and some coffee, and while they were devouring it it grew dark. Presently there was a knock on the door. Two Germans entered. They had come to collect their milk, and found themselves collected instead.

The Company Commander being killed, no one was quite sure what was happening, and getting no further orders 6 and 8 Platoons decided to come back. Max (Capt M. W. J.) Denham, the 2IC, on his way up in his Dingo to take over B Company, drove over a mine, and though his driver, Rfn Keeley, lost a leg, he himself was luckily unhurt. He took over command of B Company at this moment and reorganized them.

C Company were then ordered to relieve B Company and to hold the ground won until the Battalion was relieved by the Canadian Scottish, who were coming up behind us. It was dark, very confused, and the men were very tired indeed. They had been hard at it for two days and two nights now, with no sleep and on their feet the whole time. The going was so bad that no vehicles could get up to them, and the Kangaroos that had carried them had beat a hurried retreat with the only food they had and a great deal of equipment. But C Company had previously been issued with rations by Capt Bobby (R. A.) Henderson who had overcome his initial displeasure with his Company Commander for having 'the Company tactically dispersed'. The constant shell-fire and odd spandau had taken their steady toll of casualties, and the only thing that could be said to be fair was the weather.

Maj Toby Wake managed to collect a dozen Kangaroos together which he found near the bridge, and in the dark Hugh Elgar guided them up to Hellmanshof. Together with the carriers, they managed to carry A and B Companies back to Hebbenshof near the bridge in the small hours of the morning. C Company were not finally relieved until about 3 am, 3 March, until which time quite a lot happened. Maj Roly Gibbs took Bobby Morrison's 10 Platoon up to the furthest house, where shortly a German patrol of six men ran into them. Rfn Bayliss killed two of them and captured two wounded and two others. Later another German patrol approached them and suffered much the same fate. Barnaby Benson's 11 Platoon was just behind 10 Platoon astride the anti tank ditch, covering their line of withdrawal. About midnight 30 to 40 men walked by 50 yards away between 10 and 11 Platoons. Barnaby was heard to say, 'Thank God! The Canadians have arrived at last.' But, being Germans, they turned off unhurt into No Man's Land and were never seen again.

Finally the Canadians did arrive, and C Company returned to Hebbenshof just before first light completely exhausted. Though we had not achieved a break-through, the Battalion had completed its task of breaching the last of the Siegfried switch lines, and we learned that the Americans to our South had entered Cologne and captured Krefeld.

Under our pressure and the American threat the Germans abandoned the Line that night.

During this action the 2nd had killed at least 50 enemy and had taken over 150 prisoners almost unaided, since our armour was hindered by the appalling going. Our casualties were 5 in A, 17 in C and 27 in B, but the 49 had all come from the 9 motor platoons and therefore represented something like 20% of our dismounted strength. Saddest of all was the loss of Maj Holdsworth. Reaching the 1st Battalion in 1940 as a platoon commander at the age of 19, he was continuously in the forefront until seriously wounded at Alamein two years later. His expertise in minor tactics was passed on with all his boundless enthusiasm to a host of other officers, when he served as instructor at the School of Infantry in the year before D day. By great efforts he got away to join the 2nd Battalion in October 1944, taking over B Company. He died, as he had lived, at the head of his men, when with great gallantry they had penetrated to the heart of the Schlieffen defences.

The Allied Army Groups in the next few days closed up to the Rhine opposite and either side of the Ruhr. Bridge after bridge was demolished by the Germans in their faces, until on 7 March the Americans captured the railway bridge at Remagen intact; however, the small bridgehead thus formed led into difficult, hilly country, less suitable for exploitation than that further South. In the wake of this reverse von Runstedt was ordered to hand over to Kesselring, who for so long had held together the Italian front.

Montgomery's impeccably planned and deliberate assault over the Rhine, using both British and American troops, was due to take place on 23/24 March 1945. However, Bradley and Patton, unwilling to play a secondary role, saw an opening, and their divisions, racing Southwards over the hills, took the Rhine on the run the previous night in the Mainz area. Montgomery's massive artillery and air bombardment, combined with commando and parachute landings, was successful, and, apart from one village held by German parachutists for three days, the Rhine bank was rapidly cleared in the Wesel area. Sadly, Lt C. A. Selwyn, who had transferred from our 10th Battalion to the 13th Parachute Battalion to get into action, was among those killed parachuting into the enemy gun lines. There was an elaborate track network into our assembly areas on the West bank, and all movement was necessarily under strict traffic control; this was particularly needed to handle the hundreds of vehicles of the armoured formations, including our two battalions, which were next to.be filtered over the Rhine, before starting the race North of the Ruhr to the great North German ports.

After their junction with the Americans three weeks earlier our 12th Battalion had concentrated in Goch. There was much maintenance and preparation to be carried out, now under the new Commanding Officer, Lt Col G. W. White, MBE, who had relieved Lt Col the Hon M. G. Edwardes, MBE. Reorganization particularly affected D Company, who exchanged their twelve 6-pounder anti-tank guns, for six self-propelled (SP) 17-pounder anti-tank guns and a platoon of 4·2-inch mortars; a stray German shell, however, knocked out one of the new Wasp flame-throwing carriers, and the other was never in fact used. Meanwhile the 2nd Battalion had pulled back to near Bourg Leopold in Belgium for rest and to train much-needed reinforcements after their stiff Schlieffen Line fight; Maj Mellor rejoined the 2nd as 2IC and Maj Vernon took over B Company. On the eve of the Rhine crossing the 2nd moved forward to Üdem; officers of the two Battalions, under their Commanding Officers, played an excellent game of Eton football, Lt Col Consett touching down the winning long rouge by leaping over a barbed-wire fence behind the goal, which confirmed the Regimental reputation for light-hearted eccentricity in the minds of spectators.

On 27 March the 12th was called forward to a marshalling area just short of the river, and crossed over a Class 40 bridge at 1700 hours. They moved into a large field outside Rees with no attention from the enemy.

Maj Coleridge's account continues:

For the next two days we stood by, prepared to do various jobs on the left flank of the British activities, but somebody else always succeeded in doing them first, and we forgot all about the operation orders so carefully prepared in Goch. But on 30 March we started. With one Squadron 4/7 Dragoon Guards and one Battery of the Essex Yeomanry under command, the Battalion formed the flank guard for the 30th Corps break-out from the bridgehead at Anholt. We were given a pretty free hand, though one or two points were mentioned as desirable places to include in our centre line. Information about the Canadians some way to our left was scanty. It was thought unlikely that we should make any contact on the first day. On our right the main force consisted of 43 Division and the rest of 8 Armoured Brigade. A Company were the first away from the milling multitude in Anholt and set off along the road to Silvolde (in Holland). They bumped into enemy fairly early—in fact some time before the tail of the Battalion had disentangled itself from the many competitors for the use of the only road from Anholt. It was a poor road at the best of times.

The enemy, nearly all parachutists, were at first unwilling to give ground. They were supported by a number of guns (S.P.) and were not slow to shoot. However, A Company got them on the move, and B Company were then sent out even further on the left to get into Silvolde via a place called Nieudorp. By evening both A and B Companies had gained a footing in Silvolde and the village had been more or less cleared. C Company and the remainder of the

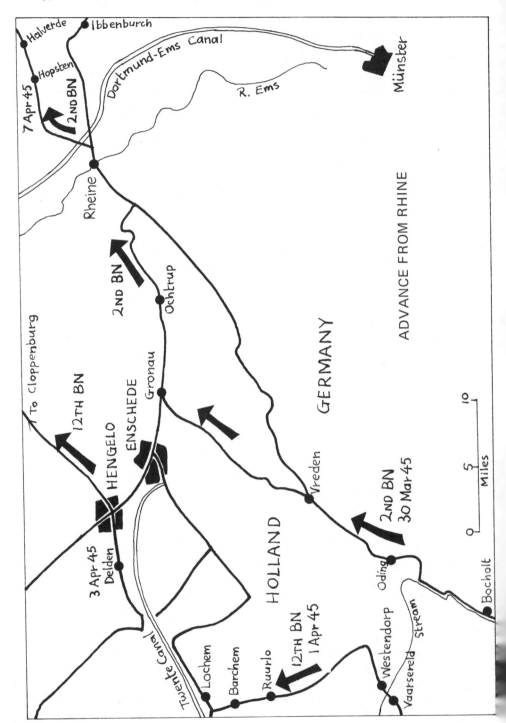

Halverde
Ibbenburch
Hopsten
Dortmund-Ems Canal
R. Ems
Münster
7 Apr 45
2ND BN
Rheine
2ND BN
Ochtrup
To Cloppenburg
12TH BN
HENGELO
ENSCHEDE
Gronau
GERMANY
ADVANCE FROM RHINE
Vreden
2ND BN
30 Mar 45
3 Apr 45
Delden
HOLLAND
Oding
2ND BN
1 Apr 45
Westendorp
Bocholt
Lochem
Barchem
Ruurlo
12TH BN
Twente Canal
Vaarsereld Stream
0   5   10
Miles

Support Company were then brought up to assist in the hours of darkness. The enemy, who during the day lost some 70 prisoners to the Battalion, became increasingly active with his guns as the day wore on. Nor did he stop at night. It was a trying time and cost the Battalion two carriers and two half-tracks. However, there is no reason to suppose the enemy enjoyed himself—and certainly some of the prisoners made one think that perhaps the end was not so desperately far away.

The plan for the morrow was to continue as flank guard for 43 Division, who would be forcing a water obstacle at or near Vaarseveld. To do this we were to clear the woods between Silvolde and Vaarseveld, then turn Westwards to Westendorp. After that nothing definite was laid down. One squadron of SRY was also put under command. The Battalion started off soon after daylight, when C Company disappeared into some large woods. There were a few enemy who were not very determined, and C Company got on appreciably. A Company were then sent off further to the flank in a direct line for Westendorp. Somewhere near the railway the enemy still clearly had O.Ps who could observe the Silvolde area. Sure enough, A Company bumped them on the line of the railway. They had at least two 20 mm. guns firing enthusiastically in a ground role, and there may have been more. A concerted attack by A Company and the 4/7 Squadron was arranged, and B Company, with the SRY Squadron, were held in readiness to exploit direct to Westendorp. Meanwhile C Company, emerging from the woods nearer the town, had also found the railway line fairly strongly held.

A Company's attack was most successful, and the enemy had obviously had enough. Prisoners were collected, and B Company were about to be loosed on Westendorp when orders came to concentrate all our effort in the C Company area. We were to push through to the river quite close to Vaarseveld to protect a bridge-building operation during the night. A thrust straight to Westendorp would have left the Germans a chance of playing about between us and 43 Division.

This meant collecting A and B Companies in the middle of a chase, moving them across by bad roads to the C Company area, and planning a Battalion attack. This was done in two hours, and C Company started to advance. The opposition now seemed less determined, and B Company passed through C Company, who had secured their start line, and made very short work of their objective. Over 100 parachutists had been rounded up during the day, and we sat down for the night protecting the west flank of Vaarseveld. Hopes were running high that a real 'swan' might develop on the morrow. It had been a most successful and extremely busy day for all.

During the night the leading troops of 43 Division and 4/7 Dragoon Guards had sailed forth from Vaarseveld bound for Ruurlo and Lochem. They made excellent progress. So the Battalion, following along in daylight, had an easy run. By the evening we were all concentrated in some woods near Barchem, not far from Lochem, where the leading battalion had found some enemy who put up a stiff fight. News came that away on the right Guards Armoured Division was getting on well. To our left the Canadians, though still some way behind, had also got their whips out.

Next morning at 0430 hours when the pursuit was resumed, the Battalion was under command of the SRY, this Group forming the advance guard to 43 Division. The intention was to force a crossing of the Twente Canal either South or Southwest of Hengelo. C Company and a squadron of tanks were in the lead. South of the canal there was no opposition, and the whole column went bowling through the countryside at a surprising speed. The bridge on the main road was found to be blown, and hopes that the Hun had not had time to demolish the others were soon brought to nothing. Reconnaissance by our own forward elements and by some troops of the Household Cavalry, who had done a quick cast along the canal, suggested that an immediate assault at a lock about a mile off the main road might easily succeed. The enemy had shown no signs of life, and various reconnaissance parties had been quite close to the canal without attracting attention. Nor had there been any shelling. The approach was bad, but offered a possible route for an armoured formation. At this point the canal ran between very high banks, making approach to the canal itself easy, but denying observation of enemy lay-out on the far side. The bridge was in two halves, linking an island between the locks with either bank. The gap was on the German side and spanned by a piece of duck-board. None of this detail could be seen until attacking troops went over the top of the canal bank.

B Company were brought up to do the assault and A Company were to follow through them and exploit the bridgehead. All likely enemy positions were given considerable attention by the Essex Yeomanry and our own 4·2 in. mortars for a quarter of an hour. As soon as the first Riflemen went over the canal bank the enemy reacted with a vengeance. A dreadfully accurate cross-fire from Spandaus swept across the bridge and its approaches, and the area was very unhealthy. With great determination, the leading two platoons fought their way to the island and the neighbourhood of the first bridge, where they were pinned. By now the enemy had his mortars and artillery firing back and the attack was dealt a crippling blow, when the third platoon was caught in the dead ground by the canal bank just as it was about to assault. Their casualties were so high that they ceased to be a decisive force and the whole assault had to be called off. But B Company's difficulties were not over. Once more they had to go through the cross-fire by the bridge—and this time they had some wounded men to help along. Nor was it easy for the Gunners to keep up an unlimited supply of smoke.

The withdrawal was carried out with methodical coolness. The example of Maj Bill Deedes and Lt Andrew Burnaby-Atkins was a great inspiration.

The action cost the lives of Lts Roger Green and Barry Newton, Sgt Hennessey and Cpl Reeson. Lt Roy Garner and 25 other ranks were wounded.

B Company had done all and more than could have been expected to press a daylight attack forward in such an exposed situation, thanks to the gallant leadership of the two young platoon commanders, great friends, who were buried together near by. The 12th now spread out along the canal, under orders to simulate preparations for further crossings. Next morning 43 Division moved round the end of the canal at Enschede, captured by the Guards. The 12th turned back Westwards as flank guard, moving through Hengelo to the area North of the canal where they had attacked the day before. The enemy were pulling out, but wood-clearing towards Delden produced some prisoners. That town was taken by the Canadians, and, after a two-day rest, companies joined their armoured regiments for 43 Division's advance on Bremen; the role of Battalion HQ and D Company was to protect Divisional HQ. The advance started on 5 April, and the enormous number of demolitions was more of a problem than the straggling parachutists, from whom prisoners were taken daily.

However, pockets of resistance were encountered unexpectedly:

On April 11th, C Company made a spirited Company attack to clear a large wood which covered the centre line. They disappeared at remarkable speed into the jungle, and it was not long before their blood-curdling yells seemed to indicate that they had run the enemy to the ground. They reappeared with 20 Parachute prisoners of war led by a CSM, and the road for the advance was once more open. It was quick work—appreciated by the General. On the 13th, B Company became involved in clearing parts of Cloppenburg, which contained some tiresome houses. John (Lt J. H.) Peyton, having dealt faithfully with one of these in the failing light, was killed as he tackled a second in a brave effort. During the advance Lt D. N. F. Wilson, working with 4/7DG, skilfully infiltrated through the enemy rearguards to seize a town, and was later awarded the MC.

By now various Divisions were getting reasonably close to Bremen, which necessitated certain movements and re-grouping. A Company and 4/7 Dragoon Guards went off to 3 Division, South of Bremen; 13/18 Hussars and B Company remained with 43 Division in the Cloppenburg area, while C Company, unwanted for the present by the SRY, returned to the Battalion control.

From 16 to 23 April the 12th, less A and B Companies, came under 3 Division with the task of watching the flooded area between Leeste and the Southern suburbs of Bremen. D Company weapons harassed the city without reply and Lt R. W. Gilliat and his patrol brought back valuable information on flood depths for later use by Buffalo crews in the amphibious assault. The city was bombed on 22 April, and on the evening of 24 April the assaulting Buffaloes surged through our positions and successfully crossed the flooded Weser. The 12th and its motor companies crossed the river further upstream and rejoined 43 Division, who were breaking into Bremen from the East. For a few hours the 12th found themselves alongside the 2nd, and the usual visits were exchanged for the first time since leaving the Rhineland a month earlier.

The 2nd had been grouped with the Greys, 4 Armoured Brigade being in support of 15 Scottish Division initially. The Battalion moved into the successive Rhineland marshalling and assembly areas on 24 March. The next day the motor companies were rafted over on The Greys' tanks, and arrived after the half-tracks on the Class 9 rafts and the carriers and jeeps on the Buffalo ferry. The anti-tank gunners enjoyed having their six-pounders manhandled off the rafts by German prisoners.

The next few days were a saga of abortive advances. On 27 March the 2nd advanced with The Greys, clearing woods astride the muddy tracks in what had been the German gun lines; the empty half-tracks were brought up at night to join their companies with great difficulty. A regretted loss during the break-out

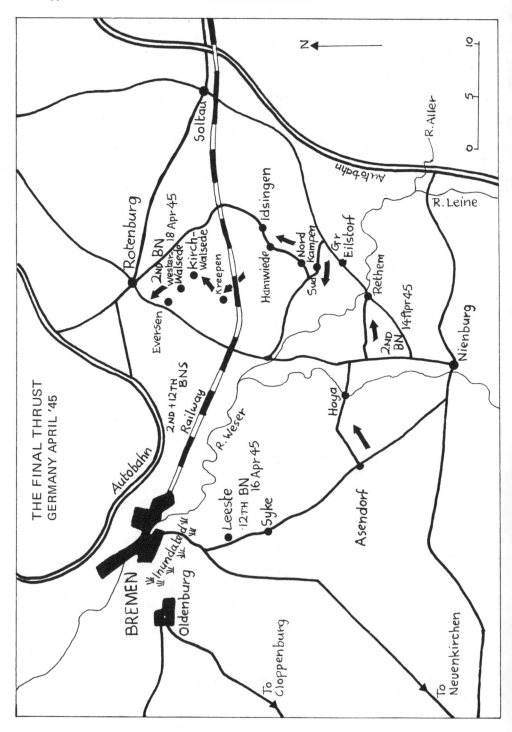

THE FINAL THRUST
GERMANY APRIL '45

was Lt D. G. Podmore, who while commanding a carrier platoon, was killed by a shell. By the end of 28 March the Group was out into the open country South of Bocholt, leaving 53 Division to clear that town of parachutists. On 30 March, while going to Bocholt for orders, Lt Col Consett's Dingo went over a mine; the driver, Rfn Tinley, lost a foot, and the Commanding Officer was deafened by the blast. Directed on Vreden, the Group cleared as far as Oding, being delayed by a succession of road blocks, but finding the scattered enemy anxious to surrender. On 31 March it became clear that 7 Armoured Division had already reached the Vreden area, so the Battalion concentrated near Oding. 1 April, Easter Sunday, was spent resting, with a Church service; that evening the Medical Officer had to evacuate the Commanding Officer, who was suffering from delayed blast effect, and Maj Mellor took over Command.

On 2 April the Group was ordered to advance and secure Ochtrup. Apart from road blocks and the consequent delaying diversions there was no opposition; indeed, the Brigade Commander, Brigadier R. M. P. Carver, led the race. Just South of the town Capt Phillips came under Spandau and bazooka fire in his carrier, and B Company were ordered to secure up to the railway line silently that night, as a start line for a formal attack. The latter was cancelled and next morning patrols linked up with 53 Division, who had entered the town from the West.

4 April saw a move East to guard against a rumoured but mythical counter-attack. The next day the Brigade transferred its support to 52 Lowland Division, to assist in expanding their bridgehead over the Dortmund–Ems Canal at Rheine; the 2nd was to operate separately from The Greys. On 6 March the 2nd entered the bridgehead and cleared up to the railway line 6000 yards to the North without opposition. The next day the 2nd, grouped with 44 RTR, moved round to the right to find a route round Hopsten, where stiff opposition was holding up the advance. B Company with a squadron cleared the woods, using flame-throwers, up to the line of the stream. The gap was, however, too wide for the scissors bridge, but while reconnaissances were carried out the two Commanding Officers joined the officers and men of B Company in 600-yard target practice with rifles at enemy moving on the edge of the Hopsten woods; 20 Germans eventually came in to surrender. Maj Mellor takes up the story:

> In the late afternoon the Battalion and 44 Royal Tank Regiment were ordered to pull back, by-pass Hopsten to the South and to secure the village of Halverde. As has often happened, there was considerable shelling and mortaring in daylight, but as soon as darkness fell the noise of the tanks was too much for the enemy, and Halverde was reached with little opposition. On entering the village, C Company in the lead discovered 60 enemy collected together in one house. Maj Roly Gibbs started to negotiate surrender when one German was rash enough to fire his revolver. The resultant small arms fire from the tanks and our Brens taught many their last lesson, but so scattered the remainder that we were still collecting the odd straggler when morning came.
>
> By the morning of the 9th another route had been found, and we were ordered to side-step East and then advance North to capture Neuenkirchen, Lintern and Uffeln. The start was delayed by road cratering, but we finally moved off with two Company/Squadron groups up, B Company right, and A

Company left. Lt David (D. J. C.) Weston, with A Company's carriers, were the first to move, and within a very short time were heavily engaged with enemy who had no intention of withdrawing, but made every effort to surround and bazooka the carriers. However, the carriers were able to pull back but not before Lt David Weston had been slightly wounded in the leg, a fact he made every effort to conceal. [Lt Weston had already been wounded a year earlier in Italy.]

Soon the two groups were well on the move, and from prisoners we learnt that we had an officer cadet training unit against us. B Company on the right had a sharp engagement for a small hamlet, which was finally cleared by a very successful platoon attack led by Lt David (D. M.) Goddard. Cpl Long led a gallant section charge, killing four Germans himself, for which he later deservedly received the Military Medal, and the final count produced 25 dead and about 40 prisoners. Meanwhile A Company on the left were meeting the same type of resistance, but the mounting total of prisoners and burning farms showed that we were breaking its back. Fighting all the way, A and B Companies entered Neuenkirchen just before dark, and C Company were ready in rear to push straight through to our two final objectives, every indication showing that we had broken through the final crust of resistance. However, orders came from Brigade that we were to stop in Neuenkirchen, and the London Yeomanry passed through to reach Uffeln without opposition. The day's fighting produced 120 prisoners and at least 60 enemy killed at a cost to the Battalion of nine casualties, a figure that says much for the skill of the junior leaders.

On 10 April orders arrived that the Brigade was now to come under command of 53 Division, with the task of supporting the Division in the bridgehead over the Weser and Aller rivers at Rethem, and the protection of the right flank as the Division turned North to capture Verden. The Brigade was to move straight away to a concentration area at Asendorf, West of Hoya, where we would have a few days' rest and maintenance before the bridge was built at Rethem.

The Battalion moved off at 1100 hours for a run of nearly 100 miles, a very severe test on our vehicles after a long period with little opportunities for maintenance.

Comfortable billets were found for the 2nd at Asendorf, where the only diversion from vehicle maintenance was shooting roe under the auspices of Lt Trenchard, acting Forstmeister.

On 14 April the Battalion moved through Hoya, across the Weser, and after a pause till midday, crossed the River Aller at Rethem. The enemy facing us was 2 Marine Division, fresh troops, and, as we soon learnt, determined fighters. C Company, with their squadron of tanks, led and were soon halted on the edge of the woods, with the Wasps proving our most formidable weapon. When it became clear that no quick progress could be expected through the woods, B Company were ordered to move up on the left and to attack along the main road to Gr. Eilstorf. Progress was again slow, but by dark B and C Companies were both within 1000 yards of the village. It was decided to wait till first light before attacking the village, and so the men got a few hours sleep. It had been a hard day; over 100 prisoners and many dead, but the enemy were still fighting stubbornly.

At first light on the 15th the attack went in, with A Company passing through C Company on the right and B Company on the left. Resistance was not as strong as the day before, but much of the village was destroyed before the resistance ceased. From Eilstorf the Battalion was ordered to attack North to secure the village of Sudkampen and Nordkampen. A Company led, and without much difficulty secured Sudkampen; B Company were then passed through to hold an important road junction 2,500 yards Northwest of the village. A propaganda van was used to persuade the village to surrender, but, in spite of the frantic efforts of the Burgomeister and his daughter to secure this, their efforts failed, and the village was attacked, with the usual resultant burning farms. Altogether nearly 200 prisoners were taken during the day, and it appeared that we were starting to get through the main crust of resistance.

On 16 April the 2nd Battalion and 44 RTR moved quietly up to Hamw*e*ide and Idsingen, already captured by the Greys. Hopes for a quiet night were dashed when orders came through for a night attack. As soon as the Greys had advanced North up to the railway line, the Battalion was to turn West and capture Kreepen and an intervening village.

Company commanders and others, arriving in their Dingoes for orders at a prominent cross-roads, were greeted by a hail of accurate shells. The little group round Lt Col Hopkinson, 44 RTR, broke up in disorder, the Colonel vanishing to the bottom of his Dingo, one of his Squadron commanders, the Commanding Officer, Intelligence Officer and Capt Max Denham, disregarding all dignity, vanishing underneath. The pathetic voices pleading from underneath for a postponement when Lt Col Hopkinson announced that he was 'getting out of here', were comic, but finally a pause enabled everyone to get on with the job in a slightly less obvious place.

B Company took the first village. 'Capt Max Denham and Lt R. A. Lloyd both claimed a "bird" to their revolvers, but Lt R. M. Wigram won with a brace.'

Kreepen was a potentially nastier affair for A Company. The leading platoon, commanded by Lt C. A. Humphreys, met heavy shelling and then fire from three Spandaus as they approached. When his very tired Riflemen checked, he made his own plan of attack and encouraged them forward again. His platoon took the village with 2 enemy killed and 35 prisoners, and, in excess of orders, he pressed on to clear the surrounding woods. Despite direct artillery fire from four field guns under a mile away, he accomplished this by 0500 hours, taking 20 more prisoners. For his excellent leadership, the culmination of much earlier good work, Lt Humphreys was awarded the MC.

On 17 April silence reigned throughout the two villages, with the Greys ahead of us and the Battalion sleeping the sleep of the just. The Brigadier, never over-generous with his praise, had told the Battalion they had done a really good job of work, and all agreed it was worth the loss of sleep. In this very successful night attack, with both villages captured, the 2nd Battalion sustained no casualties and took 100 prisoners.

On 18 April the Battalion/44 Royal Tank Regiment Group were ordered to attack North at first light to capture Kirchwalsede and then Rotenburg. The advance started with B Company and B Squadron taking advantage of the good going and moving straight on Kirchwalsede across country. A Company and C Squadron were to clear the centre line from Kreepen onwards. As soon as the advance started prisoners started coming in, and very soon B Company were in Kirchwalsede, which turned out to be a hospital town and undefended. As A Company were meeting opposition in the woods, C Company were passed through, by-passing Kirchwalsede and moving West on to the high ground North of Westerwalsede. B Company had captured a large number of prisoners, including sixteen majors and a colonel who tried to shoot his way through the town in his car, accompanied by his girl-friend who was immediately reported as a big Gestapo figure.

It was now evident that we were going to have to fight for Westerwalsede, and A Company, who had finished clearing the centre-line, was ordered to clear through the woods South of the village and advance on the village from that direction. As the leading tanks, with A and C Companies, approached the village, 88 mm. guns opened up at short range, knocking out two tanks in each Squadron. In the North C Company had met these guns at short range. Lt Hugh Elgar had been tragically killed only a few hours before news of his having won the Military Cross came through. Maj Roly Gibbs had had a very narrow escape and was very deaf from the blast of the shell. In the South, A Company had seen two of their tanks knocked out, and the pace was very slow in the woods. However, Maj Roly Gibbs, in his own inimitable way, was soon leading Lt Tom Trenchard's platoon through the village, and with the 4 RHA and Company mortars doing some pin-point shooting on the guns, and A Company closing in from the South, the village was soon cleared. The bag included five 88 mm. and many 20 mm. guns knocked out.

B Company were now passed through to capture the hamlet and bridge over the railway 2,000 yards North of Westerwalsede. Almost immediately the Company ran into accurate short-range fire from 105 mm. guns, and a complete battery was discovered lining a hedge on the objective. Lt David Goddard had one shell burst 3ft. from him, but soon the tanks started knocking out the guns, and when the carriers and two Motor Platoons arrived, after a wide flanking movement, the fight was nearly over. The clearing of the few houses followed quickly, Sgt Oake being very proud of his bulls-eye with the 2in. Mortar on a German coming in with spandau at the hip.

It now remained to get astride the main road to Rotenburg. Owing to the open ground, it was decided to do this at night, and C Company were ordered to advance North through B Company, keeping East of the railway, and to seize the road bridge over the railway on the main road. A Company were to pass through after C Company and seize the cross-roads Northwest of B Company. Both attacks went off without incident, and the Battalion was firmly established by first light across the main escape route left to the enemy Southwest of us.

In the early hours of the morning of the 19th orders came through that the Brigade was now coming under command of 52 Division, and the Battalion would not be relieved on their objective but were to clear South towards 52 Division who were still about 10 miles Southwest of us. It took very little persuasion to get the Brigadier to fight the no relief order, as it would have been a great disappointment to all if the hard fighting we had had was to be wasted and our position astride the main road given up. 53 Division agreed to take over the position, and so at first light B Company passed through A Company, turned South and started clearing the woods. There were still many enemy about, and one tank was hit before a blown bridge was met and the advance was halted.

The plan was now changed, and the Battalion waited till the relieving battalion arrived and then moved back to Westerwalsede preparatory to attacking Eversen from the East. The preliminary carrier patrols of A and B Companies had already met and dealt with some enemy, and D Company medium machine gun platoons had taken 50 Hungarian prisoners while getting into position to support the attack, when at 1630 hours orders came through to halt the attack and prepare to move into a concentration area in Deelsen to the South, where we might expect a few days' rest.

So ended a continuous 36 hours battle which the Battalion had every right to be proud of. Altogether 35 guns had been captured or destroyed and heavy casualties inflicted on the enemy. Though all were very tired towards the end, no one had any doubts that the attack on Eversen would be a success.

No one realised it at the time, but this was the last serious battle the Battalion fought during the war. For the remaining weeks of the European War we were holding a flank against light opposition.

Since we had crossed the Rhine we had had some very hard fighting, and we felt we had gone a long way along the road to perfecting the art of Infantry/Tank co-operation.

On arrival in their rest area it was found that an RASC company had originally occupied the village and had been raided by enemy from the local woods; indeed, a battery passing through had lost two 25-pounders. B Company encountered no opposition, and Lt Phillips recovered the missing guns; meanwhile the 2nd received the needed reinforcements. The next few days saw the Battalion successively moving up from village to village until Bremen fell.

After a few hours in contact with the 12th Battalion, the 2nd moved to Amelinghausen just short of Lüneburg to await the crossing of the River Elbe.

Every wave-length on the wireless was dominated by Radio Hamburg to the exclusion of every other station, but much major news kept coming through; first the death of Hitler and the fall of Berlin; then the reported comings and goings of Himmler with surrender offers; then the surrender of the Germans on the Italian Front to Field-Marshal Alexander, and finally the surrender of Hamburg, shortly after the Battalion had been given orders for its part in the attack on the city. Soon after this news the Battalion crossed the Elbe and took over the wealthy residential suburb of Hamburg called Bergedorf. At once the problems which were to occupy us for the rest of our stay in Germany started—the rounding up and disposal of German stragglers and displaced persons.

On the morrow, 5 May, came the beginning of the end. The German forces opposing 21 Army Group surrendered, and although the war was not officially over, that night was VE night for the Battalion and everyone else in the area. During the day inquisitive members of the Battalion had discovered a large wine cellar in the town, and thus every Rifleman had more than enough to drink. Lt Jimmy Stow drove to Hamburg, and the products of the cellars of the Hotel Atlanta still further enhanced the beauty of the occasion. Very large quantities of ammunition were discharged, and, after three rounds of high-explosive mortar shells had landed near Brigade Headquarters, there were anxious telephone calls enquiring if all was well. It is to the credit of Brigade Headquarters that they did not believe the Battalion report of an attack by Werewolves. The next day was spent in clearing up the mess. This chiefly entailed dealing with the hundreds of displaced persons swarming round the town. A day or so later the Battalion learnt that it was to move to Pinneburg, North of Hamburg. Shortly after this news came the final announcement from the Prime Minister that the war was over and that VE-day proper was to be celebrated the next day. The Battalion celebrated again, but not quite so hecticly as before. During the stay at Bergedorf the appointment of Maj Fred Mellor to the command of the 1st Battalion came through; he left, but in fact never took up the appointment. On account of this, Maj Dick Vernon took up his old job as 2IC, Capt George Palmer returned to B Company as officer commanding, and Capt Tom Trenchard became Adjutant.

On 9th May the Battalion moved to Pinneburg and immediately started the serious business of clearing up the area. The German stragglers were organized by the German military authorities, which helped everyone considerably as it left more time for dealing with the displaced persons. Lt Dick Burton's platoon from B Company was sent off to look after the local German Corps Headquarters. Every German travelling around the country-side had to be escorted—a necessity, because alone they would certainly have been put in the bag by one of the many check-points in operation throughout Schleswig–Holstein.

Between the Elbe and Weser the 12th had to help clear the peninsula towards Bremerhaven. The advance was made very difficult by innumerable demolitions, but by the time the war ended on 8 May 1945 the Battalion was scattered in the general area of Bremervorde.

In the 11 months' active service from D Day to VE day, from Normandy to Bremen, the 12th Battalion lost 11 Officers, 4 Sergeants and 90 Riflemen killed in Action or Died of Wounds; 16 Officers and 230 Riflemen were wounded and 10 Riflemen were taken prisoner. Eight MCs, with an MC and Bar to Lt A. G. Burnaby-Atkins, among other awards, were some recognition of a battalion whose young leaders had kept up their drive and initiative to the end. Particularly well earned was the MBE to Capt R. Broad, REME, who had done so much to keep the Battalion mobile during its long advances.

Since the 12th remained the longest in Germany, a brief indication of their part in the duties of an Army of occupation, soon to be known once more as the British Army of the Rhine (BAOR), will be given. On 19 May 1945 the Battalion moved to Hannover, where it was billeted on the edge of that much-bombed city. There was a night curfew on all German movement, and patrols had to be found to enforce this, and in so doing to arrest German servicemen who had evaded prison camps. Two prison camps, containing 15,000 German prisoners of war, and such vulnerable points in a ruined economy as an alcohol factory and oil

12 2nd Battalion Officers and Visitors at Crowborough on 22 September 1945, before departing for Tripoli

Left to Right

Top Row—Lts P. R. Smalley, E. B. Taylor, J. R. Tillard, M. W. Ponsonby, E. Cowell, C. T. C. Tatham, D. C. W. Bampfylde, A. C. Burnaby-Atkins, T. N. Thistlethwayte, P. Hazlehurst, M. D. K. Paterson, R. M. Parker, G. J. Jamieson, P. F. Povey, F. H. Scobie.

2nd Row—Lts E. H. R. Craig, R. J. Gould, C. E. W. House, Capts E. H. Spooner, T. E. St. Aubyn, Lts R. O. Lewin, M. J. F. Morrison, H. R. M. Porter, R. M. Goddard, R. H. Burton, R. Lloyd, I. M. P. Evans.

3rd Row—Lts J. L. Poe, J. E. Shirley, R. C. Stephenson, Maj J. H. P. Curtis, Capt P. Pardoe, Lts C. A. Humphreys, R. M. Wigram, D. J. C. Weston, Maj G. S. Palmer, Capts E. C. Phillips, A. C. Swetenham.

Seated—Capt Hon T. Trenchard, Maj E. D. Shafto, Col E. A. B. Miller, Maj Gen Sir Hereward Wake, Lt Col E. G. V. Northey, Maj Gen Sir John Davidson, Marshal of the Royal Air Force Lord Trenchard, Maj Gen G. Dalby, Maj Gen J. F. Hare, Majs H. A. Hope, M. J. Gilliat, C. S. Madden.

13   Lt Gen Sir Evelyn Barker, Col Comdt and GOC in C Palestine, addressing the 2nd
Battalion at Tripoli on 11 October 1946

Left to Right—Lt Gen Barker, Lt Col E. G. V. Northey, Rfn Chaplin by Jeep, Capt A. C.
Burnaby-Atkins.

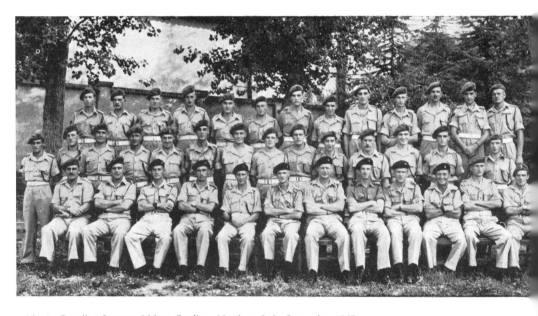

14   1st Battalion Sergeants' Mess, Gradisca, Northern Italy, September 1947

Left to Right

Back Row—Sgts G. Smith, R. Pope, R. Garner, D. Robinson, K. Churcher, K. Taylor, T. Deere, E. O'Brien, T. Hutchin
P. Vigar, N. Brooks, E. Pullen, F. Fellows.

Middle Row—Sgt A. Smith, C/Sgt J. Brown, Sgts E. Nunn, A. Lamb, P. Patchell (R.Sigs), S. Smith, C/Sgts R. Wood
Phillips, S. Green, R. Spikesley, Sgts G. Fox, E. Reynard, K. Wilkes, P. Coonan.

Seated—A. S. M. Myers (REME), C/Sgt G. Missen, CSMs W. Joyce, T. Abbott, RQMS J. Condon, Lt Col T. L. Timpson, F
F. Voysey, Capt T. E. St. Aubyn, CSMs L. Eveson, J. Woods, ORQMS R. Robbins, CSM1 T. Cameron (APTC).

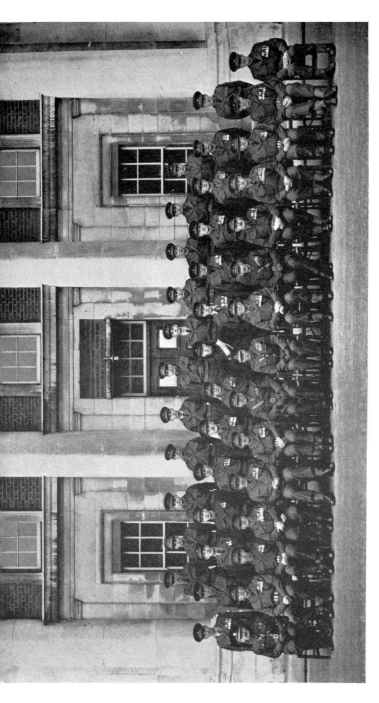

15 Inspection of the 1st Battalion, The King's Royal Rifle Corps, by His Majesty King George VI, Colonel in Chief, Winchester, 3 November 1950

Left to Right

Back Row—2/Lts C. G. N. Campbell, J. E. Oxley, A. C. Butler, R. T. Whiteley, P. M. H. Pollen, N. Eden, G. R. Cornwall-Jones, J. D. Eccles, R. F. Cavendish, Lord N. Gordon Lennox, J. J. N. Wyatt.

Middle Row—Capt J. L. Poe, Lts R. R. Cornell, J. C. S. Mills, G. W. Barker, H. R. M. Porter, Capt H. P. Edwards, C. F. Martin, 2/Lt M. B. L. Fuller, Capts A. C. Burnaby-Atkins, G. R. Seymour, E. B. Taylor, Lts R. M. Parker, J. A. Molesworth St Aubyn, R. K. Guy.

Seated—Maj M. Adeane (Equerry), Capt G. H. Mills, Majs J. A. G. Le Coq, R. H. Keeling, J. F. C. Mellor, M. A. Johnson, Maj Gen H. O. Curtis, HM THE KING, Lt Col C. T. Mitford-Slade, Gen Sir Evelyn Barker, Majs J. M. White, J. A. Hunter, P. H. Parker, Capts D. G. House, R. V. G. Elwes.

(Photograph by Salmon, Winchester)

16 Her Majesty Queen Elizabeth II, Colonel in Chief, with Officers of the Regiment at the Bicentenary Parade, St Cross Ground 25 July 1955

Left to Right

Back Row—2/Lt R. K. Erskine, Capt R. H. Underhill, Lt A. E. K. Karslake, 2/Lrs M. J. K. Miller, R. W. Snow, J. R. Leon, C. E. R. Benson, E. P. Coulman, Capt R. R. Cornell, Lt P. E. Willis-Fleming, 2/Lrs E. C. Winter, D. L. Mitchell-Innes, P. E. Cornwall-Jones, Lt C. J. Adami.

Middle Row—Capt R. K. Guy, 2/Lt The Hon J. P. F. St. J. Grenfell, Lt J. W. G. Pirie, 2/Lt C. J. Holroyd, Capt M. P. Hills, 2/Lrs R. D. Carver, J. G. Studholme, Capt E. B. Taylor, Maj J. G. Harrison, Capt F. N. Voysey, Lt M. J. Calvert, Capts H. R. M. Porter, J. A. Molesworth St Aubyn, C. G. N. Campbell, R. F. Cavendish.

Seated—Majs E. N. W. Bramall, E. C. Phillips, R. C. Gibbs, J. F. C. Mellor, Sir Anthony Eden, Gen Sir Evelyn Barker, Lt Col E. A. W. Williams, HER MAJESTY THE QUEEN, Lt Col R. F. L. Chance, Lt Gen Sir Euan Miller, Majs H. R. G. Howard, C. S. Madden, R. F. Nixon, N. J. Warry, Capt R. M. Parker.

refinery, had to be guarded. Initially nearly 180 men were on guard every night. A ceremonial guard was also mounted at the Rathaus, but more promisingly work started on restoring the Hindenburg Sports Stadium. During its remaining short existence the 12th was to prove as fine a sporting and shooting Battalion as it had been proficient in war.

On 21 June the 12th had to move at short notice to concentrate and guard 25,000 German prisoners while Russian troops moved West over the Elbe to occupy Magdeburg Province, in what is now East Germany. On 24 June the Germans were shepherded for their own protection into a tight and uncomfortable concentration area, ringed by the Battalion. On 1 July the Russians passed Battalion HQ and 500 prisoners of war of Russian origin were handed over to them. It was, however, decided that the remaining PWs would have to remain in British hands; they were accordingly moved into the British Zone and despatched North to the 43 Div camps; on 7 July the 12th moved back to their Hannover billets. They found that the PW camps had been closed, but they took their part in the Brigade quota of escorts for PW working parties, security checks and searches and an increasing number of train guards to Berlin. On 20 July a draft of 11 Officers and 256 Riflemen, those with the most service remaining before release, was sent to the 2nd Battalion, who were preparing to move to the Far East; 7 Officers and 255 Riflemen came to the 12th in exchange. The 12th had been busy painting their vehicles and rehearsing with the Regimental Band, over from England, for a parade held for Lt Gen Sir Evelyn Barker, KBE, CB, DSO, MC, Commander VIII Corps and senior 60th officer in Germany. This took place on the airfield on 4 August, with a quick and double march past, followed by an impressive drive past, in which the SP anti-tank guns played their part for the only time in the Regiment's history.

From August onwards the 12th began to enjoy the somewhat delayed fruits of victory. For those staying on, duties became lighter, and Brigade amenities in Hannover had become excellent, while sporting activities were at their peak. The earliest age and service groups went on release, led by Maj F. J. R. Coleridge, who returned to a distinguished further career at Eton after excellent service at Battalion HQ, having taken over command in action on more than one occasion. A useful series of pre-release courses was run by the 12th for those Riflemen returning to civilian life, after doing so much to maintain the Regiment's reputation.

On 13 October Maj T. L. Timpson joined as 2IC, having been a Prisoner of War since he held the same appointment with the 7th Battalion at Calais in 1940. Lt Col G. W. White, MBE, who had commanded the 12th since the Rhineland, left the Battalion on 15 November; with a brief interregnum of command by Lt Col F. Stephens, DSO, The Rifle Brigade, it was left to Lt Col Timpson, now as Commanding Officer, to wind up the 12th's active service in January 1946.

Before leaving for his next command, that of the 1st Battalion in Italy, he took tremendous care over the posting abroad of all who still had some time to serve. Officers went mainly to staff and liaison posts, and a high proportion of the Riflemen to Rifle Brigade battalions. In the next few years the spirit of this fine fighting battalion will be seen to have been passed on by its former members, who helped to recreate the Queen's Westminsters so successfully at Buckingham Gate.

The 2nd Battalion had fought a very varied war. Reformed after its fight to the end at Calais in 1940, its Riflemen had been in action all along the North African coast lands from Egypt to Tunisia. It had exchanged those burning sands and Khamsins for the icy rain and mud of Italy. Finally it had advanced from the summer bocage of Normandy to endure the chill fogs and mud of Holland and the Rhineland. Now, deservedly, it was literally to be put out to pasture for the summer of 1945 in the green, unblemished land of Denmark.

On 14 May the 2nd was delighted to hear of this move from Germany, with its problems of displaced persons and the boredom of the non-fraternization policy.

Lt R. H. Burton takes up the account:

In the afternoon of 16 May the Battalion crossed the Danish frontier. Crowds lined the road, and we were at once greeted by the gay red flag with its white cross which we were to know so well. It was fine to be in a friendly country again, and to have cheering crowds throwing flowers at our half-tracks.

We were soon greeted by the news that we were not, after all, to go to Copenhagen, that city which we had heard so much about, whose gaiety was proverbial. We were to do frontier control and take over from B Squadron of The Royals. However, any Denmark was better than none at all, and no one was really desperately disappointed. Companies were spaced out a long way apart—A Company, at Skaerbeck, being some 50 kilometres from Battalion Headquarters at Aabenraa. B Company was in Tonder, C Company in Krusaa and D Company in Rodekro. Denmark fulfilled all expectations, and was a veritable land of milk and honey, or alternatively of schnapps, women and song. The Battalion duties were not exceptionally exacting, and consisted of arranging the exodus of the German forces in Denmark, some 250,000 men. Everyone managed to find plenty of time for Danish liaison duties in the evenings.

Companies changed their location several times and most spent a period in Copenhagen. Because of the long distances a number of captured German staff cars were authorized to augment Battalion transport.

There was a considerable social side to our job, both private and public. Most officers made numerous speeches at local functions and even inspected and took the salute at Danish Army and Resistance parades. Every man was entertained in the most royal fashion throughout the whole of our stay. Danish hospitality is proverbial, and in this their hour of liberation they opened their homes and their hearts to the soldiers who had freed them. Friends were quickly made, and officers and other ranks dined out most nights, eating food which we could hardly remember existed—butter, eggs, ham and cream piled high on every table. At first our tummies suffered with so much unaccustomed fat, but we were able to enjoy it to the full.

Every Company ran numerous dances, and football matches were in great demand; the match of a Company v. the local town usually proved quite even. Perhaps the high-light of the Battalion's stay was a football match, the Battalion against Copenhagen (in which we were beaten), followed by a dinner and dance given by the Colonel in honour of Lt Gen 'Bubbles' Barker—a completely pre-war affair of champagne, lobsters and smoked salmon, magnificently organized by Maj George Palmer, Capt Teddy Phillips and Rifleman Harris. Everybody who was anybody in Copenhagen was there, and the event featured strongly in the Copenhagen Tatler.

However, after two months well-earned rest, it was time to go before their welcome was outstayed. There had long been rumours of a move to the Far East, and this was confirmed in early July. The 2nd was to reorganize as an Infantry Reconnaissance Regiment on Far East light scales of equipment. D Company had to be disbanded, and over half every other Company changed. Drafts of a sufficient number of eligible officers and men to complete the Battalion to strength were negotiated with our 12th and 8th Rifle Brigade. The Adjutant, Capt T. Trenchard, made all the arrangements with great efficiency, and when the 2nd boarded the train at Flensburg on 19 July it was up to strength except for the draft from the 12th, which was to join at Assche, eight miles North of Brussels. With the large draft of ineligibles going to the 12th, inevitably went many of the older Battalion characters. Lt Col Consett had been appointed to the British Military Mission in Cairo, and the new Commanding Officer, Lt Col E. G. V. Northey, who had commanded a company in the 1st's early desert days, was waiting for the 2nd at Assche. Before the 2nd left Belgium the Commander 4 Armoured Brigade, Brigadier R. M. P. Carver, later a distinguished Chief of the Defence Staff and Life Peer, flew down from Kiel to talk to the Battalion for the last time. He paid the tribute of calling the 2nd Battalion 'the finest fighting troops in the British Liberation Army and complete masters of the art of infantry and tank co-operation'.

On 28 July the 2nd arrived in Dover and moved to Warren Camp, Crowborough, in Sussex, whence they all went on leave. During this period three major events which affected their future took place: the Russians entered the Far Eastern war, the first atomic bombs were dropped and finally Japan surrendered. With the ensuing cancellation of the 2nd's move to the Far East we have brought the history of our Battalions in North West Europe to a close. We shall now turn back to the Mediterranean, where there is much still to tell of the actions of the 1st and 11th Battalions.

CHAPTER V

ALGERIA TO THE ADVANCE UNDER THE APENNINE FOOTHILLS

(Maps: pages 8, 12, 108, 114, 118 and 130)

We left the 1st Battalion in early August 1943, toiling up the single road from Tripoli to Tunis, passing the great Roman arena at El Djem and ending up in the damp heat of Medjez el Bab. There, overlooked by skeletal hills of evil memory, such as 'Longstop', and ringed by old minefields in the parched yellow grass, they resigned themselves to guarding Italian prisoners of war.

The 1st had been overseas since 1922. From India they had gone to Burma, before arriving under command of Lt Col 'Strafer' Gott in Cairo in 1938. Despite the casualties of three years of fighting, up and down the Desert, there was still a hard core of pre-war Regulars, who knew nothing of wartime England except through home letters and the reports of the more recently joined. Stripped of transport—which was given to formations bound for Italy—their few vehicles included a motley collection of German and Italian booty, all painted the desert yellow. It was a battalion whose base, mentally and in fact, was still Egypt; reinforcements came from 2 Infantry Training Depot, Geneifa, in the Canal Zone, and it was to that country or to Palestine that individuals went on courses or local leave. Parties not on guard were away ferrying vehicles up the single, pot-holed coast road from Alexandria to Tunis, so no training could be done. The official dress of the 1st was KD shirts and shorts, hose tops, boots and short puttees, with webbing scrubbed white; officers wore their green side-hats rigidly straight fore-and-aft. It was in this kit that the officers paraded to meet the new GOC, in early September; he injudiciously asked the QM, Capt B. Ryan, whether he had got over his Gippy Tummy yet, to receive the curt answer that he had got over that sort of nonsense in India in the 30s, and how was the General progressing? The Riflemen wore shorts, socks and boots at all work except guards; they were burnt deep brown and the habitual conversation was a jumble of Urdu and Arabic, interspersed by pithier expressions of boredom. One tactical lesson had been learnt well, the importance of reverse slope positions, and a battlefield tour of the May 1943 actions, overlooked by the grim Kournine, evoked bitter memories of comrades lost in the last fighting, as old trenches and tattered battledress with black buttons were seen again. A welcome interlude was the visit of Maj Gen T. N. F. Wilson, DSO, MC, late 60th, recently appointed the first Director of Infantry.

The one bright spot had been the tour by A and B Companies at the greener monastery town of Thibar, and it was with relief that the concentration of 1 Armoured Division 30 miles South West of Algiers was announced. The 1st was the Motor Battalion to 2 Armoured Brigade, Maj A. G. L. Goschen's A Company working with The Bays, Maj D. Karmel's B with 10th Hussars and Maj J. B.

Cunningham's C with 9th Lancers. These Motor Companies were to be on a three-motor-platoon establishment, with a carrier platoon; D Company, eventually under Maj H. R. G. Howard, was to be a support company of three six-pounder platoons, towed by inadequate Carden Lloyds, and two Vickers MMG Platoons in carriers. The 1st Battalion was under the command of Lt Col W. D. Keown-Boyd, with Maj E. A. W. Williams, MC, shortly to be 2IC, when Maj J. N. Hogg was posted to England; its move to Algeria was guided by the efficient staff work of Capt J. P. Waterfield as Adjutant. The rail move in very ancient cattle trucks brought out the rugged individualism and sense of fun which were Battalion characteristics. When a battle-worn carrier-platoon sergeant, protesting that his small platoon was overcrowded in a cattle truck, had the notice 'Chevaux 8, Hommes 40' pointed out to him, his reply—'But that's just for Frogs, sir'—carried a deep conviction of righteous superiority. The French station-master at Setif, who wished the 60th to move off in their train before the line of breakfast brew cans on his platform had boiled, was kept busy by an inspired chant of '*Il est coccu, le chef de gare*'. The OC Train, Maj Cunningham, in his Hebron sheepskin coat, and his C Company preferred a more substantial breakfast and waved the train good-bye, catching it up again at a later halt, thanks to a convoy of passing Americans.

1 Armoured Division was allotted the green plain, so admirably drained and planted by French colonists, centred on Boufarik. The Atlas Mountains, with great broom- and heath-covered foothills and crowned with cedars, stretched along the South side. Companies each occupied a farm, where wine vats provided large and fortunately empty buildings. All around were ripening oranges and tangerines, and the last desert sores began to heal. The indifferent wine, vermouth and cognac were drunk with gusto if not discrimination; and the movements of officers could be detected by sugar on the nose—the Cercle Interallie's Bronxes—or the smell of Bénédictine from Bouzarea.

A new sense of purpose began to build up from the 1st's arrival on 13 October 1943. A large draft arrived from England, and a complete issue of new vehicles and much 1098 equipment flowed in. The carriers and B vehicles were English, but the motor platoons and Company HQs received American White scout cars. A darker khaki Battle Dress, shirts with collars, and blankets of American manufacture arrived to replace the KD, dhobied white. An excellent programme of progressive training started, including the evolution of all arms drills. Particularly close work on mines and explosives went on with 1 Field Squadron RE. This admirable body of Sappers, under Maj (and future Engineer in Chief) R. Clutterbuck, MC, was always referred to, in the radio jargon of the day, as 'our very good friends' on the many joint patrolling missions in Italy.

The Foreign Secretary, the Right Honourable Anthony Eden, who had won the MC and been Adjutant at a very young age in World War I, twice managed to visit his old Regiment. In November, on the way back from the Teheran Conference, he assured the 1st that all at the Conference 'had been working hard so that they could work harder'. In January 1944, when he watched the 1st win the Divisional Boxing in the great circular wine vat (known in honour of the trainer, Sgt Montague, MM, as the Montague Arena) he made it even clearer. Back from Moscow with Mr Winant, the American Ambassador, who with Eden had been the architect of the scheme for the 60th to receive American officers, Anthony

Eden received the roar 'When are we going home?' from the large number of Riflemen, pre-war or early wartime Desert veterans, who were aggrieved at 7 Armoured Division's return home without them. He slowly answered, breaking a dead silence, 'You are all going home . . . but you've got a job of work to do first!' His reputation for pre-war resistance to dictatorship and his moral courage as a leader won him, as he stood alone in the centre of the boxing ring, a storm of cheering from the whole Brigade, and not least from his old Regiment. As the PYTHON scheme began at last to move home the pre-war Regulars, some of the feeling of isolation began to leave the Battalion, but there remained a host of separation problems, which home mail often did little to help. It was yet another divided Christmas for most of the older men.

However, at least, the 1st was based on reasonable billets rather than in the mud of Italy and able to explore the little cafés of Algiers and the surrounding villages. Their good fortune was emphasized, when, after the Battalion had acted as enemy to the Division's 18 Lorried Infantry Brigade, on an exercise, the latter was moved across into the desperate defence of the Anzio beach-head. During this period the Battalion brought the art of mounted march discipline to a very high state, which was to be a feature of its work until leaving Italy in 1947; as part of this B Company were used to provide convoy scenes for David Niven's film *The Way Ahead*.

A Brigade tented camp was set up in January 1944 for Armoured Regimental Group training on the rolling plateau between the High and Saharan Atlas ranges at Bouira. So long as the weather was sunny and crisp, the sight of first 9L and then 10H Groups fanning out with their new Shermans across the plain and hills was inspiring to Riflemen, learning to get their armoured Whites over wadis and up rough tracks. However, the February rain and snow turned the camp into a sea of mud, and General Galloway's decision to close the camp was extremely popular. The final shake-down in command appointments took place amid a wave of jaundice, which hit the Mediterranean that winter. Brigadier R. Goodbody, late RHA, took over 2 Armoured Brigade, and Lt Col E. A. W. Williams, MC, relieved Lt Col W. D. Keown-Boyd as CO, having as 2IC been responsible for much of the training, particularly of officers and NCOs. He had been Adjutant to the 2nd Battalion at Calais, and had escaped while a prisoner on the march through France.

On return from Bouira, all the Battalion except B Company (who were already in that area) moved into the old 18 Lorried Infantry Brigade billets North of Boufarik. A certain amount of patrolling went on to find escaped German prisoners and to counter gangs of Arabs, organized to steal from camps and dumps, it was thought by American and British deserters. As March brought in drier weather the Battalion moved down to Sidi Aissa, on the edge of the Sahara, for field firing, coupled with an inspection of the famous Ouled Nail dancing girls at the Bou Saada oasis. On return C Company successfully restored order in a mutiny of British military prisoners without having to use force, and further field firing took place in the pines and dunes of Zeralda.

The marvellous spring flowers of April and anti-malarial precautions along the ditches in the Battalion area were a reminder that mobile operations would soon be possible for armour in the Mediterranean. A much-admired old 1st Battalion officer, Maj J. C. Hope, MC, arrived back as 2IC in time to watch the

GOC, Maj Gen A. Galloway, take the salute at a Battalion parade on a green meadow. Riflemen were sent under protest to spend a Brigade rest week near the sea in Surcouf; they thought it a cheap preparation of lambs for the slaughter by 'Them', the higher authorities, which a nation of individuals, reluctantly in uniform for the duration, detected as pushing them around at every turn.

It was time to get into action after a year of waiting; the last six months re-equipping and training had brought the 1st to a high state of efficiency. It had given a good team of young platoon commanders time to get to know their older NCOs and Riflemen—the average age in a platoon was 24—and to remind them that desert drills and customs would not all fit the new terrain. Lt J. Anderson, the new MTO, left by sea for Italy to take over reinforcements for the 1st, and it was clear that it was to that country that the Battalion was bound. The 1st moved with its Brigade into a reception camp at Blida on 12 May 1944, but despite the disappearance of the Adjutant's secret move papers in a dust 'devil' which engulfed his tent, security prevailed.

The vehicle ship left for Taranto on 16 May and the 1st Battalion, less its advance party and drivers, embarked at Algiers on 23 May 1944 at a strength of 33 officers and 659 men. One of the preoccupations was to smuggle aboard the canine comrades of the Desert years. Riflemen had been training their dogs to lie silent inside bed-rolls and kit bags while carried aboard. In this way a little black curly-tailed bitch called 'Tich', owned by Cpl Sainsbury of B Company, was enabled to have pups at sea and bite the inspecting CSM Tyson; she will reappear later in the story, earning the Dickin Medal, the Animal VC.

On 27 May the 1st disembarked in the filth of Naples Docks and marched nine miles through the heat to Afragola. Green plots between great trees were the camp site, and the QM had to draw and ferry all the tentage in one truck; it was not an impressive example of Italian rear area staff work, but Riflemen, as always, set to work cheerfully and had a primitive camp going rapidly; guards watched with mistrust the professional thieves ringing the camp.

Maj Hope, commanding the advance party, had taken most of the reinforcements on to Matera, an old town cut into the barren hillside a few miles North West of Taranto, where the vehicles had disembarked. After marching to Caserta, the main body moved to Bari by train and then on to Matera, a sunny journey made pleasant by fresh cherries in the open-doored cattle trucks. A pleasant contact was made with the 11th Battalion, when Lt Col J. Hunt paid a visit, as the 11th moved to Egypt after their long winter in Italy.

On 9 June the 1st marched to a Brigade bivouac area in oak scrub near Gravina. It was time to adapt training to the summer countryside, for Rome had just fallen, as the Normandy landings were about to start; the Allies, who had finally burst through the Cassino barrier, were streaming North after the retreating Germans, who were using every possible obstacle to delay their pursuers until they could stand on the Gothic Line. Companies were hard at work, firing on an improvised range. In view of the great number of ·45 Thompson Sub-Machine-Guns (TSMGs), nine to a motor platoon, emphasis was placed on single-shot firing, kneeling, at up to 200 yards; hard tiles off an old barn came in useful as targets. Three-inch mortar sections in each company tested the new base plate, and on the administrative side a Divisional baggage store was set up at Taranto. The last of the pre-war Regulars and the reservists left at this

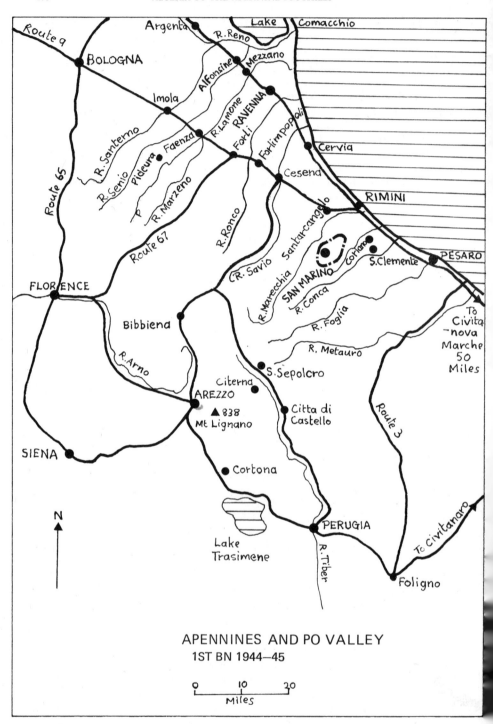

APENNINES AND PO VALLEY
1ST BN 1944—45

point; the Battalion was now a mixture of Territorial and wartime Riflemen.

On 29 June everything started to happen with a needless rush. Lt Gen Keightley, Commander V Corps, visited the Battalion, and the CO and Adjutant contacted HQ 8 Army. The authorities, who had sufficient armour forward but insufficient infantry, as the foothills of the Apennines approached, seized a fresh and highly mobile battalion from its parent formation, along with the Sappers. In this way the 1st was eased into the battle, while the rest of 1 Armoured Division was later to be thrown in cold with serious results. Receiving a warning order at 1800 hrs to move next day and an executive order 30 minutes later to move forthwith, the CO agreed to move at 0600 hrs 30 June. The pursuit was encountering stiffening reistance astride Lake Trasimene, and 61 Brigade, comprising the 2nd, 7th and 10th Rifle Brigade, with which our 1st Battalion ended the war, had distinguished itself with the capture of a series of hills North West of Perugia. All this was unknown to the 1st, who set off on a drive of some hundreds of miles North in ignorance of destination or task. The first night was spent in the hills near the Foggia airfields; next day, apart from a brief removal of dust in a mountain stream, the drive continued endlessly, crossing the Apennines to the West coast. The stench in the green slime of Cassino's craters was only equalled by the sinister stare of the ruined Monastery, looking down on the road to Rome. Passing through the shelled houses and burnt-out equipment of the Hitler Line, the 1st reached the outskirts of Rome for a few hours' sleep after midnight.

The next evening, 3 July, saw the Battalion moving into leaguer just South of Perugia, after a most efficient march; the best outcome was that the Carden Lloyds had proved as inadequate as Riflemen knew them to be and were abandoned. Thanks to rapid work by the CO and Adjutant a new demi-official establishment for D Company was implemented; it reduced the six-pounder anti-tank platoons to one, and gave the Company three motor platoons. To build up strength elsewhere, all carrier platoons were reduced to two sections. It was clearly going to be a motor-platoon war in this terrain.

On arrival in Umbria another early Desert veteran left in the shape of Maj Karmel, who handed over B Company to Maj L. A. Mackay, with Capt H. Crookenden as his 2IC. Maj Karmel sportingly learnt to parachute with his batman, Cpl Barnes, and went into Jugoslavia on special forces work with the partisans. Severely wounded towards the end of the war, he survived to resume a distinguished legal career with all that zest and love of forensic skirmishing which had made him the Riflemen's favourite defending officer.

On 5 July A Company took over a hill feature North East of Trasimene and Lt R. J. A. Darwin of C Company took out the first daylight patrol. Two days later the Battalion less D Company concentrated in the woods West of the lake as part of Sackforce—units of 9 Armoured Brigade, commanded by its 2IC, Colonel Stopford-Sackville, and under 6 British Armoured Division.

Having moved the 1st Battalion to the front, a moment must be spared to indicate in outline the strategy on both sides. June 1944 was taken up in heated Allied debate. General Alexander, Commanding 15 Army Group, considered that the best aid he could give to Normandy was to rush the Gothic Line before it could be systematically occupied; he wanted to do this in conjunction with an amphibious landing further up the Adriatic, threatening the approaches to

Austria and the Balkans and the cutting off of the rich Milan–Turin area, so valuable to Hitler. Eventually, President Roosevelt insisted on Operation 'Anvil', a landing in the South of France, as being of more direct influence on Normandy and opening up another port for US reinforcements from the States. To allow 'Anvil' to take place on 15 August 1944, Alexander had to release three US divisions and four French divisions, so experienced in mountain work; in addition 70% of the tactical air support and many specialized logistic units were to leave, reducing 15 Army Group to 18 divisions, with only a US Negro and a Brazilian division in the eventual offing as replacements.

In contrast Hitler, as Alexander had forecast, sent Kesselring eight more divisions and individual reinforcements, with orders to hold the Gothic Line from North of Pisa to Pesaro. Alexander was thus being required to exert pressure to help Eisenhower with inadequate resources in a country which was ideal for defence.

Although the Trasimene Line had been cracked, a new position presented itself to the Germans astride Arezzo. The approach from the South to this old, walled town is by a road, whose left flank is cramped by a canal; to the right three mountains overlook it. Monte Maggio lies close above the road, Monte Camurcino is more remote, but the highest, Monte Lignano, 1800 feet above the plain, runs down in a great spur across the road. On 5 July companies of 10 RB had seized footholds on Lignano and Maggio when their armour was held up. They were later relieved; 2 RB, less a company committed to the 2½-hour climb as porters, held a shoulder somewhat South West of the crest on Lignano and managed to see off a German attack; the weakened 7 RB were eventually pushed 500 yards down Maggio and consolidated with 10 RB.

On 8 July 1944 the 1st Battalion moved into close contact with the enemy for the first time since May 1943. The day started with a battlefield TEWT, run by the KDG for the Battalion on the site of a recent skirmish above the lake. The CO was called to the wireless and, placing companies at two hours notice to move, went to Sackforce for orders; as none knew the task, little could be done to get ready. At 1800 hrs officers of A and B Companies down to platoon level went forward to HQ 2 RB; the only information given was that the highest hill in sight was Lignano, and that those companies of the 1st were to relieve 2 RB near the crest that night. There was the promise of D Company as porters, but, since no mountain warfare drills had seemed appropriate to a motor battalion in an armoured division, Maj Goschen spent his time in the White, moving slowly to reduce dust and shelling, dictating a shopping list of ironmongery to be carried up.

Dusk fell immediately on return and the Whites crept forward as far as enemy harassing fire allowed. The few maps were sketchy, and twice the wrong side track was taken before the hamlet to be the Battalion command post was reached at the foot of the hill.

Overladen in the hot night, many Riflemen emptied their water bottles, little knowing that they would spend the next day waterless on the scorching hillside, as the only spring had dried up. The steep goat track was climbed at last, and the noise of equipment rattling drew down mortar-fire, which killed two A Company Riflemen. The batteries for the main radio set soon ran down, and the Battalion Line Corporal, Cpl Wilson, was later awarded the MM for daylight reconnaissance under fire and laying a double line in a more sheltered re-entrant.

2 RB had little time to hand over, and only just managed to be clear by dawn, so that local information was negligible. The companies improved the shallow rocky trenches in the few pines and low scrub, conscious that they were overlooked by the two mountains to the rear. Lignano itself seemed to have a pimple crest with a hut and one clump of low pines; this otherwise bare crest was immediately above our position, and far away down the spur our tanks could be seen firing forward towards Arezzo. Lt G. H. Mills was ordered to take out a small patrol from 7 Platoon, B Company, that night to find out the location and strength of the enemy. Trying to work round North of the crest, the patrol found itself continually forced South by slippery rock faces; fortunately, the pouring rain covered the noise of scrambling with studded boots. Lying alongside the commander, at what was found to be the crest, Sgt Potton suddenly realized that there was a figure in some low pines at his elbow. What turned out to be the German section commander of 10 men around the crest was rapidly bundled down-hill away from the pines, on which B Company's covering fire was laid. This first prisoner was briskly questioned and proved to be from 305 Division, saying that there was at least one German company on the reverse slope and that the OP on the crest was protected round the clock.

The patrol stimulated the enemy into accurate shelling next dawn, which killed L/Cpl Dowling. Even more serious, during the previous night, 9/10 July, the relief of A by C Company sustained 18 mortaring casualties, including some of the D Company porters. The goat track was clearly too exposed and the next night Maj Mackay took B Company down a steep re-entrant and across country, avoiding all track junctions, arriving in leaguer without loss. C Company had been reinforced by Lt Ricketts and his platoon of A Company, and had extended itself across the narrow strip of cover on the barren slope; thence they could watch with some cynical enjoyment the shelling of the Battalion command post below. Capt P. Wake, 2IC A Coy, was one of those wounded at this time, and an American ambulance driver, attached, died of wounds.

Lt A. Twigge, C Company, had detected a German night patrol position on the East slope, and Maj Cunningham resolved to have it ambushed on the evening of 11 July, as it moved into position. Lt Twigge successfully killed the enemy patrol's advanced elements, but unluckily was himself killed, with some of his patrol, by their covering party; since there was some indication of a larger forward movement by the enemy DF fire was put down at intervals during the night. The Company was supplied by mule on two occasions up the Western spur, and Sgt Laws, the Intelligence Sergeant, firmly led them forward despite the muleteers' reluctance; for this and much later good work he was awarded the BEM.

German patrols from Monte Camurcino were probing down to the main road, and a screen had to be put out by platoons from the leaguer. A Coy downed one of the two Germans they saw, but Lt D. G. House found his ·38 pistol inadequate on meeting another in the scrub.

Since Monte Lignano was clearly the key to Arezzo, the New Zealand Division decided to take it before the main attack struck North. On the night 12/13 July their companies relieved ours without casualties, and the 1st Battalion was once more concentrated South of Cortona. The Echelon naturally came up with PRI supplies, to pay for which companies in turn had drawn up cash and signed acquittance rolls. That well-known character 'George the Greek', as Rfn Dimitrios was known, toured platoons, administering haircuts and the latest Battalion gossip to taste. Mobile baths, usually sited in a river bed, were used, but exchanges of underclothes did not work out if the previous unit had been of Gurkha size.

The New Zealanders took Lignano after a fierce battle on the reverse slopes, and, with a Guards Brigade attack, Arezzo fell; as 6 Armoured Division pushed North West down the Arno valley for Florence against many demolitions, the 1st was ordered on 16 July to hold the North face of Arezzo and patrol forward. Inside the town Battalion HQ busily followed the CO's precept on acquisition of property—'only from houses abandoned by Fascists and then only useful articles', having stationed companies outside the walls. A Company found the sad scene where SS had bayoneted civilians, and in patrolling forward lost a Sergeant and a Rifleman, when a carrier went up on a mine. On 19 July the 1st Battalion was relieved and drove back to Cortona.

Although Leghorn had been abandoned to the Americans that day, and Ancona on the East coast to the Poles, 5 Army was directed on Florence, since the shortest route into the Po valley was from there to Bologna. There was, therefore, a call on Infantry formations to clear the hills on the right or North East flank of the Florence thrust, which took the city only on 4 August. The requirement was accordingly for the 1st to take over a brigade front, and by active patrolling to keep the enemy tied down on the Apennine slopes.

After a pleasant period of rest, the 1st Battalion was ordered to move to under command of 9 Armoured Brigade near Citta di Castello on 27 July. This town lay over the hills to the East, in a little plain where the Tiber rises, and the whole Battalion stripped to wash in its pale waters on arrival, the CO inheriting the soap suds. The Germans were holding San Sepolcro to the North and the rim of Apennines to the East, and their demolitions in this area formed the local outworks of the Gothic Line running West from Pesaro. After D Company had got their carriers by night up a precipitous track to the East, the other three companies relieved a Brigade of 10 Indian Division facing the hills North East of Citta. The enemy positions had not been located, so there was much probing forward. Lt A. J. Round worked his A Company carriers well forward along a ridge, and virtually all the motor platoons patrolled deeply on foot in daylight, 7 Platoon locating a German OP dominating the valley from a towered farm, which was successfully shelled by a Newfoundland battery. It was hot and tiring work in maize and on scrubby hillsides, but the peaches were a compensation. The friendliness of the Italians was overwhelming, and, with no Italian LO yet to hand, Capt Crookenden and Rfn Meadows, the Colonel's Dingo driver, found themselves unable to cope with all the information coming in, to which they alone could reply fluently.

On 1 August the East flank passed to 12L, who retained B Company for the moment. The remainder of the 1st moved West over the little plain to the Citerna area, looking down on San Sepolcro, but in turn under the majestic gaze of the towering Apennines to the North. Patrolling and exchange of artillery fire occupied both sides, and 12L relieved the Battalion on 4 August. A warning order, to form a mobile force to advance up the upper Arno valley North of Arezzo as far as Bibbiena, was received; on the night 4/5 August the tricky hill drive was made successfully and the Battalion concentrated just West of Arezzo. The operation, which would have been abortive against demolitions in a narrow valley, was cancelled, and the companies spent the time field firing. Most important of all, sensible Light, Medium and Heavy Scales of equipment were laid down, based on the experience on Monte Lignano. Light Scale was for quick action from vehicles in skeleton order. Medium, the normal dismounted scale, was based on the haversack and digging equipment, and its tin of bully and two packets of biscuits per man were designed to allow 24 hours away from vehicles, if rations could not be sent forward. Heavy Scale, with its greatcoat, was used with modification in winter. The benefit of the scales was that short warning orders could be issued, giving the scale less or plus certain items, when previously the Desert-minded companies and individuals had carried what they felt like, with no uniformity and a great deal of idiosyncrasy.

On 16 August the 1st Battalion received the news that it was reverting to the command of 1 Armoured Division, which was concentrating in secret on the Adriatic coast; that evening they left Arezzo and leaguered in the Foligno area. On 18 August the Battalion arrived to join 2 Armoured Brigade, hidden in trees and farms along the Chienti valley West of Civitanova Marche; washing in the cool torrent and visiting old cavalry friends filled in the time, as no movement of men in the open was allowed after early-morning fitness training. Henceforward the 1st Battalion was to fight in 8 Army on the East and North of the Apennines; the dust and heat of Umbria would seem a golden dream amid the mud and sleet of the Romagna, with its embanked rivers running down from the foothills to the coastal marshes.

Alexander, with reduced resources, was forced to make a new plan. Instead of concentrating both his armies on the direct route to Bologna, he decided to adopt General Leese's suggestion that 8 Army's strength in armour and artillery would be best employed in breaking the Gothic Line in the Adriatic foothills near Pesaro. Once Kesselring's reserves had been drawn East, Clark's 5 Army could thrust at Bologna. In briefing 1 Armoured Division, under its new GOC, Maj Gen Hull, the later CIGS and CDS, there was bold talk by 8 Army and V Corps of sweeping over the Plains of Lombardy to the Ljubljana Gap and on to Vienna. So far as Riflemen were concerned, paying an infantryman's attention to their 1:50,000 scale maps, 'the Plains' were the Po valley, with one of the most highly developed water systems in Europe. There was a network of blue with only Route 9, hugging the foothills from Rimini to Bologna, and Route 16 North to Ravenna and the Po itself; even if there was just a handful of German engineers with some Spandaus and Panzerfausts left, every blue line would have to be fought for.

8 Army's attack started on 25 August 1944 without the Germans realizing that it was not just a continuation of the Polish Corps' advance up the coast. The Canadian Corps, including 5 Canadian Armoured Division, advanced on the coastal flank, with V Corps, finally employing both 46 and 56 Divisions, inland; up in the mountains 4 Indian Division was slanting in from the San Sepolcro area. In a brilliant stroke the Infantry divisions defeated the enemy South of the Gothic Line defences, and hustled them through the minefields, tank-turreted emplacements and cleared fields of fire without giving them a chance to rally. However, German reserves, in the form of 26 Panzer, 1 Parachute and 98 Division, started to appear from the Bologna area, but even these in their turn

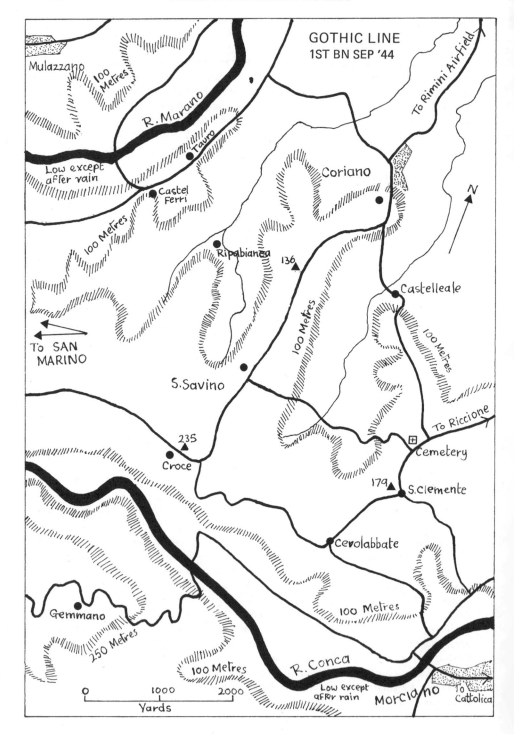

GOTHIC LINE
1ST BN SEP '44

were pushed back over the River Conca. The Poles, after taking Pesaro, went into reserve, and the Canadians seized a bridgehead over the River Conca on the night 2/3 September. In V Corps 46 Division was up to the Conca, but the remainder were echeloned back as the hills rose higher towards the Apennines in the West.

Ahead of 8 Army were only two small rivers, the Marano and Ausa, and three main ridges, before the River Marecchia heralded the Po Valley's start. With the breaking of the Gothic Line's defences, success seemed within the Allied grasp to the strategists, but at the tactical level there were features which the Germans seized on with all their talent for defensive improvization. In this area the gap had narrowed, and was entirely overlooked by the theoretically neutral diadem of peaks in San Marino, in fact containing German OPs. Looking down the Conca valley was Gemmano, a small mountain with villages and spurs, which was by-passed by 56 Division; bitterly defended by 100 Mountain Regiment, it was for the next fortnight to carry something of Cassino's malevolence about it. A ridge ran across the front from Croce to San Clemente, and slanting out North East from it was the San Savino–Coriano ridge, which ran down to the killing ground of Rimini airfield and its tank-turreted defences; behind that in turn were the old Italian coastal defences on San Fortunato hill.

Steep ridges and wadis, inadequate tracks and bare slopes, all overlooked, made this a setting for Infantry by night rather than massed armour by day. The 8 Army reserve was, however, 1 Armoured Division, and at 0420 hrs on 2 September, when the 1st Battalion moved off, it was some 70 miles South as the crow flies, and much more as the Division crawled endlessly through blinding white dust, day and night, largely on its tracks. The first leg lasted until noon, with a temporary leaguer until 1700 hrs; after two hours for replenishment and a doze on the shingle of the River Metauro they followed 10H on till 0500 hrs. Some carriers had started to break down in the blinding dust, and D Company had two Riflemen badly burnt, when a carrier and half-track were sprayed by flaming petrol, vapourized as it was shaken and heated on the march; Capt D. G. Rhodes and others did well to save much of the equipment from the blaze. At noon on 3 September the 1st Battalion crossed the River Foglia and leaguered with the rest of the Brigade near to medium-gun lines in action among the Gothic Line defences.

The lessons from the next 24 hours were later usefully passed on by Maj J. Hope to 6 Armoured Division, when General Murray was studying how such a formation should be launched from Army reserve. If the COs of the Armoured Brigade had been sent forward to the Infantry brigade through which they were to pass they would have seen the ground and been in fresh touch with the enemy situation. The armour should have been staged up gently in a series of bounds by day to allow proper sleep and maintenance. Enemy air activity was limited to night only, and in any event some tanks were on the move in daylight and could not be hidden in the bare countryside, even if camouflaged. As it was, the Brigade was launched exhausted and without any useful information.

Orders were given for Maj J. Hope with some provost and sappers to lead the Brigade to a concentration area, which in fact was dominated by the enemy. The route through our gun lines, under attack by enemy aircraft, was a tortuous nightmare of tracks, and lack of march discipline by Main and Rear Division HQ, who had somehow got into the lead, delayed the Battalion; companies finally crossed the River Conca at 0600 hrs on 4 September and dispersed in the narrow valley, suffering 15 casualties from enemy shelling in the process. While the exhausted armour poured in, Maj Hope, on the San Clemente ridge beyond, saw from the wary attitude of the few 46 Division infantrymen around that he was in the front line. 1 Armoured Division huddled in this crowded valley for the next two weeks, the Field Cashier and the over-optimistic G3 (Intelligence) learning to dig in under the intense shell-fire directed from Gemmano to the West, described by old hands as heavier than that at Anzio.

At 1330 hrs orders were given out by 2 Armoured Brigade for an attack North West over the Coriano ridge, directed to seize crossings over the River Marano, with Bays left and 10H right, each followed by their motor companies, A and B. The exhausted crewmen found that the start-line was not even secure when they finally crossed at about 1600 hrs. Maj W. Hibbert of The Bays had a culvert blown behind him, as he led his squadron up a narrow track but gallantly pressed on into hostile territory until knocked out at dusk; his MC for evading capture during his difficult return on foot was well earned. 10H had casualties at RHQ when the CO's tank was hit, and troops moving down the forward slope from San Clemente found themselves under fire from San Savino, obscured by the low sun. But it was the exhaustion of drivers which brought the advance to a halt, as one tank after another bogged down in unseen wadis. The advance was called off and the motor companies did their best to protect the leaguers, as Butterfly bombs were dropped on the gun lines, deploying next day just in time to avoid the first-light shelling. A Brigade attack by the Lorried Infantry would probably have succeeded that night, but on the wretched track allotted to the Armoured Division throughout this period the infantry could not be moved forward.

On 5 September the IO, Lt G. M. Graham, was wounded while reconnoitring a track forward for the rest of the Battalion to support the 9L Group effort; 9L with C Coy had been ordered to seize San Savino. The armour worked forward towards a white house on a spur short of the village and came under fire from bazooka teams in the rows of vines strung along low fences every 20 or 30 yards. Because of the vulnerability of their vehicles to tank-fire on the forward slope, the C Company motor platoons dismounted, but after Lt Darwin and others were wounded, the Company became pinned down; communication with the tanks was interrupted when Maj Cunningham's Dingo received a direct hit. Lt D. G. House managed to work his carrier platoon up to help the leading troop of 9L. Dismounting with his few men, who carried a variety of automatic weapons, he advanced in short bounds, spraying successive vine rows. In a short time he had rounded up over 50 enemy with no casualties to the dozen in his party; the enemy were Panzer Grenadiers but included a medley of nationalities, who, though well armed, had little stomach for this heavy fire. Lt House hastened to disarm them before they realized the disparity in numbers, but he could do no more, since there was no armoured follow-up; the award of an immediate MC was, however, appropriate recognition of the one bright spot in another unsatisfactory day. Lt M. P. Lee took a D Company patrol in daylight under heavy shell-fire to assess the state of the San Clemente–San Savino road. He found it mined and blocked by a tank and armoured cars. That night his platoon and that of Lt T. E. St Aubyn protected 1 Field Squadron RE, who cleared nearly 3000 yards of road, including the vehicles, for an attack by 1 Buffs, which did not succeed against stiffening opposition.

On that night, 5/6 September, 18 Lorried Infantry Brigade relieved the armour, since it was now seen to be an infantry battle, and the 1st Battalion concentrated back on the reverse slopes. For the next week the German strongholds of Gemmano and round Croce, which enfiladed the Corps, were to take up all the remaining efforts of 56 Division and then 46 Division. It was at this time that a splendid 60th Rifleman, Brig G. H. G. Smith-Dorrien, DSO, was killed when commanding the Queen's Brigade in 56 Division.

First A and D Coys took up positions in the San Clemente area under heavy shelling, and then B Coy relieved 10GR at the cemetery, whose dominance attracted no less than a dozen Gunner OP parties. 43 Lorried Gurkha Brigade, the 2nd Battalions of 6, 8 and 10GR, had recently joined the Division under Brig 'Tochi' Barker, and were a very welcome addition.

Rfn (later) Cpl Walker was awarded the MM for his gallantry in evacuating Gurkha wounded from Castelleale, an outpost under continual and intense observed shelling by day. He was a Geordie of great resolution, whose gentleness with the wounded was only equalled by his little dog 'Tich', who licked the faces of his patients; he had inherited her from Cpl Sainsbury when the latter went home. She went everywhere with him and was even wounded, but survived to receive the Dickin Medal after the war for gallantry under fire and her good effect on Battalion morale.

When A Echelon moved forward into the old Battalion HQ site, some casualties were sustained. Capt J. Anderson, the MTO and an upright and brave Territorial, Lt Pinkerton, a young Rhodesian who had joined the day before, and Cpl Hughes, the B Company cook NCO, were all killed in night shelling.

It had started to rain spasmodically, a serious warning that time was running out. On the night of 12 September the two Corps attacked all along the ridge astride Coriano to the thunder of 300 guns. The attack was successful, and, as the 1st moved up these slopes next evening, the grim work of the Gurkhas could be seen. After a useful patrol by Lt C. P. Lindsay of A Company gained information on the wadi crossings beyond Coriano, A and C Companies pushed forward on foot on 14 September towards the Ripa Bianca feature. They were working in front of our armour against severe opposition from Tigers and SPs, taking some prisoners but having some Riflemen wounded; Lt P. D. Way gallantly led the infiltration of C Company down the exposed slope to the wadi, but sadly lost Sgt Austin to one of the incessant mortar concentrations after digging in.

That night B and D Companies passed through to take Castel Ferri and Monte Tauro on the last ridge overlooking the River Marano, from whence the enemy tanks had been shooting all day. D Company reached their objective unopposed, but 2IC B Company's carrier went over a mine, as Capt H. Crookenden started to lead the Company forward; two Riflemen were less seriously wounded with him, but Capt Crookenden, who lost both legs, survived for many years, and took on active Chairmanship of the KRRC Association, besides a mass of work for other people. The destruction of the only detailed map did not help, but Lt A. H. Cagby led the Company up to Maj Mackay. During the night advance a flanking farm exploded into flames amid heavy firing; an impromptu flank patrol by Lt A. A. Lane found this to be a 56 Division attack, but it was typical of the lack of

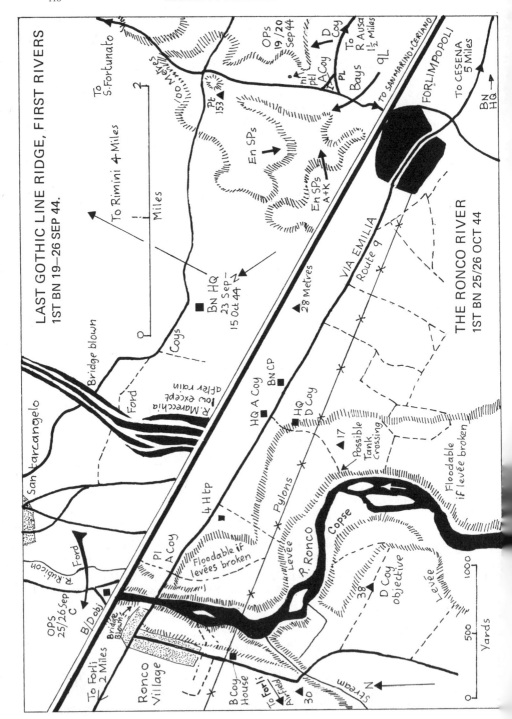

LAST GOTHIC LINE RIDGE, FIRST RIVERS
1ST BN 19—26 SEP 44.

THE RONCO RIVER
1ST BN 25/26 OCT 44

information and co-ordination from higher formations throughout this period. B Company arrived at Castel Ferri at first light, just in time to pounce on the last enemy straggling back. Supported by brisk MMG fire from Lt R. F. Kershaw's platoon on targets across the valley, the ridge was held until the Gurkhas attacked through at last light over the dried-up Marano and on to the next ridge. During the week of the Coriano attack 8 Army suffered nearly 1000 casualties each day, and in particular the infantry were steadily draining away. The Germans suffered equally, but their communications were shortening and the dust would shortly turn to mud, as the trickling rivers became roaring spates. Meanwhile our platoons digging in found cover and refreshment along the vine rows, heavy with unpicked grapes.

The Companies were relieved in turn and moved back into the cratered countryside East of Coriano, stinking of the recent battle, where a church service for the fallen was held by Capt G. Barton, MC, the Padre. Despite the omens, planning was still going on for an armoured dash to the River Savio, the first main obstacle in the Po Valley. After an abortive move on 18 September, the 1st Battalion on the next night drove out behind The Bays, with whom A Coy was already grouped. The area between San Marino's rocks and the sea was at its narrowest, and as usual Corps had given the Division only one track. With the armour leading, no possibility of getting infantry up quickly existed, if enemy opposition proved more than the over-optimistic estimates. The night crossing of the Ausa was drenched with Nebelwerfer fire; 3 Platoon HQ White was hit, killing Sgt Heath and wounding Lts Lindsay and G. H. Maufe. Farms were blazing all around, and artificial moonlight from our searchlights was some help to vehicle movement. D Company sustained casualties when mortared in a sunken road, and little information was forthcoming.

The picture as it appeared to 8 Army on the night of 19 September was that 4 Division and the Canadians were threatening San Fortunato at the end of the last ridge overlooking Rimini and the start of the Po Valley. At the other end, under San Marino, 56 Division was thought to be firm near Ceriano, but, to the undoing of our armour, this had become but a platoon toe-hold under pressure from 90 PG Division. The task required of 2 Armoured Brigade was to advance up a T-bone spur with houses at the junction and wheel right to seize the dominant Point 153. Owing to steep slopes on the East, the tanks would have to make this wheel on the forward slope in view of a series of spurs below. It was about this time that an ironic catch phrase began to circulate within the 1st, expressing a Rifleman's view of Higher Command—'Push on, old man, there's nothing on the high ground.'

Assured that both flanks were firm—and indeed the right was—A Company probed forward to find out the situation in the narrow strip of ploughland allotted the Brigade. Lt Ricketts made firm contact at the houses, and, after losing Rfn Digman—who later was liberated from Santarcangelo hospital—in a brisk exchange of grenades, he reported the armour's start line strongly held—by the enemy. An armoured reconnaissance in force up to the ridge at first light confirmed that there were SPs and 88-mm anti-tank guns well down their reverse slope, shooting the crest from over the 56 Division boundary. Nevertheless, the staff's illusory chinagraph map-markings were preferred to the harsh realities, confirmed by the three combat arms on the spot: The Bays, now reinforced by a squadron of 9L, were, on orders from 8 Army, committed to the attack. All the 27 tanks, including the Gunner OP from 11 RHA (HAC), which moved over the crest were caught as they wheeled on the slope below and knocked out. Many crewmen were Spandaued from the houses they had by-passed as they struggled back; some survivors lay out under fire until they contacted our A Company patrols after dark. In search of a more direct way to the objective from the right, D Company made a dismounted probe forward, but were pinned by intense mortaring. Lt N. J. Warry received a well-earned MC for rescuing Lt St Aubyn's casualties, making several trips through very heavy fire in a White driven by Rfn Huntingford. Saddest of the casualties in the Battalion were Rfn Bumford and Hill, MM, the latter an old soldier who had refused to go back to England, both of A Company's carrier platoon. Rfn Austin was killed and Maj J. Cunningham wounded when his Dingo was hit, and L/Cpl Annan, the CO's driver, was also wounded under the intense enemy fire, despite 11 RHA expending all their smoke. In a brilliant stroke to the East the Canadians, wisely using four infantry battalions and allowed more elbow room, took San Fortunato, but a warning order still came through on our front for 10H and B Company to repeat the unprofitable performance next day. However, in the night a drenching downpour bogged all vehicles down for 24 hours, just after 14 Foresters had taken over our front, and in the first mists of Autumn the Germans slipped away from Rimini and the ridge to beyond the Marecchia.

On 22 September the CO informed all officers that 1 Armoured Division was being disbanded owing to lack of infantry reinforcements, but that 2 Armoured Brigade would continue independently under a new Commander; Brig J. Combe, DSO, late 11H, who had escaped after capture in the desert, had relieved Brig Goodbody. It was with very great pleasure that the 60th watched the rise of Brig Goodbody to be Adjutant General after the war, since he had nothing but help and understanding for Riflemen, and the unsatisfactory commitment of armour had not been his fault. Although the Battalion had little respect for the staff work and Higher Command in the Gothic Line battles, it was to regret the future lack of Divisional protection as it was loaned (with little comprehension of its lack of dismounted manpower) from one infantry formation to another. It was not until it passed next Spring into 6 Armoured Division, and under the aegis of 61 Brigade, that it could count on being properly employed once more. In the interval our one 60th 'friend at court' was BGS V Corps, Brig A. R. W. Low; he was later to become the Rt Hon Lord Aldington, PC, KCMG, CBE, DSO, TD, DL.

However, this was all in the future, and the main thing was to get all the vehicles out of the mire; appropriately eight half-tracks were issued, on a scale of two to a motor company and two to Battalion HQ. On 23 September the Battalion moved into the low ground just South of the Marecchia with a counter-attack role in support of the Gurkhas, who were battling for the town of Santarcangelo on a knob overlooking a stream known as the Uso, but really the Roman Rubicon. B Company moved forward over the Marecchia the next night, to set up a patrol base; from this Lt Mills led a patrol over the Rubicon to cover sappers making a silent lift of wooden mines astride a ford and as far as the lateral the other side. The next day 4H and C Company, now under command of Capt W. E. Channing, one of our American officers, used the ford to probe forward, taking a prisoner but sustaining some casualties to heavy shelling.

Further back careless driving by other units raised dust and attracted enemy SP fire. To the whole Battalion's sadness the Padre, Godfrey Barton, who had been with us for over two years and won the MC, was killed by a shell splinter through the RAP's doorway.

C Company had consolidated in farms beyond the lateral, but was very isolated when the 4H tanks pulled back over the ford at last light.

That night, the 25th, C Company reconnaissance group was moving laterally with the officers, before taking up a new night covering position for a 56 Division advance next day. The Company itself suddenly came under heavy shelling and machine-gunning and suffered casualties (by the end of the day it was down to 45 men). This was later diagnosed as German aggressive patrolling to cover a withdrawal, but at the time appeared to be the start of a counter-attack. Capt Channing decided to pull back by stages this side of the river, as progressively more of his small force, including Lt Way, became casualties under the accurate fire.

However, the Battalion was pledged to secure a start-line for the Queen's Brigade advance next day, so the CO came forward to regain the lateral road with a formal Battalion night attack. B Company, which had been up all the previous night, were turned out into the rain with D Company, and with considerable difficulty crossed the two rivers and innumerable vine fences before reaching the objective, by this time unopposed except for harassing fire. The Battalion's reputation remained intact, but it was as well that Queensmen, slogging forward over their start-line next morning, did not hear the commentary of dripping Riflemen, who badly needed warmth and sleep, on what seemed their pace-stick rate of advance.

The 1st Battalion concentrated behind the Marecchia and, despite the warming sun, the Autumn nights and frequent rain put a premium on seizing billets; apart from a roof, a farm-yard was proving to be the only hard-standing for vehicles in the low country where any digging rapidly reached water. The very steady drain of casulaties caused concern, which V Corps solved on paper by reducing the establishment to 30 officers and 700 men, ignoring the equipment held. Capt P. Wake was evacuated with pneumonia to everyone's regret, and there were other changes. Maj Goschen now had Capt M. P. Lee as 2IC A Company, Maj Mackay had Capt A. H. Cagby as 2IC B Company, Maj F. W. Hodges took over C Company with Capt D. G. House as 2IC. On a reorganization of D Company to reduce vehicles, Lt R. F. Kershaw took over 7 Platoon, B Company, Lt G. H. Mills becoming IO, having been trained as such a year previously. Capt W. E. Channing took over HQ Company.

A first leave party went to Rome, and the first three officers availed themselves of 61 Brigade's kind hospitality to brother Riflemen in the Florentine Villa Capone. On this 5 Army front Alexander's hoped-for opportunity, created by the 8 Army attack, had been seized by Gen Clark. By the end of September the Gothic Line had been broken in the mountains North of Florence and a thrust had only just been held from reaching the low lands near Imola. A month later, when the 5 Army offensive halted in the face of a concentration of German divisions, the Americans had superbly fought to the heights only nine miles from Bologna itself. Kesselring, hurt in an accident, had handed over to von Vietinghoff, who was determined to repeat his Gustav Line performance.

From 1 to 21 October 1944, except for a few days when our aircraft could put in tactical strikes, the rain was more or less continual, and, in the area of principal concern to 8 Army, there was only one metal road, Route 9, from Rimini towards Bologna. Athwart it were half a dozen heavily embanked rivers, capable of rapid spate as they drew on the Apennine watershed to the South. In between them was a network of streams and vehicle-proof ditches between sodden clay fields; movement forward was like a game of snakes and ladders over winding tracks, which only intense sapper effort kept usable. The 1st Battalion moved forward over the Rubicon, glad even of primitive farms, crowded with Italian refugees, where a dry berth might be found in a cornstore or byre, emptied by the Germans of its great white oxen. Khaki drill was still being worn in the 1st well after the Autumn rains broke, since battle dress was back with Divisional baggage at Taranto and 8 Army administrative problems were legion.

General McCreery took over 8 Army at this time, and his experience commanding X Corps in the hills showed in the new deployment. The excellent Polish Corps and 10 Indian Division were brought up into the hills on the South or left flank; although track problems made the advance slow, they could successively threaten the flank of the German defences on each river-line, which eventually had to be crossed near Route 9, since that single good road was needed by the logisticians. The Army was, however, about to be weakened by the first of three more divisions, this time drawn away to fight the Communist attempt to take over newly liberated Greece. The beginning of a serious artillery ammunition shortage was also making itself felt.

The 1st Battalion moved forward, under direct command of HQ 4 Division, to good billets in the apple orchards just short of Cesena on 21 October. A Squadron (Maj J. Vaughan), 4H and a troop, 1 Field Squadron RE, were under command and A Battery (Maj D. Smith), 11 RHA in support; this force was assembled with a view to taking over the Cesena bridgehead and then breaking out to clear Route 9 towards Forli, with 10 Brigade on the left. On the night of 24 October C Company relieved the Black Watch, and D Company started the advance on foot up Route 9. Mines and demolitions were thick, but the enemy had clearly only just gone, his unmistakable smell lingering in houses and stragglers being picked up. At 1000 hrs on 25 October 1944 A Company passed through D on foot, when the latter had cleared up to a ridge running down to the road. By 1530 hrs A Company were passing through the town of Forlimpopoli; prisoners indicated that the enemy had withdrawn across the Ronco to hold there. By 1700 hrs the forward platoon and 4H troop were observing the main road bridge, of which two 50-foot spans had been blown in their faces, and was now covered by fire. Sgt Bowden, A Company, moved his carriers down to a river bend to the South and himself waded across, withdrawing when engaged from a house a few hundred yards beyond. By 1800 hrs Battalion HQ and the three other companies were moving into the Forlimpopoli area.

Unknown to the Battalion, there was considerable excitement radiating downwards from 8 Army to Divisions at this time; there were signs of a general German withdrawal to the Po, and on the 5 Army front the Allies seemed poised to cut Route 9. Greater realism would have shown Intelligence that Hitler had never been known to authorize strategic withdrawals of this kind, and that tactically the German commanders rightly imposed delay on every major defensible line, such as the River Ronco afforded. However, at HQ 4 Division there was euphoria at making an unprecedented eight-mile advance in a day, and our eventual enemy, 278 Division, was ignored, concentration being on the weakened 1 Parachute Division's withdrawal. Extracts from the 4 Division Intelligence summary, based on information received up to 2200 hrs 25 October 1944, give the background in which 2 DCLI to our left and our 1st Battalion were launched across the river to form bridgeheads incapable of mutual support:

Enemy situation

The last 48 hours have brought the enemy to his big decision, and from the fact that contact along the Corps front since early morning 24 Oct has been practically nil, it seems probable that the time has come for a very considerable change in the relative positioning of the German 14th and 10th Armies.

With scarcely a pause on the FRANZISKA line [a stream], the enemy finds himself tonight back on the GUDRUN line [the Ronco] with our fwd troops close on his heels at SELBAGNONE and the village of RONCO on Route 9. So far we have not crossed the river RONCO but *it seems that the enemy's resistance here*, incidentally the first encountered since the withdrawal started during night 23/24, *is no more than an understandable inability of the Paratps to have a river between them and ourselves without stopping to make some use of the opportunity*. By early afternoon this action had developed into something like a counterattack, but it was successfully broken up shortly afterwards.

In view of the situation South of BOLOGNA, where our Allies are within 4 miles of Route 9 at a point roughly equidistant from BOLOGNA and IMOLA, *it seems unlikely that tonight's German intentions are designed to do more than slow us up on the line of R. RONCO with outposts of about section strength, so that the main bodies can continue their withdrawal during the night.*

Prisoners taken today are mostly deserters and odd types left behind in the withdrawal, so that it is not possible to form any accurate impression of the troops actually in front of us. However, it is highly probable that 1 PARA DIV still have Route 9 as their axis of withdrawal, although as soon as FORLI is reached the Paraboys' line of retreat will probably turn abruptly North to Northwest.

278 DIV being the right hand Div of 76 PANZER CORPS is also likely to conform with this change in direction, but those divisions of 5 MTN CORPS immediately to the West of 278 DIV will probably not strike North from Route 9 until FAENZA is reached.

A civilian report today suggested that FORLI had already been evacuated by the enemy, but that there was a defence line just North of the town. It is unlikely that FORLI has been vacated already, as the town must form the main point of departure from Route 9 for the right flank of 76 PANZER CORPS. As regards the defence line, this might well apply to the GERHILD line which is the first delaying line on the new N.W. axis. GERHILD runs N.E.—S.W. through CORCOLIA 4925 which would bring it down just N. of FORLI. *As soon as the German left flank consisting of 76 PANZER CORPS* (162 TURCOMAN DIV, 114 JAEG DIV, 26 PZ DIV, Elts 90 P.G. DIV, 1 PARA DIV and 278 DIV) *has reached GERHILD the stage will be set for the big trek back to the VENETIAN line* with suitable breathing spells on the river RENO and the PO.*

*The River Adige North of the Po.

NOTE: Portions italicized by this Volume's author.

On the terrain side the Divisional War Diary says: 'By 1800 hrs reports from both KRRC and DCLI spoke of the river as not a serious obstacle . . .' but, since this impression is not contained in our log it must have emanated from the DCLI who were reported as having found fords. The Ronco Valley, though narrower and steep-sided at the Route 9 bridge site, widened out upstream. The river itself was contained by the usual grass embankments, but the floodable plain on the home side widened to half a mile. On the enemy side there was a lateral road before a plateau opened out to the open airfield area. This road started in Ronco village on Route 9, and houses lined it for a short distance before opening out into scattered farms. At the bend, where Sgt Bowden had found it wadable, there was a copse on the enemy side, below the embankment. Our side was throughout overlooked from the line of the lateral road, but contrary to Divisional belief our tanks could not see to support us from the home side.

The trouble was that the Battalion was under the direct command of HQ 4 Division, which was not geared to fight this sort of battle. Unlike a Brigade operation, no senior officer came forward to assess the ground or the enemy in conjunction with the CO, and dependence at the critical time was on very bad wireless communications or LOs. At 2010 hrs the 1st Battalion reported to Division 'One company patrolling to river. Remainder in Forlimpopoli. Patrols under small arms fire from other bank. Recce to bridge previously impossible owing to small arms fire but recceing as soon as possible.' Yet the Divisional War Diary says: 'At 2030 hrs the intentions were sent out—briefly that bridgeheads would be secured tonight over the River Ronco.' Mesmerized by the day's advance, and the fact that some spans of the long bridge still stood, Division's eyes were on Ronco village as a bridgehead, with no experience of how seizing such a built-up area would eat up the small dismounted strength of a motor battalion. Lt Col Williams already appreciated that the Ronco Line was held and needed to know more about enemy strength by patrolling before launching his battalion into a very black night. His dilemma was that the only place where tanks might cross was upstream well out of sight of the bridge and it would have needed a brigade to hold the area including both the possible crossing and the bridge.

With a better appreciation of the need for a bound by bound approach than the Divisional staff, Maj Mackay sent forward a platoon to establish a firm base on the home bank South of the bridge. By 0030 hrs he had brought B Company to it and sent the next platoon to establish itself across the river in a large, rather isolated house by the lateral road; it was likely to be identifiable on a dark and rainy night, because there was a line of pylons to it. The Divisional War Diary then says: '26 October 0100 hrs. A report from our LO returning from the KRRC that it was their intention to patrol to the river only that night caused some consternation and orders were despatched by all possible means ordering the battalion to occupy the village of Ronco on the west bank without fail.'

The actual written message from the GSO1, to be regarded as personal from the Divisional Commander, Maj Gen D. Ward, said: 'It is essential that you establish your battalion across the Ronco tonight. Unless this is done bridging operations cannot take place and the advance will not be able to continue either. All priority has been given to bridging in your sector and in any event your tanks can support your battalion from the South bank of the Ronco.' This was signed at 0030 hrs and received at 0140 hrs.

It will be noted that no mention was made of reported enemy opposition, that the supposed ability of tanks to support us from the home bank was untrue, and should not have been assumed when the staff had not seen the ground, and that the Route 9 bridging dominated the issue as if it were a mere technical exercise.

The CO was in a dilemma. His instinct told him that opposition could be serious, but he could not prove it. Leaving aside PIATS, his only defence against armour at first light would be via the possible crossing upstream, if the river had not risen too far, and he allotted D Company to secure this. He had two uncommitted companies, B and C, to try to gain a foothold in Ronco village, although B was dispersed forward patrolling. The hope was that 4H could get to them via the crossing as early as possible, and at worst that those companies could fall back the short distance to the river banks if pressed. The unknown factor turned out to be the rain's effect on the river.

The account of what followed is taken from Maj Mackay's report, written immediately after the action, and a note by Lt Kershaw of that Company, who was wounded and captured, and therefore was able to confirm what happened to the bulk of B and C Companies.

At 0145 hrs Col Williams went forward and gave orders to Maj Mackay; he told him that Maj Hodges, the new commander of C Company, would be following up, to pass through B and thence Northwards into Ronco village, as soon as possible. By 0230 hrs Maj Mackay had reached Lt M. duV. Allix, who, after an exchange of fire, captured the big house and some prisoners, although others escaped to pin-point our advance.

Lt Kershaw noted: 'We had crossed the river, which I remember was only deep enough to wet one's thighs, and had captured the house, B Coy objective. The telephone rang and Leslie Mackay replied in German much to our surprise, but I didn't think he was able to fool them. Instead of digging in, the whole company remained inside the house. We had captured the odd German when we arrived there, and it was obvious to me we were "sitting ducks" while we remained in the house.'

In fact B was more dispersed, since they occupied another house immediately to the North, and one platoon sent a patrol North into Ronco village and another wading party to sound the river bottom. Maj Mackay decided to base himself on houses where he could retain control in the dark, because the next part of the operation, planned as best they could off the map, would be a series of leap-frogs by C and B up Ronco village to that part covering the bridge. In any case, any trenches in the open clay yard would have been rapidly unusable in the pouring rain.

Soon after 0400 hrs it was certain that no tank crossing could be found in the immediate B Company area, and that, although the houses on the lateral seemed clear, the enemy knew enough about us to engage our positions. The fact that the house had been a German position, probably a platoon HQ, pin-pointed its location, and it was just clear of the village proper. However, C would at least be able to follow up the line of pylons in the drenching night and ensure that their passing through B was co-ordinated.

Lt Kershaw said: 'At about 4 a.m. grenades were lobbed at us, but it was very difficult for us to fire back, as it meant poking our bren guns and rifles through the windows, and thereby becoming easy targets. I heard tanks moving up, and then a spandau opened up, its bullets penetrating the front door of the house, down the passage and out of the back door.'

By 0500 hrs Maj Hodges arrived to join Maj Mackay, and in the next hour platoons of C started to clear houses Northwards on the East side of the lateral. However, they had not gone far when a German counter-attack started to develop at 0600 hrs, in the form of yelling Germans clearing houses down from Ronco village, backed by a tank. Simultaneously as C platoon fell back on the B Company house, that was engaged by an SP using solid shot from the West.

With masonry falling everywhere, and phosphorus smoke and dust limiting the view, it became clear that the position should be evacuated before all became casualties in the storm of high-velocity and machine-gun fire. It was quickly agreed that Maj Hodges should lead both Companies back to the river and try to take up a defensive position behind the embankment; Majs Hodges and Mackay checked all their men out of the house in the dim light. Then Maj Mackay and Capt D. Henderson, the 11 RHA FOO, remained behind to evacuate Rfn Rutherford, a difficult stretcher case. Arriving at the bank about 10 minutes later there was no sign of the Companies, and the sound of firing had died away. Rfn Dien, although at risk as a Jew, volunteered to stay with his comrade, the immobile Rutherford. Thinking the Companies had crossed to the home side, Maj Mackay swam the fast-rising river, now over six feet deep, under fire, and was joined by Capt Henderson, who had shot up a Spandau crew on the bank with his pistol, which attracted further fire. He worked up and down the bank for some time without seeing the Companies themselves, although individual Riflemen were spotted, machine-gunned on the far bank's muddy verge. Maj Mackay reported to the CO at A Company HQ, which had been used as a Battalion Command post all night, hoping that he would find Maj Hodges and the missing Companies there.

What happened to B and C Companies as they fell back to the river was unknown at the time, and is even now difficult to piece together. The enemy had sent forward cut-off Spandau groups, whose fire drove the Companies South; followed by the enemy, the nearest cover they found on the West bank was a narrow wadi, where a stream flowed into the river. Pinned by fire, many wounded or bruised by falling masonry, their weapons clogged with mud and all their ammunition expended, the only hope was to escape after dark, but darkness was many hours distant. In the event the enemy from 278 Division surrounded them at their leisure and marched them off into captivity. Only Lt Allix, although wounded, escaped and managed to hide in an outhouse till flooded out; he then swam to safety over the swollen river and flooded land, being washed hundreds of yards downstream. It was a very fine effort and a wonderful feat of endurance, for which he received a Mention in Despatches.

The account of Lt Kershaw, who had been injured and concussed by flying debris, confirmed what happened to the Companies, and to some of the wounded:

I was standing half way up the stairs at the time, when the tanks started shelling, which must have been at about 4 a.m. I have been told that when we were ordered to go back across the river and leave the house, I jumped out of a window and landed on top of a rifleman, but I know nothing about this myself. That is really all I remember until I found myself lying in a muddy stream about 200 yards from the house. There was no one around to tell me what had happened, except for Sergeant Disbery, who said we had been ordered to withdraw across the river. This was now impossible, as the river was covered by the Germans, and it was getting light. In front of me was a small wood, so I crawled up the stream: I could see tracers going over my head but luckily I was in dead ground. When I reached the wood, I found Simon Towneley (Worsthorne) of 'C' Company, my wife's cousin and later High Sheriff of Lancashire, and Sergeant Major 'Nobby' Clark, also of C Company. We decided to lie doggo in the ditch, and try to recross the river at dusk, but it was then only early morning and there were Germans all over the place. Our only weapon was a ·38 pistol! After about an hour or so we heard a shout, and saw a number of Germans around us, with their rifles pointing straight at us. There was literally nothing we could do about it, and I well remember Sergeant Major Clark saying to me 'Go on Sir, you are the senior officer, you have to go first!' We were all taken prisoner and taken to Forli—eventually I was given something to eat, and taken to a dressing station. I remember noticing a distinct lack of shelling by the British, presumably because it was realised that we might be the target! I was then taken in an ambulance with Nick Warry further behind the German lines. The ambulance kept breaking down with a jolt, due to water being put in the petrol tank by partisans! Unfortunately the jolting only added to poor Nick Warry's discomfort, with a bullet in his lung. We eventually reached the river Po, which we crossed by means of a raft staked in the middle of the river: the flow of the river floated the raft across. I was then taken to an Italian Hospital organised by Germans at Battaglia, near Padua. I shared a room with John Notley DSO, a Major in the DCLI who had been captured at the same time as me. We were to stay together until our eventual transfer to Oflag VII B in February 1945. After about six weeks at Battaglia, where a German doctor of the Ski Division attended me—Dr Benno Stampfll (now a leading doctor in Munich), we were taken in a Red Cross train through the Brenner Pass where we saw slave labour being used to repair it. After a night at Merano, to Dresden where we were taken to a German lazarett at Koenigswarther about twenty miles away. We spent Christmas 1944 there. In February 1945 we were taken by train to Dresden, packed in cattle trucks with refugees fleeing from Breslau to escape the Russians. We spent a night there in the air raid shelter, then the next night in Nurenberg and then to Eichstat Oflag VII B. There were a mass of old friends there from the 60th and other regiments. You have no doubt heard all about the tragic march from Eichstat to Moosburg near Munich in April 1945, when we were machine gunned by Thunderbolts and about thirty to forty prisoners of war were killed including Philip Denison, 60th, taken on Crete, who was at Eton with me.

All this was unclear at the time, and it was thought that the Companies might be contactable from the possible crossing further upstream where D Company was endeavouring to establish a bridgehead. Lt G. L. Paget's platoon was giving covering fire from the home embankment, when this gallant officer, the second of two brothers to be killed with the Regiment, was sniped. Lt N. J. Warry, MC, pressed on down the copse over the river, but eventually was severely wounded at close quarters and was lucky to survive his captivity. Lt I. M. Mollison, MC, who had returned to the Regiment after distinguished work with the Jugoslav partisans, penetrated to the farm beyond, which was his objective, but even his courage could not turn an automatic pistol into adequate defence when counterattacked overwhelmingly. He escaped from the railway truck heading North over the Po Valley, but his boots had been removed; trying to limp Eastwards towards Jugoslavia, he was betrayed by Fascists and rounded up. No tanks could climb the slippery levées nor engage the ground behind them, and, with the primitive wireless communications failing everywhere, the river—rising to spate level under the incessant rain—was forming a barrier, covered by machine-gun and shell-fire, to all who had already crossed. It has always been thought that German demolitions far upstream exploited the spate.

By 1100 hrs 26 October, since the Ronco was no longer crossable, the remnants of D Company fell back to a farm. By the afternoon the river had burst its banks and the flood plain South of the Route 9 had become a sea of water. In the D Company farm only the first floor was out of water, and in the shelling Capt Rhodes, the 2IC, had been wounded.

It seemed too bad to be true, and for three nights a boating party, with Sappers and Bugler Ganderton to blow the Regimental call, stood by to ferry survivors back. The spate, however, continued, and it was later found that all the living had been rounded up during 26 October. The Battalion's total loss across the Ronco amounted to 7 officers, 1 WO, 16 Sergeants and 91 Corporals and Riflemen. The officers were Maj F. W. Hodges, Lt G. C. E. Whiddett, Lt S. Towneley (Worsthorne) and Lt J. R. F. Smalley, RB, who later died of pneumonia, all of C Company, with their CSM Clark. Of B Company, Lt Kershaw was a prisoner, with his platoon sergeant, Sgt Disbery, but other veteran leaders, Sgts Goode and Chable, had been killed; D Company officers captured were Lts Warry and Mollison. Sadly, among the killed and captured were many of those NCOs with longest Desert service due for repatriation in the next few months. The sight of the White Scout cars, normally filled with cheerful faces, being driven empty back to Cesena by section drivers who particularly felt the loss of their friends was a grim one.

The 1st Battalion, however, knew that all its Riflemen had done their best under the Divisional orders, and that the DCLI upstream had suffered a similar fate. The whole episode, including lack of assistance to the Battalion when relieved, had been a warning of what befell units on loan to strange formations. But more important to Riflemen, it seemed a point of honour not to let the

Germans get away with this success, in which weather had played a major part. Under the leadership of Lt Col Williams, and backed by the training expertise of Maj J. Hope (who had been a tower of strength throughout) a very active programme of rebuilding the Battalion took place as soon as it got out of the 4 Division area and into better billets at Santarcangelo on 2 November.

First, Capt Waterfield, as Adjutant, cleared the Corps Reinforcement Unit of all fit Riflemen and the Light Anti-aircraft Gunners, who, with the disbanding of some regiments under the diminishing air threat, became our helpful but untrained reinforcements from now on. This gave us 100 riflemen; and 40 more trickled in later to bring the 1st to the reduced establishment of 725. By running two cadres and spreading experienced men across the Companies, the lost motor platoons were somehow recreated within three weeks. Maj J. M. Christian, who had been attached, now took over A Company from that splendid Desert hand, Maj A. G. L. Goschen. The latter had joined the 1st in 1940 as a Sergeant with the great party of Rhodesians, had been commissioned in the field by General 'Strafer' Gott and had won his two MCs with a very special tactical flair; he was now posted as 2IC to the 11th Battalion in Greece. Maj H. S. Killick, who as mentioned earlier, had won his MC while attached to the Hampshires, took over C Company, and both Maj Christian and he were to hold their commands until after the war ended. Lts W. A. Love, G. E. Anderson and A. A. De C. Cussans took over platoons, but from now on, as platoon commanders, leading from the front, became casualties, there would always be some platoons commanded by Sergeants.

Within 15 Army Group, 5 Army had fought itself to a standstill in the Apennines, but badly needed the town of Bologna as a winter shelter and base before any Spring offensive. 8 Army would therefore have to keep the pressure on up Route 9 to open as many Apennine laterals as possible; its own future base, Ravenna, would have to be taken as well.

Up Route 9 the Ronco Line had finally been outflanked by a crossing well upstream and Forli had been taken. During our cadres, 2 Armoured Brigade had twice ordered help sent to 12L; first the Company mortar sections under Lt Round fired 2000 bombs on a specific task, and then A Company was used to carry out dismounted patrolling North West of Forli. The first leave party of 1 Officer and 10 Riflemen left for England at this time, and, to spend one month at home, would have to be away nearly three.

On 20 November the 1st Battalion moved forward to the area South of Forli, where it picked up A Company and prepared for operations wherever loaned by 2 Armoured Brigade, who were themselves under 46 Division. Crossing river lines was inevitably involved, and, after the recent experiences, the IO was set to work with orders of battle and stereo pairs of air photographs to get a better feel of things than seemed likely to be gleaned from above. 26 Panzer Division's presence called for the assurance that tanks would be with us across any future obstacle, for the steep embankments never allowed anti-tank gun rafting. Long study of the probable axis road and the River Marzeno, beyond the Cosina canal where fighting was currently in progress, showed a glimmer of hope. There were two small lateral roads parallel with the Marzeno, and a faint snake of track winding down to the river from farms opposite each other revealed a possible ford; a shadow and some white immediately upstream of the ford indicated a

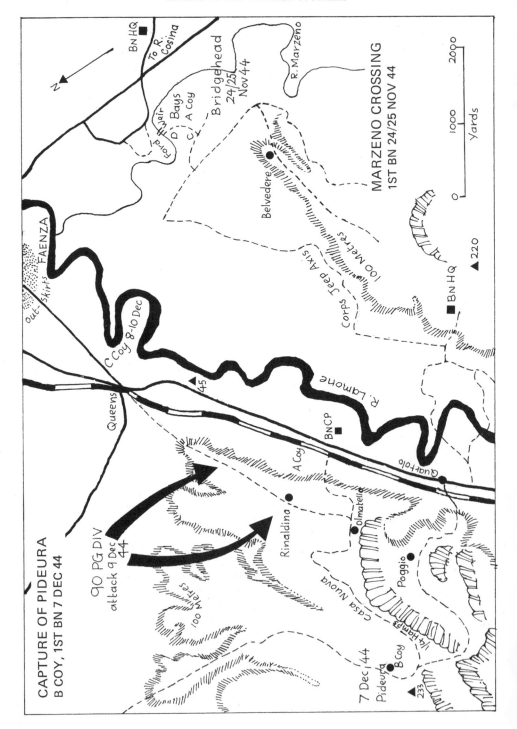

MARZENO CROSSING
1ST BN 24/25 NOV 44

CAPTURE OF PIDEURA
B COY, 1ST BN 7 DEC 44

probable weir—all something to bear in mind when fixing future objectives. This crossing, ignored by Division, was later seized by the 1st Battalion and became the Corps axis for the operations which took Faenza.

South West of Forli, where the Cosina canal forms a salient, 46 Division had used some good weather to put down tactical air strikes and artillery fire, which turned the bare spur into a brown wilderness with few intact buildings. Moving to the area of Villagrappa just short of this, the 1st found that vehicle movement forward drew harassing shell and SA fire from the Northern salient flank close by. Early in the evening of 22 November 2/5 Leicesters stalked and captured the canal bridge at Ponticello intact, and were reinforced in the village by 10H tanks. The 1st Battalion was ordered to support the Leicesters on this axis, so B Company worked forward on foot and made contact with the bridgehead during the night, moving over the canal next morning. D Company, who followed them, lost a carrier and half-track on mines. When, sure enough, 26 Panzer attacked the bridgehead at 1030 hrs on 23 November, they were seen off, losing two Mk IV tanks to our armour, one tank being captured intact. During that evening A and C Companies filtered forward on foot to just South of the bridge and the Battalion O Group snatched a little sleep in the filthy straw at Battalion HQ near by. A Company meanwhile patrolled forward up the morrow's axis with Sappers until German voices were heard.

128, the Hampshire Brigade on our right, set off in a swift advance for Faenza at dawn on 24 November; by 1100 hrs they arrived on Route 9 to find, inevitably, all the Lamone bridges blown in their sector. The 1st Battalion's task, with The Bays, was to act as left-flank protection, clearing a minor road under the foothills, leading to the Marzeno, a Lamone tributary, and to cross if possible. Starting at 0630 hrs, Maj Killick's C Company—dismounted, since all transport had initially to be held back because of bridge and hard-standing difficulties—advanced at an increasingly rapid pace as it became clear that 26 Panzer had pulled out. Only sniping and the odd long-range mortar and SP round were met. To their relief they found the hoped-for ford, detected in the air photograph, just passable to tanks, and by 1300 hrs C Company complete was firm in farms on the other side with two Bays troops. Lt Way's platoon engaged Germans starting to dig in on a lateral road parallel with the river at 1400 hrs. The CO and D Company joined them as the surprised enemy started to react with MGs and shelling. A Company joined shortly afterwards with more tanks, but carriers found the ford too difficult; the weir top could be used, however. SPs were active, and in another thwarted counter-attack prisoners were taken; their identification was of interest, for they were from the German Corps' last uncommitted reserve in this area and had been rushed down Route 9; the 1st Battalion's unexpectedly brisk crossing had caught them before they could reach the river or dig in. 128 Brigade now gladly took over what had been the subsidiary thrust, and companies of 5 and then 2 Hampshires passed into the bridgehead; this was shallow, but the Ronco experience had taught us—when we were allowed to run our own battle—to have a tight, mutually supporting defence, well backed by armour, by this time two Squadrons of Bays, and 11 RHA OPs.

The enemy was now reacting furiously to the reverse, and, knowing that vehicles could only get off the tracks into farm-yards, if they were not to become bogged, was raining down Nebelwerfer salvoes. At Battalion HQ the 2IC's Jeep and a motor-cycle were hit, but more importantly the RAP in a farm across the road was struck by two AP rounds from an SP after dark. Our new and excellent Padre, P. Richards, lost a foot, as did a civilian, the Provost Sergeant was wounded and others battered by masonry; in the absence of Capt Green, the MO, who had established himself in the bridgehead, Cpl Walker took control excellently until the Bays' MO arrived. Throughout that Autumn and Winter CSM Proberts, a pre-war bugler, carried out an RSM's field duties at Battalion HQ, since RSM Nichols had been repatriated from Arezzo after nine years overseas, including three as RSM.

Many of the Riflemen were dripping wet in the bridgehead, having waded the river, but the Battalion was not relieved by 46 Division. An ARK tank bridge was precariously in use at the ford and a Bailey bridge by 46 Division was planned upstream. Operations on 25 November were for part of the Battalion to act as flank guard in the foothills between the Marzeno and Lamone rivers, until the Poles linked with 46 Division from the hills above. B Company with two troops of Bays were to clear a parallel track. With great difficulty on a poor track and against enemy rearguards, B Company pressed on in the mist to Belvedere, where a troop leader was killed and Lt J. P. G. Wathen wounded by a shell; contact with Poles on the high Southern flank was however made. Lt Round with C Company carriers and a troop was thwarted by demolitions on another track, and a potential C Company operation was pinched out. Even tanks could not leave the tracks, and the few enemy SPs had imposed considerable delay.

That evening permission was given to withdraw, as 128 Brigade, aided by Polish pressure in the hills to the South, was fanning out for a foot advance by night towards the Lamone. After great Battalion efforts all companies were got under cover from the rain in crowded billets in Forli; only the carriers had failed to get over the ARK before the rising water closed the crossing and had to be replenished later, until a Bailey bridge was built. Two killed and 29 wounded were the total casualties for the operation, and it was with a feeling of pride that the Battalion viewed the achievement. Within one month after its Ronco losses it had reformed, retrained and partially re-equipped, and had successfully repeated a similar river crossing with a drive which was of great use to 8 Army's next operations.

Faenza could only be taken by pushing on West over the wider Lamone and seizing the high ground, whose peak was at the little hamlet of Pideura. Thence it should be possible to extend successively North East down the great ridge and threaten the Faenza garrison with being cut off, getting them to withdraw over the River Senio. The ridge running from Pideura was very steep on our side, and the greasy clay shoulders had very few tracks up to link the primitive hamlets. The lateral road below and parallel to the river on the West bank was metalled, but any bridgehead would be very shallow, and untenable if the ridge's crest was occupied by the enemy. There was only one narrow road from the Marzeno crossing, and to prevent its disappearance metal tracking and bricks from ruined houses had to be laid throughout; it was one-way, and 46 Division ran a divisional Jeep train, with an eventual turn-round time only just within the 24 hours, between the single Bailey bridge over each river. Whenever it was least wanted, heavy rain fell, and the raw cold was numbing; food consisted of any tins which could be moved forward, usually eaten cold, and the few shell-pocked farms were at a premium to provide shelter from the mud.

From 28 November, without a chance to carry out proper maintenance, B Company was at the usual short notice to reinforce the Hampshires of 128 Brigade. Thus began a bad period when 46 Division flung our companies about, despite their uncomprehended small assault strength, to be used as Brigades thought fit. Our Armoured Brigade did nothing to protect us, and throughout November and December 1944 only the combined efforts of Lt Col Williams and Maj J. Hope prevented the 1st Battalion being written off piecemeal. In fairness to 46 Division, it had suffered over 4000 casualties since August, mostly in its Infantry, and every expedient was used to maintain the offensive, demanded of a dwindling 8 Army.

In extracts from a letter to HQ2 Armoured Brigade, dated 7 December 44 during this final action under 46 Division, the CO made certain points forcibly. He summarized Battalion soldier wastage as:

	WOs	C/Sgts	Sgts	Cpls	Rfn
Python 1944	4	–	9	13	71
Battle casualties 1944	2	–	32	29	255
Python Dec 44–May 45	2	3	6	10	60

To a Rifleman, knowing that Italy was receiving no external reinforcements, these figures speak for themselves. He went on to say that the Battalion had only been reformed after the Ronco by spreading the remaining cadre as best he could. The Gunner reinforcements, however, had no knowledge of the motor role nor any proper infantry training.

He ended:

Summary of Effect of Wastage

Unless these two conditions are fulfilled for a time, i.e.
(1) Light casualties.
(2) Working more or less as a Motor Bn, the experience, knowledge and traditions of Motor Bn work which the 1st 60th has won in five hard years will fade away in a few months.

Effect of dismounted action:

A Motor Bn is a balanced force of supporting weapons, carrier borne weapons, motor infantry tactically mounted in hard-skinned vehicles, communications and administration. The number of any branch alone is small but the strength of the whole is very great. Its strength lies in its speed, great radius of action and fire-power; its weakness in its small numbers and mass of equipment if it is brought to battle confined in too small an area. A further weakness is the long time and training it takes to make a first class Rifleman.

It is, therefore, most undesirable and wasteful to overwork any one part of the Battalion. Motor Platoons divorced and pooled as infantry are small, weak, soon expended and hard to replace. If they are used as scratch adjuncts to Infantry Brigades their casualties are liable, or even likely, to be high. That applies particularly when, as in this Battalion at the moment, so many of the men are still only semi-trained.

Role of Motor Bn:

To the best of my knowledge and belief it is the firm intention of Higher Authority to preserve this Battalion as a Motor Bn.

In my opinion it is well organised and equipped for its primary role. Given reasonable opportunities it will be trained to the pitch required by that role, in spite of Python losses, and it will be fully capable of doing much useful work in the meantime.

If there is no 'suitable' job to be done this Battalion is normally only too willing to tackle 'unsuitable' ones. I must, however, report that in our present rather weak state we cannot afford to have men frittered away. Furthermore, the policy of completely dismounting motor Pls and using them as extra infantry will undoubtedly cause casualties, and will confine the casualties to what is already the most hardly hit part of the Battalion.

Sooner or later this policy will undoubtedly involve the whole or part of the Battalion in the main infantry battle. It is already in the edges of it.

I submit that it is fairly short-sighted to cripple the Motor Bn that will be vital in March in order to put 180 extra untrained infantry on the ground in December.

That this letter needed writing to an Armoured Brigade HQ after so many years of motor-battalion work was regrettable, but it had its effect in other quarters and Lt Col Williams's efforts just managed to preserve his Battalion from destruction through thoughtless attrition.

Meanwhile, after much rain and extensive patrolling to find bridge and crossing sites, 128 Brigade assaulted over the Lamone on the night of 3 December. B Company, with a platoon of D Company, had gone forward with the CO that afternoon on foot. When the Hampshires assaulted successfully over the Lamone and seized a shallow bridgehead on the East face of the ridge, B Company took over left-flank protection in a quiet sector facing South. On 5 December, as the Hampshires extended the bridgehead West up the terrible hillsides, our Company was withdrawn into reserve and back under Battalion command. 1/4 Hampshires had successively taken Casa Poggio and, with tank support, the higher Casa Nova. However, the remnants of a company, after battling their way exhausted into Pideura, were pushed out by a counter-attack on the evening of 6 December. On that day, back in Forli, the remainder of our 1st Battalion was warned to move on foot over the two rivers into the bridgehead, taking only 12 vehicles. It was pouring with rain, and exposure to the raw cold out of buildings would soon cause casualties; B Company in reserve were therefore asked to secure as many farms in the valley as they could, and dispersed their platoons to do this. Suddenly Maj Mackay, down in the valley, was taken from under Battalion command to that of 1/4 Hampshires, and received the orders to retake Pideura. There followed the reassembling of the platoons and a desperate night climb up unreconnoitred spurs to the main ridge at Casa Nova.

Maj Mackay received a good briefing at the 1/4 Hampshire HQ, for their exhausted men had at least seen Pideura in daylight before being ejected from it. The key seemed to be a large house on the crest, out of which the Germans had driven them.

Despite the climb he had just made, Lt Love took out a small reconnaissance patrol, which found the best Infantry route to the objective, across a saddle on the right. The 9L tanks would only be able to use the difficult track on the exposed left or Westerly flank, and could only therefore try to join B Company in daylight.

An FOO from B Battery 11 RHA was with Maj Mackay, and the very close liaison of the last year proved invaluable; although it cut across Gunner channels, Maj—now Sir John—Charles insisted on supporting B Company throughout the day's fighting, and made an invaluable contribution.

Thanks to Lt Love's excellent patrol, B Company worked up unseen across the saddle in the dark, and at first light, on 7 December, as accurate RHA concentrations came down and covered by a perfect two-inch mortar smoke-screen of their own, the Riflemen swept into the objective with fixed swords. The German garrison of the house was surprised and captured; throughout the day Maj Mackay evacuated prisoners rapidly under minimal escort into the saddle and back to the Hampshires as soon as taken.

The sixty Riflemen thereafter found themselves pinned inside the house, which appeared to share a very thick party wall with its neighbour; at any rate the HQ of the Germans in the hamlet was next door, although they could not be heard talking. Attempts to assault it had to round an outside wall, forcing them into cross-fire from the enemy house and some outhouses on the enemy's reverse slope.

Sgts George and Woolnough dashed round to try to assault the doorway, but the latter was badly wounded and the former captured. Surprisingly, German stretcher-bearers brought back Sgt Woolnough a little later under a Red Cross flag.

It was clear that he would die without treatment, and Capt Green, our MO, typically braved the fire to come forward and evacuate him; approaching under an improvised Red Cross flag, he urbanely made his professional call, finding to his concern that he had come to the German door, and only backed away from a huge Spandau gunner with difficulty. Thanks to his rapid evacuation Sgt Woolnough recovered, and meanwhile Sgt George was unobtrusively per-suading some of his captors that further resistance was useless. In the next counter-attack he sheltered himself among the advancing Germans, dodging their officer (who was trying to shoot him), and managed to bring in the leading 14 as deserters; he was awarded the MM for his work.

The battle raged till noon at the closest quarters, four counter-attacks being beaten off from the ground floor; a cellar was used for casualties, but the top floor had a damaged staircase and was exposed to SP fire and shelling from the enemy reverse slope. The enemy had the benefit of a road up to the crest on their side.

The 9L tank troop had lost two tanks to bazookas on the exposed Western track, but about noon, on his own initiative and against orders, Lt O. Thwaites fought his tank up to the crest; thinking it would help in the house fighting, he had brought explosive up, but it proved somewhat of an embarrassment. However, his arrival freed the beleagured B Company from further attack, since he engaged the neighbouring house and the troublesome outbuildings with solid shot. His gallantry was beyond praise, and the Company, Battery, and Lancer cooperation made all the training in Algeria worthwhile, the 11 RHA Forward Observation officer providing the only effective communications.

45 prisoners were taken during the day, and about 20 enemy killed or

wounded; the enemy were from more than one battalion of 305 Division, last encountered by B Company on the peak of Monte Lignano. As that mountain had been to Arezzo, so was Pideura to Faenza. The observation gained was critical to our artillery, when, within days, the great 90 Light Division attack had to be broken up in the re-entrants to the North East. 60 Riflemen, after a terrible night climb, had seized and held the key peak and inflicted more casualties than their own strength. Maj Mackay was later awarded the MC for his leadership in this isolated company action, which was one of the most notable feats of endurance and determination of the 1st's Italian operations. No awards were sponsored by 46 Division, however, who at the time were less than generous about anything we did. That night 25 Indian Brigade relieved 128 Brigade, and B Company came down from the ridge.

On the same day the rest of the Battalion moved from Forli over the Marzeno on foot with 25 vehicles. C Company unfortunately lost L/Sgt Whent and two carriers to Nebelwerfers, and, an embargo being placed on further carrier movement on the one road, some mules were supplied. B Company finally rejoined the Battalion at dawn on 8 December, just as the CO and IO moved West over the Lamone to set up a command post, followed by A and C Companies motor platoons on foot. Supply West of the river was from compo ration and ammunition dumps, built up by Jeep and mule; to the East the Battalion had used its initiative to develop an illegal and tenuous supply line through the Polish area.

At 0630 hrs on 9 December extremely heavy and accurate artillery concentrations were put down on every farm in the bridgehead. This heralded a major counter-attack by 90 PG Division, aimed at thrusting up on to the ridge and thus dominating the lowlands below; the shallow bridgehead, dependent on a single bridge and one approach road, could not long have held out under direct tank fire.

Thanks to great gallantry by 138 Brigade and the continuous close support of our artillery, the enemy were beaten back from the ridge; indeed, an enemy order was later captured criticizing their infantry/tank co-operation, not in the old 90 Light style. A Company later moved up to give depth to the KOYLI position; C Company had already on 8 December moved North East to the outskirts of Faenza to hold the right flank of the Queen's Brigade, on loan from 56 Division, and 10 Platoon suffered casualties in a tank duel at close quarters. B Company were moved back as a last reserve into the bridgehead. Our only vehicle in the bridgehead was the CO's Dingo, and the IO had to build up the Company's ammunition and rations with it from mule-supplied dumps. Even Commander 8 Army had to walk back between the rivers as the Divisional Jeep train crawled forward, and hours of route maintenance were put in. The presence of Maj J. Charles (B Battery 11 RHA) at the Battalion command post was as always reassuring.

Gradually the New Zealand Division relieved the medley of Brigades that was left to 46 Division. On the night of 10 December C Company started to march back; the others followed on 11 December, marching until they could meet vehicles East of the Marzeno, and by that night all were back in their old Forli billets. It was not entirely peaceful even there, for a Junkers 88 bombed the workshop and a 170-mm gun shelled the town at night down Route 9, hitting two of our vehicles. For those who liked it, the New Zealanders had discovered a vermouth factory near Route 9, and hospitably insisted on all passers-by, water trucks and all, filling up. Luckily, the 1st Battalion was not on the road at the time, for the situation rapidly sobered up when General McCreery happened to pass, and the biggest concentration of 'Red Caps' ever seen rapidly secured the area.

This was our last service under 46 Division, who left for Greece, and almost the last under the wartime 2 Armoured Brigade, whose DAA & QMG, Maj H. A. Hope, MC, late of the Battalion, had been our one contact with motor-battalion or indeed infantry experience. Faenza did not fall until 16 December, and the 8 Army's Route 9 offensive had to be halted on the Senio, if any preparations were to be made for the Spring offensive. On Route 16 North from Rimini, the Canadians had seized Ravenna on 4 December, establishing a bridgehead over the lower Lamone at Mezzano. The 1st now received a welcome warning order to pass under its old summer friends, 9 Armoured Brigade. Col Stopford-Sackville was commanding in the Brigadier's absence, and Maj R. Maudslay, 60th, later to be Treasurer to the Royal Household as Sir Rennie Maudslay, KCVO, MBE, was the most helpful Brigade Major.

The 1st had sustained casualties enough, but before they had entered Italy, and while they were there, brother officers of the 60th were killed in action away from the Regiment.

Lt J. M. A. Ridley was killed while escaping through the enemy lines after excellent service with the 2nd. A distinguished group of young Riflemen, for whom no place could be found in the 1st or 11th Battalions at the time, were attached to the Royal Fusiliers. Capts R. F. Perceval Maxwell and D. W. Holliday, and Lts R. L. Bowring and G. C. E. Cumming, were all killed in Italy, the latter two at Anzio. All had made great reputations for bravery, skill and care of their men, but a special mention must be made of Lt Cumming, one of our American officers, to whom exceptional tributes were paid by his soldiers.

Others killed in the maelstrom of Anzio were Lt. D. W. M. Carus-Wilson with the Oxfordshire and Buckinghamshire Light Infantry and Lt C. W. Newton with the Green Howards, while Lt. H. S. Shillidy had served with the Middlesex from Sicily to the Apennines before his sad death.

As the 1st Battalion moved to the Adriatic coast, it must be remembered that British teams, were active on the far side, aiding Tito's partisans. A particularly sad loss was that of Capt J. Lees in March 45, killed in destroying the local Gestapo HQ on an island. Joining the 60th just before the war, he served with the 2nd throughout the Desert, being wounded and mentioned in despatches. He then joined the Special Boat Service, and had been on many operations in the Aegean and Adriatic before falling at the head of his raiders.

CHAPTER VI

THE WINTER LINE NEAR RAVENNA, ITALY, TO VICTORY IN AUSTRIA

(Maps: pages 108, 140, 152, 156 and 166)

To its great relief the 1st Battalion moved on 16 December 1944 Eastwards away from the barren hills and spate rivers of Route 9. Up Route 16 the ground was even more waterlogged, but the swift capture of many farms and buildings had left them hardly damaged; there would be no hills here to overlook positions, and armoured friends of the Sackforce period at Arezzo would understand how to use our capabilities. A much-needed rest was in store in the neat, but cold, seaside villas of Cervia, reminiscent in its pines of a Bournemouth suburb. Lt D. E. Rae, the Signals Officer, had been also acting as Adjutant since November, when Capt Waterfield was evacuated with jaundice. After a brief return the latter suffered a relapse, and Lt G. H. Mills, the IO, carried out both duties until being confirmed as Adjutant in March 45. In view of this the MTO, Lt A. Round, was brought in as watch-keeper at Battalion HQ.

29 Riflemen were warned for return home under Python after Christmas, but only 10 reinforcements were forthcoming from 8 Army. The CO decided to reorganize to three motor companies, A, B and C, less their mortar sections. D Company would now have one MMG platoon, one Anti-tank platoon (six-pounder), one mortar and WASP flamethrower platoon and one sniper/PIAT platoon. Under a new Padre, the Reverend J. Head, Christmas preparations were made; celebration was wisely to be on 24 December as the 1st were to relieve 12L in the line on Boxing Day. News of a limited offensive by the Germans against 5 Army trickled through, but this paled against the von Runstedt offensive in the Ardennes, and in the Apennines the enemy was rapidly pushed back. Companies of widgeon battling through snow flurries along the wave-tops out to sea warned that in the meadows and marshes towards Lake Comacchio the winter was likely to be hard. They did not know it at the time, but the 1st Battalion was due to spend 62 days in the line without relief.

To relieve Infantry divisions being pulled out of the line for re-equipment, reinforcement and retraining before the Spring offensive, 9 Armoured Brigade was holding a very wide front North of Ravenna. Inland from a strip of sand and pines along the coast towards Comacchio there was an area of inundation. Popski's Private Army, 27L, 7H and an RAF Regiment Squadron, backed by a Squadron of 4H, held that area. The 1st Battalion was to relieve 12L, largely dismounted, in the key area astride Route 16 at Mezzano; this formed a shallow bridgehead when the Lamone, canalized between high banks, turned North for a mile and then continued North East. The main enemy base opposite was in Alfonsine, but 114 Jäger Division were forward of the next small canal, Fosso Vetro, over which a railway bridge still stood intact. The whole area was completely flat, but unless you laid down visibility was limited by the rows of mulberry and willow trees along shallow ditches. Anything but the shallowest scrape filled with water, and the damp cold penetrated to the bone; every reason pointed to a defence based on houses. Once the Germans had been pushed North into the water meadows by the Canadians they had to live in the canal banks, and, passing the area next Spring, it was interesting to see how they had revetted and lined their dug-outs, using whole cupboards where possible. To begin with Mezzano still had civilians in it, but later, in February 45, after the demolition cables on the Bailey bridge had twice been cut at night—sapper firing parties varied from Canadians to Sikhs, who discussed demolition orders in primitive Italian—the small population North of the Lamone was evacuated. In all such contacts Lt Pallavicini, the new Italian LO, and his charming successor, Lt Giuseppe Tecchio, who remained with us until 1946, were a great help.

On 26 December 1944 the 1st relieved 12L in the line, with Battalion HQ in their RHQ South of the river. C Company were on the left towards the North end of the village and Lt Way confirmed with a recce patrol on the first night that the rail bridge was intact and firmly covered. A Company were in farms along a lateral track between there and the river bank on the right. D (Support) had anti-tank guns out, but the mortars and HQ concentrated in the village. B Company were finishing their training South of Ravenna, having had the heaviest operations round Faenza. A feature of the Ravenna area were the active partisans (strongly against Fascist absentee landlords), a 15-strong detachment of whom were allotted to each Company. When, on 28 December, B Company came up into the line to take over the area on the left of the village from the Canadians, we were holding 6000 yards of front with no Battalion reserve; partisans had to be used as sentries to give the Riflemen, patrolling day and night, some rest. The lack of sleep during the vigil of the long night became critical.

By a general effort the new static drills came to be established. Platoons learnt to get in shell and mortar reports rapidly, on which 24 Field and later 142 Field, the Devon Yeomanry, based their counter-bombardment. Artillery concentrations on enemy patrol targets were moved around to follow reported enemy movement, rather than give-away DFs fired blindly. Wireless was opened automatically under shelling, as lines were always cut. A pattern of a daily afternoon conference for Company Commanders and the Battery Commander evolved, to give them some morning rest and to allow the IO to analyse the previous night's work for the CO. Air photographs were in general use to give the fine detail needed in country where cover, particularly under a bright moon or the artificial moonlight of searchlights, was scarce.

During the first week the Jäger probed our positions and tended to get away with it, as standing patrols fired too early. Two troops of 4H were in support for counter-attack purposes, but our position was a thin screen only just linked by fire. When Commander 5 Canadian Armoured Brigade came to plan his attack through us he was very grateful for all the intelligence the 1st Battalion was building up about enemy positions and routines. Reconnaissance patrols had crept up to watch German ration parties, with ox or horse vehicles, being greeted by enemy forward troops, and subsequently to engage them with mortars. But the CO forcibly warned our Brigade Commander that any enemy attack by night

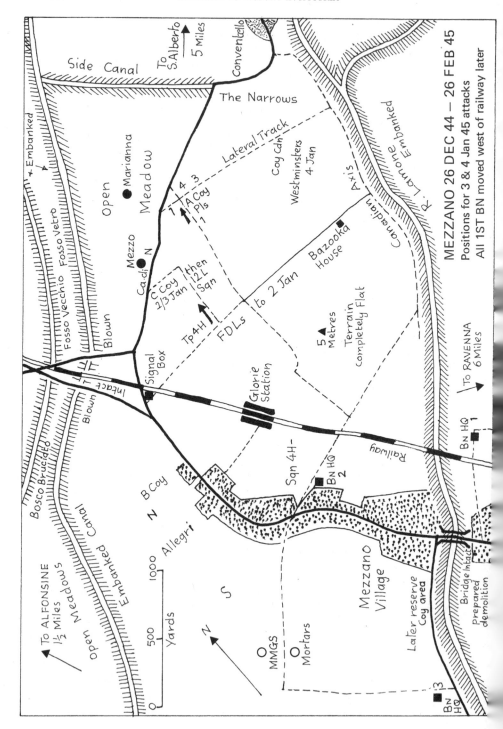

MEZZANO 26 DEC 44 – 26 FEB 45

Positions for 3 & 4 Jan 45 attacks

All 1ST BN moved west of railway later

could pass between our positions, that we had no reserve left and no infantry in the main part of the village. The enemy could be at Mezzano bridge within an hour, and this would of course cut off the Canadians after they had passed through. Squadrons of 12L and 4H were promised, and the Army Commander was informed.

A feature of this right flank of 8 Army was that posts on both sides were wide apart, and so there was considerable agent, evader and deserter traffic. One night a very gallant old partisan agent set off Northwards, only to crawl back much later having lost a foot on a mine; interesting deserters came through, from whom the enemy's routine was built up.

On New Year's Eve the Jäger took advantage of the very isolated platoon positions we had inherited. Under a cover of festively drunken singing, they put forward a strong fighting patrol on the A Company front. The flank of this was detected at midnight, but after standing to until 0215 hrs the companies reverted to doubled sentries. Half an hour later the enemy patrol fired three bazookas at the flank of 2 Platoon's farmhouse; by bad luck the volley struck the corner and collapsed the house on the occupants. Luckily, Cpl Quill was in a post outside, and, although the wire was partially cut, kept the patrol from rushing the ruin and capturing the dazed survivors. He was eventually reduced to firing his Bren single shot using loose ammunition, but bloody wire cutters in the gap and the body of a Jäger Corporal showed the effect of his cool defence, for which he was awarded the DCM. 1 Platoon's advance drove the patrol off, but not before they had captured Cpl Brown and a Partisan in a listening post; it was afterwards learnt that Brown in his black buttons was asked 'Ah, the King's Royal Rifles. How is Sandy Goschen?' by a Jäger officer, presumably a Carinthian skiing or stalking acquaintance of pre-war days. The fate of a captured Partisan was likely to be grimmer once in Fascist hands, and the assistance of the Northern Italians to our cause must be recognized. Lt M. R. Ricketts and six others were wounded in this action, to which the CO gave very serious thought. He rapidly worked out a system—which was never later beaten—using our only assets, the completely flat land and our firepower and communications. The area of every house held was treated as a killing zone, with listening posts kept well forward of it. Every platoon post had the bearings for fixed lines of any other post in range, and the very large number of Brens, Vickers and Brownings on their tripods were permanently laid on these. Within a farm positions were sandbagged round and in the building, and kept as low as possible, with ground-floor ceilings reinforced. On the approach of the enemy the platoon, under cover, called for fire by wireless; all available guns, mortars and MMGs fired at the threatened house, and another platoon in depth swept the area on foot for dazed or wounded enemy as the fire lifted. Round the MMG Platoon cowshed on the extreme left, Lt T. E. St Aubyn put up Somerfeld tracking to defeat bazookas. Like Lt C. B. H. Ryrie, MC, with the mortar platoon in an adjacent barn, his massed weapons could fire enfilade right across the front, since they were protected by a vast open meadow over the canal to the North, which both sides avoided. Strangely—perhaps because they were screened from enemy detection by the unoccupied canal bank to the North—they were never properly located and accurately engaged.

1 January 1945 continued to be inauspicious. The Battalion had not been warned of a programme of air strikes in preparation for the Canadian attack. It

was therefore somewhat of a surprise to find US Thunderbolt aircraft attacking our Bailey bridge at Mezzano in mistake for the Alfonsine bridge. Some Canadians and civilians were killed by a bomb on a house 20 yards beyond the bridge, which was undamaged, and companies got yellow smoke ready rapidly to mark the front line.

8 Army was poised to exploit the frozen meadows and the last chance of using the Canadians, before that Corps too was moved round to reinforce the Canadian Army in North West Europe. In anticipation of the Spring offensive the ground between the rivers Lamone and Senio was to be cleared with tanks and Kangaroos near Faenza. In the East, Mezzano bridgehead was to be used for a drive North East between the Lamone and the canal, Fosso Vetro; the drive was aimed at clearance as far as San Alberto and the mouth of the Reno, where it flowed into Lake Comacchio. These drives would provide the jumping-off places for the two Corps thrusts in April; the 1st, as it turned out, would be involved North of Alfonsine in the Argenta Gap break-out.

The first phase of the Canadian operation was an infantry attack on the Conventello hamlet held by the Jäger opposite our right Company, A. Initially the only axis was a cart-track hugging the bottom of the high Lamone embankment on the enemy side, until it joined the road running North East for San Alberto. The road through Mezzano to Alfonsine branched off in this direction across our front, but, since this was a bare 500 yards from the strongly held Fosso Vetro canal it was unusable in our sector; there were two groups of buildings astride this lateral road, known collectively as Casa di Mezzo, of which the one on the North side commanded all the meadows South of the canal. It would enfilade the Canadian advance, and so must be taken before their attack by C Company; thereafter it was the key to holding off any German attempt to attack the Canadians' flank and rear, as they rolled away across the enemy's front.

During the afternoon of 1 January very accurate air strikes were put down by Desert Air Force Spitfires on Jäger positions located by our patrols, and civilians reported nine casualties in one farm alone; nevertheless a patrol still tried to raid our forward positions ineffectually. While A Company sent forward strong patrols to secure the Canadian start-line on the right, C Company crossed their start-line at 0500 hrs 2 January after 10 minutes' concentrations on selected targets. Despite one gun firing short and the fuse on the pole charge becoming disconnected, Lt P. D. L. Way and his platoon broke their way into their Casa di Mezzo South objective, and covered 2/Lt F. E. Carr-Gomm's men into Casa North, from which a section of Germans had bolted after firing briefly. With Casa di Mezzo, where two 4H tanks had joined C, secure on their left, Canadian Infantry Brigade captured the village of Conventello, where the Lamone swung North East at its closest point to the Fosso Vetro canal. When, after air strikes on that canal's banks, the Canadian armour turned the Conventello corner they were leaving behind them, as warned by Lt Col Williams, an axis of a muddy cart track overlooked by the Lamone bank and just a mile from the enemy canal positions, where the railway bridge was still intact. Once the Canadian infantry moved off there would be only the 1st Battalion, holding a 6000-yard front, and it was known that 16 SS Reichsführer Division had just taken over Alfonsine. The Canadian GOC, in view of the risk, ordered the Mezzano bridge prepared as a tactical demolition, to be blown on his orders. So serious was the ammunition state in Italy that the Battalion's last 180 rounds of three-inch mortar were being sent up that afternoon, and the Mark VIIIZ state for the Vickers was equally bad; the artillery regiments were also severely limited.

After sapper mine casualties as they cleared the cart tracks, and the wounding of Cpl Jeanneret in the same way, the battle was heard moving off to the North East. The local German reaction had been heavy shelling on B Company in Mezzano, which had killed Rfn Brench. However, at 0600 hrs on 3 January heavy enemy concentrations were laid successively South West down the lateral road to Casa di Mezzo. C Company fired their DF on the canal bank, but as first light came Lt Way and 2/Lt Carr-Gomm saw figures approaching the farm-yards at Casa di Mezzo from the canal and the huge meadow with its lone farm, Marianna, to the North East. After a brisk exchange in which L/Cpl Izzard killed a bazooka party, 15 survivors were captured and many more killed by small arms, mortars and guns; the lines of infantry behind were driven by C Company fire, and that of the Canadian Perth Regiment on the right, back to the Marianna farm or over the canal bank. C Company alertness and the delay of the attack into daylight cost the Assault Machine Gun Battalion Kesselring, an élite unit, dear. Its two left-hand companies were caught in the isolated farm, which was reduced to rubble by our MIOs, while 4H tanks, which had joined C Company, silenced machine-guns and infantry, moving on the canal. The Canadians refused diversion of air effort on to the canal, but at last 400 rounds of mortar were released to the 1st. As the Perths and other infantry moved off the Westminster Regiment, a Canadian motor battalion, moved into Conventello, and providentially their MMGs were parked on their tripods in a farm-yard under the Lamone bank.

Early that night A Squadron 12L came under command and relieved Lt Way's platoons of C Company in Casa di Mezzo, allowing them to pull into reserve behind A Company; the latter had in turn relieved the Perths on the lateral track East and South East of Casa di Mezzo. Sadly one 12L officer lost a foot and another and a Sergeant were wounded on Schu mines, undetectable wooden horrors which began to become active as the ground thawed somewhat. General McCreery, 8 Army, called at Battalion HQ that afternoon, in view of the importance of Canadian success to his future operations.

A troop of MIOs of 310 Anti-tank Battery (SP) RA was placed in support of A Company at that HQ. A Squadron 4H was also in support of the 1st Battalion, and was in depth in Mezzano behind B Company, owing to hard standing and night-protection problems. One of its troops was assigned to a counter-attack role in support of 12L, and was located to the East of the village in a farm, from which a track led direct to Casa di Mezzo. Its excellent commander, Lt Jackson, reconnoitred the track up on foot to the Lancers, and was to play a critical role in the next few hours.

At 0200 hrs on 4 January a B Company listening post ominously reported working parties on the railway bridge over the canal, and at 0415 hrs very heavy artillery concentrations were brought down North East of Casa di Mezzo, presumably to isolate us from the Canadians, since the road North East at that point passed through a very narrow gap between the Lamone and a side canal from the Fosso Vetro. The SS made the fatal error (despite having seen the Kesselring machine-gunners fail in daylight) of not following up their artillery fire. Since the operation order for their attack was captured later that day and translated by the IO, their plan became clear in retrospect. It was a brigade attack by Brigade Group Maier, with right 1st Battalion 35 PG (SS), centre 16 Panzer SS Recce Battalion and left rear 26 Panzer Recce Battalion, all élite troops, excellently equipped; 114 Jäger Recce Battalion attacked the Canadians further North East. Their aim was to cut off the Canadians, as Lt Col Williams had forecast, with as a first objective the lateral road to Conventello, and thereafter to cut the Canadian axis by reaching the Lamone. The start-time in the order was given as 0300 hrs, and the cause of the infantry's delay (other than that they had been left miles back in reserve) is not known; if they had started the battle that early and passed some armour over the railway bridge it would have been hard to stop them. 16 SS Recce attacked with three companies up in arrowhead formation, using the thin vine row cover between Casa di Mezzo and the road from the railway bridge towards Mezzano; it must be assumed that the 35 PG SS Battalion crowded initially into this area also, as their right flank never extended into Mezzano. At all events, when the attack came it took the form of human waves, which started to take cover in every vine row, hedge or ditch as flares went up and our fire went down. Their advance was first heard by listening patrols at 0515 hrs, and with inexorable precision the well-planned DFs were fired, and dropped 100 yards by 100 yards to keep pace with reported enemy progress. In the buildings astride the road at Casa di Mezzo was A Squadron 12L, whose dismounted strength of 40 was that of a weak half-company. Such a garrison, jokingly known to the Battalion as 'F Company' for fear of confusion with our A, could not long have withstood the weight of a brigade attack of that nature, if the conscience of a fellow-cavalryman had not come to their aid. Entirely on his own initiative, Lt Jackson led his troop of Shermans up the track in the darkness, and, losing one tank to a bazooka as they turned in, reached the Casa di Mezzo farmyard at 0535 hrs; later a cut-down Honey tank ran the gauntlet with much-needed ammunition. There, with main and secondary armament continuously firing at the SS, until their Brownings became red-hot, they denied the shelter of buildings to the enemy and delayed them, while our artillery pounded the railway bridge area, Battalion MMGs fired in enfilade along the Fosso Vetro and the mortars concentrated round the farm. Lt Jackson's extremely gallant leadership—for which he was awarded the MC—coupled with the determination of the Lancers, delayed the attack and forced it to split; each follow-up wave was engaged by the Casa di Mezzo garrison, or more importantly DF fire was brought accurately down on it. Lt Taberer, an able South African, who commanded the Lancers, was deservedly awarded the MC, and his Cpl Wilson the MM.

Nevertheless, 26 Panzer Recce, five minutes later, was approaching the A Company positions. From the fork of the road with the Conventello track, 300 yards East of Casa di Mezzo, the left-hand farm was held by the two forward carrier sections of 1 Platoon. With the carriers forming a 'waggon ring' behind the house and their platoon of automatic weapons and ammunition, these sections created a ripple of fire which soon split the advancing enemy. Our DFs had been put down between Casa di Mezzo and the Marianna ruin, and, after the enemy fired green Verey lights, counter-fire came down on A Company.

The next house East was held by 4 Platoon, commanded by Lt I. V. Askew, with Sgt Williams a tower of strength as Platoon Sergeant. Rifle grenades were now fired into buildings, and Spandaus and Schmeissers were ripping away across the front. Riflemen fought back fiercely, as the dead round their houses showed. Particularly good work (for which he was awarded the MM) was put in by Rfn Bailey, who stalked a troublesome machine-gunner and knocked him out with a grenade.

By 0635 hrs ammunition was running very low in 4 Platoon, as reported on the wireless by Sgt Williams to his old Platoon Commander, Lt G. Maufe. That officer, who had commanded a platoon from the Desert on, and longer than anyone else in the 1st, was with his carrier platoon HQ and reserve section at a farm in depth; this had been engaged by 20-mm fire, but the assault was moving East just North of it. He had earlier reconnoitred the cart track to Lt Askew's farm, and felt sure that he would be bazookaed en route. Nevertheless, when there was just a glimmer of light, he decided he must bring ammunition up to 4 Platoon, using a carrier in one of its originally intended tasks. His driver got up maximum speed on the track forward, while Lt Maufe fired his Bren at the SS lining the ditch alongside it; Rfn Waller, an old Desert hand, meanwhile tossed grenades out from the rear compartment. Achieving full surprise, they caught the Ofenrohr (long bazooka) crew as they loaded their weapon, made the right and left turns and skidded into the 4 Platoon yard with the vital ammunition, leaving a line of dead in the ditch. In the half-light Lt Maufe had engaged Rfn Bailey and others alongside the farm, but fortunately missed. Later Rfn Waller, and he, in search of loot, flushed another group of enemy from the road ditch and located many wounded there. Both officers were awarded the MC, because holding and supplying this position—which linked Casa di Mezzo and the other A Company ones—was essential to keeping the enemy exposed to our DFs in the open.

No farm held by Lancers and Hussars or by Riflemen fell to the enemy, but they occupied one empty building along the lateral between A Company and the Lamone bank. Fortunately, the remnants of the leading wave of Germans finally blundered into the Westminster support company whose Vickers were standing in the yard and terrible execution was done before the enemy went to ground.

At 0715 hrs another attack was beaten off at Casa di Mezzo, which was then heavily shelled. It was now light, and C Company motor platoons, supported by a 4H troop, started to sweep Northwards through A Company, while a Canadian company which had been sent back did the same from the North East. 4 Platoon engaged the enemy flushed from the building, and from 0800 hrs onwards the SS began to pay an even higher price. From Mezzano B Company carriers and 4H tanks fired into the vine rows and at the canal bank, while from the East an MIO came up to join Lt Askew, shooting the enemy out of houses and ditches as it went. The SS desperately put down a smoke-screen to cover their retreating men, but the route back was so narrow that mortars and artillery fire could follow them as they went; our mortars fired 380 rounds in three hours and the MMGs 30,000 rounds on pre-registered tasks.

At 0900 hrs C Company had cleared right up to the A Company lateral track, flushing 30 more Germans into Canadian hands. Back at the Echelon Capt Ryan, the QM, was for the first time in his long career desperate for SAA, and the Battalion HQ dump was empty. However, the enemy had taken more than enough; by any standards 16 SS Reichsführer Division had suffered a costly defeat. 132 prisoners were taken by the 1st Battalion Group, and of the four leading company commanders, two were captured and two killed; at least 70 lying casualties were later observed in the vine rows between the Casa di Mezzo road and the canal, and four German stretcher parties worked continuously under a white flag till nightfall, though, when a 4H armoured ambulance tried to help, it was fired on. The total German casualties, including walking wounded, were probably 200, which with the prisoners taken by the 1st Battalion Group and the Canadians, amounted to about a third of the assaulting troops. Intelligence reports shortly after told of the court-martial of Maier, the inept commander, and it was particularly satisfactory to defeat the arrogant SS in their camouflaged smocks, their title 'Reichsführer' making it seem like a personal affront to Hitler himself. Our casualties were very light in the farm strong-points. Sadly, the Lancers suffered our only fatalities when the SS shelled the prisoners they were escorting back after the action.

Given a 6000-yard front with three weak companies and a dismounted squadron, and with the only obstacle at our backs, success had come from an admirable all-arms team effort. There had been sound battalion layout, with every weapon sited for best fire-protection; cool heads at company level for fire-direction; but above all great gallantry by troop and platoon commanders, whose NCOs and men had produced a resolute defence. This was a defence of which everyone—Lancers, Hussars, Riflemen and Gunners—was rightly proud, and for which the congratulations of General McCreery and others poured in. The Canadian GOC was delighted, and no doubt relieved, but, in the unsatisfactory passing of the 1st Battalion from one brigade command to another, the recognition of Lt Col Williams for the defence of the Mezzano bridgehead and the earlier Marzeno crossing was regrettably omitted.

A Squadron 12L, which with Lt Jackson's two Hussar Shermans had held Casa di Mezzo, was relieved by C Company in the evening of 4 January, and after a quiet night the news came that the Canadians had reached their San Alberto objective. On the night of 5 January C Squadron 7H dismounted took over the C Company sector, while the latter established a North-South barrier fence in depth, to screen the Lamone track, with long-awaited danert wire and shrapnel mines. A thaw had now set in, with rain and mud, and a general stand-fast on vehicle movement was necessary. The many enemy dead in exposed areas could not be buried, owing to shellfire as soon as parties went forward. The relief of our partisans by a new group of 30 involved more trouble than a battalion relief, but with all platoons at low strength they were essential as sentries paired with Riflemen.

During the next week snow fell and the ground froze again, allowing the 7H and 12L dismounted Squadrons finally to be relieved with their vehicles. Immense quantities of telephone cable were laid to support platoons, and on our right front the enemy's hardly won knowledge of the farms we held enabled them to reduce them slowly to revetted ruins by intense shelling. Our gunners were only allowed to fire DFs owing to ammunition shortage, but after a heavy snowfall the air cleared and the Thunderbolts returned to attack Alfonsine bridge, losing a plane to the large number of 20-mm Vierlings held by the SS. On 9 January 45 27L took over part of the 1st Battalion right front, with a view to easing in the Italian Cremona Gruppo. Assisted by the ILO, the Italians were given every help to settle into the Conventello area, and the acting Adjutant responded to their elegant flower appointment code by announcing himself and the battalion tactical number on the phone as *Cyclamina cinquanta sei*, from the new Battalion HQ in Mezzano, North of the Lamone. Every night our patrols lay out in the snow or rain, or reconnoitred with the anticipation of a Schu mine in the matted grass. With constant stand-tos the rum ration was voluntarily exchanged for extra brew materials; a Rifleman newly returned from a patrol was found to shiver and drowse if turned out again after rum, whereas the comfort of hot cocoa stayed with him. In C Company, Rfn Bass, a preacher in peacetime, held evening platoon prayers before patrolling, while Capt Head, the Padre, indefatigably toured platoons. The work of Sgt Willey as a wise and patient platoon commander at this time must be particularly mentioned.

The 1st's front was narrower now, from just East of the railway, across the North end of Mezzano, to the farms and canal on the West.

On 16 January an enemy platoon raid on our forward post, North Allegri, West of Mezzano, at night was seen off with no casualties to us by the defensive drill indicated earlier, despite three bazooka rounds. The patrol dropped off a well-dressed Italian civilian, whose story was broken by the IO and ILO, and who was sent off to counter-intelligence as an enemy agent. Three nights later a German fighting patrol bazookad another A Company house, causing four blast casualties, but losing one man and a prisoner from 35 SS Regiment themselves. By day the new D Company sniper platoon was coming into its own, Rfn Mead shooting a particularly arrogant officer as he majestically surveyed Mezzano from the railway bridge area. They removed two more SS, finding the carrying forward of a shrouded 'casualty' in daylight under the Red Cross as incongruous as the revealed ammunition boxes, which fell off the stretcher when the bearers were shot. This led later to an SP demolishing the signal-box on the railway, the only building high enough to view the German lines within SA range through the veil of bare willow branches; regrettably Rfn Walsh, C Company, died of wounds under this fire.

A dismounted Squadron of 9L had come under command, as 2 Armoured Brigade units moved into the line in the salient on our left, long held by 1 Welch. A troop to the left of our MMGs killed two Germans and took a prisoner when it was raided; our mortars and MMGs had as usual made it most unpleasant for raiders caught outside a strong-point in the open. An unusual German intervention was to fire a mass of shells, containing leaflets giving rather inept advice on how to malinger; they were treated with derision by Riflemen, but a well-advertised copy was passed to the MO, Capt O. Green, MC. Sadly, he left us in February 1945, with the best wishes and the gratitude for his unfailing courage and concern, of all in the 1st Battalion. Prompted by gynaecological uncertainty when faced with the accouchement of an Italian peasant girl—who was back at work before his medical books arrived from the Echelon—he felt that after two years of gunshot wounds he must revert to hospital work once more.

Across the front and behind the forward Companies a winter line was being developed under Maj Howard of D Company; Basuto labour dug vast holes ('This for a very big machine-gun, Baas' referring to a crater big enough for a 17-pounder), and Sappers and Riflemen erected a wire barrier. All this effort would have been very useful weeks earlier, as would the 20 snow suits which were now in constant use by patrols; the patrol boots were ineffective, as the frozen crust was very noisy under all footwear. Theatre shortages now included dry batteries of all types owing to intensive night use. Lipstick from Florence made up for a dearth of red chinograph, but rations consisted invariably of meat and vegetable stew or bully, since compo rations were largely a North West Europe luxury. Breakfast was brick-hard oleomargarine, specially made with a high melting point for desert use, with soya link 'sausages' and virtually meatless bacon; there were no pigs one cared to eat after obscene rooting in no-man's-land, and the poultry had long since gone from the ruined village and farms, except for some remarkably wary guinea fowl. To supplement the sodden battledress, many Riflemen sacrificed a US blanket to make sleeves for leather jerkins, and Maj Killick installed his cherry badge on a black velvet cap, as worn by the local peasantry. Only the Mobile Bath Unit showers, set up in a sugar factory, and the opportunity for enough sleep made the 48 hours as reserve company any different from the longer tour in each forward position; houses were still under shellfire and the exposed demolition guards on the Mezzano bridge still had to be done.

It was with regret that a tired 1st Battalion found itself once more under 2 Armoured Brigade on 30 January 45; the Commander and G Staff of 9 Armoured Brigade had been particularly helpful in a constructive way during a most active period, but the weight which had fallen on a low-strength battalion was not appreciated by the incomers. There was daily raiding between the Canadians and Germans on our right, but our nights were largely a round of patrols observing Spandaus firing tracers high on fixed lines and probing and harassing enemy posts; our MMGs and mortars fired constantly. Work went on daily on repair and revetting of house strong-points, with sandbags at a premium, and even the Wasps were called in to burn the remaining haystacks. Brigade added maintenance of a long but unimportant stretch of road to the day and night defensive tasks and the Battalion's carefully planned minimum vehicle movement was interfered with.

By 6 February 45 a thaw had set in, making men sink in up to a foot as they moved across country. However, life was made unpleasant for the Germans by listening patrols in return for increased shelling, heralding the move away of 16 SS and the ranging in of 42 Jäger's guns. One farm, Bosco Bruciato, which was known from deserters of Polish origin to be an enemy patrol base, was engaged by our mortars, MMGs and guns in one intense shoot, as a listening patrol, wireless-linked, reported the German colour sergeant's squeaking ox-cart arrival; the enemy blew up the farm as too costly to hold shortly afterwards. Extra mortar ammunition was now allotted for Brigade counter-mortar work. Having received reproof for frivolity when the 1st reported passage of migrant wildfowl in large numbers, Riflemen were delighted when the target of secret deployment of radar and LAA forward—to pick up and shoot down 'enemy gliders'—turned out to be the duck wheeling and departing in the misty nights. However, a Brigade demand for yet another summer's Khaki Drill returns sobered those hoping for a swift return home.

Apart from a sudden deluge of over 200 mortar bombs and shells on the night of 18 February—possibly the Jäger firing off dumped SS ammunition without inflicting a single casualty—the month was spent countering every German attempt to infiltrate, without needlessly risking Riflemen across the canal on completely bare meadowland. It was also a time of repelling boarders from the rear. Polish truck-drivers were continually trying to remove beams from shelled houses for firewood, and finally two partisans were attached to check any civilians trying to re-enter the empty Mezzano village. US pilots from the Thunderbolts which had mistakenly attacked Mezzano were brought up by Lt T. S. Lucas, MC, of the Regiment, and were given an insight into infantry life in the line. The 1st Battalion endured eight weeks and six days and nights of snow, mud and lack of sleep, beat off major attacks and dominated the winter darkness, so close to the enemy that none of the 400 Riflemen of F Echelon, including Battalion HQ, were ever out of shell, and often machine-gun, range. Finally the Battalion was relieved at 1700 hrs on 26 February 45 by 1 Welch, and joined the well-established A and B Echelons in the billets of Ravenna.

Many changes had been in the air for the last few days. First, Lt Col E. A. W. Williams, MC, on posting as GSO I, AFHQ, handed over the Battalion he had commanded with distinction for over a year. Riflemen owed him more than they could guess, for without his personal stand the 1st would long before have been thrown away by companies to save the infantry of other formations. Though the Ronco losses under 4 Division had weighed heavy, he had resolutely followed the 60th Rifleman's precept to build on past experience. He had showed his mastery of field tactics both in seizing the Marzeno opportunity and in the defensive layout at Mezzano, and this should have been recognized. Fortunately, his successor was his 2IC, Maj J. C. Hope, MC, known and loved by the 1st Battalion after over four years spent holding every appointment in it.

To the 1st's great pleasure it was to join an Armoured Division once more, 6 Armoured of the Mailed Fist sign, and within it would serve under Brigadier A. Gore, DSO, late RB, and his hitherto wholly RB 61 Brigade. Unfortunately, in December 44 2 RB had suffered at Tossignano, in the Apennines, the same sort of losses that our 1st Battalion had sustained on the Ronco, but by that date any Gunner reinforcements had been used up. It was therefore necessary for the weakened 2 RB to amalgamate with 10 RB under the former's name. 1st King's Royal Rifle Corps and the new 2 RB were organized as simplified motor battalions; motor companies consisted only of motor platoons carried in pooled White scout cars, driven by RASC drivers; to ensure future tactical mobility 30 of our most experienced Riflemen drivers were left out of battle, as sure enough the brief essay of the RASC into tactical driving ended in a few months, although the drivers themselves settled in well and took some casualties. Our D Company continued in its support role, with the carrier platoon of Lt Maufe, MC, containing the oldest carrier hands, two MMG platoons in carriers, a six-pounder and a mortar platoon. 7 RB was carried in three-tonners initially, but the energy of Lt Col D. Darling, DSO, MC, ensured that any armoured vehicle passing was rapidly requisitioned to get into the armoured battle. Also in the Brigade was a Green Jacket Heavy Support Company of 4.2-inch mortars and MMGs. The Brigade, apart from the Gunner DAA & QMG, was wholly Green Jacket, and many old friendships were renewed. On the Divisional staff, two 60th Riflemen were to be found, Lt Col Q. V. Hoare, OBE, as AA & QMG and Maj N. P. Lee, MBE, as DAAG. Capt A. H. Cagby also joined that staff after bringing the 1st's portion of Regimental property from Taranto to Bari, en route for England; there it was unfortunately later off-loaded and suffered from being blown into the harbour when an ammunition ship went up. Personal baggage in kitbags was moved by Capt House from Taranto to a Divisional store in Morciano, near Cattolica, where a NCO and two Riflemen could keep an eye on it.

Our new GOC, Maj Gen H. O. Murray, DSO, was a very experienced Infantryman, with a flair for blending all arms teams successfully; one of his first actions was to ask Lt Col Hope to run an officers' discussion on the San Clemente ridge, near our rest area in Cattolica, to put over the lessons of how an armoured division might be better launched from Army reserve than 1 Armoured had been in September.

Joining a new and proved Division and brother Riflemen brought the 1st Battalion under friendly but critical eyes, and gave just the sense of being on their mettle that companies needed to refresh them. Capt J. Waterfield came back from hospital in time to clear up a mass of administrative detail before formally handing over the adjutancy to Capt G. H. Mills, who had been doubling that post and IO since Christmas. He took over HQ Company, as Maj H. R. G. Howard, the most senior Regular officer, became 2IC, handing over his D Company to Maj Mackay, who had commanded B since July. Maj Christian received a new 2IC in A, Capt R. H. Willis-Fleming, and Maj G. P. Shakerley arrived to take over B Company, with Capt M. P. Lee as 2IC. It was nice to welcome some Rhodesian officers once again in Lts B. Lake and J. M. Kidd, and after a nine-month gap WO1 Waldron was appointed RSM from the 11th Battalion. While over 90% of F Echelon Riflemen went on leave to Rome, small parties of officers went for the last time to the Rifle Brigade villa in Florence, run by Capt E. M. Voules, 60th.

On 4 March 1945 the 1st Battalion moved for the last time in the vehicles it had drawn up new in Algeria in Autumn 1943, and had well maintained, backed by the resources of Lt M. G. Turner, Technical Adjutant, and Capt W. Gledhill REME. It met the Jewish Brigade heading North, many of whom would use their training against the British, including the 2nd Battalion, in Palestine all too soon. The 1st's destination, Cattolica, was a small seaside town at the mouth of the Conca valley, where it had fought through the Gothic Line. Canadians had burnt all available wood, including doors, during the winter, so self-help was needed on all fronts. Drill and other cadres were started, particularly for reinforcements received from other regiments during the winter and those who now arrived from LAA; a mass of checking, cleaning or replacing had to be done, while baths, canteens and messes were organized. However, 8 Army, on the night of 6 March, ordered a company, which had to be a composite one under Maj Killick, to leave next morning to defend an airfield near Ancona against a possible sea or airborne sabotage raid; as expected, this was a false alarm, but a tiresome interruption to a tight programme. The weather was getting sunnier, so the medical authorities started to fuss about malaria precautions, although all knew that the Battalion would be up front again, or the puddles dried up, before any mosquito felt like breeding. On 24 March Maj Gen Murray inspected the 1st Battalion, which marched past in Rifle style, despite the newness of the pace to many converted Riflemen; battle dress was hopelessly unmatched, and the lack of headgear meant that one rank wore green side hats, another khaki berets and the third the lamentable cap GS, brought in by reinforcements from elsewhere. A great loss to the 1st were 40 Rangers from the old 9th Battalion, including almost the whole Orderly Room staff, who went home on Python at this time. It was a very different Battalion in human terms from the one which had moved to Italy just under a year ago. Its casualties had so far been 62 killed, 188 wounded and 137 missing or prisoners, the latter largely at the Ronco river; in addition 2 officers and 292 Riflemen had gone home after $4\frac{1}{2}$ years overseas.

However, in the finer weather there was much training to be done by way of marching and shooting. In particular the excellent 16/5 Lancers, with which the 1st was to work, carried out well-executed field firing schemes with A and C Companies, which built up mutual confidence. Commander 8 Army held a briefing for all his COs: it is now time to follow them in looking at the opponents in what was to be the final battle. Unlike the battle in North West Europe, there was little direct effect in Italy between the operations of the Western Allies and the Russians, although political ends were equally involved. The Allied Air Forces by day and the Italian partisans by night had now virtually isolated the German Army Group C South of the Alps. The Balkan Army Group was withdrawing slowly Northwards through Jugoslavia, harried by Tito's partisans. A brief reappearance of Kesselring had ensured that, of the four divisions withdrawn, only 16 SS was a mobile one, and that had been mauled by us, as earlier recounted. Von Vietinghoff had four corps, totalling 23 divisions, in his two armies, but owing to needless anxiety about landings on the rocky Ligurian coast (which led nowhere) and the head of the Adriatic (with its shallow lagoons and marshes) he had only 19 divisions in the Po valley, and only one of these in reserve. Against him Alexander had 17 divisions, with only 6 British Armoured Division in 8 Army's reserve. As well as total air superiority, the Allies had a preponderance of artillery and armour, but this advantage was not large in infantry; the effective bombing of all Po bridges somewhat isolated the battlefield, but the Germans made brilliant use of night ferries. We had to face a series of formidable embanked river lines, South of the Po, on which work had gone on all winter. It seemed quite likely that the very experienced German divisions—the best and strongest now left to the German Army—could dictate the pace once more behind formidable demolition belts, as their attackers strained to cross the wide meadows astride that great river. From Bologna the River Reno swept in a wide loop before reaching Lake Comacchio; within it were four embanked rivers, running at right angles to any 8 Army advance, and areas of inundation and marsh. After a narrow gap of dry land at Argenta, the inundations linked with Lake Comacchio.

Alexander was now Supreme Allied Commander Central Mediterranean, with US General Mark Clark at 15 Army Group. The plan was for 5 Army, using IV US Corps' new IO US Mountain Division to strike North towards the Po, keeping West of Bologna and the River Reno; this contained an element of surprise, since the obvious threat was from II US Corps, which all winter had been on the heights just South of Bologna. This attack would only be launched when 8 Army had firmly engaged the enemy's attention on the East.

8 Army had a more difficult task, in that the narrow Argenta Gap had somehow to be forced, in order to threaten the hinge of a German retreat, which would otherwise wheel back, first to the Po, and then to the prepared short line between the Alps and the sea along the River Adige. A combination of flame-throwers and dummy runs with tactical aircraft was to be used to get assaulting infantry over the honeycombed Senio banks, but a series of right hooks by V

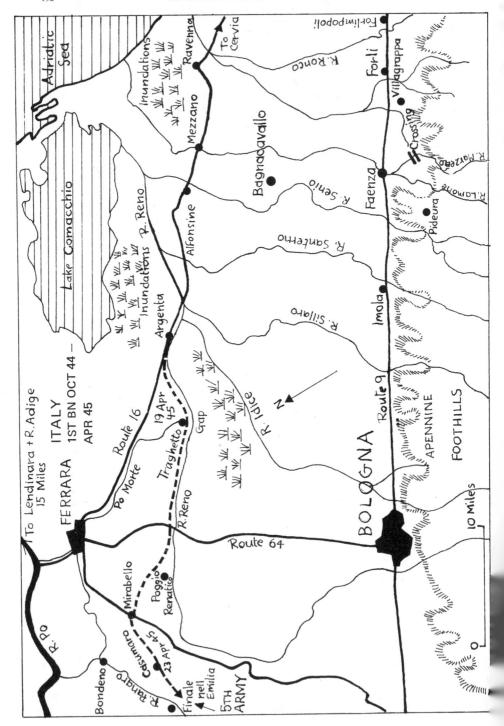

Corps for the Reno bridge and Argenta was the surprise element, using amphibious Buffaloes from Comacchio. If this failed to seize the Gap the subsidiary advance by XIII Corps parallel to Route 9 towards the Bologna area would have to become the main 8 Army thrust.

The role for 6 Armoured Division, as the only 8 Army reserve, was to be ready to exploit the success of either Corps; but with preference for the V Corps Argenta Gap operation. General Murray's planning was meticulous, and his Divisional organization ideal for his task. The Derby Yeomanry were his armoured reconnaissance in fast, early-mark Shermans and Honeys. Brigadier N. Mitchell's 26 Armoured Brigade, containing 16/5L, 17/21L and the Lothian & Border Horse, had Shermans with improved 76-mm guns and platypus track extensions, slowing the tanks but allowing movement over soft meadows. Each armoured regiment—in our case 16/5L—was grouped with a motor battalion of 61 Brigade, nominally under armoured command; in fact Lt Col Hope travelled in Lt Col D. Smyley's turretless Honey command vehicle, so that joint planning was continuous, and took over dismounted or night action if companies left their Squadrons. Behind each armoured regimental/motor battalion group followed a battalion of 1 Guards Brigade, in our case the Welsh Guards. Already General Murray had pointed the eyes of 16/5L and 17/21L Groups at a small marshy canal, Po Morte di Primaro, which ran South from Ferrara to the Reno and would bar any attempt by 6 Armoured to carry out its most desirable role—that of wheeling West after the infantry divisions and commandos had captured Argenta, and cutting across all the German escape routes to the Po. No one knew whether the Allied drive North of the Alps had allowed the threatened garrison of fanatics to slip into the proclaimed Nazi Alpine Redoubt, but bitter Apennine experience told 15 Army Group that it must at all costs prevent enemy veterans like the Parachute Corps and the Panzer and Panzer Grenadier divisions from installing themselves in the passes. The COs of 16/5L and our 1st Battalion, allotted the left in planning, were particularly enjoined to seize the dry gap, a track running on a narrow shelf between the South end of the Po Morte and the towering Reno bank above; the gap had the straggling houses of Traghetto on its North and the ferry from which it was named over the bank. For the first time in its Italian experience the 1st Battalion had absolute confidence in all the higher commanders and staffs and the all-arms teams at all levels with which they were to work.

On 8 April 1945, profiting from the Gothic Line fiasco, 6 Armoured Division moved closer up behind the line to the Ronco area near Forlimpopoli, and the 1st found itself bivouaced in green fields with a network of dusty tracks. The Archbishop of York, Dr Garbett, earlier of Winchester, visited the Battalion, where the saintly old man to the dismay of his padres responded to a Rifleman's ''Op in, Guv' and made a whirlwind tour in a carrier. The next day the CO returned from a 61 Brigade conference in Florence and briefed company commanders on our part of the 8 Army plan. As 25 reinforcements arrived straight from the 10th Battalion at Strensall, the first UK reinforcements for one year, shoals of silver aircraft were flying Westwards to attack with sensible fragmentation bombs the enemy's artillery and reserves; the infantry attacks over the Senio just before last light on 9 April, preceded by a brilliant orchestra of confusing artillery and live air attacks and a final dummy run, succeeded and continued on in a night lurid with flame within a pall of dust and smoke. The next night the formidable Santerno river was forced, while in the bivouac area companies evolved tactics for advancing by roughtly 300-yard bounds between farms and rows of trees; using arrow head of platoons, screening a central tank troop from bazookas, they found the view lying down very restricted by rapidly growing grass and crops.

On 14 April 5 Army successfully attacked North from the mountains West of Bologna, but against stiffening opposition it was still not clear whether 8 Army could force the Argenta Gap. 6 Armoured Division therefore moved North West to Bagnacavallo and just South West of its winter line at Mezzano; here it could inspect the grim fortified embankments of the Senio just above it. The 1st now came under command of 26 Armoured Brigade, and was leagured in the 16/5L Group, with companies alongside their squadrons of the same letter; two FOOs from 104 RHA and a troop of MIOs joined the Battalion, and echelons split, A2 under Capt Waterfield remaining in the old area, while A1 under Lt Round joined A1 of 16/5L.

On 18 April it was clear that the Argenta route would be ours. West of Bologna 10 US Mountain Division had brilliantly fought its way down to the last Apennine foothills, while direct pressure was now being exerted on the heights above Bologna; 90 PG Division had been drawn in from the enemy's reserve. North of Route 9 the Sillaro river had been crossed by Polish, New Zealand and Indian troops against fierce opposition, and after securing a Reno crossing 78 Division had entered Argenta, but was held up by bitter resistance from the Reno banks directly above Route 16. 56 Division and 24 Guards Brigade were endeavouring to cut back on to Route 16 from the East after amphibious landings. Moving through Alfonsine's enemy winter positions, 16/5L Group was brought forward to South of Argenta during the evening of 18 April, while the CO and Lt J. Wathen, as IO, gleaned the latest information from 78 Division; wireless silence was broken for the first time since leaving Cattolica. After Commandos had stormed the Reno banks in the night 16/5L Group moved through Argenta in the morning; after a pause, leaving 78 Division to advance North up Route 16 towards Ferrara and the Po, the Lancers and Riflemen wheeled West on the extreme left of their Brigade at 1400 hrs. Leaguer exits had been awkward, and the Group was too late to follow up napalm air-strikes on Traghetto Gap. Having the towering Reno bank on their far left flank, the Group moved into an assembly area at Trombone for final orders amid vast pear and apple orchards. Although it was 5000 yards to Traghetto Gap, which the Group was to seize and exploit through North West, the assembly area was also the forming-up place, since the start-line was the orchard edge only 300 yards West. The embanked road from Route 16 was a potential tank obstacle, as it ran first West and then South West to Traghetto across the Group's front; 78 Division reconnaissance troops and common sense indicated that the Po Morte was held. To see the armour off to a good start, it was decided that companies would dismount to lead their squadrons at least as far as the embanked road; A Company on the left were to make for the Traghetto Gap and B for the North end of that hamlet, where there was a possible crossing—no visual reconnaissance was possible in that dead flat country. Because the Divisional artillery had been employed earlier on Army tasks, it was now South of the

Argenta traffic block and out of range; the air-strikes had gone in to a rigid timing, so the Group would have to work forward using its own resources.

A Company on the left moved on easily at first over open ground, but soon ditches held up the tanks and farms had to be cleared, with a few prisoners taken; however, they reached their more remote stretch of the embanked road against shelling but little direct fire.

However, as was discovered later, a withdrawing German artillery battalion, leaving its guns South of the Reno, had crossed the ferry that morning; in the usual thorough German way it had put out Spandaus in farms on the open East flank, while it rested behind the road embankment opposite B Company. Within 300 yards of crossing the start-line a Spandau opened up; this was dealt with by the tanks, when the target could be indicated in the closer country on the right, using prearranged drills with 38 set, two-inch mortar or tracer. However, from then on there was a flank and rearguard action by the enemy, based on the embankment and houses alongside, to cover their withdrawal North West. This action in turn alerted the SPs of 26 Panzer over the Po Morte, who with the remnants of 362 Division were responsible for guarding the East flank of the still intact Parachute Corps, as it started to withdraw to the Po. Unfortunately Lt W. Love, who had led his 7 Platoon admirably at the taking of Pideura, was killed by SP shelling while seizing the embanked road. Maj Shakerley, despite his exposed position on the skyline, then personally saw B Squadron, tank by tank, up and down the narrow ramps, and into the somewhat less exposed fields below on the West side. Mortaring had been heavy at times, and an SP had put accurate fire down on to the A Company assembly area, knocking out two Whites and wounding three men, including two RASC drivers. As darkness fell B Company, covering its squadron, had just managed to reach the railway line parallel to and beyond the embanked road, but the left-hand platoon under Lt O. Montgomery, MC, was isolated, and enemy were in contact on the right front and open right flank. It was not of course known at the time that the first enemy encountered had been a chance battalion, passing across the front, and not the Po Morte forward screen. A Company, secure between the Reno bank and B Company, had moved forward to the railway with A Squadron, and was about 1500 yards from Traghetto at that point. The two companies had been caught without their Medium Scale rations and had no food, other than what the Lancers shared with them, because CO 16/5L judged it unacceptable to bring forward A1 Echelons, including vulnerable petrol three-tonners, with parties of enemy moving around the leaguers. Nevertheless, A Company sent a patrol forward to see if the Traghetto Gap was still held. Lt Lake, one of the newly arrived Rhodesians, in his first patrol action, realizing the importance of the information to our future operations, pressed forward until two of his men were wounded in a sharp exchange with a Spandau post. The enemy were heard to suffer casualties from his grenades, and he was awarded an immediate Mention in Despatches for his skill and courage in bringing back prompt and accurate intelligence. On the right, B Company patrols concentrated on reconnoitring the tank-going forward, for until our artillery could be moved through Argenta's traffic jams the tank guns were our only support, although ineffective against mortars from across the Po Morte.

Despite the CO's opposition, orders came in the night for a Bailey bridge to be

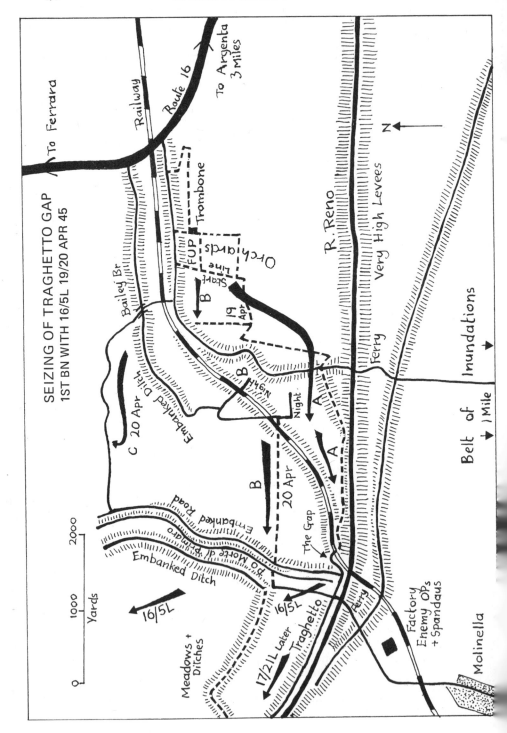

SEIZING OF TRAGHETTO GAP
1ST BN WITH 16/5L 19/20 APR 45

built over a demolition on the road running North West to the Po Morte, so that the C Company/Squadron Group could move up it at first light. Since there was no ready-made crossing there, and the strongest enemy opposition was on the right, it seemed an unnecessary diversion of the reserve, when Traghetto was the key. Owing to some topographical confusion, the C Company platoons found later that they were protected by rather than protecting the unwittingly daring sappers.

When the Battery Commander reported that his guns would be in range a simple plan was made for action by the two companies, lying hungry and uncomfortable in slits round their leaguered tanks. A Company would make for the Traghetto Gap itself, but since Lt Lake's patrol had indicated that the built-up area was firmly held, B Company was to make for a possible crossing over the Po Morte where the houses thinned out 400 yards to the North. Their actual objective was the road running along the Po Morte's Eastern levée, which dominated the West side and any escape route from the gap, as well as enfilading A Company's opposition.

At first light on 20 April 45 our artillery concentrations went down on the gap and levée objectives. B Company was advancing only 200 yards from the levée, with Lt Hawes's platoon and a troop of tanks leading and the other platoons covering the flanks, when an enemy mortar DF wounded Lt R. B. Hawes and seven men, of whom L/Cpl Whitty later died. The advance looked like stalling, when Cpl Crompton, true to his resolute Geordie character, ran forward alone through the DF and reached the road just as our artillery lifted. Slipping on to the far side of the levée, he pounced on two Spandau crews with his Tommy-gun before they had got their heads up, and was then rapidly joined by the rest of B Company. On reaching the canal, Maj Shakerley (who was awarded the MC for his gallantry on both days) took one of the flank platoons over the canal and seized a house on the far bank. Altogether B Company took 40 prisoners, including two officers, several Spandaus and a 75-mm gun. Cpl Crompton was awarded a richly deserved DCM, since his gallant leadership by example undoubtedly saved many lives as well as ensuring rapid seizure of the Traghetto Gap. For, shaken by this threat to their flank and withdrawal route North West, the enemy, instead of fighting it out in the village, only harassed the A Company advance with sniper-fire; there was, however, shelling, in which Rfn Goldberg was killed and five wounded. Enemy, trapped in tall factory buildings South of the Reno by our cutting of the ferry escape route, continued to Spandau movement on the Reno levée road, which vehicles were forced to use to circumvent a demolition; infantry, however, could safely move dismounted in the lee of the Reno levée. As A Company secured the narrow passage forming the Traghetto Gap, A Squadron 16/5L passed through, wheeling right Northwards over the meadows and running down the escaping flank guard in the open. Over 100 prisoners were taken, mostly from 262 Division, but our companies could not follow mounted, since the many drainage ditches were obstacles to the wheeled Whites.

This was the moment when the C Squadron/C Company Group should have been nicely in hand to race through. However, just as Lt Col Hope had feared, the simultaneous advance of that Group, ordered from above to be carried out up a minor road leading North West to the Po Morte, where there was small chance of crossing, had run into trouble. The first 1500 yards by Lt Darwin's platoon had gone all right, but in passing through in the closer country Lt E. M. Spencer's platoon bumped the rearguard of the previous day's enemy. He was killed by an SP shell at the head of his platoon, and his body was only recovered with much difficulty by Maj Killick personally under small arms and shellfire. Thus when C Squadron were ordered back and round through the gap C Company could not be extricated in time to move with them. The loss of Lts Love and Spencer, older married men, who had worked their way up to Sergeant before commissioning and who had been a shining example of devotion to duty, was keenly felt; Sgt Robertson took over the platoon and withdrew them with calm efficiency from under fire. The previous night's inability to replenish A and B Squadrons in their forward leaguers now began to tell, and C Squadron, after making good progress North West, also ran out of petrol, as approaching darkness and the loss of tanks to SP rearguards slowed things up.

Behind them D Company carriers had reconnoitred wheeled routes forward, and Battalion HQ and D Company had moved forward to Traghetto station. Well to the North, 2 RB and the Lothians had also crossed the Po Morte, but strong opposition, causing the loss of Lothian tanks, forced the Riflemen to consolidate in a tight bridgehead. Division's preferred thrust had always been from Traghetto towards Finale, with its Reno flank protection for the road running just below the levée, and in the afternoon 26 Armoured Brigade passed through the reserve; 17/21L, with a 7 RB Company on the rear Squadron, roared through the gap, held by the 1st Battalion, and screened by 16/5L to the North. The race across the escape routes of the crack Parachute Corps to the Po was on.

During the late afternoon the Welsh Guards came forward to relieve the 1st Battalion, and, receiving the overthrows from the harassing Spandaus over the Reno, moved forward tactically. One Rifleman, shaving in his carrier in nicely calculated safety a few feet below the top of the Reno levée, was heard to say to a WG section commander, moving forward with his men bent double: 'All right, chum, you can stand up now, even if you are 6 foot——all in your socks.' The Guardsmen's efficient relief of the 1st by nightfall was appreciated by A and B Companies, but the latter's Whites had to be commandeered to run replenishment up to the 16/5L leaguer, because three-tonners were vulnerable to the sniping of determined stragglers. Two overturned in a bomb crater in the dark and others went astray; it would have been an easier operation for Lt Round with our own experienced drivers, for it was the first RASC effort at forward area work. C Company, prudently crouched below their armour while motoring unscathed along the Reno night skyline, had already joined the 16/5L and dug in around their leaguer; Sgt Freeman led a patrol, protecting troopers collecting documents from knocked-out Shermans—yet another motor-battalion task.

On 21 April the whole 1st Battalion joined the 16/5L, where they had leaguered, and spent a quiet day. Far-away Berlin had been entered by the Russians, but in Italy the two sides were too intent on the next moves of their experienced opponents to know or care. Although Bologna had fallen at last to the Poles, von Vietinghoff's co-ordinated swing back to the Po and Adige, despite the air situation, still seemed the sort of operation which the Germans, using darkness, obstacles and rearguards, had pulled off time and again. He had sought Hitler's permission to withdraw earlier, and was refused on 14 April; however, when he again sought the Führer's clearance on 20 April it would be too late if 6 Armoured Division could strike boldly.

7 RB, thanks to the forcefulness of Lt Col Darling, had been ferried up on all available tracked vehicles to join 17/21L. A canal bridgehead had already been forced when on the afternoon of 21 April the Group, moving forward between the Reno and a canal, seized the Route 64 bridge over the latter intact, cutting the Bologna–Ferrara road to the Po. By nightfall 17/21L and a company had raced on to block the South and East outskirts of Poggio Renatico, which town was strongly held as part of the enemy supply area, and dominated the surrounding bare meadows in daylight.

It was clearly imperative to relieve the rest of 7 RB for an attack on the town, but the Welsh Guards, who were responsible for taking over ground won, could not be moved forward in time. When orders came to the 1st Battalion at 1930 hrs A Company were moved up quickly on the troop of MIOs, since only tracks could get forward. They took over a Reno ferry crossing site, while B and C Companies, moving first on foot, then on tanks, protected the Bailey bridge being built on the axis and the Route 64 intact bridge respectively. The Carrier and MMG platoons of D Company, being tracked, moved forward to support A and C, who spent a cold but mosquito-ridden night taking some prisoners.

In the early hours of 22 April, 7 RB started an attack, which left them in command of Poggio by 0900 hrs, though still under heavy indirect fire. At first light on 22 April 16/5L and our forward companies moved off, less B, still by the Bailey bridge; A moved on their MIOs and C behind them, also using the unloaded D Company MMG carriers. At first the ultimate objective was Bondeno, but this was soon allotted to the Lothians and 2 RB, who had moved round through Traghetto, when our 1st Battalion encountered stiff resistance in the town of Mirabello on the next main escape route. The significance of this was that all ferry or bridge sites over the River Reno had been seized by 6 Armoured Division, but that great obstacle now turned South towards Bologna. There was therefore a 10-mile open gap between the Reno and the River Panaro at Finale Emilia; up this corridor was the last escape route to the Po immediately West of Ferrara, and across the Panaro the enemy would have East-flank security for their race to the Po ferries. This partly explained the German resistance at Mirabello, but although a powerful enemy radio was continually calling 'Richard Ulrich Gustav . . . Komme' on the 1st Battalion net, it was not then realized that the Parachute Corps HQ and its main supply area lay just to the West at Casumaro. Mushrooms of smoke indicated the blowing up of ammunition dumps, but the parachutists were still full of fight.

A Company managed to clear the North East end of Mirabello without too much trouble, but suffered continual sniping from the buildings at the South West end, after two platoons and a troop of tanks had made a lodgement. Regrettably Sgt Williams, a fine leader of long standing, was mortally wounded here. When Cpl Cromwell's Wasp carrier was later brought up by Maj Howard it exacted a terrible retribution; the flame-thrower lost pressure, however, after three rounds and had itself to be covered out by 16/5L smoke. C Company had taken over the Northern end as A cleared on South Westwards.

Earlier, back around a cross-roads in vast open meadows West of Route 64, the 2IC, Maj Howard, had prudently insisted on dispersing all vehicles. The Allied bomb-line had clearly not kept up with 6 Armoured's advance, for one US aircraft had attacked the 16/5L column earlier. Now, as Capt Mills, freed momentarily from the command vehicle, moved forward with Lt Wathen and Rfn Partington towards Poggio to contact the 17/21L Group four US Mustang aircraft knocked out two turretless Honeys they had just passed on the open road. Quick driving, a created dust cloud and an even quicker bail-out only just saved the three Riflemen. Surprisingly, despite several aircraft runs apiece, the sloped armour of the IO's Humber scout car allowed them to limp away, when the Mustangs expended their last ·5 ammunition on the 16/5 reserve squadron, colourful with hastily exposed recognition panels.

To the North West the Lothian Group in a splendid run had managed to get one tank over the Panaro at Bondeno before it was blown, losing a dozen in the process. In Mirabello Lt Darwin's platoon on the North side could harass individual parachutists, as they played the game of dodging greatcoated and helmetless Westwards across the open, posing as unlikely civilians—for the Italians were safely under cover. Salvoes of Nebelwerfer, sullenly fired by cut-off enemy to the South and from the West on to Mirabello, indicated that they had abandoned it. A perfectly timed relief by the Welsh Guards allowed the 16/5L and our 1st Battalion a few hours sleep East of Mirabello, bur from the Colonel downwards the Riflemen were very tired, and the inadequate feeding arrangements forced on the Battalion, first by RASC transport pooling and then the inability of wheels to keep up, had begun to tell. It was still far from clear that the battle had been won, and manners were curt. During the night the Germans lost their main Po ferries to air attack, and desperation was felt in all their acts.

The task for 23 April 1945, St George's Day, was for 16/5L Group to advance to the original Divisional objective, the Panaro at Finale. Starting at 0530 hrs, the Group moved off West through Mirabello, B Squadron leading, followed by B Company. Tanks drove at top speed along the road, until the country closed in at Casumaro, another important road junction, where two enemy SPs were knocked out. They were later found to be protection for the abandoned Parachute Corps HQ in buildings opposite, where the Adjutant found the nominal roll of the Intelligence and Signal sections, who turned out almost complete on roll call. The CO of 16/5L boldly decided to race through Casumaro without waiting for Infantry clearance, relying on shock action. B Squadron seized the bridge over a canal parallel but just short of the Panaro intact, but then found the road to the river bridge blocked by an indescribable carnage of burning vehicles and dead Germans and horses, caught nose to tail on the causeway by Allied aircraft soon after dawn.

At 0930 hrs Lt Col Hope was confering as usual in Lt Col Smyly's turretless Honey, which they shared, at the West end of Casumaro; the 16/5L Corporal driver was dismounted. A sniper shot Lt Col Hope through the back and then with a second shot killed the Corporal; he continued to fire on a marked ambulance vehicle which tried to come up. Lt Col Smyly then, under wireless guidance, drove the Honey back to a point where our new MO, Capt H. Burrell, could evacuate the Colonel; but the imposed delay had caused much loss of blood and he was very tired. The 2IC, Maj Howard, being at Battalion HQ and fully in touch, at once took over command, calling up Maj Mackay from the less committed D Company to act as 2IC.

The first order was for B Company to mop up the village. This was Lt Col Hope's old Company, and their search for the sniper was rigorous. When he was flushed, striving to disguise his parachute uniform under a looted overcoat, but still carrying his rifle and telescopic sight, he received short shrift.

The trickle of prisoners now became a flood, and posed an escort problem. As well as parachutists—the defenders of Cassino, for the first time losing some of their cockiness—there were men from our old Ronco opponent, 278 Division, whose self-congratulatory pamphlet with a picture of *Gefangene Tommies auf dem Weg nach Berlin*, was now an ironic touch. 16/5L tanks rightly concentrated on destroying the masses of vehicles and guns overrun in their camouflaged rows along the lines of trees North of the village, ensuring that no major equipments could be remanned by the parties of Germans concealed in the growing crops. Draught horses were everywhere, in a scene more like a panorama of Waterloo than a modern mechanized battlefield.

First contact with II US Corps of 5 Army, in the form of 6 South African Armoured Division, was made at 1000 hrs 23 April; by 1230 hrs the appearance of American infantry on our left, who had advanced due North from Bologna, ensured that no more escape thrusts would come from enemy pockets to the South. There was much sniping and salvoes of Nebelwerfer from over the Panaro. One rocket landed on B Company command half-track, concussing Maj Shakerley and killing two of the oldest Riflemen, Hand, a signaller, and North, Capt Lee's batman. Maj Howard had reconnoitred the ground with an escort and then sent out patrols to report the state of the Panaro bridges. 5 Platoon found an unmarked Northern trestle bridge intact but blocked by burning vehicles, and brought back 170 prisoners. Lt R. W. Walter's platoon were soon pinned down by Spandau fire at 100-yard range; a dangerous deadlock was only broken when a troop of the South African Special Service Battalion gallantly routed the enemy group, losing a tank in the process, but were unable to push on to the bridge itself. The II US Corps, informal liaison with whom had prevented an attack on us, were to advance North West towards the Po, West of the Panaro. As the Americans moved silently off to attack across the river, the 1st Battalion received orders to pull back from the 8 Army boundary, their mission achieved. The A1 Echelon was picked up en route, having lost the MT Sergeant, Sgt Taylor, wounded when driving off a harassing enemy Spandau group. Three officers and 30 enemy were picked up by an Echelon sortie, the crews of yesterday's Nebelwerfers.

Unknown to us, 10 US Mountain Division were crossing the Po well upstream, having encountered little opposition, as German 14 Army's westerly Corps withdrew to cover Milan and the immense numbers of depots and troops in Italy's industrial North West. To our North the Lothians had reached the Po from Bondeno, but that formidable mirage of the previous summer was now just one more obstacle to be taken in 15 Army Group's stride. The combined work of the Allied ground forces had flushed the enemy into daylight movement, and hence destruction of their vehicles by our air forces and armour. Although resolute soldiers of 1 and 4 German Parachute Divisions swam the Po like their commander, Heidrich, they were, thanks to the linking of 6 Armoured Division's tanks and riflemen with II US Corps, and to Allied air power, without any equipment to make a stand in the Alps. The lateral link of the parachutists with

26 Panzer and 29 PG Divisions had been cut at Bondeno, and on 24 April, after a gallant stand, the latter were smashed by 78 Division and 2 Armoured Brigade; although individuals swam the Po, they too were without their equipment, and their Corps Commander surrendered next morning.

The 15 Army Group aim of destroying the German Army Group South of the Po had been achieved by skilful Allied generalship, courageous leadership in all arms, and by the Germans' enforced inflexibility, caused by Hitler's refusal to allow withdrawal until it was too late. By 25 April the Americans had five divisions over the Po, racing to block the Alpine passes by fanning out East and West from Verona. The Italian Committee of Liberation ordered a general insurrection the same day, which made further German movement almost impossible, although the sight of synthetic 'partisans' waving newly made coloured scarves, firing abandoned weapons in the air and pushing around German stragglers before whom they had fawned a few days earlier was somewhat sickening; the proper partisans would be met in the hills later. When on 28 April 90 PG, the old 90 Light of Desert days, surrendered after a gallant rearguard action, and Graziani gave up with his Ligurian Army, the small number of Desert men still in the 1st Battalion felt the final breaking of a long chain.

However, as the Battalion, concentrated in Casumaro, trekked back East in the Lancers' dust to the old Mirabello leaguer one concern transcended even the longing for food and sleep—the fate of Lt Col Hope. Moved to 5 CCS at Argenta, he had been seen by Rfn Lashmar of the Echelon, but the next day Maj Howard and a party, including his driver and batman, were told at the CCS that he had died in the night. Lt Col J. C. Hope represented, even to the most newly joined, the 1st Battalion itself. Trained as a·solicitor, he had received an emergency commission in 1940 and joined the 1st that September, where his younger brother, H. A. Hope, was already a Regular company commander. He had been Intelligence Officer and then Adjutant at Sidi Rezegh, where he won his first MC bringing ammunition forward under fire. Escaping from the German armour there, he had commanded C Company in the Knightsbridge ebb and flow until he was wounded, but was back in time to fight a rearguard action at Alam Halfa in command of B. Active at Alamein, he ran down in the open and captured an Italian divisional commander and staff at pistol-point after that battle. Refusing convalescence after a wound, he hitch-hiked from Alexandria to take over B Company again, receiving a bar to his MC for his gallantry throughout 1942. His judgment and skill saved lives at Wadi Akarit, and his leadership maintained his company, exposed to heavy fire at Kournine, near Tunis, until he was again wounded. His return to the 1st in North Africa in Spring 1943 was the greatest help to Lt Col Williams, for he inspired enormous confidence at Battalion HQ, combining his tactical flair with kindly common sense in training younger officers. Dispelling all tendency to flap ('Take a deep breath . . . now take another. Good, now start to think your way logically through this problem. . . .'), his warm sense of fun and Christian leadership were to be badly missed in the peace after the approaching victory. The award of a DSO recognized the excellence of the 1st Battalion's work under his command at the Traghetto Gap, but it was a saddened battalion who saw him buried on 25 April 1945 in the Argenta military cemetery, as Rfn Ganderton sounded the 'Last Post'.

Far-away Vienna, the goal so cynically hailed by Riflemen the previous August, had fallen to the Russians on 13 April, and their troops were now sprawling South West towards Carinthia, spreading rapine and rape down those pleasant valleys. From the mountainous hinterland Tito's partisans, following up the retreating Germans and the Royalist Chetniks, were thrusting towards Klagenfurt and Trieste, while partisans of a Communistic nature were very active in North East Italy. If the Western Allies were not to find themselves presented with a *fait accompli* far exceeding any Yalta concessions, they had better hurry. This 8 Army did, wheeling V Corps, and XIII Corps on the left, round to the North East after they established crossings over the Po on 24 April. Since it had raced across the front of XIII Corps, 6 Armoured Division now came under that HQ. 1 Guards Brigade made our crossing near Ferrara, but for 26 Armoured Brigade with their platypus tracks the drive to the Panaro was their last action. What was wanted now was speed in the shape of motor battalions and the Derby Yeomanry, so Maj H. Baring, BM 61 Brigade, came to tell the 1st Battalion on 24 April that they had reverted to command. Leaving 16/5L, for whose drive and friendliness Riflemen had great respect, the Battalion moved a short distance up the road to an unspoiled area, where all three battalions were standardized with two companies in Whites and one in three-tonners.

Surprisingly Capt Waterfield's A2 Echelon crossed the Po first on the night 26/27 April and it was not until the early hours of 28 April that the 1st Battalion crawled over that great river, as Bofors pounded every floating object for fear of any further fluvial mines; the floating Bailey had been gapped by one, causing a two-hour delay to add to that caused by New Zealand queue-jumping. At Lendinara the 1st caught their Echelon up, but after watching Lt Col Darling blow his 7 RB out of covert on his hunting horn the New Zealanders crowded the 60th off their Adige bridge approaches as priorities changed. The CO went forward to join Maj Mackay at St Elena, near Monselice, where the rest of 61 Brigade were, but the 1st, after a bad night on the pavements of Lendinara, only reached there by the better-controlled V Corps bridge at Rovigo during the night 29/30 April. After a few hours' sleep in the park of a Gothic mansion the 1st Battalion moved on, impatient at having been the reserve battalion of 61 Brigade ever since leaving Mirabello.

For the first time Riflemen lifted their eyes to see the foothills of the Alps, with the knowledge that two great rivers, the Po and the Adige, were at last behind them. The countryside was increasingly beautiful with the promise of summer, and unlike the rest of Italy the Germans had had no time to despoil it; eggs, flowers and cheers were appreciated in that order, but everyone was driving too fast on the splendid roads to engage in the social exchanges of the 2nd and 12th Battalions on their run-up to Belgium. Padua and later Venice had been captured on 29 April, and the New Zealanders were thrusting Eastwards as rapidly as possible towards Trieste, as it became clear that Tito was claiming not only that port but the North Eastern province of Venezia Giulia. Partisans of every political persuasion, moreover, were in a ferment of excitement, and it was important to keep the situation in hand, particularly as there were large numbers of armed Germans—the survivors of both 15 Army Group and Tito operations—being squeezed towards the Alpine bottlenecks.

The 1st overtook its A2 Echelon in Padua and reached Treviso at noon, 30

April; Maj Mackay, on ahead to reconnoitre the town, had found II US Corps, last seen at Finale, skirmishing with Germans in the streets, and the dead were still unburied as the Battalion drove in. Companies concentrated on the North of town, but after much-needed sleep B Company was despatched North East on 1 May in a vain effort to catch up 7 RB at San Vito, and come under command of Col Darling, who was racing for Udine; C Company meanwhile formed a block on the East of Treviso until a German force was confirmed as being in New Zealand hands. 2 RB were directed North from the town, and Lt Col R. Fyffe later arranged the surrender of the remnants of a German corps. At last, however, the 60th were to be given a task. Crossing the Piave on the afternoon of 1 May, with the CO well on ahead, the column moved South of Route 13 by side roads, once encountering a concrete roadblock and having to turn on a causeway to the Riflemen's cynical cheers; there were only two maps available, and it was with relief that the German concrete ford alongside the bombed Tagliamento bridge was found. However, there had been a storm in the mountains and there was a fast-rising spate; led by the Technical Adjutant in pouring rain, motor-cycles were lifted on to bonnets, Jeep fan belts removed and, finally using tow and winch, the 1st Battalion and its Echelon just made it across. The best prize was to have the only full petrol vehicle East of the now impassable river, Lt Round thus ensuring the 1st's mobility.

Concentrated at Bertiolo for the night with B Squadron Derby Yeomanry (DY) in support, the CO gave out orders for operations on 2 May. The 1st Battalion had been given the task of clearing a large triangle bounded by Route 13 on the South and East and by the Tagliamento on the West; its Northern apex led into the gorge near Gemona, where the river and road are forced together. Nothing was known of the enemy, other than that they were probably from the Trieste area. It was important to cut them off and open the passes up into Austria. The initial plan was therefore to work a 'stop force' of a DY troop and both MMG platoons under Lt Ryrie, MC, forward along the East bank of the Tagliamento to sit in the apex, while the rest of the Squadron moved up Route 13 from Udine, and the Carrier Platoon under Lt Maufe, MC, screened the Battalion forward to Coloredo, which was to be the firm base for the drive. With great speed the various detachments shot off into the early-morning mist, driving along airfield runways still strewn with bombs for projected demolition. However, although the right and centre progressed rapidly it was the 'stop force' which came up against a rear-guard of tanks and infantry; they were probably some of those with whom 7 RB, unknown to us as distances had made wireless inoperative, had had a brush between San Vito and the Tagliamento ford the day before.

Accordingly C Company, with two anti-tank guns, the Carrier Platoon, and a troop DY, were sent North East from Coloredo to establish a stop covering the Route 13 road junction below the hill town of Gemona. However, a squadron of 27L, despite all advice, brushed aside DY, saying they were acting on 8 Army orders, and entered Gemona; their big Staghound armoured cars rapidly got into difficulties with Germans in the narrow streets. On orders from above to use all resources in their aid, part of the C Company force had to be diverted to cover the 27L crews, leaving Gemona on foot, having lost six vehicles and a dead trooper (found next day in the morgue among the bodies of many civilian hostages shot by the SS). To the 1st Battalion's anger this rash foray allowed a formed body from 24 SS Jäger Division to slip past the abandoned road junction and to block the defile at Ospedaletto, where the Gemona spur comes down to the river. Sergeant Bowden's carrier section was temporarily trapped under the gun of a petrol-less Mark III tank; after delicate negotiations by Capt House the remarkably unpleasant crew blew it up and surrendered. In this country of little green hills and copses Lt G. Anderson managed to shoot up a truck-load of Germans with his tommy-gun, but Rfn Mitchell, a DR, was captured on a side road; the discovery of his motor-cycle with a bullet in the tank seemed ominous, but he was released later by the SS at Tarvisio, having been armed with a Luger for protection against partisans. By nightfall 2 May 45 about 600 prisoners, including administrative troops, were being marched South under escort, but the 1st Battalion, as it concentrated in Artegna, paid little heed to the BBC announcement that von Vietinghoff's South Western Army Group had surrendered. They were now up against General Löhr's Balkan Army Group, and the enemy in the gorge ahead, which they had been ordered to open as soon as possible, included die-hard types such as officer cadets and marines as well as 24 SS. The only local good news was that Gemona had been abandoned. This was brought by Maj Macpherson, who had parachuted in to organize the local red-scarf and pro-Tito Garibaldi partisans during the winter, aided by an escaped New Zealand prisoner of war; right-wing green-scarf partisans liaised from the West but were less effective.

7 RB had bumped our SS opponents the previous day North of Udine, when Capt J. A. S. Keith, originally 60th, was badly wounded by treachery; now they just managed to interpose themselves between Tito's advancing forces and the retreating Chetniks, our original allies, at Cormons, to the South East. The Chetniks, still fully armed and with their families, slowly moved West until they were in our Echelon area and surrendered to General Murray. On the same day the New Zealanders entered Trieste and found themselves in the midst of an international dispute, which lasted until the 1st Battalion left Italy in 1947.

On 3 May A Company closed up to the gorge just South of Ospedaletto, while C Company and the DY moved into partisan-held Gemona. A fine feat of driving up hill tracks took the DY tanks up on to a spur above Gemona, from which Venzone and Route 13 between it and Ospedaletto could be overlooked. After C had dug in on the reverse slope, the DY moved over the crest. Four old Italian M13 tanks, driven by Germans, were knocked out down below, which prompted a riposte of 88-mm HE fire on the spur. At 2000 hrs an SS Corporal arrived to ask for terms; from this time on the Adjutant, almost the sole speaker of very basic German, added interpretation to his other duties. Our guns were now up and the Corporal was told that a terrific concentration would be put down if a white flag was not hoisted by 0600 hrs 4 May.

At 0630 hrs 4 May A Company occupied Ospedaletto unopposed after 5 minutes' intense fire from a field and a medium regiment; after firing what turned out to be the last ground-action shots of the campaign, the enemy had withdrawn at 0530 hrs without putting up a white flag. This was to be typical of the SS, who shot a local priest who volunteered to seek a parley with them; they also killed many male hostages as reprisals against the partisans, who had knocked out much transport in the last few months.

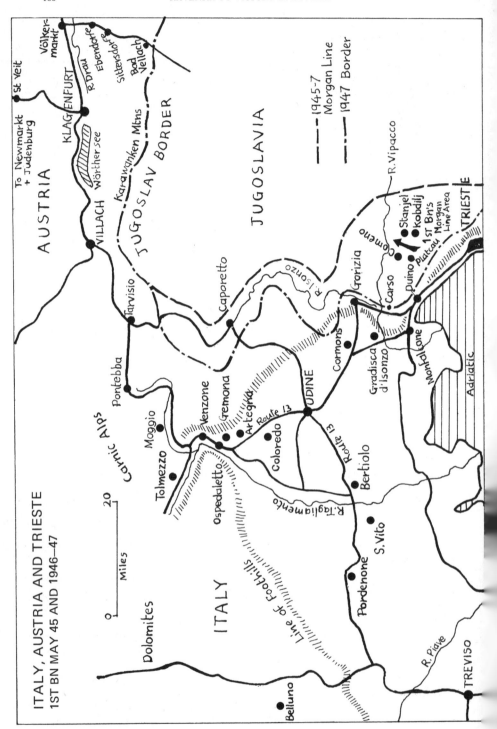

ITALY, AUSTRIA AND TRIESTE
1ST BN MAY 45 AND 1946—47

B Company passed through A and managed to get half-way to Venzone by the afternoon, before halting when the ground opened out astride a stream. Good information on enemy locations, some in flanking caves, was gleaned from civilians. There seemed to be about 300 SS in the Venzone narrows, which with its stone walls and flanking river and cliffs made a nasty position to force. An air OP was engaged by Spandaus when flying over no-man's-land.

The 1st's orders were now only to shoot if shot at, but nevertheless to try to arrange to pass through to Austria. At last light an SS officer came through to parley, and Maj Howard, as CO, and Maj Mackay courageously went forward blindfolded to the SS regimental HQ. In view of the fate of the priest and others, there was much misgiving in the Battalion, but they returned with the promise of an answer from HQ 24 SS Division at 1100 hrs 5 May.

The written reply came promptly by an emissary, who was met by the CO and Adjutant at the stream on Route 13. When it was delivered to General Murray and Brigadier Gore at Ospedaletto it was found to refuse surrender while we were allied to 'communist bandits'. General Murray, keen on saving life but anxious to advance into Austria, replied that it would be better for them to surrender and let British, rather than less 'kid-glove' forces, into Austria. If there was no answer by 0500 hrs next day, Venzone would be blotted out. Although there would be very heavy artillery support, any advance by the motor companies was likely to meet resistance in caves and cellars, so the outcome was anxiously awaited.

On 6 May a note arrived at 0600 hrs in time to stop the fire of two heavy batteries, two medium and three field regiments on Venzone. The SS Divisional Commander met General Murray and promised to get an answer from his Corps Commander; the 1st guaranteed not to open fire before 1800 hrs in return for all bridges being left intact. Meanwhile on 4 May 2 RB had been moved from Belluno to the parallel Caporetto road, now in Jugoslavia, which joined Route 13 at Tarvisio on the Austrian border; similar negotiations were in progress there, with the advantage of being nearer the German Corps HQ and the frontier.

From 1200 hrs onwards the 1st were forced to watch the deceitful SS, under cover of our guarantee, streaming North up the road. At 1600 hrs B Company occupied Venzone and A was then dropped off at the Carnia road junction to guard the left flank from large forces known to be in Tolmezzo. Another delaying parley between SS and a German officer of von Vietinghoff's late staff, loaned by V Corps, proving abortive, C Company led the 1st, less A, into Moggio over the river.

At first light on 7 May B Company and a troop DY set off for Pontebba, finding that the road had been blown twice by the SS in the night; but rapid work on the blows allowed transport to catch up B, who had reached Pontebba on foot, that night. With less tricky opponents on the other road 2 RB were able to furnish the carrier escort to General Murray on the border and thus be first British troops into Austria; 7 RB were the first battalion to enter on 8 May, and, by racing to Klagenfurt, forestalled Tito's claim to the Carinthian capital by four hours. The 1st Battalion, moving forward at first light to occupy Villach, were instead ordered to relieve 2 RB in Tarvisio; they, though denied these local honours, loyally played their part, not only securing valuable food dumps from looting but, by a mixture of bluff and diplomacy, preventing with a D Company platoon the only Jugoslav armoured column from invading Austria. Commander

V Corps expressed great satisfaction with their execution of his personal orders on this. Although, as 1 Welch relieved the 1st that evening, crowds in London were celebrating VE day, it was clear to Riflemen that only tireless and intelligent work in the absence of any political briefing would prevent the seeds of another war being sown in that area. The 1st's recce parties moved to Klagenfurt later in the day, finding it a milling mass of still armed SS and all the races of Central Europe, displaced under German rule.

On 9 May the 1st Battalion drove via Villach to Klagenfurt. Tito's troops were much in evidence, and thousands of armed German soldiers were wandering aimlessly about. With so many old scores to be settled in this meeting-place of East, West and South, the country was like a powder keg.

From the East, Wehrmacht troops and their Hungarian allies were fleeing from the Russians and Bulgarians, who were now very near. They, and the German-led Cossack troops, were unwilling to disarm until in British hands, and 6 Armoured Division had insufficient troops to handle the situation. Infantry divisions were urgently needed up from Italy, and until then, with little guidance, but a rapidly increasing knowledge of Balkan and other politics, 61 Brigade's Riflemen must do the best they could.

Croatian Ustashi, hated by Tito's men for their actions in Axis-occupied territory, were shot down by them if overtaken. Distant shots and abandoned corpses indicated that other old scores were being paid off. Everywhere displaced persons or forced labourers, whose world had been upset by the Nazis, were moving in the direction thought safest; in very few cases was it Eastwards. The Austrians themselves, disciplined by seven years of Nazi control, were orderly and pathetically reliant on British justice; both sides found it difficult to adhere to the official policy of non-fraternization, foreign to their natures.

Formed bodies of armed Germans were desperately marching North over the Karawanken passes from Jugoslavia and were refusing to surrender to Tito's troops, knowing that hard labour in return for their past conduct was the best fate which could befall them. As the Jugoslavs saw it, they had captured General Löhr, and he had theoretically surrendered his Army Group to Tito, regardless of whose area they were in.

B Company was sent a few miles South East of the town to try to locate and disarm SS troops, while the renumbered 7 Platoon of C Company guarded a power station by the Gurk bridge on the Völkermarkt road. Lt P. Way found himself the next day the umpire in a tense situation, where his platoon were vastly outnumbered by the Jugoslav troops, who were stopping all transport at the bridge; their aim was to strip all surrendered personnel, arrest wanted individuals and take over vehicles. Part of an SS Division, with whom the Rifle Brigade were also having trouble on another road, refused to lay down their arms until they were across the bridge and in British hands. Both sides lined the ditches with Spandaus at the ready, but accepting Lt Way as the unarmed umpire. General von Pannwitz, German commander of XV Cossack Cavalry Corps, which had been formed by the Germans in 1943, arrived to announced his determination to fight his way through the Jugoslavs into British hands if need be. Lt Way left Sgt Freeman as a token against violence and drove off to HQ 61 Brigade with General von Pannwitz, followed by the Jugoslav brigadier. By the time the CO and he had returned the SS had solved an incident which seemed likely to turn into a blood-bath by passing the road block as it was opened for a 27L troop, and had thrown away their arms on the far side.

On this same 10 May Battalion HQ, A Company and an MMG platoon had been sent East to Völkermarkt, where the Graz road joins one from the South over the wooden Drau bridge. Tito's troops were setting up their local government and issuing edicts to the bewildered Austrians, and were blocking the defile by looting the stream of German trucks and carts passing through the town. The CO and Adjutant visited HQ 14 Jugoslav Division; they were told that the Jugoslavs would continue to stop armed Germans passing, and we replied that the Graz road must be kept open and free of blocks. A Company occupied food-shops and the administrative buildings, and the next day picketed the road to push the mass of German vehicles through and on to St Veit. In the evening the Jugoslavs diverted part of the column South over the Drau, and their claim to take prisoners could not be disputed in the absence of guidance over the Löhr surrender.

On 12 May the 1st Battalion position in Völkermarkt, where they had been heavily outnumbered by both the Jugoslavs and the passing Germans, became stronger. D Company moved into barracks at the West end of town, and B Company, who had finished their SS task, into meadows, soon to be filled with horses, by the important Drau bridge. It was here that Capt M. P. Lee acquired the Cossack mare Maroushka, whose eventual movement to England, and grazing requirements, led him to his future wife. One of B's platoons went with Jugoslav agreement further South to Ebendorf, where their prisoners were being collected, to ensure that no shooting took place.

That morning Maj Christian, acting 2IC, started organizing disarmament of the first battalion of the Cossack Corps, who had arrived with their mounted band on the hill to the East. Under V Corps authority, it had been agreed that the Cossacks would be disarmed by us and that Jugoslav troops would guarantee their safe passage through the town. However, as soon as the first disarmed Cossack files began to trot through behind the last Wehrmacht the Jugoslavs broke their word and diverted them down a side-street to the Drau. Apart from stealing horses, reprisals for anti-partisan action seemed certain; the German Brigade Major, for whom Colonel Wagner, his Divisional Commander, came back to look, was never seen again. Carriers were used to herd the stampeding Cossacks back through the Jugoslavs, and the latter had to be threatened with use of tanks.

All day on 13 May the stream of Cossacks in their red-topped fur hats, riding every variety of quadruped from ponies to fine-looking horses, some with foal at foot, clattered through town. On the hill the separate dumps of weapons by category, including German, Russian, Italian and even captured British, grew under the eye of A Company, who also picketed the route. Carelessly cleared machine pistols ripped off a last wild burst when thrown on a heap, incurring a final Teutonic scream of rage from the German battalion commander. By late afternoon the two regiments commanded by Germans had passed on towards St Veit, but the third, entirely officered by Russians, with priests and women in their little carts, had refused to disarm. General von Pannwitz was brought up, and persuaded them to obey his orders. However, for fear of further Jugoslav intervention, orders came for that regiment and the remaining two Cossack divisions to be disarmed further East and move by a northerly route to St Veit.

C Company had moved up from Klagenfurt and was sent down to Ebendorf, on the road South from the Drau to the Jugoslav frontier.

For the next week the situation in Völkermarkt was tense, as the Jugoslavs claimed all this part of Carinthia, and locally tried to impose their military government from the town hall they had seized before our arrival. Looting of supplies and deportation of Austrians was stopped with difficulty, and carriers were stationed alongside key stores. On one night the removal of medical stores from the local hospital was only stopped by the rapid deployment of one of the 17/21L tanks from the troop under command.

In retrospect it must be said that the Jugoslavs had suffered greatly since their entry on the Allied side in 1941 and the rapid Axis occupation. They no doubt saw the British presence as a tiresome intervention, when they had a chance to remove supplies and forced labour South to rebuild their country. The local style of doing this under a Town Major and with an intractable commissar was, however, bullying and unattractive, and even Maj Owen, who had been British Liaison Officer with them for 18 months, now found their conduct as unpleasant as did the Riflemen. Their behaviour towards women, however, was throughout absolutely correct. It contrasted starkly with the situation of blazing hillsides, drunkenness and looting which the Adjutant found when moving gingerly with an ambulance into the area occupied by the Russians' Bulgarian allies; he succeeded in bringing out a Hungarian officer's wife, who had been raped many times, with her husband.

Part of 78 Division and 7 Armoured Brigade had moved through towards Graz, and now 46 Division arrived from Greece, moving into our area just East of the town and rapidly expelling the 1st's Echelon from a Schloss, earlier occupied by Ukrainian SS. The 1st now came under 26 Armoured Brigade and continued to keep roads open and maintain law and order.

On 20 May the Jugoslavs started to move South over their border, to the pleasure of the Riflemen, who had found their rough methods distasteful. On 23 May 45 C Company established themselves in villages down to the border at Bad Vellach. For the next few days the 1st concentrated on searching its large area of woods and villages, rounding up SS or other German stragglers, and helping the repatriation of prisoners of war; the French eventually left on their own initiative, but a considerable number of Poles and Russians were lifted East at their request. The first day's search for people, arms, ammunition and vehicles showed that a company took three hours for each half square mile, so that in one sense it was a relief to be ordered back to 61 Brigade in Klagenfurt. Völkermarkt was, however, annexed by GOC 46 Division personally for his HQ, and the 1st knew that all good accommodation at Klagenfurt had long gone. On 25 May Riflemen started, with the help of German PW, to clear up the bombed Jäger Kaserne, Austria's Rifle Depot equivalent, and that evening B and C Companies received a warning order for an even more distasteful task.

Unknown to anyone concerned within the Division, the Allied war leaders at Yalta had agreed on the post-war repatriation of all nationals, without apparently securing the position of those that did not wish to return, or those who had emigrated from Russia after the Revolution. The disarmament of the Cossacks had been based on their being taken into British captivity, but the 1st was now told that it had not been guaranteed that they would stay there. The

Cossack division still under 6 Armoured was now to be dehorsed, concentrated and then, without officially being told its fate, to be handed over to the Russians. No doubt, from the stark Soviet point of view, those who had become Soviet citizens after the Revolution were traitors. If they had responded, however, to German propaganda after capture, Communist treatment had given them small cause for loyalty. The 1st believed that they had not fought on the Russian front against their former masters, but had been used for internal security duties in Jugoslavia, no doubt having been glad to move under German protection after suffering under Stalin's collectivization programme. Whatever the rights and wrongs, it needed no imagination to divine what awaited the Cossacks after handing over; a bald announcement on 17 January 1947 of the Soviet hanging of General von Pannwitz, who loyally stayed with his Cossacks, for falsely alleged SS war crimes, was all that the Battalion ever heard.

The operation was under Brig Usher, the CRA, but both Maj Gen Murray and he had dropped broad hints which enabled Col Wagner and all his Germans to escape. The CO spent a day with the two company commanders, reconnoitring the hilly area North West of St Veit to see where the Cossacks were camped and how they might be brought down to the concentration area. B and C Companies and the carriers moved to the Cossack area on 27 May, and the movement of the horsemen down the next day took place as planned. The Welsh Guards then dehorsed each party and separated officers from men, while 12 RHA ran the concentration areas. By night many officers and some men took to the hills, but two platoons sent to the passes North intercepted and returned half a dozen officers and 30 soldiers. It had been particularly insensitive to detail the 1st Battalion(which had originally been ordered to disarm the Cossacks) for this duty, and the Battalion, which had carried out its unpleasant duties with strict self-discipline, heard with disgust accounts of the handing over of these simple horsemen to Soviet troops. At least under Maj Gen Murray no lies or deception had been used within 6 Armoured Division, and Maj Howard had played a considerable part in finding a formula to save those who had emigrated before the war and were not Soviet citizens.

The last major task associated with the war was relief by B Company on 1 June of 2 RB, on guard duty at the Divisional PW cage South of the town; most of the 2000 SS were moved by 2 RB to Italy next day, leaving 500 Wehrmacht prisoners for us; this camp, run by Capt Lee, was in addition to guards on VPs all round Klagenfurt.

Personnel problems were legion, since the Python scheme now removed our last longer-service soldiers, including all the Orderly Room, at a time when the paper war intensified. Over 200 more recent arrivals, who should have provided the key replacements, were transferred to 2 RB, who were being built up like our 2nd Battalion, for Far Eastern service which never took place. No UK reinforcements came out, only 80 came from 2 RB, and spasmodic drafts from the CRU were largely AA and RASC with no useful specialists. Welcome to all—except the struggling Battalion HQ staff—was the start of a month's home leave, LIAP, by an overland route efficiently organized without help from our forces in Germany; it achieved its stated promise of rotating everybody home before Christmas, and early truck trips over the Alps, later replaced by rail from Milan and Villach, were a great feat.

For the companies, now back in KD, life began in a simple Austrian way to look good. A pleasant rest area by the Wörther See was occupied by each company in turn. A Divisional Race Club was organized on the green meadows, where Maj Shakerley acted as starter and Capt Waterfield rode our best horse, 'Vienna'. Riflemen went in turn to 61 Brigade's excellent rest camp 'The Green Man' at Velden on the lake (again run by Capt Voules), and in Klagenfurt cinemas and the odd show started up.

Capt. B. Ryan, the Quartermaster, arrived back in time for a move North. RQMS Knief, who had loyally done both jobs to let the QM go home, now left himself on Python. On 24 July the 1st joined 26 Armoured Brigade, who had taken over the Judenburg area as the Russians withdrew to the delight of the cowed populace. Battalion HQ was at Neumarkt on the Vienna road, but it took a day to tour companies, who were tucked into villages in valleys to the West and North.

In one of the most sensible postings of the period, Maj A. G. L. Goschen, MC, was appointed to run military government in Klagenfurt, based on the family home at Schloss Tentschach, where he was a kind host to old friends. Another and more senior Desert leader arrived back with the 1st Battalion in August, when Lt Col S. C. F. De Salis, DSO, took over the command he had held up to Sidi Rezegh in 1941. Maj Howard, who had taken over command in the Finale action, when Lt Col Hope was mortally wounded, and had handled the operations North of Udine with skill, reverted to 2IC. The new CO must have looked on this motley collection of young officers and men—many of the latter inevitably ignorant of Rifle style and standards—and inwardly sighed for his Desert 1st Battalion.

However, he gave every encouragement to the young leaders, who would soon share the task of rebuilding the Battalion, as older men left on release. In return, his patent probity and unselfishness, as he endured yet another family separation, won respect. It was with great regret that the 1st Battalion heard that it had been ordered to move back into Italy to rejoin 2 Armoured Brigade once more. When the Battalion left the green Austrian hills—soon to be snow-covered—on 16 September 45 it viewed with distaste the noise and dirt in the parched brown lands of Italy. The little town of Lonigo, South of the Vicenza-Verona road, and Cologna, next door for C Company, provided only rough billets, but at least those who cared about the Battalion's future, knew that they had a Commanding Officer who would fight his hardest to look after them.

CHAPTER VII
THE LIBERATION OF GREECE

(Maps: pages 176 and 180)

While the 1st Battalion had been fighting on the road to Bologna in Autumn 1944, it will be remembered that first 4 and then 46 Division disappeared from the order of battle of 8 Army, at a time when infantry were desperately short. Their destination was Greece, and this chapter will concern itself with the activities of our 11th Battalion during the two years spent there.

Britain and France had guaranteed the integrity of Greece in 1939, and the Greeks' successful defence of their soil against the Italian invasion from Albania in 1940 had captured the British imagination. The fighting withdrawal of 1941 from Greece to Crete, including our 9th Battalion, the Rangers, had left us a score to settle with the Germans. However, the attempt to take the islands of Kos and Leros, when the Italians collapsed in 1943, had merely rubbed home the old lesson that amphibious operations must have air cover, and served to convince the Turks of their good sense in remaining neutral.

Behind the scenes the Greek Communist Party, KKE, were already laying the foundations of a future bid for power. In September 1941 they set up and thereafter controlled the National Liberation Movement, EAM, in the guise of a left-wing coalition. By April 1942 EAM, under KKE direction, decided to raise a guerrilla army, the National Popular Liberation Army, ELAS; some communist guerrilla bands already existed, of which the one led by Aris was particularly flourishing. In the same year another guerrilla movement, the National Republican Greek League, EDES, was set up with British support in the Epirus; it was run by former officers of a republican background with Zervas as its leader.

In 1942 the British were anxious to cut one of the principal supply routes from the Balkans to Rommel. In an effort to secure British arms, both Aris and Zervas took part in the blowing of a viaduct on the main railway line to Athens; the leaders in this sabotage were a British team, which was then enlarged to form the British Military Mission. Thereafter ELAS, while eagerly receiving arms, could not be persuaded to engage in guerrilla warfare against the Axis occupying forces, who, outside Athens, were largely Italian. Instead Aris turned on the band led by Saraphis, another republican former regular officer; after capture Saraphis secured his freedom by agreement to become the military commander of ELAS, working with Aris.

In 1943 Saraphis concentrated on expanding the ELAS bands into divisions, backed by a reserve in the form of a home guard in each village. When Italy capitulated the Germans took over as the principal occupying power—the Bulgarians had occupied Macedonia—but ELAS, with much Italian equipment, unsuccessfully turned on EDES in Epirus, in the first round of a civil war. Six German divisions were tied down in Greece, but restricted their control to the towns, except when they conducted damaging sweeps against the guerrillas; they formed Greek security battalions to assist them in internal security duties. After another attack by ELAS on EDES, our Military Mission got both sides to accept an armistice in 1944. EDES, within its restricted area in the Epirus, was particularly backed by our Mission, which by 1944 realized that it was the only force standing in the way of a complete EAM/ELAS take-over when the Germans left. One fine 60th Rifleman, Maj D. J. Wallace, was at the forefront in Epirus from 1943 on. A brilliant humanist, who had earlier spent four years in Greece, he died alongside his Andartes, storming a German-held town in August 1944. Their epitaph to him, 'The soil of Greece is proud to offer hospitality to this hero', might stand also for his brother Riflemen, who were shortly to fall in defence of democracy in Hellas.

In noting the inactivity of the guerrillas against the occupation forces, it must be said that German retribution, in the form of blowing up villages, shooting hostages and deportation of slave labour, was brutal. Apart from survival, however, the main concern of ELAS had been to keep its forces in existence and build them up for ultimate take-over. When the withdrawal of the Germans from Greece in Autumn 1944 took the Allies somewhat by surprise, ELAS concentrated on the acquisition of arms rather than any more major harassment; the Germans deliberately sowed the seeds of further civil war by leaving behind undestroyed dumps of arms, ammunition and explosives, including many mortars.

Available to General Scobie, the Commander of the Liberating III Corps, were only some commandos, 2 Parachute Brigade and 23 Armoured Brigade. The former moved unopposed into the Peloponnese in early October 44, and the parachutists advanced into Athens on 13 October from a near-by airfield. By early November the Germans had left all of mainland Greece; behind them was a looted and starving countryside, dominated by ELAS, since III Corps had only enough troops to be in Athens, the Peiraeus and a few other towns.

Little of the background was initially known to our 11th Battalion, who had spent the period since June 44 resting and retraining in Egypt after their long winter in Italy. They had received a minor foretaste only of the complication of Greek politics, when in June they had been ordered to take over a Greek camp in Egypt. They had cordoned it to allow the Greek CGS to address his mutinous troops, only 50 of whom out of 6000 remained loyal in the face of organized jeering; the remainder had had to be moved into internment.

Lt Col C. F. G. Henshaw, a pre-war Queen's Westminster, had become Commanding Officer, when Lt Col J. Hunt took over an Indian Brigade. His 21C was soon to be Maj A. G. L. Goschen, MC, from the 1st Battalion; the Adjutant was Capt P. H. Lawrence, MC, with Lt The Hon H. M. Ritchie as IO. For the liberation of Greece, under 23 Armoured Brigade, the 11th had reorganized, leaving a large Echelon with most transport in Egypt; it included a small Battalion HQ and HQ Company combined. Rifle Companies were: (A) Maj J. A. H. Powell, MC; (B) Maj R. A. Baring; (C) Maj O. Stobart; (D) Maj M. B. Harman; but Maj Powell soon handed over to Capt J. R. C. Radclyffe on posting to the Far East. E (Support), under Capt J. C. H. Beswick, consisted of one carrier platoon, two MMG platoons in Jeeps and one three-inch mortar platoon in carriers.

Embarking on 13 October 1944, the 11th Battalion arrived at Peiraeus in the cruiser *Black Prince* on the evening of 15 October, after the Royal Navy had swept a new channel through minefields when some ships were lost. Their task was to secure the port, while remaining troops passed through to Athens, the Germans being already far to the North. Former Rangers in the Battalion remembered a few Greek phrases to meet a welcome which was overwhelming in the port and city. Relations at this stage were cordial with ELAS, as the 11th rounded up Axis deserters and checked on installations. The first three weeks of November were spent on widespread guards, which provided knowledge of Athens, to be useful later. This included ceremonial and house guards for one distinguished Rifleman, in the form of Field-Marshal Sir Henry Maitland Wilson, and a welcome for another, Mr Eden, as Foreign Secretary. There was a country-wide shortage of food, exacerbated by the terrible roads and many demolitions, and Riflemen had to be very alert if dumps were not to be pilfered.

On 15 November the internal situation showed signs of deteriorating, and General Scobie gave orders that no ELAS troops should be allowed armed into Athens. The 11th formed a mobile force in the city, and watchful check-points on the approaches did the best they could. Unfortunately, as it later turned out, the fact that a large demonstration had passed off peacefully on 19 November was taken to signify an improved political situation. The 11th was therefore ordered North to disperse over a very wide area, relieving 6 Parachute Regiment.

The tasks were twofold. First, to maintain law and order, particularly by assistance in forming the new National Guard and preventing ELAS from intimidating would-be recruits; secondly, to assist distribution of relief to the hungry and cold population, particularly by providing trucks and drivers. A Company was at Trikkala, B 40 miles East at Larissa, Battalion HQ and E 70 miles South at Lamia, and the Echelon a further 85 miles South at Thebes, with C and D at Khalkis and Amfissa respectively, roughly 25 and 70 miles East and West of Thebes.

Each Company Commander became 'Mayor' of his town, dealing with the chaos left behind by the Germans. The latter had only occupied the main towns, leaving the countryside under the dominance of ELAS. People had over four years become used to a state of virtual anarchy, in which the threats and weapons of ELAS had the last word; it was at once noticeable that the population was sulky, compared to the friendliness in Athens, and had been ordered not to fraternize by EAM.

Lamia, where Lt Col Henshaw had his HQ, also housed that of EAM and ELAS. On a pretext of looking for billets the buildings occupied by EAM were entered, and a complete range of shadow Government departments, dominated by KKE, was found; in ELAS there was a political commissar down to platoon level. It was now clear to the Battalion that KKE was using EAM and ELAS as its tools, and its power was growing daily by propaganda and terrorism. Capt Beswick sought an interview with General Saraphis, Commander in Chief of ELAS, whom he found unimpressive and entirely dominated by his commissar, Aris; the latter appeared an evil figure, matching his bad reputation, and particularly suspicious when Saraphis conversed in English.

Meanwhile relief supplies were being guarded and distributed, but the organization in districts not supervised by the International Red Cross was more or less non-existent. Back from a typical carrier patrol, Lt J. G. Harrison reported that, after German burning, there were only 14 houses left out of 200 in the village visited for a population of 2100. This village was the supply centre for

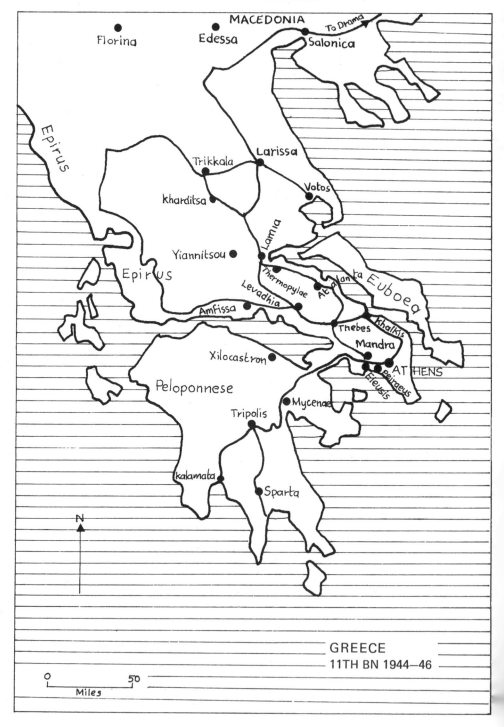

MACEDONIA

To Drama

Florina

Edessa

Salonica

Epirus

Trikkala

Larissa

khardltsa

Votos

Lamia

Yiannitsou

Epirus

Thermopylae

Atalanta

Euboea

Levadhia

Amfissa

Thebes

Khalkis

Mandra

Xilocastron

ATHENS

Peiraeus

Peloponnese

Eleusis

Mycenae

Tripolis

Kalamata

Sparta

N

GREECE
11TH BN 1944—46

0   50
    Miles

25,000 people, living as much as three days away up paths, and mules were short. The main diet was beans, and other items had not been distributed for over a month; clothes were desperately short. 80% of the people had malaria, there was no quinine and no doctor. Building materials were desperately needed if the people were not to die of exposure; Red Cross grain had mostly had to be planted to raise next year's crop.

It might have been thought that everyone would have concentrated on these problems of survival, but the hard-faced men, ambitious for power, were pressing on towards a second round of civil war. In the South of the 11th's vast area the KKE were using every effort to intimidate potential recruits for the National Guard, which would be the only obstacle to ELAS take-over; an alternative ruse was to pack it with KKE recruits. C Company at Khalkis shared with ELAS the guard on a prison camp, originally holding a surrendered security battalion but now augmented by the EAM's political prisoners, accused of collaboration. When ELAS ringed the camp with mortars and machine-guns one night it looked as if a massacre was intended. Sgt Parker solved the problem in a Regimental way without a clash with ELAS. Parties of Riflemen were sent to instruct ELAS in friendly fashion in weapon-handling, while at the same time ridiculing the siting of the posts until ELAS withdrew them in embarrassment.

The outbreak of the second round of the civil war was supposedly occasioned—after the withdrawal of the EAM Ministers from the Government—when, on 3 December 44, the police fired on KKE demonstrations in Athens. In fact, as the 11th, alongside EAM and ELAS HQ, were best placed to see, all the movements to effect a coup were in train before that, and obviously well prepared.

Just after midnight on 1 December Capt F. L. Knight reported that all ELAS troops were packing up in Thebes, and that up to 2000 were moving off South on foot with horse transport; their commander used the pretext of a three-day exercise, which was later seen to be the general cover plan. In Khalkis their troops had also turned out and were heading West for Thebes. On 2 December in Amfissa the chief of the EP, EAM's own police, refused to hand over to the National Guard commander; the build-up in numbers of the Guard, despite ELAS harassment, may have been one factor in the KKE's anxiety to take military action. In Lamia the General commanding 13 ELAS Division cancelled a dinner for E Company officers, as he had orders to take his division South 'on manoeuvres'. Key moderates started to be arrested by EP and disappeared, not to local prisons, but to some ELAS camp in the mountains.

On the early morning of 3 December the National Guard barracks in Thebes was surrounded by ELAS troops, and they were called upon to surrender; acting under duress but with some fifth-column connivance, the National Guard handed over to ELAS their newly issued British arms. Acting entirely on his own initiative (since no orders had been received by the 11th from Athens) Capt Knight took the strongest line in ordering the return to British hands of the 500 rifles and ammunition; by evening he had regained over half the arms in a very tense situation, where he had had to threaten the use of force. In the same way, and presumably to a general plan, the National Guard in Khalkis deserted with their arms; Maj Stobart half closed the swing bridge to bring traffic and shipping to a halt, while he endeavoured to recover the arms. Maj Harman in Amfissa managed to secure the National Guard's rifles by guarding their billet; the weapons had later to be burnt since there was not enough transport to move them to Athens.

On 4 December the Commanding Officer called on General Saraphis and Commissar Aris to protest about the firing by ELAS on a British ambulance. Unfortunately, no orders were received by the 11th, authorizing the arrest of these two key figures; later that night they slipped away with their HQ. Meanwhile the ELAS Cavalry Regiment, which had arrived at Larissa on 30 November, was on its way South; 500 mounted men and some infantry were backed by two old Italian armoured cars, a German Mark II tank and a 37-mm gun. At public meetings the Allies were cheered, but the British were warned not to meddle in Greek politics. Although no political guidance was received from Athens, HQ 23 Armoured Brigade issued a codeword, which concentrated the 11th Battalion in three defended localities on the line of the main road to Athens. A and B moved into Lamia, D to Levadhia and C to Thebes, and this was executed on 6 December. Further North 6 Platoon was under command of the Sikhs at the port of Vólos. During the day a sad loss occurred, when its excellent commander, Lt J. C. Armitage, MC, was killed as a Dingo overturned taking him North from orders at Lamia; Lt M. H. Partridge took over the platoon, which was not to see the 11th again for 6 weeks.

On 7 December, as ELAS troops continued to move South towards Athens, a patrol returning to Amfissa found that the EP, the EAM police, had been busy since our departure in making political arrests. The CO spent much time with an ELAS general, who thought he might be able to assist in a last-minute settlement. However, although discreet signals were sent to HQ 23 Armoured Brigade, a more significant one was received from Athens that day.

'Fighting in Athens began first light. Desultory fighting in most parts of the city with main concentration below Acropolis in Stadium, earlier in area South West from Goudhi. Own casualties light. ELAS very considerable. Reaction not yet clear. Very effective strafing from RAF during later afternoon. KKE Headquarters occupied.'

Despite the very small number of troops in Athens, no order to move in was received by the 11th Battalion. 8 December was spent in trying to locate the ELAS HQ. An alert relief truck-driver had reported a new road block, covered by a 25-pounder, West of Lamia. Intelligent deduction by Capt Beswick, based on knowledge of earlier resistance hiding-places of Aris, led a patrol, consisting of 2/Lt H. McAdam and a Greek doctor in a Jeep, to Yiannitsou; under a cover story of making a routine medical visit, a bodyguard freely told them that both Saraphis and Aris were in the village. Unfortunately, an urgent order to move South came from Brigade at 2015 hrs before action could be taken. By 2300 hrs the 11th Battalion set off in one of the quickest moves ever from billets, in view of a 70-minute turn round-time for outlying Company Commanders. They were to use the main Thebes-Eleusis road and were to engage snipers from vehicles without stopping. The order of march was B, A, Battalion HQ, E and the Echelon, with a tactical HQ behind the leading carriers of E Company. Unfortunately, at 0230 hrs 9 December a B Company three-tonner blocked the road, when it overturned as the route collapsed. The main part of the column had to turn back and take the coast road via Thermopylae and Atalanta. It was not, therefore, until last light 9 December that the column had reassembled a few miles South of Thebes.

Meanwhile other elements had been nearing the city. C Company, being South of the block, had pressed on, but were stopped by ELAS at Mandra; Maj Stobart, however, bluffed his way through and, passing Eleusis without trouble, arrived to take up positions round Constitution Square to cover the Battalion in. The 2IC, Maj Goschen, who had also gone on to find out likely dispositions and tasks for the 11th, was detained by ELAS for two hours in Eleusis, before being allowed to go on into Athens.

The main column—now swollen by other detachments, including 40 RASC trucks—set off again at 2030 hrs 9 December and to their surprise passed through these places unchallenged. Once in the city, however, they met a warm reception from side-street snipers and were hindered by dangling electric cables, being lucky to assemble in Constitution Square by midnight without casualties.

Inevitably there had been straggling vehicles in such a rapid move over the terrible roads. Most of these had been brought on by Capt P. W. Wilson in time to join the column at Thebes, having only had L/Cpl Plant lightly wounded, when returning fire in an ambush. Two carriers, two mortar carriers, the B Company office truck and the E Company ration truck were, however, missing. Considering the number of ELAS ambushes and road blocks set up behind the Battalion, it was a wonder that no one was killed. All the crews gave good accounts of themselves, C/Sgt Smith being wounded in the arm by a policeman; Sgt Eveson and Rfn Overton blasted their way through a telegraph pole and a wall in their carrier, getting through one unfriendly village. It seemed likely at one moment that ELAS would pass them on into Athens, being content with their arms and equipment—Riflemen had sabotaged their vehicles on capture. However, in the end they and other British prisoners were forced to move the 150 miles North from Eleusis to an improvised camp near Kharditsa, mostly on foot and towards the end over snowy mountains.

6 Platoon, B Company, just taken over by Lt Partridge, had been ordered to rejoin the Battalion from detachment in Vólos. Moving with a White in the lead, but with four vulnerable trucks, one carrying petrol, behind, they came under machine-gun fire outside a strongly held village North of Lamia. Lt Partridge went forward on foot to contact an ELAS officer, in the hope of persuading him to let them through. L/Cpl Fox and Rfn Hamling were, however, killed and Rfn West wounded, as the vehicles moved forward into the village on ELAS direction; hopelessly vulnerable on the one road and under overwhelming odds, there was nothing left but to surrender. The platoon, having sabotaged its more important equipment, met up with C/Sgt Smith's party on Boxing Day and were finally freed together from the same camp.

Returning to the situation in Athens, the 11th Battalion found itself concentrated in Constitution Square for the night 9/10 December. Battalion HQ, A and B Company (less 6 Platoon) were in the former KKE HQ on the South side, and D Company were in and around the Old Royal Palace on the East.

On 10 December the Battalion was ordered to conduct two operations. The first was for A Company, under Capt J. R. C. Radclyffe, to force their way into the beleagured Military Academy with a view to covering 46 RTR out; entry was achieved that afternoon, with three Shermans firing along one flank and RAF

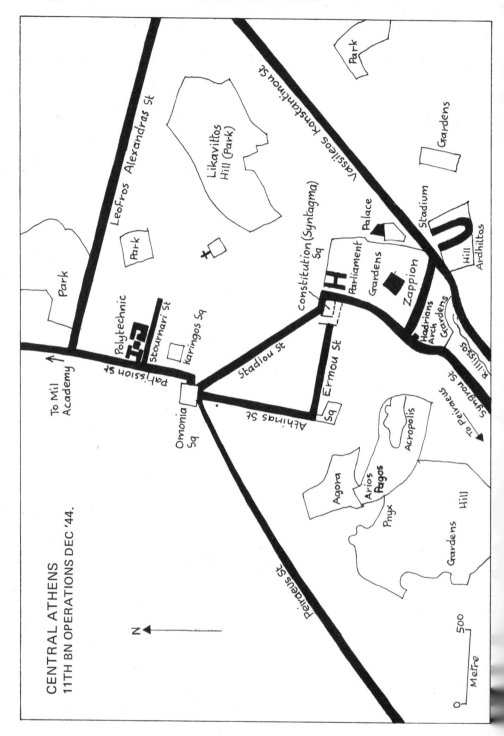

CENTRAL ATHENS
11TH BN OPERATIONS DEC '44.

17　The Rt Hon. Anthony Eden by the *Warren Hastings* Bell at the 2nd Battalion Guard Room, Münster, West Germany 1952

Left to Right
Capt J. G. Harrison, Adjutant, Lt Col The Hon M. F. Douglas-Pennant, DSO, MBE, Commanding 2nd, Mr Eden, RSM L. Grout 2nd, Lt Col K. H. Collen, Commanding 1st Battalion.

18　2nd Battalion Army Inter-Unit Team Boxing Champions 1956
Left to right
Back Row—Rfn Whiter, Ridley, Sliney, Moss, Lucas, R. Benson, Woodall.
Middle Row—Rfn Maynard, Lucas, G. Lowe, Flinn, Burford, Gardner, Macdonald, Thomas.
Seated—Rfn Dodd, 2/Lt E. Fergusson, SSI Collins, Lt Col Mellor, Capt G. Carter, Sgt Smith, L/Cpl George.

19 Officers, Warrant Officers and Sergeants of the 1st Battalion who visited Sid Rezegh, Libya, in July 1957

Survivors of the 1941 battle, present in the group, are the Commanding Officer, Lt Co H. A. Hope, OBE, MC (wearing shorts), with on his right Sgt Cheshire and on his left Cp Featherstone.

20 The Delhi Centenary at the Rifle Depot, Winchester on 14 September 1957

Maj Gen Loftus-Tottenham, representing the 2nd Goorkhas, hands a copy of Major Reic Diary to Lt Gen Sir Euan Miller, flanked by Gen Sir George Erskine, and with Col the Ho M. F. Douglas-Pennant in rear.

The 60th third of the Delhi Table is in front.

Beaufighter support on the other. The principal opposition throughout the fighting in Athens was to take the form of small-arms fire and mortaring, backed by a liberal use of explosive; the problem was that the preponderant ELAS knew the city well, were often hard to distinguish—since British Battle Dress, old Greek uniforms or civilian clothes were worn—and had no compunction about employing women or children in the forefront.

The same evening C Company relieved 6 Parachute Battalion in the Polytechnic area in a second operation. During the night both 9 and 10 Platoon houses had their front doors dynamited, but after close-quarter fighting in the entrances both attacks were beaten off. On the afternoon of 11 December Lt A. J. Richardson's 10 Platoon came under pressure from a dominating house, which the police had been forced to evacuate after a gallant fight, when their ammunition had nearly run out. A troop of Shermans engaged houses in their support and there were soon blazing buildings around the Company area. After dark C Company evacuated 150 prisoners or suspects, one a woman, whose respectable appearance was marred when a grenade fell out of her bag.

The same afternoon the carrier platoon under Lt J. G. Harrison patrolled the area below the Western end of Likavittos hill. There was much sniping, and houses held by ELAS were engaged by Bren and PIAT. The worst fire came from an ELAS hospital, where nurses in Red Cross uniform were throwing grenades from the windows. A troop of Shermans came up to assist the carriers, and a white flag was put up from the hospital after PIAT fire. However, from the window where the white flag was hanging a 50 RTR officer was killed immediately afterwards. To ensure the safe withdrawal of his platoon—vulnerable in their open vehicles—Lt Harrison forced two of the nurses on to his carrier and pulled back. In the same unscrupulous ELAS vein, C Company had found that two of the individuals killed by booby traps when trying to cut their perimeter wire were women. Lt B. E. D. Collier of 9 Platoon had to order a Rifleman to fire at a young woman approaching his house with a tray of food and wine. The Rifleman obeyed, and then begged not to be given such an order again, until the German stick grenade in her right hand was pointed out.

Meanwhile A Company, supported by two Shermans, covered 46 RTR back into the British-dominated area with all their stores. The Company then withdrew, the tanks engaging snipers en route, down Patission Street and via Omonia to Constitution Square, where they went into reserve. For five wounded their own snipers claimed six hits, and the build-up in proficiency of company snipers was an important factor in this street fighting.

During the night two platoons of B Company came under command of 50 RTR, taking up positions just East of the junction of Athinas and Ermou Streets; in front was a KKE quarter and behind were streets liable to sniping. The next day B Company snipers claimed 19 hits, including two MG crews.

The general plan was now to hold a tighter perimeter, centred on Constitution Square, until larger forces arrived from outside Greece. However, Singrou Avenue, the route to the sea, had to be kept open by constant armoured movement; a nightly convoy, of as many as 300 vehicles escorted by a troop of armoured cars, was essential for maintenance. Accordingly Lt C. E. W. House's platoon of A Company moved down with two Shermans to secure and hold the Singrou bridge over the River Ilissos on 12 December. This exposed position outside the perimeter was never properly attacked by ELAS, although dynamite charges had to be removed from the bridge, the most vulnerable point on the supply route.

On 12 December, after two platoons of A Company had cleared blocks of houses in the B Company area, a similar force from A was ordered to reinforce the HLI platoon on Likavittos hill by night. Shortly afterwards these platoons moved up to positions on the Western crest, which they held until relieved on 16 December.

In the early hours of 13 December ELAS put in a full-scale attack on the Infantry Barracks, occupied by 23 Armoured Brigade Rear HQ, a Supply Company and 463 Battery RHQ, the only 25-pounders in the city. The 11th's Mortar Platoon had their base plate position inside in the barracks with an OP in a house just outside the North wall. An alarm being given, Sgt Rutherford telephoned the Battery Command Post for orders, and was told to fire the DF on an ELAS block of flats. While firing the DF they saw large parties closing in on them, but, since they were wearing British helmets, battle dress and equipment, thought that they were friendly Greek troops they had been warned to expect that night. The base plate position was thus overrun without a fight; the OP party, after lying up for some hours, was given away and also captured. These prisoners were moved North to join the others previously mentioned, leaving only three men and two mortars in the Platoon (since Lt W. H. Tankard had been wounded the previous day). However, the Battalion was scoured for trained mortarmen and the two mortars were back in action that evening.

The ELAS attack, 1000 strong, had seized half the barracks, but in stopping to loot supplies failed to take the guns. The damage was bad enough; total Brigade casualties were 6 officers and over 160 soldiers, and 2 King's had to be put in to clear the barrack area. Capt E. T. Jones, the QM, in contrast made good use of the opportunity to look after his Riflemen, one occasion when he was able to draw supplies for the 11th without a signature.

The next four days were the low point in the defence, because any buildings cleared could not be held, with strengths so low, and every exposure caused more casualties. Water had been cut off, latrines had to be dug in what little unexposed ground was free of concrete and bread was a memory. Tanks were reduced to 5 rounds a day and mortars to 25 bombs a day. In the Old Palace Lt J. C. Brownlow's MMG Platoon looked like a naval gun turret. The MMGs were well back from the windows on mahogany tables, ready to fire; in striking contrast those not on watch were typing away at their letters home on Greek Government typewriters.

Daily the B Company snipers, Rfn Clarke—who was later awarded an MM—and Rfn Pettit took their toll. On one occasion Lt H. W. Fowler, one of our American officers, and Rfn Clarke crawled on to a roof-top which overlooked an ELAS Spandau post less than 100 yards away. Having despatched two of the men manning the gun, they waited; in about a quarter of an hour two men arrived, hauled the corpses out of the way and took up their positions. They departed the same way as their predecessors, but over-eagerness on our sniper's part only got one of the next pair as he came through a hole in the roof. On another occasion a sniping pair put paid to a well-concealed ELAS sniper; one Rifleman gave the communist call 'Koo Koo Ay' and the other shot the ELAS man, as his head came out of his hole like a cuckoo from a clock.

On 14 December C Company were ordered to withdraw from their completely isolated outpost at the Polytechnic, which they had held against every form of attack; even their supplies had to be brought up in armoured vehicles. Withdrawing successfully on foot and bringing 300 police and all the police records with them, the Company was required to take over part of the Southern perimeter at the Zappion.

For the next three days it was a question of holding on and engaging any threatening enemy move, but then 4 Division, which had arrived from Italy, began their attack up from the sea. There had been threatening movement from Ardhittos hill; it was hoped that its seizure would allow us to dominate this troublesome area on the South East, and in particular the Stadium on its reverse side. After C and then A had made preliminary moves, D Company under Maj Harman moved over the River Ilissos early on 18 December, and were dug in on Ardhittos hill by first light. Unfortunately, despite our requests, the RAF had dropped flares in the night, which had revealed D Company's advance to an ELAS patrol, and Cpl Halford had been killed. As it grew lighter it was found that no observation could be gained on to the Stadium and the already alerted enemy could overlook and sweep the Ardhittos crest from the buildings to the South. The operation had served to divert the enemy from the 4 Division advance—indeed, it had caused great alarm—and the A platoon position on Syngrou bridge had been relieved by the Hampshires. However, if the Ardhittos position gave inadequate observation and could only be maintained by heavy supporting fire effort, there was no point in retaining it; accordingly D Company was ordered at 1315 hrs to pull out at last light. Then at just before 1500 hrs a strong enemy attack started to come in on both flanks. The position was held, but seven Riflemen were captured when a section of Lt P. F. Cobbold's platoon was overrun. The withdrawal was brought forward and, covered by tanks, MMGs and mortars, D Company was back inside the perimeter by last light. Our casualties had been three killed and eight wounded, with many more on the enemy side, and the area had been identified as an enemy stronghold.

On 19 and 20 December the 11th's deployment was altered to allow greater concentration. B Company was moved to near Hadrian's Arch, A to the Zappion building, C to houses near by and D around the Old Palace. With the help of tanks from 46 RTR the troublesome houses South of the Ilissos were softened up. PIATs and Brens engaged those nearest, while tanks took on the further targets, often against enemy using explosive bullets. The MMGs and mortars went for streets still further back, the latter firing bombs, cap on, to penetrate the flat roofs and burst inside. Enemy in the former house of General Wilson were particularly active, but they were harassed until forced to demolish it, a fact which amused Mr Eden, when shown the area from an OP. The Prime Minister, Mr Winston Churchill, arrived in Athens on Christmas Day, celebrated otherwise only by the QM's plum puddings. The sewer under his hotel was found to contain nearly a ton of ELAS dynamite, so Lt The Earl of Sondes was put in command of the 'Sewer Rats' to conduct deep patrols down those unpleasant labyrinths.

The day before Christmas 50 RTR had recaptured the seven D Company prisoners, taken on Ardhittos. They were now isolated in a broadcasting station just East of Athens, and their arms were dropped to them by parachute. Rfn Fink, a devotee of the PIAT, was delighted to be rearmed with it. That night, hearing an armoured car approaching as part of a big enemy attack, he ran through the perimeter wire and took up position by the road. His second shot revealed that the armoured car was full of dynamite; for his courage and initiative Rfn Fink was awarded the MM.

On 29 December large scale operations were started to clear Athens. The 11th's task in this was to clear the previously troublesome area across the Ilissos. At 0700 hrs A right, and D left, crossed the river and by soon after 0900 hrs, having encountered only light opposition were on their objectives, the dominant houses South of Ardhittos and its slopes; behind them B and C systematically cleared the houses. Over 70 prisoners and suspects were taken and many weapons and much ammunition found, with only one Rifleman wounded. It was evident that ELAS had pulled out, leaving their makeshift hospitals in an appalling condition; the local population gave British troops an enthusiastic welcome despite all the damage to their houses.

At noon 23 Armoured Brigade ordered the Battalion to reconnoitre the Stadium and the area to its East. Maj Goschen took a troop of tanks and a C Company motor platoon in Whites through the D Company position to the South East end of the Stadium; a foot patrol from there to the North East encountered no enemy. The next morning, 30 December, C Company with a troop of tanks and a section of armoured cars went round the Stadium to the North East and cleared back South Westwards to the Stadium wall. There was no opposition, but again a quantity of arms and ammunition was taken; the 11th were then relieved by the Somerset Light Infantry and returned to billets round Constitution Square, conscious that ELAS pressure on the former tight perimeter had been lifted. 1944 ended happily when B Company as part of an armoured column relieved the beleaguered broadcasting station and brought back the seven D Company Riflemen, originally captured on Ardhittos hill.

The clearing of Athens was going well. Resistance was stiff, and it was a slow business, but the end was in sight. On 2 January 1945 the 11th Battalion conducted the second phase of a clearing operation just South of the old Polytechnic area, supported by two troops of 46 RTR. 50 RTR and the HLI encountered fairly stiff opposition in the first phase and progress was slow, so that it was noon when the 11th passed through with A Company left and D right. A Company encountered initial difficulty from buildings on the North side of Karingos Square, where the tanks had explosives, including Teller mines, thrown at them. It took 4½ hours to clear the small area up to the line of consolidation on Stournari Street, where our only fatal casualty, Rfn Draper, was killed by a mortar bomb. 137 prisoners and suspects had been taken, and the companies, reinforced by a platoon of B on the right and the National Guard in depth, hastened to put up wire barricades and booby-trap them. This was as well, since a counter-attack was put in by 50 ELAS on the D Company front soon after 0100 hrs 3 January; covering fire on the barricades and the mortar DF stopped the attack, D losing one killed and one wounded to six or seven ELAS killed. Sniping continued throughout the day, and, although it was difficult to locate, the tanks and two-inch mortars engaged the enemy, of whom four were killed.

Sniper activity was stirred up again when on 4 January our Parachutists cleared the area on the West side of Patission Street. Enemy mortaring on the centre of Athens increased, but it was a dying effort. The tragedy of it was that the very last concentration which fell in Constitution Square killed two fine officers, Capt D. J. Symons, the Technical Adjutant, and Lt J. D. Bickersteth; Capt P. H. Lawrence, MC, who had carried a heavy load as Adjutant, and two Riflemen were wounded.

The same day a column composed of the KDG, 15 tanks, a battery and C Company moved up into the open country to block escape routes to the West and North West. Road blocks delayed the advance, but soon after noon C Company, with its mortars and MMGs, was called forward to take up position at their bridge objective. Demolition charges and blocks were removed, but the bridge was unheld and C Company dug in without interference; eight Whites full of ammunition and explosives were sent back. On 5 January C moved North East to secure another bridge, but after arrival were joined by Parachutists, who had been given the same task; the Company rejoined the Battalion on 6 January.

During the night 4/5 January A and D Companies had heard much shouting, which was discovered later to be an attempt by ELAS to send a delegation through to General Scobie. At first light civilians reported that ELAS had withdrawn North from the city, and careful reconnaissance confirmed this. Shortly after midday the 11th set out in three columns due North up Patission Street with the object of preventing any further withdrawals into the hills. Sappers cleared the mines and blocks encountered, and by last light companies took up positions covering the Northern outskirts of Athens.

Apart from sending out columns, which picked up a few prisoners of war and found large stocks of arms and explosives, this ended the services of the 11th Battalion against the communist attempt to seize power. Although fighting was later to break out again in the border mountains for some years, Riflemen took no part in it; their service had been to give the Greek people a chance in due course to choose for themselves how they should be governed. ELAS had not been entirely hostile to the British initially, but the fighting had become increasingly bitter. The Battalion's casualties had been miraculously light, considering the vulnerability of anyone moving in an urban area under sniper and mortar fire. 3 Officers and 14 Riflemen had been killed and 3 and 42 wounded. The 80 taken prisoner, as recounted earlier, rejoined the Battalion by sea on 27 January 1945, having united in enduring their long winter marches with high morale.

The excellent operational work by the 11th Battalion was recognized in the awards: the MC to Majs Harman and Stobart and Capt Cobbold, the MBE to Capt Radclyffe and RSM Cumming, and the MM to Sgt Parker and Rfns Fink, Kemp, Clarke and Wilmot. It was particularly pleasing that the firm leadership and professional competence of the Commanding Officer, Lt Col C. F. G. Henshaw, a Queen's Westminster of long standing, was rewarded by the OBE.

As the Battalion account said: 'A vast demonstration in Constitution Square again acclaimed us as Liberators. This time we really thought we had been.'

In early February 1945 representatives of the Greek Government and EAM met in the presence of the British and signed the Varkiza Agreement. This laid down that ELAS should demobilize and disarm, and that prisoners and hostages should be released. This would be followed in due course by a plebiscite on the future form of government and a general election. In fact ELAS handed in older weapons, but hid the most modern; the bulk of ELAS returned home—to the relief of those who had been forced to join—but some hard-core bands crossed into Albania and Jugoslavia, now communist states, while others hid in the hills.

In a right wing backlash from ELAS, a Colonel Grivas, later to be heavily involved in Cyprus, set up the X Organization. This harried the communist bands and among other actions gave away Aris to the National Guard; he had refused to disarm and was killed by the Guard in the summer. A weak coalition Government ruled the country until the General Election in March 1946; it filled the prisons and camps with former ELAS members, alleging that those arrested were common criminals. Although the bulk of the population wanted law and order, this gave ammunition for communist propaganda, which could be freely publicized, since the KKE had been allowed to remain a legal political party.

This was the political setting in which the 11th found itself for the next 18 months, but for the present the Battalion was concentrating on military matters. The Support Company, E, was broken up and Capt Radclyffe took over command of HQ Company. Patrols from billets in Athens found arms and explosives and noted that villagers tended still to be under the fear or influence of ELAS. The 11th now found time to go over the lessons of recent fighting and started learning how to be a motor battalion again.

In February the 11th moved to a summer resort in the hills 15 miles outside Athens, where training was started in between falls of snow. A reminder of the Italian Campaign was the return of Lt D. J. Longstaffe, MC, who had been badly wounded on patrol there, and the mention in despatches of Lt H. W. Fowler, CSMs Fowler and Jones and Sgt Tidy, for gallant and distinguished services in that theatre. The war against Germany was still continuing, and much time was given to TEWTS and demonstrations, particularly covering operations with armour. Each platoon in turn went off on a three-day march round the countryside, and now found themselves very well received by the villages. In the same vein of showing the flag, B Company, under Capt Knight, spent a week at the end of March, visiting the fishing villages in the Southern half of the island of Euboea by caïque. The opportunity was taken to discuss the security situation, where there were National Guard detachments, and to see if relief was getting down to village level. Reports of ELAS bands in the hills seemed substantiated when Lt Fowler was held up for a short time by armed men in one village; there was in fact a guerrilla band in the central mountains of the island.

Meanwhile the 11th was ordered to relieve the Hampshire Brigade of 46 Division, who were returning to Italy. They were to take over responsibility for the Southern half of the Peloponnese, with a Gunner regiment in the North. Staying a night near the historic site of Mycenae, the Battalion, less B Company, arrived on 3 April. C Company was at the port of Kalamata and A at Sparta, but the road between had many demolitions; Battalion HQ and D were at the communications centre of Tripolis, while B moved to Xilokastron on the North coast. The companies patrolled constantly to assess the security and relief states of the Southern Peloponnese. A particularly interesting patrol was carried out by Lt M. L. Lejeune, A Company, down the centre promontory of the peninsula, with a motor platoon and a section of carriers. In increasingly wild country, whistle signals were heard and two men were picked up, one with a pistol and the other with an ELAS badge in his pocket. Just as the KKE were ready to denounce all political opponents as former Axis collaborators, the National Guard were filling the local prisons with former ELAS men; despite Battalion protest, the prison conditions were very bad.

The CO was ordered to gauge the effect on public order of a gradual British withdrawal, and to this end C Company left Kalamata, but remained in a hide with access to the main road. Since the National Guard was seen to have a firm grip, the Battalion withdrew by stages, and on 3 May the 11th was concentrated in Xilocastron; here VE day was prematurely celebrated on 7 May 45 with a *feu de joie* of tracer and flares over the sea, and leave successively for all the Battalion in Athens.

At the end of May A Company sent a caïque patrol down the Eastern promontory of the Peloponnese, to gauge the security position in villages inaccessible by road from Sparta. Some had not seen British troops since 1941 and gave a very friendly welcome, but there was much talk of armed bands in the hills. It is now known that, when ELAS was resurrected as the Greek Democratic Army in February 46, two areas of considerable activity were in fact the mountainous Peloponnesean promontories, which A Company patrols had regarded as suspicious. Other vestiges of war still lingered, for a B Company patrol had two men injured when their armoured vehicle went over a Teller mine by a road verge. Our patrols found evidence that some National Guard detachments had been issuing arms to civilians against the much-talked-of third round of communist military action, which in fact broke out the following year. The 11th itself was running a series of cadres for the officers and NCOs of the Greek National Army (GNA), which was starting to form with the call-up of certain classes of young men.

For the next month, however, it was its own internal personnel affairs which occupied the 11th. Maj A. G. L. Goschen MC handed over as 2IC to Maj The Hon M. M. C. Charteris, and left to run military government near his old battalion, the 1st, in Carinthia; Capt P. H. Lawrence MC was relieved after a successful tour as Adjutant by Capt The Hon H. M. Ritchie, Capt J. D. W. Hunter taking over as IO.

In July the 11th was warned that 8 officers and 200 men, those with over three years abroad, would be going on LIAP in the immediate future; since the Battalion had come overseas in 1942 the majority of men were affected. The CO accordingly decided to break up D Company, who would then hold all leave men on paper and document them; this would allow A, B and C Companies to be maintained at operational strength. Organizational changes were also afoot, as the 11th was warned to relieve 50 RTR in the Salonica area. Carriers were to be replaced by armoured cars in each scout platoon, A having Daimlers and the other two Companies the American Staghounds. To the very great regret of the Battalion, Capt D. J. Longstaffe, MC, died suddenly in hospital after running a series of successful cadres for the GNA. He was a most modest and gallant officer, who had only been welcomed back to the 11th in February after recovering from wounds received in Italy. Further memories of two difficult wartime winters had recently been rekindled by the mention in despatches of Lts C. E. W. House and B. E. D. Collier, RSM Waldron, now with the 1st, CSM Seldon and others for excellent work in both Italy and Greece.

During the war Macedonia had been occupied by the Bulgarians with German sanction. On their departure, having joined the Russian side, the whole area passed under ELAS domination, but the Communist guerrillas had left Salonica without fighting the small British garrison at the end of the second round of the civil war. With communist regimes now set up all along Greece's Northern border, 4 Indian Division was stationed in the North to ensure Greece's integrity while the GNA was building up. The 11th Battalion was to come under this Division as its armoured reserve, with for that purpose its own armoured cars, and the tanks of B Squadron 50 RTR, which came under Battalion command.

Moving by road on 7 October 45, A Company went direct to Florina, near the Albanian and Jugoslav borders and only a few miles West of the scene of the 9th Battalion's actions in 1941. Arriving simultaneously in the Salonica area was the rest of the Battalion, which until the return of LIAP parties consisted of B at operational strength only, with the new R as a reinforcement training and reserve Company. Constant road patrols were sent out by A from Florina to Edessa to discourage guerrilla activity against civilian traffic in this mountainous area. At the end of November B Company moved East to Drama opposite the Bulgarian border, and in December Maj Knight took a patrol even further, to near the Turkish border, where there had been civil disturbances. A pleasant feature was the presence of 1st/2nd Goorkhas near Drama, and old regimental friendships were renewed at all levels. At the New Year Maj M. J. Gilliat was appointed 2IC, allowing Maj M. B. Harman, MC (who had held that appointment since September) to take over A Company. Capt C. E. W. House was now Adjutant, and the staff duties of a long Battalion move were about to absorb him. The Companies and their Riflemen had become self-reliant in meeting the challenge of the intense cold and icy road conditions, but it was time for the Battalion to concentrate once more. Apart from R Company, which found the Lamia pass blocked by snow, the move to Kifissia, a summer resort nine miles North of Athens, took five days. There the 11th found itself in pleasant hotels, with Officers and Sergeants Messes for the first time since October.

The first military duty was to stand by in case of trouble during the long-awaited Greek general election on 31 March 46. Observed by the USA, Britain and France, it passed off quietly, however, the right wing in the form of the Populists winning a majority; the KKE, unwilling to have its low support revealed, declined to take part.

The day-to.day work of the Battalion consisted of an unremitting round of guard duties in Athens and Peiraeus, coupled with its own local guards against some of the most expert thieves in Europe. During the Spring many of the best-known wartime leaders and specialists left, and continual cadres were run to fill key places, some Riflemen managing to reach the rank of Sergeant in six months. A May draft of 90 Riflemen from 7 RB, disbanding in Egypt, was all the more welcomed.

Maj Gen H. O. Curtis, newly appointed Colonel Commandant, visited the 11th at the end of March, seeing the Battalion in its enlarged form, with R Company back at strength. In April the Battalion, which was now under 13 Division, took part in the farewell parade of 23 Armoured Brigade; the 11th had served happily in the brigade since Alamein, and its commander, Maj Gen Arkwright, now took Capt P. B. Tillard to the Far East with him as ADC. Another end of an era was the departure of Lt Col C. F. E. Henshaw, OBE, on 3 June 46. He had been in the 11th Battalion for more than eight years and had been its Commanding Officer throughout the Greek tour, coming to the Middle

East with it in 1942. He was a fine example of the strength brought to the Regiment by its pre-war Territorials. His successor was Lt Col D. R. C. Boileau, DSO, who had taken command of the 9th Battalion (Rangers) in action during the withdrawal down Greece in 1941. During the summer Capt M. L. Lejeune, the last American officer serving with the Regiment, left the 11th, which had been privileged, in the person of him and of Lt H. Fowler, to have enjoyed the American presence far longer than any other Battalion.

Now particularly busy with a major pre-release education scheme for Riflemen, the 11th had one more duty to perform, when it stood by during the Greek plebiscite of 1 September 46. Over 60% voted for the return of the King, and on 28 September George II returned to Greece. The next month the 11th, which had already had to break up A Company for lack of reinforcements, was placed in suspended animation; very great care was, however, taken to place nearly all Regulars within the Regiment, and characters like Capt J. G. Harrison and CSM Eveson were very welcome in the 1st Battalion.

By accident of fate, the 11th Battalion had been denied the more exhilarating roles of a motor battalion. Having taken part in the dog-fight at Alamein, it missed the break-out and advance. In Italy it held wide fronts on the Garigliano and in the East Coast hills, enduring the winter cold without the summer's pursuit. In Greece it had helped to liberate a ruined country on the brink of civil war and suffered casualties at the hands of a race which was normally friendly to Britain. Yet it was a very happy Battalion, the happiness depending not a little on the knowledge that it had performed every task given it and more, combining the professional approach of the Rifleman with the irreverence of the Territorial. For it remained more Territorial than any other Battalion, thanks to its first-class team of Officers, Warrant Officers and NCOs. It is good to think that the Battalion was raised again within six months as The Queen's Westminsters, once more under the command of Lt Col C. F. G. Henshaw, OBE.

CHAPTER VIII
ITALY, TRIPOLI AND PALESTINE AFTER WORLD WAR II

(Maps: pages 166 and 202)

This chapter covers the services of the 1st and 2nd Battalions while overseas after the end of World War II.

The problems that faced Lt Col De Salis on arrival in Lonigo with the 1st Battalion were great, and none more so than in personnel. Rightly all Green Jacket resources had been concentrated on building up both 2nd Battalions for the Far East, and, although that role had disappeared with the Japanese surrender, the key men with some service left could, of course, not be recovered. Apart from Capt Ryan, the Quartermaster, there was virtually no one left in the 1st with any experience of peacetime administration, which now came to the forefront. A proper draft of Riflemen did not in fact arrive from England until the next summer, so that the majority of men were due for release within the year. With the departure of Majs Mackay and Killick and Capt Waterfield, Companies were commanded by those who had been commanding platoons in the Gothic Line battles of a year earlier. Maj M. P. Lee commanded A, Maj A. J. Round, B; the newly arrived Maj H. B. W. Long, C; Maj P. H. Parker (who had been taken prisoner at Calais) D; and Maj D. G. House, MC, HQ. Appropriately Capt G. H. Mills as Adjutant, with his Assistant, Lt I. V. Askew, MC, dealt with the increasingly tiresome statistical returns in the former lunatic asylum. Their one major victory was to organize a smooth, covert dispersal of vital resources, against the arrival without notice of the Army Inspectorate of Equipment. Unlike their more flamboyant cavalry neighbours, the Battalion thus retained the captured typewriters, phones and other equipment not on War Establishment, but vital to winning the peace.

The first thing was to organize a really efficient pre-release education programme. Capt P. Way—later to be a distinguished Housemaster and Head of English at Radley after winning the Newdigate Prize—did this with the same care that had made him one of the best platoon commanders. This ensured that all those Riflemen who wished it would have something of a start on return home. Companies were at too low a strength for training while LIAP parties were away, and indeed the 200 vehicles had to take next priority. Centralized around the plane trees of the town park, Capt M. G. Turner and Lt J. Saunders, REME, did their best to keep engines turning during the damp winter ahead; a proof of effectiveness was the success of the drive to Naples and back the next summer.

It could have been a gloomy winter in the dank, raw cold of the Po Valley, but Lt Col De Salis gave every encouragement to sporting activities, personally taking on the CO of the Camerons in many a hockey duel. Horses brought down from Austria were well looked after by Cpl Smythe, and the next Spring

'Vienna' did well chasing, ridden by Maj Parker; Capts Le Coq and St Aubyn and Lt J. White gave a lead in the first show-jumping entries. Meanwhile the winter season culminated in an excellent paperchase, run by Majs Round and Lee. The distant mountains could be seen on one of the brighter winter days, and Rfn Hibbert discomfited the rest of 6 Armoured Division by winning the downhill after only a week's skiing experience. Nearer home, the excellent football stadium saw the 1st battling it out against the more stylish Lonigo Town, while a near-by range began to crackle under the example of RQMS Condon, severely wounded after capture in the Gazala fighting, and now a most timely reinforcement. Others warmly welcomed on return were three Ronco survivors, Capt N. Warry, MC, Lt I. Mollison, MC, and Lt Lt S. Towneley (Worsthorne); Capt J. Le Coq, who had been captured with the 2nd in the Desert, was able to make his mark in all sporting fields. For those for whom a night journey in an open Jeep on the bomb-cratered Autostrada held no terrors, Venice lay not far to the East. It was a Venice to which Lt 'Joe' Tecchio could open the mysteries, aided by the favourable exchange rate. To sit on a warm morning outside Florian's clad in a local heavy silk shirt, to end an evening of incomparable food with a visit to an uncrowded Harry's Bar, and then waft gently along the canals in a gondola, was a rare privilege and compensated for the discomfort of cold billets.

If there was a centre to Battalion life at this period, it was the little Lonigo piazza. In the Municipio the Padre, the Rev J. Head, indefatigably maintained the canteen and every possible welfare activity; in the piazza itself the locals would discuss politics in their dark capes or on a Monday scan the masses of cages holding the migratory birds, netted or limed over the week-end, for a fat fieldfare or a meagre sparrow. Opposite, in the Albergo Croce Verde, was the Mess, where the officers to their great good fortune had recruited an Italian Mess staff, presided over by Gigi, the chef, who were to remain with them for the next two years. If there was one noise to typify the period, it would be the steady drumming of a diesel and water stove, improvised to heat larger rooms; explosions followed maladjustment, and on this altar the prodigious moustache of Capt Turner was at last sacrificed.

Maj T. Trotter arrived out in the Spring as 21C after an interregnum. Shortly afterwards Lt Col De Salis left the Battalion on appointment as Officer in Charge of Rifle Records, Winchester. Denied the support of experienced Regulars or any drafts of young Riflemen, Lt Col De Salis had kept the 1st Battalion going and had set standards of integrity which were to be useful on the guard duties which followed. In a country and at an era where rackets were widespread, the 1st kept a high reputation for probity and readiness to tackle any task set it with efficiency.

Under the pacifying eye of Lt T. St Aubyn and his MMG carriers the Italians took part in March 1946 in the first free local elections for many years. And then it was suddenly off on the road once more, with officers and NCOs supplementing the drivers on the mass of vehicles. B and D Companies went off to near-by Verona, still in the favourite Soave wine country, while the remainder of the Battalion moved over the Po to Bologna, the unattainable objective of 1944. Tasks consisted of an interminable round of guard duties, relieving the Polish Corps and Territorial battalions, now moving to England. In this continual juggling of duties, which kept Riflemen on 24-hour guards every alternate day for most of the summer, the arrival of RSM Voysey, formerly of the 2nd Battalion, was an enormous help. With CSM Poscha in HQ Company, he provided a fund of pre-war experience, and the authority and knowledge to train young NCOs, when drafts began to arrive. It was at this moment that Lt Col T. L. Timpson arrived to take over command. A pre-war Regular of crisp reputation, he had been taken prisoner as 2IC of the 7th Battalion (Queen Victoria's Rifles) at Calais. An officer of high standards like his predecessor, he took immense pains to build up the 1st and to give future young Regulars their heads when commanding companies. His arrival was swiftly followed by that of the new Colonel Commandant, Maj Gen H. O. Curtis, who thereafter took a great deal of trouble to keep in touch with Battalion affairs.

Having among many other duties managed the Bologna Town Guardroom— through which flowed most of the professional criminals still left from wartime conscription—without permanently losing a prisoner, the 1st was ordered in May to concentrate in Vicenza. Rejoining 2 Armoured Brigade, they were promised a summer free of guard duties for training, based on a well-built but unfurnished barracks. Fortunately, the Battalion had concentrated on essentials like bedsteads and education stores when arriving alongside Nazi property in Austria, so that Riflemen were not sleeping as rough as the staff would have complacently let them. A Company, reinforced by most of B, had at the last moment been moved direct from Bologna to Rome, with a detachment in Florence; Maj Lee set himself up as the benign successor to Mussolini in the Villa Torlonia. The cynical were therefore not in the least surprised when within a month of arriving at Vicenza the staff warned of an impending move South by the rest of the Battalion on guard duties. It took a visit from the Divisional Commander and future Adjutant General, Maj Gen Loewen, in person to extract destination and tasks from higher authority; that forceful Canadian told them to honour the road and rail movements already organized by the Battalion unaided and not to interfere.

The Colonel flew down to Naples, the destination of Battalion HQ and D Company, while the Battalion road party dropped off C at Rome on route. Lt Maufe was left to run the rail party of horses, tracked vehicles and accommodation stores, and the wheels made Naples in four days with only one vehicle down at the end. The arrival at 'the first town of Africa' in the height of summer on yet more guard duties was a depressing reversion from Austria's green hills, but everyone buckled down to work.

For initial security a camp was established on a precipitous spur above the Posilippo cliffs, and the battle against the most expert thieves of the peninsula started. Having justified the hurried move by watchfulness during the elections, which passed off smoothly—the Neapolitan habit of saluting political and ecclesiastical events with fireworks was alarming—guards took on a 48 hours on, 48 hours off rhythm for the rest of the summer. Of particular note was D Company's security control over the Naples Docks; it was probably the only time that the local fraternity failed to make a profit. Under Capt Warry petty thieves were offered the seamy docks or a high-pressure hose; a more resolute raider was shot and, despite attempts at framing, the locals learnt to hold back till the 1st Battalion left. A great assistance was the attachment of Chetnik guards for our own local security. These Jugoslavs, who had had to leave their country as described in an earlier chapter, were smart, honest and reliable, which made them conspicuous in Southern Italy.

Gradually the companies in Rome moved down to Naples, where the Battalion was now occupying Piedmonte Barracks in the city; Capt Le Coq now commanded B and Maj Round C. The strength of the 1st was down to 400 all ranks present, and it was like a shot in the arm when a draft of 150 young Riflemen, some of whom were to stay on as Regulars, arrived from England, the first for over six months. This was a time of change, for Lt R. Darwin, a first-class cricketer, who had spent most of his three years in the Battalion with C Company, now went home. Maj D. G. House, MC, left on release, but to the good fortune of the Regiment and the Army (which he finally left as C in C Northern Ireland some 30 years later) rapidly decided that civilian life was not for him. Capt G. H. Mills, the Regiment's last wartime Adjutant, handed over to Capt T. E. St Aubyn after 18 months of protecting the Battalion from higher staffs, and took over HQ Company. Some had enjoyed the bathing, among whom was Cpl Roots, who received the Royal Humane Society's Testimonial for very gallantly rescuing a drowning airman. Others had visited Pompeii, Amalfi or Capri, but all were relieved when orders come through to move North out of the steamy heat and smells of the port to an unknown destination. For a moment it seemed that the Battalion would go to Mestre and be under Brigadier R. A. T. Eve, CBE, late 60th and now commanding Venice. On 24 August 46 the wheeled column headed North for the last time, and a party of officers carried out a battlefield tour from San Clemente through the Gothic Line en route; the monotony of driving at 22 mph prompted a song *Attenti al Treno*, based on road signs and slogans, which was sung to *Lilli Marlene* for many an evening afterwards. On the afternoon of the fifth day the column, without a breakdown on the 600-mile journey, pulled into their final Italian base, Principe Umberto Barracks in the small town of Gradisca on the Isonzo. They were once more in 2 Armoured Brigade, now commanded by Brig N. Duncan, and glad to be back in the relatively green and clean Venezia Giulia. The 1st Battalion now found itself in an area bedevilled by the unresolved problems of two World Wars.

The former Italian Province of Venezia Giulia was originally removed from the Austro-Hungarian Empire after World War I. It consisted in the South of Trieste and the Istrian Peninsula, and in the North of the Isonzo valley and the Julian Alps, between which and the sea lies a desolate and waterless limestone plateau known as the Carso. East of the river Isonzo and outside the towns of Trieste, Monfalcone and Gorizia the people of this section are almost wholly Slovenes; they had suffered economically and culturally under Fascism and had no cause to love the Italians. Their resistance as partisans in World War II had caused the Germans to destroy their villages and deport many as slave labour.

At the end of World War II it will be remembered that the Rifle Brigade had only just managed to interpose between the Chetniks and Tito's forces West of the Isonzo, while the New Zealanders entered Trieste. After forty days the Jugoslavs were pushed diplomatically Eastwards and a provisional boundary fixed dividing Venezia Giulia into two zones—Zone A to the West being under Allied Military Government, with locally recruited police, and Zone B to the East under the Jugoslavs. West of the Morgan Line there was a Jugoslav Army detachment on the Carso near Comeno in what was known as the Enclave, and

Jugoslav convoys were allowed across to supply their troops, who formed there a base for local propaganda and subversion.

The provisional boundary—which was to be effective until such time as the Italian Peace Treaty should be ratified by the wartime Allies—was known as the Morgan Line. It was only demarcated on the ground where it was crossed by roads and tracks; on the roads there were check-posts manned by British or American troops opposite Gorizia, and on the tracks there were sometimes notice-boards, not necessarily agreeing with the official maps. Its vagaries in hilly and wooded country had much in common with the Ulster border, but the Jugoslavs were very quick to take advantage of uncertainty in the areas away from tracks, as the 1st was later to find out.

However, the Battalion was at last able to put in some proper training, since they were back under General Loewen's Divisional control and within Lt Gen Sir John Harding's XIII Corps, last seen in the 1945 advance from the Po. C and D Companies shared a barracks with 9L, and by October A and C were ready for an exercise with 6 RTR on the flat country West of Udine, supported by British and US artillery; this was the first time many of our younger Riflemen had seen or worked with other Arms. Cadres of all kinds were run in Gradisca, and shooting started with the newly arrived short No 5 rifle, designed for jungle warfare. The first of many liaison visits with the US 88 Division at Gorizia was started by an Officers' Mess night for its commander, General Bryant Moore, his deputy, General Gaither, and their wives and daughters. General Moore afterwards died on active service in Korea and General Gaither commanded the Panama Canal Zone.

This was a period when families at last started to enter Regimental life again. Maj A. Round, after nearly four years' in the 1st, went home to be married and became Adjutant of Queen Victoria's Rifles, but Capt Warry brought out his wife, the daughter of our Area Commander in Naples. Until now CSM Proberts had been the only member of the 1st accompanied by his wife, but successively in 1947 Maj J. H. P. Curtis, MC, and Maj J. A. H. Powell, MC, increased the small married circle, a far cry from the 300 families of 20 years later. Gradually under the prompting of Lt Col Timpson the tenets of peacetime administration were inculcated throughout the Battalion. The re-establishment of an effective Orderly Room was greatly assisted by ORQMS Robbins, returned from Burma; under him L/Cpl Maynard, the operator in the CO's scout car throughout the 1st's part of the Italian campaign, was notable in a team of most competent clerks. Lt T. M. L. Marke, who had been Assistant Adjutant but was training as an accountant, took on the PRI and other accounts. Capt M. G. Moss, who was a first-class wicket-keeper in the Battalion side and Entertainments Officer, reigned as Technical Adjutant next door to the MTO, Lt J. C. S. Mills, brother of the HQ Company Commander, and an endless programme of inspections and repairs kept the Battalion reasonably mobile.

The first of a series of operational tasks, which continued until the 1st left Italy, started at the end of November. Route 55, which cut across the Carso plateau to link Gorizia with Trieste, had been closed to night traffic since an American Jeep had been ambushed with a fatal casualty. The task was by patrolling to convince the Slovene villagers on either side that armed wanderers would risk trouble. Companies took turns in patrolling in icy winds until on 18

December 46 the road was declared and remained fully open. The only incident was in a guard post shared with a Jugoslav detachment, when an apolitical Rifleman saw a picture of Marshal Tito and enquired why they had a picture of Goering. Thanks to a mischievous interpreter, this gaffe reached Governmental level before tempers cooled. Great benefit, however, was derived by training all the young Officers and NCOs in night patrol leading.

Christmas was a success, largely due to the poultry collected by Capt Ryan from Lonigo. The inspection by Maj Trotter of these and the Battalion pigs was a feature of daily life; as a noted gastronome he very sportingly devoured a roast dabchick served to him by Capt St Aubyn as a teal. This came from one of the poaching forays on the Corps Commander's snipe shoot at Lago di Doberdo. On one occasion General Harding was encountered in the reeds, but, like a good Light Infantryman, merely apologized for getting in the way. On the slopes across the Isonzo guns picked up the odd partridge, a woodcock and other lesser game, but the winter's chief relaxation was the winter sports at Cortina. There Capt Voules, as 1 Armoured Division Welfare Officer, reached the high point in service to all ranks, but particularly to Riflemen, which had started in Florence in 1944 and had operated in Austria, Venice and the Italian Alps. He ran a group of hotels, in which Riflemen could find the warmth and comfort, as well as good sport, which they lacked on the Morgan Line; even at Gradisca a drought and local inefficiency meant that electricity and water could never be depended on, and Duino or Trieste were often the nearest baths. On 14 January 47 the 50th Anniversary of the *Warren Hastings* was appropriately celebrated, the first Regimental occasion young Regulars had taken part in since the war; the CO announced on parade that the 1st would not be going with 1 Armoured Division to the Middle East, but probably to Germany.

Brig N. Duncan, who had been a most popular and helpful Commander, now handed over 2 Armoured Brigade to Brig D. Dawnay, DSO, but it was under Brig Erskine of 24 Guards Brigade that the 1st started to take over a sector of the Morgan Line.

As in England, that winter was to be very severe, but the bitterness of the Bora—the North East wind known to the poet Horace—excelled all experience. At Gradisca the EME, Lt Saunders, watched spilled anti-freeze freeze solid. At Duino Castle the rear wheels of three-tonners lifted from the ground as the wind got under their canopies, but on the Morgan Line it made life almost intolerable. Maj P. H. Parker took B and D Companies combined up on to the Line in January 47 to find that the dilapidated Nissen huts were barely habitable. Steel hawsers were needed to hold them down against the Bora, fountain pens froze in the pocket and water (which had to be brought 20 miles from Trieste) was frozen on arrival. By much hard work a somewhat improved series of quarters was handed over to A Company at the end of January, but Lt G. G. Thornton of B, a cricketer and ballad-singer of note, had found the supply line from Gradisca through ice and snow very hard work to maintain. Simultaneously C Company under Maj J. H. P. Curtis, MC, acted as caretakers of Duino Castle on the Trieste road, which was later taken over by GHQ. D, on relief, moved down to the shipyards of Monfalcone, where Italians and Slovene workers were at loggerheads. They were soon joined there by Battalion HQ and B, and later by A, so that for some time only a diminished HQ Company, really the Echelons, held Gradisca.

During the first Morgan Line tour the B Company platoon at Comeno had raided a suspicious meeting in a lonely village and arrested some subversive characters from over the Line; this may have prompted the activity which A encountered. A Company HQ was in the railway yard of the primitive village of Kobdilj, overlooking a gorge. Just South was one platoon check post, another just North in Stanjel and the third in a mill on the River Vipacco; a B Company platoon under Lt S. J. Symington was at Comeno, near the Jugoslav Enclave, where the American Military Governor, Maj Larson, was a good friend of the Battalion.

A Company's task was to check the passes, search and keep a record of traffic across the Line, being alert for illegal arms moving West or political abductees being taken East. Since illegal traffic obviously avoided the roads, patrols were sent out to watch tracks, establish the position of the Line and to make friendly contact with Jugoslav posts. This was successfully done until the Knoj, politically conscious and tough military police, found their soldiers fraternizing. Knoj patrols at once gave a very hostile reception to any efforts at friendly contact.

One afternoon Maj Lee and Capt R. V. G. Elwes, his 2IC, found a newly laid field telephone line on the hill just East of Kobdilj, leading between that village and over the Line into Zone B; it was presumably for use by communist agents, so that night Capt Elwes and two Riflemen followed it in the snow, establishing that it went well into Zone B; by cutting it they probably alerted the opposition.

The sequel is taken from Maj Lee's own account:

Therefore at 0330 hrs a patrol went out again consisting of Peter Lee, Robin Elwes and Rfn Gormley to find the western end. After an exhausting climb up the steep and slippery hill (during which they cursed their padded clothing) the line was found, and followed along the crest through the woods to the west, the patrol being certain from their own maps that they were some 300 yards inside Zone A. They had gone barely a quarter of a mile and had climbed over a low stone wall when from the darkness of some bushes about 40 yards in front there came a blood-curdling shriek and the challenge, 'Stoj, illi pucam!' (Halt, or I fire).

Now the year 1947 was one of peace and not war, and the patrol considered they were on a reasonable law-abiding mission, so their natural reaction to this rude development was to halt. They immediately thereafter felt remarkably foolish and endeavoured to declare themselves by calling out 'Tovaris, zavezniki, angleski' (Friend, Allies, English), and such other outlandish words as could be recalled at 4 am on a frosty morning. But nothing seemed to happen, save that the sentry continued to gibber unintelligible imprecations, and they grew cold and dispirited, till after what seemed an age Peter Lee decided that either this ridiculous impasse was to continue until dawn, when the patrol would be put in the bag, or else they must make a dash for it. Not being prepared to make a complacent entry, he turned and whispered to the others to make a break (luckily for them they did not hear). He then edged towards the stone wall, jumped over it and plunged through the bushes out into the open snow on the far side to find that he had, so to speak, been flushed straight into the beaters—a Jug patrol had been sent round to the flank as a cut-off. This moment was like a scene from a Dennis

Wheatley thriller, as the Jugoslav soldiers in their long grey coats, dimly silhouetted against the snow, ran forward, raising their guns, and the 'fugitive' jinked to the right, slithered down the frozen slope and tripped up in an outcrop of very hard rock. Then the Jugs put up a flare and opened fire with sub-machine guns; but he scrambled out, and more slid and rolled than ran down the hill till he was probably lost in the darkness. Sporadic firing continued, and a Spandau burst went zipping through the bushes, and then only an eerie silence broken by the wind in the trees and the nightmare imagined sound of the hunt following through the snow. But it was thawing now and the mist had thickened into a blanket, and the Jugs were content with capturing the other two.

Capt Elwes and Rfn Gormley, who would have been killed if they had attempted to run, made the mistake of trying to speak to their captors in German. They were lashed tightly with cable, beaten up and kept standing in the snow for two hours before being taken on a long march over the hills for a series of interrogations. They were kept in filthy conditions, and Capt Elwes had his spectacles smashed by a soldier and was thus virtually visionless. Nevertheless, they said nothing and word must have reached higher authority, because after a few days they received excellent treatment in Ljubljana. Mr Bevin had to intervene as Foreign Secretary before their three-week captivity was ended by delivery to the Americans at Gorizia.

Later in February a section patrol led by Sgt Collins were inspecting a Vipacco footbridge when they were ambushed and abducted by a Jugoslav platoon. They were released after a week, but their disappearance prompted a memorable order from Higher Authority that the 60th were only to patrol 'sidewards or backwards'.

This incident coincided with the signing of the Italian Peace Treaty granting much of Zone A to Jugoslavia, and it seemed possible that the Jugoslavs might anticipate the cession by sending troops over the Line. The newly returned Capt D. House had come forward as replacement 2IC with Lt M. R. Pennell, and the latter, on carrier patrol, had seen Jugoslav soldiers West of the Line in a village where grenades were regularly thrown. Maj Lee had just left Maj Larson's HQ at Comeno, after discussing the implications, when Maj Larson's secretary was killed by an automatic burst into his office, and policemen wounded by grenades. Lt Symington's patrols later detected a recently vacated rendezvous in a church. A Jugoslav officer without a pass was arrested, with Maj Larson's communist housekeeper, but had to be released; all the signs, including a Jeep which had clearly been used in the raid, led to the Jugoslav Enclave but nothing could be proved or done. However, when the next missile was thrown at our night sentry such a burst of fire came from him and the police that the post was not troubled again. On 22 February as the icy weather turned to rain, A Company joined the others in Monfalcone.

Capt B. Ryan, whose MBE was richly deserved after 12 years with the Battalion and being QM for most of the war, went home. In the other direction a draft of 100 had arrived, bringing the 1st Battalion up to establishment. Capt House took over HQ Company again from Maj G. H. Mills; Capt Le Coq handed over B, which he had commanded for a year, to the latter and spent much of the

Summer on a reconnaissance of 2 RB's barracks in Germany; sadly our horses were sent up there and, apart from 'Maroushka', not seen again. In April Maj Lee and Maj Mills ran a battlefield tour for all Regular officers from the Gothic Line to the Ronco and Marzeno crossing; it ended at the Traghetto Gap after the potent wine of the friendly Mezzano farmers had nearly proved too much for some. Maj Weld, Bays, covered the armoured side, while Capts House, Warry and St Aubyn stepped in to cover particular actions.

On the sporting side, the boxing feats of Algeria were repeated. With CSM Joyce and Cpl Walker, both former Army boxers, as trainers a respectable team was built up which beat The Bays in the Brigade Novices by a hair.

The foundation of an athletics team was also laid at this time, and at Battalion HQ level Lt M. J. H. Walsh was an outstanding sprinter. Thirty years later, after much-regretted transfer to the Parachute Regiment, he was a Divisional GOC with a DSO.

It was hot again, and KD was welcome as A Company set out once more for the Morgan Line, to find the accommodation vastly improved by the Americans.

The Morgan Line was completely transformed from the icy wilderness of the Winter. Cherries were ripening in the orchards, to the delight of orioles, and green lizards basked on the walls. The black *vino feruginoso*, whose potency was normally used to sustain a bridegroom on his wedding night, was opened for visitors who now made the pleasant pilgrimage. A great deal of valuable carrier experience was gained on the numerous patrols led by Lt R. R. Mackenzie, since recovery and breakdown problems were inevitable on the mule tracks across the Carso.

The Jugoslavs thought that they had the last word in this round of a one-sided hostility. Five Riflemen walking back from HQ to a post were ambushed and abducted in a deserted area. Six weeks later they were returned seriously ill with typhoid, gastro-enteritis and the general effects of under-nourishment and ill-treatment in the hands of the Knoj. They had, however, loyally remained silent on military matters and morally the victory was theirs, for they had refused to be either cowed or impressed by the bad treatment or the propaganda of their captors.

On 26 June 46 A Company rejoined the Battalion, which was largely back in Gradisca. B Company had remained in case of internal security problems in Monfalcone, but C Company had returned from duties on the mainland near Venice. While on petrol depot guard there, Cpl Collins earned the GOC's commendation. Italians had attempted to bribe him, but instead were caught, with a vehicle and a large sum of money.

The former 6, now 1, Armoured Division had sailed for the Middle East, where our 2nd Battalion was due to be its Motor Battalion. 2 Armoured Brigade had handed the 1st over to Brig Bull's 3 AGRA while awaiting the Ratification of the Peace Treaty, our final Italian task. Restrictions were imposed which limited training, but each Company found its own way of keeping busy and fit. Maj Lee took A Company up hill-walking in the Julian Alps, while B concentrated on night and early-morning training to allow full time for the beach. It was at this time that Lt Symington's prowess at the table, which has made him the successful organizer of Regimental Dinners for the 30 years since, was first noted.

Maj J. A. H. Powell, MC, had taken over D Company from Maj P. H. Parker, when the 1st heard to its dismay that it was to go to the UK, not to Germany, as soon as the new frontier was handed over to the Italians and Jugoslavs. The compromise accepted was the line proposed by the French. It gave the upper Isonzo round Caporetto—where Capt Harrison took a last party to catch a trout—to Jugoslavia. From Gorizia the whole of the Carso East of Route 55 went to that country, leaving a Free State of Trieste in a corridor East of Monfalcone to Trieste itself; this has since been incorporated by mutual agreement in Italy.

After many changes the 1st Battalion contingent, under Maj Lee, manned the new frontier South of the Vipacco on 16 September 47. There was some difficulty in persuading the Italians to come forward to face their redoubtable opposite numbers, whose columns, advancing from the old Morgan Line, had seemed at one moment in no mood to stop. However, the hand-over was at length arranged and the 1st Battalion stepped aside, conscious from the congratulations of their Commander that they had been helpful in the setting up of a new frontier. It is a great satisfaction that soon afterwards the strongly Stalinist climate changed in Jugoslavia, that the border disputes of 1945–7 have long been amicably resolved and that friendly relations with Jugoslavia, which seemed impossible in 1947, have been developed by the West.

Simultaneously Monfalcone had become part of Italy again and B Company rejoined the Battalion at Gradisca, where a ceremony of lowering the Union Jack and Stars & Stripes was held. Allied Force HQ now disbanded and the 1st started to pack up. Vehicles which had served us so well up and down Italy were handed in and stores were backloaded by Lt G. Newton, the QM. Finally in the early hours of 30 September 47 the 1st Battalion wound in its train through the pass at Gemona, scene of the last fighting in 1945, leaving away to the South some of its best for all time in Italian soil.

Rejoined by D Company on 2 October at the Hook of Holland, the 1st was helped on its way by Lt Col Sir John Maclure, OBE, whose 60th eye saw that Riflemen passing through his Transit Camp had nothing but the best. Capt House on the advance party could get no firm indication of tasks or destination, and it was not until mid-Channel that Lt Col Timpson summoned Company Commanders to give out orders. Battalion HQ and HQ Company would go to Salamanca Barracks, Aldershot. A and D, now under Maj G. T. Campbell, MC, would go to Bramley, near Basingstoke, and B and C to Bordon. The Battalion was to go to work as pioneers, breaking up dumps, and then be broken up itself. HM The King said in a telegram to the 1st Battalion 'As their Colonel in Chief I am proud to welcome them home after a quarter of a century of continuous service overseas.' Both Colonels Commandant and the Band came to welcome the 1st and, thanks to good work by Capt D. E. C. Oxley-Boyle, the Officers' Mess paid enough duty to free all individual Riflemen from Customs inspection. It was, however, a bitter blow as companies entrained for their dreary destinations, without ever meeting corporately again. In that grim Autumn, where mismanagement had brought even worse rationing than during the height of the war, the one bright spot was the cheerful drive of the Riflemen, led by the young officers, on all the tasks given them. As they manned fork-lift trucks or ran gantries, depots found output far exceeding normal despatch. While (in step with a Royal example) marriage was much in the air, Lt Col Timpson, whose efforts had succeeded in rebuilding the 1st to an efficient and happy state, was now busy in placing all the Regulars with the greatest care. Many owe a start in their careers to the pains he took, which were followed by many years of excellent work in charge of the Military Secretary's Confidential Reports Section. On 18 February 1948 a much-diminished 1st Battalion finally moved to Barton Stacey to take over the Army Basic Training Unit role, which will be covered in the next chapter.

Having followed the 1st Battalion from its post-war low point, through its build-up, to yet another reduction, it is more than time to return to the 2nd, now the only Battalion on active service. It will be recalled from an earlier chapter that the 2nd had returned from North West Europe to the UK in 1945, and had been made up to strength as a reconnaissance battalion for Far Eastern service; however, the Japanese surrender altered that, and the 2nd Battalion finally embarked at Southampton on 18 October 45, bound for the Middle East on an infantry battalion establishment and at an unprecedented strength of 45 officers and 966 men. Lt Col E. G. V. Northey was Commanding Officer, Maj H. A. Hope, MC, 2IC, and Capt the Hon T. Trenchard, MC, Adjutant. Company Commanders were HQ, Capt P. Pardoe; A, Maj J. H. P. Curtis, MC; B, Maj G. S. Palmer; C, Maj M. J. Gilliat; D, Maj C. S. Madden; and S (Support) Capt R. C. Stephenson; RSM Pendry and RQMS Slater were the senior WOs. After transhipping at Malta the 2nd Battalion arrived in the dilapidated Gialo Barracks, Tripoli, on 27 Oct, some two years after embarking for the Italian campaign.

The 2nd was the only British unit in Tripolitania, the other units being Sudan Defence Force; the country was not yet independent but under British administration. They had been warned of Arab hostility towards the Italians, but all was quiet until 4 November. Then the Arabs of the Old City rose and attacked, not the Italians, but the Jews with whom they had lived in peace for 500 years; it was a complete surprise to the Administration, but in after light was not unconnected with worsening relations in Palestine, the wave of rioting following similar events in Egypt.

The 2nd was not called out until 5 November, when Battalion HQ and the four Rifle Companies were all deployed in the town, with Support Company operating from barracks. In Tripoli and the surrounding areas they were too late to prevent an appalling massacre of unarmed Jewish families by Arabs, using knives, clubs and arson to horrible effect. Initially the Battalion was not encouraged to open fire, but on the next day was ordered to fire on all looters, curfew-breakers who would not halt, and on any crowd of more than five persons which would not disperse. Companies were deployed so as to occupy a large area of Tripoli excluding the Old City.

The death roll was 124 Jews, many of whom were women and children; many more were wounded and homeless, whole Jewish areas having been razed to the ground. The 2nd, called in too late, killed two Arabs and one Italian and wounded several Arabs; more importantly several hundred Arabs were arrested and a clear warning given that no repetition would be tolerated. Platoons and sections operated independently on patrol by day and night, and, in circumstances which called for very high standards of leadership and control, teams got to know each other very well. The bearing and behaviour of the Riflemen earned the respect of the Arabs, who took pains to keep out of their way.

The Gordon Highlanders augmented the garrison at the end of November, and although stand-by duties and guards made some inroads on time, range courses were fired and other training started. While the other battalions of the Regiment had been losing men steadily from already low post-war strengths, release only started to hit the 2nd (made up with all the younger Riflemen) in February 46; nevertheless by April S Company had to be disbanded, and a draft from the disbanding 7 RB were the only Riflemen received that year. Left to themselves the 2nd started a proper Rifle Team and carried out much field firing, as well as playing a lively part on parades, with band and bugles contrasting with the Gordons' pipes. The presence of many experienced Desert hands ensured that good use was made of summer Camp sites along the coast, although D, under Capt E. H. Spooner, suffered badly from malaria, since medical information on malarious areas was not accurate. Distinguished fathers descended on the Battalion in the form of Maj Gen H. O. Curtis, Colonel Commandant 1st Battalion, and Marshal of the RAF Viscount Trenchard. The most important visit, however, was from their own Colonel Commandant, Lt Gen Sir Evelyn Barker, KBE, CB, DSO, MC, accompanied by Lt Col C. T. Mitford-Slade and Maj Madden, with Capt J. N. Butterwick as ADC. General Barker had taken the 2nd to Palestine in the pre-war emergency and was now GOC-in-C there, so that the news he had to give was all the more welcome. The 2nd was to become the only motor battalion in the Middle East, and would move to Palestine under his command, supposedly to join 2 Armoured Brigade of 1 Armoured Division, which as recounted earlier was due to leave the Trieste area. In the event the Brigade never moved to Palestine, so the 2nd Battalion found itself under a variety of Infantry and even Gunner HQ.

On 22 October 46 the 2nd left Tripoli, but this was not the last contact with the country since the 1st was to spend two years there a decade later. Left behind with regret were Capt the Hon T. Trenchard, MC, later to be a 'Captain of Industry', Capt Spooner and many WOs, NCOs and Riflemen difficult to replace; sadly the splendid QM, Capt J. ('Biffer') Green became ill, having just managed to march the Battalion out. After a short spell in Egypt to pick up motor battalion vehicles and equipment, the 2nd began its move to Palestine on 27 November 46. Capt M. J. W. Harker successfully assumed the onerous task of Adjutant for the next year.

When the 2nd Battalion had previously served in Palestine the task had usually consisted of trying to prevent Arabs raiding the Jewish settlements. Now the Jewish population was constantly rising, many being illegal immigrants from Europe, whose treatment under Hitler had convinced them that never again would passive resistance be enough. Terrorist organizations, such as the Stern Gang and the Irgun Zvei Leumi (IZL) sought by many hostile actions, usually against the British, to impose their policies on the Administration. These actions included kidnapping, whipping, stealing arms, ammunition and military stores, mining roads and railways, and murder. The British task was difficult and onerous, and by the end of the year our Government announced that it would lay down the Mandate in favour of United Nations (UN) authority.

Throughout its time in Palestine the 2nd, as a Motor Battalion, served in the coastal plain. The first camp was at Rehovot on a main road and railway South of the Jewish city of Tel Aviv; it lay in close orange groves within a tight perimeter, which on one occasion allowed a terrorist to throw three grenades over the wire, lightly wounding some Riflemen in the beer garden. Starting under 3 Parachute

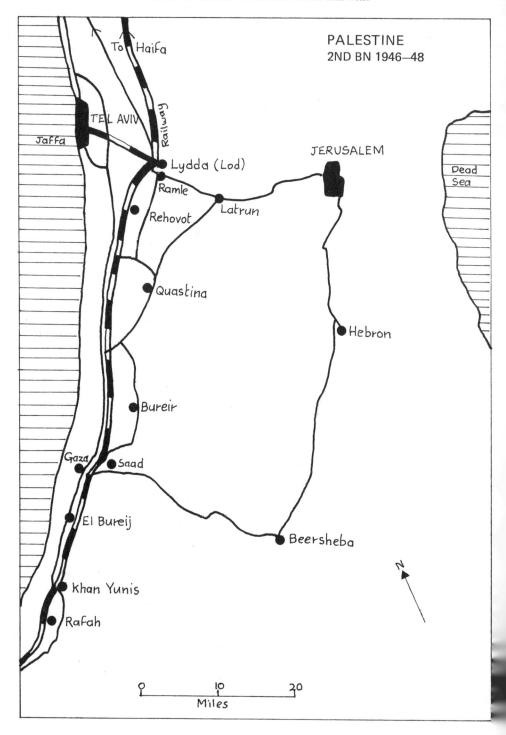

PALESTINE
2ND BN 1946—48

To Haifa

Railway

TEL AVIV

Jaffa

Lydda (Lod)

Ramle

Rehovot

Latrun

JERUSALEM

Dead
Sea

Quastina

Hebron

Bureir

Gaza

Saad

El Bureij

Beersheba

N

Khan Yunis

Rafah

0   10   20
Miles

Brigade, the Battalion passed under command of 1 Guards Brigade, which unusually was for a short period commanded by a Rifleman, the new Commanding Officer, Lt Col C. H. Gurney, OBE.

Starting with the guarding of an airfield, the Battalion then took part in Operation Elephant. This was the cordoning off of Tel Aviv from the rest of Palestine, in response to increased terrorist outrages; in theory only doctors and essential foodstuffs would be allowed to pass. For the 2nd, it started with the deployment of A Company under Maj E. G. B. Davies-Scourfield, MC; as it was 1 March (St David's Day) 1947, they had to protect a police station threatened by the IZL, normally a Welsh Guards task. As they set off into the darkness, with Rehovot Police Station under mortar fire, other explosions and LMG fire could be heard in the distance. A blinding flash down the column was found to be a White going up on a demolition charge, injuring Lt N. W. S. Yonge and a Rifleman; the demolition kit but not the terrorist was found in the orange groves. Operation Elephant was shortly ordered, and Battalion HQ, B and C Companies set out in a great column of half-tracks, Whites, carriers and Dingoes, headlights shining, for their sector of the cordon. C Company on the right were in open country, but B Company's sector of orange groves, gardens and buildings had to be wired; section posts were established and linked by patrol. B Company also blocked the main Jerusalem–Tel Aviv road, using two half-tracks as the main block. This night cordon inevitably divided farms and families, but special cordon passes were soon issued. The IZL reacted against the Coldstream Guards inside Tel Aviv, and a party under Capt H. R. M. Porter was involved in the firing, while grenades thrown at B Company HQ wounded two Riflemen. Capt J. Armstrong (RB), the Company Commander, lost his best go-between when in a nocturnal brush he wounded an individual who turned out to be the man's son. The operation, which ended on 17 March, had its uses because it flushed a number of terrorists out of Tel Aviv, who were picked up during searches made simultaneously elsewhere in Palestine.

The remainder of the Spring and Summer of 1947 were spent in necessary but unspectacular tasks. The principal one was the clearing of mines and protection of a seven-mile stretch of the main Haifa–Cairo railway line. Village and town searches were interspersed with a detachment just East of Tel Aviv. Protection of Jewish VPs against their own terrorists and regular patrols and road-blocks were all in the day's work, and one guard was on a workshop in the Levant Fair, which had been the 2nd's billets in 1936/7.

On 1 August 47 the 2nd moved to an RAF camp, Qastina, further South, where they were in more open country and came under 61 Lorried Infantry Brigade, in which the 1st had served at the end of the war. Apart from a road-block, duties were lighter, since the area was largely Arab and further from Jewish terrorism. It was also a period of relative calm while the UN Special Committee on Palestine was preparing its plan for a Palestine solution. The opportunity was seized to carry out company training; cadres had been run as often as possible to replace NCOs and specialists, because there was a steady rundown to a strength of 750, due to release and Python. Despite the many duties the 2nd used its ingenuity to improve both its military and its sporting standards. A Battalion Rifle Team was led by that fine shot Capt (QM) R. Keeling, who first came to notice with the 1st Battalion in India 20 years earlier.

RSM Cannon and he represented Palestine in the NRA Colonies Shoot, and the 2nd won matches as far away as Transjordan and Iraq. More local shooting at Rehovot had been the flighting of doves in the orange groves, and there was hunting with the Ramle Vale. At Battalion level Capt C. A. Humphries, MC, could be relied on as a polished cricketer, but none had to work harder than CSM L. Grout to win a race in the Sarafand Donkey Derby. This was one of the many light-hearted events of Christmas 1946, of which the ingenuity of the Battalion vehicle parade was the highlight, carriers and half-tracks as always proving a most stalwart basis for disguise. When the 2nd moved to El Bureij, South of Gaza, winter wild-fowling on the Wadi Gaza and to the North on the great Lake Huleh (now largely drained) reached a peak not to be seen again.

In October 47 the 2nd Battalion was sent to El Bureij, six miles South of Gaza and the site of General Murray's HQ in the World War I Gaza battles. The camp itself, being in the drier South, was bare and sandy, but a Rifleman's touch soon made it reasonably comfortable. Lt Col C. T. Mitford-Slade commanded the 2nd from October to December 47. Lt Col J. L. Corbett-Winder, MC, who had relieved Lt Col C. H. Gurney, OBE, in August 47, commanded the 2nd Battalion from December 47 until its final break-up in England on 11 September 48. He will be remembered as the most experienced CO of the 1st Battalion at the end of the Desert war.

A motor battalion was ideally suited to Southern Palestine, with its open, sandy country, where mobility and communications could be used to the full. Initially and until 28 February 48 the 2nd was in 61 Brigade, but under CRA 3 Division for Internal Security (IS) operations, his HQ being conveniently inside the camp. The area was predominantly Arab, with scattered Jewish settlements; it was the supply of these latter by Jewish convoys which usually caused an outbreak of shooting. The problem was initially seen as being one of maintaining law and order until the Mandate was handed over to another responsible authority on 15 May 48. The first period of calm was broken when the UN decided on 29 November 47 to partition Palestine into an Arab and a Jewish State. In early December this was greeted by the stoning of Battalion vehicles, attacks on Riflemen and theft of weapons. To impress both sides that they had the intention and strength to maintain order, six columns of all arms, including motor platoons, toured the countryside in mid-December. Reception was friendly, and it proved most useful later to have got to know both the desert routes and the leading personalities in each village or settlement. Attacks on Jewish vehicles started soon after Christmas, so that they tended to move in convoy. To remain impartial the British did not provide escorts, but standing patrols were put out to cover vulnerable areas; although it was intensely cold in the early hours of the morning, these provided excellent training for junior commanders, drivers and wireless operators, as well as a form of battle inoculation. Occasionally, as near Beersheba, patrols were forced to fire to break up attempts by Arabs to destroy a convoy, but persuasion was used where possible. Ingenuity had to be used too, as when a party of 10 Jews lost their way and drove into the bitterly hostile town of Gaza, only just gaining refuge in the police station. To avoid their murder much deception work was necessary, before they were driven out under tarpaulins in a platoon half-track.

On 8 February 48 the Gunners withdrew, leaving all Palestine South of the

Gaza–Beersheba road to the Battalion. Empty camps were stripped bare within hours by the locals, who also increased their attacks on and thefts of British vehicles and equipment. It was clear that Gaza District, through which the British had to withdraw to the Canal Zone, must be held till the last, if the bottlenecks of Gaza and Beersheba were not to be closed to us; equally a breakdown of order there would have had serious repercussions elsewhere. Accordingly, when 61 Brigade withdrew to Egypt on 28 February 48, the 2nd Battalion was told that it would remain until the end of the Mandate, and augmented, would constitute Southforce. The CO, with Mr C. W. Wright, the Superintendent of Police, and Colonel R. J. Thorne-Thorne, the District Commissioner, would control Gaza District.

Southforce consisted of the 2nd Battalion with under command C Squadron The Life Guards (Maj Turnbull), a self-propelled anti-tank battery, an Air OP detachment rising to five aircraft, and detachments of Sappers, Signals and Medical personnel. It was under direct command of Maj Gen H. Murray, CB, DSO, late GOC of 6 Armoured and now GOC 1 Infantry Division.

The task was to keep open the main road and rail communications, while assisting the Civil Administration to maintain law and order. The District contained 33 Jewish settlements, and the threat to peace came from Arab attacks on supply convoys or Jewish firing on Arabs from them. The Jews had now fitted many vehicles with metal sheets and used improvised armoured cars; the Arabs responded with electrically detonated mines or ditches dug across roads. Southforce had permanent patrols on the roads, consisting usually of an armoured car, an SP anti-tank gun, and a motor section or more in half-tracks or Whites; Air OP Austers were particularly useful for gaining quick information or patrolling the railway line.

Since the Arabs were in the majority, the roads could only easily be kept open by maintaining close contact with them; the line taken with them was that we had no quarrel with the Arabs, but that they must obey British instructions until the end of the Mandate. Since there was no central Arab organization, liaison was with local mayors and sheikhs, and unofficially with irregular guerrilla leaders. Contact was quicker with the Jews since they had a permanent liaison officer, who could issue instructions to all settlements.

During 1947 there had been a steady turnover of Field officers, among those not previously mentioned being Majs G. De Pree; R. C. Gibbs, DSO, MC; E. C. Phillips, MC; and J. L. Poe. The final team until after the evacuation of Palestine were Maj H. R. W. Vernon, MBE, as 2IC; Maj G. A. Campbell, MC; Maj N. H. Cooke (RB); Maj C. M. Archer and Maj G. R. Seymour, with Capt P. W. Colman, who had relieved Capt M. J. Harker, as Adjutant. Capt R. M. Parker had relieved Capt R. O. Lewin as Technical Adjutant in a Battalion whose vehicles latterly covered up to 90,000 miles a month, and while Capts C. P. Hazelhurst, M. W. Ponsonby (bound for the Foreign Office), J. R. Tillard and E. B. Taylor among others had left, there were successors like Capt J. C. Slater and C. H. Tidbury, who could more than hold their own. If there was one Regimental character with whom the last days of the British Mandate in Palestine could be particularly associated it would be Capt H. R. M. Porter. In the months of March and April he interposed as umpire on three major occasions between a fire-fight of Arabs and Jews at great personal risk, and by bluff, diplomacy and force of character restored the situation. On one occasion at Saad his threat of using a PIAT eventually parted a fight between Arab and Israeli armoured cars and many dismounted Arabs. On another he evacuated badly wounded Jews after securing a truce, but finally in stopping a fight with heavy casualties at Bureir he was wounded by a Jew. His excellent work, carried out with a very personal and dashing style of leadership, was later recognized by the award of an MBE and a Mention.

All junior commanders were soon or later involved in trying to keep the peace, but some instances stand out. Sgt Birdsall, returning with a small convoy from the North, found guerrillas from Hebron attacking an RASC convoy. Dismounting, he immediately opened fire, accounting for three attackers and recovering the stolen weapons. 2/Lt R. N. Farrington (RB) was awarded the MC for gallant work in intervening in an armoured-car action and persuading the Jewish commander to withdraw. 2/Lt C. P. G. Chavasse (RB) received a Mention for very effective work in stopping heavy fighting, recovering Arab wounded and picking up arms. When Jews cut the railway line the local Arabs could be enjoined to see to its protection, and the 2nd Battalion in parting the combatants did much humane work in recovering the wounded of both sides. During the final period C Company maintained a detachment in an isolated police station, where Capt J. C. Slater followed Capt Porter.

Meanwhile Maj C. M. Archer's A Company had relieved B on detachment in Beersheba, with one platoon detached to the South. Originally the Jewish settlements in the desert had only been supplied with difficulty. These well-sited hamlets now began to turn to the offensive, using armoured cars, and tied down the Arab population in Beersheba; the Arabs suffered from a lack of co-ordination between Gaza and that town, and would have run out of supplies if not escorted. As the police left, OC A Company became entirely responsible for such order as could be maintained in the area, using road patrols. On one occasion 2/Lt P. J. H. Whiteley managed to regain 13 weapons for the Argylls, but both sides were clearly building up an armoury against the British withdrawal.

As 15 May 48 approached the 2nd Battalion gradually allowed events to take their natural course in areas away from the main roads, so that they could concentrate on keeping open the latter. The Egyptians began to make their presence felt, first by an irregular company, who had to be stopped from mining the road South of Gaza, and by their build-up of Regular forces South of the frontier for an invasion of Palestine. A Spitfire of the Egyptian Air Force provided the only incident on evacuation day. It made an entirely unjustified attack on the 2nd Battalion camp with bombs and machine-guns; in this disgraceful affair Rifleman Gelling was killed and eight members of Southforce wounded, three Austers being put out of action. Apart from this, 1 Infantry Division and much of HQ Palestine were covered through the District and by nightfall Southforce was at Rafah and the force disbanded. On a parallel route from Beersheba A Company covered the Jerusalem convoy out, so that apart from an enclave left in Haifa until July, the 2nd Battalion were the last British troops to leave an area which saw three major battles in World War I and which unhappily has been the scene of periodic Arab–Israeli fighting ever since their departure.

The last word on the 2nd Battalion's performance will be left to GOC 1

Infantry Division, Maj Gen H. Murray, who had also held a high regard for the
1st Battalion in Italy. In a letter to Lt Col Corbett-Winder, he said:

> I am writing to congratulate you and your Battalion on the magnificent way in
> which you conducted operations in Palestine during the period you were
> under my command.
>
> The decision to keep you, together with a Squadron of the Life Guards and
> two self propelled anti-tank guns in the South was, as you know, made so as to
> prevent lawlessness in that area which might easily have spread to other parts
> of Palestine. It required a Regiment of great worth to carry out a task which
> had previously taxed the resources of a brigade.
>
> That the Regiment should have carried out this mission for nearly three
> months in the face of overwhelming difficulties with complete success was a
> measure of your quality. It was a privilege and pleasure to have had you
> serving with us during those fateful months and you leave behind with us a
> memory which none of us will ever forget.

Very properly Lt Col Corbett-Winder, who had borne a heavy burden of
responsibility, was awarded the OBE and a Mention. Apart from those already
identified, Sgt T. Rundell was awarded the BEM, and Maj G. R. Seymour, Capt
(QM) R. Keeling, MBE, Capts R. M. Parker and C. H. Tidbury, 2/Lt J. E. R.
Wauchope and nine NCOs and Riflemen received Mentions.

To the great disappointment of the whole Regiment, this very fine Battalion
was broken up soon after arrival in Egypt on 16 May 48. Only 75% of Regulars
were allowed to return home. Some were dispersed throughout the Middle East,
many going to Cyprus. Three transport platoons were made up under 60th
officers and NCOs and attached to an RASC Company, where they were rapidly
used for backloading stores from the frontier they had just crossed.

After handing in vehicles and equipment the remaining 300 sailed for home,
being greeted by their Colonel Commandant and band at Southampton on 3 June
48. Based on the 1st Battalion at Barton Stacey, near Winchester, the 2nd
Battalion, with a detachment of 120 under Maj Seymour, ran the Devon ACF
Camp at Penhale, Cornwall. It meant the complete reconstitution of a neglected
camp, but with such staff as Capts Tidbury and R. M. Parker and CSM Grant, and
backed by the Quartermaster, Capt Keeling, yet another success was scored
before the 2nd Battalion was placed in suspended animation on 11 September 48.

The individual initiative and self-reliance, based on their experience as young
officers on patrol, was to be a feature of Regulars who had served with the 2nd
Battalion in Palestine. Through the accident of posting and the linking of the
motor-battalion role to armour in BAOR, they were also marked as virtually the
only 60th holders of the General Service Medal until the Borneo operations with
which this Volume will close.

A good many found protracted service in BAOR or at home unsatisfying after
the excitement of wartime or Palestine operations, and retired early. Among these
one must mention C. H. Tidbury, who later rose to be Chairman of Whitbreads,
G. R. Seymour, prominent in that company, and M. W. Ponsonby, who earned a
later CBE and Ambassadorship in the Foreign Service. The Regimental view has
always been that in attracting the service, however short, of good Riflemen both
sides benefit, and their subsequent advancement does their Regiment honour.

CHAPTER IX
NATIONAL SERVICE AND
THE REFORMED
BATTALIONS

Since from 1948 to 1950 the sole work of the 1st and only surviving Battalion of The King's Royal Rifle Corps was training, it is as well to start with a brief review of the work of its predecessors.

The Green Jackets OCTU, started largely through the percipience of Maj Gen Sir John Davidson, one of the 60th's wartime Colonel Commandants, was commanded at York by Lt Col E. Northey from July 43 to November 44, when Maj T. Trotter, also 60th, took over. It moved down to Bushfield Camp near Winchester in April 45, and by the time it had disbanded in December of that year had commissioned about 1000 officers into the two Rifle Regiments. As well as preparing cadets for motor-battalion work, instructors inculcated the best Green Jacket traditions into a generation of future young Regulars, which brought great strength to the union when they were called upon to form The Royal Green Jackets a quarter of a century later.

Vital to this system was the technique of getting in touch with young potential officer candidates at an early stage, preferably at school. The Green Jackets Colonel Commandants' office was inaugurated at the Rifle Depot in 1940, and throughout the war Capt the Hon J. R. Ritchie, 60th, and Capt R. P. Cave, RB, were responsible for initial selection, enlistment and posting of successful officer candidates for the two Regiments to the OCTU. This logical system, based entirely on a Rifleman's infinite pains over individuals, has won the admiration, and indeed envy, of the rest of the Army, and is now enshrined in Light Division practice for both the Light Infantry and The Royal Green Jackets. Part of this system depended on care taken over potential officers on arrival, and this will be referred to later.

With the arrival of the US Army in the Rifle Depot in 1942 there remained only a tiny holding party, of which Sgt Phillips as Pioneer Sergeant was the chief 60th member; he later was awarded the BEM, and died after holding the same position at Sennelager. In January 47 Maj Sir David Hawley, Bt, descendant of a famous Commanding Officer of the 1860s, reformed a small depot, based on Serles House, in the Lower Barracks at Winchester, now the RHQ of The Royal Hampshire Regiment. Although primarily responsible for the administration of those between appointments, he put in much valuable work on building up the Bands with Bandmasters Jarvis and Baker, and on moving the Museum. Maj C. J. Wilson retired in October 47 to start a long tour as Administrative Officer, giving continuity to Regimental affairs and a stimulus to cricket, rackets and other sports, of which he himself had earlier been a protagonist.

It will be remembered from earlier chapters that our 10th Battalion and the

Rifle Brigade's 9th, at Strensall, near York, and Ranby respectively, had inherited the roles of the 1st and 2nd Motor Training Battalions, giving continuation training to recruits passed on by 27 Primary Training Centre at York. In November 45 they in turn came South to form two joint units.

The first, 27 Green Jackets Holding Battalion under Lt Col N. Blockley, OBE (RB), was at Ogbourne St George, near Chiseldon, Wiltshire. Although primarily a drafting unit, it was given also a training function. Maj E. J. Hawxwell as WTO and RSM Starkey were some of the older pre-war Regulars, who were confronted with the task of training Royal Netherlands Army contingents, reforming after wartime Nazi occupation to fight in the East Indies.

Towards the end of 1946 this unit disbanded, its functions being merged in the other joint unit, 27 Infantry, later Green Jackets, Training Centre, with Training Companies at Bushfield Camp and Holding Companies at the Rifle Depot, Winchester. Gradually the arrival of other units had forced the unit's redeployment to Barton Stacey, North of Winchester, where it continued to train recruits for both Regiments under the command of Lt Col W. Heathcoat-Amory, a former CO of the 2nd and 8th Battalions, with Capt J. R. C. Radclyffe, MBE, as Adjutant. To try to preserve the Regimental system the Infantry were divided into 15 Groups in October 46, of which the Green Jackets, long used to supporting each other, were one. With the further run-down of the Infantry in the next year, a Regular battalion from each Group was designated to take over the Training Centre, now with the passing of the National Service Act to be a Basic Training Unit. In this way a cadre of the 1st Battalion found itself moving to Barton Stacey in February 1948, to take over the Basic Training Unit role from the former Training Centre and man it entirely with 60th Riflemen. The permanent staff was fixed at 24 officers and 295 men, which meant that increasingly large numbers of Regulars had to be placed extra-regimentally. The experience of older pre-war Regular NCOs was, however, particularly valuable at this period. The expertise and sharp humour of such veterans as C/Sgt Whiting and Sgt Murray, MM, were of help to young Regular officers and Riflemen alike.

Although this seemed a dreary task to give to a Regiment with an outstanding fighting record, the grounding in the organization of training, of shooting, of potential officer training and of peacetime administration was to stand the Regiment in very good stead. That this task was well done and done with spirit was very largely thanks to the leadership of Lt Col C. T. Mitford-Slade; his work laid the foundation for the expansion which followed, for he commanded throughout the period, with Capt J. Le Coq as his Adjutant. Maj M. F. Douglas-Pennant, DSO, MBE, was 2IC and the Company Commanders were Capt R. F. Nixon, HQ; Maj J. A. H. Powell, MC, A; Maj C. R. Scott, B; Maj R. F. N. Chance, MC, C; Capt E. N. D. Bramall, MC, was Officer in Charge of the OCTU Platoon, and nearly all the other officers, WOs and NCOs were to be found in increasingly responsible posts as the Regiment took on an active role again.

Briefly, starting in March 48, the first intake of National Servicemen (NS men) were called up for a period which varied during the NS era, but never exceeded two years. Since they later had a TA obligation after Regular service, our NS men came largely from the London area where our TA battalions had reformed. Sixty men would arrive on the 1st and 3rd Thursdays of each month in civilian clothes, and after the usual preliminaries, completed a 10-week programme. The two Training Companies, A & C, received intakes alternately and divided them into a 60th and a Rifle Brigade platoon. B was the Holding and Drafting Company, but since only 22 men a month could be absorbed by the Rifle Brigade in Germany, once the 2nd Battalion no longer required drafts, the remainder had to be drafted outside the Regiment. Because of our high Regular recruiting rate, by 1949 no less than 580 were thus placed. In 1948 some RAOC and REME recruits came to us for initial training, but in 1949 two-thirds of our intake were earmarked for the RAEC, due for promotion to Sergeant Instructor soon after leaving.

Since some of the RAEC had already gained University degrees, this increased the number of potential officers for advanced training. The excellence of this system, inaugurated by Capt E. N. W. Bramall, which was carried on by Lt S. J. Symington and Capt G. H. Mills, was of great benefit to the Regiment. Parents and schoolmasters, some remembering Green Jacket OCTU days or with wartime service as Riflemen, hearing of the great care taken over individuals, requested a son's or pupil's attendance, so that the 1st Battalion received far more potential officers than any other Infantry Group; this tradition was inherited by the Rifle Depot, when the 1st became active once more.

It was for all ranks very pleasant to be back in the Winchester area again, and that ancient City, the home of Rifle Regiments since 1858, had granted them its Freedom on 18 July 1946. Strong Guards of Honour under Lt Col W. Heathcoat-Amory, DSO, and Lt Col V. Turner, VC, had represented the 60th and Rifle Brigade, with marching detachments of past and present Riflemen with their Bands. The City entertained 400 all ranks to lunch in the Assembly Hall after the ceremony, and gave a ball for 600 guests in the evening. Now, on 12 October 48, the 1st Battalion exercised its Freedom privileges by marching past the Mayor on moving back to Bushfield Camp. A tea party was given in Abbey House, and a silver cup presented to the Mayor and Corporation to commemorate the occasion.

The gradual assembly of much pre-war expertise and regular access to Chilcombe Range laid the first foundations of the shooting successes of the next two decades. The Rifle Brigade on German ranges had been able to lay down a vintage somewhat earlier, but Lt R. L. S. Mather and CSM Dixey as the WT staff worked tirelessly behind the scenes to ensure success. Sweeping the board at the 1949 Aldershot District Meeting, the 1st went on to win the Small Arms and Rifle Brigade Cups and the Britannia Trophy, losing our own KRRC Cup to the Rifle Brigade by a mere half point. With a lead given by Lt Col Mitford-Slade and Capt Keeling, it was nice to see younger Riflemen like Rfn Dalby and Cpl Airey running 1st and 2nd in the Rifle Brigade Cup. The year's successes were crowned by the Queen Victoria Trophy, the Royal Irish, Prince of Wales and Young Soldiers Cups in the Non-Central Matches.

In 1950, the last year in the training role, with Lt R. R. Cornell as WTO, good results were once more gained at the District rifle meeting. At Bisley the meeting developed into a tremendous match against a somewhat more experienced Rifle Brigade team, and the KRRC Cup was lost to them by two points. However, the Britannia Trophy was again won, and we were 2nd in many cups. The pleasing thing was the development of the younger shots. Cpl Airey won the Manchester Cup, and he, Cpl Solomon and CSM Lamb were among the six in the Army

Hundred, which included Lt Col Mitford-Slade. We did less well in the Non-Central Matches, but here again the team events for younger soldiers showed promise.

However, it is a Rifleman's precept not to produce gladiators for one skill only, but to encourage as many as possible to take part in a wide variety of sport. No major successes were scored against the large UK training establishments of the Services, who retained professionals (called up as NS men) to pack their home teams for a particular sport, rather than post them off to field units. Much was learnt by young officers about the organization of team training, which was to stand us in good stead later. Capt D. House began a long career as a most active Sports Officer, with Lts Walsh and Mather as active athletes; special mention must be made of the 800-metre running of Capt E. Kenney-Herbert, who, among other achievements, held the BAOR record and was third to two Olympic runners in the Army Championships. The boxing team, run by Lt Symington, found the packed teams too much for them, but our contact with the London Clubs was quietly laying the seeds of future success. Football, under Capt J. R. Tillard, an Oxford Blue, was improving, and in many other sports great fun was had. Casting back to 1946, there was the first post-war stirring of renewed interest in rackets, when Maj Gen T. N. F. Wilson and Capt A. J. Marsham won the Army Doubles, but it was to be some years before, under the prodding of Maj C. J. Wilson, the Regiment was to be once more at the top. The classic Hampshire sport of dry-fly fishing was introduced to many through Mess rods on the Itchen at St Cross, and the Barton Stacey shoot was particularly profitable in partridges.

Although it was a time to make contact again with England, struggling slowly out of its post-war depression, to see old friends and to get married, the professional aspects of soldiering were brough home to Regular officers by the need to work for the reintroduced Staff College examination. Many young Regulars had been forced into Grade 3 staff posts by the lack of Battalions, and, remembering their field experience, found a satisfaction in serving units better than they had sometimes been served themselves by the Staff. With the consistent encouragement of post-war Commanding Officers, officers of the two old Rifle Regiments who intended to soldier on worked to overcome this hurdle, and a very good number succeeded each year. It was also a convenient moment for those who found that their best fun had been gained at platoon level to leave, if they (and often their wives) wanted to try civilian life; often they moved about more in civil jobs than they would have done in the Army.

Post-war crises had passed the Regiment by, in its training role. 1948 had seen the start of the Malayan Emergency, where our patrolling skills could have found employment, and we were not among those rushed to face the advance of Red China towards Hong Kong in 1949. However, in Summer 1950 the communist invasion of South Korea finally persuaded all but the most naïve admirers of our former Soviet ally that nothing except the nuclear deterrent was keeping them out of Western Europe. With the rise of the North Atlantic Treaty Organization (NATO), so our commitments built up; the threat was from Soviet armour, so British armoured divisions were called for in BAOR, and they in turn would need motor battalions.

But this was all in the future when the visit of the Colonel in Chief, HM King George VI, was planned. Preparation for it started with a series of very necessary

Adjutant's parades. The rapid National Service succession of 2/Lt the Earl of March by his younger brother had confused most Riflemen and caught out Capt. Le Coq, who on dressing the officers, invited him in a bellow to 'get up on the extreme left, Mr Gordon-Lennox'. A very satisfactory whisper rippled down the line of Captains of very similar seniority to the Adjutant 'Lord Nicholas, you fool . . . Sir!' By an infinity of pains the first, and sadly last, post-war visit of the Colonel in Chief was organized, despite the inadequacy of Bushfield and the need to move on to the Rifle Depot for lunch. 3 November 1950 was a bitterly cold and windy day, but 1000 spectators kept warm under blankets providently loaned by Capt Keeling. After giving a light-hearted rocket to one Colonel Commandant, wearing a black Sam Browne, the King inspected the companies, made up for the occasion into small guards of 3 officers and 48 men. Dress was battledress, anklets and web belts, with the dark green beret distinguishing Rifle and Light Infantry Regiments from the dark blue of the rest of the Army. Officers wore SD hats and carried short black leather canes. However, Lt M. B. L. Fuller as Orderly Officer wore the new No 1 Dress of rifle green, as opposed to the pre-war black patrols, with black shoulder knots and the scarlet collar piping; the cross belt and silver-scabbarded sword, many of which were now loaned or given to the Regiment by generous retired officers, were a foretaste of our ceremonial dress for the years ahead. After a march past by companies in quick and double time, the Colonel in Chief, while inspecting, spoke to many of the 230 Veterans under Maj Gen T. G. Dalby and visited the Warrant Officers' and Sergeants' Mess. In Upper Barracks, the King spoke individually to all officers, presented to him outside the Mess, and then endeared himself to all by inviting the distinguished retired Riflemen to stand aside, saying 'Now come on, let us young chaps who've been on parade have a look at the fire.' The Colonel in Chief's eye missed nothing, and he was particularly interested in the picture of HM King George V in 60th full dress, in the silver and afterwards in the Museum. It was a happy coincidence that Lt Col Mitford-Slade, whose son was among those newly arrived recruits addressed by the Colonel in Chief, had commanded the wartime 8th Battalion during its Royal guards at Sandringham. Before the Royal visit it had been announced that both the 1st and 2nd Battalions would be reformed, respectively as motor battalions in 11 Armoured Division in BAOR and 6 Armoured Division at home, and the Colonel in Chief must have sensed the high spirits of a Regiment once more on the move.

This was a period when much time was given to Regimental affairs. Maj Gen Sir Hereward Wake and Maj W. F. Deedes, late 12th Battalion and by now an MP and 'Peterborough' in the *Daily Telegraph*, edited and produced *Swift and Bold*, based on the Chronicles, as a condensed history of the King's Royal Rifle Corps in World War II. This was a tour de force against paper shortages and other difficulties. Contacts with our Allied Regiments were built up by visits from both sides. To our great pleasure the one which had helped us most by reinforcements to the 1st Battalion now became the Royal Rhodesia Regiment. Lt Col J. de L. Thompson, ED, who had commanded a company with us, took over their 2nd Battalion, while Brig C. H. Gurney, Lt Col C. Consett and Maj J. Powell kept the alliance alive at that end and Col N. S. Ferris OBE, ED, paid the first of several family visits to the Depot.

In Canada Lt Col P. B. Earle, MC, who had been a Liaison Officer to Field

21   HRH The Duke of Gloucester, Colonel in Chief of 3rd Green Jackets, The Rifle Brigade and Colonels Commandant at the Parade at Winchester on 6 November 1958 to mark the formation of the new Green Jackets Brigade.

Left to Right—Lt Gen Sir Euan Miller, Col Comdt 2nd Green Jackets, The King's Royal Rifle Corps; Gen Sir George Erskine, GOC in C Southern Command; HRH, Gen Sir Montagu Stopford, retiring Col Comdt 3rd Green Jackets, The Rifle Brigade; Maj Gen Sir John Winterton, Colonel of 1st Green Jackets, 43rd and 52nd; Gen Sir Francis Festing, new Col Comdt of 3rd Green Jackets, The Rifle Brigade and CIGS.

22 Colonel Commandant's Visit to 2nd Green Jackets, The King's Royal Rifle Corps, at Ballykinler, Northern Ireland, in October 1960

Left to Right

Back Row—2/Lts R. R. Montague-Johnstone, M. H. Eustace, R. M. Gamble, D. C. Gascoigne, A. S. G. Drew, A. N. Allan-Smith, R. P. L. Knight, D. H. Mead, C. J. D. Bullock, Capt J. R. Miller, RAMC.

Middle Row—Lts J. R. E. Nelson, G. R. Shreeve, Capts A. E. K. Karslake, J. V. Keyte, R. C. F. Leach, M. H. Mossop, RAPC, G. E. Slater, J. W. Mason.

Seated—Capt C. G. N. Campbell, Majs J. St. C. Simmons (and Simba), J. A. Molesworth St. Aubyn, J. R. C. Radclyffe, Lt Col T. H. Acton, Lt Gen Sir Euan Miller, Majs G. H. Mills, E. W. Newton, T. N. Thistlethwayte, Capt V. F. West.

Marshal Montgomery in the latter part of the war, after working in the CIGS's office, did much to revive the old alliances by visits in 1949 to the Royal Rifles of Canada and the Victoria Rifles of Canada; gradually contact was built up with the other Rifle Regiments of the Canadian Militia, some of whom, like the Dufferin and Haldimand and the Brockville Rifles, had been converted into artillery. For historians a useful summary of their history is in the 1949 Chronicle. Only distance put any obstacle in the way of closer ties with the Sydney University Regiment, whose officer-producing role, based on undergraduates, had trained such notable leaders as Sir Roden Cutler, VC, the future Governor of New South Wales.

It was, however, from even further that a new alliance, that with the Fiji Regiment, came in 1950; this was based on recognition of the outstanding service of Fiji volunteers with The King's Royal Rifle Corps in World War I. In World War II the Fiji Regiment had distinguished itself against the Japanese in the Solomon Islands, gaining a VC in the process. On 4 December 1950 the Secretary for Fijian Affairs, Ratu Sir Lala Sukuna, KBE, Médaille Militaire, BA, LL.B, one of the most distinguished Fijians and their Regiment's Honorary Colonel, arrived at the Rifle Depot to cement the alliance. After inspecting a guard of honour with all the crispness of an old soldier, wounded and decorated with the French Foreign Legion, he presented the 1st Battalion Colonel Commandant, Maj Gen Curtis, with a *tabua* (pronounced 'tambua'), a sperm-whale tooth, now in the Museum, as a mark of particular respect and goodwill. The flowering of this alliance will be found at the end of this Volume in the commissioning of 2/Lt M. Yasa from the ranks into the Regiment.

With the partition of India our old Delhi friends, the 2nd King Edward VII's Own Goorkha Rifles (The Sirmoor Rifles) had become a regiment of the British Army, stationed in the Far East. Despite some War Office murmuring that British Regiments could not be affiliated, our long connection, reflected in a common approach to dress, drill and customs, was formally recognized as an Affiliation. Although only their 1st Battalion, serving in 4 Indian Division, had been contacted during the war, exchanges of officers and the use of the Rifle Depot as a home for those in the UK brought the Regiments increasingly closer together.

By 1950 the Adjutant, Capt E. C. Phillips, MC, and several WOs and NCOs of the Kenya Regiment Permanent Staff were found by us, and our connection was to be increasingly close during the next decade, which included the Mau-Mau Rebellion.

Before launching the two Regular Battalions into their motor-battalion role once more, a word must be said about other valuable work on the home front. The Territorial Army was reformed in July 1947, and our contribution was to lie in the London-based 56 Armoured Division. In the Queen Victoria's Rifles, based on the bombed 56 Davies St, W1, Lt Col P. J. Bradford, DSO, MC, was the first post-war CO. He had reinforced 8 RB in August 44 with a splendid company from our 8th Battalion, and had commanded their H Company with distinction. Capt A. J. Round was Regular Adjutant, and the number of wartime officers now joining the TA (some of whom will be seen again) included Maj R. M. Snagge, MBE, and Lt C. C. Gregory. Lt Col C. Henshaw, OBE, recently CO of the Queen's Westminsters in its Grecian 11th Battalion guise, reformed them at the undamaged 58 Buckingham Gate HQ. While Capt Phillips was Regular Adjutant, before joining the Kenya Regiment, with Capt B. Ryan MBE as QM, the pre-war Territorials or wartime officers were there in strength despite the struggle to begin their civilian careers once again. The Regiment owes a debt of gratitude to the two COs and to other experienced officers, such as Majs P. Daniell, O. Stobart, MC, A. Swetenham and H. Wise; Capts L. A. Mackay, MC; and F. L. Knight and Lt J. Butterwick, for providing an immediate cadre on which to build up the Battalions with the magnificent lot of young NS men shortly to join them. Since the Rifle Brigade had lost the Tower Hamlet Rifles, the Rangers now joined the London Rifle Brigade as the TA battalions of that Regiment.

It was clear that the Army Cadet Force was to be given better backing after World War II than in the period between the wars. The 1st Cadet Battalion KRRC had originally been formed in 1890, and was granted the Battle Honour 'South Africa 1899–1902' in recognition of the 100 cadets who served as volunteers for that war. Lt Col P. Mortlock, the wartime CO, had almost unbroken service with the unit since 1903, and was relieved by Lt Col J. Hutchinson, MM, in 1947; in 1950 Maj E. Dyball, whose classic wartime MT report 'I opened the bonnet and the moths flew out' became a Chiseldon catch-phrase, took command with Maj G. Hanson, both RARO, as 2IC, at the Sun Street HQ in Finsbury. In 1942 a 2nd Cadet Battalion KRRC had been started by the Home Guard, based on Regent's Park Barracks and with a Queen Victoria's Rifles link. In 1947 Lt Col R. G. H. Sutton took over command, now in Albany St, NW1, starting a long period of service to the Regiment. Although there have been links with closed units in various London schools, it has been through its own KRRC Cadets that the Regiment has drawn a steady trickle of good Riflemen, some reaching senior rank.

Turning back to the Regular Battalions, the first thing was to assure the continuity of training on which our expansion would depend. This was relatively simple because the Depots of the two Rifle Regiments in Upper Barracks, Winchester, were augumented by Bushfield permanent staff and became at a stroke of the pen The Green Jackets Depot, commanded by Col D. R. C. Boileau, DSO, late of the Rangers, as Brigade Colonel. The Depot, consisting of HQ Company, for a time a Holding Company, and the all-important Training Company, had a fully integrated staff from both Rifle Regiments. The two Colonel Commandants' representatives were now found by senior Majors, in our case Maj M. Gilliat, MBE, since the forward planning of Regular Officers' careers needed a mature eye and the trust of Commanding Officers and individuals as well as of the War Office. Lt Col Mitford-Slade, having served his Regiment unsparingly, later became a principal figure in Somerset affairs, and in due course the Lord-Lieutenant. During the summer and autumn he had used two very experienced Company Commanders in Maj J. A. Hunter, DSO, MBE, and Maj J. F. C. Mellor, DSO, to run TEWTS, reminding younger officers and NCOs of motor battalion drills. Fortunately, many of these had themselves served in the war or in Palestine, and there was a fair knowledge of the vehicles and wireless, which were to be the same as those held at the end of the war. It was, however, to be much less easy to extract the Regular Riflemen from extra-regimental employment (ERE).

When the 1st Battalion marched through Winchester, past the Mayor at the

Corn Exchange (now the Library) and on to the station on 10 January 1951, it was a more historic occasion than anyone knew. The Regiment was for the last time to be two battalions strong and to be in the motor-battalion role. Apart from a brief interlude for the Bicentenary in 1955, the 1st Battalion was not to see England again under that title, or to be stationed in this country for a decade. But all that lay in the future, and there was an immense amount of work in BAOR for the 1st and their new Commanding Officer, Lt Col K. H. Collen. He had handed over Queen Victoria's Rifles to Lt Col J. M. White, OBE, just as Lt Col M. A. Johnson took over the Queen's Westminsters. When Majs Mellor and Hunter returned to the UK in April Maj G. Campbell, MC, became 2IC, with the following Company Commanders: Maj J. Radclyffe, MBE, HQ; Maj C. Martin, A; Maj J. Le Coq, B; and Capt E. Taylor, C until the arrival of Maj H. R. W. Vernon, MBE. On arrival at Dempsey Barracks, Sennelager, near Paderborn, Westphalia, there was a desperate race to draw up half-tracks, carriers, wirelesses and other equipment and run cadres to train all the specialists. Luckily, on the vehicle side Capt J. C. S. Mills, having been recalled as a reservist at the time of the Korean emergency, took a Short Service Commission to use his previous MT experience as the Technical Adjutant, and Lt R. K. Guy, the first of the post-war Sandhurst Regulars, started a distinguished career with his appointment as Signals Officer. The Captains largely had World War II or Palestine experience, and the platoons were commanded by the first of an excellent succession of National Service officers.

But a few of the earlier officers can be selected to show the wide spread of talent and interests. N. Eden (now The Earl of Avon), rose to command Queen Victoria's Rifles; P. M. H. Pollen rowed, ran and galloped a mile successively in a record 14 minutes at Oxford before rising to the Board of Sotheby's (with Capt J. A. Floyd at the top of Christie's); R. T. Bosanquet became a familiar face in television, Lord Nicholas Gordon-Lennox a discreetly eminent presence in the Foreign Service and N. F. Althaus Master of the Skinners Company. A. W. Drysdale, G. M. Nissen and a good many others displayed their initiative and acumen in the City, while A. C. Butler, P. C. Goodhart and P. M. Hordern were active as Members of Parliament and D. A. H. Wilkie-Cooper in Winchester affairs.

Capt G. R. Seymour as Adjutant and RSM Starkey kept a watchful eye on discipline, since the strength of Export beer and the immense number of British and Allied troops, visiting the nearby All Arms Training Centre and swamping local Gasthaüser, could have been a problem. In this they were admirably backed by the firm and fair Sgt Johnson, probably our best post-war Provost Sergeant, who later transferred his talents to Customs and Excise.

The Rhine Army training cycle, which had already absorbed the newly formed 11 Armoured Division and its 33 Armoured Brigade, to which the 1st was Motor Battalion, had become fairly immutable, owing to the dictates of agriculture and climate on higher formation training. Large manoeuvres across country could only take place after the corn harvest and before the Autumn rains waterlogged the plough, usually by mid-October, although in some years much earlier. Collective training from platoon and troop to brigade level had largely to be carried out on the one pre-war permanent manoeuvre area on the Lüneburg Heath, known as the Soltau Training Area. A tented camp site lay at its edge on the bleak grass airfield at Reinsehlen, but the florid delights of Hamburg were accessible by Autobahn. For those units, like our 1st and later 2nd Battalions, who were not stationed in the North, this meant a series of visits, with tracks moving by train, usually over a week-end, and the armour too had to carry out their firing on the near-by tank ranges at Hohne. The 1st was lucky in being able to fire its classification and ARA matches on the English-style ranges on the Sennelager Training Area, and then use the excellent field firing facilities there, but most units, like the 2nd, when at Münster found 300-yard German tunnel ranges, and again had to leave barracks for classification. With range work, collective training and the constant round of signal exercises, to practise communications and staff work, with sets inadequate for the distances involved, it was quite possible for individuals or teams in companies to spend about three months out of four out of barracks between March and August. Coupled with an intense round of visits, demonstrations, special organizations or equipment for trial—all in the end depending on unit resources—it would have only needed a ruthless and over-ambitious Commanding Officer to make a nightmare of the 'Rhine Army rat-race'.

Fortunately, our successive Commanding Officers, in true Rifle style, protected their battalions and saw that there was always some light-hearted venture afoot in which kindred spirits could join. Although the continual training and replacement of young National Service officers and Riflemen placed a heavy burden on Regulars, particularly platoon sergeants, who rarely left the battalions, the reward was the stimulating and irreverent company of a splendid cross-section of the nation's youth. There were the reluctant characters, whose sole contribution was to cross off the days on their bedside calendars, and those for whose problems of low pay and separation from struggling families no Army solution could be found. But as we shall see in summing up at the end of the period, it was an era from which the Green Jackets derived as much benefit as the thousands who became Riflemen. The Rifle style of man-management contrasted pretty favourably with the latter-day resurgence of rigid formalities, which could still be observed in some other units in the 50s.

The secret to not letting Rhine Army get on top of a battalion was to plan a year ahead, to know what one wanted to do and make sure that higher formations firmly understood the facts and reasons. If a battalion was then forced to take on some unwanted task, at least any benefits which might contribute to its own needs could be squeezed out with a good grace. However, in 1951 the 1st Battalion, arriving in mid-January, found half the winter had gone; thus the season, traditionally consecrated to individual training, cadres, and administrative inspections, was curtailed. As indicated, cadres were rapidly run; then platoons and companies, map-reading desperately over ground already well known to their affiliated armoured regiments, flew into the field. By the end of the September BAOR exercise it was clear that the shortage of mobile infantry was causing motor companies to be overworked. The lorried infantry brigade was slow and vulnerable, now the West was seen to be in an adverse air situation. Working with the tanks by day, the motor company was used as a screen or on other duties at night. B Company solved their HQ security problem with Maj Le Coq's Jagdhund and Capt R. Parker's even more formidable 'Max', a Boxer brought back from Palestine; but even that old Desert hand CSM Abbott, who had surveyed some curious deployments with an indulgent eye in his time, found 2/Lt Wyatt's marooning of his batman to find a missing dog in mid-manoeuvres somewhat excessive. Straight off that exercise, the 1st moved South by train to the Niersteiner vineyards, and crossed the Rhine in Royal Navy craft as part of large French Army manoeuvres, where, if the interpretership of 2/Lt M. E. Shone was to be trusted, the French C in C commended the Battalion on its ardour and flexibility.

Despite the pressure the 1st, with Lt R. Cornell as WTO and Maj (QM) R. Keeling as expert, had managed to be runners-up at the BAOR Rifle Meeting and at Bisley had won the KRRC Cup for the first time since 1935, as well as many other trophies. Among the older shots CSMs Hooper and Murray were still well placed, but a younger generation of Regulars like Cpls Airey, Baird and Lawrence were moving ahead, particularly on the Bren. It was splendid to see the Green Jackets Depot winning some of the main competitions, particularly 2/Lt A. C. Butler as joint winner of the Worcester Cup, showing that the foundations laid earlier at Bushfield and in Palestine were sound. The moving of the 1st from Bushfield half-way through the football season had sadly come when the team had reached the Army quarter-final. With Sgt Lunn as captain, the work of Cpl Alcock, 2/Lt R. F. Cavendish, and Capt R. M. Parker and Sgt Hurlock as backs must be mentioned, it being very rare among professional sportsmen during National Service for Regular officers to earn a place in a battalion side.

Leaving the 1st Battalion to clean and repair their overworked vehicles and equipment with the advent of Autumn 1951, the equally hectic raising of the 2nd Battalion must now be recounted. The War Office, bent on raising seven 2nd Battalions from regiments with the largest element of Regulars, were also mindful of the loss of the 3rd and 4th Battalions by both Rifle Regiments in 1922. It was decreed that the 2nd Battalion The King's Royal Rifle Corps would be the Green Jacket contribution, and that it would be badged to us, but would be manned on a fully integrated basis so far as Officers and WOs and NCOs were concerned. Getting the 1st formed up for BAOR took first priority, so by 1 March 51 there had assembled at the Rifle Depot only Lt Col the Hon M. F. Douglas-Pennant, DSO, Capt T. Wallis RB as acting Adjutant, Maj B. C. Ryan, MBE, as QM and some 50 all ranks. It then seemed impossible, but the aim of producing a fully trained motor battalion by the end of October was achieved by excellent leadership and hard work at all levels. Maj the Lord Dunalley as 2IC, and Majs A. Palmer, MC, and R. A. Flower, MC, came in from the Rifle Brigade, joining Maj J. A. Hunter, DSO, MBE, MC (60th but wartime commander of 8 RB), and P. Pardoe as the experienced team of Company Commanders. RSM Grout headed a very happy WOs and Sergeants' Mess.

Maj P. Pardoe commanded the Guard of Honour at Calais on 2 June 1951, in which were included his fellow-survivors from the old 2nd Battalion's stand there in May 1940, Cpl Williams and L/Cpl Hill. The 1st Battalion Band under Bandmaster Jeans and Bugles under Bugle Major Silver were on parade, and the French authorities and their Army were strongly represented. Over 850 relatives and friends travelled over to watch HRH The Duke of Gloucester unveil the memorial to those 204 Green Jackets who fell at Calais. The Cross stands on the waterfront where some of the bitterest fighting took place, and can be seen by the thousands of Frenchmen and Britons who daily use that busy port.

Before leaving Winchester, the 2nd managed to classify on the range, and then A and B Companies were already off to join their armoured regiments. Launched from a now overcrowded Rifle Depot, the 2nd Battalion moved to Assaye Barracks, Tidworth, the first to be built on modern lines, with small rooms and bedside lamps.

While collective training to Battalion level was pushed ahead, the 2nd, like our two Territorial battalions, was given for a fortnight a vast injection of 'Z' Reservists. It had been decided that, to fill the gap while the Regular reserves built up, a proportion of those who had served in World War II and immediately after should be called up for retraining, in our case officers and men who had all served in a Green Jacket battalion before. While the 2nd received 350, the Territorial battalions at Camp were allotted about 800 each, and some help had to be given by the Regular battalions. Thanks to the enthusiasm and determination of all concerned, and the fact that the Reservists were interestingly employed in field training, the scheme was a great success.

In Exercise 'Surprise Packet', some 25 years since the pre-war 2nd Battalion first experimented with half-tracks, the Battalion successfully showed its paces. This was to be the last large-scale manoeuvres in England, with the newly formed 6 Armoured and 2 Divisions attacking Maj Gen Lathbury's 16 Airborne Division TA. To the four 60th officers forming part of the Staff College team of umpires, the greatest interest lay in the performance of their late Commandant, Lt Gen Ward, and his newly formed HQ 1 British Corps, over from Germany. Impeccable movement tables—designed to allow the Divisions to cross each other's axes, so that inexplicably the Infantry could take on the bare Marlborough Downs while the Armour was plunged into Savernake Forest—faltered as saboteurs dealt with the unsecured Test bridges. The Army was paying the penalty of having been run down to a point where no practical trial of tactical concepts or staff procedures had been made since the war, because there had been no uncommitted field formations with which to experiment. The Army's performance improved steadily as the new Divisions successively reached BAOR.

However, the 2nd was now fortunately allowed a period in which to run cadres and tidy up administration before the move to Germany. One task which had to be taken on from scratch was the formation of a Band, and it is to the great credit of Bandmaster Rodgers that this was accomplished before leaving England, by dint of great personal exertion. By his efforts and those of Bandmaster Jeanes of the 1st, the Regiment regained its musical reputation and was able to attract and hold first-class musicians.

A Band made all the difference to the drill programme, started in February in preparation for a most successful later Colonel Commandant's parade, on which Rfn Challis received a rare bar to his Long Service and Good Conduct Medal. Regretfully, however, this training was to be needed more rapidly than that, for the Regiment received the very sad news that HM King George VI, our Colonel in Chief, had died. The Colonels Commandant, Maj Pardoe and 18 Riflemen marched in the funeral procession, and the 2nd Battalion, the Rifle Depot and the Territorial Battalions lined the London streets. In Germany the 1st Battalion formed part of the Brigade congregation in Paderborn Cathedral, offered by the Roman Catholic bishop as a mark of rare respect in those pre-ecumenical days.

The recent Royal visit to Winchester had made the Regiment particularly conscious of its loss.

On 8 March 1952 the 2nd Battalion arrived in its new home, Oxford Barracks, Münster, in the same Westphalian plain as the 1st, 40 miles East at Sennelager. The two barracks should be briefly described as typifying the accommodation to be occupied by British troops for many years in Germany. The 2nd had moved into a former Luftwaffe Flak battalion barracks, nicely planted with trees, between individual company blocks and garages. Following Goering's precepts, a fine Officers' Mess lay over the road, and the barracks was well separated from Brigade HQ and other units, being on the edge of town. It had all possible amenities except playing fields, which were rapidly made, but took time to mature.

By contrast the 1st Battalion's Dempsey Barracks dated from the Kaiser's day, with iron rings on the walls for horses and high blocks shared by companies or converted into Messes. A vast barn known as the Robertson Hall was the icy venue of many a Staff and Promotion Exam, until it conveniently took fire just before the 1st Battalion left in 1955. The sad thing was that owing to continual financial obstruction, the two Battalions were not officially allowed to send teams to each other for the natural round of joint sporting and social events which should have seen the best facilities at each end shared. It is needless to say that, as when Mr Eden visited the 2nd, a party came over from the 1st, but every contact depended on improvisation, often in private cars, which few except officers owned.

The team in the 2nd Battalion had changed somewhat. Capt J. G. Harrison had become Adjutant in England, the 2IC was now Maj R. F. L. Chance, MC, with Majs R. F. Nixon, MBE, and J. H. P. Curtis, MC, arriving as Company Commanders. Among the subalterns 2/Lts P. M. Welsh—later to command a Green Jacket battalion—and M. R. Coulman won the Army Rackets Pairs, and the latter went on to win the Singles, a very fine feat. In 1953 they repeated this excellent performance, Coulman beating Welsh in the Singles final, and added the Combined Services Past and Present Doubles to their trophies. A mention must also be made of 2/Lt R. M. Burr, whose fine play was denied us with the end of his National Service. In the 1st Battalion there had also been changes, when after some gap-filling, Brevet Lt Col E. A. W. Williams, OBE, MC, its wartime CO in Italy, arrived as 2IC. Maj H. R. G. Howard commanded HQ, with Maj E. G. B. Davies-Scourfield MBE, MC, A; Maj G. H. Mills, B; Maj H. R. W. Vernon, MBE, C; and Maj H. A. Hope, MC, D, newly formed with Motor Platoons from the other Companies.

Both Battalions were on the old simplified establishment of Scout and Motor Platoons, without MMGs or anti-tank guns. The inability to defend oneself against armour if caught on the vast open fields of North Germany gave a feeling of insecurity not only to Desert veterans, and Energa Grenade and American 3·5 Rocket Launcher were clearly only for close protection. Clothing, with the loss of gas capes, was worse than in the war, and small pools, such as that of Canadian rubberized boots, did little to keep Riflemen, dependent at best on a leather jerkin, dry or warm. Individuals bought or acquired odd items of waterproof clothing, and the aspect of Riflemen in the field was somewhat piratical throughout the '50s and until the issue of the first green combat clothing.

The operational problem of sharing a long frontier with the East or Soviet Zone of Germany called for rapid turn-out of all troops. Every unit had its Alarm Scheme and platoon stores were set up in the deep cellars common to all barracks to allow more rapid loading. If 1952 was the year at highest level of practising defence on a wide front, it was for motor battalions the year of the bank post to watch wide sectors on a river line. The 1st became heavily involved, and, after trial, selected a standard model. A train-load of 150 tons of timber and corrugated iron arrived at Soltau and the Battalion dug in and stayed in position for five days to pinpoint crossings for dawn armoured counter-attack. However, it was to be the defending 2nd Battalion who watched the Weser on the Corps exercise while the 1st infiltrated across, Lt R. H. Underhill deceiving the opposing Brigadier into giving away his battle plan. Sgt B. Rimmer of the 2nd, however, captured his elder brother Sgt Rimmer of the 1st on the Weser bank.

One of the benefits of BAOR service to young Regulars was the opportunity to work with all arms and with Allies. A welcome encounter at this time was with a composite Canadian Rifle Battalion, made up from Regiments allied to us. However, the Green Jacket Colonels Commandant had become concerned at the tying down of both Regiments to Germany while in the motor-battalion role. Regular recruitment was suffering, and younger Regular officers such as Capts Seymour and Tidbury and Lt Fuller, who all successfully entered Whitbread's, were leaving the Army. It was arranged that the Sherwood Foresters should share the Motor role, and that 1st Rifle Brigade should be relieved first. That Battalion was thus able to take part in operations in Kenya and Malaya, but the Regiment again missed the opportunity. Lt Col G. Campbell, however, commanded the Kenya Regiment at this time, with his twin brother as 2IC, and Capt R. Guy was awarded a well-deserved MBE for his work as Adjutant. After distinguished work in the Canal Zone, General Erskine crowned his operational career by his East African leadership, with Lt Col H. Hope as GSOI on his staff.

At Sennelager it was the year of learning to stop mass attack at long ranges, and those involved in supervising successive 600-yard fire and movement practices were grateful for the unfailing priority accorded by Miss Rosy Redgrave's mobile canteen to all Riflemen as soon as spotted. Although the 1st had conducted successful trials of the Sterling SMG, the unreliable Sten and the No 4 Rifle were still in service, and it was galling to see other Armies better kitted out and with self-loading rifles at the BAOR Rifle Meetings. However, our two Battalions shot excellently with the weapons issued to them, and an inadequate summary will now be given of some of their successes. In 1952 the 1st won the KRRC Cup at Bisley for the second year running, but the subsequent loss of CSM Hooper and other experienced shots called for the gradual rebuilding of a team. The 2nd Battalion under the expert leadership of its CO then began to build up a team which was to carry it to the top. They won the BAOR Small Bore Championship in 1953, after securing the Worcester and Roberts Cups the previous year, thanks in particular to Cpl Harper. Bisley saw Lt P. M. Welsh win the Whitehead after a tied reshoot, and it was a nice riposte that in 1954 his tireless Weapon Training colleague, CSM J. Pope, won the very difficult Army Hundred Cup. Lt Welsh, an admirable ball-game player and shot, was also to be found as the effective heavyweight in the winning BAOR Inter-Unit Boxing team of 1954. In 1955 Lt Welsh became Champion Shot of BAOR in a thrilling

60th shoot off with Sgt Airey of the 1st, while the expert Bren team of C/Sgt Howard and Sgt Baird won the Worcester at Bisley. In non-Central matches each Battalion gained the Company shield, and the Hopton Cup, getting expertise down to platoon level, was also won, but it was the 2nd who gained the Queen Victoria Trophy in 1955. It may be fairly admitted that the departure for Kenya of the Rifle Brigade's brilliant team was a help, but REME now appeared to be establishing a hold on Bisley with their Corps experts, concentrated at home on long courses.

1953 was of course Coronation Year, and it was with the greatest pride and pleasure that Her Majesty Queen Elizabeth II's gracious assumption of the appointment of Colonel in Chief was received by the Regiment. Simultaneously the news that Brigadier John Hunt's expedition had scaled Mount Everest delighted his brother Riflemen. The 1st fired a *feu de joie* and doubled past at Paderborn, trained, as so often later, by Capt R. M. Parker as Adjutant. It was, however, Lt Col E. A. W. Williams who commanded the Regimental contingent in the London procession, while a street-lining contingent from the Depot and the Territorials paraded under Col Boileau. The following summer HM The Colonel in Chief accepted from the Colonels Commandant a diamond Regimental brooch in the form of a Rifleman's cap badge, to which all ranks past and present, Regulars, Territorials and Cadets, and the Ladies Guild subscribed. It should be noted here that the Regiment owed much from this time on to the wise advice of Lt Col the Hon Sir Martin Charteris as HM's Private Secretary. After many distinguished years and appropriate recognition in that appointment he was to be granted a Life Peerage and to become the Provost of Eton. A brother 60th Rifleman, Lt Col Sir Martin Gilliat, was Private Secretary to HM Queen Elizabeth The Queen Mother throughout most of the same period, and a sizeable group of retired 60th officers gradually built up as Gentlemen-at-Arms.

1953 saw the beginning of a new look in West Germany, as the relationship moved from notional occupation towards alliance within NATO; the impact on battalions was the progressive reduction of post-war privileges, concessions and amenities of all kinds. It was less felt, however, by the Regiment than by those units who had remained in Germany at the end of the war, thus profiting by escaping the rationing and restrictions at home. It was also the end of the first stage of Regimental reactivation. Lt Col R. F. Chance took over from Lt Col K. H. Collen, who left to command a Brigade, with later distinguished service in Cyprus. After long service with the King's African Rifles in Africa and the Far East, he had patiently shielded his Battalion from the more excitable commanders and staffs and had confidently left a competent team of company commanders to work out drills with their armour. Above all, this first post-war assembly of families of Regulars formed a warm circle, leading to many close friendships. At the same time Lt Col the Hon M. F. Douglas-Pennant handed over to Lt Col E. A. W. Williams, on appointment as Brigade Colonel. This was particularly appropriate as he had formed from scratch and led a most happy Green Jacket team, laying the foundation of even closer grouping to follow. In the 1st Majs C. S. Madden, R. C. Gibbs, DSO, MC, and E. C. Phillips, MC, came in as Company Commanders. The irreverent cartoons of Capt G. Bowden moved with that artist to Queen Victoria's Rifles, where Capt R. S. Ferrand had relieved Capt J. C. S. Mills as Adjutant. The latent competence of Lt C. G. N. Campbell, unofficial

Jester to the 1st, was emerging in his new appointment as MTO. In the 2nd Majs Bassett, MBE, MC; O. H. J. Foster, and A. R. Faulconbridge, MC, had arrived from the Rifle Brigade and Maj P. H. Parker had rejoined his Calais battalion. Maj H. P. Edwards, having commanded a company at Sidi Rezegh, had relieved Maj B. C. Ryan, MBE, who had been Quartermaster at Regimental duty for 13 years. Capt Symington, as lively an officer as ever served in the Regiment, took on the austere mantle of Adjutant with great competence.

1953 had seen fewer higher manoeuvres, partly because of financial costs but also because the arrival of United States tactical nuclear weapons on the potential BAOR battlefield made every level start to think about concepts, doctrines, tactics and drills. When the 2nd took part in, and the 1st umpired, the largest manoeuvres ever, 'Battle Royal', in Autumn 1954, it was clear that the Divisional organization, equipment and drills were inadequate—not least logistically— when a dispersed Corps Maintenance Area could not yield up its supplies within the hours of darkness.

In 1955 mixed battle groups of armoured squadrons and lorried-infantry companies began to appear, and some of the rest of the Army began to realize what the Green Jackets had long known—that only a motor battalion or something like it could hope to survive alongside the efficient Centurions in an adverse air, armoured and artillery situation. The 1st had conducted trials with Saracen six-wheeled armoured personnel carriers, but it was clear that only a tracked vehicle with a ditch-crossing capability could really keep up across country. Lt Col Williams, faced with the need to produce a fourth motor company for trials, borrowed one by friendly agreement from Lt Col A. Read, DSO, MC, commanding the 1st Battalion The Oxfordshire & Buckinghamshire Light Infantry. This happy co-operation between Light Infantrymen from the country and Cockney Riflemen was repeated in 1956, when 100 of the former, ineligible to move with their Battalion , joined our 2nd Battalion. It was a good augury for closer co-operation between Regiments from 1958 on and the later assumption by both officers of Colonel Commandant posts.

Before the two Regular Battalions of the King's Royal Rifle Corps separated for the last time in 1955, the Bicentenary Year of the Regiment, a vignette of their other less martial activities should be given.

A combination of enterprising young officers and experienced riders, ready to pass on their knowledge, made BAOR in the 1950s a golden age for all kinds of Regimental riding. For better-class horses there were German races; in British events under our rules, our horses were graded according to ability, allowing much fun even for relative beginners. The 1st Battalion improved a rough-hewn point-to-point course in the Lippspringe heather and held the first meeting in 1952. With the disbandment of the local hunt, point-to-points had to become official race meetings, and in 1954 the BAOR Committee took over a new course on the Lippspringe airfield made by the Battalion; a polo ground was also established alongside it.

Capt G. R. Seymour had brought out the versatile 'King Harold', ready to race, show jump or take part in hunter trials. Often ridden by Capt T. E. St Aubyn, he won steeplechases at Hannover as well as Regimental races. Maj P. Pardoe brought out 'Mr Price' with the 2nd Battalion a year later, which proved an excellent steeplechaser. He then bought the beautiful thoroughbred mare 'Royal

Mint' from the 11th Hussars, which won him four races, including the Mounted Infantry Cup, in 1953, and another three in 1954. In the same year he beat the best Cavalry horses on her to win the Grand Military Chase. 'Squirt' won a two-mile hurdle race for Lt Col J. A. Hunter, with 2/Lt P. F. Barbour up, but the owner had extremely bad luck with this and other good horses, until importing 'Golden Plume' for the flat.

In 1954 the happy coincidence of five officers with suitable experience serving simultaneously in the 1st Battalion prompted a resurgence of polo for the first time since 1939. Lt Col Chance, Majs R. Gibbs and E. Phillips and Capt T. St Aubyn made up the team, and, although it never quite came up to expectation, much fun was had. Although this renewal of the Mounted Infantry spirit of an earlier era was cut short by the 1st Battalion's move in 1955, Maj Phillips and 2/Lts E. C. Winter, C. J. Holroyd and the Hon J. P. F. Grenfell just had time to win the Rhine Army Team Race. All through this period the Regimental March was frequently played for winners at the races; the last comment should be left to the Commanding Officer of a famous Cavalry Regiment: 'When the 60th go, we shall be losing one of the best Cavalry Regiments in BAOR.'

As evidence of this, during each of these years a Green Jacket Race was run at Lippspringe, Regimental riders being awarded the customary cups. Since the 9th Lancers and 3rd Hussars were in the Division and stationed near by, these two Regiments and the 1st Battalion arranged various other activities such as hunter trials and dances in the same week. Married officers were very conscious that their bachelor brother officers could neither easily make nor follow up contacts with possible future wives during short home leave from BAOR. So during such social weeks wives tirelessly put up parties of girls out from England, night clubs in the cellars and picnics were organized, and happily for the Regiment some excellent matches were clinched at this time. The 1st Battalion were 'at home' to the 2nd for racing or range firing, but the 2nd too were hosts on many other occasions, their greatest asset being the Mess and its very experienced doyen, C/Sgt Pierce. This isolation was largely a problem for younger Regular officers, since National Service Riflemen or three-year Regulars did not usually marry until leaving the Army, and the long-service Regular cadre of WOs and senior NCOs were virtually all married, with their wives in quarters near by.

There is no doubt, however, that the Rhine Army training cycle, with its Summer pressure and frozen Winter tedium, led many good younger Regular officers to leave at this time. Many were those who had just experienced the excitement of the last months of the war or in post-war Palestine, and who found the prospect of being administratively employed as a Company 2IC, with work for the Staff College examination ahead, less attractive than a chance to prove themselves in civilian life. There was little prospect of a Company to command until the best pre-war Regulars had moved once more through the posts of 2IC and CO, although the great number of Green Jackets of Staff College quality, employed away from the Regiment, allowed some Temporary rank, unknown in many other Regiments.

With hindsight, more decentralizing to the excellent WOs and senior NCOs and more risks should have been taken, to get the restless younger officers off to operational attachments and secondments overseas, but priority was given to full manning of the two Battalions. The repetitive training cycle and the bachelor existence in a foreign land was found as tedious by the three-year Regular Riflemen, the best of whom just reached Cpl in that span, so it was very rare for a young Regular to extend. The Regiment, and the Army, were thus living on borrowed time, depending largely on wartime and immediately post-war WOs and NCOs, who were not being replaced. These bore the brunt of training the continually moving Riflemen, and experience had taught them not to rely administratively on happy-go-lucky young NCOs. In the words of a later CIGS, National Service might have been good for the nation's youth, but it was in process of killing off the Regular cadre.

While the Regiment was held in BAOR, every effort was made to use the facilities. Many Riflemen first launched themselves on skis off the wooded slopes of Winterberg, and later took part in patrol races. Rfn R. Hooper of the Rifle Depot was in a different class, and in 1953 won the Army Downhill and Slalom, being the Army Ski Champion and 2nd in Inter Services skiing; 2/Lts M. J. Miller and R. P. Williams-Ellis from the 1st Battalion were well placed. In 1954 the 2nd took up the challenge with Majs J. H. P. Curtis and P. H. Parker, and Lts J. R. T. Eve and D. W. R. Bedford. They won the Alpine Combination, being 1st in both Downhill and Slalom, and Rfn Hooper was both Army and British Ski Champion.

Officers and their Riflemen took part keenly in every form of sport offered, and the 2nd Battalion even won a Sapper regatta in assault boats. That Battalion also captured the BAOR Inter-Unit Cricket and Golf; the play of Capt Symington and Lt Col Mellor and those distinguished Rifle Brigade performers Capts T. C. Gore and F. E. Hughes-Onslow and Lt S. J. Pitamber come particularly to mind. The greatest shooting and boxing triumphs of the 2nd Battalion will, however, be left until after we have described the Bicentenary celebrations of 1955.

The defeat of General Braddock near Fort Duquesne on 9 July 1755 had been the occasion leading to the formation of the 60th Royal Americans; it was appropriate, therefore, that the Bicentenary should be celebrated in that same month 200 years later. Planning started in Spring 1954 under the two Colonels Commandant, General Sir Evelyn Barker of the 2nd and Lt Gen Sir Euan Miller of the 1st. In London the staff work was done by Capt C. Timson and Mr Siddle at the 32 Eccleston Square office of the Celer et Audax Club, KRRC Association and Riflemen's Aid Society; arrangements in the country were made by the Depot staff under Maj J. F. C. Mellor. Since the 1st Battalion was to be at Tidworth en route to Derna, its Adjutant, Capt R. M. Parker, was responsible for co-ordination of drill. To ensure enough space, and provide a finer setting than the then rather run-down buildings of the Rifle Depot, the Green Jacket Club ground at St Cross was loaned. It was vital that when the Colonel in Chief decided to hold an inspection in person our arrangements for Her Majesty's first visit to Winchester should be in the closest co-operation with the Mayor and Corporation, who were celebrating the 800th anniversary of the granting of the City's first Royal Charter. In the event the Royal Visit consisted of a programme arranged by the City and Winchester College in the morning, ending with a City Luncheon to which the Colonels Commandant and the Depot Commander, Colonel the Hon M. Douglas-Pennant, were invited. After lunch Her Majesty visited the 60th Museum at the Depot, while HRH The Duke of Edinburgh changed into Field Marshal's uniform, before driving on to St Cross for the parade and tea.

The drill for the parade, commanded by Lt Col R. F. L. Chance, was evolved in conjunction with Lt Col E. A. W. Williams from that used on an admirable Colonel Commandant's parade by the by the 2nd Battalion. It was based on what was known of pre-war Green Jacket ceremonial, drum beat and bugle call largely replacing word of command, and from this concept has stemmed all Green Jacket and later Light Division major ceremonial occasions. The Bands of the 1st and 2nd and the Bugles of the 1st were massed on parade in No 1 Dress of Rifle Green with scarlet collar piping and wings, but with Bandmasters and Bugle Majors in 1902 pattern 60th officers full dress, and with buglers in the sealskin Riflemen's caps, of the same period. Officers on parade wore No 1 Dress, cross belts and swords, while the men wore Battle Dress, green berets, and the disliked blancoed belts and slings, since during the rapid turn-over of National Servicemen it was too costly to issue smarter clothing.

The parade consisted of the Royal Salute, Inspection, and the speeches, of which the Royal Address is given in full:

'General Sir Evelyn Barker, Officers, Warrant Officers, Non-Commissioned Officers and Riflemen, past and present, of The King's Royal Rifle Corps.

'I was very glad at the time of my Coronation to become your Colonel-in-Chief, and on this, the first occasion that I have met you on parade, it gives me great pleasure to join with you in the celebration of your Two-Hundredth Anniversary.

'In the two centuries that have passed since you were first raised you have served your country in peace and war in many lands. Wherever you have been you have always brought honour to the name of England and fame and distinction to that of your Regiment.

'The roies which you have been called upon to play have been as varied as the countries in which you have fought. But whether it has been as Scouts in the forests of North America, as Infantry of the Line in the trenches of France, or as Motor Infantry in the desert of Libya and in Europe, you have always held true to the motto—Swift and Bold—given to you by General Wolfe at Montmorency Falls below Quebec. That is the spirit that has made the name of 'Rifleman' one well calculated to bring comfort to your friends upon the field of battle, and has earned for you the respect of your enemies wherever you have met them.

'The honours you have gained for your country, and your Regiment have not been earned without loss and I think it is right that, on this day—although it is one of rejoicing—we should also remember with pride and gratitude those who have given their lives, or their health, whilst serving in your ranks.

'I am confident that in the future you will maintain and enhance the fine traditions of service, courage, good conduct and initiative which have been so strongly built by you and by your predecessors. I wish you all success and happiness.'

For the first time the Colonel in Chief saw a Rifle Regiment's march past in column of companies in quick time and a march back in close column in double time, with the 'Eyes Left' and 'Front' given to the bugle. The line was reformed and the Parade advanced in review order, before marching off.

Commanding the Parade, which was from the 1st Battalion except for No 4 Company, was Lt Col R. F. L. Chance, MC, with as 2IC Maj C. S. Madden, Adjutant Capt R. M. Parker and RSM J. Garside. Senior ranks of Companies were:

No. 1 Maj E. C. Philips MC, Capt C. G. N. Campbell, CSM T. Lyttle, CSM K. Evans

No. 2 Maj N. J. Warry MC, Capt H. R. M. Porter MBE, CSM R. Robbins, CSM W. Price

No. 3 Maj R. C. Gibbs DSO, MC, Lt J. W. G. Pirie, CSM G. Hallett, CSM T. Byrne

No. 4 (2nd Battalion) Maj R. F. Nixon MBE, Lt A. E. Karslake, CSM G. Shreeve, C/Sgt J. Sanderson

The total strength on parade was 16 officers and 486 men.

It is sufficient to state that on 25 July 1955, a glorious Summer day, the meticulous drill, the speed and smoothness of movement to the inspiring music and the air of informal gaiety admirably conveyed to the new Colonel in Chief the spirit of the Regiment, in a manner worthy of the 200 years and all the Riflemen who had gone before. Their presence was signified by four officers in old uniforms, of which the 1792 uniform, given by Mr Welsh, the Regimental Tailor, and worn by Capt R. F. Cavendish, is in the Museum. More recent service in two World Wars was represented by the 500 Old Comrades, who paraded for inspection and gave three loyal cheers. Among those presented as former 60th Riflemen to Her Majesty were the Prime Minister, Sir Anthony Eden, and 5 of the 18 Americans who had been commissioned into the Regiment through their own gallant initiative and his help before the United States entry into World War II. Four, R. Cox, J. Brister, G. Cumming and L. Mosseri, had been killed and four seriously wounded. Presented on this occasion were W. Channing, H. Fowler, S. Alsop, T. Ellsworth and J. Tuttle, and they conveyed in a unique and living way the connection of the Regiment with the land where it was first raised and had served. It was very appropriate that Her Majesty's visit ended at the Cathedral, when Dean Selwyn pointed out the Book of Remembrance, containing the names of 14,014 Riflemen, including his own son, who had fallen in the two World Wars. Thanks to much careful preparation, allowing a relaxed atmosphere on the day, and to the light touch of the Colonel in Chief, it was a most happy occasion and a splendid reunion of old friends.

Sadly, 1955 was also the year when it was confirmed that the 2nd Battalion, only raised again in 1951, was once more to be placed in suspended animation. It lasted longer, however, than the reformed second battalions of other Regiments, and its prowess was certainly unequalled. Before taking up the role of the single battalion left to us, we shall review the 2nd Battalion's last years.

1956 in BAOR was yet another year of Divisional trials in a tactical nuclear environment. The effect on the 2nd Battalion was again to see the concept of the half-tracks being driven by the RASC, as in 1945 in the 1st Battalion. Carriers were removed and an MMG platoon in Champs formed, with a Section of two vehicles often loaned to companies to provide some reconnaissance element. The tactical concept up to Armoured Regimental Group level that year was the night infiltration of armour, with the Motor Company escorting the wheels and then joining the leading Squadrons by first light. Motor Company Commanders were Maj D. House MC (A), Maj G. H. Mills (B), Maj W. Amoore (6 GR) C; Capt R. K. Guy MBE was Lt Col J. F. C. Mellor's Adjutant with Maj O. Foster, RB, 2IC. The projected Divisional exercises were, however, cancelled, since Nasser had nationalized the Suez Canal Company and our reserves had been called out in August. What was to come was still unsure when the 2nd Battalion, thanks to good work by Maj (QM) H. Edwards, handed over smoothly to the Royal Hampshires and left Münster for its old barracks, Assaye, in Tidworth on 15 October 56. The 2nd's only part in the crisis was, however, to run a transit centre for refugees from the Hungarian rising of that year.

The 2nd Battalion ended its service on a high note. In shooting, it won the non-central Queen Victoria Trophy for the third year running in 1956, being 1st in the King George, Company Shield and Hopton Cup competitions. With a Battalion strength of only 250 by Summer 1957 the team went to Bisley determined to win, although there were only 30 young soldiers to complement their very experienced elders. By an outstanding team effort the KRRC Cup was won with 128 points out of a possible 130; Capt Welsh gained the Silver Jewel and Cpl Gridley was runner-up in Class B in the same competition, while 2/Lt Hayman won the Young Officers' Cup. As their own new Colonel Commandant, General Sir George Erskine, Commanding Southern Command, presented the trophies, it was, with the Depot's five wins, very much a Green Jacket affair.

Boxing was the other sport for which the 2nd Battalion will be particularly remembered. Thanks to good planning and devoted hard work by Capt G. Carter RB, SSI Collins APTC and the excellent team, the BAOR Team Championship was won in 1956, our bugles effectively suppressing the Ulsters' pipes in the final. Owing to the concentration of boxers in certain larger training establishments in the UK, no Infantry battalion had won the Inter-Unit Team Championship since the war. The 2nd Battalion, however, won convincingly against a strong Gunner team; as usual in a Cockney battalion the lighter weights, Rfn Maynard, Gardner and Macdonald and Lane, had a clean run of wins, but Rfn Burford, boxing in a higher weight than usual, produced a surprise knock-out and L/Cpl George clinched the match even before Rfn Dodd's final win. The latter won the BAOR Individual Championship as Welter, and Rfn Maynard became the first 60th Army Champion, at bantam-weight, since Rfn Thorne's 1933 success. Best of all was the good sportsmanship of all the team, to which 2/Lt E. A. J. Ferguson, fighting heavyweight against his preference, contributed; a Scottish Rugger international, he, Lt D. C. Pitman and others defeated some very good Rugger sides by their sheer zest, which was typical of a Battalion prepared to turn their hand to anything. Divisional motor-cycle trials were won, and enterprising sides played cricket in Berlin or golf in Holland. In the final year individual boxers won many successes, Rfn Whelan becoming our first International Representative at featherweight.

The 2nd Battalion had been a very happy Green Jacket enterprise during its five years' existence up to the official suspended animation date of 31 December 57. It owed much of this to its three very experienced Commanding Officers: Lt Col the Hon M. F. Douglas-Pennant, DSO, MBE, and Lt Col E. A. W. Williams,

OBE, MC, had each held wartime commands with distinction and had been post-war 2ICs. Lt Col J. F. C. Mellor, DSO, had been a wartime 2IC and acting CO; the 2nd Battalion, shrinking steadily but a sporting force to reckon with, ended up on a high note thanks to his own light touch.

The 2nd Battalion's demise soon saw the ending of another era. 6837905 Rifleman Bert Challis, BEM, had enlisted on 10 August 1914 and served through two World Wars. Captured in the Desert when the 1st Battalion in 1942, he had returned to Regimental Duty in the QM's Stores after the war and was awarded the BEM in the Coronation Honours of 1953. On the running down of the 2nd Battalion he refused a Depot post as being an old man's job and returned to the 1st at Tripoli. When he died in February 1959 he was aged 63 and had been the oldest private soldier in the Army, with over 44 years service in the Regiment.

CHAPTER X
FROM SERVICE IN NORTH AFRICA TO THE REGIMENTAL REORGANIZATIONS

When the 1st Battalion left Rhine Army on 15 June 1955 for a brief sojourn in Tidworth it had completed its last four and a half years of working in an All Arms team within an armoured division. When younger Riflemen returned to BAOR as Royal Green Jackets in the mid-1960s they would find that all the Infantry there had become mechanized. Although the process started needlessly more or less from scratch, as though there had not been 25 years of motor-battalion experience in the two old Rifle Regiments, a rising generation of Riflemen and Cavalrymen, as commanders or on the Staff, had an image of the quick and flexible thinking and action of motor infantry by which to judge and test those Infantrymen gearing themselves to fight at faster than walking pace. Just as man-management techniques, the 'Shoulder Arms' and many old Rifle working traditions have now been adopted generally by the new all-Regular Army, so the old Rifleman of the earlier motor section would be entirely at home in the armoured personnel carrier of his mechanized counterpart; he would merely envy the tracked mobility, the overhead armour and communications, which would have made him so much more effective than when in the 15 cwt truck of the Desert war, or even the later half-track.

It was full circle, back to North Africa for the 1st Battalion when after playing a major part in the Bicentenary Parade at Winchester Lt Col Chance took them overseas on 2 September 1955. Moving by troopship via Malta to Tobruk, they arrived at the little seaside town of Derna, known to the CO and some of the Company Commanders from the war. The Battalion suffered the disadvantage of being split three miles apart, astride the town, the larger East Barracks being more adequate than the West. For the next five years, until Berlin, the 1st was to be in single-battalion stations, with a professional lack of other arms' experience and, on the social side, of large garrison amenities; this at least encouraged self-help and in the usual Rifle way the Battalion determined to improve conditions they had found. The vehicles and equipment, left for months in the hands of a small rear party, needed a thorough overhaul, and by urgent Sapper work a first-class classification range was completed by the following April. Gradually families were brought out as the inadequate number of hirings and quarters were expanded. It was, however, a particularly poor station, the worst for 10 years, for Riflemen, with limitation on transport use preventing much contact with the RTR at Barce, 130 miles away; the best that could be done was to encourage much sport within the Battalion and a wide range of activities, led by officers, of groups sharing similar interests. Even bathing had to be carefully organized, in view of the dangerous currents, and even so two Riflemen were drowned. Thanks to the Colonel's leadership, and hard work by Maj Phillips and Capt J. E. Oxley in the stables, a lively Saddle Club was well patronized by all ranks, some of whom learnt to play polo.

Inundated by senior visitors, who had owing to remoteness to stay the night, the 'Bar Roma' was usefully created behind the Officers Mess as a pleasant venue on hot nights. Most officers of that period would particularly remember the shooting, the wild duck and snipe on the coast, the elusive Barbary partridges among the juniper scrub of the Djebel, but above all the pigeons, living in the deep holes of Cyrenaica, rising like teal and returning to dive home, often unscathed.

The 1st Battalion was in 10 Armoured Division, which was strung out from Akaba to Tripoli, but separated by an Egypt from which the last British troops had just gone. Since the 1948 war with the emergent but unrecognized state of Israel, the tide of Arab nationalism was rising to stir the apathy of centuries. The 1st's role, beside that of motor infantry, already practised in the desert on exercises, was to be the 'fire brigade' battalion of the Middle East. Very soon after arrival, Maj N. J. Warry, MC, was ordered to take his C Company to Sharjah (now part of the United Arab Emirates), 2000 miles away on the Trucial Oman coast. The aim was to dissuade the Saudi Arabian Government from occupying the Buraimi Oasis with its potential oil, and in so doing to back up the newly formed Trucial Oman Scouts. Warned to move on 25 October 55, the Company was en route to El Adem by midnight and was flown on by the Royal Air Force the next day via Jordan, Iraq and Bahrein, all then linked by treaty to Britain. During their flight, the Scouts were securing the oasis from Saudi sympathizers. Thus C Company had time to form a firm base at Sharjah and become mobile in Land Rovers, before the CO—who had flown out with them—went back to Derna. Maj Warry then established a platoon patrol base 200 miles inland, using oil company resources; the remainder of the Company's stay was passed in desert and other training, and organizing an active Christmas, in which donkeys, camels and boat-borne carol singers played their part.

On 3 January 1956 Maj R. C. Gibbs, DSO, MC, left Derna with his D Company to relieve C; and in so doing was to spend the first of many tours on the Persian Gulf, latterly with the Parachute Regiment, until being the last British GOC of that area. Although his Regiment was denied a period of command by this first-class Company Commander, his later work as Colonel Commandant and rise to CGS have given much pleasure.

Behind the relaxed style lay determination, calm courage, and clear-cut commonsense. So often in the wartime 2nd Battalion, his interventions—which had won him the MC in North Africa and the DSO as a Company Commander in North West Europe—had restored confidence under fire. Similarly, in peace it was found that on his arrival, in command or on the staff, the problems which had weighed down others seemed to melt away; as a great Rifleman, he is held in high regard by his brothers of all ranks.

On 11 March there were political demonstrations in Bahrein, and five Arabs were killed when the police opened fire. D Company flew at one hour's notice to the island, followed two days later by A Company, and their presence alone steadied the situation without need for military intervention. After pleasant contacts—particularly with the Royal Navy and the local oil company—D returned to Derna in April and A in June. Meanwhile, despite these detachments, cadres had just managed to keep up with the training of NCOs and specialists, but few soldiers were signing on in a station where the duties in the two barracks were inevitably so heavy, and recreation so limited.

With Nasser's nationalization of the Suez Canal, in July 1956, the 1st was put at 24 hours' notice to move, and remained on call for several months. 300 Regular Reservists from the Regiment, The Rifle Brigade, the DLI and DCLI arrived in batches during August, producing enough NCOs and men to bring A, C and D Companies up to strength, B remaining the training company. As the Battalion was working up to a pitch of readiness in September, Lt Col Chance handed over command to Lt Col H. A. Hope, MC, after a tour which had seen a major move and his command of the Bicentenary Parade. He had done much to secure improvement in the very poor facilities which the Battalion had found on arrival in Derna, and could hand over an efficient team to his successor, a brother company commander at Sidi Rezegh 15 years earlier. Another change over the year had been the relief of Capt J. G. Harrison as Adjutant by Capt I. Grahame of Claverhouse, and it had been Capt F. N. Voysey—so long a steadying influence as RSM of more than one Battalion—who had borne the brunt of the Sennelager–Tidworth–Derna move as Quartermaster.

Lt Col Hope, no stranger to the 1st Battalion or the Desert, threw himself into the Battalion exercises in preparation for whatever role might be allotted in a situation clearly moving to a crisis. General Stockwell and other commanders came to see the Battalion, but in November internal security started to pose a threat. Egyptian propaganda finally moved some Libyans into action. Vehicles were stoned, and Capt R. H. Underhill badly cut as a result. One bomb did some damage to the Officers' Mess, and four parked vehicles were damaged by others. When news of the advance of Israeli forces into Egypt reached the Battalion it was on exercises in the desert, and D Company had to be rapidly sent on internal security duties to Tobruk. In the end it was decided that it was politically unacceptable to use 10 Armoured Division against Egypt from Libyan soil, and the 1st played no part in the abortive Suez operation. In the welter of political propaganda which followed the withdrawal from Egypt, the reservists, left with a sense of wasted time and effort, were susceptible to agitation. As in many other units, an agitator worked on an alcoholic NAAFI group in the remote West Barracks, but a well-directed round over their heads by the cool Guard Commander brought the bemused men to their senses without any harm done. The reservists had worked well and sensibly while there seemed a job worth doing, and the authorities at last took the hint and returned them back to their homes and jobs. From the realization that Britain, with large forces based on National Service, had neither the equipment, organization nor modern training to engage in large-scale operations came the Defence White Paper of 1957. This, however inaccurate in some of its forecasts, allowed the Army to progress away from its existence as a pale shadow of its 1945 reality.

Because of political and military inconclusiveness after Suez, 1957 was spent by the 1st Battalion in a state of uncertainty over its future. In the early part of the year the recent departure of the reservists, and the unexpected prolongation of the life of the 2nd Battalion at Tidworth, confined the Battalion to maintaining its mass of vehicles and equipment with its very few Riflemen. Eventually it was announced that, with the break-up of 10 Armoured Division, the 1st would become an Infantry Battalion. Although to leave the Motor role so close to the scene of its wartime triumphs was a cause for nostalgia, the simplification of training, the release of specialists to fill up sections and the ability to be employed more widely than linkage with armour had permitted brought a sense of freedom from a role, which in peace had become a shackle. Individuals went home to learn about the MMG and anti-tank gun, while the Battalion learnt how to march. Lt Col Hope used a last opportunity to take all officers and senior NCOs over the 1941 Sidi Rezegh battlefield. He had commanded A Company in the centre of the attack, and Sgt Cheshire and Cpl Featherstone were present to give section views of the battle.

Other desert expeditions took place in April. Maj Warry took a small party down the old frontier wire to Giarabub to visit the Grand Sennussi's tomb by that former Italian fort. A more ambitious column, after much planning and training, advanced on Kufra Oasis under Maj E. N. W. Bramall, MC. Moving via the coast road to Agedebia, Lt J. W. Mason, an imperturbable Regular officer from Australia, who served originally with the Sydney University Regiment, was left to maintain an advanced base with C/Sgt Fowley, and the party pushed on towards the Sand Sea. Encountering more soft going and heavier petrol consumption than calculated, the difficult decision was taken to thin out further by leaving Capt C. J. Adami, the administrative officer, on the North side of the Sand Sea. Maj Bramall, 2/Lt G. P. R. Crossman as navigator with the sun compass, and 2/Lt C. C. P. Williams, a later Green Jacket cricketer of note as well as an MP and Chairman of the Prices Commission, led the way on over the Sand Sea, but the honours must go to AQMS Rodigan, REME, and Sgt Fee, who achieved almost impossible repairs to the vehicles. Having reached Kufra and enjoyed the oasis—visited at that time by few Englishmen except the wartime Long Range Desert Group—the expedition successfully returned across the desert via Mechili. 2/Lt Crossman's developing passion for the desert, its tribes, and their activities, from falconry to camel expeditions, was given full rein, when he assisted Maj T. E. St Aubyn as officer in charge of mounting and running the War Office sponsored Cambridge University expedition to the Tibesti Mountains in the heart of the French Sahara. This was most successful, lasting from June to September, and Maj St Aubyn used the experience to lead annual private expeditions all over the Sahara for many years after he had retired from the Army.

Changes of senior officers had been taking place during the year. Maj J. H. P. Curtis, MC, relieved Maj P. Pardoe as 2IC, both contributing much on the sporting side. The latter's predecessor, Maj C. S. Madden, had in 1955 led a winning King George V Cup team with a fine personal score well supported by Capt M. J. Calvert. While Maj J. R. C. Radclyffe, MBE, continued his long reign in HQ Company, Maj C. A. Humphreys, MC, and Maj T. E. St Aubyn took over C and A Companies respectively. Maj M. P. Hills had recently transferred into the Regiment, at a time when a very good lot of younger Regular officers were leaving. Among those leaving as the 1st sailed to Derna was Capt R. F. Cavendish, who was sadly later to suffer almost total paralysis. Backed by a gallant family, he has remained a central figure at many Regimental gatherings, and the more recent award of an MBE for services to his fellow-disabled gave much pleasure to all Riflemen.

After many months of uncertainty it was finally announced as late as October 1957 that the 1st Battalion would move to Gialo Barracks, Tripoli, in December to finish its overseas tour; this had been the barracks occupied by the 2nd Battalion in 1945. The last few months under District were unsatisfactory, and there was the added complication of closing down Derna on handing Cyrenaica to the Libyans. However, the Summer's infantry training had culminated in both a landing from the sea and a very tough counter-insurgency exercise across the Djebel West of Derna. Finally in mid-November parties moved West to Tripoli, some by road, others by LST and the main body by troopship from Tobruk; D Company was left there as rear party until January. Gialo Barracks had to be acquired on a temporary lease, but the main thing was that, once in, no one managed to push us out.

The 1st Battalion, under the Libyan treaty, had no internal security commitment, so was able to get on with a proper cycle of infantry training, interrupted only by visits at short notice, often by ships of the Royal Navy. After an ambitious desert expedition, led by Capt Grahame of Claverhouse, with Capt C. J. Holroyd and C/Sgt B. Rimmer as other senior members, which crossed the central Sand Sea from Gatrun to Mourzouk, the highlight of May was the company camps at Tarhuna, South East of Tripoli. Both the CO and Maj Curtis knew the Tripoli area well, and the presence of a spring-fed pool made the field-firing even better, despite the Arab tendency to remove targets for fuel more or less under fire.

To vary the training, a very ambitious Queen's Birthday Parade, based on the Bicentenary drill, was rehearsed under Maj R. M. Parker and RSM Shreeve. 3000 spectators, including the complete Diplomatic Corps, saw HE The British Ambassador take the salute at a splendid parade, on which The Colonel in Chief afterwards expressed HM's satisfaction through diplomatic channels. The Battalion wore Khaki Drill bush jackets, shorts, hose tops and puttes, but the Band and Bugles in No 3 Dress (Whites) dominated the parade under the experienced team of Bandmaster Jeanes and Bugle Major Silver. It was the last great Regular parade on which the red cherry and the black Maltese cross on the red ground—which had carried our battle honours on so many fields of action—were to be worn.

For the six subsequent weeks a trial was conducted in which the Battalion was made completely mobile on a Land Rover and trailer basis. Starting this new concept from scratch, the 1st successfully worked up to a 200-mile sortie into the desert. However, just before the final July 1958 exercise the Iraq crisis, whose aftermath was irreversibly to alter the Arab scene, demanded that all the vehicles should be withdrawn as British garrisons all over the Middle East went on alert. A lighter touch was the participation of a platoon in the film Sea of Sand, based on Long Range Desert Group exploits. C/Sgt Lennox made himself useful as adviser on desert brewing skills and sartorial fashions of 1942.

Lt Gen Sir Euan Miller, KCB, KBE, DSO, MC, as Colonel Commandant, and Lady Miller had paid a welcome visit to the Battalion in April, and saw how well the Battalion had adapted to its new station. Under the successive lead of Mrs

Chance and Mrs Hope as much as possible had been done to draw families together, living as they were in fairly primitive surroundings. One particular family tragedy struck hard in June; Maj R. J. A. Darwin, who had recently taken over his first company, D, was killed by a civilian car when on training. He had served in the Desert with 7 RB and had been wounded with the 1st 60th, his parent Regiment, in Italy. A fine cricketer and good Rifleman, he tragically left behind a widow and two small girls.

The time has come to sum up the last tour in—though not the last visit to—North Africa of 60th Riflemen. Derna and Tripoli had been poor in amenities, although the latter had provided more international and inter-Service contacts through the Royal Navy and the United States Air Force base. Although competition shooting was dominated by the 2nd Battalion at home, the 1st had had its successes in the Non-Central Matches abroad. 11 Platoon C Company won the Hopton Cup, with 1 Platoon A Company 2nd; with the King George and Royal Irish Cups, won by the two Messes, they secured the Queen Victoria Trophy abroad in 1958. Shooting in that year under the difficult conditions of Tripoli, the Messes won their Cups again, and again the Queen Victoria Trophy abroad was secured in 1958-9.

Boxing was a sport in which the Battalion was never defeated as a team during its tour, and won the majority of individual contests. Swimming, as might be expected, was worked up to a general high standard to win the District Inter-Unit competition, and the District Athletics were also won. Excellent cricketers like Majs Bramall and Humphreys, Capts Guy and I. H. McCausland, Lt C. J. H. Gurney and 2/Lt C. Williams spread enthusiasm for the game down to company level, and hockey was equally popular; during the short Tripoli season sand grouse provided some excellent game shooting, and the stables built by 2/Lt P. B. Mitford-Slade formed a base for an active Saddle Club and polo.

The Battalion had taken—indeed, had created—every opportunity to keep Riflemen interested, but the problem had been the run-down in strength and, with the disincentive to prolong service, the lack of new talent to train on as NCOs. Both Commanding Officers had suffered under local staffs who tended to use the uncertainty of our Libyan stay for doing little administratively, yet proving adept at misemploying Riflemen on duties, if not resisted. Lt Col Hope's last protective action, backed by the District Commander, was to threaten to march his Battalion off the troopship, when Movement Control looked like marooning half the Battalion baggage. He saw the 1st into a temporary camp at Piddlehinton near Dorchester, before retiring early to be a most successful Personnel Manager of Whitbread's. With singular ineptitude the War Office, having allowed the 1st to run down to a cadre, instead of posting it to England to recruit the Regulars vital as the end of National Service approached, warned it for onward routing to Ballykinler, Northern Ireland, in the New Year.

With the end of this Middle East tour, it is time to turn back to England and to review the considerable activity at the Green Jackets Depot and among the Territorials and Cadets.

When in July 1958 Col the Hon M. F. Douglas-Pennant, DSO, MBE, retired he had commanded the Depot for four very active years, binding the two old Rifle Regiments closer together. Despite changes of drafting and other policy he had to build up successively the 1st Rifle Brigade and our 1st Battalion for overseas service, while the life of our 2nd Battalion was prolonged beyond expectation. Under the CO the key Depot role is played by Training Company, since apart from training recruits to take their place in a Battalion, its staff have to put over the Green Jacket style of discipline to recruits from in many cases difficult urban backgrounds, where the authorities are seen as hostile. A good many 60th Riflemen made their contribution to the Company; Majs Bramall and Mills, Capts Welsh and Mason and CMSs Hinett, Garner and Fowley were all involved in the Company. RSM J. Pope and ORQMS R. Robbins, rare 60th veterans of the Burma campaign, communicated expertise in shooting, drill and clerical training, as well as much practical Rifleman's lore to the newly joined, while QMSI Lawrence, SASC and late of the Regiment, juggled the Aldershot District and Bisley Rifle Meeting teams between training and other commitments on the permanent staff. In 1956 his predecessor, QMSI Thurston, admirably supported by Capt G. Wemyss and Sgt Young, both RB, had led the Depot to a magnificent seizure of the KRRC Cup and 17 other trophies. Col Douglas-Pennant, who laid great emphasis on the importance of recruit Riflemen being trained by the best shots in the Army, himself captained the successful Army Team. In the following two years, while not reaching that peak, the arrival of Sgt Harper compensated for some of the loss of other experienced shots and the Royal Ulster Rifle Cup was twice won, besides the Worcester and several other trophies.

On the administrative side it was during this period that Brigadier T. I. Dun, DSO, MC, late RAMC, started a long reign as Medical Officer. Of particular value over many years was the excellent co-operation between him and Training Company Commanders when assessing the physical potentiality of recruits or the need for speedy discharge.

In these years the Depot was the scene of successive parades. On 14 September 1957, exactly 100 years since the Guides, the Sirmoor Regiment of Goorkhas and the 1st Battalion 60th Rifles turned to the offensive outside Delhi, the Centenary of the Friendship then established was celebrated by the Regimental Association of the 2nd King Edward VII's Own Goorkha Rifles and the Green Jackets Depot. At a parade, dressed in No 1 Dress for the first time and commanded by Maj G. H. Mills, a special copy of the diary of Maj Reid, Commandant of the Sirmoor Regiment at Delhi, was presented to us; appropriately, it was laid on our third of the Delhi Table. Simultaneously in Singapore, Capt V. West, 60th, seconded to 2/2nd Goorkhas, was presenting them with a Truncheon sling from the Regiment. After a Centenary Service in the Garrison Church, when Goorkha memorials were dedicated, and their Association lunch in the Guildhall, the day ended with the planting of a Deodar at St Cross by sergeants of the two Regiments. This symbolized the close bond between them of which the presence of Queen's Gurkha Orderly Officers and others, using the Depot as their English home, had for some time been evidence.

In 1958 the Centenary of the Rifle Depot's establishment at Winchester was celebrated by a parade in No 1 Dress under Maj E. C. Phillips, MC, in front of the Guildhall, where the Brigade Colonel handed over a commemorative shield to the Mayor in token of the very happy relationship with the ancient City over the years.

The most important parade was, however, that held on 6 November 1958 to mark the Inauguration of the new Green Jackets Brigade cap badge and the assumption of the new Regimental titles. The move to a much smaller all-Regular Army of 165,000, whose commitments later raised it to 182,000, meant many amalgamations, particularly in the Infantry, where Counties could no longer sustain one or more Regiments.

The Royal Hampshire Regiment now was to train its recruits at the Depot of the Wessex Brigade in Devon, leaving only its RHQ and Museum in Serle's House. Lower Barracks for the next 20 years was occupied by the Medical & Women's Services Record Office.

Green Jacket success in Regular recruiting, both in numbers and in quality of officers and men, untied to a County but with traditional areas—of which London was the principal—had, however, made our viability clear. It was thought, nevertheless, that the new Brigades should be of a minimum of three Regiments and that eventually these in turn might become Battalions of a Large Regiment. Accordingly The Oxfordshire and Buckinghamshire Light Infantry, who as the 43rd and 52nd Light Infantry had formed admirable supports to the 95th or Rifle Brigade in Sir John Moore's Light Brigade, (later Division), were to join us as Green Jackets. From the first this natural union was given an unreserved welcome, and much careful thought went into making the transition easy. When the Light Infantrymen wished to adopt the style of Riflemen, Maj Mills, working at the War Office to Cols J. Mogg and A. Clarke-Browne of the 43rd and 52nd, was able to pronounce after research that the style depended only on the Queen's pleasure and the custom of the Service; the first was graciously given and the custom was immediately observed, their black button stemming from this process. Regimental titles showed the unity of the Brigade, ours becoming 2nd Green Jackets, The King's Royal Rifle Corps. The new cap badge, a silver Maltese cross within a wreath under the crown and 'Peninsula' was not unlike our cross-belt badge, when The Duke of York's Rifle Corps, or that of the Rifle Brigade. The large superimposed bugle horn was a direct application of the Light Infantry pattern to the cross, but unbalanced the design. As will be seen, the older and neater version, with the bugle curled into the centre, was adopted by The Royal Green Jackets. For the present 1st Green Jackets, 43rd and 52nd, retained Colours, but did not carry them on parade, and wore their double Sam Browne belt. All wore a red 'Green Jacket' flash on green in Battle Dress, but each Regiment retained its own dress distinctions, apart from the cap badge and those mentioned above. However, a unifying spirit was already at work among serving officers. The 'back to back, and fire outwards' philosophy which had made the original Green Jackets so formidable if harried by authority, at once extended its defensive power to the third component, and in return a very talented group of senior 43rd and 52nd Light Infantrymen were to strengthen the alliance throughout the next decade or more. General Sir Gerald Lathbury, Colonel Commandant, Quartermaster General and Governor of Gibraltar, General Sir John Mogg, Representative Colonel Commandant of The Royal Green Jackets and Adjutant General, and General Sir Antony Read, Colonel Commandant The Light Division, Quartermaster General and Governor of the Royal Hospital, come particularly to mind.

The Parade itself was taken by HRH The Duke of Gloucester at the Rifle Depot. The new standardized drill included the automatic reversion to the 'At Ease' position after all movements, in Light Infantry style, but the cautionary order was 'Look to your front' in 60th style. Colonel J. F. C. Mellor, DSO, who had become Brigade Colonel, experimented with a Carry, like the High Port, for use when doubling with the new 7·62-mm self-loading rifle (SLR) of Belgian Fabrique Nationale origin. In fact, though the rest of the Army now copied the Shoulder, which we had always used for sensible and protective carriage of our rifles, we subsequently retained the Trail for both Quick and Double March.

Although we were sad to lose our traditional and distinctive cap badges with the touch of scarlet, our original badges had been silver; the formal acceptance by the Army Dress Committee of the cross belt and silver scabbard, even if supplied largely through the kindness of retired officers, was more significant.

A cast back to the earlier part of the decade must be made to review the progress of our Territorials and Cadets, as they built up after World War II. Just as 1951 saw the two Regular Battalions reformed and active as Motor Battalions once more, Queen Victoria's Rifles were also in the same role and the Queen's Westminsters Lorried Infantry in 56 (London) Armoured Division TA, each forming an additional company. To ensure preservation of the Regimental connection and closer linkage with our Territorials the 1st and 2nd Cadet Battalions, KRRC, amalgamated, and moved from the City to the County of London TA administration, with Lt Col R. G. H. Sutton now in command; Maj G. R. B. Hanson was 2IC and Maj C. C. Gregory, QVR, gave much support.

1952 saw the long-awaited opening after its bombing of the rebuilt Queen Victoria's Rifles HQ at 56, Davies Street, Mayfair, by HRH The Duke of Gloucester, Colonel in Chief, The Rifle Brigade, but originally gazetted into the 60th. The kind patronage of successive Dukes of Westminster, whose Grosvenor Estates are benevolent landlords of the free site, has been a constant feature since the previous Drill Hall was opened in 1890 by the then Duchess. The new 1952 Drill Hall was for many subsequent years in the care of Sgt and Mrs Johnson. This was a period in which Territorial officers started to take over command from Regulars, for Lt Col P. B. Earle, MC, originally a Regular, relieved Lt Col J. M. White, OBE; company commanders included wartime 60th officers like Maj M. G. Turner, TD, but the Subalterns were all found from National Service officers, who had completed their full time service with Regular Battalions, and were thus also experienced. In the Queen's Westminsters Lt Col M. A. Johnson handed over command to Lt Col F. L. Knight, TD, who had been a company commander in the 11th Battalion in Greece. Majs J. N. Butterwick and G. S. Palmer, for instance, had also seen war service with the 12th and 2nd Battalions respectively. It was also in 1952 that Maj The Rt Hon Anthony Eden, PC, MC, became the Honorary Colonel of the Queen's Westminsters, following service in and much close contact with battalions of the Regiment in two World Wars. General Sir George Erskine, KCB, KBE, DSO, was Honorary Colonel of Queen Victoria's Rifles. The Queen's Westminsters began to show the form which made it one of the best shooting Territorial Battalions throughout this period. Simultaneously Lt C. J. (Chris) Chataway was making world records on international running tracks. Both battalions had been filled out by 'Z' Reservists at camp for three years, but from 1953 National Servicemen doing their part-time service made up the numbers and showed the benefit of their Regular training with the Green Jackets.

In 1954 the 1st Cadet Battalion, KRRC, originally founded as a social experiment by the Reverend Freeman Wills at an HQ in Finsbury Square, celebrated its Diamond Jubilee at Davies Street with one of the original members and many subsequent Cadets present. In 1957, at the first camp of all Green Jacket Cadets at the Depot, the Battalion won the all-round Section competition against strong CCF contingents. The Davies Street HQ, with much historical research by Lt Col Earle, was developing a worthy display of Queen Victoria's Rifles history. Photographs of COs back to 1885, old uniforms back to 1803 and many pictures and prints had been assembled; a Calais and 1939–45 Memorial was unveiled in 1956 by Lt Gen Sir Euan Miller, a Colonel Commandant and Calais survivor. At 58 Buckingham Gate, long the Queen's Westminster HQ, the portrait of the Kaiser continued to gaze sternly from the wall on many a lively evening in the handsome Mess, and the Annual Church Parade was held as usual in Westminster Abbey.

1956 saw a major change for our Territorials. The TA Armoured Brigade was disbanded and both Battalions converted to Infantry. However, the new 169 (Green Jackets) Brigade TA was formed within 56 (London) Division, consisting of our two Battalions and The London Rifle Brigade Rangers (TA), with Brigadier G. W. White, MBE, late 60th, as its Commander. Training was to include light rescue and first aid for Civil Defence. Shortly afterwards, part-time service for National Servicemen was cancelled, so that Battalions were entirely dependent, as pre-war, on building up their strength with Volunteer Territorials, using the current cadre of Officers, WOs and NCOs as a base; this was a very difficult task in the sour aftermath of Suez. In 1957 a much smaller Queen's Westminsters was honourably beaten by the Seventh Regiment, New York National Guard team, which for the first time since 1926 shot shoulder to shoulder at Bisley for the Howard Vincent Shield, inaugurated in 1904. The team from the American Regiment, whose history can be traced to 1806, was accompanied by Lt Col Knight and Capt P. D. C. Richards, BEM, who had done so much for Queen's Westminster shooting, to audiences graciously given by HM The Queen and HM Queen Elizabeth, The Queen Mother. However, our Battalion was good enough to sweep away the opposition in many TA competitions, winning the Quartet Cup and the China Cup with a team entirely composed for the first time by members of one Regiment. Capt Richards and Sgts Witt, Priestley and Walton were among those Territorials who the next year won the Volongdis LMG Pairs and other trophies, and beat the 7th Regiment in the usual Cable Shooting Match.

1958 was the year of the Territorial Army's Golden Jubilee, and contingents from both our old Territorial Regiments marched past The Queen under heavy rain in Hyde Park. Queen Victoria's Rifles benefited from Lt M. A. C. Drummond's membership and Maj G. Bowden's imagination in the creation of a week-end Training Centre for patrolling and assault training in the former's estate at Fawley on Southampton Water. After long and successful tours of command Lt Cols Earle and Knight handed over QVR and QW to Lt Cols C. C. Gregory and J. N. Butterwick respectively. Maj G. S. Palmer retired after many years, ending as 2IC, with Maj C. H. Tidbury, Capts G. M. Nissen, J. J. N. Wyatt, A. Drysdale and R. M. Burr as some of the more active Queen's Westminsters of 60th origin. In Queen Victoria's Rifles Majs G. P. Lincoln, TD, E. Rose, TD, and A. R. Macneal, and Capt K. N. Loudon-Shand were some of the more senior members not already mentioned. A good selection of 60th National Service officers were still joining the TA Battalions as volunteers, despite being relieved of their part-time commitment, but recruiting of Riflemen in areas no longer residential continued as a perennial problem; in both Battalions companies were, however, reformed by great effort. In 1959 Brig J. F. C. Mellor, DSO, relieved Brig G. W. White, MBE, in command of 169 (Green Jackets) Brigade, TA, after a brief tour at the Depot, and RSM J. Pope began a further improvement of QVR shooting.

These two old Territorial Regiments, with many years of separate existence before they became part of The King's Royal Rifle Corps, were nearing a considerable change. Following the announcement of a major TA reorganization in July 1960, the amalgamation of Queen Victoria's Rifles and the Queen's Westminsters was decided upon. Fortunately, with a great deal of tact and co-operation, the new Regiment emerged under the splendid title of Queen's Royal Rifles TA, using the common denominators of the Colonel in Chief and the Regular title. It was agreed that Lt Col J. N. Butterwick, TD, late QW, should command, with Maj K. N. Loudon-Shand, TD, late QVR, as 2IC; Capts M. J. Calvert and L. P. Grout were Regular Adjutant and QM respectively. Something of the admirable wartime contribution of our Territorials has been given in earlier chapters of this and the preceding Volume. During its short period in the new guise, QRR was unifying in a way which made possible successful survival in the greatest TA reorganization of all, the creation of the TAVR in 1967.

Sir Anthony Eden, shortly afterwards elevated to be the Earl of Avon, was Honorary Colonel of the new Regiment for the first year. In 1962, after long Regimental membership and connection, not least through his son, Maj The Viscount Eden, he retired. His successor, The Rt Hon Richard Wood, PC, MP, had been severely wounded with the 2nd Battalion in the Desert, but notwithstanding had been an active MP since 1950, and later Minister. To the Regiment's great good fortune his interest, encouragement and wise counsel were to be available as Honorary Colonel far beyond the scope of this Volume.

The Queen's Royal Rifles rightly gave first emphasis to recruiting, never easy in the West End of London, and successfully used the challenge of tough training to draw in young men, who in the light of abolished National Service sought a greater challenge than routine life at work and home. In 1962 Lt Col Butterwick's excellent initial year was followed on by Lt Col K. N. Loudon-Shand. A contingent of 'Ever Readies', with higher call-out and training commitments and consequent bounties, was formed, prepared to fly anywhere at short notice to reinforce a Regular Battalion. Despite uncertainty as to whether the SLR or No 4 Rifle was to be the future Territorial weapon, the QRR was in the first flight in all competition shooting.

In 1961 the 1st Cadet Battalion won the Douglas-Pennant Trophy for ·303 shooting for the fifth consecutive year. All-round excellence was further shown when the first six cadets in the County of London to receive HRH's Gold Award from the Duke of Edinburgh came from our Cadet Battalion. Some of their elders were already Riflemen in the Regular Battalion in Northern Ireland, and on that happy note our account joins them.

CHAPTER XI

2ND GREEN JACKETS, THE KING'S ROYAL RIFLE CORPS, FROM NORTHERN IRELAND TO BERLIN

When the 1st Battalion, now under its new title of 2nd Green Jackets, The King's Royal Rifle Corps, arrived home and stayed in Piddlehinton, Dorset, over Christmas 1958, it had been allowed by the War Office to run down to an inexcusably low ebb. Any recent arrivals in Tripoli had had to be left behind in ERE and there had not been enough new blood from which to find and train new junior NCOs. Fortunately, Depot Training Company under Maj J. H. Hanscombe, one of the RB officers who had served in our joint 2nd Battalion, took immense care over individual recruits, and his excellent reports had identified the most promising material.

This care was of great use to Lt Col T. H. Acton, OBE, the new Commanding Officer, in achieving his aim of laying the foundations of a happy and efficient Regular Battalion. He had been Adjutant of 1 RB at Calais and a prisoner throughout the war, but his intelligence, his concern for Riflemen and pursuit of high Green Jacket standards made him the founder of the all-Regular Battalion. As an organizer and trainer his memorial was the happy and efficient Battalion which was still identifiably of his building throughout the next decade. As a Regimental exchange a former 60th Rifleman, and another Calais survivor, Lt Col E. G. B. Davies-Scourfield, MBE, MC, simultaneously took over command of 3rd Green Jackets, The Rifle Brigade.

The setting of Ballykinler, County Down, has been described early in the previous Volume, but when the Main Body arrived in a very cold mid-January 1959 it was to find Abercorn Barracks in a dirty and cramped state. The two Messes and the Main Sandhurst Block of Hore Belisha vintage were fair, but the Dining Hall in the latter was not opened, after modernization, for a year. Fortunately, there was a wealth of Nissen huts around, which the usual initiative turned into a Corporals' Club, Ladies Club, hobby centres and even a poultry farm. There were some married quarters, and others in process of being built, but as older bachelors of the North African period started to marry the local girls, many had to live in unsatisfactory hirings in Newcastle or Downpatrick. For single Riflemen the local bus company provided inadequate transport, and only the Sandes Home, since destroyed and rebuilt, gave much local cheer. A sentry with a Bren, watching the main gate from behind a sandbagged upper window, indicated that another round of internal security problems had been under way in

240

Ulster. Although the IRA was being worn down, there was still a heavy toll of guards and duties to greet a weak battalion.

Lt Col Acton immediately started NCO cadres, since there were no more than two Corporals in a Rifle Company. All training and leave had to be planned, keeping in mind the ability to turn out a platoon or company at short notice down on the Eire border. Some relaxation was brought to the barracks by running buses to bring Belfast girls to monthly dances run by companies in turn, and the happy accident of the local WRAC Summer camp at the TA Training Centre close by made the otherwise bleak seaside environment more cheerful. The howling wind—before the present plantations grew up, and the new quarters on the duneward side were built—was with the yelping of seagulls the most remarkable feature of the camp.

That year the Battalion was equipped with the Self-Loading Rifle (SLR), and already held the excellent Sterling sub-machine-gun, on which it had done trials in Sennelager; but the Bren, the Vickers MMG and three-inch mortar, the latter two in platoons incorporated within Rifle Companies to keep up their numbers for internal security, were of pre-war vintage. The greatest boon was the admirable line of gorse-flowered ranges the other side of the equally well-turfed playing fields from barracks. After classification on the new figure targets, Capt A. T. R. Shelley and CSM Solomon, as the Weapon Training pair, settled down to work. The Brigade and District meetings saw our team improving steadily. We won the Northern Ireland Queen Victoria Trophy, the first time Queen's University, Belfast, had been defeated since the war; the performance of Cpl Habbershaw (who had done so well earlier at the Depot) being of particular note. At Bisley the Eastern Command Cup and a second place in the KRRC Cup showed that we were once more on the way up.

Companies were encouraged to run their own camps for platoon and company training, with excellent platoon exercises set by Battalion HQ in between. Camp sites took on the characteristics of company commanders; A under Maj T. St Aubyn were usually in reach of camp and a bath, while Maj Humphreys preferred to make C too inaccessible for visiting officers. D Company under Capt Calvert combined both amenity and remoteness by camping in range of Armagh. One of the Summer's highlights was the annual District 'Army Day', held that year at Ballykinler with an infantry attack, organized by Maj Humphreys with fire support worthy of Warminster, which an unexpected 16,000 spectators saw with considerable appreciation.

One of the benefits to company commanders of service in Ulster was that block leave was taken by companies in turn. This allowed the Battalion later to move out at full strength on training to the Magilligan area in the North West, near the Foyle's mouth. Profiting from unexpectedly fine weather, Internal Security (IS) problems in a useful first Brigade exercise were well handled by the new team of junior officers and NCOs; thanks to the Brigade Commander, Brigadier V. Street, late RB, full use was made of helicopters, whose employment was new to the Battalion.

With an Administrative Inspection only a month away, Capt M. M. V. Beak as Adjutant and RSM Shreeve had to teach the Battalion the new Green Jacket drill with the more bulky SLR and put over sword drill to a whole generation of officers for the first time. Every room in the dingy barracks was painted by

Riflemen themselves, since self-help was the only way to get anything done. The work on drill paid off, as Capt I. H. McCausland was able to command an excellent Guard of Honour at the Downpatrick Assizes, where Maj W. Brownlow, late RB, was High Sheriff. All of these activities, the running of local Hunter Trials by Majs T. St Aubyn and H. J. W. Newton, the first 43rd and 52nd Company Commander to join us, and social and sporting ventures at many levels had quickly put the Battalion on the map as a lively addition to the Ulster scene. Old Riflemen were kind, and many other doors were opened. What was particularly useful was the friendly sporting and shooting rivalry between us and the Duke of Wellington's Regiment. Obviously we did not offer to take on the Duke's at Rugger, but they were tough opponents on the range, and we in turn particularly distinguished ourselves at hockey. Older players like Maj Humphreys and RSM Shreeve were joined by Capt McCausland, Lt C. L. G. Henshaw, son of the CO of 11 KRRC in the war, 2/Lt G. B. C. Hopton and some excellent Band players. Since Lt Col Acton's aim was to lay foundations, both training and sport laid much emphasis at individual, platoon and company level work. Athletics were a case in point, where L/Cpl O'Hara already began to distinguish himself with the hammer and 2/Lt J. R. E. Nelson became Battalion Victor Ludorum with javelin and 880-yard successes.

The Winter and early Spring period of individual and cadre training saw a number of changes. Maj R. F. Nixon, MBE, handed over as 2IC to Maj G. H. Mills, prior to taking over command of the Malayan Reconnaissance Regiment. He took that unit to the Congo (now Zaïre), and commanded it with distinction under the very difficult circumstances of the United Nations intervention. To the Regiment's great good fortune he later became its Retired Officer at RHQ The Royal Green Jackets, where he has looked after its many activities and interests with intelligence and care. Not the least of his contributions has been to lend his experience as wartime Adjutant of the 2nd Battalion, The King's Royal Rifle Corps, to the writing of this and more particularly the previous Volume of the Annals.

Maj Beak, on going to the Staff College, handed over to Capt V. F. West, who had returned from a good tour with the 2nd Goorkhas. Two first-class Regimental soldiers, ready to turn their hand to any training or sporting project with their Riflemen, Maj T. E. St Aubyn and Maj C. A. Humphreys, MC, now left the Battalion for the last time, as did the MTO, Capt F. N. Voysey, who had done so much to uphold Regimental standards. Maj J. A. Molesworth St Aubyn, referred to hereafter in abbreviated form, and Maj T. N. Thistlethwayte took over A and C respectively, their two Weimaraner pointers named 'Otto' and 'Blotto' serving to confuse Riflemen even further. It will be remembered that a whole age group of 60th officers commissioned in the late '40s left more or less simultaneously after the last BAOR tour. There was thus to be a gap in company commanders throughout the '60s, admirably filled by a succession of Rifle Brigade and 43rd and 52nd officers until the common roll of The Royal Green Jackets made the spreading of such resources less identifiable. Maj J. St C. Simons, 43rd and 52nd, later to do excellent work at the Rifle Depot for which he was awarded the OBE, was one of these. The strength of the Battalion had now risen to a point where Rifle Companies could form a third Rifle Platoon. Maj Simmons therefore formed B into a Support Company of MMGs, mortars and MT, with Lt

(QM) G. Shreeve as the MTO, RSM Byrne, descendant of several generations of 60th Riflemen, having succeeded him. Thanks to a lot of hard work in 1959, the Battalion began once more to look like an operational unit after its run-down.

Major H. J. W. Newton, MBE, 43rd and 52nd, had arrived to take over D Company, complete with West African grey parrot to prove his overseas service; its discreet 'Kiss me, darling' startled unwary visitors, just as Honk, the abandoned seal pup (raised by Rfn Halpern of zoological bent) distracted inspecting officers by the Guard Dog kennels. Maj Newton and D Company were given an important task so often demanded of a Rifle Regiment, when professional skill and care are needed—that of carrying out trials on Fabrique Nationale's General Purpose Machine Gun (GPMG). All Officers and NCOs of D and Lt Gurney's MMG Platoon were trained by the Small Arms School Corps (SASC) at Hythe. They in turn trained their Riflemen, who now received an advance issue of the comfortable 1958 Pattern equipment, needing no blanco, and the new green showerproof Combat clothing, much what Henry Bouquet envisaged 200 years earlier. After exhaustive and exhausting trials all Summer Major Newton made a full report, which led to the replacement of both Bren and Vickers by the GPMG in 1964. Its reliability and belt-fed, rapid rate of fire have been only offset by its weight, which has made it a clumsy patrolling weapon.

In Spring 1960 the Battalion fired its final classification with the ·303 Bren, which was then recalibred to ·762 mm, and its first on the SLR; the new courses were too easy and a rather unrealistic number of double Marksmen's badges were to be seen. It was a year of increased tempo, where outside commitments could only be met if our own priorities were skilfully juggled. A particularly welcome visitor was a Rifleman CIGS, Field Marshal Sir Francis Festing, late Rifle Brigade, whose wisdom as Colonel Commandant later led the three old Regiments into a voluntary and most successful union. Training progressed from TEWTS, through Section field firing among the sand dunes to Company Camps, both near Ballykinler and at a very rainy Magilligan. A cloudburst in the Sperrin Hills was used to test Battalion and Company administration, when pulled 'out of the line'. On the main Battalion exercise an active enemy from the local Depot provided action for all, until the companies located and surrounded their camp one dawn. Alerter and fitter and with a better standard of section leading since leaving the motor role, the Battalion dealt with the problems set on a Brigade exercise in half the time allotted.

It was not all field training, however. 'Army Day' was held in Belfast at Palace Barracks, and our display contribution on the square was an excellent A Company squad, showing off every aspect of 60th drill, largely silent, under CSM Hawkes. It provided a crisp contrast to the stately Irish Guardsmen of Maj G. Alan, whose Rifle Brigade father had long been a kind host to Riflemen at the Depot. The production of displays was run by Maj Mills and CSM Massingham, and included massed bands, flown over to outflank a shipping strike. This included our Band and Bugles, who had been taken to New York by Maj J. R. C. Radclyffe, MBE, as Band President, to take part in the British Military Tournament and Tattoo.

1960 was indeed a year in which the British invaded the United States, for the Queen's Westminsters team were only just beaten in a shoulder to shoulder match against the 7th Regiment. However, the scene of the principal invasion was Governor's Island in New York harbour, 60th Royal American Regimental

HQ from 1756 to 1783, where a service was held in the Chapel of St Cornelius the Centurion; a 1788 60th Colour, which was presented in 1921, is displayed in the chapel and Maj Gen Sir Hereward Wake, former Colonel Commandant, laid a wreath beneath it. Brigadier R. A. T. Eve, Sir Hereward and their wives had come over to represent the Regiment at a round of festivities. These included a splendid Regimental Dinner in New York's Knickerbocker Club, largely organized by John Waterfield, late 1st 60th and of the British Consulate-General there. Mess silver had been sent over by the Battalion, and 10 out of the 12 surviving American officers had come long distances to be present and to greet Sir Hereward. He had sponsored their gallant wartime volunteering for the Regiment, and at an advanced age was sportingly making his first visit to their country. 17 representatives of Allied Canadian Regiments and those of the 7th Regiment were also present at a dinner, to which the Colonel in Chief sent a gracious telegram. George Thomson and Harry Fowler, on their home ground, gave lunch parties in the country, and the others present were John Tuttle, Charles Bolte, Bill Durkee, Tom Braden, Heyward Cutting, Ted Ellsworth, Stewart Alsop and Bill Channing; Stewart's later courageous resistance to a fatal blood disease was to be the admiration of his brother Riflemen. When the award of the Meritorious Service Medal to Bugle Major Silver was announced one evening at the Tattoo, the impact which the Band and Bugles had made on New York audiences stimulated maximum enthusiasm. The value of the visit to the Regiment was further enhanced through its extension by Brigadier and Mrs Eve to Canadian Allied Regiments thereafter.

Back in Northern Ireland our athletes were excelling themselves, the cool running of Capt J. V. Keyte finalizing our win at Command level. To our surprise we romped home against the Corps teams of Western Command at Oswestry, but at Aldershot we had to be content with 5th place in the Army Championship—nevertheless, the first time a 60th team had competed there within memory. The Javelin had been won by Lt Nelson and L/Cpl Gunner, and Cpl Seaman and Bdsm Atkins had pole vaulted very well. At Boxing there were many good performances, particularly by Rfn Webster, who represented the Army at featherweight, and L/Cpl Griss, who won the Command Individual at light heavyweight.

The WTO was now Capt J. W. Mason, backed by the experienced CSM Solomon, and thanks to good planning we had a clean sweep at the 39 Brigade and Command Meetings. C/Sgt Airey was Champion Shot, but other names such as Cpl R. Smith and Cpl York were beginning to join Sgt Harper and Rfn Habbershaw at the top. However, at Bisley a REME team put us again into 2nd place, drawing in a legitimate but somewhat thwarting manner on the shooting resources, particularly armourers, of that Corps while they were on long courses. However, it was interesting to see all three Green Jacket battalions in the first five, since the 43rd and 52nd, with Maj M. Pennell of 60th origin, were moving ahead and the Rifle Brigade were back in BAOR.

The Summer would have been restricting socially, if training and other activities had not been at a peak, for the Riflemen had been 'gated' by Command for three months from recreational visits to Belfast, and no officers wished to go where their men could not. The cause was that a Rifleman had been badly beaten up in that divided city, and that mistakenly a party of his friends had beaten up a young civilian the next night. It was in fact a warning, which was very useful later in training young Regulars in self-discipline, but meanwhile Lt Col Acton drew as usual on the talent within the Battalion to make life amusing at Ballykinler. Thanks to the first broadening of the use of the Battalion funds, one of the earliest Go-Kart Clubs in the Army was formed. This was one of the last contributions of that imaginative and amusing fourth-generation Rifleman Capt C. G. N. Campbell before retiring, and the Club was carried on by Lt M. L. E. Phillips, later *Times* Racing Correspondent. Maj Simmons had played a similar role with his organizing of water-skiing on the Strangford Lough, and the two together had stimulated much Mess activity, presided over successively by Sgts Skinner and Owen. The latter and Lt Shreeve were to be found on the shore, with flighting or sea-fishing in mind, but the shooting generally had been disappointing, consisting of little bogs with one teal, two snipe and three owners apiece.

Field sports came to the fore in mid-October 1960, when Lt Gen Sir Euan Miller paid his visit as Colonel Commandant. After a splendid dinner the previous night, the sword drill of all four company commanders was impeccable, even though they had just returned from a successful dawn flight. This sporting venture was thanks to the kindness of Maj J. R. Perceval-Maxwell, late 60th, who had lost one of his sons, commissioned into the Regiment, after a gallant patrol action in Italy. The parade and lunch afterwards was used to thank our many kind hosts over the last 18 months, and the salmon was provided by Lt Col Acton, who had generously taken many younger officers to fish on the Owen Killew.

The period spent in Northern Ireland had been usefully employed, thanks to Lt Col Acton's leadership and the good team of Officers, WOs and Senior NCOs under him. The Battalion was happy and more efficient, thanks to greater continuity and less equipment, than for some time. With 2/Lt R. N. Allan-Smith's departure we had said good-bye to the last of a long line of splendid National Service officers; all officers were thus on a minimum of a three-year Short Service Commission. Of the men, 50% were Regulars, but in Regular Riflemen we were still only 45%, with less than two years in which to build up a complete Regular team.

The Battalion's destination was Berlin, and fortunately Lt Col Acton, in making a reconnaissance, had formed a sharp impression of the possibilities and difficulties of service in that confined Garrison. There were many ridiculous or unattractive aspects to life there, which the CO classed as 'Berlinery'. These included the goldfish-bowl visibility of every aspect of Battalion life to the two-tier commanders and staff, which, if the Commanding Officer and his Battalion were not robust and positive, could lead to bullying over trifles until morale reached a low ebb. Unbalanced anxiety about what Berliners or Allies in the three Western Sectors might think, coupled with a frozen acceptance of all the 15-year-old procedures and standards, led to waste of manpower, unrealistic training and unsatisfactory conditions. 'But this is the way it's always been done, and no-one has challenged it before' was the staff's continual cry. Lt Col Acton correctly diagnosed that battalions, once forced on to the defensive, gave up the struggle and broke up their company and platoon structure. The temptation lay in concentrating on turning out impeccable Spandau Prison and ceremonial guards, allowing the German civil labour to replace Mess and other specialists and, under heavy pressure of duties imposed from above, neglecting NCO training. 'Funny, we seem to have very few NCOs', said the CO of the outgoing battalion to our 2IC in the Advance Party. Next day he pointed out an NCO's cadre—with numbers worn by individuals, as names were apparently not known—and hailed it as the first run during their 18 months in the Garrison; it is not surprising that Regiment is no longer in the British order of battle.

Ours was the first Rifle Battalion ever to serve in Berlin, and Lt Col Acton used this to shake up a station where the staff were apt to interfere in the internal details of units; even in the Mess the civilian caterer had to be told, when he said 'But the Brigadier always insists on Hasenpfeffer when he dines here,' that the host, not the guest, drew up the menu. Riflemen were encouraged to buy the new black plastic waist belt to go with the new Khaki No 2 Dress, resembling a simplified officer's Service Dress, thus obviating all blancoing; the cap was now a Rifle green peaked cap for ceremonial occasions; 120 black plastic slings were bought as a pool against all ceremonial parades. To avoid the wasteful large Quarter Guards, which had crippled training in other regiments, the rapid production of a Bugle Section in No 1 Dress, to sound a fanfare for the constant stream of visitors, became the drill. Because the frequent Guards of Honour were typically always of Royal rather than correct strength in Berlin, the older soldiers of B Company's Support Platoons were warned and drilled for this. Since any attempt to shake out tactically before entering the Grünewald was anathema as 'straggling on the Heerstrasse' (even cross-country runs had to start in threes), an unobserved route to the forest training area in the dead ground below the Brigadier's house was found. Above all, the CO was determined that the field chain of command and organization would be maintained on all tasks. Unlike predecessors, the large Spandau Prison Guard was found by a Rifle Company, rather than a guard specially picked in apprehension of yet another high-level rebuke.

The Battalion's move was the last to be made before the introduction of air trooping, and was thus a nightmare journey by bus to Belfast, boat to England, train across our island, boat to Holland and then train on to Berlin, arriving late at night at the end of 36 hours' travel. To ensure the maximum complications the Main Body and families were to move in mid-December 1960 into the extreme cold, blowing from Eastern Europe.

Clearly this was to be a full test of Battalion organization, since it was important to show the rapidly increasing number of families of young Regulars that the Regiment cared about them in a practical way. Luckily, one of the greatest improvements in the emerging all-Regular Army was in the quality of training of the Army Catering Corps; Messing Warrant Officers, trained in catering management and in the control of the excellent new equipment, now provided for the first time a full range of dishes, meeting both Regimental, local and individual tastes. WOII Everton, the first of this calibre, accompanied the 2IC on the Advance Party, and pre-stocked with food all the large number of new quarters, secured with immense care by the Adjutant, Capt West. The newly appointed Families Sergeant took over quarters in advance and placed a Rifleman in those immediately due to be occupied, responsible for heating them and providing a welcome for a family arriving out of a snow flurry at midnight.

The QM, Capt G. E. Slater, BEM, after brief detention by the Russians at

Helmstedt, had to take over poorly maintained equipment, for which few spares had been secured, and accommodation below Regimental standard. So that the obligatory and expensive 'Protocol Cocktail Party' could be combined with Christmas hospitality, invitations were rapidly sent out and the Messes fully decorated with all our possessions, from the Royal pictures and those of Buller and Grenfell to the *Warren Hastings* wheel. Meanwhile, late at night, a full range of Alarm Scheme drills was worked out, including the new problem of rousing and bringing in married men from scattered quarters two miles away. Berlin traffic regulations, on which a test had to be passed before drivers could take the wheel, were flashed back to Battalion.

The problems and solutions to such a move are now well known, but it may be said that many of the subsequent Regimental drills were first successfully evolved at this time. The need to get the Battalion off to a good start, particularly since a whisper of our Summer 'gating' from Belfast had unhelpfully been passed on from Northern Ireland, was shown when the Brigadier and a dour posse of Military Police formed up at Charlottenburg Station to deal with what they clearly imagined would be a scruffy and riotous Rail Advance Party. With a Rifleman's quiet order Capt Keyte led his immaculate party and their baggage away, while the uninitiated were still awaiting the first pace-sticked scream of command. With a grudging grunt of 'They'll do' the first potential confrontation was over, and subsequent alarming encounters with the fixed swords of alert tactical sentries rapidly cured a tendency to snoop around platoon positions at night.

The need to move straight from rustic Ulster tempo into top Garrison gear was apparent from the moment Maj Newton, accompanied by his parrot, spaniel 'Bugler' and the Main Body descended into the bitter cold of Spandau Station on 7 December 1960. Luckily, Wavell Barracks was well heated, although Riflemen were not allowed in it for long. Immediately after a good Christmas, the Battalion was pitched headlong into a six-week test of many of its capabilities. A first Spandau Guard, on the three Nazis Hess, Speer and von Schirach, was accomplished without the telephoto lenses of the Press or the scouting of the other three Powers revealing any improprieties. Platoons moved into the large, snow-bound Grünewald, whose confusing rides demanded good compass work, to prepare for the Berlin Brigade Battle Tests. Six of our platoons competed, but in the time available we could not defeat local knowledge and an element of packing, gaining an honourable second place overall.

Our neighbours to begin with over a dividing fence were the most pleasant King's Own Scottish Borderers, under Lt Col Robertson-Macleod, whose son later was commissioned into The Royal Green Jackets. Their more restless successors were 1 Welch, but when it was made clear that the Commanding Officers knew each other and would impose similar and heavy sanctions on any raiding parties an uneasy truce prevailed. At Gatow it was a relief when Lt Col J. Burgess, later to be first Divisional Brigadier of The Light Division, brought in the Durham Light Infantry to replace their predecessors, who had been going through a tiresome phase of strident public relations, using the *Berlin Bulletin*. A Guard of Honour for Lt Gen Sir Charles Jones, Commander 1 Corps, and father of a later Royal Green Jacket CO, was followed by winning the Brigade Boxing, for which Sgt Wigger had got our team wonderfully fit. Although just losing the next round, the match was notable for the number of contestants knocked out, of which Cpl O'Hara's despatch of his officer heavyweight opponent was the highlight. The Alarm Scheme turn-outs worked up to a crescendo of three in one week. The final one was at 10 pm on a pay night, but loyal Riflemen were seen running from all over town, and it was with pride that the Battalion was able to move out of barracks well before the rest of the Brigade. The 2IC, as acting CO, had to drive himself, as his driver operator was lost in the American Sector with the vehicle key; back in barracks the stragglers were sobered up under a shower by the experienced Capts G. E. Slater, BEM, and A. J. Lamb, before being despatched to their companies. As will be seen, it was fortunate that the operational drills had been taken seriously from the start.

Berlin had many possibilities, however, for everyone who had soldiered in the social backwaters of the previous few years. Lt Col Acton had wisely advised Riflemen to abandon their informal jeans and to invest in a good suit, overcoat and gloves, if they were to make any headway with the local girls and avoid the Town Patrols. He had placed the greatest importance on making the Battalion Welfare Committee a well-prepared means of securing views and putting over policy, run by the 2IC, with the Adjutant and RSM present to answer or note points and the QM to deal similarly with the Q side. He himself took the meeting on important occasions, such as first arrival in a new station, to ensure that Battalion routine, such as timings, jarred as little as possible with the reasonable needs of the individual. The minutes were published widely and care was taken to explain the factors when requests could not be met. Equally concerned for the training of the new young Regular officers, as well as covering the normal subjects, he patiently instructed them in the art of being good hosts, a quality which was often remarked on by Allied visitors, contrasting pleasantly with an earlier Regimental reputation as the 'rude Rifles'. In March 1961 Lt Col Acton's excellent tour of command came to an end. In every department and activity he had indeed laid the foundations. He had courageously risked his reputation by running the Battalion on a very light disciplinary rein in order to build up a family of high-spirited Regulars; this was a point which would need future care, if the required self-discipline were to be engendered. The affection and respect which all felt for him was well expressed in the stirring send-off by all Officers, Warrant Officers and Sergeants at Charlottenburg, with Irish coffee and the full weight of Band and Bugles to lighten the occasion.

The continuity was well maintained, since his successor was his former 2IC, Lt Col J. H. P. Curtis, MC, a lively company commander in the wartime 2nd Battalion. It was a nice touch that the skin of the splendid tiger which his father (later Colonel Commandant) had shot 30 years earlier was hanging in the Mess to greet him. Before going further, it would be as well to describe the organization of the Battalion which he had taken over. First, its vehicles were a medley of German trucks of poor cross-country value. A, C and D were Rifle Companies under the same Commanders, but B now contained a Reconnaissance and Assault Pioneer Platoon under Lt G. C. B. Hopton, as well as the mortars of Lt J. R. E. Nelson and the anti-tank Guns (120-mm Mobat recoil-less guns) of Lt A. E. Berry. During the year a Support Platoon of a mortar and an anti-tank section was posted to each Rifle Company. The Company Commander of B, until he took over as 2IC, was Brevet Lt Col D. G. House, MC, whose considerable experience and attention to detail played a great part in establishing professional standards at all levels.

Lt Col Curtis had a considerable reputation as a tactical thinker, and had been the first GSO I of the newly created Army Combat Development cell; he had also a keen sense of the Regiment's contribution to tactical experiment throughout its existence. With the move from the motor-battalion role, in which we had created our own drills, we had taken on the accepted tactics of the Heavy Infantry, based on the deliberate and formal drills established by 1944 for a conscript Infantry. Lt Col Acton had purposely instilled these, so that there was a basis of simple command and control in the field on which to build. Fortunately for Lt Col Curtis his arrival coincided with the first issue of an effective family of radio sets (wireless had gone out as a term), by which vehicle and man pack sets could be on the same net and with improved dismounted range. His first question was 'Are we good at skirmishing?' The answer was that the Battalion had no clear idea of what he meant, but were at a stage when all were keen and ready to experiment. In essence skirmishing, as Lt Col Curtis saw it, was running a dismounted battle on armoured lines. Given a series of report lines and adequate communications down to platoon level, with a battalion axis, sections, platoons and companies could freely use mutually supporting fire and movement in advance or withdrawal. In the former it should often be possible to manoeuvre the enemy out of a position, without the need for a costly assault, by threatening his rear and engaging in accurate selective shooting. Massive and wasteful random artillery concentrations, no longer available, would have to be replaced by accurate fire based on quick intelligence; and open order 'partridge driving' must be abandoned, so that alert and fit Riflemen could use every bit of cover available. It was in summary the tactics of the Peninsula, with radios replacing bugles, rather than those of Passchendaele. The new Combat Dress, now issued to all, with its showerproof green material would have delighted Bouquet and de Rottenburg; its tactical practicability gave an added zest to field training.

Within days of his arrival, Lt Col Curtis's chance came. After a 15-mile dismounted approach march, the Battalion concentrated in the extreme South of the Grünewald, preparatory to advancing North on an exercise set by Berlin Brigade. The directing staff, by setting up formidable opposition in a narrows, had confidently expected that a routine series of ponderous deployments from one taped start-line to another would take at least 48 hours to clear an axis for the armoured squadron through the forest. However, dawn found Maj T. N. Thistlethwayte's C Company, towed in secrecy by the Sappers in assault boats up the Havel lake, very active in his rear. Majs J. A. M. St Aubyn and Newton, supported by the mortars, infiltrated, hooked and thrust until after 24 hours the armour was forcing the last remnants of a bewildered enemy across the open under Staff College hill. The Battalion had been under perfect control throughout, and its morale was excellent after just displaying the first modern infantry tactics seen in Berlin and still unrecognized at Warminster. It was the Regiment's and the Army's loss that political developments in Berlin prevented Lt Col Curtis from experimenting further until the Battalion had returned to England 18 months later.

Change was at work on the human side too. Lt Gen Sir Euan and Lady Miller paid a final visit before he handed over as Colonel Commandant to Gen Sir

George Erskine. His wise advice and insistance on high standards had been a consistent help to successive COs.

There were also internal changes in the Berlin team, as Maj J. A. Molesworth St Aubyn handed over A to Maj R. M. Parker; he will be seen again, after a busy tour as DAA and QMG to the Gurkhas when confrontation started in Borneo. Maj Newton, whose experience had been of great value, handed over D temporarily to Maj M. P. Hills, but the 1st Green Jackets link was later provided through Maj G. C. Stacey in B Company. Maj J. A. Wilkinson, 2 GR, attached to complete his last year with us, the Affiliated Regiment, in command of HQ Company, had done great work from the Advance Party on; his work as PRI in organizing a very successful "Appy 'Ampstead', conceived by the CO, was first-class.

1961 was the year when a long and successful partnership in the Band and Bugles broke up. Sadly, Bugle Major R. Silver died suddenly of a heart attack in April. His father had died serving with the 1st Battalion in World War I, and his two older brothers and he joined the Regiment between the wars. BM Silver was selected as a bugler by Bandmaster McBain, later the celebrated Director of Music and composer of *Mechanised Infantry*. Captured at Calais with one brother in 1940, BM Silver was the founder of the post-war Bugles, and those trained to his superb standard have since provided a hard-core of Bugle Majors across the Royal Green Jackets and indeed the Light Division. The funeral in the Garden Military Cemetery in Berlin with full Jewish rites was made even more poignant by his 15 young buglers sounding a *Last Post*, which would have met even their trainer's high requirements. His dapper figure was replaced on parade by Cpl Green, who, in the next 16 unbroken years of service with the Battalion established his own high standards and style as Bugle Major. He later was to lead Massed Bands and Bugles on many great ceremonial occasions such as the 1967 Royal Review and the 1974 Light Division Retreat on the Horse Guards, and was to be awarded a well-earned BEM.

The founder of the 1st Battalion Band in 1949, Bandmaster E. Jeanes, left later in the year, becoming eventually Director of Music of the Blues, for which appointment he sportingly learnt to ride. His Band had been graded 'Outstanding' in a Kneller Hall inspection in Autumn 1960, and he and his wife—who among other activities had run an excellent Kindergarten for the Battalion in many stations—were much missed. Band continuity was well maintained by Band C/Sgt Barker and the two athletic Band Sgts, White and Washington.

Before the Bandmaster left, however, there was the Queen's Birthday Parade in the Olympic Stadium to be tackled. This was a replica of the Trooping with the addition of a vehicle screen of jeeps and tanks, firing a salute. After rehearsals under Maj R. M. Parker a workable compromise between Heavy Infantry and Rifle drill was reached. We gave the other guards a start in arms drill, and quick marched at exactly double the remainder's slow march. Maj Thistlethwayte, mounted as Parade Major on a police horse, showed off our Regimental saddlery to good effect. At the end our Double March of guards under Maj Hills and Capt West, coupled with the Rifle style and tunes, identifiably of Jäger origin, drew particular applause from the 60,000 Germans present. Mr Jeanes not only conducted the Massed Bands but produced a Massed Retreat in the evening, and our Glockenspiel came well to the fore in its homeland.

After this parade there were two months when the pressure on companies lifted somewhat. The Battalion athletes, after tying in a thrilling final relay, were adjudged winners at Brigade level, but team training could not be maintained effectively until July. However, the resolute running of Capt J. V. Keyte and Cpl Gazzini, as well as the magnificent hammer-throwing of Cpl O'Hara, who with Sgt Wigger beat the Army team record, were of a high order, and many other young athletes were performing well.

All over the Battalion small parties were dispersing to follow their particular interests. Rifle platoons camped in turn near Lüneburg and offered themselves to act as enemy, those with 3rd Green Jackets having a most active time. Riflemen had been making canvas canoes under Sapper guidance, and canoeists were dropped off in pairs by Lt C. J. D. Bullock and 2/Lt M. C. Swann to descend the Weser tributaries; L/Cpls Impey and Mitchell resolutely marched the last 50 miles to the Bremen rendezvous, when their canoes were irreparably ripped. Lt M. L. E. Phillips was in charge of cyclists who toured round the whole of Southern Scandinavia, calling in on Maj C. Humphreys in Oslo en route. Others under Lt Nelson sailed, canoed and trekked in Southern Norway, and parties walked in the Harz Mountains. That Summer the end of an era was approaching in Berlin, but none knew it.

On a more martial note, Lt Col Curtis held a lunch for the whole Battalion in the cookhouse to celebrate our many shooting successes. The aim was to let young Riflemen see the team members, regardless of rank and age, at the top table, to identify their trophies, distributed round the dining hall, and in so doing to encourage others to realize what the title of Rifleman stands for. The Battalion in the 1960 non-central matches had again won the Queen Victoria, C Company the Company Shield and Hopton Cup, the Warrant Officers and Sergeants the Royal Irish, with the Officers runners-up in the King George. In a harder classification the Battalion had maintained its marksmen, Sgt Fry winning the Gott Trophy although Brevet Lt Col House gained the highest individual score. After winning the Berlin Brigade meeting, we had to yield to 3rd Green Jackets in the BAOR competition, although Cpl Jenkins won the Roberts Cup and our team the falling plates.

At Bisley the Battalion won the KRRC Cup, with 1st Green Jackets third and 3rd Green Jackets fifth; the Depot won the Minor Units Championship, and a Green Jacket team the Methuen Cup. Cpl Hunt as a young soldier won the Rifle Brigade Cup and Cpl Jenkins was again very well placed. It had been an excellent first year for Capt (QM) A. J. Lamb as WTO.

In August 1961 it suddenly looked as if the shooting might really start. Ever since the West German currency reform of 1948, the disparity of living standards and political freedom between the East and West Zones of Germany, the so-called Democratic (DDR) and Federal Republics, had increasingly become more blatant. Millions of refugees from the East literally voted with their feet by escaping to the West; West Berlin, comprising the French Sector in the North, the British in the centre, and the United States in the South, was a focal point for escapes and a show case of Western European progress. The East Germans, backed by the USSR, resolved to stop this and to use access to an isolated West Berlin as a lever against the three other Occupying Powers, and hence NATO; they had tried this once before and had been defeated by the air lift.

On arrival the Battalion, in lengthy security briefings, had been told by Intelligence staff, who in some cases had been in Berlin since 1945, that ample warning would be gained of any Soviet or East German moves. However, on the night of Saturday 12 August 1961, somewhat after Lt Col Curtis had picked up his duck after a most successful flight on the sewage farm, Soviet armour started to move unseen from its training area on the West of the city. Laying a floating bridge over a lake, it moved into East Berlin behind DDR troops. The latter meanwhile had ringed West Berlin unnoticed with single coils of wire—the infamous Wall was not built until November—sealing off the West Sectors' borders. On a sleepy Sunday morning word of this trickled very slowly down to Battalion level, and the CO's children, visiting the Brandenburg Gate, the British Sector's main access to the East, were the first to report it to their father.

The Battalion was only able to riposte in a minor key. The Soviet War Memorial lay in the British Sector, just West of the Brandenburg Gate, and the Soviet Guard was relieved daily by bus. On the grounds that the East German action had enraged Berliners and that he was responsible for the Guard's safety, the GOC, at 2200 hrs on 16 August, ordered the War Memorial wired off by dawn the next day; the wiring was to be executed as rapidly and unobtrusively as possible. The Sapper squadron was away on training in West Germany, with all the compressors and wiring gloves in the Garrison. 'Field Engineering All Arms' was hastily read to convert 1000 yards of triple danert wiring into three-ton loads, and rags and woollen gloves used to blunt the barbs of rusty wire. Fortunately, the whole Battalion had spent a week with our new Assault Pioneers on wiring and mines under Lt Hopton and Sgt Horsley in March. Nevertheless, the driving of pickets into concrete pavement and much other work had to be done by the more experienced Officers and NCOs. Two Companies and the Assault Pioneers had linked the first coils on time, and before a sleepy Soviet officer noticed anything. The unpopularity of Soviet troops and the need to protect them was blandly explained to him in answer to his protests.

Later that day the Guard was permitted to be relieved, travelling through the later well-known 'Checkpoint Charlie' in the US Sector. If Lt Col Curtis' suggestion, that a checkpoint should be opened opposite the War Memorial to prevent the bus running the gauntlet, had been adopted some of the tense confrontations at 'Charlie' might have been avoided, and greater direct leverage imposed on Guard access. Border patrols were started in our Sector and anti-tank guns deployed, while the value of recasting archaic defence plans, which Lt Col Curtis had recommended on arrival, was now apparent. The military situation gradually settled down as the politicians took over, but Brevet Lt Col Mills, relinquishing 2IC to become AMA to CIGS, was able to see massive signs of recent Soviet armoured deployment as he made the lonely journey to Helmstedt. In Berlin the Battalion manned an OP at the top of the old Reichstag building, which was later a favourite viewpoint over the Wall of many important visitors.

On the training side the Battalion disappointingly could not take part in the large-scale exercises in West Germany. We had taken part in no collective All Arms training since 1954, and junior Officers and NCOs and specialists badly needed this experience. However, the Olympic Stadium at least provided a magnificent covered pool, and under Lt M. H. Eustace our team won the Brigade meeting. Two well-known characters, ORQMS Robbins and C/Sgt Jackson, returned to their specialist Orderly Room and MT niches, and in Signals C/Sgt F. Williams was making the most, with Capt P. B. Mitford-Slade, of the new radios. RQMS Fowley replaced the most efficient RQMS Sanderson on the latter's successful departure into industry, and yet another group went off to the Kenya Regiment on what was sadly to be a last tour.

The pressure on a Battalion in Berlin has always been great, as has been explained, but the political situation called for even more guards and duties than usual. The news that the Battalion was to move to Colchester in Summer 1962 to join the Strategic Reserve allowed everyone to get their second wind and resolve to complete the tour on the highest note possible. Thanks to very careful and systematic preliminary training, the Battalion swept the board in the rigorous Berlin Brigade battle tests, held in wintry weather; the Trophy and four out of five platoon plaques were won. Much of this was due to pre-test training organized by Brevet Lt Col D. G. House, MC, as 2IC. He handed over to Brevet Lt Col E. N. W. Bramall, MC, in March 1962, and went on to command 1st Green Jackets with distinction on operations in Borneo. After later being Colonel Commandant The Light Division and Director of Infantry among other appointments, he ended his military career as Lt Gen Sir David House, GCB, CBE, MC, GOC in C Northern Ireland during the protracted resurgence of civil disorder and terrorism; he followed this by being appointed Black Rod to the House of Lords.

In March 62 the Battalion was the first unit to move complete out of Berlin since the building of the Wall. Despite an ominous hold-up of the Advance Party, the Main Body was cleared in record time thanks to immaculate previous staff work, and the Battalion's professional bearing and the speed and precision of Rifle drill visibly impressed the Soviet officers at the checkpoints. A hard week's field firing followed at Sennelager, ending with a Battalion firepower demonstration, and the firing of an Honest John rocket, showing young Regulars some of the support available on operations. D Company had now been taken over by Maj R. K. Guy, MBE, and Capt McCausland had relieved Capt Mason, who had had a strenuous tour as Adjutant thanks to the paperwork and restrictive disciplinary practices of Berlin. Just as the rest of the Army was moving towards a less rigid style of discipline, that in beleagured Berlin, with its curfew and exaggeration on prestige grounds of what would elsewhere have been minor offences, would have made a third Winter intolerable. Since spirits could be obtained easily and relatively cheaply in bars out of barracks, Army policy now permitted their NAAFI sale to junior ranks for the first time. Young Riflemen were encouraged in every way to learn their capacity inside barracks; the Corporals had instituted an excellent Bierkeller of their own on arrival.

However, it was now Spring and the tempo was increasing as the long, cold nights gave way to sunny days of ceremonial. Gen Sir George Erskine paid his first visit as Colonel Commandant in time to see the Battalion move from a practice alert to a full exercise and watch a farewell parade for the outgoing GOC. The June Queen's Birthday Parade, this time organized by a Green Jacket, Major G. Carter, RB, took the same form as in 1961 and the Rifle contribution was equally well appreciated.

On the Sector borders a surge in the rate of escape attempts to the West stimulated fire by the East German police, to which the West Berlin police often replied. The Battalion patrols and OPs, forbidden to join in, managed to emerge unscathed by ricochets, and the CO had to restrain our police on one occasion from engaging their own side across a tricky salient.

Competition shooting was at least permitted us, and, after winning the Brigade meeting, our team went on to Sennelager. There they swept the team and individual board, winning the Rhine Army Shield, Wavell Trophy and Sterling March. Lt D. C. Gascoigne became Champion Shot of BAOR, with Cpl Jenkins second, and Rfn Stanger won the Young Soldiers' Cup. At Bisley a disastrous Britannia shoot just denied us the KRRC Cup, but individual performances were particularly good. Sgt York won the Roupel, and Maj Welsh the Whitehead from a TA staff post. Sgt York and Cpl Jenkins secured the Worcester, and Capt Lamb's final season as WTO was crowned by our non-Central successes. In the same series, the Queen Victoria was again won, although we only completed three matches, the Company Shield and 1st Army Cup going to C and the Hopton to D.

Liaison with the United States Garrison had built up, using the Royal American connection; Col Philbin had known John Waterfield during post-war service in Moscow, and an unofficial affiliation with 3rd Battlegroup, 6th US Infantry, flourished. Before the Battalion left they did us the exceptional honour of giving a farewell parade and dinner for us and presenting a plaque. Their crest bore the alligator, denoting the war against the Seminole Indians in 1837, in which by coincidence an American ancestor of the writer was severely wounded leading a company of the 6th Infantry.

The period in Berlin had been useful to the Battalion. It had learnt to hold its own in a Brigade, exposed to the glare of publicity, and it had developed a professional attention to detail at all levels, which had not been a pronounced characteristic during the rapid turn-over of the National Service period. The delights of a big city had been fully tasted after rustication in Derna, Tripoli and Ballykinler, but self-discipline had yet to be fully understood or practised by high-spirited young Regulars. The atmosphere in Berlin had become more claustrophobic since the building of the Wall, and the Battalion was not sorry to leave, this time by air, for Colchester in the first week of July 1962. The new Brigadier, R. H. Whitworth, a Guardsman, was highly complimentary in his special order, of which the following are extracts:

> Their time in Berlin has included some of the most critical months in its eventful story since the end of the war.
>
> I would like to thank the Battalion for its faithful, efficient and cheerful service, and to congratulate all ranks on the way they have exemplified the highest standards of the British Army in the eyes of their Allies and the Berliners. They have maintained the highest reputation of their Regiment in the exacting circumstances of the Berlin Crisis of 1961/62.

With the Battalion's return to England, something of the activities at home and overseas in the interim must be recounted. The new Green Jackets Brigade Depot came officially into being on 1 January 59, under Col R. A. St G. Martin, OBE, late 43rd and 52nd, with Lt Col R. A. Flower, MC, who had been one of the Rifle Brigade officers in 2nd 60th, as Depot Commander. In 1959 and 1960 the Depot worked hard to fill up Battalions with the last NS men, to give more time for Regular recruiting efforts to take effect, and families started to attend Passing-out Parades on a larger scale. The standard of shooting was maintained, the Minor Unit Championship at Aldershot being regularly secured under the lead of QMSI Lawrence, late 60th, and under QMSI Beasley the same event was won at Bisley in 1961, 62 and 63.

In 1961 all the effort began to pay off as 700 Regulars were recruited for the Brigade, but in the next year infuriating restrictions were placed on the Brigade by the War Office, when battalions were still 30 short of establishment. The long-overdue modernization and partial rebuilding of the Depot had forced a move back to Bushfield, where two 60th officers who had been in the Calais action, Col Davies-Scourfield and Lt Col Pardoe, were Brigade Colonel and Depot Commander respectively; Maj Hanscombe, after four admirable years of active recruiting, good man-management and sound training, finally handed over Training Company on retirement; he then became an active member of. our Territorials. A feature during this period was the gradual build-up of the Junior Soldiers' Wing, comprising at first Junior (originally Boy) Bandsmen and Buglers, but eventually expanding with non-specialists into Junior Rifleman's Company; potential NCOs still went to the Infantry Junior Leader's Battalion.

Older Riflemen had been hard at work on the administrative side, and in 1963 Maj H. P. Edwards, MBE, ended his long and distinguished service as Quartermaster, just as his son was starting to work his way up from his second stripe. The Colonel Commandants' office, invented by the old Green Jackets, had in effect been recognized by the authorities in the 1958 reorganization. Officer-recruiting was handled in retirement by Lt Col A. Palmer, MC, late RB, with Majs T. E. St Aubyn and C. A. Humphreys, MC, both 60th, as successive Brigade Adjutants. Another initiative was also recognized, that of the organization which had run the Riflemen's Aid Society and other essential welfare. Each Regiment was authorized to have two Retired Officers and supporting Clerical Officers. Maj C. J. Wilson continued to handle sporting and museum affairs, while Brig R. A. T. Eve, CBE, led the way in a rationalization of funds and recording of property which put not only the 2nd Green Jackets but the later Royal Green Jackets for ever in his debt. Its strength was that, unlike other Brigades, the RHQ of the three Regiments was centralized at the Depot, in touch with affairs, visited by those on leave and working as a team on joint matters. It was the same strength which we derived from appointing a succession of first-class officers, often COs designate, to run recruiting for the Brigade as a whole, rather than leaving it to each Regiment's retired officers, based on some remote former depot, as the remainder of the Infantry tended to do.

One of the duties of RHQ was to keep in touch with Allied and Affiliated Regiments, and among these the connection with the Kenya Regiment (Territorial Force) was one of the shortest in years but closest in affection. That Regiment had been formed on 1 June 1937 by Col A. Dunstan-Adams, OBE, MC, TD, who was still Honorary Colonel when disbandment unhappily took place in 1963. Its dual role was to provide a unit which could be used in time of emergency as an aid to the civil power, and which could also supply leaders for the King's African Rifles (KAR), when it expanded in time of war. As an officer-producing unit its contribution to the KAR for the East African and Burma campaigns of World War II was very great. After the war the Green Jackets were allotted the pleasant task of providing the permanent staff, in a colony renowned for its beauty and the hospitality of its inhabitants; this fell particularly on the 60th when in the routine ABTU role at Bushfield, and later when the Rifle Brigade were preparing for an overseas tour.

In Autumn 1952 the Kenya Colony Emergency scheme was implemented against Mau Mau terrorism, and, despite an initial lack of all administrative backing, the Regiment deployed by companies, separated by vast distances and moving constantly. They pioneered many new patrol techniques, particularly in the densely forested slopes of the Aberdares, but their work took them from 14,000 feet up on Mount Kenya down to the Southern border, co-operating closely with the Police Reserve pilots. Those who wish to read a fuller account must turn to the KRRC Chronicle for 1954 and subsequent years, but it must suffice here to say that when the active phase of the Emergency ended in 1956 the Kenya Regiment (TF) had played a central role in restoring peace.

The Kenya Emergency had brought together an effective group of 60th Riflemen. Gen Sir George Erskine as Commander in Chief East Africa was architect of victory, and sheltered the Kenya Regiment when its lack of orthodoxy caused official concern; Lt Col H. A. Hope, MC, was his GSOI earning the OBE. The Kenya Regiment itself was commanded by Lt Col G. T. H. Campbell, MC, throughout the Emergency, earning a well-deserved OBE for his leadership; for part of the time his twin brother, Maj E. F. D. Campbell, Black Watch, was 2IC. Capt R. K. Guy earned an MBE for his onerous task as Adjutant, trying to maintain control in a Regiment where initiative was the most highly prized characteristic. Capt R. R. Cornell organized the training, while RSM Pendry made the first jungle range. A much-valued character, rising from CSM to RSM, was RSM J. Holland, DCM, MM, and other CSMs acting as Permanent Staff Instructors in the Emergency, included G. Williams, R. W. Garner, E. Eves and R. Nunn. The creation of administrative support from scratch by Lt (QM) F. Wakefield, RB was especially valuable; 1 RB was fortunate to take part in the last 18 months of Emergency tasks before moving on to Malaya.

In 1956, with Lt Col C. S. Madden as CO, Capt J. R. T. Eve as Adjutant, and Capt C. G. N. Campbell, the nephew of the previous CO, as Training Officer, the close ties established with the King's Royal Rifle Corps were recognized by the Colonel in Chief's approval of a formal alliance. Green berets and No 1 Dress and other Riflemanlike embellishments were worn by the Kenya Regiment, and 60th Permanent Staff wore their green, red and black lanyard.

With a return to its Territorial role, the Permanent Staff had to build Company HQ with timber from unwanted camps and contact National Servicemen and volunteers; training camps had to be built from scratch, and indeed self-reliance and ability to mix with every race and every degree were some of the useful attributes engendered in 60th Riflemen seconded to the Kenya Regiment. Shooting was not neglected, particularly when Capt P. Welsh was Adjutant, and CSM L. Jones even formed a Kenya team at Bisley when on leave. After a successful tour, involving much reorganization, Lt Col Madden was relieved by Lt Col H. R. W. Vernon, MBE, in 1959. Regimental HQ was administratively well served by the very experienced RQMS Eveson—later awarded the MBE—and ORQMS Sullivan, allowing Capt Welsh the chance to become yet another Champion Shot, this time of East Africa Command. Lt Col

Vernon managed with the aid of Lt Col E. C. Phillips, MC, down from Khartoum, to form a sporting 60th polo team, of whom the younger members were Capt C. J. Holroyd, seconded to KAR, and C. J. H. Gurney, Kenya Regiment Training Officer. More importantly, during his tour of command Lt Col Vernon took the lead in introducing African and Asian volunteers into the Kenya Regiment, the report of his working party being welcomed by the Legislative Council. Sadly, although the initiative was an undoubted success, the Kenya Government decided on financial grounds to suspend the Kenya Regiment in 1963. With Lt Col D. R. L. Bright, 43rd and 52nd, as the last CO, a moving farewell parade and service was held in Nairobi. Those who now visit the Regimental Chapel of the Royal Green Jackets in Lower Barracks, Winchester can be reminded of the brief but very happy alliance with a high-spirited Regiment and of service which helped to ensure the safe transition of a beautiful country to independence.

Our links with the Kaffrarian Rifles, formalized in 1927 but dating back to 1883, inevitably lapsed when South Africa—a country where the Regiment had earlier served with such distinction—left the Commonwealth. However, a natural alliance in the Western Hemisphere was approved by the Colonel in Chief in 1959. This was with the Queen's Own Rifles of Canada, whose affiliation to the Buffs, based on sharing the same encampment in World War I, was also to continue. The Queen's Own, whose home station was Calgary, besides being one of the very few Regular Infantry Regiments in Canada was also in origin the oldest surviving Militia Regiment. A detachment had served alongside our 1st Battalion in 1870 on the Red River expedition, paddling over hundreds of miles of forest waterways to reoccupy Fort Garry (Winnipeg). With their almost identical bond of Rifle dress and customs, the alliance at once bore fruit, with an officer exchange shared with the Buffs. When a decade later the Queen's Own, in a further Canadian Army reduction, were merged with the Princess Patricia's Canadian Light Infantry, the alliance was maintained, since the Rifle Brigade's long-standing alliance and exchange with the latter Regiment was now inherited by The Royal Green Jackets.

Although the Princess Patricia of that latter Regiment's title was still, as Lady Patricia Ramsay, present at joint Ladies Guild functions of the two original Green Jacket Regiments, the King's Royal Rifle Corps had suffered losses among members of the Royal Family interested in Ladies Guild affairs over the last decade. HM Queen Mary, who had been Patroness, had died in 1952. Two sisters had long been active in memory of their brother, HH Prince Christian Victor of Schleswig–Holstein, a very keen 60th Rifleman, who had died on active service in the South African War. When, after much interest in World War II Committee work for our prisoners of war and families, HH Princesss Helena Victoria died in 1948, HH Princess Marie Louise took over as President of our Ladies Guild until her own death in 1956. The Regiment's Gothic silver statue of a Knight—itself originally a gift in memory of the Prince Consort to his godson—is a reminder of the devoted interest in the Regiment of that family. It is worth recalling that it was their mother, HRH Princess Christian, who opened the Riflemen's Cottages in 1904, now modernized and expanded into the best of all living war memorials. Also in the Gothic style are Queen Victoria's swords still worn by our buglers. The King's Royal Rifle Corps was fortunate from the day of its formation, almost entirely due to the work of HRH The Duke of Cumberland, in the interest of our

Royal Family and the active part which they played in our affairs. It was accordingly with great pleasure that the Regiment acquired a portrait of our late Colonel in Chief, HM George VI, in 1962 by Denis Files, the same artist who had painted our full-length portrait of HM Queen Elizabeth II.

CHAPTER XII

THE AIRPORTABLE
BATTALION
AT HOME AND OVERSEAS

(Map: page 268)

The Army at home which 2nd Green Jackets, The King's Royal Rifle Corps, was joining at Colchester after leave in August 1962 was a very different one from that which in 1956 had moved slowly in troopships, with World War II equipment, towards Suez. The politicians had at last realized that if they were to meet the consecutive and often concurrent crises in our colonies, as they moved into independence with an internal struggle for power or threat from outside, very rapid air reinforcement of overseas garrisons would be needed. The need for shipping to use the Cape route to the East was another key factor. Southern, later to be Army Strategic, Command at Wilton had the responsibility for planning such deployment, with 3 Division at Bulford responsible for training and the command of any force above a brigade size. The Strategic Reserve was scattered by brigades round England, with the only armour on Salisbury Plain. 19 Brigade, which our Battalion joined, at least had its Infantry and Gunners all in the Colchester Garrison, but Sappers were at Maidstone. East Anglian District, also in the city, was responsible for local administration, other than discipline, which followed operational channels. Thanks to Green Jacket recruiting efforts, 1st Green Jackets was strong enough to be one of the first battalions into the Borneo emergency from Penang, and 3rd Green Jackets was also overseas in Cyprus. No other Brigade of Infantry, other than the Parachute Brigade, yet had all its Regular battalions fit for operations; the fate of weak battalions was to be District troops, often over-committed on local duties at the expense of training, with lowered morale, which made recruiting yet more difficult.

The establishment of our Battalion was that of Airportable Infantry, based on Land Rovers and trailers, to enable strategic carriage, in long-range RAF transport planes to any suitable airfield world-wide open to us. Since Suez, overflying the Arab world was always uncertain, and the Northern route via Cyprus, Turkey and Iran to Kuwait or Bahrein was the usual Eastern route. In view of the role, up-to-date inoculation of the Battalion was essential, as was the ability to travel in civilian clothes, and with weapons in baggage holds, through countries where the presence of an armed body of soldiers would have been a political embarrassment. To be ready for this, very detailed Air Movement Instructions had to be prepared from somewhat contradictory Army and RAF sources; packing, loading, lashing and manifest completion had all to be learnt, passed on and committed to writing. The division of the Battalion into 'Chalks', the RAF jargon for plane-loads, the duties of the Emplaning Officer and other mysteries had to be learnt. The success of the next year's air moves owes much to a tremendous amount of staff work put in by Brevet Lt Col Bramall as 2IC, who had led the Advance Party's excellent work. Sadly Capt (QM) G. Slater had found yet another 1098 equipment in poor condition, with many long hours of work before spares and deficiencies could be made up; there was also much work necessary on the three-ton trucks, held to make the Battalion mobile in its alternative NATO reinforcement role.

Roman Barracks itself was brand-new, built to a standard Army concept and unluckily to a tremendously tight synopsis scale, particularly in stores. To concentrate on housing soldiers, no garages were built in the first phase and the open plan with acres of grass made security and maintenance difficult. This problem was later particularly encountered by the small rear party when the Battalion was away. However, the centrally heated barrack rooms with bedside lights, Dunlopillo mattresses and good washing facilities were a great improvement, and the cookhouse and Junior Ranks' Club excellent. The two Messes once adorned with all our pictures and silver looked very handsome, and at the Guard Room the *Warren Hastings* Bell from the 1897 shipwreck once more rang ship's time. Sadly, however, the Corporals had to make do with a converted hut.

On return from leave, Lt Col Curtis could at last take the Battalion into the field. We were now up to a strength of over 600, all Regulars for the first time since 1939, and many younger Riflemen had not trained away from barracks before. Equally only half our families were in quarters, and the younger wives, in hirings scattered over Essex and Suffolk, were unused to the problems of separation.

A keen tactician—who would have enjoyed the training, and who had done much for the Regiment—Maj T. N. Thistlethwayte, handed over C Company to Maj W. S. C. Chevis, 1st Green Jackets, at this time. Before retiring as a Lt Col, he was 2IC during the Battalion's second operational tour in Borneo in 1966.

Moving by road to Otterburn, Northumberland, in September, the Battalion deployed straight into its Internal Security (IS) role against border raiders led by Capt G. P. R. Crossman, and there was much patrolling and a fine forced march by D Company before his party were rounded up. The 65,000 vehicle miles covered by Sgt Woodcock's MT gave confidence that hard work had brought the transport up to standard. Brig D. Beckett's Brigade exercise which followed at Stanford, Norfolk, was a most useful test of many of the techniques needed by an Airportable Battalion on IS duties. Starting and finishing on airfields, a simulated air move in trucks, with all the associated packing and documentation problems, tried out our newly written drills. A 20-mile advance to contact with a river crossing, although tiring, was less strange; but a subsequent very realistic setting in aid of the civil power, in which another unit had found itself overrun by a rioting mob, needed great alertness and firm handling. However, C Company's baton squad rapidly dispersed the crowd, and later 2/Lt M. L. Dunning's A Company platoon steadily exacted the ultimate sanction with blank, before they could be swamped by a charge. All the IS tasks, of gathering intelligence, patrols and cordons, which the Battalion was to need within the year, were well tested. As enemy on the final exercise our night patrolling was particularly effective, Lt R. M. Gamble, who had won the Sword of Honour at Sandhurst, running an especially good stay-behind party. Orchestrated by the final 'Advance' and 'Charge', sounded by Bugle Major Green and the earlier assault pioneer demolitions of Sgt Horsley, all teams in the Battalion returned quietly confident after a marvellously dry and amusing period of training.

Apart from preparing for a successful Administrative Inspection, the period up to Christmas was taken up with the very detailed planning necessitated by the forthcoming Battalion Group exercise in Cyrenaica; vast desert training areas were then available to us under the Libyan Treaty with the King, in return for defence commitments, which were a Strategic Reserve task. Since this was the first major Airportable overseas exercise conducted by the Regiment, it is worth recording the mounting phases involved.

First, a small reconnaissance party, of Brevet Lt Col Bramall, Capt (QM) Slater and Capt Crossman, made LO to the local population as a keen Arabist, flew to Malta and Libya; the area was known from Derna days, and the training and logistic requirements could easily be assessed.

On return companies wrestled with freight lists, load manifests and packed vehicles according to stringent safety regulations. Vehicles had to be fully laden to a precise weight before the RAF would fly them.

After Christmas leave, the QM and MTO, Lt Shreeve, flew to Cyprus to draw heavy equipment and vehicles from the strategic stockpile, established there after our withdrawal from the Suez Canal base, when the two Sovereign Base Areas were subsequently agreed. The equipment and vehicles were to be moved by landing craft to Tobruk.

The winter of 1962/3 was the worst for many years, and Exercise 'Sandstorm' was well named. After rechecking the paper work and shovelling snow at Lyneham, the Group flew to RAF El Adem, South of Tobruk, on 15 January 63. (The maps on pages 108 and 230 of the previous Volume VI show the principal places mentioned.) The Group consisted of the Battalion less Rear Party, M Battery (Eagle Troop), 2 Regiment RA, with their new Italian 105-mm pack howitzers, a Sapper troop and 19 Brigade administrative detachments. It totalled 756 all ranks, 57 Land Rovers and 40 trailers. The Group was shuttled out in Comet jets, Britannia turbo prop aircraft and Beverleys over a seven-day period, while the Advance Party collected an extra 50 vehicles and tentage from Capt Slater's ship at Tobruk. At Gazala, at the seaward end of the 1942 Line of that name, Lt Col Curtis and the QM chose a patch of ground as camp. For a fortnight the dust flew or rain scudded down, and at night ice sometimes formed on bivouacs and windscreens.

For the first week, Companies and the Battery learnt desert navigation and leaguering drills and fired weapons, always wary of wartime minefields. The main exercise, involving a series of actions, covered 300 miles in a week, a round trip via Tmimi, Mechili, Charruba and Derna, so often mentioned in the Desert fighting. One of the best features was the involvement as enemy of our Queen's Royal Rifles platoon of 'Ever Readies' under Capt D. A. H. Beddard, an imaginative production of evidence that our Territorials, now commanded by Lt Col K. N. Loudon-Shrand, TD, could rapidly reinforce their Regulars. Pre-positioned by helicopter at Mechili with an infantry company from Benghazi, the enemy were located by OPs preceding the Group in open formation just before last light. Attacking Westwards at dawn to blind the enemy, the C and D Company Riflemen skirmished on to the dominant feature, as Lt J. A. F. Graham-Wigan, the Forward Air Controller, directed RAF Hunters in realistic dummy runs.

For two days thereafter the Group pressed Westwards over the same difficult ground met by those cutting off the Italians in the 1940 Wavell Offensive. The recovery team under Lt Shreeve did magnificent work in repairing trailers and springs as they advanced. At Charruba our anti-tank guns and the Battery fired operational quantities of ammunition for the first time, as the Companies conducted intensive field firing. It ended with A and C Companies working forward, supported by all guns, mortars and Hunter aircraft available.

On moving North East to Derna Lt Col Bramall was put in command of the next phase on the 'Castle', a precipitious peak last assaulted by the Battalion in 1957. C and D Companies took it frontally by night, while A Company hopped over in helicopters at dawn to cut off the bandits' retreat.

On the return to camp heavy rains caused flash flooding in the wadis. Only hard work by the Assault Pioneers allowed the CO's vehicle to return from a favourite duck marsh. Capt Holroyd was marooned in mid-flood, until D Company at the rear of the column welcomed the arrival of Maj R. M. Parker in a Scammell, bearing rum and whisky. Meanwhile far to the South East, in the lonely hills where the frontiers of Libya, Egypt and the Sudan meet, an expedition from Kenya led by Capt C. J. H. Gurney had achieved the amazing feat of making a rendezvous, exact in time and space, with Capt Crossman's reception party from Gazala. After climbing Kilimanjaro, traversing Kenya, Ethiopia, (where they were assisted by Ewan Ferguson, a 60th Rifleman now in the Foreign Service) and the Sudan, the party reported to El Adem in time to return by RAF aircraft to England as planned.

When the aircraft returned to a still frozen England, meeting with the inevitable diversions, it was the end of yet another phase in the rebuilding of the Regular Battalion. Lt Col J. H. P. Curtis, MC, was the last pre-war Regular Commanding Officer, in that he had just entered Sandhurst in 1939 and had anyway been brought up in the Regiment. He was also the last with wartime Desert and Company Commander experience. These strands had all combined, with his flair for operations and tactical training, and his interest in history, to make Exercise 'Sandstorm' a valuable demonstration for young Riflemen of the Battalion team at work, as well as the last ever expression of desert mastery by a Regiment which was not to be seen in Libya again. An older pre-war Rifleman was also leaving shortly. Capt G. E. Slater, BEM, had first established his reputation when he had retained a firmer grip on his Section than any other patrolling the Mandalay bazaars in 1938. He had worked himself to the bone in the Berlin and Colchester moves, and his last gift to his Battalion was the return of all equipment to the Cyprus stockpile without incurring a single bill. A second Quartermaster had recently been authorized to deal with the mass of costly equipment; in parallel many overworked Infantry appointments such as Signals, MT and Officers' Mess had now been raised to colour-sergeant rank. Lt Col Curtis had cast his fresh eye over the special problems of a Regular Airportable Battalion flying away in emergency, including the enormous number of married junior ranks. His case, taken to the Adjutant General, for a new Battalion appointment, was eventually to lead to the invaluable establishment of a Families Officer. Meanwhile he wisely recommended to his successor the use of the senior or Home Quartermaster, soon to be Capt A. J. Lamb, on static and home base duties, such as accommodation, in-barracks messing and families. The junior or Field Quartermaster would handle 1098, and supplies and messing on operations or exercises. This was later discharged by Lt Shreeve, who handed over MT once more to a young Regular; in this way Capt P. Treneer Michell—previously renowned for running cadres and amateur entertainments —started to learn the administration and staff work which was to carry him 15 years later to a Brigade Major's post and command of the Battalion.

Casting back, it was indeed the end of an era when Lt Col Curtis left, for within a year his father Maj Gen H. O. Curtis had died, preceded by Maj Gen Sir Hereward Wake, severing two old and valued 60th family connections. Invaluable continuity in Battalion command was maintained, for his successor was Lt Col G. H. Mills, who had been 2IC in both Ballykinler and Berlin and had known and actively worked to implement the policy of his predecessors; indeed, for the last six months the filling of officer and NCO appointments had been in full consultation with him. Lt Col Mills had been wartime Platoon Commander, IO and Adjutant in 1st 60th in Italy and had since commanded motor companies in both 60th Battalions and at the Depot, and like his predecessor and successor had the great advantage of the Regimental system, in that he knew and was known by most of the senior ranks in the Battalion. Simultaneously Brevet Lt Col Bramall was relieved as 2IC by Maj the Hon R. M. Parker, whose A Company was taken over by Maj D. M. Stileman, RB, last seen in 2nd 60th at Münster; the latter was at first known to few, but rapidly made his mark in the respect and affection of all ranks. After a successful tour, Capt I. H. McCausland was relieved by Capt P. B. Mitford-Slade as Adjutant, whose Signals Section was taken over by Capt C. L. G. G. Henshaw. RSM Byrne was relieved by RSM T. Fowley, and in the Orderly Room ORQMS Beardon, the most senior of the former KRRC Cadets, dealt with the undiminished flood of paper until the arrival of ORQMS Sullivan from Kenya. Part of this paperwork was concerned with airportability, and, in a Regimentally invented appointment of 'G' Adjutant, Capt Crossman worked under the 2IC on training planning or as Emplaning Officer, foreshadowing the later Operations Officer, used in Northern Ireland.

Lt Col Mills, in the first of a frequent series of informal talks to individual Companies—who were now developing clear personalities of their own— started to put over his aim. Having played some part in laying the foundations and building a happy and efficient Regular Battalion, it was to develop the professional Rifleman in that Battalion. National Servicemen had received six months rather crude training and were then expected to use this veneer of knowledge for the remaining 18 months in a section, or as a basic specialist; it was hoped that civilian skills might save some of the latter training. Little time for professional training could be spared for Corporals and above and for officers, although it had been a source of present Green Jacket strength that more effort in this line was made than elsewhere in the Infantry. Because training was inevitably repetitive there was no incentive for three-year Regulars to sign on and start a full career. The NS Army had been living on borrowed time, for few young NCOs were staying on as Regulars. Now Riflemen were enlisting for six or nine years, with monetary advantages in commitment to the latter. The CO, therefore, saw it as a duty to bring all Regulars on as rapidly in their profession as their individual potential and enthusiasm allowed. Some would naturally develop faster than others, but all who earned it would get a chance to move ahead, whether as a specialist, as an NCO or both. To encourage development meant envolving a method of measuring achievement, so that a Rifleman could move on from basic skills to an à la carte menu of skills and specialisms appropriate to the Battalion's role, equipment and station and to his personal needs. Riflemen would be coached in basic skills until they had passed individual tests. All would receive refresher training, if tests showed that it was needed, but trained Riflemen need never again do repetitive individual training.

The basic theme in the training directive to cover the next two years was simple. All Riflemen had to be fit enough to get to any objective, alert enough to spot the enemy and marksmen enough to hit them, shooting selectively. Clearly, Physical Efficiency (PE) Tests and Range Classification, which were completed in February 63, were part of the process, but alertness needed more sense of adventure. Lt Col Mills introduced his system of 'scalps', by which, on field training, each officer and man carried a slip of paper, giving name, rank and number, signed and stamped by the CSM, who alone could replace it. An officer or NCO could lose his scalp for idle or unwary leadership. Two or more Riflemen ambushing an individual, stalking a sentry or picking up a straggler could gain his scalp, or, if outwitted, lose theirs, and a final scalp count ensured beer for the wariest platoon and rewarded initiative, as scalps gained counted double.

Before alertness could be tested on Salisbury Plain, the period immediately after the hand-over by Lt Col Curtis was spent on 'Spearhead' duty. This meant that the Battalion was taking its turn on stand-by on the Strategic Reserve roster at 72 hours notice to fly overseas. The lightweight wooden packing cases were assembled and all equipment grounded for trial packing, but no final work could proceed towards one of the countless contingency plans without definite earmarking for an operation. In any case the Army Department had so far fought shy of committing an actual 'Spearhead' battalion, always hitherto misemploying some District battalion at low strength, to husband its reserve. Time was not wasted, however, for the Buglers learnt their new operational role of air and helicopter reception of supplies, while all Companies carried out training with helicopters, drills which were to be so useful later in Borneo.

The first tactical training under the new directive was Section, Platoon and Company training at the Tidworth end of Salisbury Plain. Known to few in the Battalion, the limited training areas allotted were used to a programme laid down by Battalion. This was essential to ensure a common tactical doctrine, since, through the Company Commanders, 1st and 3rd Green Jacket experience was also represented. Each platoon moved tactically long distances by night to new positions, known only to the Company Commander and themselves; heavy equipment was dumped for them, so that full advantage was taken of operational atmosphere on the Downs and many scalps changed hands in ambush and counter-ambush. Valuable infantry/tank co-operation drills, the first in open country since 1955, was carried out with 5 DG, and at Sandhurst Lt Gamble commanded an excellent Infantry demonstration with the accent on Support and Specialist platoons. The new 81-mm mortar with double the range and twice the accuracy of the old three-inch mortar was demonstrated. The Commandant and brother Rifleman Maj Gen J. Mogg was warned that there would be realistic simulation of a 'short' bomb, thus joining the other Green Jackets, who alone did not scrabble for shelter in the mud.

After a tricky platoon test exercise, the Companies moved round the North Circular in the early hours. They left the Colonel and 2IC to watch a chilly dawn over Stonehenge, before moving on to Wilton for training meetings. The one drawback of Colchester, as will later be seen, was the requirement to go to the Plain for Command or Divisional briefings in a period when helicopters were so rare.

The latter half of May was spent on Adventure Training, the War Department having only recently given official support for what the Regiment had been doing ever since Bouquet's injunction that 'the men should take it in turns to go on hunting expeditions with their Officers and remain out of camp for some weeks at a time. . . .' Hunting was not always available, but the spirit of enterprise was. In A Company, platoon commanders had to plan and execute their expeditions; 2/Lt J. P. O. Beddard took his men canoeing on the Seine, Sgt Copping's team cycled to Caen and Lt Gamble took climbers to Skye. Maj Chevis took C Company to radiate from a base camp in Snowdonia and Maj R. K. Guy, MBE, sent parties on battlefield tours from Calais to the Low Countries. General Erskine, as Colonel Commandant, listened to briefings for this development process in the fitness, self-reliance and initiative of young Riflemen, and delighted many Riflemen and their families by his warm interest.

The Battalion dispersed on block leave till the end of June, knowing that Company, Battalion and Brigade training had to be crammed into July before Spearhead duty again in August. The climax was to be a 3 Division/38 Group RAF joint exercise, set by Southern Command in Libya in September, on which a great deal of emphasis was being placed within the Division. Brig Beckett was designing a testing Counter-Insurgency (COIN) and Internal Security (IS) Exercise near Tidworth, but at the same time, in anticipation of the Libyan exercise, required the Battalion to do further armoured/infantry work on the Plain. The CO spent part of his leave designing an interesting exercise for the Battalion astride the Avon at his old family home, before the move to the Plain.

However, events suddenly began to move very fast. Just as the Battalion was due to return from its month's leave at the end of June, Lt Col Mills was told that they were to take up Spearhead duty on 1 July 63; this was out of turn, but apparently to avoid any commitment of the Parachute battalion earmarked for it. He then received warning of a possible operational commitment in British Guiana for one Rifle company and a skeleton Battalion HQ. This was not helpful, since he was forbidden to tell anyone else in the Battalion. Further complications were that, if the whole Battalion was not committed, a skeleton HQ would not include the necessary administrative teams to maintain a force in a turbulent and primitive setting 5000 miles from home. To increase the variables, Brigade were insisting that the complete series of exercises must be carried out on the Plain, despite the fact that it would be impossible within the notice to meet the continuously changing and increasingly rigorous RAF packing and loading requirements, if all the 1098 equipment was dispersed.

However, with the official reduction of notice to 24 hours for D Company and the Battalion HQ party—which the CO had decided to risk making more an Advance Party than a Tactical HQ—and with the rest of the Battalion at 72 hours notice, leave was given to tell a minimum number of people of a possible British Guiana (BG) destination. Very little was known of that remote South American colony, except that it was tropical, and light trousers, a shirt and bathing trunks were among items added to personal packing lists. It was typical of the lack of information that the fact that the entire coastline was mud or mangrove swamp was one of the many facts not recorded. No support weapons were to be included in the operation, if ordered, and the fly-out strength would be 450 including attached. A draft Battalion order of battle was drawn up, based on each Rifle Company using the older and better trained men of its Support Platoon to reinforce Rifle Platoons, ensuring that they were brought up to a minimum strength for IS duties of 27, with Sections of two NCOs and six to provide 24-hour patrols and guards, if necessary. Rifle Companies were each to fly at a strength of about 100, including attached. The remainder were B Company's Recce and Assault Pioneer Platoons, Battalion HQ and a combined A & B Echelon under OC B Company, Capt C. J. Holroyd. The Rear Party under Maj M. P. Hills, OC HQ Company, would include the Home QM, Capt Lamb as previously described, and those ineligible for reasons of age, medical category or domestic or other problems. In the rush of events and the eagerness of Riflemen to be included, some of those with problems slipped in. Since the new barracks had no large buildings or sheds, the immensely costly and vulnerable equipment, particularly radios, had to be strewn over the grass round barrack blocks as Colour and Platoon Sergeants seized those just returned from leave and started trial packing as best they could. In everyone's mind was the fact that within 10 days it would all need to be unpacked and redistributed, if Battalion and Brigade training was to continue as directed.

Brigade was insistent on this, and indeed put little weight on the BG contingency plan being implemented. There was, after all, 1 Coldstream out there as Garrison Battalion, about to be relieved by 2 Grenadiers, and the fact that the Colony was suffering a three-month General Strike with tempers at snapping point—to which the humidity at the end of the long rains contributed not a little—was not appreciated. While Rifle Platoons practised IS drills, which had just come out in clear form for the first time in admirable new pamphlets, called *Keeping the Peace*, the CO was warned on 2 July 63 to attend a routine administrative briefing at Wilton on 3 July for the Grenadier CO. This meant a very early start by train from Colchester to Salisbury in time to listen to the problems of the other CO as BG Garrison Commander, including the running down of the stockpile during the strike, which had closed Georgetown as a port. It seemed incredible that, after 150 years of colonial rule, the medical authorities present could not decide whether BG was still a malarious area. Lt Col Mills determined that he would treat it as such with strict paludrine routine, since although the coastal irrigated strip had been temporarily cleared in the post-war DDT spraying, the jungle was too vast and loggers, 'pork-knockers' (the casual prospectors for alluvial gold and diamonds) and others seemed to emerge from it with malaria in their blood.

Over lunch the Command Chief of Staff stressed that any deployment of our Battalion to BG was remote. An afternoon visit to 3 Division at Bulford strengthened this impression. General Carver, later CDS, said that training for the Libyan exercises was top priority, while Lt Col R. E. Worsley—then GSO I, and in process of moving from the Rifle Brigade via the Royals to higher command—showed photographs of a Middle Eastern airfield, which he was certain was of operational significance.

Somewhat confused and jaded, the CO returned to Colchester soon after 8 pm to be met by Mrs Mills, who said 'I suppose you know?'—'I never seem to know anything.'—'Well, you're off at midnight.'—'I just don't believe it.'—'I think you ought to go—it'll look a bit odd if you're the only one left.' Unknown to all, and especially to the Battalion, tempers had finally snapped in BG; the occasion was alleged rape of a young Indian girl by an African with inter-communal reprisals, leading to the cane-knife choppings and arson which had bedevilled BG over the years. Mindful of an earlier occasion when troops had not been called in rapidly enough and the centre of Georgetown, the capital, had been burnt and looted, the Colonial Ministers appealed to the Governor. 1 Coldstream were overdue for relief after a tiresome nine-month tour, and it was not thought that the Grenadiers could take over, straight from London duties, and meet the IS commitment simultaneously. The Chiefs of Staff had therefore for the first time committed those at 24 hours notice to move on Spearhead duty. With the costly equipment programmes, particularly of the Royal Navy and RAF, under constant threat, all strategic deployment had become a tiresome virility test, with the RAF indicating that Transport Command would only be held up by the slowness of the Army. Instead of being allowed the customary 15 hours in barracks, from receipt of the move order at 1945 hours Wednesday 3 July 63, before moving off to RAF Lyneham, D Company and the Advance Party were told to move as soon as possible. Khaki drill (KD) had to be broken from bulk and issued, along with mosquito nets, kitbags had to be packed, boxes filled and sealed, weapons bundled and passenger manifests made out. As a first priority married men had to be called in from quarters and the many hirings in Colchester and elsewhere. The drills, worked out over the months, had been worthwhile, and there were few hitches, thanks to devoted work, particularly by Maj Parker and RQMS B. Rimmer. The CO took only two decisions that night; one was to pack a tropical dinner jacket, which he was able to use when dining with the Governor; the other was, when handing over the Main Body to the competent hands of Maj Parker as 2IC, to ask him to allow the successful Shooting Team to complete its Bisley Week at all costs, despite the number of key figures involved. Under the new WTO, Lt D. H. Mead, who had been champion shot at the District meeting, the Team had cleared the board at the 19 Brigade meeting. At Bisley the KRRC Cup was secured, along with the SMG by Sgt Jenkins, the Worcester and Eastern Command LMG Cups, chiefly by Sgts R. Smith and Fry, and the Northampton and Small Arms Cups. Lt C. R. Hill became Champion Young Officer, and only the loyal and rapid departure to his plane before the final shoot deprived L/Cpl Stanger of the Rifle Brigade Cup.

However, all this seemed remote, as Lt Col Mills and Maj Guy sat in the front of the first bus leaving barracks soon after 0100 hours 4 July. 120 men and 5 tons of freight were moving off under six hours from the first order. They wished, as they read the operational brief on BG, that they had paid rather more attention in Staff College days to uncannily similar scenarios for deployment of IS duties. However, it had not seemed much concerned with motor-battalion work. Behind them the Main Body was still at 72 hours notice, and Maj Parker was advised to carry on with local training.

Since no temporary mounting centre had been set up, the party reached Lyneham soon after dawn, to be given breakfast and pushed into a transit hut.

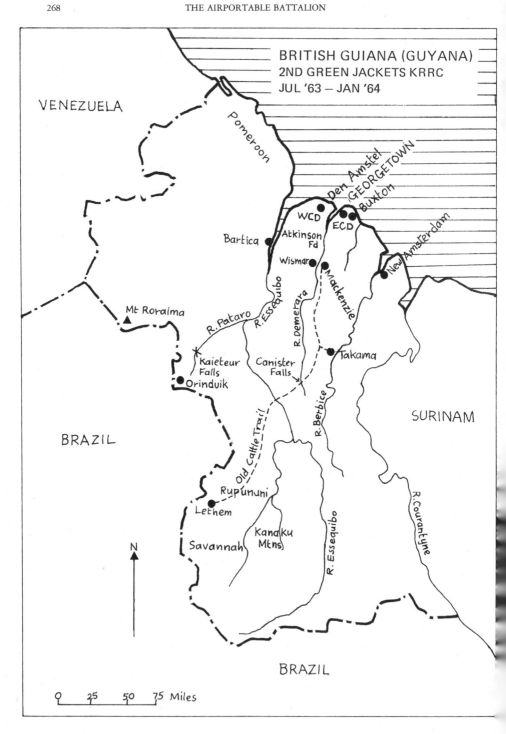

BRITISH GUIANA (GUYANA)
2ND GREEN JACKETS KRRC
JUL '63 – JAN '64

VENEZUELA

Pomeroon

Den Amstel
GEORGETOWN
Buxton

WCD

ECD

New Amsterdam

Bartica
Atkinson
Fd

Wismar

Mackenzie

Mt Roraima

R. Pataro

R. Essequibo

R. Demerara

Kaieteur
Falls

Canister
Falls

Takama

Orinduik

R. Berbice

BRAZIL

SURINAM

Old Cattle Trail

Rupununi

Lethem

Savannah

Kanaku
Mtns

R. Essequibo

R. Courantyne

N

BRAZIL

0   25   50   75 Miles

The totally strange atmosphere of another Service made a deep impression. Despite the vaunted air flexibility at Whitehall level, aircraft and crews would not be ready to fly till noon. Instead of being accorded operational priority, the move was deemed an 'unscheduled flight', treated at the lower level as an interference with the civil-airline-style trooping traffic overseas. Maj Guy's two Britannias took off on time at noon, but, following on his earlier effect on the CIGS's planes, Lt Col Mills found his Advance Party plane was unserviceable. Then followed an afternoon of inconsiderate treatment by the Air Movements Staff, basically Equipment Officers, unused by temperament and training to handling people. Six times the now tired party were paraded in full marching order and kept waiting until aircraft were pronounced unserviceable; the last time it became clear that embarkation was purely for Press benefit, as no ground or aircrew turned up. Fortunately, Brig Beckett, who had many contacts from his Parachute days, then arrived, and for the first time the Station Commander visited the party. Food and good accommodation was at last produced, and by this intervention the party could secure a night's rest before flying on.

The route was via Gander, Newfoundland, and Bermuda, where Lt D. C. Gascoigne, ADC to his uncle the Governor, was briefly contacted. Finally, after a 24-hour flight, the CO's party arrived on the morning of Saturday 6 July 63 at Atkinson Field, a wartime US strip and hospital huts on the jungle bank of the Demerara river, 20 miles South of Georgetown, BG. Unknown to them Maj Parker had already at 0800 hrs received the orders for the Main Body to move at the shortest notice; C Company left barracks within three hours. Maj Parker had noticed the glumness of Capt Crossman, who had done splendid work as Emplaning Officer. This was at the prospect of having to put down his saker falcon, acquired in Libya on the winter exercise. With typical sang froid, Maj Parker despatched him down to a falconer friend near Marlborough with the magnificent bird, phoning at intervals en route; with a desperate dash he just caught the last plane out. The Main Body's move out was uneventful, except for a Britannia containing freight. At Bermuda Riflemen noticed that liquid (which turned out to be battery acid) was dripping out of a crate. They also noticed that the crate had been loaded upside down by the RAF as marked, and this was confirmed by the local Squadron Leader. Without calling a single Rifleman as witness, and apparently preferring their opinion to that of their own officer on the spot, an RAF Board blamed the Regiment for the damage to the plane; an independent Army enquiry restored the situation, but it left yet another bad taste. Out of these lessons learnt, however, rapidly emerged improvements to operational air movement. The Army set up a properly staffed Air Mounting Centre at Corsham where soldiers could be looked after, until the Army's Air Transport Liaison Officer could call them directly forward to a plane known to be in working order. The RAF took Equipment Officers off personnel emplanement duties and trained those assigned, and leak-proof covers to batteries were issued. The arrival of the Directly Moulded Sole (DMS) Boot with its rubberized sole allowed soldiers to emplane without removing footwear, as well as providing the silent and relatively waterproof boot demanded by fieldcraft. The Regiment, which had long shunned stamping on parade as damaging and noisy, watched with amusement the rest of the Army trying to keep up the vain practice in the new boot, while the Guards and Sandhurst retained a pair of noisy ammunition boots for ceremonial.

On arrival D Company had passed under command of 1 Coldstream. They had been committed operationally with greater haste than Lt Col Mills would have allowed, if he had not been delayed. Under Maj Guy's leadership, however, the tired Company rose to the challenge.

A summary of the position in Britain Guiana in July 1963 must be given if the Battalion's work is to be understood. The country, one of three colonies on the North East coast of tropical South America, consisted of tropical rain forest and inland savannah, where the soil was sandy and only the leaf-mouid of centuries provided any fertility. Four great rivers, black with peat, flowed North from the highlands on the Brazil border and provided the only communications except by Dakota or Grumman amphibian. From the West these were the Essequibo, with its logging centre at Bartica, and the Demerara, with the capital, Georgetown, at its mouth and the bauxite mine of Mackenzie inland. After the smaller Mahaica, the next great river was the Berbice with the town of New Amsterdam at its mouth; the remote Courantyne formed the border with Dutch Surinam. Far to the North West lay Venezuela. There was one bad road along the coast from the Essequibo to the Courantyne and a little railway parallel to it as far as the Berbice; the only other road was that to Atkinson Field where the scrub jungle started on the Demerara. The only developments were the sugar estates and rice plantations East from the Essequibo in a 10-mile-wide strip along the coast. On this rich alluvial plain, built up by Orinoco mud coming down the coast, a sea wall prevented flooding, while an elaborate system of canals and dykes (dams in the Dutch) permitted dry-weather irrigation from flooded savannah.

The British had finally taken the colony from the Dutch in the Napoleonic Wars, and distinguished members of the Regiment had served there with 60th Battalions thereafter (vide KRRC Chronicle 1948). On being given their freedom and land grants in the 1830s, the African workers had largely abandoned the hated canefields and had moved into Georgetown, where they later dominated the Civil Service, the Police and other white-collar employment. Those that remained in the countryside formed isolated communities among the palm groves of Buxton in East Coast Demerara (ECD—Georgetown and the populated strip East of the Demerara river) and Den Amstel in West Coast Demerara (WCD), between that river and the Essequibo. They also dominated Wismar, the squatters' town opposite the paternalistic bauxite mining community at Mackenzie 40 miles up-river, accessible by the Old and New Sand Trails, amphibian or boat.

The indentured Portuguese and Chinese workers, who had succeeded them, had swiftly gone into trade and formed the business community with its own small political party. Then for nearly 100 years indentured workers from India, the so-called East Indians, had come from Calcutta and Madras, and, having worked out their time, tended to stay in neat rural communities among the canefields. Their thrift won them land, and they specialized in rice. Their smaller physique allowed them to be dominated by the Africans, and, until the post-war DDT spraying, the rural population was checked and debilitated by malaria. However, by 1963 their recent population surge had put the Africans into second place and a country where all had till recently gone to school and worked together tolerantly found itself divided on racial lines by ambitious politicians.

The Constitution then current was an unsatisfactory one, designed to cover a short period of transition to independence, which had, however, been halted in 1956.

The Governor, Sir Ralph Grey, a splendid New Zealander, found himself with no staff, and with the Police under Mrs Jagan, the left-wing Home Affairs Minister; the Government was entirely composed of the PPP, which her husband Cheddi Jagan, the Prime Minister, had turned into an entirely Indian party, with an activist youth organization. There was then no Defence Force, so the Governor as C in C had only the British Garrison battalion at his disposal, which could not intervene unless invited by the civil power. The largely African opposition party was the PNC, headed by Forbes Burnham, originally a Jagan colleague before the communities were urged to vote on purely racial lines. The now outnumbered Africans had seen themselves threatened by PPP policy and had fomented an effective General Strike, which had brought the colony to near administrative collapse over an 11-week period. Inter-communal incidents were leading to increasing violence and some deaths, and just before our Battalion was ordered out the Prime Minister had written to the Governor, saying that the situation was out of control and inviting him to take all steps he thought fit to restore order. The Coldstream had deployed companies to ECD and WCD and a platoon to New Amsterdam, but needed to concentrate for relief by the Grenadiers. The Police had had no leave during the strike and were very tired; their largely African composition inspired allegations of partisan treatment among the Indians. It was into this scenario, hastily read on the plane, that our Battalion found itself committed.

Immediately on arrival Maj Guy found himself directed to take over security in co-operation with the Police in ECD; he wisely concentrated D Company in the cramped quarters of the District police station 15 miles East of Georgetown to ensure good liaison from the start. By the time the CO, accompanied by Commodore Ashmore (later Admiral and CDS, but at that time Commander, British Forces Caribbean Area) visited D Company on the afternoon of Saturday 6 July, Maj Guy had done his best to make a new and effective presence felt by maximum patrolling at Section strength. It says much for the fitness of the Riflemen that, despite a month's leave and being dumped dog-tired into a temperature of 90° Fahrenheit and about 95% humidity, they kept going on foot along the grassy canal banks among the dense and airless canefields. Swords were fixed on patrol, because, although both communities were basically friendly to the British, everyone carried the long, razor-sharp machete, known as a cutlass, used for cutting cane or grass; it was never sheathed, and the scars and missing appendages, from children upwards, showed its potential effect if arrest were resisted. Although the single coast road could be controlled, there was a network of tracks and footpaths along the dams, along which Indian youths could speed silently in gangs with the ubiquitous airgun; coconut shells filled with paraffin and petrol made effective incendiaries, if lobbed at night into the unglazed windows of the universal wooden huts on stilts. Many of the Indians were furious with the Africans for running an effective strike against the PPP Government, and the two isolated African communities were at risk. If they were attacked the African majority in Georgetown and Wismar could exact, as they had before and would do after our tour, a terrible retribution on the Indian minority. In a country exasperated by shortages and at the most humid part of the year the influence of irresponsible demagoguery from both sides, coupled with cheap rum, was on the point of leading to a tragedy.

Back in Georgetown, the CO and Capt Holroyd secured one wing of Queen's College, the only secondary school in the Colony, and used the convenient chalk to allocate classrooms to the Advance Party. A tropical rainstorm blew through the slatted wall and a starving mouse had to be driven with boots from 24-hour ration biscuits. Late that night the strike ended, since our arrival had made apparent to the PNC the intention of the British Government to intervene. Mr Duncan Sandys, Commonwealth and Colonial Secretary, was to come out to investigate the situation. However, sporadic murder and arson continued, since communal tempers had now been aroused, and it was the Battalion's task to take over the coastal rural areas and to restore order.

The CO had to draw up rules of engagement and other standing orders with Capt Mitford-Slade. Radio communications, other than those between some sugar estates or police stations, were difficult. Capt Henshaw and his signallers climbed the roof and strung aerials between palms, but companies tended to be inside the first bounce of sky wave and rather far for ground wave. Transport, other than our eight Land Rovers, had to be hired by Capt Treneer Michell from Indian contractors, who provided luridly coloured trucks without canopy or sides. Capt Shreeve and SQMS Williams, ACC, explored the markets, where pineapples, bananas and paw-paws were delicious, but many other commodities were unrecognizable. After D Company's saturation patrolling, the violence had moved across the Demerara to WCD, where Den Amstel was in a state of siege, so Maj Stileman was ordered to take his A Company over the ferry and assert control. His previous service with the robust Police Commissioner, Mr Peter Owen, when they were both in Somaliland, had already put co-operation with the police on the best possible footing. His intervention now was positive and just in time. His excellent platoon commanders made their presence felt tirelessly, but it was his own Christian leadership which won the day. After another murder and further arson, he summoned the elders of both communities and persuaded them to meet. He reminded them that, before the politicians had promoted racialism, they had all been tolerant neighbours, and that no one could profit from violence. They agreed, and asked them to put this over to their restless young men. This was swiftly done, and by the vigilance of patrols and the old-fashioned concern—described by the Governor as in the best style of the former District Commissioners—of officers and NCOs in dealing with local problems order was restrored astride the Demerara.

At New Amsterdam a Coldstream patrol had been forced to open fire on a gang, inflicting casualties, and the Berbice was a hotbed of agitation and rumour. While Maj Chevis and the rest of C Company were held in reserve at Battalion HQ, his platoon, commanded by Lt C. J. P. Miers, was detached there. Regretfully, this young officer, a Sword of Honour winner and successful artist, had to be later sent to reinforce 1 Green Jackets in Borneo where his good work won him a Mention in Despatches. Lt Graham Wigan simultaneously took the Recce Platoon as far as the Courantyne border, using the local capacity for rumour to increase his numbers a hundredfold. After the violence stopped, the next thing was to get the sugar cut, but all the workers were chary of passing the cane brakes at dawn and dusk for fear of ambush. Maj Guy pioneered an escort system, followed by other Companies as confidence grew. Gradually the tall chimneys on the estates, their names telling of the colonial succession— Uitvlught, La Bonne Intention, Good Hope—began to puff smoke, and canefields blazed, to kill the snakes and weeds, before cutting. The police were encouraged to join patrols, and gradually the cane-workers were weaned of escorts, which appeared randomly and then imperceptibly dwindled away.

Brig K. Trevor had brought out a skeleton 2 Brigade HQ from Plymouth as part of the emergency deployment, and has assumed command of the Garrison as the Coldstream left. It was he who informed the CO that, although their work had restored order, the Battalion—having left at the shortest notice—was to stay on for six-month tour; this would see the Colony through constitutional talks now scheduled for the Autumn. The CO toured companies to break this unwelcome news. One of his tasks was greatly eased by the agreement of three officers, Capts Henshaw, Mitford-Slade and Gurney, due shortly to be married, to remain in the Colony as an example of solidarity with the 40 Riflemen in the same predicament; the latter could not, of course, afford to fly home. The very great number of young Riflemen, with even younger wives and small children, isolated in hirings for miles around Colchester or with their parents posed a problem encountered for the first time. Mrs Mills and Mrs Fowley formed a team which visited families; helped by experienced wives and backed by Maj Hills and Capt Lamb, the needs of families were assessed. The arrival of some reinforcements and baggage in September allowed those individuals with greatest family problems to be flown home, and the introduction of a newsletter served also to keep families in touch. On another occasion, shortly after arrival, companies had to be informed of a sad event. A very careful briefing, after reconnaissance of the town and talks with the police, had been given by the IO, Lt Gamble, to all those in HQ or in reserve in Georgetown before they were allowed to walk out in pairs. Unfortunately, a Rifleman left his pair and died from injuries received; it says much for the discipline of the Battalion that neither on this nor at any other time during the tour were Riflemen involved in retaliation, violence or other crimes in a colony where these were endemic, and not a single court-martial had to be held.

The generosity on sugar estates had allowed companies in ECD and WCD to occupy empty quarters, usually at platoon strength. The facilities were good and made up for the inability to walk out, except in Georgetown. Regular contact at daily joint meetings was, however, maintained with the Police. In the same way the Brigadier and the two COs, with the Police Commissioner, had reported to the Governor each evening. It was soon possible to draw up a programme of company reliefs. Small Officers' and Warrant Officers' and Sergeants' Messes were temporarily established in Georgetown. To get the Junior NCOs Cadre completed, Maj Parker reconnoitred Takama, the old volunteer force training camp 150 miles from Georgetown. Finding the track almost impassable, the cadre under Capt C. J. H. Gurney was routed by boat up the Berbice river, with C/Sgt Lerwill in charge of administration, including the revival of his butchery experience on local livestock. Tactics and field firing were well executed in an area of savannah, which had formerly been the goal of cattle drives down the jungle trail from the great Rupununi savannahs far to the South West.

By the end of August the Grenadiers had run their cadres and were ready to relieve our Battalion, which managed to squeeze into the old hospital, the rest house and other accommodation at Atkinson Field in early September. Before leaving the coast the flag had been shown in remoter areas—by Capt J. V. Keyte on an island in the Essequibo, by Lt Dunning across that river and by 2/Lt A. D. McGrigor at a mine near the Venezuelan border. It was a matter of pride that strict weapon-handling drills had prevented anyone being killed or injured by accidental discharge throughout operations.

Lt Gamble, an experienced leader of expeditions, was thwarted to find himself organizing a successive wave of projects for others. However, he went on the first of these, to the Kaieteur Falls, at 741 feet sheer the third highest in the world, and a magnificent sight as the great Potaro river plunges over a sandstone lip into the 15-mile gorge cut over the centuries. The CO and his party went the easy way by amphibian aircraft, which landed above the Kaieteur. Promotion nearly accelerated when a canoe containing the Adjutant, MTO, IO and him almost sped over the falls thanks to Amerindian inefficiency in high water. Maj Stileman and 17 of A Company pioneered the route by ferry to Bartica, truck through the jungle and by boat portage and foot up the Potaro. By the time the Battalion left BG, 150 all ranks had made the expedition to the Falls successfully.

The concentration at Atkinson Field, with a pleasant Echelon of Grenadiers, allowed centralized messing. It was also an opportunity to put over the concept of self-discipline to a very young Battalion. There was only one road to Georgetown 20 miles away and a special shift of liberty truck drivers was organized nightly. To the relief of the Battalion the very few tiresome characters soon found themselves restricted to camp as IS risks, where they could swim and see a film, but not annoy their fellows by unpunctuality on return transport, drunkenness or misconduct.

Once concentrated, training was developed in a progressive and interesting series of phases. The first was the perfection of IS drills, culminating in a Brigade exercise in Georgetown. Moving by night to Queen's College, the Battalion had rapidly to set up control points, disperse mock riots and organize cordons, all carried out in traditionally restive parts of that primitive wooden city; our speed and efficiency clearly impressed the observant local populace. This phase was deliberately repeated at the end of October, during the Constitutional Conference, when realistic inter-company IS drill competitions were run in daylight by Brigade, in which each of our Companies won their round conclusively after careful preparation.

During September a change-over of certain key figures took place, to fit aircraft movements, bringing in some reinforcements and a dance band, which enlivened the evenings. Maj Parker left for a staff appointment in the Far East, having been very largely responsible for the smooth emplanement of the Battalion for the move out. He later brought the Battalion back from the Far East, and, with his motor-battalion experience, took it into its successful assumption of the mechanized role. His successor for the rest of the tour was Maj R. S. Stewart-Wilson, MC, 3rd Green Jackets, who expended much imagination and energy on training and expeditions before going off to command the Staffords. Maj Guy also left at this time, and, since he later commanded the 1st

Battalion The Royal Green Jackets, he leaves this story. One of our best post-war officers, he was awarded the DSO when in command in a key sector of Belfast and currently is a Major General, as Chief of Staff HQ BAOR. His relief in D Company was Maj J. A. Molesworth St Aubyn, who nobly returned straight from a separated tour on the staff in Borneo, and whose company on bird-watching sorties was much appreciated by the CO.

The opportunity was taken to send Capts Holroyd and McCausland home to work for the Staff College exam, which they passed. Meanwhile, despite considerable pain (which later necessitated removal of a kidney), Capt Keyte took over the combined HQ and B Company.

By this time the Battalion knew that it was at long last due for an overseas accompanied tour, relieving 1st Green Jackets in Penang, with operational tasks in Borneo, starting in early 1965. All training that the CO set his Battalion thereafter was with this working up for operations in mind. In particular, the development of individual self-reliance and the building up of platoon and company teams within a Battalion frame-work was given high priority. Basic jungle training drills could be practised in BG, and fortunately Maj Stileman and Cpl Cahill had Malayan Emergency experience. A cadre was run for company instructors, and then each Company was deployed in the higher jungle along the creeks not far from Atkinson Field. Platoons patrolled against each other, based on camps where the perimeter vine and track, the water point and the silent routine dominated all, the latter only broken by the dawn roaring of howler monkeys. Hammocks, whose use originated with the Amerindians, to keep men off the damp, ant-infested jungle floor, were improvised from lightweight blankets until many brought their own local cotton ones. Since there were no 24-hour ration packs, rice and curry were bought locally and, with bully beef, individual jungle rations were created in plastic bags. The great benefit of this was that all learnt to navigate confidently in jungle, where even the map was improvised from an old logging sketch and brought up to date by the Intelligence Section.

In parallel with this the first individual tests were being prepared for and passed to allow more progressive training thereafter.

Before the long 12-hour tropical nights spent in a hammock became too tiresome, Companies took on the problems of savannah operations. The weather had become drier since August, and with the temperature in the 80s and cooler at night, the breeze rippling the scrub perfectly tempered the sun. The only landmarks were distant jungle strips along widing creeks, the only water in a sandy plateau. Contact had been made by the CO with Arawaks, the peaceful original Amerindian inhabitants, and expeditions were made to play cricket there; on one company exercise an Amerindian bitten by an alligator was contacted and evacuated. Nearer camp a good jungle range and section field firing range were created to bring out quick ambush drills. Sufficient mortars and anti-tank guns had been flown out in September to allow specialist cadres to be run.

The culmination of the jungle and savannah training was a Battalion exercise, in which Inkerman Company of the Grenadiers and our Recce Platoon were the enemy. Skirmishing drills were applied to the terrain, in which companies had first to open jungle trails before breaking out into the savannah. C Company had been landed in the enemy's rear by river boat, but Maj Chevis's Riflemen paid for this luxury in having to hack a path across a jungle creek by night to cut off the enemy retreat. The final assault was made to the cackle of waking guans and parrots, as an American B50 accurately bombed the enemy camp with flour bombs. The Battalion, supported by only one Land Rover per company, had literally been fighting for its water across the sandy plateau, and the 35-mile foot advance in 90° Fahrenheit was a most creditable performance. The use of buglers to indicate the progress of skirmishing wings in scrub too dense for small radios had lent a touch of the Peninsula to the energetic tactics.

Thanks to Maj Stewart-Wilson and Lt Gamble, expeditions were always out from the Battalion. The former pioneered an informal survey of wild country on the Brazilian border at Orinduik, whence Lt Mead brought back blowpipes. Others enjoyed the breezy Southern savannahs of the Rupununi. This area normally accessible only by air was largely owned by a legendary ranching clan, who sadly found themselves in revolt against the government a few years later. The founder had opened a Cattle Trail from Lethem to Takama at the end of the first war, which was in use till 1957. It was decided to send a small expedition up the trail from Mackenzie to see if it was still usable for surface movement of troops; a lavishly equipped University party had used it in 1957, and two years previously the Public Works Department had opened it for some engineers. However, no British troops had since even got over the first river.

The Recce Platoon under Lt Graham Wigan was given the task, with Cpl O'Hara and Rfn Coyne of the Assault Pioneers. The latter under Sgt Horsley had also constructed a bridge from jungle materials to aid local traffic, and were to help the expedition as far as the Canister Falls on the Demerara. The myriad deadfalls encountered had to be cleared by axe and saw, since there were no power tools. 55 miles out from Mackenzie, the upper Demerara was crossed by making an Irish bridge of rocks. The 21 miles to the upper Essequibo river was traversed with much difficulty on greasy steep slopes. Amerindians were encountered, and, since the radio communications by sky-wave were working, the 2IC managed to contact balata (wild rubber) boats upstream to improvise a ferry. Time was running out, however, since the Platoon had to be back for operational reasons by a fixed date, and the Trail beyond the river was found to deteriorate rapidly. After a Grumman amphibian had flown in much-needed spares, the expedition returned to report conclusively: 'The Lethem Trail can no longer be considered a practicable surface route to the Rupununi, except in the dry season and with much time and route preparation.'

It was important to retain the confidence of the two communities during the move towards constitutional and electoral change, so companies were covertly despatched to potentially restive areas on the coast. A dawn cordon would quietly be found ringing known trouble-makers as they awoke, to the amusement of their more respectable neighbours. The community as a whole much enjoyed the accompanying dance band at a subsequent party. As a pleasant way of demonstrating the presence of highly disciplined and efficient troops, the first Tattoo ever held was staged on Georgetown Cricket Ground by 2 Grenadiers and our Battalion. A D Company drill squad, trained to a high standard by CSM F. Williams, was complemented by an amusing A Company IS action, in which Capt Keyte played a realistic Sheikh on a donkey. While C Company took part in the

23   Bugle Major R. Silver, MSM

Before his death in Berlin in 1961 he had completed 30 years of admirable service and had laid the foundations of post-war Green Jacket bugling.

24   Cpl D. Hunt, A Company, 2nd Green Jackets, The King's Royal Rifle Corps, with The Rifle Brigade Cup

He was Champion Young Soldier in 1961 and rose to be RSM of the same Battalion in 1978.

25 The Commanding Officer, 2nd Green Jackets, The King's Royal Rifle Corps, gives out orders on training in Cyrenaica, January 1963

Left to Right—Maj Elliott RA, Lt G. R. Shreeve, Maj R. M. Parker, Lt Col J. H. P. Curtis, MC.

26 The Team which won the KRRC Cup, Queen Victoria Trophy and many other events, and which provided the Queen's Medallist, in 1964.

Left to Right
Back Row—Cpl Winkworth, Rfn Child, Sgt Jenkins, Cpl Clarke, Sgt Fry, Cpl Witham, Cpl Stanger, Sgt R. Smith (Queen's Medal), Rfn Ball.
Seated—CSM Airey, S/Sgt Tuttiet, REME, Lt D. Gascoigne, Maj P. Welsh, Lt Col G. H. Mills, OBE, Lt D. Mead, Lt R. Hill, CSM Coram.

PT display and did the stage management, Lt Graham Wigan made a risky free-fall descent in a high wind, which at the last moment took him over the pavilion, fortunately unscathed.

After a lively Christmas, the Battalion finally flew home, without the expected relief by Queen's Own Buffs, between 2–13 January 1964. That their vigilance had been necessary was highlighted when a final outbreak of violence later took place before the colony moved to independence as Guyana. However, their swift and sudden arrival had produced a calm, which lasted a year and undoubtedly prevented a slide into widespread inter-communal violence. Few who served there will forget the friendly and normally easy-going people or the sight and sound of parrots and toucans flighting over the jungle at dawn, but it was more than time to go home.

Before leaving Lt Col Mills received the following letter of appreciation from HE The Governor, Sir Ralph Grey:

> As you are about to take your Battalion back to the United Kingdom after completing a six month tour of duty here, I write to thank you for all that 2nd Green Jackets have done in and for British Guiana during your time here.
>
> You came to us at very short notice, when we were in unhappy difficulties and the Battalion showed their quality at once in their immediate readiness for duty in aid of the civil power. On the same afternoon that the first troops arrived, they were on duty on the East Coast Demerara. In spite of strange conditions all ranks quickly adapted themselves and exercised a wise, calm and helpful influence in restoring calm in a troubled area.
>
> In all parts of the country where Riflemen were deployed on duty they made themselves quietly useful; but I should specially mention the success in impartially keeping the peace that was achieved on the West Coast Demerara. Communities at odds with one another quickly learnt to respect and to value the unifying influence of the Green Jackets.
>
> I am grateful to you personally and to all officers and other ranks for your help. I share your relief that it was never necessary for the Battalion to fire a shot here save in training; but there were many instances in which an obvious quiet readiness for duty was effective and I must pay tribute to the discipline and efficiency that have been maintained in months of standing by, when boredom and the effects of peace-time service far from home might have dulled the Battalion's edge.
>
> Please give my grateful thanks to all and my best wishes for happiness and success in your next duties.

Sir Ralph Grey was later to be Governor of the Bahamas before becoming the last Governor-General of Northern Ireland under the old constitution, in a crisis which saw splendid service by all three Royal Green Jacket Battalions, including many of the Riflemen to whom he was now saying farewell. The seal of official approval on the Battalion's work in British Guiana was finally set by the award of the OBE to the Commanding Officer in the 1964 Birthday Honours.

The emergency tour had been an invaluable step in the consolidation of the Regular Battalion. The Riflemen who returned home were matured as well as bronzed; self-confidence was soundly based on achievement in everything to which they had set their hand, including self-discipline. Teams who had worked and played together knew and trusted each other, and among the young families the ability of the Regiment to look after its own was appreciated. A very small number of disruptive men had been identified, isolated and discharged, to the relief of their fellows.

During a well-earned leave several key appointments changed hands. Maj Stileman took over as 2IC and settled down to formalize the previously described system of Battalion Tests, which had been tried out in 1963. His A Company was taken over by Maj G. R. W. Carter, MBE, 3rd Green Jackets, last seen in 2nd 60th. Maj P. M. Welsh took over C from Maj Chevis, and Capt McCausland took over D from Maj J. A. Molesworth St Aubyn for the Summer. The latter, after much valuable training work for the Regiment, ended his Green Jacket service as 2IC with the 3rd on yet another emergency Far Eastern tour; he then retired as a Lt Col to the South West, holding the office of High Sheriff of Cornwall among other appointments. Maj R. A. Pascoe of the 1st was OC HQ Company until taking over D in the Autumn, while Maj M. Hills and Capt G. Crossman retired after most useful last tours.

Our new Brigade Commander was Brig D. Fraser, late Grenadier Guards and one of the keenest intellects in the Army. A very rapid understanding was reached between him and the Battalion by means of his training directives and personal visits. He made the much-appreciated comment to the CO after an excellent administrative inspection, that the Riflemen on parade in full kit—as for Spearhead deployment—portrayed for him an old Peninsula battalion of Rifles. The climatic change was met by vigorous PE Tests and run-downs on the range, as the Battalion classified. This was as well, for the Battalion was to find itself deployed from the tropics to beyond the Arctic Circle before mid-summer. In March the Battalion was suddenly allotted the Allied Mobile Force (Land) role, the NATO Fire Brigade. The newly appointed Commander was luckily the delightful Maj Gen The Hon Michael Fitzalan Howard, late Scots Guards, and the CO, whose French, German and basic Italian were fully used, found himself at short notice at Heidelberg for briefing. After training to platoon level, Companies practised deployment drills for all phases of European warfare in a Battalion setting at Stanford in May. A useful Battalion Group exercise, including a Battery, Sapper Troop, and all units of the British Logistic Support Unit under Maj Pascoe, followed, for the next time all would meet was in Northern Norway.

Very little could be found out about the potential operational deployment area, except that in 1963 June had been very hot. Luckily, the CO had ordered full winter clothing to be worn, since there was snow down to tree-level on the hills round Bardufoss Airfield, 70 miles North of Narvik, as the Battalion flew in. The vehicles and heavy equipment were moved by sea to a fishing village near by, and Norwegian Army trucks were provided for our three-ton drivers. In the pine groves of the concentration area we got to know our allied Norweigian, Alpini and Belgian Parachute Battalions and practised special skirmishing withdrawal drills evolved by the CO for the steep glacier-worn valleys. In a company, two platoons were thrown forward well up the scrubby hillside, overlooking any threat to the third blocking the road to the rear. The aim was to force a continual series of laborious and costly deployments uphill and was very effective. In the dusk of an Arctic summer's night C and A Companies crept forward to the Battalion's selected forward positions covering a narrows in the great

Lyngenfjord, itself a critical sector where a Finnish salient comes in from the East. Every team in the Battalion Group was well exercised as the full weight of Norwegian Brigade North advanced. In our sector we had useful intelligence from the Norwegian Home Guard. The enemy Commander told the CO afterwards that although they knew the ground backwards they were continually surprised. Submarines and PT boats were enfiladed by Mobats, and Maj Carter's A Company devastated a US Marine landing from unlocated positions and again when they tried to outflank us over the mountains. Just evading flank thrusts by ski troops, the Battalion blew the main bridge and fell back behind a low wire barrier, long prepared by Sappers and threading unseen through the birch woods. Prisoners were taken but none lost by us in aggressive patrolling, until Alpini moved over the peaks, the Belgians by assault craft and the Norwegians by helicopter into the enemy's rear. It had been great fun, and a most valuable test of drills and communications; not least had been the evident competence of the Battalion, judged by critical Allied eyes, and the ability to maintain operations, including watchkeeping at all levels in a day which lasted 24 hours—self-heating tins of soup were invaluable in the chill of the Northern small hours. The most remarked feature had been the friendliness of the Norwegian Army, many of the older officers having served in Britain in World War II; in particular Colonel Lund, a former Defence Minister, who had commanded the battalion on our flank, was a mine of helpful local information.

The Allied parade at the end of the exercise was in fact the last physical deployment with the AMF(L), since another exercise, which Maj Stileman had reconnoitred in South Eastern Turkey, was cancelled because of a Cyprus crisis. However, July was very busy, since NCO and specialist cadres were run, while the remaining Riflemen completed the conversion course to the GPMG, on which D Company had conducted trials four years earlier. Meanwhile at Bisley the Battalion team put up what was arguably the best performance in the history of the Regiment. Under very close pressure from the Parachute Brigade, whose commander Brigadier R. C. Gibbs, late 60th, was present, the team shot supremely well to win the KRRC Cup, the Small Arms and the Northampton. CSM Airey and Sgts Jenkins and Fry did well, but three members shot outstandingly. Sgt R. Smith won the Queen's Medal as Army Champion and the Army 100 Cup. Maj Welsh was 1st in Class A of the Roupell, while Cpl Winkworth won that cup and that of the Manchester Regiment, besides being 1st in Class B of the Whitehead. With Depot help we won the Methuen, using the SLR against the other Services with their more accurate No 4 Rifle. Shooting for the Army in the National Meeting, Maj Welsh won the Green Jackets Cup and together with Sgts Smith and Jenkins won the Hamilton Leigh, besides several other 2nd placings in both meetings. A Battalion lunch was held outside the inadequate Dining Hall to congratulate the team and display their trophies. To be the best shooting battalion in the Army and to have its Champion Shot gave a feeling of confidence to all Riflemen; a year later they were to exact a devastating toll on any enemy within range.

In its last year in England the Battalion was to be found at the top in many other fields. Capt J. R. E. Nelson and Lt M. Dunning won the Army Rackets Inter-Regimental Doubles in fine style. They went on, with Maj Welsh, and Capts McCausland and Hopton, to win for the first time the Army Squash against a confident School of Artillery. The District Cricket and Athletics were also won, and some excellent local performances were put in on the Rugger field. This was thanks to Maj Stileman, who had stimulated great enthusiasm in British Guiana despite the climate. Our two Fijians, Cpl Yasa and L/Cpl Buliciri, were particularly hard to put down, and the former had even played for BG against Trinidad.

After block leave in August, the Battalion, under command of Maj Stileman, became enemy on the Salisbury Plain and Stanford phases of a large 19 Brigade exercise, to which Lt Col Mills was Chief Umpire and Assistant Director. The exercise was a most imaginative period of six weeks, with pauses for field maintenance and rest, and ranged as far North as Otterburn. From the Battalion's point of view it provided much-needed work with armour, artillery and aircraft.

In the first phase, after Lt M. H. Eustace's Recce Platoon had acted as a useful screen with the armour, Capt McCausland's D Company were flown in Royal Naval helicopters into an intermediate position. There were excellent tasks for tank and anti-tank gun alike, while A and C Companies swept the skyline from reverse slope positions. The *coup de main* seizure, by a patrol led by Sgt R. Smith, of an unsecured Avon bridge caused much alarm. The Battalion was glad, however, to leave the Plain, which it had crossed from Warminster to Tidworth, because airportable infantry in daylight had little scope for survival against armour.

The last phase at Stanford, where the Battalion was aggressively probing a Brigade 'box', was more fun. After the Brigade's attention had been firmly drawn towards the North, the whole Battalion slipped round in daylight under the noses of an unwary but truculent Commando. To their fury the Marines were suddenly and overwhelmingly skirmished out of their company positions, and Maj Pascoe, who had taken over D Company, overran their HQ, just as the evening meal was being issued. Forced to withdraw, their return for revenge after dark ran into more trouble before the Battalion slipped away. It had been a good last work-up for the future Borneo team, and the Battalion marched past Lt Gen Darling in Rifle time with considerable panache, from its traditional position on the left of a great Brigade Group parade.

For five weeks from mid-October, until the Far Eastern Advance Party left on 20 November 64, a final drive was made on Individual Training. Capt Hopton ran continuation training for the large drafts from the Depot, while Maj Carter ran three progressive courses for Trained Riflemen, covering as many skills and drills appropriate to the Far East as could be taught without a jungle. Lt Dunning ran an Anti-tank and Mortar Cadre, while Capt Nelson and Lt Mead trained the Signallers and Drivers of their new appointments. Capt R. P. Montgomery, MBE, who had transferred to the Regiment from the King's African Rifles, trained senior NCOs who might find themselves platoon commanders or Sergeants on detachment. Meanwhile, many younger officers were away on courses, in particular 2/Lt M. M. K. Yasa. Having been a very popular Corporal in A Company, he had passed the Mons OCS Course and been accepted as an SSC officer in the Regiment, the first commissioned Fijian. Lt Col Mills, determined to get him off to a good start as the best token of our alliance with the Fiji Regiment, sent him on ahead to learn Malay and then meet up with Maj Welsh, his Company Commander, on the Jungle Warfare course; he would then be two skills ahead of everyone else when the Battalion arrived.

On the administrative side Capt Shreeve, who had had very little leave, slaved over the mountain of paperwork then necessary to disperse the equipment after the close of training, for the barracks was not being immediately taken over. By much hard work the Battalion in the event marched out leaving everything in excellent order, but by that time Capt Lamb was already in Penang starting to take over the barracks and quarters from 1st Green Jackets. There the 2IC, Maj O. Pratt, would fill the same appointment for the first six months in our Battalion, communicating his knowledge of the Far East most helpfully. Maj Stileman, after an intensely active and useful period organizing an excellent training cycle, later commanded the Rifle Depot, where his innovations earned a richly deserved OBE. Capt Mitford-Slade ended a most efficient Adjutancy of 18 months when he handed over to Capt Nelson.

It had long been mutually arranged that Lt Col Mills and this outgoing team would make all arrangements for UK training, administration and the emplanement of the Battalion, allowing Lt Col E. N. W. Bramall, MC, the new Commanding Officer, to concentrate on Far Eastern training and future operations. During the Autumn these two good friends had worked together on composing the best possible Platoon and Company teams of Officers, WOs and NCOs, and on the handling of family separation and other problems, for which the BG tour had been a rehearsal. The legacy which Lt Col Bramall inherited was a happy Battalion, as well trained individually and collectively as the Airportable role allowed, and confident that it could turn its hand to anything. It had matured, and a new style of self-discipline made it a natural partner at work or relaxing with other Arms, Services and races, while wives had become part of the larger Regimental family.

It was fitting that Lt Col Mills's leaving present to the Regiment was a portrait of Brig Gen Henry Bouquet, the first commanding officer of the Battalion, copied from an original primitive painting which he had traced in the States. Both Mrs Mills, who had done so much for the families, and he were descended from Americans active on the frontier of Bouquet's period. He therefore encouraged a study of the great Swiss and his Royal Americans to mark the 200th anniversary of Bushy Run and Bouquet's subsequent penetration to the forest bases of the Indians. Lt Col Bramall was now the right officer to lead the Battalion into a similar encounter. His predecessor was fortunate in being able to carry his interest in the careers of officers and soldiers successively through appointments at HQ The Royal Green Jackets and The Light Division to that of Director of Manning (Army). He was later the first Rifleman to be nominated for the post of Resident Governor of Her Majesty's Tower of London and Keeper of The Jewel House.

CHAPTER XIII

REGIMENTAL
REORGANIZATION AND
RIFLEMEN IN
THE BORNEO JUNGLE

(Maps: pages 298 and 302)

In the England from which our Battalion flew away at the end of January 1965 great changes were imminent. If at the end of this Volume Riflemen are seen to be well poised to tackle and surmount the problems occasioned by a waning interest in defence commitments at home and overseas, it will be because of wise leadership at the head and the enthusiasm, efficiency, and flexibility of those serving.

The three Colonels Commandant, under the Chairmanship of Field Marshal Sir Francis Festing, late CIGS, could see that a wave of Defence cuts was likely. Since they believed the Green Jackets to be one of the most forward-looking, viable and efficient organizations in the Army, they were determined that a situation must be created in which it would be impossible for Riflemen to lose their rightful place in the Order of Battle. It had been hoped by the Army Board that Brigades of Infantry would form large Regiments, thus sharing sources of recruits and of trained officers and men in a way which has, as this story has shown, long been the practice within the Green Jackets. Much amalgamation in the late '50s had made many of the surviving Infantry regiments reluctant to do this. However, our Colonels Commandant resolved—entirely voluntarily, and under no official pressure—that a New Regular Regiment, The Royal Green Jackets, should be formed, the Battalions numbering as before and initially with the old titles in brackets. In this way the old and valued traditions and unique heritage of the former Regiments could be preserved and held in common, and the priceless assets of some of the best officers in the Army and the Riflemen they had trained could be shared.

The full effects of this wise and courageous act will be best analysed by historians of The Royal Green Jackets. The preliminary announcement was made by Field Marshal HRH The Duke of Gloucester, when as Colonel in Chief 3rd Green Jackets he reopened the Rifle Depot on 29 May 65. The building in both Upper and Lower Barracks had been initiated by our Colonel Commandant, General Sir George Erskine, when he was C in C Southern Command, before his last appointment as Lieutenant Governor of Jersey. This splendid Rifleman was dying, and knew it, but courageously worked on as long as possible for his Regiment. Active in the formation of the new Regiment, he had formulated a more flexible policy for using Regimental funds to help those genuinely in need, and had been a source of wise advice to Commanding Officers, based on his own distinguished service in war, internal security operations and peace. In harness with him Lt Col A. G. Bennett had been a valuable Chairman of the Riflemen's Aid Society, as well as Secretary of the ARA, while Brig R. A. T. Eve, CBE, had done much thoughtful work on trusts, funds and property at Regimental HQ. One of the latter's sons, Maj J. R. T. Eve, had inaugurated the Parachuting Club, leading to the Display Team, and the first TA entry into Army Skiing, in which Lt J. J. Palmer-Tomkinson won the Giant Slalom; the other, Capt A. J. T. Eve, had organized the generous gift of a modern silver clock from all former 60th National Service officers in gratitude for the kindness shown to them by Regular Riflemen.

It was in fact the TA, including the Queen's Royal Rifles, in which those two were then serving, which was to be first under threat. 1965 saw the announcement of a major reorganization, to be effective on 1 April 67, by which the strength would be reduced from 110,000 to about 50,000; the old TA of Haldane's Act would go, and a Territorial and Volunteer Reserve (TAVR) would be established under a new Act. Although the old TA had been too large to equip properly, and its Order of Battle and state of preparedness did not match the Regular Army's needs for instant readiness against attack without long mobilization, the brusque methods used were ungracious. By chance Lt Col G. H. Mills took over the original plan, and was able behind the scenes to humanize as many details as possible in the next year of heated debate, both inside Parliament and in the country at large.

The QRR under Lt Col Loudon-Shand had been well recruited and efficient, and this was recognized in his promotion to Brevet Colonel and the award of an OBE. The mixture of former NS and Regular officers had made for imaginative leadership, and the wisdom and efficiency of Maj L. Grout and Maj A. Lamb as successive QMs gave a sound base from which Capt C. Henshaw could organize training. The lively 'Ever Ready' platoon had trained with the Queen's Own Rifles of Canada in 95 degrees of frost, including the wind chill factor. Luckily, there was, to take over at this juncture, an experienced Territorial CO, Lt Col The Viscount Eden, TD, with many useful contacts, not least with the Honorary Colonel, the Rt Hon Richard Wood, PC, DL, MP, whose wise counsel was invaluable throughout a critical period. The other Green Jacket COs concerned, Lt Col C. Humphreys, MC, formerly 60th and now commanding the Oxfordshire & Buckinghamshire Light Infantry TA, and Lt Col T. Wallis, London Rifle Brigade Rangers TA, were well known to him, and a unanimous approach could be taken. Lt Col Eden had recently played a part when his father, the Earl of Avon, had laid a wreath during a moving ceremony at Calais on 22 May 65, 25 years after the Defence. Lt Gen Sir Euan Miller, Maj Gen E. A. W. Williams (soon to be our Colonel Commandant), Maj Gen T. H. Acton and Lt Col Ellison-Macartney were among the survivors of the action in an Allied and inter-Service commemoration.

A Territorial Home Defence component of the new TAVR was rapidly abandoned as soon as the Government secured a larger majority. The Volunteer deployment secured by our obvious viability, however, saw companies in Oxford, Buckingham Gate and Sun Street, three old TA Battalion HQs, while Battalion HQ and HQ Company was to be at Davies Street. By unanimous wish the old Territorial names were to be superseded by the title of the 4th (Volunteer) Battalion The Royal Green Jackets, emphasizing the unity of the Regiment. The increased liability was matched by the improved equipment, and for the first time a steady trickle of Riflemen began to join the Volunteers after finishing Regular service, visible evidence that the new Regiment was binding itself even closer together than ever before. After stepping down to allow Lt Col Wallis the initial command, Lt Col The Viscount Eden later earned an OBE and a Brevet Colonelcy for his work with the new Battalion. He ensured the continuance of historic links with the Livery Companies and with Lloyds, and the support of the former Regiments' Trusts. A further personal service to the Regiment was his creation of the Royal Green Jackets London Club at Davies Street, which has been the greatest asset, not least in displaying to visitors a Rifleman's special brand of informal comradeship. His successor as Club Chairman, M. H. Glazier, a respected Queen Victoria's Rifleman of Calais 1940 vintage, has continued to do much for Regimental affairs, not least in ensuring his brother officers wore impeccable headgear on many a ceremonial parade.

The undeniable efficiency and happiness of the 4th (Volunteer) Battalion was able to speak for itself when the TAVR was later reviewed in the '70s. The Battalion was asked to raise Volunteers in Buckinghamshire and to expand further in the traditional Rifleman's area of West Ham. As Buckingham Gate was affected by near-by demolition, a move into the better recruiting area of Fulham was made. Although this story has trespassed into that of the Royal Green Jackets, it is right that Riflemen should see as a whole the steady and natural progress of the originally independent Volunteer Regiments, first into the broad and invaluable alliance of Territorials with Regulars, forged in two World Wars, and finally to a full union, voluntarily conceived, of all Green Jacket Regulars and Volunteers in one splendid new Regiment.

The story of Regimental support in the Cadet field is of loyal perseverance despite the many changes of policy throughout the period. Col R. G. H. Sutton was awarded a well-deserved OBE and continued his support as Honorary Colonel to our 1st Cadet Battalion, commanded by Lt Col G. Hanson, in North West London. With Colonel The Viscount Eden, OBE, TD, DL, as Honorary Colonel, the 1 (Royal Green Jackets) Group, North East London, finally united all Cadet Riflemen in that most traditional of areas.

Though the Rifle Depot had always been a Green Jacket affair, the 60th had made a particular contribution during the early 1960s. The Brigade Colonel, succeeding Col R. A. St. G. Martin as previously mentioned, was Col Davies-Scourfield, but in 1963 Lt Col P. Pardoe handed over to Lt Col R. Workman, 1st Green Jackets. Other 60th Riflemen was RSM Massingham, ORQMS Robbins and RQMS Evans, followed by RQMS Solomons, while Maj J. Radclyffe commanded HQ and Capt C. Adami the Junior Riflemen's Company. Bandmaster R. Rodgers trained junior Bandsmen until 1964, when, to everyone's pleasure, he was awarded the MBE and granted a Commission. A particularly experienced RB team on the training side in Maj G. Wemyss and Capt J. Foley led to a shooting zenith at Bisley in 1963, when Cpl Notley won the Queen's Medal, Gold Jewel and Manchester Cup, and the Worcester with Cpl White. The Rifle Depot won the Staff & Schools Match and the Minor Units Cup for the third and, in 1964, fourth years running; our recruits as well as trained Riflemen could have the utmost confidence in their instructors in the prime Infantry skill.

Turning back now to the Regular Battalion, it must be remembered that The

King's Royal Rifle Corps had not been on full operations since Palestine, just after World War II. Held in BAOR by the motor-battalion role, the Regiment had missed the Korean War, the Malayan Emergency and the Mau Mau Rebellion. When relieved of the motor-battalion commitment, which had once afforded such a field for the swiftness and boldness of our motto, the 1st Battalion had served in Libya without seeing action. Northern Ireland in a peaceful phase, and Berlin during the building of the Wall, had brought only a hint of past or future thunder, and the very speed and effectiveness of our intervention in British Guiana had doused the embers before they could become a flame. There were thus many senior ranks in 2nd Green Jackets who were three-quarters of the way through their service, and who by staying loyally with their Battalion found themselves without even a General Service medal, unlike the 1st or 3rd, and indeed the Infantry as a whole. Not only was this personally a matter of concern to professional Riflemen, but it was particularly unsatisfactory to a Regiment whose roll of Battle Honours was the longest. They had successfully met every peacetime challenge, but, counselled by successive Commanding Officers to beware of mutual admiration or hubris, had even in the hour of triumph kept a certain modesty, always conscious that only the oldest had been submitted to the ultimate soldierly test in action. The exhilaration of the younger Riflemen was unlimited in the prospect of the Far East, a good base in Penang and tours of action in Borneo. Those who would command from section level up were also conscious of the responsibility for the lives of these young men and for the good name of the Regiment, resting in their hands. As we shall see, intelligent leadership discharged all tasks with remarkably low casualties.

The first task was to fly the 600 all ranks and 165 families out to Penang. Despite some delay through unserviceability of aircraft all the 24-hour-long flights, with short stops at Istanbul and Bombay, were completed by 2 February 65. Capt A. Lamb and Sgt Alsop had been taking over married quarters since before Christmas, and assuring the local Amahs that they would be taken on by our families. At the same time Rifle Company and Platoon Commanders and Sergeants had arrived at the Jungle Warfare Course in Southern Malaysia, so that a cadre of instructors would be ready to train their Riflemen. Carefully concealing their knowledge of basic jungle work, learnt in British Guiana, the cadre was found to make remarkably quick progress by the School.

The take-over from 1st Green Jackets, commanded by that former 60th Rifleman Lt Col D. House, OBE, MC, was particularly smooth, and his 2IC Maj O. Pratt, remained to fill the same appointment in the 2nd, to start off the first Borneo tour. Penang is an island 5 miles off the West coast of the Malay Peninsula, only 60 miles South of the Thai border. There is only one town, Georgetown, largely Chinese and a free port. The island has its own hill station reached by cable railway; with its friendly inhabitants, recreational facilities and the palm-fringed beaches for picnics it was the ideal station for all ranks. In particular, the spacious Minden Barracks on a hill overlooking the straits, its Messes shared with Garrison staff and much visited by the Royal Navy and other friends, was, despite its five-mile perimeter, an ideal situation in a climate which was, though humid, less enervating than Singapore.

There was, however, a very intensive programme ahead for the men, since the 2nd was to take over an operational area near Kuching, Sarawak, by the end of

April 65. Rifle Company Commanders were Maj Carter (A), Maj Welsh (C) and Maj Pascoe (D), as in 1964, so that they knew and were known by their men particularly well. Support Platoons had been used to bring Rifle Platoons up to a full operational strength, and the latter benefitted by the leavening of more experienced Officers, NCOs and Riflemen. B Company, commanded by Capt R. Montgomery, contained the Assault Pioneers and a Tracker/Recce Platoon. The latter was in fact commanded by Capt Montgomery in person, with Sgt Batey, a future RSM, as Platoon Sgt; it was trained to work with both Infantry Patrol Alsatians and tracker Labradors and Iban trackers of Borneo, following up enemy infiltrations and assessing the size and time of passage of the enemy party. The other addition was the Air Platoon of two 3 seater Sioux helicopters, 'Celer' and 'Audax', piloted by Capt R. Adshead, 1/6 Gurkhas, and Capt C. Harrison, 3rd Green Jackets. Well maintained by a team led by CPO Nesbitt, RN attached, they were known as 'Rifle Green Airways' and fulfilled a key role on recce, casualty evacuation and as CO's rover. Maj J. Radclyffe, who had taken over HQ Company, was to be OC Rear Party, backed by Maj A. Lamb as Rear QM, Capt G. Shreeve being Forward QM as in Guiana. The Band, under Bandmaster Tonks, with Band WO Barker, and Sgts White, Washington and Ashby, was to move over in part to Kuching for the last month of the tour, but Bugle Major Green and his buglers were fully employed in Borneo throughout. At Battalion HQ, under Lt Col Bramall, was Capt J. R. E. Nelson as Adjutant, Capt D. C. Gascoigne was Ops Officer, Capt A. S. G. Drew Signals and Lt R. M. Gamble as IO; RSM T. Fowley continued in that post until he was commissioned as QM in September 65, when RSM B. Rimmer took over as RSM from QRR (TA).

Jungle training started for Companies in the uncleared areas of Penang island, where basic skills were taught. Thereafter the Battalion went down to the Jungle Warfare School for three weeks, of which the final week was spent on a Battalion exercise. Companies trained hard on patrolling, harbouring, ambush drills and all the other techniques so important in the jungle. Returning to Penang at the end of March, there was under a month before the tour started, so fitness and marksmanship were pressed forward; even so, on the last 72-hour platoon exercise many realized their need for greater fitness. Once in Borneo, the constant patrolling produced a physical peak, which allowed the actions later described to take place.

The operational setting into which the Battalion was about to move must first be examined. The newly independent state of Malaysia—which then included Singapore—had incorporated the former British-administered territories in Borneo as East Malaysia in 1963. Running from the East, these were Sabah (British North Borneo) and Sarawak; the Sultanate of Brunei with its oil revenues lay in the middle, and had a direct relationship with Britain. Sarawak had been under the Brooke family from 1841 to 1946, when it was handed over to the Colonial Office, and all three territories were much less developed than the larger Southern part of Borneo, which had been properly mapped by the Dutch, and which Indonesia had now inherited. The Dyaks on the coast had links with Malaysia, but the original Iban and other tribesmen in their long houses tended to trade across the ill-defined international border running through dense jungle along the hilly and mountainous spine of the great island; on the cleared coastal lands were groups of Chinese. Not all of these welcomed Malaysian control, whether for the same Marxist reasons that had launched certain local Chinese into the long Malayan Emergency, or because the then Indonesian leadership saw a last chance for expansion as the British handed over. The tribesmen themselves were very vulnerable to terrorist pressure, if not protected in their remote jungle clearings. Winning their hearts and minds was to be a continual and delicate priority task.

The first action started in Brunei in the early morning of 8 December 1962, when there was an attempt to seize power in the rich Sultanate. 1st/2nd Goorkhas were flown there within the day, and their swift action nipped this coup in the bud, but not before Lt D. E. Stephens, who had been one of our NS recruits at Winchester and had served in the Queen's Westminsters, was killed in ambush. 1st Green Jackets moved rapidly into Borneo from Penang, as the British Government and Commonwealth responded to the wish of both the Malaysian Government and the majority of the local inhabitants that the territories should not pass by default into the hands of local terrorists or of the Indonesians, raiding from over the border as part of the so-called Confrontation. Gradually operations passed into a struggle to protect the local inhabitants from Indonesian Regular troops, or from raiding parties trained by them. The Indonesians had the initiative, since the British action was strategically defensive, and in the 1st Division of Sarawak its capital, Kuching, was only 25 miles from the border. They had the added advantage of a major river parallel to the border, whose Northward tributaries gave them administrative backing to base camps opposite many points of access. Hampered by maps which showed only the water courses and a spider's web of contours with few heights, the British had none the less the precious mobility afforded by the RN and RAF Wessex and Whirlwind helicopters, once an Indonesian thrust was detected; but this intelligence could only be gained by troops on the ground and the Iban Border Scouts working for them.

The Advance Party of 2nd Green Jackets left by air for Kuching on 28 April 65, followed closely by the Main Body, who travelled by sea. The four and a half months meant family separation, but at least there had been time to think problems out, and backed by members of the Ladies Club, Mrs Bramall, Maj Radclyffe, Maj Lamb, Mrs Fowley and others could provide advice and assistance. The sector taken over from 1st Scots Guards was a large one, stretching back from a 20-mile strip of the Indonesian border as far as the North Coast. Before giving details of the actions, it is useful to study the Commanding Officer's reflections written at the end of the tour; there is a reminiscent ring of Bouquet's training concepts in them.

Background

When the battalion arrived in the 1st Division of Sarawak in April 1965, shortly after a substantial British and Commonwealth reinforcement of the Borneo territories, the threat across the border from Indonesia was considerable. The enemy regular strength had trebled in the last six months and, only a few days previously, regular Indonesian troops had made a skilfully planned and bravely executed attack on a forward patrol base held by the 2nd Parachute Battalion; and only great gallantry on the part of the defenders had

prevented the post being overrun. There was indeed a very real threat that the
Indonesian Army might make a concerted thrust against the town of Kuching
which lay only 25 miles from the border.

Had this occurred the Brigade Commander intended to take the fullest
advantage of the mobility provided by the helicopters of the Royal Navy and
Royal Air Force. He planned to hold on securely to the forward patrol bases
along the border, maintaining them as necessary by helicopter and with the
help of airdrops. From these forward bases offensive patrols would be
launched to harry any enemy columns, firm bases or subsequent reinforcements which might be part of the drive towards Kuching. With these barbs
firmly planted in the enemy side, reserve companies of forward battalions and
any other reserves the Brigade Commander could muster would be moved by
helicopter to block and, with artillery and air support, destroy any enemy who
were threatening to break through. Given a good measure of air support
which we would have undoubtedly received from the Royal Air Force Tactical
Group—No 224 Group—this plan should have been successful in preserving
the integrity of Sarawak. It was the classical pattern for defence under limited
war conditions when there is little heavy equipment, but where the three
Services are obliged to work in close harmony and when we possess the
priceless mobility and ability to resupply provided by helicopters.

As it was the threat never developed. Our own build up of ground and air
forces deterred a major effort by Indonesian regular units, and the constant
and aggressive activity of our patrols limited the infiltration across the border
to manageable proportions. Subversion in the rear areas, which were
inhabited by Chinese near Lundu, Bau and Kuching itself, remained a serious
problem, for there any infiltration which did penetrate to any depth could
be given a refuge from which to carry out assassinations and sabotage; and
later on considerable military effort had to be put into supporting the
police, in resettlement operations, cordon and searches and following up
reports of terrorist bands. The primary task of each battalion remained
however to deter, by active patrolling, any would-be infiltration across
the border and, should this fail, to get the maximum information of the
enemy's movements so that he could be cut off and destroyed by helicopter-
borne reserves.

All this was an Infantry task 'par excellence', requiring skilled patrolling,
good platoon and sections tactics, accurate shooting, robustness and
endurance and a steady nerve. The fact that it was so successfully carried out,
and the Indonesian efforts rendered virtually ineffective, was a great tribute to
the British and Gurkha Infantryman. The excellence of the Gurkha soldier for
this type of warfare is taken for granted but, once he had been given time to
adjust himself and carry out adequate training in this new and very strange
environment, the British soldier proved himself capable of the same high
standards.

The patrol base

To achieve their aim, battalions adopted a fairly set pattern of defence behind
the border, the first important element of which was the forward patrol base.

This was established comparatively close to the border itself, anything from 1000–5000 yards, and had two main aims in view:

a. To provide a springboard from which patrols could operate, and a haven to which they could return, in comparative security, in order to receive a reasonable minimum of good administration (proper meals, showers, etc), without imposing an undue strain on helicopter resources.

b. To provide protection for border villages and a focal point for the gathering of intelligence on the activities of the enemy on the other side of the border.

Helicopter flying hours would not have stood up to mounting every patrol from a main base perhaps 20–30 miles to the rear, as well as meeting such other vital tasks as routine maintenance and movement of reserves. Moreover, by moving patrols forward from these bases on foot, not only were flying hours saved but also surprise was maintained by avoiding the rather flamboyant approach characteristic of a helicopter-borne operation.

The second aim was part of the important process of building up the confidence and winning the hearts and minds of the local Dyaks and Ibans. This was vital if the flow of intelligence (by means of a certain number of both legal and illegal border-crossers) was to work to our advantage. Later on, as confidence in our activities and reports of successful ambushes increased, it became possible to provide this confidence more indirectly, by maintaining patrols in the area at irregular intervals in such a way as to keep the enemy guessing. Initially, however, the protection had to be seen to be provided, and any adjustment of bases which had to be made from time to time on the grounds of economy had to take full account of local feeling.

The minimum economical size for these patrol bases turned out to be a company. Anything less than this would have been vulnerable to a determined enemy supported by mortars, and would only have allowed for a very few men to be out patrolling along the border at any one time. In many ways, two companies were ideal. This allowed adequate protection of the perimeter with at the same time, a reasonable ratio free for patrolling. The living accommodation and defences were therefore usually designed so that, although up to two companies could be accommodated temporarily, the defences could still be effective, if the resident garrison fell to 2 or even $1\frac{1}{2}$ platoons. Platoon bases such as Sapit, which only allowed 10 men to be out on patrol, were run down, as soon as the question of confidence amongst the local people could be resolved.

The bases had to be prepared to withstand attacks by a battalion group supported by mortars, and much attention therefore had to be paid to field works, fields of fire and defensive devices to hinder an assault. All troops slept protected by overhead cover, or at least by thick blast walls, and all were within easy reach of their fighting trenches where sentries manned LMGs, fixed line GPMGs and the normal range of illuminations. All trenches were linked by telephone to a central command post. To the observer the finished article looked like a cross between a sector of a World War I trench system and a 'Wild West' fort occupied by the United States Cavalry in some past Indian war. Most of the bases could, however, have withstood a heavy mortar bombardment, and would have been extremely difficult to overrun without a large number of casualties. They would certainly have been able to buy sufficient time in which to bring reserves into the area to encircle the attacking forces. The important thing was to maintain constant vigilance because, with the border so close, the risk of surprise attack was considerable.

In a Vietnam-type of situation, where the threat would be much greater, any such bases would have to be much larger and stronger, in range of more substantial artillery support and with larger cleared areas outside the perimeter and even possibly perimeter lighting.

Apart from patrolling, life for rifle companies in the forward patrol bases was always varied and interesting. To make life secure and as comfortable as possible required imagination, industry, discipline and good organization. Field works had to be dug, fields of fire and helicopter pads cleared, obstacles and devices invented and constructed, and local civil labour had to be recruited, organized and paid to help with this work under supervision and thus release soldiers for active patrolling. Finally, locally recruited Border Scouts working direct with the Battalion through the patrol bases had to be integrated into the defence plan in an early warning and reporting role.

As I have already mentioned, the patrol base was also valuable as a focal point for gathering intelligence. There was a certain amount of legal cross-border trade, and in any case the border itself was in places very vague and undefined. The practice amongst the local people of visiting relatives 'on the other side of the hill' had never properly ceased, and there were plenty of free-lance agents ready to give information, if the money was right and they approved of our methods. There was always, of course, a risk that such agents might be working for both sides, but by carefully graduating the tasks given to each, checking the credibility of the information against other more reputable sources and, above all, by picking and paying well, we gained more than we ever lost.

All this kept everyone on their toes, with company second-in-commands and support platoon commanders fully engaged respectively on adminis-tration and on the task of battle adjutant with special responsibility for Intelligence. Despite the full complement of mud and rats, which always characterizes such fortifications, the British soldier quickly adapted himself to the very primitive conditions. Safely out of the orbit of Battalion Office and the RSM, he seemed cheerfully prepared to live in the jungle indefinitely.

Patrolling and ambushes

The second and most important element in the pattern of defence were the offensive patrols operating from the patrol bases. Indeed, as the defence of the patrol base got progressively stronger, it became increasingly important to resist any temptation to Maginot-mindedness. The bases were in no sense blocking positions because of the ease with which the enemy could circumvent them. The enemy could only be deterred, harried and destroyed by continuous patrolling along the border, which was carefully planned and resolutely executed. The patrols had three tasks:

a. *Reconnaissance.* To discover, with the help of experienced trackers, if certain routes had been recently used by the enemy and, if they had, to follow up these tracks and report on the enemy's movements.

b. *Ambushing*. To anticipate the enemy's likely movements, possibly based on information received in carrying out the first role, and to move into a position where an effective ambush could be laid.

c. *Harassing*. To destroy any enemy patrol or firm bases or bivouac areas which the enemy might be inclined to establish on our side of the border.

Patrols varied in size from 6 to 10 men for comparatively local reconnaissance, to a full company strength for large patrols, when contact with the enemy was likely. In the case of large patrols the end product was, where possible, a carefully sited ambush or, in exceptional cases where an enemy bivouac area was located and could be approached, an assault using maximum fire power. The ambushes which were sited on infiltration, escape or communication routes demanded stamina and immense patience on the part of those who had to remain silent, concealed and alert for anything up to 72 hours. The British Infantryman showed that he was robust, reliable and adaptable enough to do this, while the Indonesian, although extremely brave when cornered, contributed to his downfall by his fortuitous habit of making the same mistakes over and over again and giving insufficient attention to planning routes and formations of his patrols.

By no means a complete company was required in the ambush itself, which probably only called for 10 riflemen to cover the main killing area at any one time. Allowing for rest and relief, stops and warning parties on either flank, subsidiary ambushes and firm bases in depth on the routes to and from the ambush, a whole company could be quickly absorbed. The technique of inserting a well-placed ambush is not dissimilar to placing an assault party on top of a mountain. Here the final party is relatively small, but camps and carrying parties at ever-increasing heights are essential to give support, strength and confidence. On the way to the ambush site, the company, moving in bounds and providing flank protection where necessary, would be well balanced to meet the unexpected. Once the ambush was sprung, the ambush party could fall back through a series of support areas and firm bases, gaining increasing strength as they went. These reduced to the minimum the likelihood that the enemy would be able to outflank them and cut off their withdrawal.

Another golden rule was to ensure that whenever possible an ambush was planned to lie within the range of our Battalion's mortars or supporting field artillery (105 mm How). Because of the length of a battalion's front (anything between 20–50 miles) and the sparsity of forward bases, this was not always so easy to organize. Special sites in inaccessible jungle had sometimes to be cleared, and the guns and mortars then flown in by helicopter. The support given was, however, invaluable. FOOs and MFCs with the ambush, or more usually at a forward firm base a short distance away, could direct fire on to the enemy escape routes, on any attempted follow-up, or on enemy mortars, which intervened once the ambush had been sprung. This fire covered the subsequent withdrawal of the ambush party from their exposed position.

Much of the country in both Sarawak and Sabah, the other Borneo territory, was immensely hard, with jungle-covered hills rising to 4000–5000 feet, knife-edge ridges and precipices, and rivers in the valley capable of becoming raging torrents five to six feet deep in a few hours after the invariable heavy afternoon rain. Wherever there had been an old habitation, cultivation or a logging area, the primary jungle would have deteriorated into the most unpleasant secondary jungle, where visibility was often down to a few feet and where a few hundred yards of movement took an hour or more. In these areas—and this particularly applied to the valley floors—there was a great temptation to use the established tracks and jungle paths in order to speed up movement and reduce effort. However, never can the old Infantry saying that 'sweat saves blood' have been more applicable. Until a track had been blocked near the border and fully proved to be unheld or unmined, there was always a risk of ambushes and mines and of giving away surprise. Indeed, even if a physical block had been established, there was no certainty that the enemy had not circumvented it and cut in behind. Initially, and until patrols became really familiar with the area, it proved sound policy to avoid established tracks and to cut in on these at intervals from a flank, even if this involved an extremely arduous cross-country move. Jungle can be singularly unpleasant, but it is seldom impenetrable.

How basic techniques might be incorporated into a hypothetical operation is outlined below and can be applied to actual operations discussed later. An ambush site would have been chosen as a result of Intelligence or perhaps intuitive anticipation, and the route there and back carefully selected to avoid tracks and gain maximum surprise. The distance from the patrol base would vary considerably along different parts of the border, but patrols usually prepared to go out for 8 days. Great care had to be exercised getting into position and as much as 3 days might be needed for this alone. The ambush had then to be maintained from 2–3 days if it was to have the best chance of being sprung successfully. Withdrawal would take less time, but basic precautions were still needed and the going might be slow: another 2 days would therefore have to be allowed for this. The patrol would probably carry a further day's ration (a 9th day) for emergencies. The route both out and back would avoid tracks and any river would be crossed at a point distant from any established crossing place, in order to increase surprise. Firm bases would be placed at such a crossing place, in order to safeguard the withdrawal, and on any high ground above the ambush site. The Company Commander and FOO would probably base themselves at this second firm base. The ambush itself would probably be about 500–1000 yards further forward, depending on the ground, and within this span the ambush platoon would set up an additional support or administrative area, which would also act as a rendezvous for the withdrawal. This would be the place where the members of the platoon not actually in a fire position would rest, and it would also provide a measure of flank protection against an enemy trying to roll up the ambush from a flank. It would be reasonable for this support area to be about 200 yards away from the ambush itself.

Once the ambush had been sprung, the troops would withdraw through the RV to the company firm base, and then together the whole party would move back to any river, crossing under the protection of the platoon left behind. Under certain circumstances patrols might be picked out by helicopter from one of the suitable landing pads, which would have been built along the border and periodically checked. This would save a long march back and spare fatigue, and additional troops might be sent to secure this LP before the main body arrived. Helicopters, however, would not be used to introduce the patrols into the area, unless it was certain that the pattern of helicopter movement and the configuration of the ground made it possible to retain surprise.

When planning these patrols a commanding officer had to consider a number of factors. First, every effort had to be made, by studying the Intelligence available, to anticipate the enemy's next move. Often this was a matter of backing a hunch, because other pointers were misleading and contradictory. Then the tasks allotted had to be matched to the state of experience and local knowledge of the troops and their commanders. This was a very strange environment for British troops, and it was necessary to graduate the tasks in order to build up confidence and ensure the steady progression of successes, which does so much for morale. Next the best way of applying the techniques which I have described to the particular piece of ground had to be worked out in considerable detail, after careful discussion with the company of platoon commander who was to carry out the operation. Finally, the risks had to be weighed most carefully to see whether they were justified in the context of Confrontation and in the light of the situation at the time. Nothing would have been achieved without some degree of risk, but the risk of losing British lives had to be weighed against the urgency of the enemy threat and the possibility of political settlement. Although the Indonesian threat was pernicious and serious enough if unchecked, it never materialized in so drastic and urgent form as to justify really heavy British casualties. The initiative had to be won along the border and the enemy's aggression blunted, but the real challenge which faced commanders at every level was to do this without sacrificing valuable world opinion, without escalating the conflict beyond our resources, and above all without incurring large casualties on our own side.

Air mobility operations

The last element in the defensive plan was the reserve company or companies which were moved into battle by helicopter to block and encircle located enemy infilitrations. Sometimes the reserves would be moved to reinforce or relieve forward companies in their patrol bases so that the tactical deployment could take place from there, thus taking advantage of the short helicopter turn-round and the local knowledge of the forward troops. Sometimes reserves were deployed direct from a base area. In either case, if the response was to be quick and the operation successful, six conditions had to apply:

a. Troop-carrying helicopters (RN, RAF or in certain cases 'Scouts' of the Army Air Corps) had to be made available urgently and outside the normal tasking programme. This was a matter for the Brigade Headquarters and the RAF.

b. A joint plan had to be made at Battalion Headquarters by the CO and an airman who could speak both for the helicopters and, when applicable, the fighter ground-attack aircraft.

c. The helicopters which were to be used had to assemble with the companies they were going to lift at a base airfield or at a forward company's landing zone, sufficiently early to receive a common briefing and together work out their loading and priorities.

d. A landing zone or roping-down area had to be selected, which was both adequate for getting the troops on the ground quickly and unlikely to be strongly held by the enemy.

e. If there was some likelihood of enemy resistance in the area a proper plan for suppressive fire had to be made, co-ordinating artillery, fighter ground-attack, armed helicopters when these exist, and the arrival of the first lift of helicopters.

f. The CO with an FAC who might also be the pilot of his Sioux helicopter, plus the affiliated battery commander of an FOO, had to be prepared to command the operation from an airborne command post. This might be lifted in one or two aircraft of his own air platoon or in a Scout helicopter of the brigade flight which was ideal in size and performance but not as well endowed with communications as the Sioux. The role of the command post was to synchronize the attack and bring in the infantry assault immediately after the fire plan had stopped.

No-one will pretend that all these conditions were always met, or that these techniques—many of them still in the development stage—worked perfectly. There were a number of lessons to be learnt, and I will mention them later. Although we could have done with more of them, helicopters certainly proved their value and gave the British Commonwealth Forces a mobility completely denied to the enemy. Without them far less would have been achieved.

Lessons for the future

I have said more than enough to indicate that the campaign in Borneo, and especially in the western parts of Sarawak known as the 1st Division, was a very satisfactory campaign from the point of view of the Infantry soldier. There was a clear-cut and worthy aim, for we were helping friends who had asked for help. The physical challenges imposed by the country and the climate were tough and demanding, and the successful surmounting of them correspondingly rewarding. There was plenty of opportunity for young men to prove their nerve and endurance in contact with a tough and brave enemy, and there was considerable scope for initiative and intelligence as well. There were short moments of high excitement, and even when there were no contacts the business of patrolling and living in forward bases was never dull. Above all, although the risks and hazards were real enough, not too many soldiers got hurt, and fewer still lost their lives.

Perhaps even more significantly, Borneo was an encouraging example of military force contributing to a political situation. Instead of the progressive escalation that was often so inevitable, military force intelligently employed produced conditions which helped and perhaps even promoted sensible negotiations. It did this by decisively rendering Confrontation ineffective, while not using more force than was necessary to achieve this and retaining the sympathy of world opinion throughout—no mean feat, which reflected great credit on the skill and sagacity of the higher command.

But having made this slightly smug assessment, what real lessons does the Borneo campaign hold for the future? It is not really an argument to say that Borneo was an unusual campaign, being neither a limited war—because of the reduced threat, and the considerable restrictions imposed on our use of force—nor a full-scale revolutionary war—because the degree of subversion was never advanced enough—nor yet an internal security problem, because of the inroads of the Indonesian Army from across the border. Most campaigns are unusual, and nearly all of them unexpected. Nor should one be unduly influenced by the British Government's declaration that its aim is never again to get involved in a campaign of the scope and duration of Borneo; for who can tell as long as we have any British presence overseas? Certainly with the balance of power hanging over us, and world opinion ever watching us, campaigns of partial and controlled involvement in which the political and military factors have to be carefully balanced seem to represent a definite trend. It would be wrong to read too much into the experiences in Borneo, for the enemy effort was indeed small, and in any case there is nothing so deadening to original military thought as a thoroughly successful campaign which may establish false principles. Equally, it would be wrong to take too little notice of this experience, particularly in the field of patrolling and Joint Army Air operations.

I believe Borneo confirmed that British and Gurkha troops had a very real talent—perhaps genius would not be too strong a word to use—for this type of campaign, in which aggression, robustness and successful anticipation had to be subtly blended with restraint, humanity and sensitivity to the aspirations and the hearts and minds of the local people—a point UNO might be wise to note.

On the Infantry equipment side the picture was encouraging. The Infantryman was clearly well equipped and armed for operations in the jungle. The US Armalite rifle was popular, and more than offset its range and possible penetration limitations by its significantly lighter weight, and the lightness of its ammunition which enabled so much more to be carried. The GPMG was invaluable in static patrol bases and in ambushes, where there was little preliminary walking. It was, however, too heavy for long-distance patrols, and for this a lighter fully automatic and stable weapon was required. This role was met by retaining the Bren LMG. The M79 rifle grenade was ideally suited to the role of patrol support weapon. It also provided a useful punch in an ambush. Given a smoke capability, it might well replace the 2″ mortar. The Infantry got its main support from the 81-mm mortar, which was excellent and highly flexible, having the capability of firing a bomb at the useful minimum range of only 80 yards, and from the 105-mm Howitzer with its heavy and lethal shell and its ability to be lifted into position by helicopter. With the wide frontages involved, however, it would have been useful if this latter weapon could have had 4–5000 yards extra range. Finally, in the Sioux helicopter we had a magnificent aircraft which did much to enhance the capability and flexibility of the battalion. Robust, unsophisticated and easy to maintain, each aircraft was invariably in the air for its full 45 hours a month and, in the spacious and isolated environment of Borneo it is difficult to imagine what we would have done without them.

The training, too, thanks to the effort of the Joint Warfare School at Johore Baru, was on the right lines; although I believe that still more can be done right through an Infantryman's training to make him more confident and capable of moving and fighting in rather smaller groups than the normal Infantry section. The risk of the individual British soldier getting lost and unable to find his way back to base if separated from the main body of his company or platoon was naturally always greater than in the case of the Gurkha soldier. Because of this commanding officers and company commanders were reluctant to send out really small parties on the lines of SAS patrols, although tactically these could have been very valuable in certain cases. The SAS can, of course, call on a much higher standard of man that the average Infantry recruit, but it would nevertheless be wrong to underestimate the ordinary Infantry soldier, provided he is given sufficient training in this sort of patrol work and the confidence that goes with it. I am sure even more must be done to build up self-reliance in the individual if we are to be fully up to the challenge of Revolutionary war. [This was written well before the emergency in Northern Ireland had put a premium on the thinking individual soldier.]

On the organization side, a number of modifications were needed at Battalion Headquarters to compete with the autonomy brought about by large fronts. As well as planning operations, controlling the widely dispersed companies, obtaining intelligence, liaising with Border Scouts and Police and tasking the daily helicopter lift in conjunction with the RAF, Battalion Headquarters—through its administrative base—often had to run its own complicated chain of supply, using road, river, helicopter, air drop, or a mixture of all these methods. Battalions which were on a $2\frac{1}{2}$-year Far East tour also had the commitment of leaving a substantial rear party at their main base in Peninsular Malaysia (Malaya) or Hong Kong. A Battalion Headquarters in which the Adjutant was the jack of all trades and had to do both G and A work could not possibly cope. Instead it was necessary to have separate officers to handle each of the different functions: e.g., A matters (the Adjutant), Intelligence (the IO), Operations and Plans (G Staff Officer), Helicopter tasking (MTO), Q matters (the QM or his representative at Battalion Headquarters, who might be a second QM, a Regimental Officer or the RSM), and Communications (RSO); the whole operational centre being under the control and direction of the Second-in-Command, who was Chief Operations Officer and co-ordinated the various staff functions. It is comforting to note that the new Establishment proposed for the Infantry Battalion makes provision for this increase in Battalion Headquarters Staff. The Training Company Headquarters, which in my battalion absorbed the reconnaissance and pioneer platoon from Headquarter Company, was sometimes used to run the Battalion Headquarters area, sometimes employed on a special fourth company task, and sometimes used to command the Battalion Reserve; for Borneo proved what had been apparent so often before, that only with four companies is a Battalion a properly balanced force.

On the whole the Infantry Battalion proved itself a flexible, economically organized unit which could quickly adapt itself to any tactical situation or administrative layout. [Extracts from Lt Col Bramall's reflections on the Battalion's tour, written on its conclusion.]

The Battalion, with Company and Platoon fortified camps sited to afford protection to local longhouses and Kampongs, was initially deployed between 2 Para on the left and 3 Royal Australian Regiment (3 RAR) on the right or West flank, facing South and South West. Maj Carter's A was on our left in depth at Padawan, with Lt M. Dunning's 1 Platoon well forward at Sapit, 200 yards from the ill-defined border. Maj Welsh's C on the right was based on Pang Tebang with two forward platoon detachments, the one under Lt C. Wallace being at Tringgus. Battalion HQ and HQ Company were at Semengo Camp, near its airfield, with B's Tracker Reconnaissance and Buglers and Maj Pascoe's D near by. Responsibility for camp and airfield defence was the Battalion's, with most of an armoured-car squadron, a company of the Singapore Guard Regiment, a Light Air Defence Battery, the bulk of a sapper squadron, an AAC flight and RAF elements. A feature of the only road from Kuching was that a bazaar and attendant Kampong had been set up at virtually every other milestone, so that later internal security problems revolved around these bazaars and detached Chinese living in groups near their fields.

On 5 May 1965 the Battalion Main Body disembarked at Kuching and their Sioux flew to that airport from the ship. By 7 May the Scots Guards had been relieved, and command assumed by 2 Green Jackets. That night the first trip flare went off at a C Company forward position and dawn investigation, revealing no human tracks, indicated the passage of some jungle animal. DFs were next registered by our mortars and the single field guns, positioned to support forward platoon fortified camps.

Already on 9 May sources warned of a possible attack on Sapit in the next few days, and by 11 May this had hardened to a 100-strong party moving NE. However, by 16 May the thrust had turned out to be on the 2 Para front, whose forward position would have been overrun but for the gallantry of a Warrant Officer. The lack of depth within Sarawak around Kuching had rightly demanded that reserves be kept in hand, and D Company was called upon to redeploy rapidly in an attempt to head off and ambush the Indonesians as they moved from the initial contact.

16 Platoon under Lt C. Brinkley was airborne in two Belvedere helicopters with 45 minutes of Brigade giving the order, and secured a Landing Pad (LP) for Maj Pascoe's HQ and 14 Platoon, who moved under command 2 Para later that day. By nightfall four platoons under 2 Para were 1000 yards from the border, but contact had been lost, although a half-prepared enemy ambush site was spotted.

However, 14 Platoon, under Lt M. Robertson, had an eerie night encounter in the jungle. They had been working all day on clearing a helicopter LP on a knife-edge ridge, at a point where a track from the North joined a game trail running along the crest. Power saws, necessarily used on the huge trees, had made their continuous irritating whine, and towards nightfall, the job nearly done, the platoon had an uneasy feeling that they were being watched. Acting on this sixth

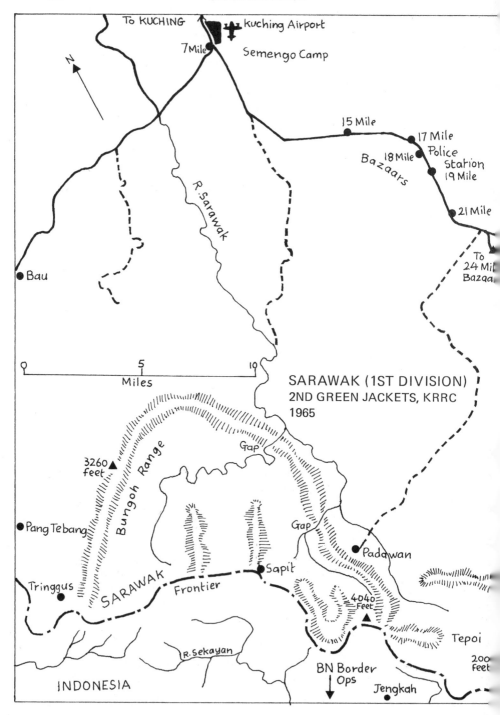

sense, well known to field soldiers, Lt Robertson made his jungle camp astride the track just North of the crest.

Suddenly his NCO sentry, watching the track from the supposedly friendly North, alerted by far-distant MG fire, sent a message to say that lights were coming up the track and that he could hear movement. Just before the Platoon Commander reached the sentry, the latter opened fire with his Bren, appreciating that the enemy were too near for him to risk the danger of being rushed; he reported that he had seen the lights disappear off the track about 50 yards away. No friendly elements were on the move after dark, so it had to be treated as a part of the Indonesian raiding force. Lt Robinson and Sgt Hunt consulted the map by torch under a poncho, and then called on the nearest gun to put a round down on the track; after correction, he called for three rounds of gunfire, which arrived perilously close as airbursts.

A careful patrol forward after first jungle light found the Bren's bullet-holes in trees but no dropped equipment or other sign of enemy casualties. The deep leaf mould of primary jungle, cleansed daily by downpours, rarely offered footprints; a worn place on an exposed root was usually the only trace, and nothing could be seen in this instance. If it was a party of returning enemy, they had to go home the hard way across terrible country; at all events the platoon drills had been well tested.

The inestimable value of good radio communications with each position and the ability of our Sioux to pick up casualties emerges clearly from the signal logs of the period. On 19 May a C Company signaller was badly burnt when a charging engine exploded in its pit, and was evacuated rapidly. An A Company Rifleman, painfully bitten by a spider, had treatment dictated by radio, and other mishaps included falling on panjis, sharpened bamboo stakes forming part of post defences, in the dark. A very tense moment came when virtually the whole A Company O Group was missing in a helicopter. The pilot had, however, managed to crash land safely on the Border and they were picked up.

On 20 May the Battalion was ordered to extend its front, to take over Tepoi with D Company, less a platoon. This was roughly SE of Sapit, covering a longhouse and valley, whose head was dominated by a jungle peak 3000 yards West; occasionally the slow beat of a Russian heavy machine-gun in Indonesian hands would be heard firing from there without effect, but Tepoi on its cleared spur, bristling with defences, above the Kampong was to be the base for our most successful forward actions. Lt R. Hill's 15 Platoon, first in, put down mortar and LMG fire on lights seen to the North, followed up by artillery fire, without detectable result; it must be remembered that the steaming jungle was full of phosphorescent growths and creatures, but subsequent events made this look like enemy infiltration. Enemy mortar-fire next day on to where our mortars had fired might have been an irritable attempt to catch our clearing patrol; it did not succeed. Unfortunately, a faulty artillery round during registration later caused casualties in the Tepoi Kampong, which required rapid helicopter evacuation.

On 30 May the first fatal casualty was sustained by the Battalion. 16 Platoon, under Lt C. Brinkley, was making its way towards Tepoi when Rfn Godfrey, whose body was brought into Tepoi next morning, was unfortunately killed. Immediate return to the contact area by his comrades, leading in the tracker Platoon, found all trace and scent erased by rain.

A remote counter-strike was made on 3 June, when Lt R. Winwood's 3 Platoon on patrol between Tepoi and Sapit saw 12 enemy 800 yards away on a bare slope and brought down accurate artillery fire. Intelligence (thanks in part to the winning of the border tribesmen's hearts and minds) was swift, and reasonably accurate, from a well-assessed blend of sources; by 7 June we knew that two enemy dead had been carried into the local Indonesian base camp. Sapit itself was an old, dilapidated fortified camp, dangerously exposed to any border thrust, and Lt Col Bramall exerted continual pressure for its abandonment; the political view was that the local Kampong had been earlier under Marxist propaganda and needed a presence to ensure stability.

The next actions were, however, in a very different quarter—in the rear whence the CO's reserve D Company had been whisked away. Luckily the Semengo Airfield alarm scheme had been recently tested and communications sharpened, for just before midnight on 27 June Lt Col Bramall's force in the cultivated plain was called into action. 18 Mile Police Station (the Kampongs at two-mile intervals will be recalled) had been attacked; simultaneously an attempt had been made to blow 24 Mile bridge and a civilian murdered. At 2325 the CO was told to form a company at Semengo by 0800 hrs, and that 1/6 Gurkhas were being moved to join him. At 0100 hrs 28 June C Company was warned for a move to Padawan to join A as cut-offs against an enemy withdrawal South. By 0220 hrs the Police had recaptured their station with three police and four civilian casualties. The enemy, 100 strong, had been reported withdrawing West, leaving as usual no detectable tracks. At 1100 hrs the CO moved his Tac HQ to Padawan, and deployed A and C Companies as cut-offs, while the Police and two platoons of 1/6 Gurkhas searched the 18 Mile area onwards; the curfew area was now to be extended.

Although on 29 June the Battalion was largely facing North against the thwarted enemy operation in its rear, patrols were still out to watch for border incursions. That afternoon Cpl Steward of D Company was badly wounded by an Indonesian anti-personnel mine left behind by an earlier enemy patrol. It must have been a bitter blow to an excellent athlete to lose a leg, but the writer was able, more than a decade later, to admire Steward's philosophic courage at a Reunion. He was evacuated by helicopter from an LP marked by smoke in a very difficult operation. Command problems had not been diminished by the earlier killing by C Company of a curfew-breaker, who failed to respond to three challenges. Luckily, his family, who identified him as a mental case, were completely understanding about the need to obey rules stringently in the emergency.

That evening A and C were ordered to concentrate, when a company of 2/2 Goorkhas arrived as a reserve at Semengo. By now Brigade had identified the enemy band responsible for the attack as a group of Chinese communists, trying to start an insurrection on the pattern of the Malayan emergency of 1948. Terrorist pressure on Chinese settled away from the road Kampongs would provide them with a base, unless concentration of families on Malayan lines was rapidly effected. On 1 July deployment was as follows: A Company was back at Padawan, having never abandoned Sapit, and D at Tepoi less two platoons at Semengo; C was at a Kampong to the North East of A, but was relieved by B Company, 2/2 Goorkhas, on 3 July.

Under Operation 'Hammer' the Battalion was ordered to cordon 15, 17, 19, 21 and 24 Mile Bazaars, while the outlying Chinese were regrouped into camps at these Kampongs: although a punitive measure against the supporters of the disgraceful attack, it was a beneficial act of security for those of good will or waverers, in that they could thereafter be shielded from terrorist pressure. 2 Green Jackets had under command two platoons of A, C Company, B Company 2/2 Goorkhas, B Company 1/6 GR and C Sqn 4 RTR for the operation; this started at 0600 hrs 6 July 1965 with troops moving to helicopter pick-up points. 45 minutes later the cordon was in position, and the grouping of Chinese continued all day without incident. Eventually numbers were 700 at 17 Mile, 300 at 19, 450 at 21 and 1050 at 24 Mile Bazaar camp. That afternoon 1/6 Gurkhas and our 1 Platoon found an area showing traces of a political meeting and deserted basha (jungle camp) for about 30 to 40 people; the Chinese houses near by were destroyed. Arrangements were made for representatives to leave camps daily to feed livestock in the morning only, and the 24 Mile camp was under particular restriction.

On 8 July the cordon was withdrawn, and apart from reports of uniformed Chinese and subsequent abortive search of caves, the rear area was now secure, thanks to premature action by the terrorists and our swift riposte. One happy feature of this period was working with the Gurkha Company of Maj G. Johnson, who later on transfer was to command 1 RGJ.

It was now time to turn back to border operations. The Indonesians, having started the policy of Confrontation against Malaysia, had of course the initiative in the early part of the campaign. From the safety of camps set up near the headwaters of boatable rivers they could raid North over the border at a time and place of their choosing. Although their incursions had been progressively less successful, our tribesmen in their longhouses could never feel at ease while living under this uncertainty.

On the Battalion front a very satisfactory feel of the enemy over the Border's razor-sharp watershed had been gained from many types of intelligence source. However, owing to our inadequate maps of Indonesian territory—which only indicated water courses and rough shapes of high ground without contour or spot height—the ground could only be assessed by moving over it. The recent picture built up was of a new and more efficient Regular Indonesian unit in the area, which unless it could be quickly shaken would soon increase the pressure on our longhouses and Kampongs; coupled with the recent Chinese communist rear security problem, this could be serious, and must be averted by preventive action. The first thing was for each Rifle Company to leave its camp in turn, and carry out the more offensive drills of establishing platoon ambushes from a company firm base, as described earlier by the CO. By working over the Border, the essential reconnaissance could also be made. To assist in this Capt Mead, as MTO, relieved 1 Platoon in Sapit with the Buglers, a reversion to their old Peninsula forward deployment.

The critical area for Indonesian incursion over the Border was due West of Tepoi. There the boatable River Sekayan, 50 yards wide and parallel with the Border, ran South within 4000 yards of it. The side-valley of a winding tributary, the River Jengkah, ran East to within 400 yards of the Border watershed and thence parallel to it; over the crest the shallow Tema led straight down the 4000

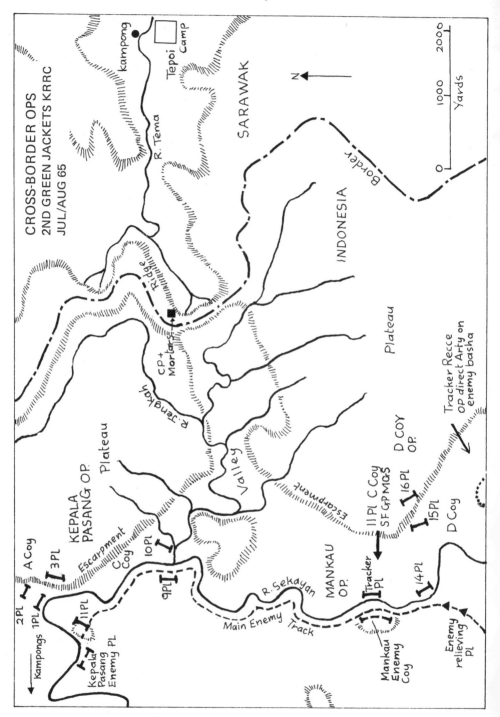

CROSS-BORDER OPS
2ND GREEN JACKETS KRRC
JUL/AUG 65

yards to Tepoi. 3000 yards South of the Jengkah's confluence the Sekayan ran below a bluff on the West bank, on which stood the Indonesian military camp of Mankau, close to a Kampong site. This was the base camp for an Indonesian Regular company and their armed irregulars.

4000 yards North, intelligence told us that a camp for a detached platoon, Kepala Pasang, had recently been set up where the river valley turned West. It could dominate the Kampongs across the river, and would be well placed to use infiltration routes East, between Tepoi and Padawan. A Company's first cross-Border patrols confirmed the location of this unmarked camp and found the best way to the Sekayan just downstream of it, where communications with Mankau could be cut; no crossing over the Sekayan was found, however. C Company was meanwhile reconnoitring the Jengkah valley approach to the Sekayan from Tepoi; ambushes found that no Indonesians were at present moving up the valley to the Border. Maj Welsh managed to get one man over the Sekayan, without which prelude the CO would not have risked a company across. The CO and Lt Gamble as IO carefully debriefed A and C after their successive working-up missions, and 15 Platoon found there was no easy way south of Tepoi up on to the plateau leading to opposite Mankau. Visitors like Maj Gen Hunt, Divisional Commander, and Maj Gen Carver, DASD (both future CGSs), could be shown something of the brains and sweat which would shortly be expended to save blood in getting the Battalion secretly into position to dominate the forward enemy opposite.

All this time, besides their efforts in trying to track contacts, Capt Montgomery's Combat Trackers had been in contact with the Border Scouts, formed from local tribesmen in our area; they had been busy building up the picture, as well as relieving a platoon at Tringgus in June. It was during this period that Capt Montgomery, with his long African experience, and Lt Gamble, an excellent patroller, who had patiently and admirably discharged his duties as IO in British Guiana and now Borneo, were unleashed by Lt Col Bramall. They had located an Indonesian detachment on our extreme left, South of and overlooked by the plateau leading to Mankau. As a preliminary flank precaution and to get some 105-mm and 5·5-inch shells registered on the ground over the Border, but well away from immediate operations, the Trackers led an FOO into position above the camp, which was then intensively shelled; intelligence later confirmed a number of enemy casualties, with all the problems of their evacuation without helicopter, and the desired feeling of insecurity. This registration was later to be most useful in covering Lt Robertson's ambush party out.

On 29 July the CO held an O Group for Operation 'Gun Runner', and somehow found time two days later to accompany the Resident of 1st Division, Sarawak, and the District Officer, Kuching, to Sapit; their task was to explain to the tribesmen why at long last our position there could be destroyed without their position being endangered. 'Gun Runner' was designed to assist in this, since the CO had decided as a first step to undermine the morale of the enemy platoon in the isolated Kepala Pasang.

If the enemy had been in our territory, they would of course have been removed by assault. However, as the CO wrote:

There were two factors which militated against a direct attack on the enemy post. One was that, by placing themselves very close to a village, it made it very difficult for us to make a full-scale attack on them without inflicting casualties on innocent civilians and, secondly, the enemy defences were so sited that it could have been difficult to have overrun the camp without suffering very heavy casualties, which, with the circumstances prevailing at the time, was not considered to be justified. However, there were things which could be done to harass and isolate the enemy and to force him to withdraw from the threatening position. After reconnaissance it was decided to mount an operation which would isolate the enemy camp, ambush anyone going in or out, and, if this failed to achieve results, involve a very selective attack by fire against the known enemy huts and positions with a view to inflicting military casualties and creating alarm.

It must be remembered that, to avoid warning the Indonesians of an approaching operation, helicopters could not be used over the border, either to move troops in or to supply them. Thus every Rifleman had to follow new tracks in virgin jungle, cut by the leaders, carrying a heavy load, including several days rations as well as ammunition, up incredibly steep and slippery slopes and over a multitude of rivers and streams in perpetual spate.

To ensure control and fire co-ordination, dependent on first-class radio communications, Lt Col Bramall had just had a helicopter pad cut at the Western tip of the Border salient, on the high ridge West of Tepoi. Since the CO was expressly forbidden to enter or fly over Indonesia, a command post was set up there; from there also Sgt Gazzini established a base plate position bringing both Kepala Pasang, Mankau and the river between just within extreme range.

A Company, on this occasion under Capt C. Leach, since Maj Carter had injured an ankle, moved South from Padawan by helicopter to a helipad 5000 yards North of Tepoi. That night they crossed the Border and two evenings later 1 and 2 Platoons were at the foot of the escarpment, with Company HQ and 3 Platoon on top, looking down into the camp from 1000 yards East. The Company's tasks was to isolate the camp on the North Eastern side from across the Sekayan, ambushing exits and approaches and covering the river, used for patrols and supplies from Mankau. Lt Dunning's 1 Platoon were to move down to the river; Lt S. St Aubyn's 2 Platoon was in support, 500 yards back up a creek below the 500-foot escarpment to the North East.

Maj Pascoe's D Company moved out from Tepoi behind C and ambushed approaches to the Jengkah valley from the South, in case the Mankau company tried to cut C off by advancing over the plateau. They provided a valuable insurance in depth, but in fact had no contacts. Sadly, Rfn Newton died of a ruptured appendix before he could be evacuated.

Maj Welsh led C Company up the Tema valley and past the mortars; thence he followed the winding Jengkah almost to its mouth. His task was to cross the Sekayan in that area and isolate the camp from Mankau to the South. After ambushing the approaches for 24 hours, if there was no contact, the Company was to work its way forward to where it could bring controlled and selective fire down on to the enemy position.

C Company established 2/Lt Harrisson's 10 Platoon as a firm base on the last creek before the Jengkah's mouth, but had a highly difficult crossing of the

Sekayan. The river was swollen by rain to a depth of eight feet, and every man had to swim across with his weapons and equipment in a fast-moving current and with the continuous danger of enemy interference. That this was very real was brought home when a wide much-used main track from Mankau was found to run parallel only 15 yards across the Sekayan. It should be remembered that, apart from one man, C Company had never been as far forward as this, and the exact location of Kepala Pasang itself could only be conjectured on the primitive map. Leaving an OP and ambush party from 10 Platoon to watch the Sekayan from the East bank, Maj Welsh next established 2/Lt M. Yasa's 9 Platoon, with Sgt Lloyd as the excellent Platoon Sergeant, in ambush astride the Mankau track; he remained with it himself, as if the Mankau Company intervened a very difficult fighting withdrawal back over the river would need his personal leadership.

He had assigned to his most experienced team, Lt C. Wallace and Sgt R. Smith 84, and their 11 Platoon, the task of isolating the Kepala Pasang camp from the South. The Platoon, like others, was divided into two Patrols or strong Sections for jungle work; these were under Cpl Stanger, Bisley shot and later RQMS, and Cpl Taylor, Captain of the Battalion Football team and later CSM. Let us take up the story in Cpl Stanger's words:

We headed North up the track from Mankau in the pitch dark of early morning in the jungle; as usual an Iban tracker led, covered by two scouts. One Section covered the front, moving in single file, and the other the rear; the secondary jungle was too thick to leave the track. My Section was leading when, after we had advanced over 1000 yards, we reckoned we must be getting fairly near the camp. We had just climbed over a little hill, which dropped very steeply on the North side, when the track took a sharp turn West and I found myself in the greying light on the edge of the camp itself. Luckily there was no sentry in sight and we hurriedly backed away, sweeping out any possible traces with branches. Lt Wallace decided to site the ambush on the North East of the track as it crossed the hilltop about 150 yards from the camp, with the rest area in dead ground behind. Sgt Smith put the Claymore anti personnel mines on stumps alongside the track and we lay down to wait; a little later we heard voices and the noise of the camp waking up.

Radio communications were working perfectly, and A Company had reported in position, with Lt Dunning covering the river North East of the camp, when 2/Lt P. Harrisson's OP at the Jengkah mouth reported three Indonesian irregulars coming upstream from Mankau in a boat, patrolling and presumably with supplies for the camp. They spotted and landed to investigate the ineradicable trail where Maj Welsh's two forward platoons had swum across and clambered up the far bank. If they had turned back to raise the alarm at the larger Mankau garrison they would have had to have been engaged on the spot, but, boating on upstream, they were allowed for the moment to proceed.

The contact was reported, and the CO in his CP back on the Border ridge had to decide whether to engage this party or hope for a better opportunity later. On the principle of 'a bird in the hand', and because they would raise the alarm in any event, and by accurately locating C Company make the enemy more alert and less vulnerable, the CO ordered A Company to deal with the boat patrol when it came into their ambush. The plan was made easier by the fact that the commander of 1 Platoon was Lt Dunning, a cool hand and crack shot.

Lt Dunning's ambush killed all three of the enemy on their arrival opposite, and then rapidly fell back on Lt St Aubyn's support position. From his OP on top of the escarpment Capt Leach saw an Indonesian crew in the camp get their mortar into action and start to drop bombs along the escarpment. When our artillery fired he observed a direct hit on the mortar with the second round. This action had triggered off exactly the sort of enemy reaction for which the CO had hoped, as will be seen in Cpl Stanger's account.

> I had just relieved Cpl Taylor's Section in the ambush, when a mortar started to fire from the camp. The FOO with the Platoon put down 2 rounds from a single gun, which seemed to fall just right, as the mortar was silenced. We could hear shouts and sounds of panic from the camp, and almost at once two Indonesian Regulars pounded past my nose up the very steep hill. Pausing for breath at the top, they sat on stumps alongside the track, one leaning against an unseen Claymore. The ambush was sprung by Sgt Smith firing it electrically, but even that Bisley Queen's Medallist found he had fired more rounds to despatch the two than he had mentally declared. Lt Wallace skilfully withdrew his Platoon through the jungle to rejoin the track further South. Hearing a major assault going in on his late ambush position, the FOO brought down artillery fire on it and then successfully dropped rounds down the track to catch any pursuers.

This was found later to have inflicted more casualties.

When all was quiet the A and C Companies withdrew without loss, although C, who were on the wrong side of the river, had an even more hazardous return journey because further rain had brought an increase in depth to 15 feet and an even stronger current. It was a great tribute to Maj Welsh, who was subsequently awarded the Military Cross for his part in this and other operations, that not a man or weapon was lost, although there were some very close shaves. An additional hazard in crossing a river such as this was that any immersion for a period of more than a few minutes brought a very considerable risk of infection from a rat-borne disease called leptospirosis, which is a very serious illness indeed; it attacks the liver, and involves a very high fever. In fact two officers and four other ranks subsequently contracted the illness as a result of this operation but were cured. 2/Lt Yasa, the Fijian officer, was one of these; his great strength had been of considerable use in the river, and his Platoon Sgt, Sgt Lloyd, had saved one Rifleman's life there. Lt R. Ker as C Company Ops Officer had been of great assistance to Maj Welsh throughout this period.

The journey back to the comparative sanctuary of Tepoi and Padawan took another day and a half, with C Company at least soaked through from their crossing. By 7 August 65 C Company was in Semengo and A and D back in their bases. A feature of return from all such operations was the admirable administrative welcome by Capt Shreeve and the Company 2ICs, Capts C. Leach, G. Hopton and J. Mason.

In terms of enemy casualties this operation was not a large one, although the garrison had been significantly reduced and badly shaken. For some considerable time afterwards reports filtering through from civilian sources indicated that the enemy in the area were extremely jittery and convinced that British troops were all round them day and night. This particular group of enemy never again showed any offensive inclination at all, and from then on concentrated exclusively on their own defence, later abandoning the camp.

Having created the feeling of isolation and panic in the platoon at Kepala Pasang which was to lead to its abandonment, the CO next decided to create the same insecurity in Mankau. This would be a more difficult task; the enemy was now alerted, and the camp's position on a bluff across the river with a civilian Kampong at its rear made it unassailable without heavy casualties, both to us and to civilians, if a running fight started. There were two weaknesses, however, which would allow harassment: the enemy used the Sekayan below for water and washing, and the plateau on the East terminated in an escarpment overlooking Mankau from less than a mile, within range of GPMGs in the sustained fire (SF) role on tripods. As a reward for hard work the Tracker/Reconnaissance Platoon under Capt Montgomery, accompanied by Lt Gamble, was given the task of laying an ambush on the East bank of the Sekayan opposite Mankau. 11 Platoon, C Company, was to be the Fire Platoon, forming a base on the escarpment above; they were responsible for carrying in all the GPMGs, tripods and two belts of ammunition a man.

Helicoptered to a pad 5000 yards South of Tepoi, the force approached the escarpment opposite Mankau over the plateau from the North East and 11 Platoon formed the base on top. After a radio discussion in Swahili between Capt Montgomery and Maj J. Baker, the 2IC, the Tracker/Reconnaissance Platoon spent the night in the riverside bamboo before crawling forward. Early the next morning the first two Indonesian Regulars came down to wash, and were killed when they acted suspiciously. The fire caused the duty soldier cook in his whites to run out of the foremost hut of the camp up the slope, to be despatched by L/Cpl Fraser, noted for his virtuosity on the Bren. Knowing their vulnerability in the valley bed, Capt Montgomery and Sgt Batey started to get their men out. It was as well, for a hidden enemy machine-gun post, sited to fire up and down stream to cover the North flank of the Mankau salient, opened up as soon as our movement was seen reflected in the bamboo tops. A 40 minute climb took our men unscathed, ahead of the enemy mortar fire, to the rendezvous on top of the escarpment; then 11 Platoon's GPMGs rippled over the river into the camp and its perimeter, and artillery fire searched out along the bank and up the slope. The guns were so hot after firing that the force had to wait before setting off. It was yet another long slog home, but at least 11 Platoon was lighter by many thousand rounds of GPMG ammunition. Intelligence soon revealed that Mankau, the enemy main camp on our front, had also turned on to the defensive.

Although time was getting short, as the arrival of a relieving Gurkha reconnaissance party proclaimed, intelligence revealed that there was just a chance of deepening the sense of insecurity which the Mankau garrison now felt—by threatening their communications with their battalion and flank companies. The main lateral track angled in on to the West bank of the Sekayan a bare 1000 yards South of the alerted Mankau, and C Company's experience had shown that it would be foolhardy to cross this spate river to ambush the track further back. Maj Pascoe's D Company was allotted the task of ambushing the track from the East bank.

Setting out from Tepoi, he avoided the much-used Jengkah valley and slanted South West up the plateau as he crossed the Broder. He took great care to avoid all recognizable jungle tracks and followed the successive contour lines high up the slopes, crossing ridges and fast streams; at times D Company had to negotiate vicious secondary jungle and bamboo, but once up the slope they had gained the easier primary jungle. Maj Pascoe dropped off 16 Platoon to cover a jungle track from the South East, giving an element of depth as well as flank protection. About 500 yards short of the ambush site he established Lt R. Hill with 15 Platoon and a mortar MFC at the top of the escarpment. Here by means of OPs placed in the uppermost branches of a 100-foot tree it was possible to gain observation over the Mankau area, from which mortar fire was likely to come in the event of contact. This position provided a firm base, and Maj Pascoe, after going forward himself to site the ambush, returned there to be alongside his FOO.

The ambush party itself, consisting of 14 Platoon, was commanded by Lt M. Robertson, who was subsequently awarded the Military Cross for his part in the action. The approach had already taken two days, moving very carefully through the jungle where visibility was no more than a few feet and the going liable to be very noisy; but at least another half-day was taken with the final approach to, and reconnaissance of, the ambush position. The position which was finally selected was on the East bank of the Sekayan looking across at where the lateral track joined the river at a range of about 50 yards. This position had the advantage of giving a good field of fire and at the same time a measure of concealment for the ambushers, who were able to position themselves back from the track in a way which was usually difficult to achieve in thick jungle. The river also provided some protection against a sudden assault on the ambush position. The Sekayan had of course also to be watched, as a sandbank showed traces of boat landings.

With the sentries out and weapons carefully sited, the ambush party settled down to a patient wait, keeping utterly silent, still and concealed in their very cramped positions; a small administrative area was set up about 200 yards away where members of the platoon who were not actually in the ambush position could rest. Because of the uncertain pattern of Indonesian day movement the only time that the Platoon Commander felt able to rest was during the night.

The ambush had to wait for over 48 hours with nothing happening at all, by which time most of the men in the ambush must have felt that the information had been faulty and that the enemy were not going to use the track at all.

After two fruitless days in the ambush, Lt Robertson was ordered to take a small patrol upstream to see if any other action could be taken before shortage of rations forced the Company to return. Fortunately, when nearly opposite Mankau he found a helpful civilian, who confirmed that a relieving platoon of Indonesian Regulars was expected up the track very shortly. On hearing this Maj Pascoe decided to stay out an additional day.

Suddenly, on the third day at about 11 o'clock in the morning, a scout, moving cautiously, came into view in the ambush area, wearing the usual black leather boots, peaked cap, camouflaged smock and American equipment of the Indonesian regular forces. Lt Robertson allowed him to pass through and waited until there were 10 enemy visible in the killing area. He then personally sprang the ambush, killing the centre man and, in the first volley of fire from the other

27 Winners of the Army Rackets and Squash Rackets 1964.

Left to Right—Lt M. Dunning*, Maj P. Welsh, Capt J. R. Nelson*, Capt I. McCausland, Capt G. Hopton.

*Winners Inter Regimental Rackets Doubles.

28 The Commanding Officer 2nd Green Jackets, The King's Royal Rifle Corps, subsequently 2nd Battalion The Royal Green Jackets, briefs HRH the Duke of Gloucester, Deputy Colonel in Chief, on the Battalion Air Platoon at Penang in January 1966.

Left to Right—HRH, Lt Col E. N. D. Bramall, OBE, MC, Capt C. Harrisson, Capt P. Blaker.

29 (above) Lt M. J. C. Robertson, MC, with [the]
Terence Cuneo painting of the Borneo campaign a[s carried out]
by his platoon, hanging in 2nd Battalion The R[oyal]
Green Jackets Officers Mess.

30 (left) 'The best of the old has flowed into the n[ew.']

The King's Royal Rifle Corps Brooch, presented to [HM]
The Colonel in Chief in 1953.

The Royal Green Jackets Brooch, incorporating [the]
KRRC Cross, presented to HM The Colonel in Chi[ef in]
1967.

Riflemen, six more of the enemy fell. Among the firers, unfortunately for the enemy, was Cpl Winkworth, a later CSM, who proved that the modern Bisley matches had field relevance. As soon as they had recovered from their shock the Indonesians fought back fiercely and bravely. Some of them tried to cross the river to attack the ambush, and two of them got a machine-gun into action behind a tree, firing intensely at the ambush position; it proved difficult to locate. Rfn Martin, Platoon Commander's runner, was told by him to try to draw its fire, so that it could be knocked out before those on the river bank became pinned. Gallantly, in so doing, he was hit in the leg by a burst of five shots. This allowed the Platoon Sergeant, Sgt Hunt—later RSM of the same Battalion, in which Robertson was by then a Company Commander—to engage the machine-gun with the new US M79 grenade, fired from a launcher; the gun and crew were then quickly knocked out. On our side the Bren Gunner, Rfn Campbell, had also been active in reducing enemy fire and movement. An enemy light mortar then joined in, and there was an intense fire fight for about 10 minutes, during which time Lt Robertson called for artillery support on the mortar, which was relayed through the OP a short distance behind. When there were no more targets still visible to engage, the platoon commander ordered the withdrawal of his platoon to a prearranged rendezvous covered by artillery fire of the one gun located within range. Phosphorus grenades were thrown to cover with smoke those most exposed on the river bank.

As they checked their men back through to the rendezvous, Lt Robertson and Sgt Hunt noticed the absence of Rfn Martin. Going back immediately, they found him propped up against a tree, and carried him back to the rendezvous, still under sporadic fire. Here the platoon formed up to move back to the firm base.

The journey back was no less difficult than the approach. The enemy was still mortaring the area, and this time the company had a wounded man with them, which, even with six men to the stretcher, made negotiation of the very steep ridges and streams extremely difficult. It took half a day and a night to get back to a place where the wounded man could be lifted out by helicopter. It was subsequently learnt that in the action the enemy lost 14 men killed or very seriously wounded and others with lesser injuries. D Company's only casualty was the one man wounded, who later recovered.

One of Mr Terence Cuneo's most graphic action paintings, condensed to show both the fighting withdrawal and extrication of Rfn Martin at the end of this perfect ambush action, hangs in the 2 RGJ Mess.

Although 40 Royal Marine Commando thought A Company help might be needed to deal with a platoon-sized incursion in their area to the South, this was later stood down, and within days the tour drew to its close.

During the last month the Band had joined the Battalion from Penang, and was in popular demand at all forward posts, as well as around Semengo and Kuching. The Buglers had returned from the abandoned position of Sapit in time to bring their bugling prowess up to Bugle Major Green's satisfaction. They provided a smart Bugle Guard for the unexpected honour of a visit by the Prime Minister of Malaysia, Tengku Abdul Rahman, who spoke to those at Semengo and thanked the Battalion for its good work in Sarawak. Band and Bugles combined to sound retreat in a farewell ceremony in Kuching, where the Chief Minister of Sarawak also expressed his gratitude.

A senior officer in Borneo later wrote that the war in his part of the world was largely won by soldiers wearing green berets, and it had been a happy concidence that the Gurkha and British Riflemen, descendants of those at Delhi, had once more worked together, even if only to nip embryo insurgency in the bud. Our Battalion was to conduct a final operational tour on the East coast of Sabah (North Borneo), at Tawau and up river, but only C Company was to have a small and successful patrol clash. Lt Col Bramall, 2/Lt P. Harrisson and Rfn Ryves received Mentions in Despatches for their work.

The incursions of Indonesian confrontation had been held; by the infliction of casualties and the creation of a loss of morale and feeling of insecurity among Indonesian forward elements South of Kuching the Battalion had admirably done its part. It is a happy thought that Malaysia, Indonesia and Great Britain have since been on the friendliest terms, and that the charming peoples of East Malaysia can pursue their longhouse family life in peace.

The Brigade Commander, Brigadier Cheyne, was very complimentary about the Battalion's work, and the following messages were received. General Lea, Director of Borneo Operations, said:

Congratulations on an excellent tour. I have been much impressed by the skill and zeal with which the Battalion has fulfilled its many and varied tasks. Please convey to all ranks my thanks and appreciation for all that the Battalion has done. Good luck and best wishes for the future.

General Hunt, later CGS, wrote:

I should like to congratulate you and all ranks on a very successful first operational tour in Borneo. You went from strength to strength, which is the right way to go, and at the end you were at the top of your form and complete master of your enemy.

I hope you will pass on my congratulations on a job well done to all ranks in the Battalion.

Besides the MCs awarded Maj Welsh and Lt Robertson, Maj Pascoe, Lt Ker and Sgt Lloyd in recognition of their services in Sarawak received Mentions in Despatches, and Sgt R. Smith 84 a Commendation in Brigade Orders; as always, there had been more good work than could be adequately recognized. In graphic terms the Battalion had killed 44 Indonesians and wounded many more for the loss of one Rifleman killed and three wounded, and all had fully earned their Borneo medal.

Some of the Battalion returned to Penang by air and others by LST. However, the arrival of the Main Body in one of the last troopships, with Band and Bugles playing, to be welcomed by their families, made a moving occasion in almost nineteenth-century style on an island with so many touches of that era.

A few changes were afoot, as Maj Carter handed over A Company to Maj Montgomery. Seconds in Command were in rapid succession, as Maj J. Baker, 3rd Green Jackets, who had excellently seen us through the latter part of the Sarawak tour, left to command the Cheshires, and was succeeded by Maj T. N. Thistlethwayte. When Maj Lamb left for a last tour with QRR (TA), after doing so much for the families, his place as QM was taken by Capt Shreeve, and RSM T. Fowley was commissioned, for what was to prove an excellent series of QM tours, ending sadly with his early death. WO I. B. Rimmer, a very fine 60th Rifleman, then started an admirable tour as RSM, leading to equally good work as QM. Capt Adshead, who had formed and commanded our Air Platoon so well in Borneo, now handed over to Capt P. Blaker. A popular award was that of the BEM to Cpl Windle, a Calais survivor, who had cooked for his fellow-Riflemen in such hot climates as post-war Italy, British Guiana and the Far East over the last 30 years.

Since success depends on preparation, and the Sabah tour was to start on 18 January 1966, the day after a visit by HRH The Duke of Gloucester, there was much to be done after a fortnight's leave. Administrative inspections, NCO and specialist cadres to train those whose talents had been identified on the Borneo tour, and the training of all Riflemen in their basic skill on the range kept the Battalion at full stretch. Indeed, the flexibility of the organization was yet again tested, since our element of the Tawau Assault Group had to be trained. Under the overall command of Maj G. Hopton, a skilled waterman, B Company's Recce Platoon and the Assault Pioneers under Capt D. Rowland-Jones, were to form part of an inter-Service and Commonwealth force to control the waterways through the mangrove swamps of Eastern Sabah; assault boats and outboard motors were to provide the mobility that their paddles had given 60th Royal Americans on Bradstreet's raid against Fort Frontenac in 1758 and 60th Riflemen on the Red River Expedition of 1870.

It was thus appropriately with the consciousness of operations excellently carried out, and with professional zest in tackling whatever the future might require of them, that Lt Col Bramall brought his Battalion, the Regulars of the old 60th, to that natural point on the last day of 1965 when they would voluntarily merge their identity with the 43rd and 52nd and The Rifle Brigade, already 1st and 3rd Green Jackets, in the new Royal Green Jackets. It was fitting that he should be in command at that point, for his brother Riflemen saw him as embodying the talents of all the best of our old Commanding Officers—the trainers, operational commanders, administrators and leaders whose interest was their Riflemen and families—with the flair for intelligent innovation which lies at the heart of the Regimental character.

Back in England Maj Gen E. A. W. Williams, as our Colonel Commandant, addressed the following last message to HM The Queen, Colonel in Chief:

The Colonel Commandant and All Ranks past and present of the 2nd Green Jackets, The King's Royal Rifle Corps, send to your Majesty our humble duty and loyal good wishes. We wish to thank your Majesty and your predecessors, as our Colonels in Chief, for the interest and encouragement which you and they have given to the Regiment during our long history.

We look forward to many years of loyal service to your Majesty as a Battalion of your Royal Green Jackets and are heartened by the knowledge that you will continue to honour us as our Colonel in Chief.

Her Majesty graciously replied:

Please give my warm thanks to all ranks past and present of the 2nd Green Jackets, The King's Royal Rifle Corps, for their loyal greetings and for their expressions of gratitude which I much appreciate.

I send my best wishes to the Regiment for its future service in The Royal

Green Jackets, a service which will I know be as distinguished as in the past.

ELIZABETH R

Colonel in Chief

On a tropical evening in far-away Penang the Band and Bugles of the Battalion sounded Retreat on 31 December 1965 at Minden Barracks to mark the last day of The King's Royal Rifle Corps.

It was a moving occasion, and a fine sight under both a magnificent moon and floodlights.

The whole Battalion and all the married families were there, and the Commanding Officer made the following short speech:

'Ladies and Gentlemen, the Sounding of Retreat and the Tattoo which we have just listened to and watched has a very special significance for us this evening, and I know our friends in the Garrison and our visitors will forgive me if I address a few words to the Battalion and our families. In five hours time as we enter 1966 our Regiment, the 2nd Green Jackets The King's Royal Rifle Corps, which has been in being for 210 years, will cease to exist as a separate Regiment of the British Army and instead we will become the 2nd Battalion of a new and larger regiment, The Royal Green Jackets, whose Colonel in Chief will be Her Majesty The Queen.

'In this life, if you are sensible and particularly if you are young, you look forward and not back; and indeed it is the tradition of Riflemen that they are progressive and move with the times. But we would not be human if we did not feel very considerable sadness at the passing of a Regiment with such a proud and wonderful history, and one in which so many of us have had such splendid times and such great comradeship, some, for close on a quarter of a century. The name of the King's Royal Rifle Corps, the 60th Rifles as it has often been known, the K.R.R.'s, as it has sometimes affectionately been called, will always have a very special place in our hearts and that is exactly as it should be.

'However, I want you all to appreciate this, that, although the name will go, the spirit and ideals which made the Regiment what it was—the fighting qualities, the pride in professional skill, the intelligent and humane discipline, the sympathy and understanding between all ranks, and the concern for the individual, for his welfare and for those of his dependants, all these will remain and will be equally conspicuous in the new Regiment as they were in the old.

'The motto 'Swift and Bold' given to us by General Wolfe at the battle of Quebec must and will continue to apply, and those who serve in the new Regiment can still expect things to happen, whether it be operational or other business, in an intelligent, efficient yet economical and, I hope, unpompous way. You can rest assured that the Royal Green Jackets will continue to enjoy the same extremely high reputation that the King's Royal Rifle Corps always had in the eyes of the Army, and quite honestly one cannot say better than that.

'So, as the Regimental flag comes down for the last time to the familiar tune of Auld Lang Syne, in which I hope you will join, let us remember with great pride the great and glorious past of our old Regiment, the King's Royal

Rifle Corps, the comradeship and good times we have had and the men who lived alongside us, have fought with us and in some cases have died in the service of the Regiment; and let us be grateful that we have been lucky enough to be included in such a company. Then as the band marches off, to Lützow's *Wild Hunt*, played officially for the last time as the Regimental March (though it will remain the Battalion March), I would ask you all to pledge yourselves wholeheartedly to the unqualified success of the new Regiment, and I would ask the men if they will, to dedicate themselves anew to the ideals and codes of conduct and performance which made our old Regiment great, and which will I know ensure that this new Regiment, the 2nd Battalion of the Royal Green Jackets, will continue to be in our eyes, and I hope in many others as well, the best Battalion of the best Regiment in the British Army.'

Something of our 210-year-old record of service and of what we brought as our special contribution to the Royal Green Jackets is found in the final chapter which follows.

CHAPTER XIV

THE CONTRIBUTION OF THE 60TH SINCE FOUNDATION AND TO THE ROYAL GREEN JACKETS

Heavy infantry

Many readers of this and the preceding Volume may not possess the Volumes covering the period 1755 to 1918, which are now rare. The aim of this final chapter, therefore, is to sum up for them what the 60th Royal Americans, the Duke of York's and, later, King's Royal Rifle Corps—the 60th Rifles—contributed over two centuries to the Army. It will also suggest what the Regiment contributed to The Royal Green Jackets in the final merging of identities, marked by the Colonel in Chief's Royal Review, on which this story passes into the hands of the historian of the magnificent new Regiment.

In the history of the British Infantry there are those regiments, which derived from or imitated the lower numbered regiments of the old Line, from the Restoration of 1660 to the wars against Louis XIV, Marlborough's Infantry.

The principle of assault or defence at close quarters was perpetuated for the British Private of the Line when he was issued with the flintlock musket and the socket bayonet. For 150 years, as at Ramillies, Fontenoy and Waterloo, he displayed the same stalwart courage and stolid virtues. The tactics of Waterloo were still in use in the Crimea, even though the Infantryman was carrying a rifle for the first time. Most of the subsequent Infantry Regiments tended to follow the Marlborough tradition, even though they might latterly be styled Light or Rifle. The exceptions were the four whose paths first crossed in the Peninsula and finally merged in The Royal Green Jackets.

The Marlborough concept was based on the arms issued and a view of the men who carried them. The enemy advanced or stood in mass; the smooth-bore musket could hit that mass at 60 yards and below, and since only the first loading could be fully supervised, the first volley of each rank must be held till the last moment for crushing effect, followed up by the bayonet. Men must be shoulder to shoulder so that one voice could give the orders, and under returned fire, and the inevitable casualties, all loading and other drills must become automatic, without thought. In this turning of men into a fire-production machine, obeying blindly a centralized order, no eye for ground or any other initiative must be cultivated, since central control would be lost.

The simple, uneducated soldier, under rigid discipline, must be drilled until he could load to a shouted time and march in rank; once at grips with the enemy his dogged courage would do the rest. In the open, cultivated fields of Western

314

Europe, against an enemy who followed a similar system but was often less disciplined and phlegmatic, this was for a time an effective formula.

The North American challenge

North American service was to challenge and erode this doctrine. In the forests of the Seven Years War (America's French and Indian War), the range and accuracy of weapons were less important than training, discipline and tactics. On the more open, cultivated Revolutionary battlefields along the East Coast the selective shooting of the American rifleman would be a novel feature of war.

Our story must start with the crushing defeat sustained by the much-maligned General Braddock on 9 July 1755. Although he had seen little active service, and followed regulations to the letter, he was not, contrary to some accounts, ambushed. His scouts met the advancing enemy and his vanguard's first volley killed the French leader; he had flank guards out in file at platoon strength along the column. The fault lay in the total lack of training for rapid deployment in a forest, the rigid style of fire control and the drill that beat back those who sought to advance using individual cover. Discipline collapsed because there was no bond of sympathy between the confused young Irish soldiers and the brave but remote British officers who strove to lead them. Braddock and his regiments were totally unprepared for the swiftness and individual use of ground and firepower of a few hundred Indians, despite the warning and example of the Virginian volunteers who gallantly covered the rout. His dying words 'Who would have thought it?' and 'We shall know better next time how to do it' have in a very real sense been our Regimental watch-words in the 200 years that have followed.

The origins of the regiment

The 60th Royal American Regiment (we can ignore the confusing initial numbering as 62nd) was unique.

Although the initial skirmishes of 1754, which had started the war, had been between French and Indians and the Virginians led by young George Washington, and Braddock had used the Virginian route of advance, the key to the central colonies lay in Pennsylvania. On her more Westerly settlements fell the weight of Indian raids; her farming communities of Germans and Swiss could provide the horses, waggons and manpower for future operations on a shorter route to Fort Duquesne if only they were not controlled by a Quaker Assembly.

Thus in October 1755, when Jacques Prevost arrived in London with a proposal to raise a regiment of Germans and Swiss, both from Europe and from Pennsylvania, his idea acted as a catalyst, to plans that government ministers were already discussing. Prevost, a Swiss, had been emigrating to the American Colonies after unsuccessful French service, when Lyttleton, the Governor-designate of South Carolina, and he were taken by a privateer. No doubt they had discussed colonial defence as prisoners, and his claims must have been backed by Lyttleton when they were liberated in England.

The Regiment thus derived from the need to provide a long-term solution to defence in North America, using local men, accustomed to frontier conditions, under good professional officers. Although it must not have the weaknesses of Braddock's regiments, it must be Regular to escape the whims of colonial politics.

The Regiment was a truly Royal creation, as denoted by the unusual grant of a Royal title from its foundation. A special Act of Parliament had to be passed to allow the commissioning of foreign Protestants for service in America only; in advance of this the Treasury would grant no funds for recruiting. King George II, however, personally advanced Prevost £2500 before Christmas 1755, and the Duke of Cumberland, as Commander in Chief, pushed the project through the Cabinet in January 1756. Unlike the normal single-battalion Regiment, they decided that ours should consist of four battalions, each of a thousand men. To ensure its proper administration and local recruiting—in so far as resistance to such matters by Colonial Assemblies allowed—General Lord Loudoun, the newly appointed Commander in Chief in North America, was made the first Colonel in Chief. Under him, a Colonel Commandant was named for each battalion.

By the time the Act was passed in March 1756 James Prevost had gathered together some 90 officers and NCOs, including Henry Bouquet and Frederick Haldimand, the first Commanding Officers of our 1st and 2nd Battalions respectively, and Augustin Prevost, a future Commanding Officer and defender of Savannah. These and many others came from the Swiss Guards of the House of Orange, the Princess being Cumberland's sister, and the British Minister at The Hague, Yorke, being a former ADC of Cumberland. There was also a good contingent of Germans, including NCOs and soldiers, brought over by Capt Baron Dietrich von Münster. Half the officers were, however, volunteers from the existing British Army, Englishmen and Scots. Appointments were back-dated, so that the Regiment's birthday was always taken from the Colonel in Chief's appointment on Christmas Day 1755.

The unique characteristics of the early regiment

We thus have a unique Large Regiment, created by the Royal Family and designed for a specific operational theatre, in itself most varied in terrain and climate, with a professional cadre of officers and some senior NCOs to recruit and train local volunteers.

The officers and some NCOs arriving at New York in convoys during the summer of 1756 had major problems to face. The first was recruitment in under-populated colonies, where every employer was sharply keeping his workers to their indentures; at least Indian raids discouraged the normal route of deserters towards the Western frontier. Administration was a perpetual nightmare in the face of colonial assemblies, who, even as Western settlers in the Alleghenies were scalped or carried off, would deny lodging and care of the sick to hard-pressed battalions.

In this early period we see the Regiment largely through the eyes of Bouquet, whether commanding the 1st Battalion, or as commander of expeditions, since his voluminous papers were left to his close friend Haldimand on his death, and they in turn to the British Museum. Dr Kent of the Pennsylvania Historical and Museum Commission has made it his life's work to track down, both in the States and in Europe, as much as can be found out about Bouquet and his very distinguished group of contemporaries and fellow-workers. The Regiment is indeed grateful to him and to the Commission for the publication of the successive Volumes of 'The Papers of Henry Bouquet', held by RHQ.

The great strength of the Regiment from its inception was that it was a new concept.

The Swiss for two military generations and in the two wars in America were a dominant influence, usually in command. Henry Bouquet of the 1st Battalion, Frederick Haldimand of the 2nd and the 4th, and Augustin Prevost of the 3rd and later the 1st, all reached General rank and were officers of distinction. Their Swiss upbringing and service in the regiments of Berne gave them several common attributes. Among these were true democracy, where all men regardless of rank were treated on their merits and were seen as assets, valuable when trained and not to be lightly thrown away. Probity, a sense of responsibility, a small nation's need to do business tolerantly with all men and a strong sense of family and community were all transferred to the new Regiment. Bouquet in particular had used peacetime service in Holland to improve his general as well as his military education to a high degree, and all the knowledge of the Swiss and Germans was expended with great industry in their new King's interest.

It is remarkable that, plunged into a new service in a strange and largely undeveloped country, using a foreign language, all these officers could so rapidly make such an impact. Because they could serve only in North America, the Swiss and Germans gave a continuity lacking in other regiments, whose officers were frequently transferring to forward their careers. This loyalty seems to have communicated itself to their British comrades, who served on with our battalions in many hardship stations.

The British officers—many of them Scots in the aftermath of the '45— who volunteered for the new Regiment shared certain attributes. They were anxious to get into action, and flexible enough mentally to see a challenge in new conditions and a rough life. For some the possibility of land grants in a new country was an attraction. The first 70 years of overseas service, in the field or under improvised conditions, taught our Battalions that if they wanted to survive they could only depend on their own efforts. Practical Swiss and British officers, a leavening of extremely competent engineer officers like Gordon and Des Barres—who between them did much of the Sapper work of North America before Royal Engineers arrived—and hardy American soldiers somehow overcame the ravages of climate, disease and governmental neglect. Because of the posting flexibility afforded in a Regiment which never sank below two Battalions, key officers knew each other, and a sense of the Regiment as a family was engendered.

The Regiment had the invaluable asset of successive Colonels in Chief being Commanders in Chief in North America during its formative period. Of these Lord Loudon and Sir Jeffery Amherst never spared themselves with help and sound advice. The support of the former launched the Swiss on their Regimental careers and the latter, who rose to be Field Marshal Lord Amherst, saw his old Regiment safely through many vicissitudes until, on his death in 1797, it passed into the hands of our first Royal Colonel in Chief, HRH The Duke of York.

Another source of strength in the early years was a succession of active and influential professional officers as Colonels Commandant until our own officers could reach that position; serving (usually in command of brigades) in North

America, they could see that their Battalions were properly administered and employed. Some, like Monckton and the distinguished Lord Howe, actually commanded their battalions; the professional skill of the latter—who learnt much from Rogers and his Rangers—until his tragic death before Ticonderoga, contributed much to the training of his 3rd Battalion, and indeed to the light tactics used later at Louisburg and Quebec.

The Seven Years War against the French and Indians in North America and the Caribbean

If 1757 was the year of recruiting and administration, it was also one of training, as well as the first experience, at the Fort William Henry massacre, of the horrors of Indian warfare. In 1758 all our battalions were hard at work. Light troops of the 2nd and 3rd, already wearing green, found the only landing-place, and under Lt Brown stormed ashore at Louisburg. Meanwhile Bouquet laboured on the construction of a line of communication and forts. At length his 1st Battalion was among the small force of the dying General Forbes, which paraded on the ashes of Fort Duquesne and the future foundations of Fort Pitt by the great Ohio—Braddock was in part revenged. Although in the centre Haldimand's 4th lost heavily alongside the Black Watch at Ticonderoga, Bradstreet and a small amphibious force, including two 60th Companies as the only Regulars, took the fort at modern Kingston and destroyed the French shipping on Lake Ontario. It is interesting to see so many Royal Americans involved in assault boating, for even Ticonderoga's reverse was preceded by a long paddle up Lake George. Bradstreet, despite later criticism, must be particularly recognized for his Corps of 2000 fighting boatmen.

1759 was for us the year of forest skirmishing, when the flexibility and modernity of Swiss training and tactics were put to good use. The 1st Battalion, with Bouquet as DAG to the force, kept the Fort Pitt road open against Indian ambush, wearing a preview of the favourite Regimental colour scheme in their green leggings with a red garter. Fort Niagara was taken in the centre, and the link between the Mississippi and Canada cut. Haldimand modestly gave command and credit to Sir William Johnson, the Indian agent, but it was his 4th Battalion that crushed a surprise French thrust at the expedition's Oswego base, where failure would have brought disaster.

The 2nd, commanded by Captain Oswald, and the 3rd, under the admirable Lt Col John Young, were particularly active around Quebec, charts of whose river approaches had been made by our engineer, Lt Des Barres, the previous year, and were used by Captain Cook. The Light troops and Grenadier Companies of the force were massed as at Louisburg, but our Grenadier Companies often operated as a pair. They and the 3rd successfully raided the Quebec shore 12 miles above the city, and Major Augustin Prevost, wounded in the head, survived trepanning to continue a brilliant career. It was the rivalry between two companies of the 2nd and our Grenadiers which next led them into an insanely gallant attempt to storm the heights above Montmorency Falls. The courage and skill shown by Ensign Peyton in trying to protect his dying Captain, Ochterlony, from the Indians should never be forgotten. Despite this bravado it was our Grenadiers whom Wolfe chose to clear the Canadians and Indians from that bank and earned us his motto 'Celer et Audax' – 'Swift and Bold', now the Royal Green Jacket Motto. At the Heights of Abraham the 2nd's Light Company under Lt McAlpin climbed a precipice to clear and hold a key post, while the 3rd were the link from the landing to the Plains. The 2nd, moved to cover the only dangerous flank, the left, skirmished to thwart the Canadians in the brush and defeated them, but sustained one-third of the British casualties, for the regiments in line were only asked to sustain a long-range volley and fire two in return.

Surviving a bitter winter, the two Battalions helped to blunt the advance of Levis. When our Navy arrived they then advanced on Montreal, the 2nd forming a composite battalion with the 43rd. Co-ordinated thrusts by our new Colonel in Chief, General Jeffery Amherst, who used the 4th to lead the advance from Lake Ontario, took Montreal. Col Haldimand was appointed its first Governor, and his tolerance and moderation, as well as knowledge of the language, did much to smooth the transfer of power. From this base, in September 1760, Robert Rogers of the famous Rangers set out with that wing of the 1st Battalion, separated from Bouquet since 1757, to take over France's Western forts. The main fort, Detroit, was soon garrisoned, but our last party did not reach Green Bay on the West side of Lake Michigan until Spring 1761. Thus was formalized the hopelessly vulnerable series of detachments, each of an Ensign or Lt and a few soldiers, not enough for a 24-hour guard, half starved and ill-equipped, which stretched 900 miles through the wilderness back to HQ of the 1st at Lancaster, Pennsylvania.

This was not all that was required of the new Regiment in the Seven Years War. In 1762, General Monckton took an expedition South which captured Martinique; this included the 3rd under Lt Col Augustin Prevost and its Colonel Commandant, Haviland, as a Brigade Commander. Almost at once the 3rd moved on with a force against Havana, Cuba, whose sea approach was dominated by Fort Moro. In terrible heat, with no local water, a way for the guns was cut through the rocky jungle and the siege pressed forward despite the ravages of disease. The 3rd were not only prominent in repulsing a sortie, but, wading through a swamp, broke a regiment of Spanish cavalry on the beach. It has long been believed that the words of the *British Grenadiers*, which came out as a popular music sheet just afterwards, refer to our men at Havana.

Pontiac's rebellion

Although 1763 spelled the end of the war for Britain, its most terrible aftermath was about to begin for the 1st Battalion. In a programme of retrenchment, the 3rd and 4th Battalions were being disbanded, and the other two reduced to half-strength. Despite the reports of Bouquet and officers in the posts, the resentment of the Indians was not appreciated by Amherst.

In April 1763 Chief Pontiac of the Ottawas proclaimed his revolt, and by July the detachments from Green Bay right back as far as Lake Erie had been captured by a variety of Indian stratagems. In this catastrophe—made inevitable by the stationing of tiny detachments in posts designed for peaceful trading rather than defence—the blame must be borne by neglectful authority. The courage and endurance in evading capture shown by Private Gray and the party led by Ensign Price deserve special praise. Only Detroit and Fort Pitt remained intact on the frontier, thanks to larger garrisons and the vigilance of Maj Gladwyn and Capt Ecuyer, a Swiss.

Bouquet acted with care to relieve his fellow countryman and pushed forward with some of his 1st Battalion and the 42nd Highlanders, the Black Watch. On 5 August 1763 his vanguard dislodged an ambush near Bushy Run. However, to protect the convoy of packhorses carrying the stores critically needed by the besieged fort, a fighting withdrawal was made to a defensive circle on a hill in the woods. After over 24 hours without water, two 60th Companies were pulled out of the circle under guise of a retreat. Lured on by the feigned retreat, the Indians were shattered at close range and then hunted by Royal Americans and Black Watch with a professional touch that showed we had indeed 'learnt to do it better'. Only highly trained and disciplined troops could have maintained morale and control in what the historian Parkman described as the best contested action ever fought between Whiteman and Red.

Bouquet relieved Fort Pitt, but Maj Wilkins at Niagara was frustrated, by enemy action and storm, from relieving Detroit. However, the siege—which was illumined by the extreme courage of Capt Donald Campbell and Sgt Smith among many others, and the ribald escape of Ensign Pauli from an enforced Indian marriage—was finally relieved by Colonel Bradstreet in August 1764, although Pontiac had himself moved off the previous autumn. Bradstreet, who should have known better, disobeyed all orders, by granting peace terms to any Indians he met, without insisting on their many captives being handed over. Bouquet, his superior in both the Army and the Regiment, was incensed and ignored Bradstreet's action (see his marvellously Riflemanlike letter in the Museum).

He pressed on with the task given him by the new C in C, Gage—that of advancing to the distant base villages of the recalcitrant Indians and enforcing peace. This meant an advance deep into present Ohio, a much greater risk than that required of Braddock. Nevertheless, by mid-October 1764 he had established a force of 1500 men, Virginians, Pennsylvanians, the Black Watch and his remaining 1st Battalion companies, 100 miles West of Fort Pitt on the Muskingum. He was not only a superior soldier, as trainer, tactician and logistician, but his leadership as a negotiator was supreme. By patience and firmness he enforced peace and recovered over 200 captives, many reluctant to leave the Indians. At the petition of Colonial assemblies the King granted him promotion to Brigadier General, but within days of arrival in his new command at Pensacola he had died of a fever.

Bouquet's training concepts

Still recognized today in the United States, and particularly in Pennsylvania, as a great man, thanks to the devoted work of Dr Donald Kent and others, Bouquet and his close friend Haldimand may be taken as the founders of the first modern Infantry Regiment. If this seems too bold a claim, an extract from his training concepts can be seen as perfectly appropriate to training a present-day battalion for forest warfare without helicopter support—the modern terms are listed at the end—and only the bugles or radios of later years are missing.

It may be taken for granted in warfare with the Indians, 1st that their general maxim is to surround their enemy, 2nd that they fight in extended order and never in a compact body, 3rd that when attacked they never stand their ground, but immediately give way only to return to the charge when the attack ceases. These principles being admitted, it follows 1st that the troops destined to engage Indians must be lightly clothed, armed and accoutred; 2nd that having no resistance to encounter in the attack or defence they are not to be drawn up in close order—a formation which would only expose them to needless loss; 3rd, that all their evolutions must be performed with great rapidity, and the men enabled by constant practice to pursue the enemy closely when put to flight, and not to give him time to rally.

Colonel Bouquet's suggestion was to form a battalion of 'hunters'—the exact equivalent of the word Jäger—500 strong, with two troops of light horse—mounted infantry—and a company of artificers attached, composed of frontiersmen, from fifteen to twenty years of age, enlisted for fifteen years and specially trained for the service.

Clothing

The clothing of a soldier for the campaign should consist of a short jacket of brown cloth, a strong tanned shirt, short trowsers, leggings, moccassins, a sailor's hat, a knapsack for provisions and an oil surtout against the rain. This surtout should have two coats of oil, and with the second coat it will be useful to mix some dark greenish colour to make the coat less conspicuous in the woods.

Arms

Their arms, the best that can be procured, should be short fusils and some rifles with bayonets in the form of a dirk to serve for a knife; small hatchets, and leathern bottles for water.

Exercises

The soldiers before being armed must be taught to keep themselves clean and to dress in a soldier-like manner. The first thing they are to learn is to walk well, afterwards to run; and in order to excite emulation small prizes might from time to time be given to those who distinguish themselves. They must then run in ranks in extended order and wheel in that order; at first slowly, but by degrees with increasing speed. This evolution is difficult, but most important in order to fall unexpectedly in the flank of the enemy. The men are to disperse and rally at given signals; and particular colours should be given to each company as rallying points. The men must be trained to leap logs and ditches and to carry burdens proportionate to their strength.

When perfect in these exercises the young soldiers will receive their arms and follow the above-named evolutions on all kinds of ground. They will be taught to handle their arms with dexterity; and without losing time upon trifles to load and fire very quick, standing, kneeling or lying on the ground. They are to fire at a mark without a rest, and not allowed to be long in taking aim. Hunting and the award of small prizes will soon make them expert marksmen.

The men should learn to swim, pushing before them on a small raft their clothes, arms and ammunition; they must also learn to use snow-shoes; they must be taught to throw up entrenchments, make fascines and gabions; as well as to fell trees, saw planks, construct canoes, carts, ploughs, barrows, roofs, casks, batteaux and bridges; and to build ovens and log-houses. With practice the youngest among them will soon become tolerably good carpenters, masons, tailors, butchers, shoe-makers, etc.

Light horse and dogs

In order to complete the establishment of this Corps two troops of Light Horse, each composed of 50 men and Officers, should be attached thereto. These men are to perform the same exercises as the foot soldiers, but to be afterwards taught to ride and in especial, to be very quick at mounting and dismounting with their arms in their hands. They must learn to gallop through the woods up and down hill, and to jump logs and ditches.

The horses must be strong and hardy and accustomed to feed in the woods; they must be thoroughly broken to fire, be practised in swimming rivers etc. Saddles and accoutrements to be of the plainest description, strong and light. The mounted men to have the same equipment as those on foot, and armed with a short rifle and a battle axe with a long handle for use in case of the charge. Each of these mounted men should be provided with a bloodhound who would be of use in discovering the enemy's ambush, and following his tracks. They would seize the naked savages, or at all events give time for the horsemen to come up with them; they would also add to safety of the camp at night.

The men should take it in turns to go on hunting expeditions with their Officers and remain out of camp for some weeks at a time, taking with them a little flour, but otherwise relying on the game and fish caught.

Great care is to be taken to preserve purity of manners, order and decency among the men; this will be found much easier in the woods than in the neighbourhood of towns. It would be a good plan to give the men only a small portion of their pay in cash, the remainder will be accumulated for them until discharge; then they would receive the balance due to them and 200 acres of land.

The clothing is a combination of 1965 jungle clothing and combat clothing of the 1970s. Training is a combination of the modern Physical Efficiency tests and range courses, concentrating on snap and run-down practices in a field firing environment. Turning 18th-Century rural Americans into assault pioneers would have been easier, but even urban Riflemen warm to such tasks. The reconnaissance platoon of light horse, working with combined tracker and war dogs in the form of the resolute Southern hound, links, through Mounted Infantry, with the carriers, scout cars and dogs of our own time.

Finally, the emphasis on adventure training of men with their own officers as opposed to degrading urban billet life, and the stress on savings and a gratuity show a concern for man-management which was virtually unknown in the British Army of the time. All this was later to be shared by the 60th and the Regiments of the Light Brigade, sounding lonely bugles against the administrative chaos and neglect in the long night of the 19th-Century Army.

From Canada to the Caribbean

While the 3rd and 4th Battalions were disbanded in England the 2nd under Col Haldimand relieved the 1st on the outposts; the latter under Lt Col Augustin Prevost sailed from Quebec in 1767 to Jamaica, for an Act had now been passed to include the West Indies as American service. In 1770 the rest of the Infantry were ordered to form light companies, which we had organized, independently of the improvised Louisburg Light Infantry, for the Quebec campaign of 1759. In 1772 the 2nd were also moved South, where Maj Etherington, in Bouquet style, persuaded the Black Caribs of St Vincent to cease their mountain resistance.

The American War of Independence

Somehow the two Battalions survived the ravages of disease, but there were still sufficient Americans serving to make retention in the West Indies tactful when the War of Independence broke out. However, Augustin Prevost was sent to Hannover and England to raise the 3rd and 4th Battalions once more. When the 3rd and 4th Split between Pensacola and St Augstin, Florida, cadres of officers and NCOs came over from the 1st and 2nd to ensure common training and traditions. Not the least distinguished of these was Colonel Augustin's younger brother, Lt Col Jean Marc Prevost, who acted as his 2IC when he was ordered to drive North on Savannah, Georgia; the 4th Battalion under him guarded the left flank of an exhausting advance over the rivers along the coast. After our entry into Savannah, an American force of 2000 men reached Briar Creek, 50 miles away. In March 1779 Lt Col J. M. Prevost secretly blocked the road in front and then himself led a brilliant surprise attack of the Grenadiers of our 2nd, 3rd and 4th from the rear, capturing a general, the guns and baggage, and destroying the force.

The finest moment of British defence in the South came in September 1779 when Augustin Prevost, now Maj Gen, defended Savannah with only 2000 men fit for duty against a combined force of 10,000 French under Admiral D'Estaing and his fleet, and Americans under Lincoln. The key Spring Hill redoubt was held for an hour by a small garrison including our 4th Battalion men, and the day was finally won when Maj Beamsley Glazier led our Grenadiers and some Marines in a counter-attack. The bravery of the dying Americans Lt Bush and Sgt Jasper is recalled by the colour of the 2nd South Carolina Regiment, honoured in our Museum.

On a rash expedition to Nicaragua, only the 1st Battalion and a certain Capt Horatio Nelson, RN, were effective, and loss of command of the sea allowed the French to capture St Vincent and the Spanish in New Orleans to reduce our West Florida posts at leisure. Maj Gen Prevost retired and his brother, Jean Marc, died of wounds. Finally, in 1783, when the 3rd and 4th were disbanded after a period in New York, the first Royal American period of the Regiment can be said to have ended with the war. In Georgia it had been undefeated, and on the Canadian border Maj Gen Sir Frederick Haldimand, as Governor, had successfully defended a people, against which the Regiment had been raised to fight. The Swiss and American period was over, but the experience and tradition were strong enough to carry American citizens into the Regiment 200 years later. The

United States, Canada and Britain can take particular pride in the only Regiment founded to link their histories in such a gallant way.

The French Revolution

In 1786, after 20 years service in fever-ridden Jamaica, the 1st Battalion was sent to Halifax and the 2nd in the next year to Montreal; both battalions were by this time made up of British soldiers, although Haldimand and Prevost remained as Colonels Commandant and there was a handful of original officers. In 1787, under threat of war with France, the 3rd and 4th were yet again raised from English and Hanoverian recruits; John Moore, later famous, joined as a Major, but there was a new generation of European officers among the Captains and Subalterns. The 4th was despatched to Barbados, but the 3rd was distributed round three of the other islands.

In 1793, with the outbreak of war, the 4th Battalion played a major part in the seizure of Tobago. Led by Maj Gordon, the Light and Grenadier Companies of the 9th Regiment and 60th, backed by the remainder of our 4th, stormed the fort, and forced the Governor to surrender. In 1794, due to casualties, most of the 3rd was transferred into the 4th, while recruits were sought in the Channel Islands, and the Grenadier and Light Companies of all battalions in the Windward Islands were massed and trained to conduct operations as in the American War of Independence. The 60th contingents played their part in the brilliant seizure of Martinique and Guadaloupe from stronger French garrisons. However, the arrival of the Revolutionary leader Hugues to arm the black population saw the tide swing against the British throughout the islands. Disease, the inroads of the French and their Negroes, and the Carib revolt on St Vincent wore down the 3rd and 4th, the latter commanded by Lt Col George Prevost, a son of Augustin.

By 1797 the 4th had been built up again and returned to the Windward Islands. The 1st, having handed over men to the 2nd at Quebec, had done the same, arriving in Barbados; the 2nd also detached half its companies to Caribbean islands. The source of replenishment for what was still a foreign service Regiment was to be found in the Channel Islands. There, and around the Solent, émigré French, Dutch and later Austrians and Germans, all former officers and soldiers of their armies, fleeing Revolutionary excess and later Napoleonic invasion, could be recruited by a Regiment legally constituted for this purpose. Yet another European transfusion was soon to bring with it an advanced weapon and the tactics and dress to enable it to be properly used.

Rifle Companies and Battalions

As early as 1758 a few rifles had been experimentally issued to Colonel Bouquet's 1st Battalion, and officers and some men had carried rifles on frontier operations. Indeed, his inventory on death shows him to have had a rifle and fusil among his personal equipment. In 1794 a Battalion, probably the 1st at Montreal, was officially armed with the rifle, and a Rifle Company, probably in green, was formed in each of our other Battalions. In December 1797 an Act was passed to allow a 5th Battalion to be formed. This is the Rifle Battalion, raised by Lt Col Baron Francis de Rottenburg, author of a treatise on Riflemen and Light

Infantry; the detailed account of this Battalion comes later. In July 1799 another Act allowed the formation of a 6th Battalion, but already in February its nucleus Rifle Company dressed in green had been formed and took part in a skirmish in Holland. The 6th, inspected by the Duke of York—now Colonel in Chief—embarked for Jamaica in 1800, where it joined the 1st and 4th, who were ravaged by fever. They were condemned to a terrible climate, with yellow fever and malaria, and were receiving drafts, sometimes of Englishmen sentenced to transportation, and sometimes of foreigners, often prisoners of war impressed into a service for which they felt no loyalty. It is a miracle that our Battalions survived, let alone did their duty. The threat to the West Indies from Bonaparte's expeditionary force in San Domingo held these battalions in Jamaica, the 2nd at St Vincent and the 3rd in Grenada; however, the brief peace of Amiens was soon broken in 1803 and the French, who had lost nearly 30,000 men from fever, surrendered and the survivors went to Jamaica. The British West India Regiment had been raised, and their battalions now served alongside ours, and, seasoned to the climate, gradually relieved them.

The Napoleonic Wars

The struggle was now against Napoleon's well-organized armies, and took place for the British chiefly in the Iberian Peninsula. However, there were also actions against France's enforced allies, such as Holland, where command of the sea—finally demonstrated at Trafalgar in 1805—allowed retribution against the colonies of trade rivals. Before turning to the Peninsula, let us look briefly at the Regiment in other theatres.

The West Indies and the Cape

When in 1803 we seized what was to become British Guiana from Holland, a Corps of Dutchmen was formed under Lt Col McLean of the 60th, and others joined our 2nd Battalion. Its Rifle Company and McLean's Corps then seized Surinam in 1804. In 1806 the 3rd, recruited to strength in Guernsey, returned and helped to take the Danish Virgin Islands. After being built up on a similar Jersey tour, the 2nd was diverted to Corunna in 1809, where it remained at the port and took part in the battle covering the embarkation; it was then routed back to Barbados.

In the same year, serving under Maj Gen Sir George Prevost—now a Colonel Commandant—the 3rd, commanded by Lt Col Mackie, and 4th Battalions did particularly well in the capture of Martinique, and their three Rifle Companies made a formidable cliff assault on the Saints. However, their best men must have been concentrated in the Rifle Companies, of which we have a Museum picture of a Guadaloupe patrol. Our Grenadiers, massed away from 2nd and 4th Battalion command, did badly there, for more than once General Beckwith, the expeditionary commander, protested to the Secretary of State that 'certain corps in this army be no longer loaded with men polluted by civil crimes, congregated with French prisoners and deserters', citing drafts sent to the 60th. However, Mackie's 3rd restored the balance with well-merited French thanks for rapid suppression of an insurrection on Martinique and good conduct thereafter. As

Spain rose against Napoleon and the command of the sea was secure, our Battalions were deployed all over the West Indies on internal security duties, the 2nd for instance being stationed in Demerara and, in better quarters than 2 Green Jackets, mentioned in a previous chapter. The threat was now from American privateers, as the War of 1812 had been declared, and the 60th distinguished themselves in minor naval actions as marines.

Another continent and future scene of action was opened to the Regiment. The 4th, packed with disaffected prisoners of war, garrisoned Capetown when it was first captured from the Dutch in 1806, and the 1st, properly recruited in South Hampshire, was stationed there from 1811 until it was disbanded at Portsmouth in 1819, handing over its title to the 2nd.

The period of West Indian service, from which the Regiment was rescued by the Duke of York, deserves to be summed up. Only a Regiment with first-class officers could have brought their men, recruited from so many unsatisfactory sources, through condemantion to what was then a graveyard. Deaths from yellow fever and other disease were fewer in our Battalions than in others. The connection with South Hampshire, the Isle of Wight and the Channel Islands goes back to the late 18th century, and more than justifies our Winchester home, finally established in 1858. The message of De Rottenburg must have been communicated through his writings, because it is clear that the Rifle Companies skirmished on classic lines over the most formidable country and under a deadly sun. The ability of our Battalions to work with the Royal Navy and with every race, colour and creed of the many encountered, is another characteristic from our early years.

American War of 1812

Apart from service as marines in the West Indies the Regiment was not involved at New Orleans or elsewhere on the South Coast. It was in the defence once more of Canada that 60th individuals and a Battalion showed the old mastery of forest tactics.

Colonel de Salaberry, a Canadian of Basque origin, had been commissioned into the 4th Battalion in 1793, at the instance of HRH The Duke of Kent, who was a keen supporter of the Regiment. He had distinguished himself on Guadaloupe, and killed a notorious and offensive duellist when still a boy. He had acted as General de Rottenburg's Brigade Major, and had fully understood the latter's tactics. Now in 1813 he had, with 400 of his Voltigeurs and 150 Indians, kept 6000 Americans in check for a month South of Montreal. By skirmishing and skilful use of deceptive bugle calls he finally defeated this larger force with light loss at Chateaugay. De Rottenburg, his commander, simultaneously broke a thrust at Chrysler Farm, and these two actions, well known to Canadians, saved Lower Canada. De Rottenburg was made President of Upper Canada, while the Commander in Chief (unfairly criticized later) was Lt Gen Sir George Prevost, who had successfully defended Canada for two years; the latter's memorial is in the South aisle of Winchester Cathedral.

In 1814 the newly formed 7th Battalion under Lt Col John formed part of an amphibious raid on the State of Maine. By some particularly cool skirmishing the Riflemen seized ground overlooking the Penobscot river; the action ended in the destruction of the US frigate *John Adams* and her guns, and the securing of New Brunswick's border. Although happily the nation was not again to be at war with the United States, the Regiment was long to be stationed in Canada. One can take pride in the fact that while it carried the title 'Royal Americans' (although it was by now no longer used) the Regiment never gave any but the most distinguished service in North America.

The 5th, the first rifle battalion, and the Peninsula

In 1793 our then Colonel in Chief, Lord Amherst, became Commander in Chief of the Army. He had full experience of the need for skirmishing tactics against the French and Indians, and had seen Maj Fergusson demonstrate his famous rifle in 1776. No doubt he saw the need to revive the old skills and combine them in an effective way, for there were in the service of the Crown several French, German and Austrian émigré units, trained, armed and dressed as Chasseurs or Jäger, at this time. The point was to get these combined skills into a regiment in the British Army, and since there was no British tradition like that of the Swiss and German hunters, who had been making and using rifles for many years, it must first be imported. Under him the fit men of three such foreign regiments were drafted into our 1st, 3rd and 4th Battalions, providing a leavening of skirmishers for the West Indies as we have seen. Amherst died just as the permanent move came to fruition in 1797, but to him must go the credit for the arming of the 1st with rifles and the formation of a Rifle Company in each of our Battalions in 1794. His successor, HRH The Duke of York, as both Commander and Colonel in Chief took the project further.

The second action was the Act to form the 5th Battalion in December 1797 and the order to raise it in January 1798. It was raised simultaneously in two wings, having at first separate identity. One was chiefly from Löwenstein's Chasseurs in Barbados; the distinguished officers included Maj Robert Craufurd, later to be killed when Commander of the Light Division, and Capt John Galiffe, a future Commanding Officer, who had served in the Royal French Army and the Dutch service. There is a record of the Light Horse of Löwenstein-Wertheim wearing dark green with scarlet collar and cuffs as far back as 1755.

The other wing of the 5th was raised on the Isle of Wight from three companies of Germans, specially recruited by General Baron von Hompesch, who had served in both the Austrian and Prussian Armies. The command of this was given to Lt Col Baron Francis de Rottenburg, an Austrian who had served in the Royal French Army and with the Poles against Suvaroff. He had served in Hompesch's first regiment since 1795, and later helped him to raise the German rifle companies. He was not only a skilled tactician but also won the affection of his troops through his parental care and interest in them. In a busy life he had somehow found time to write *Regulations for the Exercise of Riflemen and Light Infantry*, which covers the drill, manoeuvre and duties of Light Troops and Outposts under all field conditions. No doubt at the order of the Duke of York, the Adjutant General commended its translation to the whole Army in August 1798. In 1805 Sir John Moore, when writing to Col Mackenzie of the 52nd, said: 'I mean to make de Rottenburg the groundwork. . . . In reading over his book attentively I perceive much good in it. It only requires to be properly applied.'

One of the most interesting points is that Moore wrote in the same year that the bugle calls used by the 52nd and 95th (Rifle Brigade) were those of de Rottenburg, as of course were the 60th calls. Like Bouquet before him, de Rottenburg was one of the key founders of the Regiment, and indeed in essence of The Royal Green Jackets. Again like his predecessor, he became a naturalized Briton, sponsored by the Duke of York. The Duke of Kent was a fervent admirer of de Rottenburg, of Galiffe (whose father had been the Duke's tutor) and of de Salaberry.

The 5th Battalion's uniform derived directly from Löwenstein's and Hompesch's, being a rifle green jacket faced with red. The Riflemen were armed with a rifle and sword, with black belt and pouch and brown leather knapsack worn slung, and the badge was a silver bugle. The officers wore a black crossbelt, with lion, whistle and cross, and a sword with black leather sling, and all ranks had an embryo scarlet 'cherry' on the cap. Officers and men wore moustaches, which gave them a foreign look to English eyes.

De Rottenburg's wing, now of four companies, was rapidly in action in the Irish Rebellion of 1798. Their commander was General John Moore, whose 60th staff officer, Capt Anderson, remained with him until his death. It was the first time Moore saw de Rottenburg's principles applied in action, for he stated that in the pursuit following one of two classic skirmishing actions the Riflemen killed 60 or 70 rebels; the first casualties recorded in our Rifle role were killed here.

In 1799 de Rottenburg took his companies to Martinique, where those of Löwenstein brought the 5th Battalion up to strength in time to occupy Dutch Surinam; there further German and Austrian reinforcements were acquired. At the peace of 1802 it moved on to Halifax via Trinidad; an order was issued authorizing green jackets and pantaloons and black gaiters on sound Rifle lines, as well as a renewed issue of rifles.

Moving yet again to Hampshire in 1805 and on to Cork in 1808, it was trained to a high state by de Rottenburg. He now left to train and command successive brigades of Light Infantry, taking our Canadian officer, de Salaberry, as Brigade Major, and thence on to Canada for the War of 1812. The proficiency of our officers was to put a strain on the 5th in the Peninsula, as so many were away in key staff posts or as ADCs. Those remaining were very young, and indeed the new Commanding Officer, Maj William Davy, one of the first Old Etonians commissioned into the Regiment, was only 28.

An Army was being embarked for Portugal to help our old ally against a Napoleonic invasion, Portugal being our sole means of entry into European trade because of his Continental System. It is worth quoting extracts from Davy's Battalion Order on embarkation, foreseeing the risks of work by platoons and companies on the outposts, behind which the rest of the army expected to march and rest secure:

> . . . the Commanding Officer feels it his duty to recall the attention of the younger part of the Officers to the absolute necessity of making themselves acquainted with the several duties of the outposts, that they may be enabled to lead and instruct the men intrusted to their care. He also expects they will seriously consider that any neglect on their part before the enemy may cause the most fatal consequences (from the particular service allotted to the battalion) not only to themselves, but to the whole Army. . . .

... The men are to understand that by the maintenance of order and discipline we can alone look forward to successful opposition to the designs of an enemy. . . .

The true 'Rifleman' will never fire without being sure of his man. . . . And he will recollect that a few direct shots that tell will occasion greater confusion than thousands fired at random. . . .

It is particularly recommended to the men, and will be strictly enforced, to behave with humanity to the people in an enemy's country. . . .

It is the duty of every Officer carefully to provide for the wants of his men.

The Officers should endeavour to learn the capacities and characters of their men that they may employ them to the best advantage; this may be easily done by conversing with them, and hearing their opinion and sentiment on different subjects.

For action in Portugal the 5th—now referred to for the first time as the 60th Rifles—formed a Light Brigade with four companies of the 2nd Battalion of the 95th. The latter Regiment had been formed, as the next logical step in the creation of Riflemen, started by Amherst and carried further by the Duke of York. After yet another disastrous Low Country expedition in 1799, two military reformers, Col Coote Manningham and Lt Col the Hon William Stewart (soon to hold these appointments regimentally) proposed to HRH the assembly of an Experimental Corps of Riflemen.

Formed by selected officers and men attached from 15 British regiments, the Corps carried out an amphibious raid on Spain with three of its companies on 25 August 1800. When the Corps was formally established and recruited, largely from Ireland, that date was taken for its foundation.

In 1801 Lt Col Stewart, drew up and published in Coote Manningham's name his *Regulations for the Rifle Corps*. Bouquet and de Rottenburg had necessarily been concerned with the operations and field training of battalions always overseas and usually on active service. Stewart's 'Regulations' could only have been written by a Briton, who had full understanding of British soldiering at home and why it was imperfect. Coote Manningham's backing was necessary, because much of the Regulations dealt with interior economy and other matters which were the Colonel's prerogative.

It was a brilliant formula for establishing mutual trust and respect between all ranks; initiative and responsibility were encouraged within a clear code of discipline and chain of command. It gave the Corps, which became The Rifle Brigade, a head start of many decades over the Army as a whole, in anything from medals and Marksmen to messing; it is not surprising that the Rifle Brigade found that it had little in common with unprogressive regiments thereafter.

The Experimental Rifle Corps proposal came in 1799, the year that de Rottenburg took his wing of our 5th Battalion off to the West Indies. It is not known whether either 95th officer had seen 60th Riflemen—the Duke of York, of course, was their Colonel in Chief, and he had—for the uniform and equipment are almost identical, but the green, unrelieved by any other colour, would have appealed as better practical camouflage. In all events the Commander in Chief's two breeds of Riflemen were now on outpost duty side by side.

They were the first troops to land on 1 August 1808, and Wellesley gave orders that they should be drawn up on the exposed flank and always form the advance guard on the march. The two units each wore green jackets, and carried Baker rifles, but our Riflemen's blue pantaloons and the touch of scarlet worn by all ranks distinguished them at a distance, and on closer contact the German spoken by some officers and most of the men. Starting off with a classic skirmishing advance and withdrawal at Obidos, in the actions to get Junot out of Lisbon, the Light Brigade came into its own at Rolica on 17 August 1808. A French withdrawal was forced by continual left flanking actions in appalling country, and the two battalions earned special praise—it is in every sense the first truly Green Jacket battle honour.

No doubt this convinced Wellesley of the essential use of Riflemen in his operations, for the next day he decided to attach a company of 60th Riflemen to cover each of the seven Brigades of his Army, leaving only Battalion HQ and three in the Light Brigade. Their place in numbers was taken by the 50th in the Light Brigade, to which were added two companies of the 1st/95th; the 43rd and the 52nd also landed on that day with another Brigade. When Junot attacked at Vimiera on 21 August, the 60th were thus involved all along the scattered line, both in the Light Brigade and elsewhere, withdrawing under pressure to fire into a column's flanks but always exacting a price, sharing for the first time since Quebec with the 43rd in a gallant supporting counter-attack.

Some memorable quotations came from this battle: 'In this battle', said Col Leslie, 'the 60th Riflemen, who were all German, showed great tact in taking advantage of the ground and in dexterity in the use of their arms.' One Rifleman, offered a half-doubloon by his Brigadier for every French officer he brought down, said as he downed a third, 'By God I vill make my vortune.' Another, selecting a French officer as target rather than a marksman who was alarming a visiting officer by his accuracy, explained it coolly: 'It vas more plunder.' That frankness and realism are surely in the Rifleman's tradition. Leslie added: 'They displayed that steadiness and cool courage so essentially requisite to a Rifleman, in not hurriedly throwing away their fire until there was a positive chance of their fire taking effect.' This was particularly necessary with the slow muzzle-loading Baker rifle, and for the next fifty years Riflemen would work in pairs, as front- and rear-rank men, to keep up a comradely rate of fire. Equally Rifle Battalions were the first to break down their companies into detached platoons, where a young officer, bearing heavy detached responsibility, worked on a more permanent basis with his sergeant and twenty or thirty Riflemen, communicating by bugle with his company commander.

After this battle Brigadier Fane wrote to Maj Davy:'congratulating you and my friends of the 60th upon the flattering approbation our services have met with from our Sovereign'. De Rottenburg added: 'The Duke of York spoke to me in high terms of the Battalion.'

However, this first peak was to develop rapidly into the only trough in our Peninsula service. To make up casualties and with no reinforcements from home, Maj Davy misguidedly got permission from the C in C to enlist deserters from the French Army, hoping to secure those Germans forced into it. This had sometimes proved successful on isolated Caribbean islands when we had command of the sea, but was most risky for companies serving detached in the outposts so close to the French. In World War II the Polish Corps was built up in this way, but all Poles had a burning desire for revenge. That it seemed reasonable on the spot is shown by Wellesley's support and the approval of Burrard, the C in C and an old 60th officer. However, on the beginning of Moore's raid into Spain, ending in Corunna, five of our ten companies were detached under Captains and Subalterns, Maj Davy having a firm grip on the other five. As the five detached neared Junot again, the newly acquired men, no doubt seeing their pathetically small British force isolated against growing opposition deep in Spain, deserted back to the French service, and others misbehaved by looting in the manner prevalent in the French Army; these companies, with their hard core of loyal original Riflemen, were ordered back to Portugal. Moore sent Davy's wing back to join them, making it clear that it was to allow him to concentrate and grip the Battalion again; Davy at once brought the discipline and administration under control, being backed by the Duke of York in getting rid of 44 men, formerly from prison ships, who had been foisted on him. However, like a typical Rifleman, he kept on individuals of the same origin who showed some promise.

Although the 5th Battalion was not in the retreat to Corunna, the 2nd Battalion was in the battle at that port of embarkation. Meanwhile the 5th, purged of criminals and deserters who should never have been in it, had the rare distinction of being in the Peninsula from the first landing in Portugal to the end of the campaign in France six years later.

Despite the shortages, Davy insisted that men reduced to wearing their drawers only at least washed them, and that lost bugles and rosettes (the red 'cherry') should be replaced, and he soon had the Battalion in good shape.

Sir Arthur Wellesley, now back in command, was in no doubt of the value and reliability of 60th Riflemen, when writing in May 1809 to recommend our Companies to Brigade Commanders to which they were attached: 'They will find them to be most useful, active and brave troops in the field, and that they will add substantially to the strength of the Brigades.' This was in skill and not numerically, of course, for these companies often fell below 50 in strength, but their selective shooting of French commanders at all levels often meant that an enemy column was out of control by the time it met the red-coated Heavy Infantry. To act as Supports, on later Light Division lines—though, of course, that formation was not currently in the Peninsula—the Riflemen had the Light Companies of all battalions in a Brigade. Wellesley personally confirmed that Davy was responsible for administration and discipline of the whole Battalion, even though detached, and that he should station himself wherever most convenient for those tasks.

Although Napoleon did not believe in rifles, they were opposed by a company of picked musket-carrying Voltigeurs, small, active and intelligent, for each regiment. The French General Foy, comparing the two systems after Waterloo, noted the opinion that the English soldier of Heavy Infantry had not enough intelligence and smartness to combine regular Line duties with the individual action of the skirmisher. He particularly remarked on the use of the rifle by the 60th and 95th and their echoing horns, which directed their movements and reported enemy manoeuvres to their General. The original type of silver-bound cow horns, used by the 95th before bugles, can be seen in the Museum.

Wellesley's trust was not misplaced, either when a 60th company helped snatch a footing over the Douro or when, advancing into Spain up the Tagus, he met a French attack of two to one superiority at Talavera on 27 July 1809. When young British regiments in the 3rd Division broke under immense pressure, only a steady fighting withdrawal across six miles of plain by the 45th and the five companies of the 60th under Davy saved Wellesley from capture and probable defeat. Personally taking command of these two units, he recorded their 'gallantry, steadiness and discipline' and gave their COs his particular thanks as well as Gold Medals; the fact that both regiments had not left the Peninsula gave them continuity of field experience rare in Wellesley's Army, reformed after Corunna.

After this battle Maj Davy had to fight to retain his old establishment of Sergeants, greater than that of the Heavy Infantry, where of course they did not, with their spontoon (short pike), contribute to fire power. He pointed out that Sergeants were the best shots, that his Battalion, split up on outposts might cover a 10-mile front, and that Sir John Moore had often said to him that 'one Rifleman should be deemed the equivalent, when posted, to three sentries of the line, and that the parties must be in all cases commanded by an officer or NCO'. He won his case, having pointed out that companies were down to one officer, sometimes only an Ensign.

Early in 1810 Maj Davy, at last promoted Lt Col by Wellesley's intervention, handed over command to Maj Woodgate, who had previously commanded a detached wing. Davy, who was a later Maj Gen and Colonel Commandant, deserves special recognition for carrying the 5th Battalion through a difficult period to enhanced distinction. At the head of the 60th, in this same year of 1810, the Duke of York was forced to resign as C in C, but continued on as our Colonel in Chief.

The Light Division had now arrived under Maj Gen Craufurd, with the three 95th Battalions responsible for covering the 43rd and 52nd. The other five Divisions of Wellington's Army were covered by the 5th/60th, now commanded by a most distinguished new CO, Lt Col William Williams, who had succeeded Baron de Rottenburg, until then still technically the Commanding Officer.

By 27 September 1810 Wellington was under extreme pressure and had adopted a strong position on the steep ridge at Bussaco, with a ravine below so narrow that Riflemen could fire across. A French officer said, 'black specks indicated the sharpshooter outposts ... Riflemen, whose short rifles were so murderous. Their bugle horns ... could be heard emitting a sound so discordant and piercing...' On this forward slope Picton had entrusted Williams with a composite Battalion of three 60th companies and the four Light Companies of the Division. When 11 French battalions attacked North of the only road, the three Light Companies there were driven back, but, on de Rottenburg's principle, Lt Col Williams swung his three 60th Rifle Companies back in an extended line. From a spur overlooking the road they could fire into the flank and blunt each drive of the French columns in the old selective way, as first four and then 11 largely leaderless battalions were finally repulsed when meeting the Heavy Infantry on top. Williams, although wounded twice, was never recognized for this brilliant action; Picton did not put in a despatch because Wellington was with him, but afterwards realized his Commander in Chief had not seen the Riflemen in action in the dead ground. The better-known Light Division action on the other road to the North thus was the only one to be mentioned in the Despatch.

While in the lines of Torres Vedras, the 5th received a paltry draft from the Isle of Wight of 1 Ensign, 1 Sergeant and 37. Few companies, of whom the main were in 2nd and 3rd Divisions, with HQ in the latter, had more than a Capt or Lt and an Ensign. Former French Army prisoners of war were still being sent out as reinforcements from England only six months after their capture in Spain. In the advance Lt Col Williams continued to form a Light Battalion within the 3rd Division, led by his three 60th Companies, and succeeded in harrying and turning Masséna's left unsupported, inflicting casualties.

Although driven out of Portugal, Masséna turned to the attack with a superior force and Wellington prepared to receive him on the plateau overlooking Fuentes d'Onoro. The defence of the village itself was entrusted to Lt Col Williams. The three 60th Rifle Companies, backed by 28 Light Companies, held up a French Corps attack all day on 3 May 1811, inflicting three times our casualties, but Williams was himself severely wounded; Wellington specially mentioned his gallant defence and promoted Woodgate Brevet Lt Col for a gallant counter-attack.

On 16 May 1811, when Masséna took advantage of Beresford's faulty deployment at Albuera, our three Rifle Companies with 2 Division played their part in finally repulsing the French flank attack. Maj Galiffe and Rifleman Loochstadt, escorting artillery, had the unusual distinction of being present at both Fuentes d'Onoro and Albuera. On 12 August Williams, commanding the 3 Division light troops as usual and the 74th, was cut off over a river, but coolly found a ford and led his men out by night, capturing a French cavalry patrol en route; sadly, Capt J. Prevost, who had been wounded earlier, was killed at this time.

In the South Capt Blassiere, one of our Company Commanders with 2 Division, carried out a daring night patrol into Arroyo dos Molinos, which allowed General Hill on 28 October 1811 to surround and smash the French cavalry in that town.

1812 opened with Wellington's successful storming of the fortresses of Ciudad Rodrigo and Badajoz. At the former, General Craufurd was killed, but we suffered little loss in the storming. At the latter, Riflemen suffered when they prematurely engaged in a fire fight with sentries, but must have done well in Picton's seizure of the Castle, for both Lt Col Williams and Brevet Lt Col Fitzgerald were specially mentioned and received Gold Medals; the former commanded his usual Battalion group of 60th and Light companies, with the latter commanding the 60th element. Fitzgerald, who had been commissioned into another regiment as a child, transferred into the 60th and was to be a first-class Commanding Officer of the 5th and 1st Battalions, eventually rising to Field Marshal. His decorations are in the Museum.

Free now to threaten the enemy's communications with France, Wellington advanced as far as Salamanca. On 22 July 1812, Marmont mistakenly thought that he was starting to withdraw, and allowed his divisions to get out of mutual supporting range in an effort to turn the British right flank. Our three companies headed 3 Division, when it broke through one French division and penetrated another to a point when our heavy cavalry could break it. It was a great victory at low cost, but Lt Col Williams and Maj Galiffe were among those wounded. The former, wounded for the sixth time, later transferred into the 13th (Somerset Light Infantry) in Canada, where under General Prevost he further developed a brilliant career, which ended as a Maj Gen and KCB. His gallantry and skill had made the 5th Battalion outstandingly effective. It is worth noting that, in the subsequent 300-mile retreat from Burgos, 60th discipline and health were maintained, in contrast with the rest of the Army. Far to the North East the retreat from Moscow was heralding the beginning of the end for Napoleon.

Although Lt Col Fitzgerald was still on our strength, he formed a Light Battalion with our three companies and the light ones of 2 Division, and it was Maj Galiffe who in fact commanded and administered the 5th in all the actions of the final two years. Now aged 46, he had great experience, having first served in a Swiss regiment of the Royal Army of France until the Revolution, and as a Dutch hussar until he was a founder member of our 5th Battalion in 1797.

When Wellington left Portugal for good in 1813, the fall of Burgos allowed him to transfer his supply line to the Northern Spanish ports and thrust at the French communications over the Pyrenees. King Joseph made a stand forward of Vittoria to try to concentrate his forces, but Wellington dazzled him by successive thrusts across the river on to ground which dominated the plain and the road back to the town. In mist and rain on 12 June 1813, the Spanish seized a hill on the French left and were enabled to hold it, when Lt Col Fitzgerald held the counter-attacking French with his usual combination of Rifles and Light Infantry, supported by the 71st. In the centre a surge of Green Jackets—three 60th companies leading 3 Division and two 95th Battalions from the Light Division—swept on to the 'Hill of the English' and the 60th and 74th passed through the village beyond. On the English left 1 Division, with the 60th Riflemen and Guards Light Companies, were threatening the French escape route. When the centre collapsed, only Reille's stalwart rearguards saved anything from the debacle. One hundred and fifty guns were taken and the reign of King Joseph and the French over the oppressed Spanish people was nearing its end.

The new commander, Soult, however, launched an offensive in the Pyrenees when he saw that Wellington, occupied with two sieges, had overstretched himself on a bad road system. On 25 July 1813 the forward brigade of 2 Division, covered by its 60th Company, held on for nine valuable hours; in the withdrawal the Rifle Company of 4 Division were the rearguard. The other brigade of 2 Division made an equally valuable stand against D'Erlon. Holding the original outpost on an isolated rock with his usual grouping of 60th Rifle and Light Companies, Lt Col Fitzgerald then took over the brigade and fought a brilliant delaying action back over the pass. 2 Division's gallant stands, in which 60th Riflemen had formed the rearguard, had bought invaluable time from the three attacking French divisions. Sadly, Lt Col Fitzgerald was badly wounded and captured a few days later when leading his skirmishing Rifles and Light Infantry boldly into Soult's rearguard, when the latter was desperately striving to regain France.

French casualties were heavy, particularly in officers, owing to our selective shooting. A unique testimony to the coolness and accuracy of our Riflemen came soon after this in a report by Marshal Soult, French Commander in Chief in Spain, to the Minister of War in Paris:

St Jean de Luz, 1st September 1813.

The loss in prominent and superior officers, sustained for some time past by the Army, is so disproportionate to that of the rank and file that I have been at pains to discover the reason; and have acquired the following information, which of course explains the cause of so extraordinary a circumstance.

There is in the English army a battalion of the 60th consisting of ten Companies—the regiment is composed of six battalions, the other five being in America or the West Indies. This battalion is never concentrated, but has a Company attached to each Infantry Division. It is armed with a short rifle; the men are selected for their marksmanship; they perform the duties of scouts, and in action are expressly ordered to pick off the officers, especially Field and General Officers. Thus it has been observed that whenever a superior officer goes to the front during an action, either for purposes of observation or to lead and encourage his men, he is usually hit.

This mode of making war and of injuring the enemy is very detrimental to us; our casualties in officers are so great that after a couple of actions the whole number are usually disabled. I saw yesterday battalions whose officers had been disabled in the ratio of one officer to eight men; I also saw battalions which were reduced to two or three officers, although less than one-sixth of their men had been disabled. You can imagine that if these casualties should recur, it would be very difficult to provide for the replacement of officers even though the nominations were made beforehand.

Colonel Dumas, on Soult's staff, claimed, in support of this, that '"Les Riflemen" killed all our officers between July 25 and August 31 (1813), viz 500 officers and 8 Generals.' Whenever the Light Division was engaged, the 95th Rifles would have exacted their toll, but the 10 60th Rifle Companies distributed between five other Divisions would have played the main part in ensuring that French columns were largely leaderless and not in full control before they reached our main Line of redcoats. If the French were clear that the greatest damage came from the 60th, as opposed to the Brunswick Oels and King's German Legion riflemen, in their distinctive uniforms, we must accept their accolade.

On 7 October 1813 Wellington forced his way over the Bidassoa, the first Ally to enter France, a few days before the distant battle of Leipzig. Roughly half the 60th officers were now of British origin, but in the battle to cross the Nivelle it is our foreign officers' names which stand out.

The French Army had long prepared a line, part of which was South of that river. Maj Galiffe, now effectively our Commanding Officer, was specially mentioned as commanding the advance of 3 Division. Commanding his three 60th and the Light Companies, in the style of Williams and Fitzgerald, he forced the bridge over the Nivelle at Amotz, splitting two French Corps; Maj Schoedde, one of our most experienced officers, who was later to earn the rank of Maj Gen and a KCB in 1842 in China, commanded the three Rifle Companies at Amotz, and was awarded a Gold Medal for seizing the bridge. Lt Lerche, formerly a sergeant major in the battalion, led his 60th company at the van of 2 Division and earned special notice.

After incessant rain the prolonged battle of the Nive took place in December 1813. Our junior officers and sergeants in particular suffered casualties in the gallant stand by 2 Division, isolated over that river against more than double their numbers.

It had been a year when the value of the 60th was again recognized. Another Act of Parliament authorized four more Battalions, of which only the 7th, in green but with a 2 to 1 proportion of Light Infantry to Rifles, and the 8th, fully Rifles, were formed.

On 23 February 1814 the Passage of the Adour involved our Rifle Company with the Guards Brigade of 1 Division in a classic bridgehead defence. The 60th had led a daring crossing in pontoons over the 300-yard-wide mouth of this tidal estuary below Bayonne. Backed by the usual two Guards Light Companies and four more of 3rd (Scots) Guards, they saw off two French battalions. 'The Rifles gradually and steadily retiring', the Light Companies held the columns, while 50 gunners, who had each carried four rockets into the bridgehead, and field guns with shrapnel from over the Adour forced a retreat; the first use of the new field rocket was particularly effective. Capt Harrison, our Company Commander was, a few days later, totally blinded; in recognition of his services he received the unusual retirement award of full pay for life.

Meanwhile to the East, Wellington had been forcing the French back at Orthez; our 3 Division companies skirmished well, but pride of place must go to the 52nd Light Infantry, who under Colborne (later FM Lord Seaton) advanced through a marsh and were as effective as against the flank of the Imperial Guard at Waterloo.

In March the three 60th Companies paved the way for 3 Division in brilliant skirmishing against French *tirailleurs*, using hedges and walls, just as the three 95th Battalions led the way at Tarbes two days later.

The war ended with heavy 60th casualties. In the battle for Toulouse in April 1814, Picton wastefully threw his four Rifle Companies, under the recently promoted Brevet Lt Col Galiffe, against the strongly fortified Garonne bridge. A redoubt and flanking batteries allowed no tactical manoeuvre, and despite great gallantry the 120 Riflemen were repulsed with 40% casualties. A few days later a French sortie on the Guards at Bayonne caused both of the 60th officers and some Riflemen in that company to become casualties.

The news of the Emperor Napoleon's abdication was now reluctantly accepted by Soult and his commanders. This was the end of our 5th Battalion's most distinguished service against the French, which had lasted unbroken from the first landing in Portugal in 1808. We had only 9 officers and about 250 Riflemen remaining, but they and the earlier casualties had earned 15 Battle Honours and the general Honour 'Peninsula'. This is now shared in the cap badge of The Royal Green Jackets with the 43rd, 52nd and 95th (The Rifle Brigade), the heroes of the outposts and skirmishes over the rocks and heaths from the Atlantic coast of Portugal to the Midi.

It will be recalled that, in the War of 1812 against America, the 7th Battalion was active in Maine, and that 60th Riflemen were distinguished at all levels in the defence of Canada, which they had earlier striven to take and which without

Haldimand could easily have been lost in the American Revolution. However, no 60th Battalion was at Waterloo, although Capt Horace Seymour of the Regiment, one of the most powerful men in the Army, is reputed to have killed more enemy than any other with his sabre, as ADC to Lord Uxbridge.

The admirable 5th Battalion, having incorporated the 8th, ended its days at Gibraltar, command having passed from Galiffe back to Fitzgerald when the latter was liberated. The latter took a large draft to Quebec in 1818, and on 16 July 1818 the Prince Regent signed a Memorandum: 'That in consequence of the 5th Rifle Battalion being about to be disbanded, the 2nd Battalion of that Regiment be clothed, equipped and trained as a Rifle Corps.'

It had been decided that Line Regiments should be reduced to only one battalion and the two Rifle Regiments to two each. Thus the Rifle Brigade lost one battalion, but the 60th lost six; the ones to be perpetuated were our 2nd and 3rd, renumbered as 1st and 2nd. In 1817, the 6th from Jamaica and 7th from Maine had amalgamated with the 3rd at Halifax, Canada, and in 1819 the 1st left the Cape for Demerara and disbandment. In Guiana the 4th was disbanded in the same year.

The new 1st was referred to as late as 1826 as 'late 5th' by the Horse Guards, and was also known as '1st Rifle Corps', denoting its seniority as a Rifle Battalion in the Army. The 5th's butts up position of the 'March at Ease' was perpetuated, and the CO, Lt Col Andrews, was a Peninsula veteran.

The new 2nd Battalion was commanded by Col Mackie, CB, who had commanded it as the 3rd since 1808; the two Majors were the redoubtable Galiffe and Henry Fitzgerald, when the 2nd moved in 1824 to Demerara.

The Duke of York's Own Rifle Corps

Thanks to the Duke of York, our Colonel in Chief, and reinstated as Commander in Chief, the anomalous position by which British 60th officers were condemned to serve in bad stations overseas (because their foreign brother officers could not legally serve in England) was rectified in two important War Office letters of 1824.

'His Majesty has been pleased to direct that the 60th Regiment shall cease to bear the appellation "The Royal American Regiment" and be termed the "60th Regiment, The Duke of York's Own Rifle Corps and Light Infantry".'

A month later the 2nd Battalion was converted from a Light Infantry to a Rifle Battalion, and, with the final abandonment of colours, Ensigns became Second Lieutenants.

The last German soldiers, described as 'a most quiet and orderly set of men', were now discharged, and those officers of foreign origin who had not become British subjects were offered half pay or settlement in Canada. It must again be stressed what the Regiment owes to the brilliant Swiss, Austrians, Germans, Americans and others who as officers or soldiers led the Army in tactical innovation, skill and gallantry in the first 70 years of the Regiment's service overseas, often in action and always under active-service conditions. That the famous 5th Battalion somehow managed like all good Riflemen, to make themselves comfortable in the Peninsula is shown by their elegant decanters in the Museum.

The new Commanding Officers were to be men of influence in the important introduction to service at home. Col Bunbury, whose urbane portrait in full dress enlivens the 2 RGJ Mess, was asked to wear the Duke of York's button and was a lively character; he replied, when asked if his officers gambled, 'No, for I have won all their money!' More importantly, he was efficient, and the Duke of York was very pleased with the first sight of his new Rifle Regiment at Chatham, when he himself was wearing the uniform of his Rifle Corps. His sword, sabretasch and cross belt worn on that parade are now in the Museum. Our earliest silver dates from our move from overseas to more formal English mess life; the silver snuff box in 2 RGJ's Mess, with a straight Rifle bugle horn, was presented in 1824 by Lt Evans, and sample cutlery is in the Museum.

On October 1824 the King authorized the resumption of the 'Celer et Audax' motto, now borne as 'Swift and Bold' by The Royal Green Jackets. Regrettably, the Duke of York, who had achieved the innovation of Rifle Battalions and the conversion of the Regiment into his own Rifle Corps, based in England, died in 1827. His brother, HRH the old Duke of Cambridge, took over as Colonel in Chief. The Duke of York would have been satisfied that, from 1816 on, his Riflemen were professionally already ahead of most regiments in attendance at another of his creations, the Staff College. Under his influence and that of his Commanding Officers, good-quality English officers flocked to join the Regiment, and surprisingly soon the names of great Regimental families start appearing in successive generations on the rolls.

The 1st, operating for the first time with the Queen's Bays, were forced to kill five civilians in aid to the civil power in the desperate Northern England unrest of 1826. On 1 January 1827 it disembarked at Lisbon with an expeditionary force which successfully pre-empted the invasion of Portugal by Spain. Col Lawrence, later the distinguished commander of 2nd Rifle Brigade in the Crimea, always recalled modelling that battalion on our 1st.

The 2nd, under first Galiffe and then H. Fitzgerald, remained in Demerara until 1829, earning both the praise of General D'Urban for efficiency and good conduct, and that of Sir Colin Campbell on the Isle of Wight, by which time Lt Col the Hon A. F. Ellis, MP, was CO. Campbell had served with the 7th and again with the 5th Battalion at Gibraltar, and was later Commander in Chief in the Indian Mutiny, becoming FM Lord Clyde. 'War-worn Sir Colin' saw much of our 1st Battalion under his command against Sikhs, hillmen and Mutineers, although in an age of purchase, he did not serve long enough in a 60th Battalion to be counted as one of our Field Marshals.

The 60th, The King's Royal Rifle Corps

In 1830 King William IV, within a few months of his accession, approved the new title as 'The 60th, The King's Royal Rifle Corps', thus setting the seal of Royal approval even more firmly on the Regiment.

The Ionian Isles

During 1834 the 1st moved from Gibraltar to Malta, and in 1836 to the Ionian Isles, then British, based on Corfu or Vido with detachments elsewhere. Weber's

Huntsman's Chorus was the Regimental March, now that of The Royal Green Jackets, and the practical custom of opening the tight jacket and wearing a waistcoat in the Mess led the rest of the Army into the adoption of Mess Kit.

The 2nd Battalion found themselves alongside the 1st in Corfu in 1837. They had last met in 1802 in Tobago. The 1st went home to Woolwich in 1840 and the GOC's report to the Horse Guards said 'I have seen all the Armies in Europe, and do not hesitate to aver that more efficiency in the peculiar Arms of this Corps I have not met.' Lt Col Molyneux was a first class CO and had the advantage of having Capt Mitchell, the Rifle expert, as Adjutant from 1835 to 1844. Inspected by the Prince Consort, the 1st were armed with Brunswick percussion rifles; all the officers dined at Cambridge House with the Colonel in Chief in 1841, in what was the forerunner of our Regimental Dinners.

Jamaica

In 1841 the 2nd Battalion returned to Jamaica. Although the seasoned British West India Regiment had long taken over most garrisons, the Horse Guards were still content to condemn British battalions to the unhealthy camps round Kingston. Our predecessors had just lost their CO and 140 men from yellow fever before being moved, but the excellent GOC was allowed to send only one company to camp at Newcastle, 4000 feet up in the mountains.

Between June and August 1841, from a fit, young 2nd Battalion, 140 Riflemen and some wives and children had died before they were moved to Newcastle. Lt Col Ellis had worn himself to the bone, riding in the sun to cheer detachements and patients, and, like Bouquet before him, died of yellow fever within four days of his Battalion's move to the hills. Our total loss was 2 officers and 173 men, 10 wives and many children, about 33 per cent in all.

The Sikh Wars

In 1845, the 1st Battalion under Col the Hon Henry Dundas, CB, with Lt Col Bradshaw as second Lt Col, embarked on its famous fighting tour in India, returning only in 1860. It was the first Rifle Battalion to serve in India, and the first with a common roll of promotion for the whole Regiment.

By the end of 1845 the 1st had assembled in Poona. The Punjab was in a ferment and the Sikh Army was on the march. By 11 February 1846, the unseasoned Battalion was trans-shipped to Karachi, where Bradshaw took over from Dundas, who had been given a brigade. However, our victory at Sobraon gained Mooltan and an uneasy peace until April 1848; our representatives in Mooltan were then murdered.

Procrastination during the summer led to Afghan backing of the Western Punjab's revolt, and in October the 1st Battalion started to march and boat the 600 miles up the Indus as part of the Bombay Division, commanded by Dundas. In December the latter was ordered to clear the South side of Mooltan city and five 60th Companies seized the Ava Mundee mound. This was a key position needed by the siege guns, and their Brigadier wrote of their subsequent skilled skirmishing into the walled garden suburbs 'nothing could exceed the gallantry and discipline of the the 60th Royal Rifles'.

Bradshaw returned from leave to take over from Maj Dennis, who had been wounded, and three Rifle Companies from now on protected our guns by their sniping fire against the Sikh garrison. The tusk trophy in 2 RGJ's Mess given by Maj Maughan, RA, comes from Gullala, the great elephant who brought up the guns, but who normally carried our Officers' Mess tent poles. In the assault of January 1849 our 'steady and well directed fire kept down that of the enemy very considerably while the troops were approaching the breach'. It must be remembered that alone in the Army the Rifle Brigade and ourselves used modern weapons, camouflage and open tactics, saving many lives, while the remainder of the Infantry still advanced in the costly red-coated close-order formations of Waterloo. On 21 January, Mooltan Citadel surrendered and on 2 February the 1st Battalion was specially ordered to start its forced march of 283 miles, to bring Riflemen on to the field of Goojerat, averaging 17 miles a day including halts. On 21 February 1849 his old Battalion covered Dundas' Division forward on the left, but our use of artillery turned a Sikh Army double our number to flight before we could close in. The Rifleman's cane held by 2 RGJ lists on it the tremendous marches of the 1st Battalion at this period, for they led the infantry pursuing the Sikhs and forcing their surrender 115 miles further on. When the 1st Battalion halted on 29 March at the Khyber, up which the Afghans had been driven, they were 213 miles from Goojerat and 500 from Mooltan, all covered at operational pace on foot in increasing heat.

Rifleman Burke and Gullala's Tusk

The Punjab had been annexed, but the hill tribes refused to pay revenue to their new masters. Col Bradshaw was asked by the civil power to lead a punitive expedition, including a covering force of over 200 Riflemen from the 1st Battalion, and including the guns of Maj Maughan, who messed with us. Leaving Peshawar, they opened operations on 11 December 1849 against a village held by 2500 tribesmen. The skirmishers of the Rifles and Guides cleared the defended flanking heights and the village fell after a five-hour operation. This was a prelude to a similar success three days later, recalled in the silver figures on the top of Gullala's Tusk in the 2 RGJ Mess and in the great black Standard in the Museum, where it is recorded:

> This standard was taken in a personal encounter by Private James [really Michael] Burke, 1st Battalion 60th Royal Rifles, in which he killed two of the enemy and was himself slightly wounded at the storming of the Heights of Pullee in the Buz Dhurra on the 14th December 1849.
>
> The above Private presented the standard to Lt Col Bradshaw commanding the force, and was for his gallantry promoted Corporal in the Field by him.

Burke afterwards became RSM of the 1st Battalion.

A final operation to open the Afridi road from Peshawar occupied another 200 Riflemen in hill skirmishing before the 1st moved into a hill station. Col Dundas received the KCB, and kept in close touch with the 1st, later becoming General Lord Melville, GCB. He instituted our Regimental Dinner, based on his earlier Coldstream service. Lt Col Bradshaw became CB and Maj Dennis a Brevet Lt Col, but Bradshaw, an excellent CO, soon died. Another loss was the death of HRH the (1st) Duke of Cambridge, in 1850. HRH The Prince Consort then became our Colonel in Chief. The great Duke of Wellington spoke in his last report of much satisfaction 'at the perfect efficiency of this Corps in all respects'; the Colonel Commandant in receipt of this was his old Peninsula subordinate, Maj Davy, now Maj Gen Sir William.

The Kaffir Wars

It was now the turn of the 2nd Battalion, after a tour in England and Ireland, to recapture the Peninsula spirit; under Lt Gen Sir Harry Smith they were matched against the Kaffirs in their rocky and mountainous land, divided by rivers with rare fords. Sir Harry had been a skilled officer in the Rifle Brigade in Spain, where he had met his Spanish bride, whose name is immortalized in the town of Ladysmith. He had particularly asked for Lt Col Nesbitt's 60th Riflemen, knowing that superior marksmanship and field craft were needed against the Kaffirs, who were equal on their own terrain to the American Indian. Disembarking on 7 October 1851, Sir Harry had the 60th on operations inland from East London only a week later. Riflemen took and cleared the Water Kloof in skirmishing order, 'regarded', says the Despatch, 'by the Kaffirs as impregnable', and by Smith himself as almost impracticable.

For the next two years the increasing toil of counter-insurgency operations in an exhausting climate and terrain was excellently sustained. Harry Smith particularly noted in a Despatch the taking of Iron Mountain, where the ground finally forced a frontal assault with fixed swords (as bayonets have been called since the Peninsula) against the Kaffir assegais. 'Maj Bedford with two Companies of the 60th Rifles pursued the fugitives over declivities nearly impassable, many more cattle falling into his hands . . .', and Capt Hope and Lt Du Cane displayed especial gallantry. Despite their shrewd tactics and bravery, the Kaffirs were finally worn down. One of the pleasanter moments had been meeting a Rifle Brigade Battalion once more in the field—a series of oils is in their Museum—and a sad pride was taken in sharing with the 43rd respect for the discipline of our drafts at the sinking of the *Birkenhead*.

The Rifle Depot and reformed battalions

Many changes were taking place in the Regiment. Battalions had long had Bands and Bugles, and indeed the singing of the German Riflemen was spoken of before the Peninsula. The weapon had recently been the Minie, but the Enfield name began to appear in 1855. The shako was becoming lower, and the uniform or tunic without any Regency trimmings. As a result of Crimean lessons our 3rd Battalion was raised again, followed by the 4th, during the Indian Mutiny, at Winchester. In 1858 Winchester became the Joint Depot for the two old Rifle Regiments, well in advance of Cardwell's County connections. This anticipated by a hundred years Brigade or Division linkage of the Infantry. By chance the 3rd Battalion spent many years on active service, while the 4th had 13 years of training under Lt Col Hawley but very little action until the Great War.

The Indian Mutiny

Back in India the 1st Battalion had pioneered its own field firing. In 1854 the Commander in Chief ordered this to be adopted by all the Army in India, saying, 'in the 60th Rifles a sufficient number of targets are planted out to admit the extension of a Company. All the usual Light Infantry practice is carried out within a distance of 500 yards, and the men become thereby accustomed to judging distances and consequent range of sight.'

This field training was timely, for when the Battalion marched from Jullundur in the Punjab to Meerut at the end of 1855, the Mutiny was only 18 months distant. The new long Enfield Rifle put a proper weapon into the hands of all Infantry, but only 10 rounds per man were issued to the 1st, despite protest.

The Sepoy Revolt flowed from many causes, of which the annexation of Oudh in 1856 provided a stimulus for a planned conspiracy apparent to the more watchful. In Meerut a native regiment had refused cartridges of the old type; the mutineers were put in irons and gaoled at a parade on 9 May. By chance the Church Parade on 10 May had been brought forward, for the Sepoys had hoped to catch the British congregation unarmed. 60th Riflemen were awaiting parade in their summer whites when a Rifleman brought news of the wave of murder and arson fanning out from the native lines.

Our bugler sounded the Alarm and Assembly, and the 1st drew arms and ammunition; Lt Austin rushed the first 50 of his Company to seize and hold the Treasury $1\frac{1}{2}$ miles away, where he held on throughout the night and exacted some vengeance for atrocities there. Lt Col John Jones ('The Avenger') took command, and more ammunition was issued from the Magazine. The Brigade Commander, pursued into the lines by his own Sepoys, led the 60th, some Carabineers and Horse Gunners against the mutineers in the flaming city, dispersing the Sepoys and local hooligans and protecting the British families. Meanwhile the Subaltern of the Day, Heathcoate, cut his way through a mob and led a guard out to seize the Arsenal. All was then done locally to restore order and gather up the carnage of the men, women and children slaughtered. However, when it was found next day that the mutineers had marched on Delhi no cavalry pursuit was ordered, and in that city the Commissioner did not read the Meerut despatch until too late. Luckily, the gallant Lt Willoughby of the Artillery seized and blew up the Delhi Magazine.

Back in isolated Meerut, wild rumours prevailed, and the only native reinforcements mutinied in their turn. It was not till 27 May 1857 that, leaving two companies as Meerut garrison, Lt Col Jones marched out with his remaining six companies, totalling 16 Officers and 450 Riflemen. Besides the Carabineers, there were the Gunners, including Tombs' Battery, in a party ordered to join the Field Force marching on Delhi. Camped just short of the Hindun river, nine miles out of Delhi, on the 30th, the 1st and its Gunners combined in magnificent fire and movement. The Riflemen under immediate command of Lt Col Jones crossed a 600-yard causeway under direct artillery fire and stormed the Sepoy batteries. They then skirmished the enemy infantry out of a fortified village, routing 5000 with considerable enemy loss. They repeated a similar action next day and burnt the village, but four Riflemen died of the daily increasing heat.

The Ridge at Delhi

On 1 June a warm friendship and later Alliance started, as the Sirmoor Battalion of Gurkhas, now the 2nd King Edward VII's Own Goorkhas, joined the column. Moving cautiously by a flank march, the column joined the Field Force; 'the Rifles in particular, though they had had a long march, came along stepping out merrily and singing in chorus'. The mutineers in Delhi, now 20,000, eventually built up to 60,000, while our Force was below 4000. Grouped with the Goorkhas and some of the 9th Lancers, the 60th waded a canal North of Delhi under fire, and by a process of hooks and charges the covering batteries were captured and Sepoys broken. On 8 June we took up positions on the Ridge, overlooking Old Delhi, 1200 yards away from the North West over rocks and scrub. The key picquet was Hindu Rao's House, held, under Maj Reid, exclusively by his Goorkhas and our Riflemen; we were also at the Observatory. Almost at once the Guides arrived to join us by a magnificent 600-mile march. Each Regiment has since then possessed its third of the Delhi Table, where the blood of our casualties mingled as they were tended in Hindu Rao's House. Carved with the badges and mottoes of the three Regiments, our portion is in the Museum, and was in evidence at the Delhi Parade 100 years later at Winchester.

Every day saw a Sepoy sortie, and to resist them the picquet was built up to 300 men from each Regiment, A counter-attack of Riflemen, Goorkhas and Tombs' Gunners destroyed a dangerous enfilading battery, and kukris were put to good use. When the main camp behind the Ridge was attacked, the future FM Lord Roberts wrote: 'All was now in confusion, the disorder increasing as night advanced, when a small body of Infantry (about 300 of the 60th Rifles) came up, dashed forward and cutting a lane through the rebels, rescued the guns.' However, by 26 June 11 Officers out of 14 and 200 Riflemen had become casualties. Only the thought of what would happen to the thousands of British families if they failed kept the little force going through that terrible burning summer.

On 23 June 1857, the centenary of the battle of Plassey, the Sepoys made a great attack, confident of success. From 5 am to 4 pm its main weight fell on the Rifles, Guides and Goorkhas of the Hindu Rao picquet, who held on. They then turned to the counter-attack, taking the Subzee Mundee gate, threatening the South of the Ridge and camp, and established a picquet there. Lt Hare's Company volunteered as one man to seize the key 'Sammy' (Swansi) House in an action where C/Sgt Garvin won the VC. The Sepoys, after a most brave offensive, then retired, having lost a quarter of their men.

On 29 June Lt Heathcote wrote:

Our men are thought a great deal of, and certainly they are beautiful shots; the enemy funk us more than any other regiment, so much so that the King of Delhi has offered a reward for every Rifleman's jacket brought into Delhi.

It should be noted that, on advice of their MO, the Regiment wore their green serge jackets throughout the summer to protect against chills leading to cholera, and had only lost two men through disease, although in the camp behind officers and men were going down daily. Part of this was due to officers' and NCOs' care, particularly over water, and Maj Reid noted his admiration for the 60th Rifles and their 'discipline in the field, so different to that of any other Corps'.

Throughout July, when the heat reached 120° F and the swarms of flies spread cholera in a camp awash with monsoon rain, the attacks on the Ridge and counter-attacks succeeded each other almost daily. When Capt Wilmot's pistol missed fire in the rain, Rfn Thompson broke through the ring of Sepoys, bayoneting two, and earned a VC for saving his Company Commander's life.

The great Moslem festival on 1 August 1857 signalled another attack, when an enemy build-up of 20,000 against the 'Sammy' House was eventually seen off by Maj Reid's 900; Jones was temporarily commanding a brigade with distinction. One of our buglers on his own initiative deceptively sounded the Regimental Call, 'Retire' and 'Double', and the Sepoys, who stormed forward, recognizing the call, were mown down by our guns. Bugler Sutton, who later won a VC for reconnoitring the breached walls, dashed forward and killed a Sepoy bugler in the act of sounding.

In typical fashion a fine day called for a cricket match and pony racing in the Rifles' lines, and the arrival of the 52nd Light Infantry among other troops on 14 August was welcomed. They, six companies of the 1st Battalion 60th Rifles and the Sirmoor Goorkhas formed 2 Infantry Brigade.

Capt Sir Edward Campbell, Bt, whose family was to serve for a hundred years and four military generations in the 60th, had done much good work. On the night of 6 September the essential prelude to the bombardment and assault of Delhi was brilliantly executed by his Company, which crept forward silently without being discovered to within 200 yards of the City's Northern walls. By dawn batteries had been thrown up on the cleared ground behind and our siege guns were established; from Meerut garrison our remaining 6 officers and 200 were now released to join us, bringing us up to 390 in all. While in that garrison those Riflemen had formed a very effective Elephant Column to dominate the district.

By 13 September the breaches at the Cashmere and Water Bastions, visible to this day, as are all the landmarks around the Ridge overlooking Old Delhi, were pronounced practicable by Engineers escorted by Riflemen. For the assault our companies were to skirmish in front of the five assaulting columns and keep the defenders' heads down on the walls; another company was with Maj Reid's column of Goorkhas and Guides and one in reserve. 4000 men were to storm a City held by 40,000.

At 3 am on 14 September Col Jones inspected his Battalion minutely, before they led the assault. Soon after dawn, Campbell's Company swept forward and covered the Cashmere Gate, to allow the Engineers to place the charge; its detonation was the signal for Bugler Hawthorne to sound the 'Charge' to the 52nd column. However, to the left Hare's 60th Company had not only cleared the wall but had scaled it with ladders, to cover the main Cashmere breach.

Once inside Jones collected his Companies and held the large building assigned to him, but successive loss of column commanders led to delay and the erection of Sepoy street blocks. Our losses had been 80 all ranks, greater than those at Badajoz, and the inability of Maj Reid's column, despite Goorkha and 60th efforts—unsupported by artillery—to clear the enemy from their salient South of the Ridge imperilled the British rear. However, each day Col Jones and his Riflemen infiltrated forward and sniped at the enemy gunners, often working with the 52nd, and the tide started to turn at many points. Finally on 20 September 1857, covered by Riflemen, Engineers blew the Palace Gate and Jones and his men seized the Red Fort, where he proposed and drank the Queen's health.

If Delhi has been covered at length, it is because the 60th never fought better against overwhelming odds for such a long period and under such terrible conditions. Starting with 440 all ranks, and reinforced by 200 men just before the storming, our total casualties were 389. VCs were awarded to Lt Heathcote, two Colour Sergeants and four Riflemen, and Jones received a Brevet Colonelcy and the CB. In a final Order the Delhi commander said: 'The 60th Royal Rifles have shown a glorious example in its splendid gallantry and its perfect discipline to the whole force.' Much of the latter was due to the excellent Adjutant, Capt Kelly, who had enlisted in 1841 and was commissioned later as a reward for his education and ability. Equally fine was the performance of the Sirmoor Battalion, whose translation to Riflemen at their request was a reward for battlefield perfection, later extended to other Gurkha regiments.

The Terai

The new Commander in Chief, Sir Colin Campbell, spent the Spring of 1858 relieving Lucknow, where our Lt Col North took the silver-mounted powder horn, now in the Museum. In April Col Jones was put in command of a Brigade, which was to converge on Bareilly from the North West, destroying large Sepoy forces in the densely jungled foothills of the Terai. Led by his skirmishing Riflemen, he defeated one superior force after another, storming a city and taking 37 guns, in clearing the province. When Sir Colin cautiously entered Bareilly he found the Riflemen of his old Regiment already there in an action which was to earn Rfn Bambrick the VC. Jones was appointed KCB—rare for a Colonel. He became QMG in India, having defeated every enemy encountered, taken all towns he attacked and all guns pointed at him; he would have been the first to say that this reputation was true of all his Riflemen.

Armed with the muzzle-loading Short Enfield and commanded by a succession of Captains—for Maj Palmer, CB had also left the Battalion—the 1st took part in the final drive in Autumn 1858 to break up the 150,000 rebels still left in the bamboo hills of Northern Oudh, near Nepal. At the same time half the 2nd, which had been shipped from the Cape, took part in column work. When finally the 1st Battalion left Calcutta in March 1860, the Governor General published a very detailed General Order, recounting their long and arduous service and particularly commenting on the discipline and excellent conduct of all ranks, as well as their valour. The memorial column at Dover Harbour is a tribute by the Town Council to the survivors, who marched into their new station so bronzed that they were taken for native troops. Even so, many Riflemen had volunteered to stay overseas with the 2nd Battalion or the Rifle Brigade.

War in China

Renewed difficulties had broken out with China and a small joint British and French expeditionary force was organized to land and advance on Peking. The

2nd Battalion, under Lt Col Palmer, trudged through the mile of sea mud on landing on 1 August 1860 near Pehtang. Their only action was the capture of the Taku Forts commanding the Pei-Ho river. Not involved in the great attacks by Tartar horse, the 60th band played at the funeral of our murdered envoys. The French had seized and looted the Summer Palace, but agreed to hand over part of the spoil to the British. Capt Fletcher and Lt the Hon R. Vereker bought the enamel vases for the Regiment, which are in the Museum with the former's picture. The 2nd Battalion was the last to leave Peking, and formed part of the brigade garrison of Tien Tsin. Dressed in fur caps, boots and sheepskins, they endured a bitter winter, isolated by a frozen sea, skating and acting to pass the time. The great summer heat and disease, however, cost them 94 men, to whom a memorial was raised on leaving on 30 September 1861 for England via Hong Kong.

Eighteen years of peacetime duties world-wide

Thereafter for over 18 years the Regiment, just as after World War II, fired not a shot, but its efficiency was maintained at home and abroad. The 1st, after an enjoyable period at the Tower of London, and, surviving the volleys of ramrods accidentally fired at them in Hyde Park by the new and over-eager Volunteers, spent a dull period in Malta. It was enlivened by a few incidents, however, such as the escape by the later FM Lord Grenfell from the clutches of a great octopus during a night swim. The Battalion reached Quebec and Montreal in 1867.

The 2nd Battalion pleased the Commander in Chief, HRH The Duke of Cambridge, on manoeuvres with its modern open tactics, still not used by the Heavy Infantry. After internal security operations against the Fenians in Ireland, it used the new Suez overland route to serve, first in Calcutta and then in modern Pakistan, reaching Rawal Pindi in 1872.

The 3rd Battalion, reformed in 1855, had a frustrating overseas tour. Although very strong it was kept in Madras from December 1857 and was not involved in the Mutiny operations. A tour in Burma with detachments in the Andamans, like the 1st in the 1930s, followed until 1865. Rashly ordered to embark from Rangoon for Madras in the cyclone season, both halves of the 3rd met cyclones. One ship with 500 men and women aboard was only saved by the gallantry of Ensign Lindesay and his Riflemen volunteers, who cut away the wreckage, enabling the Captain—who was the only ship's officer sober—to regain control.

The 3rd Battalion had been formed by promoting officers within the 60th. The reformed 4th Battalion was therefore required to receive volunteers from other Regiments on the post-Crimean run-down, in particular Hawley of the 89th. The 4th Battalion was our first to be raised at Winchester, and recruited its Riflemen from London and the South during 1857. It moved via Dover to Ireland, but the outbreak of the American Civil War required it to be rushed to Canada in the SS *Great Eastern* in June 1861. During that war the 4th was in the Citadel at Quebec and Montreal, but after the War ended in 1865 it moved to London, Ontario, to watch the border against Fenian raids by Irish demobilized from the US Army. After a brief incursion at Niagara by 15,000 Fenians the threat diminished and the 4th moved to St Johns, New Brunswick, in 1868. The

1st Battalion was now on the St Lawrence, and had built the fort covering the Quebec Citadel.

Lt Col Hawley's command

In 1860 Lt Col Hawley had taken command of the 4th Battalion, which now had a good leavening of 60th officers with experience against Kaffirs, Sepoys or Chinese. A widower, he gave all he possessed to the happiness and efficiency of his Battalion, which after deep study and enquiry he modelled on all he could find about the 5th Battalion in the Peninsula. When asked his formula for success, he replied: 'By feeding the men well and giving the officers plenty of leave.' This was over-simplification, because his shrewd business sense brought messing and every other fine point of the neglected administration to the highest level. His officers he trained on Bouquet's lines by sending them with parties of Riflemen on hunting and canoeing parties in winter and summer, where they had to live off the country. A superb canoeist himself, when young Redvers Buller first wanted to shoot some rapids, and then with belated prudence suggested a portage he replied: 'No, I have come to this point for your pleasure and you must now go on for mine.' The rapids were expertly shot. His field training was based on simplified orders, including whistle and hand signals, instantly obeyed by Riflemen trained in alertness, self-reliance and self-discipline. His principles were not adopted by the Army until 1896, but meanwhile he had trained or given an example of how to create and handle a modern Battalion to many younger officers. After bringing a superbly trained 4th Battalion home to England in 1869, he finally handed over in 1873.

The Red River expedition

Back in Canada, despite the purchase of Western land claims by the Government from the Hudson's Bay Company, the French Canadians felt that their aspirations were being slighted by English settlers. In 1870 Louis Riel seized Fort Garry, now Winnipeg, on the Red River, and after summary trial an English surveyor was shot. The Government in Ottawa entrusted the DQMG (the branch then responsible for operations), Col Garnet Wolseley, who had already seen service world-wide, with command of an expedition to suppress the rebellion. Troops allotted were the 1st Battalion 60th and two Militia battalions, including the nucleus of the later Queen's Own Rifles of Canada. From Toronto 635 miles of the Great Lakes had to be crossed. From Port Arthur to Fort Garry was a further 600 miles, including a watershed of 800 feet.

Lt Col Fielden's 1st Battalion started on 14 May 1870 by train and steamer, as soon as the ice had melted, but the 1st were not assembled at Port Arthur till 21 June. Riflemen had then to cut over 20 miles of roadway in pouring rain and biting flies. A river route was pioneered by Capt Young, who led his Company in a relaxed and practical style, his matches always dry in his red night-cap. Buller, an old hand, arrived from the 4th, and managed to catch up with his men. The 30-foot boats, each containing two sections and three months' stores, had to be handled over 47 portages. Wolseley wrote: 'It was wonderful how quickly the little Londoners of the Rifles became good men in the boats and over the portages.' He also found officers and men becoming expert axemen and *voyageurs*. A century ago the Cockney style of the Regiment was already apparent! The self-confidence of the older Riflemen, many of whom had fought at Delhi, was much admired. Wolseley also praised the leadership of the officers in pitching into all physical labour. Rowing on over the Lake of the Woods, the dangerous Winnipeg rapids were shot, and the 1st slowly proceeded up the Red River. 10 miles from Fort Garry the rifles, now breech-loading Sniders, were unpacked and a flank guard company landed and mounted on ponies. When the Riflemen reached the Fort on 24 August it was found that Riel and his band had just fled, bound for the States. On the 28th the Militia arrived to take over, and by 25 September 1870 Lake Superior was regained. It was a brilliant feat, against all local prophecy, carried out in the short season between the lakes freezing. Lt Col Fielden received the CMG and two Brevet Majorities were awarded.

In November 1871 the 1st Battalion was the last British unit to leave the Citadel in Quebec, which the Regiment had helped to take in 1759. The strong links and good reputation left behind have been maintained through our Affiliated Canadian Regiments. In 1876 the 1st left Halifax for England, finally quitting its original continent.

Cardwell's reforms

The Army, thanks to the warning of Prussian victories and the efforts of Cardwell, was slowly reforming; the necessary prelude of a formalized General Staff and War Office had, however, to await the aftermath of Boer War reverses. Soldiers were now enlisted on short-service engagements and equipped with the Martini Henry of Kipling's tales. Commissions and promotions were no longer purchased, and from 1881 onwards the Army at home was treated as the reinforcement depot for battalions, usually in India, facing the supposed Russian threat.

In the linking of the 37th and 57th the new Hampshire Regiment arrived in Winchester, just as the 43rd and 52nd were linked to Oxfordshire and Buckinghamshire, now a RGJ sphere of interest. However, the flexibility of the 60th and Rifle Brigade derived from an establishment of four battalions, each one recruiting on a wider basis, and from a shared Depot; the long-standing interest in professional innovation was to keep them in fighting trim. Since the 1860s, in line with our future Volunteers and Territorials, great interest had been taken in competition shooting.

During an Indian tour of 16 years starting in 1876, the 4th saw only counter-insurgency service in Manipur and the Chin Hills on the Burma border, and acted as home Battalion during most of the South African War.

The Afghan Wars

The 2nd Battalion had reached Rawal Pindi in 1873 and had plenty of time to train in various Indian stations before the outbreak of the Second Afghan War in 1878. The Battalion was with the original advance to Kandahar via the Bolan Pass, but saw little action until a move towards Kabul was made. At Ahmed Khel in 1880 the Company detailed to protect Divisional HQ saw desperate fighting to protect the guns, when the column was charged first by swarms of Afghan horse and then tribesmen. It took part in Roberts' famous march from Kabul back to Kandahar and even harder hill work thereafter, marching 1000 miles in 100 days over the mountains, until returning to England after a brief wartime sojourn in Natal.

The Zulu War

South Africa was to absorb much of our Regimental attention. We had annexed the Transvaal, and border disputes with the Zulus turned to a war, in which we were defeated at Isandhlwana. Reports of this did not reach England till February 1879, but our 3rd Battalion embarked within a week, and reached the forward assembly on the Tugela River at the end of March. A Column was formed, in which one brigade was commanded by our Lt Col Leigh Pemberton, so Lt Col F. Northey took over the 3rd. At Ginghilovo, when the 60th covered the front face of a square waggon leaguer on a low hill, the 3000-strong Column came under attack on all sides from 10,000 Zulus. Engaged by our men from 800 yards onwards, the Zulus worked up to within 150 yards in the long grass before they opened fire. They were repulsed with heavy loss, but sadly Lt Col Northey, an excellent officer of the well-known Regimental family, died of wounds. Apart from an unfortunate incident, when our picquet outside a night leaguer was first rushed by panicking native scouts and then suffered casualties from fire from inside the leaguer, the 3rd saw little further action. Redvers Buller, who had served in Ashanti, however, won his VC against the Zulus, before taking part in many other campaigns, forming the RASC as QMG, and then becoming AG.

War in South Africa

Freed of the Zulu threat, the Northern Boers proclaimed independence in December 1880 and small British garrisons were ambushed or besieged. In January 1881 General Colley marched North but failed to force Laing's Nek or to employ our four Companies properly. However, when the Boers threatened the road to his rear he took out Lt Col Ashburnham and his five 60th Companies with four guns, two manned by Riflemen, and a mounted troop. Across the River Ingogo on 8 February, they met a Boer force which built up to 1000, and the 60th just had time to seize and ring a flat hill-top. A fire-fight between some of the best field marksmen in the world lasted from 11.30 am till dark, but despite the cover the Boers were never able to rush the plateau. RSM (later QM) Wilkins showed particular coolness and steady shooting, later receiving the DCM. After dark in pouring rain the Battalion formed a hollow square around the guns and wounded, fording the rising Ingogo with much difficulty; indeed, Lt and Adjt Wilkinson was among those drowned when caring for casualties.

Colley in his despatch wrote:

> The comparatively young soldiers of the 60th Rifles behaved with the steadiness and coolness of veterans. At all times perfectly in hand, they held or changed their ground as directed, without hurry or confusion; though under heavy fire themselves fired steadily, husbanding their ammunition, and at the

end of the day, with sadly reduced numbers, formed and moved off the ground with most perfect steadiness and order; and finally, after eighteen hours of continuous fatigue, readily and cheerfully attached themselves to the guns and dragged them up the long hill from the Ingogo, when the horses were unable to do so.

The 3rd Battalion suffered 120 casualties out of 217 engaged, but the Boers never tried to interfere with Colley's communications again.

Fortunately, Colley dropped off his three 60th Companies at points on his fatal advance with a tiny force on to Majuba. They, with a company of the 92nd Highlanders, were able to cover some of the survivors retreating from that disaster, in which Colley was killed and which brought peace.

The Egyptian Campaign

Although the 3rd Battalion moved to Malta in April 1882, they embarked for Egypt in early July. Arabi Pasha's coup threatened the new Suez Canal and the 90,000 French and British subjects in the country, and the 3rd found themselves in Alexandria to restore order from mob looting on 18 July. The Cavalry had not arrived, so Capt E. Hutton at once formed a Mounted Infantry troop, patrolling forward 10 miles in his expert way; Rfn Corbett earned a VC on valuable reconnaissance.

Wolseley's concept was to threaten to advance up the Delta on Cairo, while rapidly seizing the Canal and using the desert approach from Ismailia alongside the Sweetwater Canal's West branch. The 3rd were in due course switched there, and a fourth Brigade was formed with the DCLI under our Col Ashburnham, now CB, ADC. Redvers Buller, head of Intelligence, had reconnoitred the very strong Egyptian position at Tel el Kebir, on which an approach march started in the early hours of 13 September 1882. The 3rd Battalion were in the second line, advancing 1000 yards behind, but linked by a connecting Rifle Company to the left-hand Brigade of Highlanders; the guns were on our right. Within 150 yards at first light, the Highlanders came under heavy fire, and had considerable difficulty crossing a deep ditch and parapet with fixed bayonets. Our 3rd split to support the Black Watch and HLI, one company capturing four guns; it was an hour before all the works were taken against Sudanese opposition. However, resistance ended with an eventual Egyptian rout and Cairo was occupied, Riflemen being seen for the first time in Gezireh.

The Eastern Sudan

The occupation of Egypt eventually involved the Government in its dependency, the Sudan, where the Mahdi had started to attract followers. Successive British-led Egyptian Army efforts to control the Eastern Sudan from the Red Sea against Osman Digna and his Fuzzy-Wuzzies had led to disaster. Accordingly, the 3rd under the promoted Colonel, Sir Cromer Ashburnham, KCB, moved to Trinkitat on 23 February 1884. The Battalion fortunately found itself in Buller's Brigade, but in both actions change of front brought it to the rear face of the brigade square. At El Teb a majestic march round the enemy's left allowed the guns in the square to silence their opposing pieces, and the position was rolled up; but alas, our gallant QM, Wilkins, was killed.

Moving by sea to Suakim, the 3rd formed part of the right square under Buller, who wisely held back 600 yards from the Tami ravine, full of Fuzzy-Wuzzies, and used his fire power. Despite excellent reconnaissance by Lt Marling, 60th, who won a VC for saving one of his Mounted Infantrymen here, the other square closed up to the ravine and the General ordered the Black Watch to charge; into the gap in the square thus formed and under cover of the black powder smoke the Fuzzy-Wuzzies poured. There was no panic and much gallantry, but only the intervention of our cavalry and Buller's square relieved the pressure. Buller then advanced and took Osman's camp; over 1000 dead were seen, and the recovery of much lost equipment from previous disasters was a warning to the Mahdi of what was later to befall him at Omdurman.

The hideous spiked helmet had replaced the Rifleman's cap in 1878, and this was no doubt worn when the Queen inspected the 1st at Osborne in 1887 and at HM's Jubilee Review at Aldershot later that year; it should be remembered that the Gothic swords worn by 2 RGJ buglers were given by Queen Victoria herself.

On the North West Frontier

At the end of 1890 the 1st embarked for India and within a few months was on active service on the frontier. Starting unfit and untrained for hill warfare, they saw little close action but learnt a lot. Another expedition followed without action. The Riflemen were itching to use their new Lee Metfords, the first in India, but were crippled with malaria back at Rawal Pindi. However, they had regained their strength for the Chitral Relief Expedition of 1895, since they performed a feat of arms at the storming of the heights controlling the Malakhand Pass. Another Brigade was already half-way up when our 1st was ordered to link the Highlanders on the right and Guides on the left. They raced up the 1500-foot nearly sheer face, turning the Swat tribesmen out of sangar after sangar, and assaulted the crest, level with the neighbouring battalions; amazingly, our casualties were light and those of the armed tribesmen heavy, though of course we had a few mountain guns.

The wreck of the 'Warren Hastings'

The 1st's next challenge was in discipline and initiative at sea. Leaving India in 1896 in the RIMS *Warren Hastings*, they dropped four companies at the Cape; the remainder of the Battalion under Lt Col Forestier-Walker then sailed back for Mauritius, accompanied by four companies of the York and Lancasters and a Middlesex draft, 1000 in all with 27 women and children. At 2.20 am on 14 January 1897 the ship struck a reef off the Island of Réunion in pitch dark and pouring rain. The men fell in below in perfect discipline and silence. At first it seemed as if the families could wait till daylight to clamber down and over the rocks, and the men started to disembark. However, the ship took a violent list, and the Battalion stood fast while the families were rapidly cleared. Rfn McNamara then volunteered to swim with a line to land through the surf and undertow, and the rest of the troops made their way ashore, with many acts of gallantry. Thanks to perfect co-ordination between Commander Holland, RIM, and Lt Col Forestier-Walker, the only loss was a native cook, whom a sick Rifleman just failed to save. French officials were kind and helpful, and congratulations poured in from England. FM Lord Wolseley, Commander in Chief, issued a special Army Order with pride in the discipline shown, and HRH the Duke of Cambridge wrote of it as 'a noble example. As Colonel in Chief of the gallant Corps I feel more than ever proud of being associated with so splendid a Regiment.' Queen Victoria cabled her great satisfaction, and much regretted the loss of property of all ranks.

Parliament had to be invoked to get compensation for the men, and the officers of the 2nd Battalion generously presented a Dutch silver ship, now in the Museum, in recognition of the 1st's loss of silver. The *Warren Hastings* wheel and bell, now held by 2 RGJ, were presented to the 1st, on condition ship's time was rung on the latter, and Battalion Guard Rooms all over the world have since echoed to its notes.

General Hutton and the Mounted Infantry

In view of the Regimental reputation for innovation, and since it links Bouquet's concept of Light Horse with the motor battalions of World War II, a brief mention must be made of Mounted Infantry (MI), which for 30 years filled an indispensable gap. The great authority was a 60th Rifleman who became Lt Gen Sir Edward Hutton; he reorganized the forces of Canada and New South Wales before the South African War and founded Australia's Commonwealth Forces thereafter. From the time when he raised a corps of Mounted Infantry in Egypt in 1882, his brother Riflemen and he were always in the lead in this art, whether on camels trying to relieve Gordon, or on horses in the South African War. Hutton, while DAAG at Aldershot, simultaneously formed and ran the Mounted Infantry School from 1888–92; it was thanks to him that so many officers had been trained before the South African War broke out. In the war the 60th were the only regiment to form a complete battalion, 25 Mounted Infantry, although most battalions there at the outbreak had a company, like the 1st. Hutton himself commanded a force of 7000 Regular and Colonial MI on Roberts's advance to Pretoria and beyond. The Regular Cavalry were costly and at that period were poor marksmen, reluctant to dismount, unlike their Dragoon forebears. MI were seen by Hutton as a substitute for cavalry on colonial expeditions and 'to provide a force of selected Infantry sufficiently mobile to act as such in conjunction with Cavalry'. This latter use leads directly to our motor role with tanks.

As this brief account of earlier 60th history enters the twentieth century, where official documentation contains full details, and when the scale of action tends to dwarf that of battalions, only the highlights will be touched upon.

The South African War

By 1899 it had long been clear that the points of dispute between the Boers and British must soon come to a head. The Republic could put 50,000 armed men into the field, while British troops in South Africa amounted to only 10,000; this garrison was doubled just before war broke out. The Northern salient up the

Natal railway from Durban, over the Tugela river to Ladysmith and Newcastle, was particularly vulnerable, and the 1st Battalion was part of a brigade furthest forward, near the Dundee coalfields. On expiry of Kruger's ultimatum on 11 October 1899 Boer columns invaded Natal. At dawn the rocky Talana Hill, 5000 yards East of the British camp, was seen to be swarming with Boers, 3500 of whom had moved up in the night with seven guns. A frontal attack up a donga was held up by intense fire, but the 1st 60th, in reserve in a wood, skirmished forward to a wall half-way up the hill. This was on the initiative of Lt Col Gunning, when Maj Gen Penn Symons was mortally wounded, and the Irish regiments conformed with our movement. After two hours of heavy fire some co-ordination with our artillery was achieved, and the 60th led the final storming of the steep and rocky crest, Lt Col Gunning falling at the head of his Riflemen. 60th casualties were 5 and 23 killed and 7 and 73 wounded, but one Boer column had at least been repulsed with loss. The 1st, covered with glory, had now joined the 2nd Battalion in Ladysmith, soon beleaguered. Redvers Buller, now 60 and after many years in Whitehall as QMG and AG, was, too late in life, given the desperate task of recovering our defence neglect. He had to split his force to cover the Cape, and himself commanded the troops trying to cross the Tugela river and seize the great ridge barring our way to Ladysmith. VCs and other relics in the Museum tell of the effort by F. Roberts and Congreve, RB, to save the guns in his first battle at Colenso.

Our 3rd Battalion was in a brigade containing Cameronians, DLI and 1st RB, and took a brilliant part in relieving the pressure on Spion Kop on 24 January 1900. Crossing the river alone, they advanced for 1500 yards under increasingly sharp rifle fire, without artillery on either side. By classic skirmishing they crawled, ran and fired up the almost precipitous hill and routed the 200 marksmen of the crack Carolina Commando out of their trenches. Unfortunately, Buller recalled the troops on the crests as victory was in his hands. Lt Col Buchanan Riddell was killed when consolidating the objective, and 60th losses were 3 and 19 killed and 4 and 73 wounded, which indicates their skilled use of the scant cover. Their Brigadier said, 'I have been a Rifleman for over 30 years, and never, in the course of my experience, have I seen a finer bit of skirmishing and fighting.'

Meanwhile inside Ladysmith, 1st and 2nd 60th were in 8 Brigade with 2 RB. The defence, continuously probed, had all the perils of the Delhi Ridge, being based on a few hill-tops with no depth. In the early morning of 6 January 1900 the Free Staters crept to within point-blank range of the key, Waggon Hill, held by the Imperial Light Horse, and its Crows Nest peak, held by three Companies of 1st 60th. Their advance was just held off by a series of desperate local counter-attacks, until reinforcements, including four Companies each of our 1st and 2nd Battalions under Maj Campbell, could come up at 7 am. All available reserves were thrown in to hold the crest, until, just before dusk in a thunderstorm deluge, the Devons cleared the forward slope in a bayonet charge. Our casualties were 4 and 17 killed and 1 and 42 wounded, the close range making it a small-arms battle only; earlier casualties had meant that many of our officers were attached from other regiments. Enteric, dysentery and near-starvation existed within the garrison, but morale remained high. Bandmaster Tyler, nearly drowned in the *Warren Hastings* wreck, won the DCM for gallantry in the siege.

Under Buller the relief force was, however, making progress over the Tugela. In bitter fighting including two gallant counter-attacks, swords fixed, by day and night, our 3rd Battalion did everything possible to win through to their brother Riflemen. When on 28 February the siege (which had lasted exactly 4 months) was raised, the Warrant Officers and Sergeants of the three 60th Battalions resolved to perpetuate the memory of gallant Riflemen by holding an annual Ladysmith Ball, still observed in 2 RGJ.

Although the 2nd Battalion went to India in July, the 1st under Buller took an active part in the defeat of the Boers in the Eastern Transvaal. Thereafter the problem became counter-insurgency, met by erecting a series of blockhouses, held by infantry, who patrolled the linking wire, while cavalry and mounted infantry sweeps cleared the area inside. The 1st and 3rd remained on these duties till the end in 1902, being joined by the 4th for the last few months.

Between South Africa and World War I in 1914 the 1st served in Malta, with FM Lord Grenfell as Governor. His picture as Sirdar of the Egyptian Army is with 2 RGJ. Then, stationed in Egypt, they helped to keep order in Crete and the Sudan, before returning home, when the well-known names of Oxley and Northey are among the COs. The 2nd stayed in India till 1910, taking part in the Delhi Durbar parade of 1903 and that for the Amir of Afghanistan in 1907. The tactful Mr Dunn, the famous Bandmaster, in allowing the Amir to conduct his unscripted Anthem, earned the task of scoring it, and much money for the Band Fund. The 3rd took in Bermuda, Malta and Crete before moving to India in 1910, where they were at the 1911 Durbar.

The 4th went home from the Cape in 1904. HRH The Prince of Wales, late King George V, Colonel in Chief since HRH the Duke of Cambridge's death in 1904, authorized the 60th to resume its earlier Slow March, *The Duke of York's March*, as an inspection tune. This was no doubt played at the opening of the South African war memorial Riflemen's Cottages in Green Jacket Close, Winchester, by HRH Princess Christian of Schleswig–Holstein; her son, Prince Christian Victor, 60th, had died in South Africa and 2 RGJ holds his picture and silver Prince Albert statue. In 1909 the 4th preceded the 3rd to India and were also at the Delhi Durbar, camping by the 2/2nd Goorkhas near the Ridge.

Regimental activities and organizations

During this period the Rifle Shooting of the Regiment reached a peak, the 2nd Battalion winning the Queen Victoria Trophy from 1909–12, with 1910 being the best year, on a par with 1964's performance by a Regiment of one battalion only. Under several great Riflemen the present 60th and Royal Green Jacket institutions, stimulated by our joint Rifle Depot with the Rifle Brigade, had been inaugurated far in advance of most Regiments. The Celer et Audax Club started as a dinner club in 1859, but, thanks to FM Lord Grenfell, became the central 60th organization in 1908. The Riflemen's Aid Society was formed jointly with the Rifle Brigade in 1884, and the care and generosity of many generations of Officers towards their Riflemen has handed over to the Royal Green Jackets a most valuable legacy. Another joint effort was the Green Jacket Cricket Club of the same date, which has helped to publicize an unofficial term for Riflemen of Peninsula days until it became the obvious new Regimental title the ground and provided the new tie; the ground at St Cross, a Royal setting for parades, is of course its creation. The KRRC Chronicle was started in 1901, and by good fortune the 43rd and 52nd and Rifle Brigade used the same format, which is now perpetuated in the RGJ Chronicle, an inestimable source for historians. In 1907 the Ladies Guild was created, originally largely to provide clothes for Riflemen's families, and, after working magnificently in two World Wars, is now another RGJ institution. Finally, the KRRC Association reunions owe their origin to the Veterans' Dinners started at Davies Street in 1906 with the backing of General Buller.

World War I

World War I was on too vast a scale to cover in any of the detail, which is to be found in Volume V. There are, however, certain battalion actions which stand out, where, undimmed by poor generalship, bad staff work or the grip of mud and wire, the beacon lit by Bouquet, de Rottenburg, Hawley or Hutton can momentarily be seen.

On 10 September 1914, having retreated from Mons, the 1st Battalion, 1150 strong, under Lt Col E. Northey, found itself advancing near the Marne. At Hautesvesnes it encountered a German rearguard of 1200 in a sunken road, supported by a battery and machine-guns. Covered by our battery, the 1st Battalion skirmished over largely open ground, until at 700 yards they won a fire-fight, which had lasted an hour. The pinned enemy surrendered, with 150 casualties and 550 captured, to our 14 Riflemen killed and 4 officers and 60 Riflemen wounded, an amazing display of our markmanship and courage. A magnificent later attack by the 2nd Battalion with the Royal Sussex Regiment across the Aisne seized a key ridge and overran batteries, but at the cost of 300 casualties. In October 1914 Ypres was reached, and in nearly gaining the Passchendaele Ridge the 1st Battalion lost 6 officers and 167, including Lt Prince Maurice of Battenberg, of whom pictures are held in 2 RGJ and the Museum. Under overwhelming mass attacks the surviving old Regulars had not long left. The remnants of the 1st, surrounded when flank units gave way, were finally overpowered after a magnificent stand, with 9 officers and 437 Riflemen killed or captured. The 2nd were also effectively counter-attacking close to the 52nd Light Infantry, who broke the 1st Guards Brigade at Nonne Bosschen, and Lt Dimmer won a VC for gallant defensive actions with his Vickers. By the end of November all but a cadre of the 'Old Contemptibles' were gone, but Ypres had been held and the line extended to the sea.

Our 3rd and 4th Battalions arrived in the icy trenches from India in January 1915 and formed a light brigade (80th) of Rifles and Light Infantry. In their splendid stand at Second Ypres the Rangers and they were almost wiped out.

Notable hereafter are the arrival of our Territorial Regiments, and the distinguished work of Brigades, often composed of New Army Battalions of Rifles, Light Infantry and once the PPCLI. Eventually the 14th and 20th Light Divisions were formed; their memorial still stands as not unworthy successors, (even if less well employed) to the Light Division in the Peninsula, and predecessors to our present link of Royal Green Jackets and Light Infantry. By 1916 Rhodesians were fighting splendidly in the trenches, particularly as snipers in the 2nd Battalion. However, in July 1917 the 2nd were required to be the seaward battalion of a two-unit shallow bridgehead North of the River Yser opposite Nieuport Bains. At 6 am on 10 July 1917 an intense bombardment by heavy artillery started, which lasted most of the day without counter, until a German Marine division attacked at 7.15 pm. Many dug-outs in the sand dunes had collapsed, and Lt 'Strafer' Gott had particularly distinguished himself as IO in trying to keep contact when lines were cut. Lt Col Abdie was seen by an Australian to shoot five Germans with his revolver, before himself falling dead at the mouth of a tunnel. The 2nd Battalion was overrun when most of its members were casualties or buried in the sand. Casualties were 17 officers and 481 Riflemen out of 20 and 520; many awards were made, particularly to a party who later escaped, and the 2nd soon built up, thanks to a large draft of Oxfordshire & Buckinghamshire Light Infantry.

At Langemarck in September 1917, the 20th Light Division made a splendid series of attacks, taking all objectives and breaking up all counter-attacks, following up their August gallantry in the same area.

The 14th Light Division met the full weight of the famous German attack in fog on 21 March 1918. Our Battalions, which had averaged 600 apiece, were down in many cases to below 100 all ranks, when finally relieved during the fighting withdrawal on 25 March.

In the more open warfare of the final attacks of 1918 the 1st Battalion, under Lt Col E. G. St Aubyn, DSO, who had been gassed and wounded several times, particularly distinguished themselves in clearing up to the Canal de L'Escaut, forming a bridgehead and holding it against counter-attack. The 16th Battalion, formed originally of Church Lads' Brigade members, crowned many good actions by its crossing of the River Selle in October 1918.

Arriving in Salonika from France before Christmas 1915, the 3rd and 4th Battalions skirmished, patrolled and raided against the Bulgars and Turks in the Struma Valley's cold and heat. The 4th was rushed to France in 1918, but the 3rd stayed on, until it sailed to occupy Constantinople after the Armistice.

The King's Royal Rifle Corps Roll of Honour in Winchester Cathedral records the names of over 12,000 dead from World War I, exactly balancing those on the Rifle Brigade Roll opposite. It is fitting that the Orderly Officer, with the RSM and Bugler of the Rifle Depot to sound the calls, turns the pages containing their names and those of World War II round the year, for these Riflemen and their forebears, many in unknown graves world-wide, did their Regiment and their country much honour.

The 60th contribution to the Royal Green Jackets

When the voluntary and natural union of the 43rd and 52nd, the 60th, The King's Royal Rifle Corps and The Rifle Brigade took place on 1 January 1966, the 60th brought certain special contributions and qualities to The Royal Green Jackets.

The first was the highly prized and long direct connection with the Royal Family. It had been the creation of a King and a Royal Duke; another Royal Duke had brought it home and made it his Rifle Corps, starting a tradition of Royal Colonels in Chief dating back to 1797. A Sovereign had made it his King's Royal Rifle Corps, and since 1904 Sovereigns or their heirs had been Colonels in

Chief. The 'Royal' in the new title derived directly from this, as did HM The Queen's gracious consent to transfer her Colonelcy in Chief to the new Regiment.

The 'Green Jackets', the Riflemen and their tactics were the natural descendants of Bouquet's early concepts, formalized by de Rottenburg. The techniques and traditions of Jäger and Chasseur and their dress had first to be imported and tried out at the instance of Amherst and the Duke of York. The 60th was the only legal vehicle into which foreign experts could be incorporated in the British Army, and our Rifle Companies and a Battalion soon proved their worth.

Under the pressure of Napoleon—just as the Parachute Regiment was rapidly formed under German pressure—it was soon found that de Rottenburg's clear principles could be developed by selected British officers and men. In the Experimental Rifle Corps, the 95th, and later Rifle Brigade of Coote Manningham, de Rottenburg's concepts were developed into a complete Regimental organization and style, whether in barracks or in the field.

The two old Light Infantry Regiments, the 43rd and the 52nd, who had shared the North American experience with the 60th, built on the best Light Company and improvised Light Battalion techniques of that theatre, under famous Commanding Officers like Colborne. In the West Indies the remainder of the 60th were already formed of mixed Rifles and Light Infantry, thanks to transfer of foreign experts. Using de Rottenburg's work, Moore combined the long-range, accurate and camouflaged Riflemen with the rapid firing muskets of the active red-coated Light Infantrymen into the Light Brigade and later Light Division. The old Regiments thus combined to perfect what the 60th had been privileged to pioneer, and 'Peninsula' is our bond as well as the foundation of modern Infantry tactics. De Rottenburg's bugle calls are those the Royal Green Jackets use today, held in common since the Peninsula, like many aspects of drill and dress.

In pure fighting terms the 60th led the list of Battle Honours in the Army, but this was largely a question of keeping four battalions operationally ready to seize any opportunity of action. Just as new equipment was given us to test, as proven innovators, so commanders eagerly sought our services, as in the long campaigns of the Sikh and Kaffir Wars.

It is in a deeper matter that another great 60th contribution has become enshrined in the new Regiment, that of human relations both within and outside a battalion. For the first 70 years the 60th contained a mixture of races, Swiss, German, French, Dutch, Austrian, American and Canadian, always leavened with a good proportion of British volunteers, professionally keen to see active service overseas. For several military generations Swiss Commanding Officers set a pattern which reflected their education, culture and cosmopolitan approach, the very reverse of British 18th and 19th-Century insularity. Knowing that the Regiment and they were on trial, they welcomed any member who would loyally do his best regardless of origin. All 60th had to learn to get on externally with a medley of race, colour, language and creed, whether Delaware, Carib, French Canadian Catholic, Martinique Negro or the many European and other races contained within the Regiment. In every Peninsular Division in which they served, 60th Companies were favoured by all ranks, not least by the Guards.

By contrast the Rifle Brigade, exclusively British from the first, and removed from numbered Regiments of the Line after Waterloo, saw itself rightly as a select club. It was potentially superior to those Regiments, who were happy to soldier on with archaic virtues, and was content with the society of its own battalions. The friendly rivalry which developed at the joint Depot from 1858 onwards was very good for both sides.

When the 60th came home in 1824 its composition became British, but its style remained cosmopolitan. A combination of the care and protection of the Duke of York and his Royal successors and the fighting reputation of the 60th attracted intelligent and educated British officers. Under enlightened Commanding Officers they gave high priority to the welfare of their increasingly urban Riflemen.

The early concept of the open mind and the free and easy exchange of ideas was transferred to our British officers during the long Peninsula and Caribbean operations, and was firmly embedded in the Regimental character. It is, therefore, no accident that affiliations and alliances with the 60th were sought wherever the Regiment served world-wide, and that the Goorkha, Canadian and Australian links are in origin the oldest and in sum the widest contributed to the new Regiment. Within the author's service Americans, Rhodesians, Australians and Fijians have volunteered in war and peace for the 60th, whether in our Regular or Territorial Battalions, and were freely welcomed, individuals from all four groups receiving commissions. It was also the former 60th National Service Officers who saw fit to make a handsome presentation to the Regulars who had made them feel so much at home. 'Home' is the key-note, but the 60th family was always outward-looking and warm, as well as loyal and closely knit within.

By force of circumstances, as well as by philosophy, the 60th were useful in progressively binding the Green Jackets closer together. In World War II 1st 60th twice served in a Motor Brigade, commanded by and otherwise composed of Rifle Brigade officers and Battalions. From 1951 to 1957 2nd 60th was in fact a Green Jacket Battalion, and both sides welcomed the later return of Rifle Brigade officers for further 60th service. Because of a large number of retirements, 2nd Green Jackets needed 2ICs and Company Commanders from both the other Regiments, and provided a Commanding Officer and Platoon Commanders for the 43rd and 52nd; that the 60th had worn the red coat, carried Colours and been Light troops before they were Rifles put them historically in the centre of the new family. By a combination of selection and chance the all-important Rifle Depot had since World War II seen a preponderance of Officers and Warrant Officers in Command or Training Company appointments who were either 60th or who had served with a 60th Battalion, and without immodesty this was a warm and unifying influence.

The 1967 Royal Review

The all-important step after the formation of The Royal Green Jackets in 1966 was to seek an occasion to present HM's new Regiment to the Colonel in Chief in all its components, Regulars, Volunteers, Territorials and Cadets. In particular the support of the Old Comrades was needed to make all feel that the new was a projection of everything good that the old had exemplified.

By chance the planning and execution depended on Green Jackets with a strong 60th background. The Regimental Colonel, Col G. H. Mills, planned the Review with Sir Martin Charteris, Private Secretary to HM, and Maj T. G. H. Jackson, and commanded the Parade, where Lt Col D. M. Stileman, Maj W. S. Chevis, RSM F. Williams, Bugle Maj Green and the Key Bass Drummer Sgt Washington all had common 60th, 2nd 60th or 2nd Green Jackets service. General Sir Evelyn Barker, former Colonel Commandant, commanded the Parade of all Old Comrades, on which a former Prime Minister, Lord Avon, former Secretary of State for War James Ramsden, and the Rev G. H. Wooley, VC, were among those old 60th Riflemen who paraded under Lt Gen Sir Euan Miller. Maj Gen E. A. W. Williams and Col the Hon Richard Wood escorted The Colonel in Chief as Colonel Commandant and Honorary Colonel respectively.

HM The Queen particularly remarked that the 2nd Battalion's Guard almost without exception had double Marksmen badges. The Colonel in Chief commented on the way in which Riflemen managed to make perfect arrangements in advance, so that all could enjoy themselves in a relaxed and informal way on the day; HM's own light touch on many occasions contributed much to this.

In his speech of welcome, FM Sir Francis Festing, Representative Colonel Commandant, said:

'May it please Your Majesty,

'It is with warmth and a deep sense of privilege that Your Majesty's Royal Green Jackets welcome the first visit of their Colonel in Chief.

'Present here are also two thousand Old Comrades of the former Regiments, from which the Royal Green Jackets are proud to trace their origin. The Royal Green Jackets in this widest sense offer their loyal gratitude that the great privilege, extending over two hundred years, of connection with the Crown through Regimental Title or Royal Colonels in Chief is carried forward into the new Regiment.

'Mindful of our old foundations but always eagerly searching for improvement, we pledge ourselves to try to be worthy of the great honour Your Majesty has done us and to serve the Crown in like manner as have those who have gone before.'

The Colonel in Chief graciously replied in the following words:

'Field Marshal Sir Francis Festing, Officers, Warrant Officers, Non-Commissioned Officers and men of the Royal Green Jackets:

'When the new Regiment was formed last year, I was delighted to become the Colonel in Chief, and I am happy today to review Guards from the three regular Battalions all of which have distinguished themselves in the last three years on active service in the Far East, and from the Rifle Depot which has successfully pioneered new training standards for the Infantry.

'It is never easy for Regiments of long tradition and strong individuality to accept change and reorganisation. You have done this admirably and I congratulate the famous Regiments from which you were formed, and which are so well represented here today by their Old Comrades, on the spirit with which they entered into the new union of The Royal Green Jackets.

'I am confident that it will flourish.

'The brooch I am wearing today is your gift, and that of the Volunteers and Territorials, and I thank you all very much indeed.

'The Naval Crown at its base reminds us that Riflemen manned the rigging of Nelson's flagship at Copenhagen. Then, as now, they were always ready to put their hands to any new task—and do it well. Initiative and adaptability are the qualities upon which the reputation of Riflemen as soldiers has been built and on which it will depend in the future.

'One hundred and sixty-four years ago your predecessors were founder members of the Light Division. Next year The Royal Green Jackets will form part of this famous Division once again alongside other Light Infantry Regiments. I am sure that wherever you are called upon to serve, at home or abroad, you will add lustre to its name.

'I wish you all success and happiness.'

The brooch alluded to is at heart the King's Royal Rifle Corps brooch presented to The Queen when she became Colonel in Chief in 1953. A happy thought of Maj Gen Williams and Her Majesty's gracious consent allowed Col Mills to arrange its conversion round the 60th heart, with the bugle, wreath and Naval Crown of the other old Regiments and the common Peninsula superscription. In it, as in the music, drill, dress and style of the Parade, all were able visibly to see what the brooch enshrines—that the best of the old had flowed into the new.

Traces of the old in the new

To end this long tale of sacrifice and achievement, what would the 60th Rifleman recognize of his old Regiment in The Royal Green Jackets today? In outward form the ball and other black buttons, the Mess waistcoat with its thin scarlet lines and much of the drill, from 'Look to your front!' onwards, would ring true. The scarlet and black of buglers' plumes, the Regimental March and bugle calls, and the Motto 'Swift and Bold' would still gladden and inspire. Many useful traditions and practices, shared by the old Green Jackets from the Peninsula or developed in the 150 years thereafter, are now held in common with the Light Infantry in our Light Division. Hutton would see the flexibility that took us with distinction from Mounted Infantry through the Motor Battalion to any task the modern Infantry can be given. Hawley would recognize the care given to the training and administration of self-disciplined Riflemen, and the easy bond with their officers. De Rottenburg would marvel why it took so long for the other Infantry to become his quiet, alert, camouflaged Riflemen, shooting selectively and responding quickly to communications, practices which the Green Jackets alone cultivated for a century and a half.

Bouquet, Haldimand, the Prevosts and their Swiss, Austrian, German, American and British brothers of the earliest 60th would recognize the practical informality, the cheerful camaraderie, the attention to detail and the self-discipline of all ranks. All would be proud of their creation, and not least of Lord Widgery's remark about the 2 Royal Green Jackets barricade on Bloody Sunday 1972 at Londonderry: 'The conduct of these soldiers was impeccable despite the ugly situation which developed.'

Looking at the generation of 60th who helped to create the Royal Green Jackets, our forebears might well wonder at the magnificent succession of vintages from the vineyard they planted so lovingly in the stony soil of Braddock's defeat. In a different sense they might repeat his last words as they contemplated their old Regiment's contribution of two officers successively to hold the highest rank and position in an Army to which they themselves were only admitted by special Act. The succession as Chief of the General Staff of General Sir Roland Gibbs, GCB, CBE, DSO, MC, by General Sir Edwin Bramall, GCB, OBE, MC, both of the wartime 2nd Battalion The King's Royal Rifle Corps, is clear evidence of the high quality of Rifleman which the Regiment's reputation continued to attract during its last quarter-century.

Thanks to the inspiration of a long line of 60th—Royal Americans, Duke of York's and King's Royal Rifle Corps and Green Jackets—all Riflemen at heart, our forebears might fairly claim that we had indeed learnt to do it better the next time.

APPENDIX A
REGULAR OFFICERS 1947

Colonels Commandant
Barker, Lt Gen Sir Evelyn H., KBE, CB, DSO, MC
Curtis, Maj Gen H. O., CB, DSO, MC

Lt Colonels
Maclure, Sir John W. S., Bt, OBE
De Salis, S. C. F, DSO
Grenville-Gray, C. E. M.
Gurney, C. H., OBE

Majors
Wilson, C. J.
Eve, R. A. T., CBE
White, C. A.
Sismey, O. N. D.
Timpson, T. L.
de Bruyne, G., OBE
Herbert-Stepney, C. J., OBE
Heathcoat-Amory, W., DSO
Davies, W. D.
Boileau, D. R. C., DSO
Oxley, R. G. R.
Stafford, B. B. E. H.
Mitford-Slade, C. T.
Dalby, C.
Chapman, P. G.
Trotter, T.
Collen, K. H.
Douglas-Pennant, M. F., DSO, MBE
De Pree, G.
White, J. M.
Hunt, H. C. J., CBE, DSO
Johnson, M. A.
Williams, E. A. W., OBE, MC
Consett, C. d'A. P., DSO, MC
Scott, C. R.
Powell, J. A. H., MC
Northey, E. G. V.

Chance, R. F. L., MC
Campbell, G. T. H., MC
Corbett-Winder, J. L., MC
Keown-Boyd, W. D.
Howard, H. R. G.
Christian, J. M., MC
Round, J. G.
White, G. W., MBE
Gilliat, M. J., MBE
Mason, G. H.
Mellor, J. F. C., DSO
Charteris, Hon M. M. C., OBE
Hawley, Sir David H. Bt

Captains
Trotter, F. L.
Fetherstonhaugh, T., OBE
Whitbread, S.
Hunter, J. A., DSO, MBE, MC
Turner, A. R.
Madden, C. S.
Hope, H. A., MC
Earle, P. B., MC
Vernon, H. R. W., MBE
Parker, P. H.
Davies-Scourfield, E. G. B., MC
Pardoe, P.
O'Donovan, T. J. M.
Curtis, J. H. P., MC
Hornsby, D. F.
Gibbs, R. C., DSO, MC
Willis-Fleming, R. H.
Nixon, R. F. N.

Lieutenants
Kent, W. S.
Radclyffe, J. R. C., MBE
Le Coq, J. A. G.
Mills, G. H.

Humphreys, C. A., MC
Phillips, E. C., MC
Poe, J. L.
House, D. G., MC
Elwes, R. V. G.
Darwin, R. J. A.
Shirley, J. E.
Warry, N. J., MC
Seymour, G. R.
St Aubyn, T. E.
Kenney-Herbert, E. M. M.
Bramall, E. N. W., MC
Harker, M. J. W.
Bampfylde, D. C. W.
Lewin, R. O.

Hazlehurst, C. P.
Tillard, J. R.
Ponsonby, M. W.

2nd Lieutenants
Parker, R. M.
Barker, G. W.
Thistlethwayte, T. N.
Tidbury, C. H.

Quartermasters
Hind, Maj G. P. R.
Barker, Maj A. E.
Dracott, Capt F. E.
Keeling, Capt R. H., MBE

APPENDIX B
TERRITORIAL ARMY OFFICERS 1953

Hon Colonels
Erskine, Lt Gen Sir George W. E. J.,
KCB, KBE, DSO
Eden, Maj The Rt Hon R. A., MC,
MP

Majors
Cleaver, H. R., TD
Owen, D. G., TD
Knight, F. L.
Woodhouse, The Hon J. A. D.
Earle, P. B., MC
Hedges, R. K.
Joyner, F. H., MC
Turner, M. G.

Captains
Greenly, A. P. H.
Doley, P. J.
Palmer, G. S.
Lloyd, R. A.
Gregory, C. C.
Egleston, M. K. M. F.
Lincoln, G. P.
Watson, A.
Rose, E.
Snowden, R. W., TD
Geffen, J. L. H.
Butterwick, J. N.
Tiddy, R. M. B.
Harker, M. J. W.
Morrison, M. J. F.
Kimberley, A. W.
Maude, M. C.
Rothschild, P. H.

Lieutenants
Neale, N. H.
Garratt, J. M.

Lieutenants (contd)
Travers-Smith, I. O.
Hoskyns, Sir J. C., Bt
Macneal, A. R.
Morgan-Grenville, J. R. B.
Barnes, T. J. R.
Althaus, N. F.
Wauchope, J. E. R.
Waddington, D.
Noel, H. M.
March, The Earl of
Grant, A. M.
Gibbs, S. C.
Longrigg, R. E.
Lloyd, C. R.
Crisp, J. W. M.
Pickthorn, H. G. R.
Watney, M. B. A.

2nd Lieutenants
Trustram-Eve, D. M.
Trustram-Eve, P. N.
Johnstone, The Hon R. E. L.
Nissen, G. M.
Grenville-Gray, W. E.
Miller, E. J.
Morgan-Grenville, G. W.
Eccles, J. D.
Gordon-Lennox, Lord N. C.
Summers, T. R.
Parker-Jervis, R.
Abell, J. N.

National Service Officers
Lieutenant
Shone, M. G. T.

2nd Lieutenants
Butterwick, A. J.

2nd Lieutenants (contd)

Cornwall-Jones, G. R.

Pollen, P. M. H.

Evill, H. C. S.

Wyatt, J. J. N.

Whiteley, R. T.

Butler, A. C.

Jermain, J. H.

Simpson, M. K. O.

Wilbraham, M. J.

Drysdale, A. W.

Anderton, F. M.

Stevens, J. E. G.

Thornycroft, T. E.

Drummond, M. A. C.

Hollins, J. S. S.

Murray-Brown, N. J.

Mosley, M.

Bosanquet, R. T.

Note: Capt N. Eden was ADC to the Governor General of Canada at this time.

APPENDIX C
REGULAR OFFICERS 1964

Colonel Commandant
Erskine, Gen. Sir George, W. E. J.,
GCB, KBE, DSO.

Lt Colonels
Pardoe, P.
Mills, G. H.

Majors
Radclyffe, J. R. C., MBE
Humphreys, C. A., MC
House, D. G., OBE, MC
Bramall, E. N. W., MC
Parker, Hon R. M.
Thistlewayte, R. N.
Molesworth St Aubyn, J. A., MBE
Beak, M. M. V. W.
Guy, R. K., MBE
Nightingale, R. C., MBE

Captains
Welsh, P. M.
Calvert, M. J.
West, V. F.
Karslake, A. E. K.
Holroyd, C. J.
Shelley, A. T. R.
McCausland, I. H.
Adami, C. J.
Keyte, J. V.
Mason, J. W.
Crossman, G. P. R.
Leach, R. C. F.
Henshaw, C. L. G. G.
Mitford-Slade, P. B.
Nelson, J. R. E.
Hopton, G. B. C.
Gurney, C. J. H.

Lieutenants
Treneer-Michell, P.
Berry, A. E.
Graham-Wigan, J. A. F.
Drew, A. S. G.
Eustace, M. H.
Bullock, C. J. D.
Gamble, R. M.
Mead, D. H.
Gascoigne, D. C.
Colville, D. E. W.
Browne-Clayton, R. B.
Dunning, M. L.
Ker, R. H.
Hill, C. R.
Miers, C. J. P.
Rowland Jones, D. E.

2nd Lieutenants
Wallace, C. B. Q.
Adams, N. H. H.
Robertson, M. J. C.
Winwood, T. R.
Wells, M. E. I. A.
Brinkley, C. W.

Quartermasters
Grout, Major L. P.
Lamb, Capt. A. J.
Slater, Capt G. E., BEM

Short Service Officers

Lieutenant
Shaw, T. P.

2nd Lieutenants
Palmer-Tomkinson, J. J.

Beddard, J. P. O.
McGrigor, A. D.
St Aubyn, S. G. M.

Quartermaster
Shreeve, Capt G. R.

INDEX

In view of their constant change in rank or title officers and civilians are shown by initial or first name only. Soldiers are shown by rank where this can be traced. Formations and units are shown in alphabetical or numerical order for ease of reference, irrespective of seniority or precedence. Quotations in the text have been left unamended as to spelling or initials in case it helps contemporaries.

Chapter XIV has not been indexed, although some contemporaries may find their names mentioned. This is because the Chapter is merely a historical summary. The historian should consult the appropriate Volume of the Annals at the Museum in Winchester for greater detail.